By recovering large numbers of Wilson's letters in collections outside Princeton University, the editors have been able to reconstruct a remarkably full account of Wilson's activities during one of the most crucial periods in his career. The papers in Volume 22 fully document the monumental struggle over the election of a United States senator, Wilson's victory over the state Democratic machine headed by James Smith, Jr., his legisaltive triumphs, and the beginning of a movement to make Wilson the Democratic presidential nominee in 1912.

Letters Wilson wrote almost weekly to Mrs. Mary Allen Hulbert Peck contain Wilson's personal reactions to ongoing events. Another significant aspect of this volume is the complete account from newspapers of Wilson's daily activities, his public statements, and his speeches, virtually all of them printed here for the first time in permanent form.

The volume ends as the New Jersey Legislature of 1911 concludes its session, adopting a sweeping reform program on the eve of Wilson's first nationwide tour.

percent is given to subscribers.

Arthur S. Link is Edwards Professor of American History, Princeton University.

THE PAPERS OF

WOODROW WILSON

VOLUME 22

1910-1911

SPONSORED BY THE WOODROW WILSON
FOUNDATION
AND PRINCETON UNIVERSITY

THE PAPERS OF

WOODROW WILSON

ARTHUR S. LINK, *EDITOR*

DAVID W. HIRST AND JOHN E. LITTLE

ASSOCIATE EDITORS

EDITH JAMES BLENDON, *ASSISTANT EDITOR*

JOHN M. MULDER, *ASSISTANT EDITOR*

SYLVIA ELVIN FONTIJN, *CONTRIBUTING EDITOR*

M. HALSEY THOMAS, *CONSULTING EDITOR*

Volume 22 · 1910-1911

PRINCETON, NEW JERSEY

PRINCETON UNIVERSITY PRESS

1976

Copyright © 1976 by Princeton University Press
All Rights Reserved
L.C. Card 66-10880
I.S.B.N. 0-691-04638-7

Note to scholars: Princeton University Press
subscribes to the Resolution on Permissions of
the Association of American University Presses,
defining what we regard as "fair use" of copyrighted works. This Resolution, intended to encourage scholarly use of university press publications and to avoid unnecessary applications
for permission, is obtainable from the Press or
from the A.A.U.P. central office. Note, however,
that the scholarly apparatus, transcripts of
shorthand, and the texts of Wilson documents
as they appear in this volume are copyrighted,
and the usual rules about the use of copyrighted materials apply.

Printed in the United States of America
by Princeton University Press
Princeton, New Jersey

INTRODUCTION

AS this volume opens, Wilson, Governor-elect of New Jersey, faces a danger that threatens to plunge his party into disarray and stultify his leadership even before his inauguration—James Smith, Jr.'s determination to return to the United States Senate. Moving cautiously at first, because he does not wish to alienate the Newark boss and imperil his legislative program, Wilson, through mutual friends and then in person, appeals to Smith not to stand for election. The former senator refuses to give any assurances; indeed, there are many signs that he is quietly lining up support. Progressive editors and politicians step up their campaign against Smith and in favor of James E. Martine, who had received an inconclusive endorsement in the Democratic senatorial primary in September 1910. Wilson comes out against Smith and for Martine in a public statement on December 8, 1910—the opening move of a brief but intense battle for control of the Democratic party in the state. In a brilliant campaign, marked by speeches in Jersey City and Newark and by unrelenting pressure upon Democratic members of the next legislature, Wilson rallies his forces and detaches Hudson County from Smith. In the end, Smith is left with support from only a few faithful friends in Newark. The legislature, in a Democratic landslide, elects Martine senator on January 25, 1911.

Meanwhile, Wilson, acting like a prime minister, plans a legislative program with his lieutenants and, after his inauguration on January 17, goes into the Democratic Assembly caucus to turn back the Smith machine's opposition to his first measure—the Geran bill for a comprehensive direct primary election system. Victory in this first, crucial struggle opens the way for the adoption of the balance of Wilson's legislative program, and more—laws for the regulation of the rates and services of railroads and public utilities, workmen's compensation, stringent control of campaign expenditures, school reform, and commission government of New Jersey cities.

By the end of the legislative session in late April 1911, Wilson is not only the master of his party in New Jersey, but also the person to whom Democrats throughout the nation seem to be turning as their presidential candidate in 1912. Heartened by the response to speeches in Pennsylvania, Virginia, and Georgia, Wilson permits friends to organize a small pre-convention "publicity bureau" in New York and to plan a speaking tour for him through the Middle West, the Far West, and the South.

Official communications, news reports, texts of speeches, and public statements combine with letters to form a rich fabric of documentation for this exciting stage in Wilson's career. Only a small collection of his official papers (cited as the Governor's Files, New Jersey State Library) has survived. The balance, containing virtually all correspondence relating to state administration and patronage, was at some time removed, dispersed, or destroyed. However, enough evidence of this kind has been recovered from personal collections and the newspapers amply to represent Wilson's administrative and political concerns.

Readers are reminded that *The Papers of Woodrow Wilson* is a continuing series; that persons, events, and institutions mentioned in earlier volumes are not re-identified in subsequent ones; and that the Index to each volume gives cross references to fullest earlier identifications. We continue to print texts *verbatim et literatim*, making silent corrections only of obvious errors in typed copies and occasionally supplying or changing punctuation in transcripts and newspaper speeches when necessary for clarity.

THE EDITORS

Princeton, New Jersey
January 14, 1976

CONTENTS

Introduction, vii
Illustrations, xix
Abbreviations and Symbols, xxi

The Papers, November 10, 1910–May 4, 1911

Announcement of Joseph Patrick Tumulty's appointment as Secretary
  to the Governor, 328
Appeal for Relief for Manchuria, 416
Carnegie Foundation for the Advancement of Teaching, newly adopted
  Rule 4, 132
Interviews
  On publicity, 5
  On the problems of the Governor of New Jersey, 9
  On tariff, taxes, and corporations, 216
  On the senatorial situation, 235
  On regulation of corporations by state laws, 312
  About reform government, 354
  On political conditions, 554
  On the Democratic party, 591
Letters, Collateral
  Edward Wright Sheldon to Henry Green Duffield, 176
  Augustine Thomas Smythe to George Howe III, 34
  Joseph Patrick Tumulty to James E. W. Cook, 356
  John Wesley Wescott to Joseph Patrick Tumulty, 451
  Ellen Axson Wilson to Frederick Yates, 234
Letters from Wilson to
  Warren Worth Bailey, 523
  Ray Stannard Baker, 412
  Hiram Bingham, 606, 607
  Jonathan Bourne, Jr., 36
  John Joseph Bracken, 230
  Henry Skillman Breckinridge, 236, 525
  Robert Bridges, 12, 287, 333, 411
  Calvin Easton Brodhead, 199, 238, 308
  James Bryce, 211
  Andrew Carnegie, 515
  Harold Carrow, 25
  Henry Groves Connor, 383
  Richard Heath Dabney, 13
  Winthrop More Daniels, 25
  Cleveland Hoadley Dodge, 29, 237, 382, 438
  John Fairfield Dryden, 416
  Charles William Eliot, 78
  John Fox, 167
  William Goodell Frost, 48, 440
  Harry Augustus Garfield, 30
  Robert Garrett, 84
  Edward Field Goltra, 199
  Elgin Ralston Lovell Gould, 606
  Arthur Twining Hadley, 187

William Bayard Hale, 414, 526

John Ralph Hardin, 37

George Brinton McClellan Harvey, 13, 46, 260, 326, 435, 467

Azel Washburn Hazen, 37

Robert Randolph Henderson, 55

Jenny Davidson Hibben, 573

John Grier Hibben, 259

Henry Lee Higginson, 38

Joseph Stanislaus Hoff, 415

Harriet Hyde, 361

Robert Underwood Johnson, 126, 406

Thomas Davies Jones, 48, 154

Winifred Jones, 223

Lindley Miller Keasbey, 433

Charles William Kent, 333

Daniel Kiefer, 261

William Brewster Lee, 14

Frederick H. Levey, 136

Benjamin Barr Lindsey, 405, 525, 599

Thomas Bell Love, 25, 434, 583

Charles Williston McAlpin, 293, 358

Cyrus Hall McCormick, 29, 405

St. Clair McKelway, 134

Thomas McKinsey, 238

William Pierce Macksey, 212, 330

Isaac Wayne MacVeagh, 37, 205

James Edgar Martine, 36

Thomas Nelson Page, 30, 377

Walter Hines Page, 413, 414, 515

Alexander Mitchell Palmer, 26

Mary Allen Hulbert Peck, 139, 141, 204, 209, 292, 294, 323, 329,
      333, 362, 382, 391, 396, 407, 424, 438, 453, 477, 500, 509, 517,
      531, 543, 570, 581, 597

Clarence Hamilton Poe, 503, 509

Henry Smith Pritchett, 23, 569

George Lawrence Record, 13, 382

James Ford Rhodes, 49

William Henry Rideing, 406

Reginald Rowland, 480

Clarence Sackett, 200

Jacob Gould Schurman, 30

Thomas Berry Shannon, 598

Edward Wright Sheldon, 13

Robert W. Shultice, 99

Charles Andrew Talcott, 456

Samuel Huston Thompson, Jr., 405, 521, 523, 527, 574, 577

Henry St. George Tucker, 287

Various Correspondents, 252

Marion Jackson Verdery, 257, 553

Oswald Garrison Villard, 135, 288, 308, 454

Henry Watterson, 286

John Wesley Wescott, 206, 289, 394, 414, 516, 520, 548

William Royal Wilder, 358
Frederic Yates, 187
Letters to Wilson from
  Leon Abbett, Jr., 281
  Henry Eckert Alexander, 231
  James Waddel Alexander, 30
  Lamson Allen, 335
  Frank Rose Austin, 375
  George Frederick Baer, 215
  Warren Worth Bailey, 522
  Simeon Eben Baldwin, 15
  Allan Benny, 395
  Charles Clarke Black, 169
  Edward William Bok, 21
  Jonathan Bourne, Jr., 34
  Gamaliel Bradford, 138
  Henry Skillman Breckinridge, 213, 523
  Robert Bridges, 333
  Calvin Easton Brodhead, 22, 198, 206, 232, 294
  Oren Britt Brown, 361
  Philip Alexander Bruce, 254
  Thomas Smith Bryan, 576
  William Jennings Bryan, 307, 465
  James Bryce, 33
  Jacob L. Bunnell, 378
  Richard Evelyn Byrd, 20
  John Lambert Cadwalader, 17
  Josiah Cleveland Cady, 424
  Andrew Carnegie, 514
  Alexander Francis Chamberlain, 379
  George Earle Chamberlain, 174
  Peyton Cochran, 118
  Cook Conkling, 394
  Sherman Montrose Craiger, 428
  Juliet Clannon Cushing, 156
  Josephus Daniels, 121, 406
  Robert Davis, 26
  Joseph Albert Dear, Jr., 97
  Samuel Shepard Dennis, 23
  Martin Patrick Devlin, 128
  Thomas H. Dillow, 163
  Thomas Dixon, Jr., 96
  Cleveland Hoadley Dodge, 72, 94, 232, 377, 436
  Ralph Waldo Emerson Donges, 120
  Julius Daniel Dreher, 604
  Henry Green Duffield, 186
  Frederick A. Duneka, 21
  Maitland Dwight, 430
  John Henry Eastwood, 129
  William Simpson Elder, 17
  Charles William Eliot, 78
  Leroy J. Ellis, 116, 244

Matthias Cowell Ely, 85
Charles Apffel Eypper, 344
Robert Alexander Falconer, 45
Benjamin L. Farinholt, 587
Joseph Fels, 278
William T. Ferguson, 28
John Joseph Fitzgerald, 16
Henry Jones Ford, 84
Franklin William Fort, 27
John Franklin Fort, 53
Solomon Foster, 183, 260
Hollis Burke Frissell, 140
William Goodell Frost, 172, 214
William Cavanagh Gebhardt, 101, 162, 321
Elmer Hendrickson Geran, 18, 100, 145, 280
Robert Brodnax Glenn, 327
Henry Cowper Gollan, 14
Edward Field Goltra, 97, 197
William Elliott Gonzales, 507
Elliot Hersey Goodwin, 256
Thomas Pryor Gore, 387
James Richard Gray, 506
Philip Barling Ben Greet, 36
Julian Arthur Gregory, 245
Alexander Barclay Guigon, 383
Arthur Twining Hadley, 184
James Alphonsus Hamill, 72
George Brinton McClellan Harvey, 38, 227, 466
Charles Robert Hemphill, 21
Charles O'Connor Hennessy, 124
John Grier Hibben, 77
Francis Wrigley Hirst, 234
Samuel Colgate Hodge, 259
Hamilton Holt, 32
George Howe III, 33, 517
Robert Stephen Hudspeth, 321
William Hughes, 18, 161
George Wylie Paul Hunt, 291
Charles Henry Ingersoll, 499
William Mann Irvine, 22
Melancthon Williams Jacobus, 44
Ryerson W. Jennings, 284
Robert Underwood Johnson, 98
William Mindred Johnson, 19
Thomas Davies Jones, 126
Francis Fisher Kane, 246, 435, 486
Lindley Miller Keasbey, 422
Frederick Wallace Kelsey, 146
Charles William Kent, 326
William Kent, 31
James Kerney, 201
Daniel Kiefer, 257, 578
Anthony Killgore, 164

Clara Schlee Laddey and Mary Loring Colvin, 289
James Lafferty, 233
George Mason La Monte, 82, 174, 308
John J. Lane, 147
Adolph Lankering, 258
John E. Lathrop, 159, 247, 255, 404
Edward E. Lee, 31
John Jacob Lentz, 228
Frederick H. Levey, 125
Benjamin Barr Lindsey, 274, 387, 584
Job Herbert Lippincott, 125
Thomas Littlehales, 513
Thomas Bell Love, 122, 224, 409, 576
William Lustgarten, 570
William Gibbs McAdoo, 51
Charles Williston McAlpin, 256
Thomas Nesbitt McCarter, 83
Samuel Sidney McClure, 85
William Frank McCombs, 581
Cyrus Hall McCormick, 71, 386
Vance Criswell McCormick, 408
Charles Howard McIlwain, 165
Alexander Jeffrey McKelway, 206, 226
St. Clair McKelway, 170
William Pierce Macksey, 232
Isaac Wayne MacVeagh, 143
William Francis Magie, 79
Dudley Field Malone, 45
James Edgar Martine, 52
William Hunter Maxwell, 214, 290
Henry Collin Minton, 311
John Moody, 114
Hopson Owen Murfee, 55
Richard Cole Newton, 155
Edmund Favor Noel, 16
Joseph M. Noonan, 133, 223, 245, 377
James Richard Nugent, 49, 171, 203
Edmund Burke Osborne, 366
Harry Vliet Osborne, 181, 285, 310
Robert Latham Owen, 208
Walter Hines Page, 433
Francis Landey Patton, 404
Mary Allen Hulbert Peck, 100, 331
George Walbridge Perkins, 19
Bowdre Phinizy, 573
Mahlon Pitney, 28
George Arthur Plimpton, 209
Clarence Hamilton Poe, 437, 499
Joseph Hyde Pratt, 520
Jacob Cole Price, 325
Henry Smith Pritchett, 130, 148, 283, 365, 548
Frederick K. Pulsifer, 117
Moses Taylor Pyne, 17

Louis Irving Reichner, 450
James Ford Rhodes, 27
Lucius Thompson Russell, 137
Clarence Sackett, 215
William W. St. John, 76, 81, 155
Shosuke Sato, 139
Jacob Gould Schurman, 399
Charles Scribner, 51
Edward Wallace Scudder, 233
Wallace McIlvaine Scudder, 225
Edward Wright Sheldon, 165
James Edward Shepard, 98
George Sebastian Silzer, 243, 311, 328
Evans Griffiths Slaughter, 203
Charles F. Sleeper, 164
James Smith, Jr., 132, 154
John Walter Smith, 15
Edwin Augustus Stevens, 113, 173
Pleasant Alexander Stovall, 516, 543
August C. Streitwolf, Jr., 243
Mark Anthony Sullivan, 22
Frank Thilly, 35
Harvey Thomas, 309
Samuel Huston Thompson, Jr., 375
Charles Franklin Thwing, 53
Frederick Todd, 121, 185
John Joseph Treacy, 163
William Monroe Trotter, 50
Henry St. George Tucker, 282
Joseph Patrick Tumulty, 118, 145, 200, 233
Oscar Wilder Underwood, 95
William Simon U'Ren, 197
Francis Preston Venable, 20
Marion Jackson Verdery, 201, 552
Oswald Garrison Villard, 26, 83, 127, 287, 307
Allan Bartholomew Walsh, 29
Henry Watterson, 143, 160, 184, 212, 274, 393
John Wesley Wescott, 42, 169, 261, 413
Benjamin Ide Wheeler, 54
Edward Seymour Wilde, 41
William Royal Wilder, 361
Charles Richard Williams, 52
John Sharp Williams, 93, 197
Joseph R. Wilson, Jr., 95
Caleb Thomas Winchester, 35
Hiram Woods, 158, 175
New Jersey: Senatorial Contest
Statement on the senatorship, 153
Statement by James Smith, Jr., 166
Report of Wilson's comment on the senatorial election, 229
Proposed statement on the election prepared by Wilson for assemblymen-elects' signatures, 239

Reports on Wilson's conferences with Essex County Democratic
    delegation, 239, 253
Wilson's statement on the Martine-Smith race, 248
Report of Wilson's reply to James Smith, Jr., 272
Wilson's statement on Martine's election, 365; report of comments,
    367
New Jersey: Legislative Program
    Report of a statement about the Hotel Martinique conference, 357
    Statement on a proposed increase in postal rates, 427
    Statement on the Geran election bill, 430
    Reports of conferences with the Democratic assemblymen of New
        Jersey, Trenton, N.J., 481, 504
    A statement about an altercation with James Richard Nugent, 512
    Report of Wilson's remarks on the passage of the Geran bill, 569
    Report of remarks about the commission government bill, 574
    Statement on the work of the New Jersey legislative session of
        1911, 578
New Jersey: Inaugural Address, 345
New Jersey: Governor's Messages to the Legislature
    Veto of House bill concerning the salaries of fire department em-
        ployees, 508
    To the Legislature of New Jersey, concerning a federal income
        tax, 511
    Veto of House bill on the appropriation of moneys by the boroughs
        for the celebration of the 50th anniversary of their founding, 524
    Veto of a Senate bill to establish and regulate parks, 526
    To the Senate of New Jersey, 534
    Veto of a House bill concerning the care of wayward females, 548
    To the House of Assembly of New Jersey, 549
News Reports
    Wilson's arrival in Milwaukee, 55
    Wilson's arrival in St. Louis, 262
    Meeting of Wilson and William Jennings Bryan in Princeton, 502
    Wilson's arrival in Indianapolis, 554
Princeton University: Documentary Material
    Resolution of the Princeton University Faculty on Wilson's resig-
        nation, 79
    Report of a testimonial presented to Wilson by Princeton under-
        graduates, 322
Princeton University: Meetings and Addresses
    Report of speech to Princeton University undergraduates, 3
    Report of a talk to the football team, 4
    Two reports of a farewell address to the senior class of Princeton
        University, 149, 152
    Report of an address to a religious meeting, the Philadelphian
        Society, 159
    Response to a toast, "Princeton Ideals," at a *Daily Princetonian*
        banquet, 600
Public Lectures and Addresses
    Report of a luncheon address in Milwaukee, Wisc., 57
    Public lecture in Milwaukee, Wisc., 61
    Report of a lecture on business and government, Chicago, Ill., 74

Thanksgiving Day address, Har Sinai Temple, Trenton, N.J., 87

Address to the Conference of Governors, Frankfort, Kentucky, 102

Report of a message to the Sons of Delaware of Philadelphia, 148

Address to the Illinois Manufacturers' Association, Chicago, Ill., 178; news report, 180

Address to the New York Southern Society, 188

Presidential address to the American Political Science Association, St. Louis, Mo., 263

Report of a speech to the City Club, St. Louis, Mo., 276

Report of a speech to the Princeton Club of St. Louis, 283

Address in Jersey City, N.J., 295

Address at Temple B'nai Jeshurun, Newark, N.J., 316

Report of an address on the direct primary principle, Newark, N.J., 335

Report of a speech to the annual dinner of the Board of Trade, Jersey City, N.J., 359

Address to the Board of Trade, Newark, N.J., 367

Report of an address on civic awakening, Trenton, N.J., 379

Report of an address to the Inter-Church Federation of New Jersey, Trenton, N.J., 385

Report of a speech to the Kansas Society of New York, 389

Address to the National Press Club, Washington, D.C., 396

A tribute to Mark Anthony Sullivan, 400

Report of a speech to Stevens Institute alumni, New York, 410

Address on behalf of Berea College, New York, 417

Report of an address to the Kentuckians of New York, 421

Address to the Democratic Club of Philadelphia, 441

Report of remarks to the New Jersey Consumers' League, Trenton, N.J., 452

Report of remarks to the New Jersey Editorial Association, Trenton, N.J., 455

Address to the West Hudson Board of Trade, Harrison, N.J., 456

Address to the Board of Trade, Hoboken, N.J., 468

Report of remarks at the annual dinner of the New Jersey Senate, New York, 474

Report of an address to the Chamber of Commerce, Trenton, N.J., 482

Report of two speeches in Atlanta, Ga., 487

Address to the Southern Commercial Congress, Atlanta, Ga., 491

Remarks to the New Jersey Conference of Charities and Correction, Princeton, N.J., 528

Address to the Burlington County Democratic Club at the Jefferson Day Dinner, Burlington, N.J., 535

Address to the National Democratic League of Clubs, Indianapolis, Ind., 557

Report of remarks at the Free Synagogue, New York, 585

Report of a dinner given to Wilson by Senator Ernest R. Ackerman, New York, 588

Report of an address to the Board of Trade, Phillipsburg, N.J., 590

Reports of an address at the Pewter Platter Dinner, Norfolk, Va., 592, 594

Report of a speech to the National Democratic Club, New York, 601

Telegrams
    Peyton Cochran and Charles MaCauley East to Woodrow Wilson, 96
    George G. Feigl to Woodrow Wilson, 376
    William Cavanagh Gebhardt to Woodrow Wilson, 257
    Judson Harmon to Woodrow Wilson, 15
    James Edgar Martine to John Sharp Williams, 94
    Dan Fellows Platt to Woodrow Wilson, 86
    Robert W. Shultice to Woodrow Wilson, 99
    Hoke Smith to Woodrow Wilson, 480
    James Smith, Jr., to Woodrow Wilson, 15
    Edward Bushrod Stahlman to Woodrow Wilson, 376
    Oswald Garrison Villard to Woodrow Wilson, 101
    Woodrow Wilson to William Gibbs McAdoo, 51
    Woodrow Wilson to Dan Fellows Platt, 87
Index, 610

ILLUSTRATIONS

Following page 322

Wilson reviewing the Inaugural Parade
Princeton University Library

Wilson at his desk in the New Jersey State House
Princeton University Library

Henry Watterson
"Marse Henry," by Isaac Marcosson

James Edgar Martine
Princeton University Library

Samuel Kalisch
New Jersey, A Historical, Commercial and Industrial Review,
    ed. Ellis R. Meeker

John Wesley Wescott
Mrs. Ralph W. Wescott

Elmer Hendrickson Geran
Princeton University Archives

Walter Evans Edge
New Jersey, A Historical, Commercial and Industrial Review,
    ed. Ellis R. Meeker

Joseph Albert Dear, Jr.
The Book of New Jersey, Joseph Albert Dear

Henry Smith Pritchett
Institute Archives, Massachusetts Institute of Technology

TEXT ILLUSTRATIONS

*"He don't know where he's going, but he's on his way!" Cartoon in the
Baltimore Sun, December 12, 1910, 176*

ABBREVIATIONS

ALS	autograph letter signed
CCL	carbon copy of letter
EAW	Ellen Axson Wilson
ELA	Ellen Louise Axson
hw	handwriting, handwritten
HwLS	handwritten letter signed
MS	manuscript
T	typed
T MS	typed manuscript
TC	typed copy
TCL	typed copy of letter
TLS	typed letter signed
WW	Woodrow Wilson
WWhw	Woodrow Wilson handwriting, handwritten
WWhwL	Woodrow Wilson handwritten letter
WWhwLS	Woodrow Wilson handwritten letter signed
WWT	Woodrow Wilson typed
WWT MS	Woodrow Wilson typed manuscript
WWTL	Woodrow Wilson typed letter
WWTLS	Woodrow Wilson typed letter signed

ABBREVIATIONS FOR COLLECTIONS
AND LIBRARIES

Following the National Union Catalog
of the Library of Congress

CtY	Yale University
DLC	Library of Congress
KyBB	Berea College
MH	Harvard University
MH-Ar	Harvard University Archives
MH-BA	Harvard University, Graduate School of Business Administration
MHi	Massachusetts Historical Society
NIC	Cornell University
NN	New York Public Library
NcD	Duke University
NcU	University of North Carolina, Chapel Hill
Nj	New Jersey State Library, Archives and History, Trenton
NjP	Princeton University
PHi	Historical Society of Pennsylvania, Philadelphia
PP	Free Library of Philadelphia
RSB Coll., DLC	Ray Stannard Baker Collection of Wilsoniana, Library of Congress
ViU	University of Virginia
WC, NjP	Woodrow Wilson Collection, Princeton University
WP, DLC	Woodrow Wilson Papers, Library of Congress

[Nov. 10, 1910]   publication date of a published writing; also date
                         of document when date is not part of text
[[Nov. 17, 1910]]   delivery date of a speech if publication date
                         differs
[*Dec. 8, 1910*]   composition date when publication date differs
[- - - -]   undecipherable words in text, each dash
                         representing one word

THE PAPERS OF

WOODROW WILSON

VOLUME 22

1910-1911

THE PAPERS OF
WOODROW WILSON

Two News Reports

[Nov. 10, 1910]

WILSON SPEECH FOR STUDENTS

Governor-Elect Tells Them that the People
Are Looking for Leaders.

SPECIAL PRIVILEGE DOOMED

PRINCETON, Nov. 10.—A big parade of undergraduates, led by a band, paraded about the city by torchlight last night, winding up by serenading their former college president, who appeared at a window and bowed his thanks.

The usual campaign signs and banners were carried, among them being some like this: "How does it feel to have 45,000 majority?" "Wilson swept the State!" "Poor Vivian!" "Has anybody here seen Lewis?" But the one which caused the most enthusiasm among the students was this: "The next great event— We will beat Yale!"[1]

In response to chorused requests for a speech, Dr. Wilson said that the present time was the chance for every one of his hearers. A college man should know the history of our country and be acquainted with its politics. The country is looking for leaders, Mr. Wilson declared, and regardless of party will support the man the people have confidence in. The present election he considered a national awakening which is not confined to New Jersey.[2] Americans have turned with serious purpose to the betterment of politics. They are going after special privileges until special privileges no longer exist.

Continuing, Governor-elect Wilson said:

The thing that happened in New Jersey yesterday was nothing unusual. The very same thing was happening all over the country, but the victories were not party victories, but the triumph of a cause. The people of this country are seeking new leaders to direct them, and it is not the day of the leader who would inflame the minds of the people, but the day of intelligence and judgment.

During the campaign it was said, among many other things, that I wanted only college men to hold public office. Of course, a thing like that is ridiculous, but I do believe that the man who has had a college education ought to be ashamed of himself if he does not know how to fill public office, but a college education is not a prerequisite. Any man who has studied history knows that some of the greatest men in the history of our nation were not college men—Washington and Lincoln.

In the years to come it is to the thoughtful and enlightened men of the country that the people will look for the solution of problems that will arise from time to time. America is calling her sons to service, and America will be great or small as they live up to the spirit of this year.

If you could have seen the audiences that I faced during the campaign and watched the look of intense interest on the faces of those men you would realize that they took an interest in the questions that were brought up, because those problems affected them vitally. America longs for some one to lead and direct. The people are no longer willing to follow blindly in the footsteps of men who have deceived them.

I wish to say that during my administration nothing that is contrary to the interest of the people will pass unrebuked, and if you think that such will be the case you want to get acquainted with the man whom you have chosen as your leader. It is my ambition to be the Governor of all the people of the State, and render to them the best services I am capable of rendering.

Mr. Wilson last night spoke for a half hour to the members of the university football team in a speech that had as its keynote "Sports for sport's sake." He walked from his home, Prospect, to the field house. He said that to him it was more desirable that the team be a representative team of Princeton than that it should win. He would be present, he said, on Saturday at the Yale game, and he was very confident that Princeton would win. He expects to enjoy the game greatly, because to him the new game of football seems far more enjoyable than the old.

Printed in the *Newark Evening News*, Nov. 10, 1910.
  [1] In football on November 12. Yale defeated Princeton, 5-3.
  [2] Wilson was referring to the widespread Democratic victories in the recent elections, about which see D. Lawrence to WW, Nov. 9, 1910, n. 2, Vol. 21.

❖

TALK TO FOOTBALL TEAM

. . . In a short talk to the members of the football team at the Field Club last night, previous to his speech at Prospect, Dr. Woodrow Wilson emphasized the importance of playing the game for the game itself rather than for mere success or individual glory.

Victory, he said, is surely to be desired but it should not overshadow all else so that the game itself sinks into insignificance. Success is of course exceedingly important but honor should outweigh all considerations of success so that that team which conducts itself in the most sportsmanlike manner is the one of which to be most proud. The spirit in which Princeton teams have often met defeat is more heroic and really greater than victories might have been.

In this connection Dr. Wilson said that the new rules are doing much to bring football to a high level as a sport, for its brutal features are being done away with and the better elements retained. The absence of grinding mass plays makes the game vastly more interesting to the spectators and at the same time it is rendered more desirable for the participants. The opportunity for unsportsmanlike playing is greatly reduced and hence it is now a game in which gentlemen can successfully engage.

Dr. Wilson next spoke of the great change which is going on all over the country in the attitude of the people toward mere material success. People are now returning to the earlier ideals of America, when honor and courage were exalted above success. The universities should be the leaders in this great movement, if they are to properly serve the nation. In athletics as well as elsewhere this tendency should be reflected and the team should conduct themselves in a manner which will bring honor more than glory to their Alma Mater.

Printed in the *Daily Princetonian*, Nov. 10, 1910; some editorial headings omitted.

Two Interviews

[Nov. 10, 1910]

WILSON SAYS PUBLICITY IS CURE FOR PUBLIC ILLS

New Governor Declares Election Was Evolution, Not Revolution, and a Healthy Sign—That Public Has Become Aroused to Its Own Best Interests

"Pitiless publicity is the sovereign cure for ills of government which can be applied easily and effectively by the men whom the people intrust temporarily with executive duties," yesterday declared Woodrow Wilson, Democratic Governor-elect of New Jersey.

Dr. Wilson was sitting in the study of the president's house at Princeton University when visited by a newspaper man. Heaps of telegrams and letters of congratulation were piled high upon the table in front him, including cablegrams from many parts of the world.

The man who is soon to desert "the quiet groves of the academy" for the capital of New Jersey shows no ill effects of the hard work of campaigning which he has been doing for nearly a month. His voice has no note of hoarseness, the color of his face is healthy, his keen gray eyes sparkle with the joy and pride of triumph, and his whole manner is that of a man who is preparing to buckle on the armor for new combats.

With the candor of a boy, Dr. Wilson discussed the causes which, in his opinion, led to the sweeping Democratic victories of last Tuesday.

"Looked at from the national standpoint," said he, "our success represents the reaction or recoil of the people from the system of special privilege which is growing all too rapidly in this country. Personalities had little to do with the triumphs of the Democracy Tuesday. The people have decided to take their government into their own hands once again and find out what the matter is—diagnose the ills that are afflicting the body politic and apply the proper remedies.

"The result is not a revolution; it is more an evolution. Such occurrences in a democracy are healthy signs. They denote that when the people are aroused, when they have their attention called to conditions which afflict them, they can be trusted to take hold and change them.

"In my campaign I told the voters that if they wanted to send me to Trenton as their chief executive I would be their voice in office. In that key I pitched my campaign. It was that which won the fight, and I mean to keep faith with them. There should be no mystery or secrecy in government. The men who administer the government of a democracy should not act as though that government was their property. It belongs to the people.

"In this spirit I shall deport myself at Trenton. I want the people of the State—all of the people of the State without regard to party or class—to know this. I promise them that everything which is done shall be made known to them in the slightest detail. I want the press to freely publish and criticise everything I do. The people shall be kept informed by me what goes on in the Capitol. To illustrate: If a bill to remedy an existing abuse shall be introduced in the Legislature and held up in committee an undue 'time the people ought to know why it is being held up and by whom. This I shall endeavor to ascertain for them and report upon."

"Did national issues cut a considerable figure in your campaign?" was asked.

"National issues necessarily were a factor," replied Dr. Wilson. "National issues will continue to appeal strongly, consciously or unconsciously, to the people of every State of the Union so long as protection runs riot at Washington. In principle, the protective system is sound. I realize that it has built up our industries. But there is such a thing as having entirely too much even of a good thing.

"That is what is the matter with protection today. It tops all of our economic evils. It shelters nearly every great trust in the country.

"In their last campaign the Republicans were pledged to reduce the tariff, but at the same time they also promised to revise the schedules as to guarantee a profit to manufacturers.

"No more vicious or undemocratic enunciation than this promise in the Republican platform of 1908 to guarantee a profit to manufacturers was ever proclaimed. It practically offers a bounty to industrial inefficiency. It tells manufacturers in the same line that they need not compete with each other or with the outside world, because the Government of the United States will safeguard them against loss; indeed, that the Government will see to it that they shall make a profit.

"The voters are just beginning to understand the enormity of this plank in the last Republican platfrom [platform] and are governing themselves accordingly. They know that the party in power has violated its pledge to reduce the tariff, and they suspect that one reason the promised reduction was not made is the desire of the party in power to assure a profit to manufacturers, no matter how it may effect the cost of living."

Dr. Wilson agrees with Judson Harmon that guilt is always personal. Upon this basis he would deal with the criminal practices of the trust. While believing that a proper reduction of schedules would weaken the power of the trusts for evil, as without excessive protection no trust could long survive in the United States, he would at the same time apply the old-time principles of the common law to them. Upon this point he said:

"We have witnessed in modern business the submergence of the individual within the organization, and yet the increase to an extraordinary degree of the power of the individual—of the individual who happens to control the organization. Most men are individuals no longer, so far as their business, its activities or its moralities are concerned. They are not units, but fractions; with their individuality and independence of choice in matters of business gone they have lost all their individual choice within the field of morals.

"They must do what they are told to do, or lose their connection with modern affairs. They are not at liberty to ask whether what they are told to do is right or wrong. They cannot get at the men who ordered it—have no access to them. They are mere cogs in a machine which has men for its parts.

"Corporations do not do wrong. Individuals do wrong, the individuals who direct and use them for selfish and illegitimate purposes, to the injury of society and the serious curtailment of private rights. You cannot punish corporations. Fines fall upon the wrong persons, more heavily upon the innocent than upon the guilty, as much upon those who knew nothing whatever of the transactions for which the fine is imposed as upon those who originated and carried them through—upon the stockholders and customers rather than upon the men who direct the policy of the business.

"If you dissolve the offending corporation you throw great undertakings out of gear. You merely drive what you are seeking to check into other forms or temporarily disorganize some important business altogether, to the infinite loss of thousands of entirely innocent persons and to the great inconvenience of society as a whole. You can never bring peace or command respect by such futilities.

"I regard the corporation as indispensible to modern business enterprise. I am not jealous of its size or might, if you will but abandon at the right point the fatuous, antiquated and quite unnecessary fiction which treats it as a legal person; if you will but cease to deal with it by means of your law as if it were a single individual and also—what every child may perceive it is not—a responsible individual.

"Such frictions [fictions] and analogies were innocent and convenient enough so long as corporations were comparatively small, and only one of many quite as important instrumentalities used in business—only a minor item in the economic order of society. But it is another matter now. They span society, and the responsibilities involved in their complex organization and action must be analyzed by the law as the responsibilities of society itself, in all its other aspects, have been."

Upon the subject of [the] "new nationalism,"[1] New Jersey's Governor-elect had little to say directly. He only smiled when it was mentioned, and remarked that it did not enter into the New Jersey campaign at all.

Printed in the *Trenton Evening Times*, Nov. 10, 1910; some editorial headings omitted.
[1] See n. 1 to the report of a speech in Jersey City, Sept. 21, 1910, Vol. 21.

✧

GOV.-ELECT WILSON IS TO BE SERVANT OF ALL CLASSES.

Woodrow Wilson began yesterday to put his teeth into the meat of the problems whose solution he will seek as Governor of New Jersey. The phrase was his own, spoken beside a desk in Prospect, his Princeton home. The desk was piled high with messages of congratulation upon a victory that had seemed overwhelming enough Tuesday night, but grew yesterday to proportions twice as great.

Literally by the thousand, and from every State in the Union, these congratulations poured in on Dr. Wilson. Hundreds of them added hopes for 1912 to the rejoicings over 1910, and, tired as he was from the strain of his campaign, the Governor-elect confessed the gratification he felt because so many were glad of his success. Two of the messages in particular pleased him. One was from Vivian M. Lewis, his Republican opponent.

"Accept my heartiest congratulations," it read. "May your administration be a most successful and happy one."[1]

The other came from Mayor Hampton H. Wayt of Staunton, Va., Dr. Wilson's birthplace. It read:

"The city of Staunton congratulates the Democratic party and yourself upon your selection and election."[2]

Dr. Wilson's formal acknowledgment to his new constituents was brief.

"I feel very deeply the honor the people of New Jersey have conferred upon me," he said. "I feel quite as deeply the responsibility it imposes upon me and my colleagues on the Democratic ticket. I shall, of course, put every power I possess into the service of the people as Governor of the State. It will be my pleasure and my privilege to serve them, not as the head of a party, but as the servant of all classes and all interests in an effort to promote the common welfare.

"I must regard the result of the election as a splendid vindica-

[1] V. M. Lewis to WW, Nov. 9, 1910, Vol. 21.
[2] H. H. Wayt to WW, Nov. 8, 1910, T telegram (WP, DLC).

tion of the conviction of the Democrats of this State that the people desired to turn away from personal attacks and party manoeuvres and base their political choices upon great questions of public policy and just administration."

Dr. Wilson added to this statement later in the day in an interview given to The World.

"Unhappily," Dr. Wilson began with a smile, "I have a business mind and I must have meat to put my teeth into when I try to talk. It's a hardship at a time like this, for I can never find a place to make a beginning."

"Don't you think that that 'business mind' is the very thing that the American people are looking for just now in their public men?" Dr. Wilson was asked.

"I do indeed," was his prompt reply. "But the business mind must not be one that confines itself to a single topic or a single interest. It must be a co-ordinating mind; it must seek not to solve this problem alone or to serve that interest alone; it must look and work toward the welding together in one organism of all interests for the solving, in so far as we may, of all the problems that confront us.

"That is the job of the statesman to-day. I was struck some time ago by an announcement made at a meeting of the leaders in the tobacco trade. 'We must meet public opinion more than half way,' these men were told by their chairman. To-day's greatest need is to develop the man who can foster that inclination. It is betraying itself all around us and in quarters where we might least expect to see it, but we cannot afford to wait for the impulse that suggests or advises it.

"Every day brings to my notice some new man who wants to get away from the old way of doing things. These tobacco men had that desire, and I believe that there was more than acknowledgment of antagonism in it. Conscience had its part, the desire to do right for right's sake, but we must do more than hail these changes of heart. Public opinion, moved by fits and starts, becomes uneven and unstable, and with such a public opinion we will fail of the needed result.

"It comes back to co-ordination. The province of law is to set up standards of conduct that will preserve and enhance the common welfare. The man we need, the man we must develop, is he who can lead us to the will that is square with those standards. If that will does not come the law must be invoked to an exercise of the power with which it is invested and to the confusion of conditions that so invariably comes with that [blank] commerce clause of the constitution.

"Well," he said, "I don't believe that the Constitution shouldn't grow."

"Have you heard the latest theory regarding cancer?" I asked him. "I don't know that I have, but the latest that has been brought to my attention is that the cancer is not the result of diseased tissue but of an access of life so hectic, so excited, that it burns the tissue away, and so breeds the deadly condition."

"My business has been the study of constitutional processes, not only in this country but the world over, and the explanation of those processes. We will never get to the place toward which we all aspire by any such excited life in any one part of the Constitution. [If] It is to grow as we grow, it must be throughout its structure. The theory that child labor, for example, may be classed under interstate commerce logically leads to the inclusion of more and more of the phases of intercourse until there is no reason why divorce and marriage laws should not be put there.

"It is rational and respectful interpretation that we need, above all else. What plans I may be said to have laid already come under that classification, I hope. What I hold regarding the Public Service Commission, for example, is that regulation and legislation must not be approached in any spirit of getting even, but in a lively appreciation of justice. We must find upon what foundation rates are built—the physical valuation of the railroads, their expenses, their needs or betterments—all the considerations that properly have a part in such a problem. Having found out all this we can determine where justice lies, and justice along [alone] must actuate us.

"The older I grow the less interest I find I have in general propositions of what we ought to do about this and that. They're not debatable; they're true enough, but of what use are they? It is toward concrete solutions of the problems about which these propositions are built that I find myself turning. Very particularly is that my state of mind just now, for I believe that New Jersey's problems are only those that the nation has been facing. They are not new, they are only unsolved.

"The tumult of controversy that has been raging in the magazines and the newspapers over these problems of everyday lige [life] has been of service. The charges and the conclusions that have been drawn from them have been extravagant sometimes, but they have at least pointed in the right direction. It has been very much like the Schomburgk line in the Venezuelan controversy, which Mr. Cleveland so well characterized as a line that had been drawn far beyond the true line in the hope that a compromise line might be drawn midway between the two and so give that much of an advantage.[3]

"We're getting tired these days of those who shout that things are all wrong. We've found that it is too much like the Scotchman's claret, 'It don't set you no for'arder.' But we mustn't forget our debt to the men who have shouted us awake. They have roused us and they have served us well in doing that, even though they show that having awakened us they lack the leadership the situation needs.

"What we need in my belief may be illustrated by a discussion I had once with Senator Beveridge. I was teasing him about having brought up his child labor bill under the wing of the inter-state commerce clause of the Constitution.[4]

"As I went about the State in my campaign I told Labor: 'Of course I am a friend of labor, but because I am its friend I am not hostile to capital.' To Capital I said: 'Of course I am the friend of the vested interests, as we call them, but because I am I shall not blind myself to the rights of labor.' I want only to be the servant of all classes and all interests to seek earnestly for concrete solution of the problems that are to-day concerning them all."

Printed in the New York *World*, Nov. 10, 1910; some editorial headings omitted.

[3] Perhaps Wilson had heard Cleveland make such a statement in conversation during his years of retirement in Princeton. Or he may have remembered similar statements made by Cleveland in his Stafford Little lectures at Princeton on the Venezuelan boundary controversy on March 27 and 28, 1901 (about which see the news report printed at March 30, 1901, Vol. 12), which were later published as Grover Cleveland, *The Venezuelan Boundary Controversy* (Princeton, N. J., 1913). See pp. 1-31, especially the following remark on p. 31: "We can hardly keep out of mind the methods of the shrewd, sharp trader who demands exorbitant terms, and at the same time invites negotiation, looking for a result abundantly profitable in the long range for the dicker which he has created."

[4] About Beveridge and his child labor bill, see *Constitutional Government in the United States*, n. 4, Vol. 18, p. 186.

To Robert Bridges

My dear Bobby,   Princeton, N. J. 10 November, 1910.

Thank you with all my heart for your note.[1] It brought me cheer; for I wanted to win your approval of my new adventure.

How bully it is about Charlie Talcott! I wish our elections threw us together in the same place! I want fellows I know and trust about me to keep me straight with advice.

Affectionately Yours,   Woodrow Wilson

WWTLS (Meyer Coll., DLC).
[1] R. Bridges to WW, Nov. 9, 1910, Vol. 21.

To Richard Heath Dabney

My dear Heath: Princeton, N. J. Nov. 10th, 1910.

This is just a line of thanks and affection. Your telegram[1] gave me the deepest pleasure.

Always affectionately yours,   Woodrow Wilson

TLS (Wilson-Dabney Corr., ViU).
[1] R. H. Dabney, to WW, Nov. 9, 1910.

To George Brinton McClellan Harvey

My dear Colonel Harvey: Princeton, N. J. Nov. 10th, 1910.

Your kind thought of me conveyed in your telegram[1] gave me a great deal of pleasure and I thank you for it most sincerely. I have been sustained throughout by your generous confidence in me.   Always faithfully yours,   Woodrow Wilson

TLS (WP, DLC).
[1] G. B. M. Harvey to WW, Nov. 8, 1910, Vol. 21.

To George Lawrence Record

[My dear Mr. Record: Princeton, N. J., c. Nov. 10, 1910]

I particularly appreciate your kind letter of congratulation,[1] and thank you for it with all my heart. I shall hope to justify your kindness   Cordially Yours,   [Woodrow Wilson]

WWhwL written on G. L. Record to WW, Nov. 9, 1910, Vol. 21.
[1] G. L. Record to WW, Nov. 9, 1910, Vol. 21.

To Edward Wright Sheldon

My dear Ed: Princeton, N. J. Nov. 10th, 1910.

Your telegram[1] gave me the greatest pleasure. The confidence you have shown in me has been one of my chief elements of strength and hope and I thank you for it with all my heart.

In haste,   Affectionately yours,   Woodrow Wilson

TLS (photostat in RSB Coll., DLC).
[1] E. W. Sheldon to WW, Nov. 9, 1910, Vol. 21.

To William Brewster Lee

My dear Chang: Princeton, N. J. November 10th, 1910.

Thank you for your telegram of yesterday[1] with all my heart, sent in the name of the Princeton Alumni Association of Western New York. It was very delightful to get such a message particularly when it was conveyed through you. Please express to the Princeton men concerned my warm appreciation and keep for yourself my sincere love.

Always affectionately yours,   Woodrow Wilson

TCL (RSB Coll., DLC).
[1] W. B. Lee to WW, Nov. 9, 1910, Vol. 21.

From Henry Cowper Gollan

My dear Governor,   Hamilton Bermuda 10-11-1910

My very heartiest congratulations to you on your magnificent victory, though if I were not afraid to offend against that wonderful fetish-word, democratic, I should be much more inclined to confine my congratulations to the voters of New Jersey whom you have enlightened, and whom you have so highly complimented by undertaking the management of their affairs. My wife,[1] who is still in the States though she rejoins me at the end of this month, has kept me well supplied with newspaper reports of your speeches so that I have been a most interested though invisible follower of your campaign. Strong believer though I am in parliamentary institutions, I dont believe there is any vital force in them apart from that derived from the men who work them. I cant think with Professor Garfield who I remember telling me, a propos of the grant of representative institutions to the Philipinos, that he believed there was some mystical virtue in such institutions which tended to make men in time capable of working them; and that is why I am so rejoiced to find you taking up the good citizen's burden. For when you become President, the whole world, & none more so than the British Empire, will benefit.

I suppose your duties will for a time prevent you from running down to Bermuda; but you must not altogether forget us and some day I trust you will re-appear among some very sincere admirers of yours.

With kindest regards
Believe me   Very sincerely yours   H. C. Gollan

ALS (WP, DLC).
[1] Marie Louise Norris Gollan.

From James Smith, Jr.

Newark N J Nov 10 [1910]

The result of the election affords convincing proof of your ability to lead. Your campaign has been without precedent. You have sought to arouse the people by appealing to their convictions. Your principal advocate has been your own intense earnestness. The response must be gratifying to you as it is to your friends. To the State it will mean incalculable benefit. Every well wishes [wisher] of good government will hail the result as a personal gain. You have now earned a rest which I hope you will permit yourself to take before assuming duties that are to bring you further honor. You have my earnest wishes for an administration in keeping with your high ideals and for a career marked always by public appreciation and approval

James Smith Jr

T telegram (WP, DLC).

From Judson Harmon

Columbus Ohio Nov 10 [19]10

Congratulation. Am glad to be in such good company

Judge [Judson] Harmon

T telegram (WP, DLC).

From Simeon Eben Baldwin

My dear Mr. Wilson: New Haven, Conn., Nov. 10, 1910.

Thanks for your telegram.[1] Your victory in New Jersey makes ours in Connecticut seem small; but we had tough odds to fight against and are tolerably content.

Yours sincerely,   Simeon E. Baldwin

TLS (WP, DLC).
   [1] WW to S. E. Baldwin, Nov. 9, 1910, Vol. 21.

From John Walter Smith[1]

Dear Governor: Baltimore, Md., November 10, 1910.

I want to add my congratulations to the congratulations of the country which are, no doubt, pouring in upon you on the occasion of your successful election as Governor of New Jersey.

Your magnificent canvass and your overwhelming success have excited admiration and rejoicing among all intelligent and patriotic people, I believe, of our land.

Personally, as a Democrat I look with confident hope to a more prosperous party era, as I believe with new, conservative and honorable men taking a prominent part in party councils, that we will, as a party, regain and hold the confidence of the sane, thinking people of the United States.

Your success, I am sure, nowhere gives more pleasure than to your many friends in the State of Maryland.

With kindest regards and best wishes for a happy and successful administration in the high office to which you have been lately called, I am,

Yours very sincerely,   John Walter Smith

TLS (WP, DLC).
[1] Democratic senator from Maryland since March 1908.

From John Joseph Fitzgerald[1]

My dear Mr. Wilson: Brooklyn, N. Y. November 10, 1910.

Permit me to extend my sincere congratulations upon the result in New Jersey. Your splendid campaign and its results have done much to revive the hopes of the Democracy throughout the country.

With best wishes for a successful administration, I am,

Very sincerely yours,   John J. Fitzgerald.

TLS (WP, DLC).
[1] Democratic representative from the 7th congressional district of New York.

From Edmund Favor Noel[1]

My Dear Sir: Jackson, Miss. November 10th., 1910

I noted with much interest the progress of your campaign in New Jersey reading the newspaper extracts from your address. You made a great fight and have won a splendid victory. To you and to the Democrats of New Jersey I extent [extend] my hearty congratulations.   Very sincerely   E. F. Noel

TLS (WP, DLC).
[1] Governor of Mississippi since 1908.

From Moses Taylor Pyne

My dear Woodrow   Princeton, N. J. 10 November 1910

I want to congratulate you most heartily on your splendid victory of Tuesday. Although we have differed much of late on matters of policy, I can assure you that I have always felt that our differences were only those of opinion and that I have always had towards you the same feeling of warm friendship that I have had for the past thirty odd years.

No one wishes you more success in your new line of work than I, nor will anyone be more gratified to see your continued advance.   Yours very sincerely   M Taylor Pyne

ALS (WP, DLC).

From John Lambert Cadwalader

My dear Dr. Wilson,   New York 10 November [1910].

I sincerely congratulate you on your election, but in particular because you individually have been able to change a hostile majority so to speak into an enormous majority in your favor.

There were other attending factors of course, but you *individually*, and personally—you in the flesh—& not vicariously, or in the spirit, have done the thing. All that is most gratifying, and most valuable, because you may expect that the people who supported you at the polls will be ready again to support you, in case there is danger of good measures being blocked, or bad ones put forward—and you can appeal *to the Country*!

Your friends and and [sic] well wishers of every class—not dependant at all on party affiliations[—]will be delighted at your success.   Faithfully yours   John L. Cadwalader

ALS (WP, DLC).

From William Simpson Elder[1]

My dear Mr. Wilson: Deadwood, So. Dak. November 10, 1910.

As a Princeton man, of the class of Eighty-six, I want to congratulate you on your splendid campaign and election as governor of New Jersey. It seems that the people of New Jersey are more keenly alive to the new conditions under which we are living than are the Alumni of Princeton University, or, perhaps I should say, the trustees of Princeton University. The Progressive Republicans and Democrats alike of the West have been watching your campaign with profound interest, and hoping for your success.

If the democrats nominate a candidate in 1912 with progressive ideas, give Jefferson and Jackson a rest, quit talking platitudes, and show an honest intention of getting the Government, National and State, out of the hands of the corporations and big moneyed interests, they will receive the support of this great Western section against most any candidate the republicans can nominate, except La Follette, and he has no possible show of being nominated. Party lines are not cutting much figure any more. I believe you are the man for the work, and I wish you all kinds of success in your administration, but I am satisfied you have a big task ahead of you, in eliminating the corporations from the control of New Jersey.

With kind regards, and best wishes, I remain

Yours very truly,   William S. Elder[2]

TLS (WP, DLC).

[1] Princeton 1886, a lawyer in Deadwood, S. D.

[2] Wilson's handwritten draft of his reply, written on the bottom of this letter, is as follows: "You make the right distinction between the trustees and the alumni, and what you say of the Democratic opportunity is eminently true."

From William Hughes

My dear Governor: Paterson, N. J., November 10, 1910.

I feel very much gratified at the result, not only because we won a victory, but because I think the stand you have taken and the fight you have made will result in a tremendous lot of permanent good to the people of this state, and as a consequence thereof to our party. There are a number of things that I am extremely anxious to talk over with you at the first opportunity. I am going to Greenwood Lake for a day or two and on my return, which will be about Sunday next, I will be free. Before I go to Washington I would like very much to have an interview with you at your convenience.

With very best wishes, I remain,

Very truly yours,   Wm. Hughes

TLS (WP, DLC).

From Elmer Hendrickson Geran[1]

Dear Sir: Jersey City, N. J., Nov. 10, 1910

The slogan of the Assembly Candidates from Monmouth County was, "We will help Woodrow Wilson help you."

Now that election is over, I desire to assure you of my purpose to assist you in the enactment of those laws which shall, from time to time, in your judgment, be for the fulfillment of Party pledges and other proper and needful legislation.

I rejoice in your election because I feel the call of the citizens for honest politics, honest government, and the enactment of laws without improper suggestion and unamerican control. Though less able, I am still as free as you to do my duty. I rejoice also in the opportunity afforded me as a Princeton man and a decent citizen of the community, to follow your leadership.

Yours very truly,   Elmer H. Geran

TLS (WP, DLC).
  [1] Princeton 1899 and former student of Wilson, member of the law firm of Geran and Walker of Jersey City. A Democratic assemblyman-elect from Monmouth County, he lived and practiced law also in Matawan, N. J.

From George Walbridge Perkins

My dear Dr. Wilson: New York. November 10th, 1910.

As a dyed-in-the-wool Republican I want to extend my heartiest congratulations on your great victory in New Jersey. The example you have set to the young men of the nation and the principles you stand for in public life mean everything that is worth while to our country for the future.

As to your views on the business questions of the hour, in my judgment they are absolutely sound. The idea that a corporation can have a being and be guilty of a wrong has always seemed to me to be perfectly absurd. It is the individual who acts and who should be held responsible. I realize that this is not the view that obtains in some of the business circles where I move, but nevertheless I am sure it is the right view and must ultimately prevail.

With all good wishes, believe me,

Sincerely yours,   Geo. W. Perkins

TLS (WP, DLC).

From William Mindred Johnson[1]

Personal.

My dear Dr Wilson,   Hot Springs, Va. Nov. 10, 1910

Although I was as you know an ardent supporter of Mr. Lewis, yet I trust you will not take it amiss if I write to congratulate you on your election and to express the hope and belief that your administration will be most successful.

I left New Jersey just in time on Tuesday afternoon to escape the landslide! Yours sincerely   W. M. Johnson.

ALS (WP, DLC).
[1] Princeton 1867; Republican state senator, 1895-1900; lawyer, businessman, and civic leader of Hackensack, N. J.

From Francis Preston Venable[1]

My dear Dr. Wilson: Chapel Hill, N. C. November 10, 1910.

Permit me, first, to extend my most cordial congratulations upon your great victory in New Jersey. Your friends all through this section have been watching with the greatest interest your splendid campaign and we all rejoice in your success.

I write to ask whether you will be at home in Princeton on Wednesday or Thursday of next week, namely, November 16th or 16th [17th]. I expect to be in New York and wish to run over and talk over a matter with you.[2]

Please let me hear from you at the Shoreham Hotel, Washington, D. C.

With kindest regards,

Sincerely yours,   Francis P. Venable

TLS (WP, DLC).
[1] President of the University of North Carolina since 1900.
[2] Whether Wilson could deliver the commencement address at Chapel Hill the following year. His address is printed at May 30, 1911, Vol. 23.

From Richard Evelyn Byrd[1]

My dear Wilson   Richmond, Va. Nov 10. 1910

Your triumphant election was expected but is none the less gratifying. Accept my congratulations. I regard you as the best & most available candidate for the Presidency on the democratic ticket of 1912. Should your ambitions turn in that direction I will give you my most hearty support.

Sincerely   Richard Evelyn Byrd

ALS (WP, DLC).
[1] Member of the law firm of O'Flaherty, Fulton, and Byrd of Richmond; Wilson's friend and fellow student at the University of Virginia; at this time Speaker of the Virginia House of Delegates.

From Edward William Bok

Philadelphia
November tenth Nineteen hundred and ten

My dear Doctor Wilson:

Good work! I certainly congratulate the people of New Jersey in knowing a good thing when they see it. And how they did see it! With joyful wishes, believe me

Very sincerely yours,   Edward Bok

TLS (WP, DLC).

From Charles Robert Hemphill[1]

Dear Dr. Wilson: Louisville, Ky. Nov. 10, 1910.

I wish to add warmest congratulations from Mrs. Hemphill[2] and myself on your election to the office of Governor of New Jersey. Your own friends in the South and your father's friends[3] will have highest satisfaction in the successful issue of your campaign. I have followed your canvass with deep interest and rejoiced in the frankness, skill, and wisdom with which you have discussed the issues of the times. I cannot but indulge the hope of seeing you go still higher, advancing to the Presidency of the United States.

Do not trouble to answer this: you have too many things to engage your attention. I just wish you to know the old-time friends are thinking of you.

With kindest regards for Mrs. Wilson and yourself, and hearty good wishes for your successful and happy discharge of your new duties.   Faithfully Yours,   Charles R. Hemphill.

ALS (WP, DLC).
[1] President of the Presbyterian Theological Seminary of Kentucky in Louisville.
[2] Emma Muller Hemphill.
[3] Hemphill had been a student of Joseph Ruggles Wilson at Columbia Theological Seminary, 1871-74.

From Frederick A. Duneka[1]

My Dear Mr. Wilson: New York Nov. 10, 1910.

After all, a *Man* counts for something. We are all of us grateful to you for being elected. May all the good fairies guard and guide you.   Yours Sincerely   F A Duneka

ALS (WP, DLC).
[1] An editor at Harper and Bros.

From William Mann Irvine[1]

Dear Dr. Wilson: Mercersburg, Pa., November 10, 1910.

I have not yet met a single man in this section of the country who is not delighted beyond words by your election to the Governorship of New Jersey. Every Princeton man is proud of you. You made the cleanest and finest campaign that was made anywhere in all the States. I hope that in two years from this time the entire Nation will say to you as we used to say to the Neophytes in Whig Hall: "Step Higher!" I do not hesitate to predict for you one of the most satisfactory and brilliant administrations Jersey has ever seen.

Trusting this note will find all the members of your family well, I am, with kindest regards, in which Mrs. Irvine[2] joins me,
                    Most cordially yours,   W. M. Irvine.
TLS (WP, DLC).
  [1] Princeton 1888, headmaster of the Mercersburg Academy since 1893.
  [2] Camille Hart Irvine.

From Calvin Easton Brodhead[1]

My Dear Governor: Plainfield, N. J. Nov. 10, 1910.

Please accept my heartiest congratulations on your great victory. I am happy to say that I went in along with you on the Assembly ticket. It was generally considered impossible to elect a Democratic Assemblyman from Union county, but of course they did not look for such a tidal wave as you started.

We did splendidly in Plainfield, carrying it for you by about 137 votes. The normal Republican majority is about 2,000. Our mutual friend Mr. Ellis[2] has been indefatigable throughout the campaign and a great deal of the success of the ticket in Plainfield is due to his efforts.

With kind regards, I am,
                    Yours very truly,   Calvin E. Brodhead.
TLS (WP, DLC).
  [1] New York sales agent for the Scranton Bolt and Nut Co. and assemblyman-elect from Union County.
  [2] Leroy J. Ellis, New York agent for the Norfolk & Western Railway, who lived in Plainfield, N. J., and was president of the Plainfield Democratic Club.

From Mark Anthony Sullivan

My dear Dr. Wilson: Jersey City, N. J., Nov. 10, 1910.

I desire to congratulate you on your splendid victory. It must be very satisfying to have won, and very flattering to have such a large majority.

There can be no doubt of the temper or the will of the people of the State, and what appears to me to be the greatest opportunity that has confronted any Jerseyman, is yours. May you be given the strength to carry out the program which you have mapped out, and as a reward therefor may you be chosen to serve the whole people of our Union, as its President, is my earnest wish.   Very truly yours,   Mark A Sullivan

TLS (WP, DLC).

From Samuel Shepard Dennis[1]

My dear Dr. Wilson: Newark, New Jersey. November 10, 1910.

Only a line to wish you every success in the new office to which the people of New Jersey elected you last Tuesday by such an overwhelming majority. I do not recall that I have ever voted the Democratic ticket before, but I could not lose so good an opportunity as your election to our highest office afforded me.

In common with many other independent men, I take you at your word, and believe that you will be a Governor of the whole people, and not a Governor of any special interests; also, that you will be governed by your own views of what is right and proper, and not by the dictates of a certain set of men.

I hope I may see you at Mr. Carnegie's next Wednesday, as Mrs. Dennis[2] and I expect to go there to meet the Trustees of the Carnegie Foundation Fund[3] at that time.

With kind regards and best wishes, believe me
                    Very truly yours,   Samuel S. Dennis.

TLS (WP, DLC).
  [1] President of the Howard Savings Institution of Newark and trustee and director of several corporations.
  [2] Eliza Thomas Dennis.
  [3] That is, the Carnegie Foundation for the Advancement of Teaching.

To Henry Smith Pritchett

My dear Pritchett,   Princeton, N. J. 11 November, 1910.

Thank you sincerely for the suggestion.[1] It is a very wise and proper one, and I comply with it with pleasure. I am obliged to you for making it. I enclose the letter revised.

In haste, with warmest appreciation,
                    Faithfully Yours,   Woodrow Wilson

I value very highly your kind letter about my election,[2]—and the advice is most wise and sound. I am quite aware of the danger of the oratorical impulse and am, as a matter of fact, on my guard against it, but probably not always enough on my guard. Your letters have given me a great deal of pleasure and reassurance: and your counsel will always be needed and welcomed.

W. W.

WWTLS (H. S. Pritchett Papers, DLC).

1 As this note will recount, Pritchett's "suggestion" was made during a recent conference with Wilson in Princeton, and extant correspondence between the two men and other materials make it clear that it related to Wilson's application for a retirement pension from the Carnegie Foundation for the Advancement of Teaching. As early as November 1908, Wilson was considering "retiring" to some role in public affairs and counted on a Carnegie pension of $4,000 annually, or half his salary as president of Princeton (WW to Mary A. H. Peck, Nov. 2, 1908, Vol. 18).

Before 1909, the foundation had awarded standard pensions at sixty-five after a minimum of fifteen years of service and smaller pensions, regardless of age, after twenty-five years. The board of trustees, at a meeting in November of that year, adopted a new rule stipulating that a professor might be pensioned after twenty-five years of service before he reached sixty-five only if he were disabled. This provision obviously eliminated Wilson's chances of receiving a pension before he reached the normal retirement age.

According to a memorandum by Pritchett, dated June 6, 1932 (photocopy in WC, NjP), Wilson, at the meeting in November 1909, made two moves to protect his future prospects. The first was to introduce a resolution to the effect that when twenty-five years of service included tenure as a college or university president, the applicant should be eligible for a service pension regardless of age. Pritchett recalled that several trustees objected to this proposal because, since the board was dominated by college heads, such an action would open them to the charge of self-interest. Wilson thereupon withdrew his motion. Just before the meeting adjourned, Wilson brought the matter up again, urging the trustees to "safeguard the interests" of those whose twenty-five years included presidential service (see also H. S. Pritchett to WW, Jan. 24, 1911). He argued that a college president endured greater strain than a professor and that this ought to be taken into account, particularly in cases of heads of institutions who had served with distinction. Thereupon the trustees approved an amendment offered by Wilson to the new pension rule, stating that an award might also be granted "after the years of service . . . to the executive head of an institution who has displayed distinguished ability as a teacher and educational administrator." Carnegie Foundation for the Advancement of Teaching, *Fourth Annual Report of the President and of the Treasurer* (New York, 1909), p. 189.

On this somewhat ambiguous basis (for example, the new rule did not specify whether a retiring president had to be sixty-five years of age to receive a pension), Wilson made his application. The first documentary evidence of his contact with Pritchett about this matter is Pritchett's letter to Wilson of November 3, 1910, Vol. 21, which suggests that Pritchett was at first favorably disposed toward granting the award.

At some time between November 3 and 11, 1910, Wilson drafted his letter of application, which, as Pritchett remembered it, discussed at length his personal affairs and uncertain future. Again according to his memorandum, Pritchett found the letter very injudicious and feared that it might be used against Wilson if it was made public. Traveling to Princeton, he returned the letter to Wilson and advised him to destroy it, adding that Wilson's amendment did not cover his own case. Wilson allegedly responded that he ought to know the meaning of the amendment because he was its author. Moreover, Wilson went on, since he was embarking upon a public career for unselfish reasons and therefore exposing his family to unknown risks, the trustees should be happy to support him. Pritchett answered that the Carnegie Foundation had not been established to support former college presidents in political careers and that, in any event, he did not see how it could make an exception for a man only fifty-three years old. He again urged Wilson to withdraw his application. Pritchett repeated many of these arguments in his letter to Wilson printed at December 3, 1910. (For a similar but less candid account, see H. S. Pritchett to N. Hapgood, Jan. 20, 1912, printed in the *New York Times*, June 25, 1912.)

However, Wilson did not withdraw his letter of application. Pritchett's suggestion, to which Wilson's letter of November 11, 1910, referred, was that he submit the application through the presiding officer of Princeton University.

Neither Wilson's original letter of application nor the revised version that he sent on November 11, 1910, is extant in the files of the Carnegie Foundation for the Advancement of Teaching, in Pritchett's private papers, or in any other collection known to the Editors.

2 H. S. Pritchett to WW, Nov. 9, 1910. Vol. 21.

To Winthrop More Daniels

My dear Daniels: Princeton, N. J. November 11th, 1910.

I want to take this early opportunity to express my deep appreciation of the interest you showed in the campaign and the very important service you rendered to promote its result. I need not tell you how much I myself have valued your counsel or how much I shall depend upon it in the months to come.

With warmest regard,

Faithfully yours,   Woodrow Wilson

TLS (Wilson-Daniels Corr., CtY).

To Howard Carrow[1]

My dear Mr. Carrow: Princeton, N. J. November 11th, 1910.

The campaign is over. We have won a most notable victory. I know the important part you played in the campaign, by giving your services as a speaker, and I want to send you this word of cordial thanks and appreciation. The good old party now has a chance to re-establish itself in the confidence of the State.

With much regard,

Sincerely yours,   Woodrow Wilson

TLS (WP, DLC).

1 Former judge of the Camden District Court, 1891-96; member-at-large of the Democratic State Committee, 1898-1912; at this time practicing law in Camden.

To Thomas Bell Love

My dear Mr. Love: Princeton, N. J. November 11, 1910.

I need not tell you how deeply I appreciated your generous message,[1] but I must give myself the pleasure of doing so, if only to send in return my heartfelt thanks.

Gratefully yours,   Woodrow Wilson

TCL (RSB Coll., DLC).

1 T. B. Love to WW, Nov. 8, 1910, Vol. 21.

To Alexander Mitchell Palmer

My dear Mr. Palmer: Princeton, N. J. Nov. 11, 1910.

I need not tell you how deeply I appreciated your generous message,[1] but I must give myself the pleasure of doing so, if only to send in return my own warm regards and greetings along with my heartfelt thanks.

Gratefully yours,   Woodrow Wilson

TLS (WP, DLC).
[1] A. M. Palmer to WW, Nov. 9, 1910, Vol. 21.

From Oswald Garrison Villard

My dear Dr. Wilson: New York November 11, 1910.

To add another to the mass of congratulations you are receiving and cannot possibly answer may seem to you unkind, but I cannot resist the temptation to tell you of the great happiness in this office over your tremendous victory. Not in my recollection has the entire staff so enjoyed taking part in a campaign as it has in yours. I wish you not merely personal success as Governor, but the power to advance those true democratic American principles which so far transcend all questions of personality or party.

With warm regards,

Faithfully yours,   Oswald Garrison Villard.

TLS (WP, DLC).

From Robert Davis

My dear Doctor Wilson: Jersey City, N. J. Nov 11/10

There are a few things that I feel that I should say to you at this time.

The first is to tell you that your grand victory has done more to restore me to health than the Doctors have been able to do.[1] I feel that last tuesdays battle brought to our party what we stood most in need of, some big men. And in my humble opinion the very biggest of these is Woodrow Wilson

Much has been said, during the past campaign, about 'bosses.' Inasmuch as I have been specifically named as one of them, I feel it incumbent on me to tell you, that, if I have any influence with the Hudson delegation they will stand a unit for every measure that you deem of importance, and they will stand to the last ditch.

I see in your election the regeneration of the Democratic party in this state, and I feel that, under your able leadership, events of the next two years will enable us to go to the next National convention with a candidate for the highest office in the gift of the American people in the person of Woodrow Wilson. With the most heartfelt wishes for your future success, I am,

Sincerely yours,   Robert Davis

TLS (WP, DLC).
¹ Davis was in the last stage of a terminal illness. He died on January 9, 1911.

From James Ford Rhodes

Dear Mr. Wilson   Boston Nov. 11th 1910

I congratulate you heartily on your election.

Whether your quitting the attractions of academic life for politics (in the highest sense) is wholly self-sacrifice or not, everyone who loves study and book-learning must rejoice that you are bringing in a masterly way those influences into the field of affairs.

The American Historical Association and the American Academy of Arts and Letters are proud of their member.

With kind regards and best wishes

I am   Very truly yours   James F. Rhodes

ALS (WP, DLC).

From Franklin William Fort¹

My dear Dr. Wilson,   Newark, New Jersey Nov. 11th, 1910.

May I offer my congratulations upon the contest you waged, the position you assumed and the victory you won? While I cannot say that I am glad to see your party successful, if it had to be a Democrat, I'm mighty glad the choice is yourself. I found it exceedingly hard, fond as I am of Mr. Lewis, to make any speeches on the stump except by ignoring you utterly and talking only about him. We Republicans take it very hard that the Democrats should have nominated a man with an impregnable record and an absolute disinclination to make any helpful breaks.

In the sincere hope that your administration may be as creditable and successful as your campaign,

I am   Very sincerely your friend,   Franklin W. Fort

ALS (WP, DLC).
¹ Princeton 1901, attorney of Newark, and son of Governor John Franklin Fort.

From Mahlon Pitney[1]

My Dear Woodrow,   Morristown, N. J. Nov. 11, 1910.

Permit me, as a college class-mate, fellow-"Alligator,"[2] and personal friend and admirer, to extend my warm congratulations upon your brilliant success in the campaign just terminated. The unprecedented vote that you received throughout the state is ample proof that you have gained, as you have deserved, the entire confidence of the people.

I hope and trust you will have equal success in your administration of the office of governor. It will be to me a source of much pleasure to be associated with you in the work of the Board of Pardons, and in the other little matters that bring Governor and Chancellor into official contact. But, with your permission, I shall hope to see you, personally and unofficially, more often at least than heretofore. If I can be of service to you at any time, do not fail to command me, and I will try to respond in the spirit of Princeton and of "Old Seventy-Nine."

Very Cordially Yours,   Mahlon Pitney.

TLS (WP, DLC).

[1] Chancellor of New Jersey, 1908-12; Associate Justice of the United States Supreme Court, 1912-22.

[2] An ephemeral eating club at Princeton, of which Wilson and Pitney were members from 1877 to 1879.

From William T. Ferguson

My dear Governor: Washington, D. C. Nov. 11/10.

Accept my heartiest congratulations. I hope that your administration will be a success and prove to my colored friends that you are our friend.

I hope that you and your friends will prove to the country that the Tillman's, Vardaman's and Heflin's[1] are not the dominant factors of your party.

May good health attend you.

Very truly yours,   W T Ferguson

ALS (WP, DLC).

[1] Benjamin Ryan Tillman, Governor of South Carolina, 1890-1894, United States senator since 1895; James Kimble Vardaman, Governor of Mississippi, 1904-1908; James Thomas Heflin, congressman from Alabama since 1904. All were blatant anti-Negro agitators.

From Allan Bartholomew Walsh[1]

Dear Governor: Trenton, November 11, 1910

Kindly accept my sincere and hearty congratulations on your splendid victory of last Tuesday. I know that you will make as creditable a record during your administration as you did as President of Princeton University.

I want to assure you of my hearty sympathy with the principles for which you stand. As the sole Democratic representative in the Legislature from your home county, I would esteem it an honor to introduce bills embodying these principles.

When it suits your convenience I would be glad to visit you and take counsel on such matters as one occupying the position I do should consider with the leader of my party. Any time you may state will be agreeable to me.

With kindest wishes, believe me,

Yours very sincerely,   Allan B. Walsh

TLS (WP, DLC).
[1] Democratic assemblyman-elect from Mercer County, foreman of the electrical testing department of John A. Roeblings Sons' Co. of Trenton, N. J.

To Cleveland Hoadley Dodge

My dear Cleve: Princeton, N. J. Nov. 12th, 1910.

I need not tell you how your telegram[1] went to my heart. It is very delightful to have your confidence and affection and I thank you for the message from the bottom of my heart.

In haste,   Affectionately yours,   Woodrow Wilson

TLS (WC, NjP).
[1] C. H. Dodge to WW, Nov. 9, 1910, T telegram (WP, DLC); Dodge's letter of congratulation is printed at Nov. 9, 1910, Vol. 21.

To Cyrus Hall McCormick

My dear Cyrus: Princeton, N. J. Nov. 12th, 1910.

I need not tell you how deeply I appreciated your telegram of congratulation.[1] There is no one I would rather have believe in me than yourself and I shall hope very often to be guided by your council and advice in days to come.

Always affectionately yours,   Woodrow Wilson

TLS (WP, DLC).
[1] C. H. McCormick to WW, Nov. 9, 1910, Vol. 21.

To James Waddel Alexander

My dear Mr. Alexander: Princeton, N. J. November 12, 1910

I appreciate very warmly your very generous letter of November 9th.[1] It is delightful that men whom I have known a long time, and whom I have known as my friends, should feel as you do about my election.

Cordially and faithfully yours,   Woodrow Wilson

TLS (WC, NjP).
[1] J. W. Alexander to WW, Nov. 9, 1910, Vol. 21.

To Jacob Gould Schurman

Princeton, N. J.
My dear President Schurman: November 12, 1910

Allow me to thank you most cordially for your very generous letter of November 9th.[1] It has given me the deepest pleasure.

I need not tell you how much it encourages me that you should think as you do about my efforts in politics. I know your own deep interest in public affairs, and your own courage in the expression of your opinions, and that makes me value your letter at its true worth.

Cordially and faithfully yours,   Woodrow Wilson

TLS (J. G. Schurman Papers, NIC).
[1] J. G. Schurman to WW, Nov. 9, 1910, Vol. 21.

To Thomas Nelson Page

Dear Mr. Page: Princeton, N. J. November 12, 1910

You are very generous in your thought of me and I thank you very warmly for your kindness in sending me the cordial lines of congratulation,[1] which have given me so much pleasure.

Sincerely yours,   Woodrow Wilson

TLS (T. N. Page Papers, NcD).
[1] T. N. Page to WW, Nov. 9, 1910, Vol. 21.

To Harry Augustus Garfield

My dear Garfield: Princeton, N. J. November 12, 1910

Thank you warmly for your letter of November 9th.[1] It has of course given me the deepest pleasure. I shall wish more and

more as the weeks go on that I had you at hand to consult with,
I should turn to you so often.

Always affectionately yours,   Woodrow Wilson

TLS (H. A. Garfield Papers, DLC).
    [1] H. A. Garfield to WW, Nov. 9, 1910, Vol. 21.

From Edward E. Lee[1]

My dear Sir: New York, Nov. 12, 1910.

The United Colored Democracy of the Borough of Manhattan
and the Bronx, of which I am Chief, extends to you congratulations upon your election as Governor of the State of New Jersey.

We feel proud of the fact that the Negroes throughout this
country are awakened to the fact that their interest in the government of this country lies in their affiliation with the great
political party of which you are one of its leaders.

We feel that with such men as you and other noble men who
have been elected to office by the Democratic party in this campaign, the Negroes of this country at large can safely trust their
welfare in their hands believing that justice will be meted out
to them regardless of race, color or creed.

Hoping you a successful administration of the affairs of your
great State and the elevation, perhaps, to a higher position within
the government of this great country, I remain,

Sincerely yours,   Edward E. Lee[2]

TLS (WP, DLC).
    [1] Chief of the United Colored Democracy of the Boroughs of Manhattan and
the Bronx, who ran an employment agency for domestic servants.
    [2] Wilson wrote on the bottom of the letter: "Add: I particularly appreciate
your generous confidence in my friendship for my African fellow countrymen."

From William Kent[1]

Confidential

Dear Mr. Wilson: Kentfield, Cal., Nov. 12, 1910

I wish to congratulate the country as well as your State on
your splendid victory which was the result of a moral upheaval
and in no sense a partisan triumph

In my little campaign at the other edge of the continent I won
out against a Democratic majority given in the Governorship
fight, of 5000, with a majority of 3100. I was bitterly opposed by
both norporate [corporate] interests and the standpatters in the

Republican party. The contest for Governor[2] and the contest in this Congressional District, show that the people here are alive to the situation.

I followed your campaign with great interest and realize that we are working on the same lines. I think it is safe to say that no Republican candidate has ever taken as radical ground against the tariff as I have and I do not believe any one running on that ticket has ever played the non-partisan role as hard as I have.

I hope to see you a candidate for the Presidency at the next election and in such event, unless Pinchot,[3] La Follette or some equally progressive man is on the Republican side, I shall give you my heartiest support.   Yours truly,   Wm. Kent

TLS (WP, DLC).

[1] Heir to a traction fortune in Chicago where he had been involved in various reform movements, Kent had moved to California in 1908 and had just been elected to Congress from the 2nd congressional district.

[2] Hiram Warren Johnson, Republican insurgent and candidate of the Lincoln-Roosevelt League wing of the California Republican party, had defeated the Democrat, Theodore Arlington Bell, in a closely-contested race for governor. Actually, both Johnson and Bell advanced similar progressive views, and both strongly denounced the alleged domination of the state government by the Southern Pacific Railroad. Johnson's chief advantage in the campaign was the traditional Republicanism of California voters. See George E. Mowry, *The California Progressives* (Berkeley and Los Angeles, 1951), pp. 105-34.

[3] Gifford Pinchot, whom President Taft had dismissed earlier in 1910 as chief forester in the Department of Agriculture and who was at this time president of the National Conservation Association. For the controversy leading to his dismissal, see n. 3 to the speech printed at Nov. 4, 1910, Vol. 21.

From Hamilton Holt[1]

My dear President Wilson,   New York November 12th, 1910.

Fabian Franklin[2] of the *New York Evening Post* has written a short sketch of you which will appear in THE INDEPENDENT out Thursday.[3] I am very anxious to have you write an article for THE INDEPENDENT on the causes of the recent Democratic landslide thruout the country and the opportunities before the Democratic Party. Such an article coming from you at this time would be widely read and would undoubtedly do a great deal of good.[4]

          Very truly yours,   Hamilton Holt

TLS (WP, DLC).

[1] Managing editor of *The Independent*.

[2] Editor of the *Baltimore News*, 1895-1908, at this time associate editor of the New York *Evening Post*.

[3] "New Democratic Governors," *Independent*, LXIX (Nov. 17, 1910), 1067-74. Wilson was the first and most prominently featured in these sketches.

[4] Wilson did not write the article.

From James Bryce

My dear President Wilson   Monte Video [Uruguay] Nov. 12/10

We have just heard of your election and desire to congratulate you most heartily.

Though one can't repress some regret at the interruption of your schemes for developing new and valuable forms of life at Princeton, still the example of your selection for a post offering such opportunities of public service as the Governorship of a State like New Jersey is of such far reaching importance as to efface that regret.

Let me wish you all success in the office, and a long and honoured career of usefulness and distinction in the service of State and Nation.

With our warm regards and sincere congratulations to Mrs. Wilson, I am   Very truly yours   James Bryce

ALS (WP, DLC).

From George Howe III, with Enclosure

Dear Uncle Woodrow,   Chapel Hill, N. C. Nov 12, 1910

Tardy congratulations, but not the less sincere and enthusiastic for all their tardiness! I have been waiting to get the final reports, but can get no definite news. Your name is on everybody's lips. For some months a few of us have been speaking of you as "our next President," and others smiled at the phrase. The smiling ones are now confidently using the phrase themselves. We know that "interesting things" are going to happen in New Jersey which will give promise of the greater things that you will do after 1912.

I have followed your campaign with absorbing interest and it has been a revelation to me, both of political things and of yourself. I doubt if there has ever been another like it—so far removed from the usual tricks & intrigues of politicians, so triumphant on its basis of truth and wisdom.

But, all the same, I am sorry for old Princeton in her loss.

My best love to all, & again & again my warmest, sincerest congratulations.   Affectionately,   George Howe

They are already calling me the President's nephew, & I am even receiving letters of congratulation! I inclose a sample.

ALS (WP, DLC).

ENCLOSURE

Augustine Thomas Smythe[1] to George Howe III

Dear George: Charleston, S. C., Nov. 9th, 1910.

I write to congratulate you on the handsome election of Dr. Wilson.

While not directly concerned, or under his jurisdiction, still I watched his career with great interest, and thought it was a very good sign of the times when a man of his ability and pursuits was willing to take political office and administer the affairs of a State. It is an example that can well be followed by other men.

So please accept my sincere congratulations, and with love to Margaret,[2] believe me

Yours truly,   Augustine T. Smythe

TLS (WP, DLC).
[1] Member of the South Carolina Senate, 1880-1894, lawyer of Charleston, S. C., in the firm of Smythe, Lee & Frost.
[2] Howe's wife, Margaret Smyth Flinn Howe.

From Jonathan Bourne, Jr.[1]

My dear Sir: [Washington] Nov. 12, 1910.

I realize that it is somewhat unique for a Republican United States Senator to congratulate a Democrat upon his election to the Governorship of a state, but I take pleasure in congratulating you, not upon Democratic success, but upon the character of campaign you conducted and your declaration that you are and will be against political bosses not only in the Republican party but in your own party as well. This declaration shows that you recognize that you are to be the chief public servant of all the people of your community and not their chief dictator. Many executives have not apparently realized the true function of their office, namely, that they are the instrument and not the will of the people.

I enclose herewith a copy of an address I delivered in the Senate on May 5, last, on the subject of Popular vs. Delegated Government.[2] I trust you will find time to read it and will be glad to have such comments or criticisms as you choose to make. I feel that the country is entitled to the views of all men of national prominence, such as yourself, upon the subject of popular government,—the initiative and referendum, direct primary, corrupt practices and recall laws.

I also enclose a copy of an interview of mine appearing in the Washington Star the evening before election.[3] Would appreciate such comments as you care to make on my analysis of the political evolution that this country is now undergoing.

Yours very truly,   Jonathan Bourne Jr

TLS (WP, DLC).
    1 Insurgent Republican senator from Oregon.
    2 A clipping of a speech entitled "Knell of Bossism." It was reprinted in the *Congressional Record*, 61st Cong., 2nd sess., pp. 5823-30.
    3 This enclosure of a clipping from the *Washington Evening Star*, Nov. 7, 1910, is missing.

From Caleb Thomas Winchester[1]

My dear Governor Wilson: Middletown, Conn., Nov. 12, 1910.

Will you allow me to be one of the hundreds of people who are now doubtless telling you by letter how glad they are that they may address you in that style. Some of us old mugwumps have been pretty well pleased at the recent news from several states; but nothing has been so gratifying as the nature and the results of your campaign. A canvass conducted frankly and squarely on high political principles, without narrow partisan bias and without bitter personalities or reckless charges, and resulting in overwhelming success—that is something to make any American citizen glad and proud.

And while all lovers of clean politics and good government must be gratified at your success, you may well believe that your old personal friends have felt an especial thrill of pleasure and pride. Some of us followed the campaign in New Jersey with intense interest, and read all reports of your speeches we could find. Personally, I felt last Wednesday morning like giving an old-fashioned Methodistic shout!

You will not—must not—take any time to acknowledge this note, but only permit me me [sic] to sign myself, as always,

Yours most cordially,   C. T. Winchester.

TLS (WP, DLC).
    1 Old friend and former colleague, Olin Professor of English Literature at Wesleyan University.

From Frank Thilly[1]

My dear President Wilson: [Philadelphia] November 12, 1910

I am just returning home from the meeting of the Association of American Universities and can no longer restrain my pent-up joy over your glorious victory. You and your opponent have given the country a magnificent example of how a political campaign ought to be conducted, and it is to be hoped that the dignity, honesty, cordiality, and good humor which marked your conduct will find many imitators hereafter. With the heartiest congratulations and wishes for the success of your administration, I am   Very sincerely yours,   Frank Thilly

ALS (WP, DLC).
   [1] Former member of the Princeton faculty, at this time Professor of Philosophy at Cornell University.

To Jonathan Bourne, Jr.

[My dear Senator Bourne: Princeton, N. J., c. Nov. 13, 1910]

   I sincerely appreciate your interesting and generous letter, and wish to thank you for it most warmly. I must turn aside from a multitude of present distractions to thank you also for the speech and interview you were kind enough to send. I shall look forward with great interest to reading them.

                    Sincerely Yours,   [Woodrow Wilson]

WWTL typed on J. Bourne, Jr., to WW, Nov. 12, 1910.

From Philip Barling Ben Greet[1]

                                           Asbury N. J.
Dear Governor Woodrow Wilson   Sunday, Nov. 13 [1910]

   Im not in politics except stage politics but I want to congratulate the State in which I so often live during my vacations on your accession to its interests[.] I always remember your great kindnesses to me & mine at my favourite University—Princeton[.][2] I trust *you* will have as much happiness as you seem to give others.   Yours very truly   Ben Greet

ALS (WP, DLC).
   [1] Theatrical manager and producer who had led touring repertory companies through the United Kingdom and the United States since the 1880s.
   [2] When his players performed there in 1904. See WW to EAW, April 8, 1904, n. 1, and May 19, 1904, both in Vol. 15.

To James Edgar Martine

My Dear Mr. Martine: Princeton, N. J., November 14, 1910.

   It was a very great victory, and you were one of the most valiant fighters in it. Words of appreciation do not pay the debt; but it is delightful to speak them where they are so well appreciated and deserved. We shall now lift the old party to new success.

With warmest regards and appreciation,

Faithfully yours,   Woodrow Wilson.

Printed in the *Newark Sunday Call*, Nov. 20, 1910.

To Azel Washburn Hazen

My dear Doctor Hazen: Princeton, N. J. November 14, 1910

It was delightful to receive your message of congratulation.[1] You may be sure that it pleased me as much as any that came to me. It is a constant stimulation to me to try to deserve your generous friendship.

Mrs. Wilson joins me in warmest regards to you all.

Faithfully yours,   Woodrow Wilson

TLS (received from Frances Hazen Bulkeley).
[1] A. W. Hazen to WW, Nov. 9, 1910, Vol. 21.

To John Ralph Hardin

My dear Mr. Hardin: Princeton, N. J. November 14, 1910

I have time for only a line of thanks for your generous note of the 9th,[1] but it is a line which carries very warm and hearty appreciation of your generous kindness. It was delightful to come upon you once and again in the campaign and to know you were helping.

Cordially and sincerely yours,   Woodrow Wilson

TLS (WC, NjP).
[1] J. R. Hardin to WW, Nov. 9, 1910, Vol. 21.

To Isaac Wayne MacVeagh

My dear Mr. McVeigh: Princeton, N. J. November 14, 1910

Your letter of November 9th[1] is generous and delightful. I do not deserve the praise which it bestows but it is none the less encouraging to receive it, and it will be delightful to try to deserve some small part of it. I look just as you do upon the opportunity conferred on me and hope with all my heart that I may be able to live up to it, at any rate, in some degree.

Cordially and faithfully yours,   Woodrow Wilson

TLS (I. W. MacVeagh Papers, PHi).
[1] I. W. MacVeagh to WW, Nov. 9, 1910, ALS (WP, DLC).

To Henry Lee Higginson

My dear Major Higginson: Princeton, N. J. November 14, 1910

Thank you most warmly for your generous message of congratulation.[1]

I am deeply distressed to learn what you think of Mr. Foss. Seeing him only at a distance I had hoped that he represented what the rest of us are trying to represent. Certainly the cause of good government goes forward by irregular strides, and sometimes through disappointing means.

Cordially yours,   Woodrow Wilson

TLS (H. L. Higginson Coll., MH-BA).
[1] H. L. Higginson to WW, Nov. 9, 1910, Vol. 21.

From George Brinton McClellan Harvey

Dear Mr Wilson: New York November 14th, 1910.

Thank you for your note.[1]

I enclose a short editorial which will appear in this week's Harper's Weekly. Denials[2] would have served only as grist for the mill of misrepresentation during the campaign, but it seems to me that these few words may be said now with propriety.[3]

Everybody who contributed to the campaign expenses through me did so voluntarily, with no expectation that you would ever know of their having done so and, of course, without the slightest anticipation or desire of reward or recognition of any kind. I kept a careful record of the names and, just as a measure of precaution in the event of my falling from an aeroplane or being swallowed by a whale, I wish to put it in your possession.

The "Harveys" and "Harpers" were naturally interested very keenly and insisted upon being "in it." In this class of loving contributors were J. Henry Harper,[4] E. S. Martin,[5] F. A. Duneka,

[1] WW to G. B. M. Harvey, Nov. 10, 1910.
[2] That is, denials that Wilson was using the governorship of New Jersey as a stepping-stone to the presidency.
[3] This brief editorial, entitled "To Be Continued," consisted of a series of Harvey's endorsements of Wilson's political career from 1906 to 1910. Harvey concluded the list of quotations by observing, "We now fully anticipate the nomination of Woodrow Wilson for President of the United States by the Democratic national convention of 1912, as against William H. Taft, Republican candidate." Harper's Weekly, LIV (Nov. 19, 1910), 4. In this same issue, Harvey ran Wilson's picture on the cover, a full-page portrait of Wilson and his family, and a page of editorial reactions to Wilson's election as governor. "Woodrow Wilson's First Political Triumph," ibid., pp. 8-9.
[4] Joseph Henry Harper, vice-president of Harper and Bros.
[5] Edward Sandford Martin, one of the founders of the Harvard Lampoon;

F. T. Leigh,[6] A. D. Chandler,[7] H. S. Harper,[8] W. O. Inglis,[9] Alma P. Harvey[10] and Dorothy Harvey.[11]

Others hardly less insistent were fellow golfers and neighbors at Deal. These comprised Frederick H. Eaton, a fellow trustee of yours I think, on the Mutual Life Board,[12] Thomas G. Patten,[13] George S. Coxe,[14] Leo Schlessinger,[15] F. A. Marshall,[16] Arthur Lipper,[17] J. W. Wooley,[18] George W. Young[19] and Samuel Sachs.[20]

Others were personal friends whom I ran across from time to time and who considered it a favor to be permitted to help along, in a way however small, a movement for better government. These were: F. L. Stetson,[21] Wayne MacVeagh, who subscribed himself "an admirer," Thomas F. Ryan,[22] "a Virginia Democrat," who always responds generously to anything in which I am personally interested, Ethan Allen,[23] A. C. Humphreys,[24] Patrick

---

editorial writer for *Life*, a humor magazine, 1887-1933; and, in 1910, also on the editorial staff of *Harper's Weekly*.

[6] Frederick Tollington Leigh, treasurer of Harper and Bros. and a lieutenant colonel in the New York National Guard.

[7] Arthur Dickinson Chandler, manager of the periodical department and a director of Harper and Bros., also secretary and a director of the North American Review Publishing Co.

[8] Henry Sleeper Harper, a partner in Harper and Bros.

[9] William Otto Inglis, a member of the editorial staff of *Harper's Weekly* and one of Harvey's close associates.

[10] Alma Parker Harvey, his wife.

[11] His daughter.

[12] Frederick Heber Eaton, president and director of the American Car & Foundry Co. and a trustee of the Mutual Life Insurance Company of New York.

[13] Thomas Gedney Patten, just elected the Democratic representative from the 15th congressional district of New York.

[14] The Editors have been unable to identify him.

[15] Louis Schlesinger of Newark, who was involved in various real estate and insurance enterprises.

[16] The Editors have been unable to identify him.

[17] Senior partner in the New York investment banking firm of Arthur Lipper and Co.

[18] The Editors have been unable to identify him.

[19] George Washington Young, president of George W. Young Co., a New York banking firm.

[20] Senior partner of Goldman, Sachs & Co., Wall Street investment bankers.

[21] Francis Lynde Stetson, New York lawyer in the firm of Stetson, Jennings, and Russell and general counsel for several large corporations, including the United States Steel Corp. He was also the long-time counsel and personal adviser of J. P. Morgan and had been a close friend and adviser of Grover Cleveland.

[22] Thomas Fortune Ryan, utilities tycoon and financier, with interests in banking, the tobacco industry, electric utilities and street railways in various cities, extensive coal holdings in Ohio and West Virginia, and diamond mines in the Belgian Congo.

[23] Retired New York lawyer, Deputy United States attorney for the southern district of New York, 1861-69.

[24] Alexander Crombie Humphreys, President of the Stevens Institute of Technology of Hoboken, who during 1910 had reorganized his former engineering firm of Humphreys & Glasgow of New York as Humphreys & Miller.

Calhoun,[25] C. H. Kelsey,[26] B. F. Yoakum,[27] J. D. Crimmins[28] and J. Hampden Robb.[29]

This is my complete list. You can see that the individual amounts[30] were small and intended merely as evidences of good-will from the fact that, including my own contribution of what seemed proper and happened to be convenient, the total did not quite reach $10,000.

I think I sent you a note from my old friend Vice Chancellor Garrison,[31] proferring a contribution. I said I should be happy to receive one. When it came it was accompanied by the enclosed note.[32] I replied politely that you had insisted from the beginning upon bearing your own personal expenses and consequently I must return his check. I hope you will feel that this was right.

I do not consider it at all necessary to give you this information, but it does seem desirable to do so, first, as I have said, as a precaution, and secondly, because I do not want now or ever hereafter to withhold from you any information whatsoever in my possession that might by the remotest chance have a bearing upon your political fortunes.

One other thing: Office seekers become so eager at times that they consciously or unconsciously misrepresent matters. It was but natural that many should solicit my good offices in their behalf. To all such I have said plainly, that, under no circumstances, would I propose or recommend anybody for any place under your administration. This determination I shall adhere to with rigidity.

I feel that this also may be superfluous, but I have always found that a simple understanding of fact beats the very best of inferences "all holler."

Now, having bared my soul, I want to beg you to go away

[25] Grandson of John Caldwell Calhoun. Patrick Calhoun, president of the United Railroads of San Francisco, had been implicated in recent exposures of graft in that city.

[26] Clarence Hill Kelsey, financier and president since 1891 of the Title Guarantee & Trust Co. of New York.

[27] Benjamin Franklin Yoakum, self-made railroad magnate, who was chairman of the board of directors of the St. Louis and San Francisco Railroad, chairman of the executive committee of the Chicago and Eastern Illinois Railroad, and chairman of the board of the Rock Island Co., a large holding company for several railroads in midwestern, western, and southern states.

[28] John Daniel Crimmins, New York financier who made his fortune in the construction business and was at this time president of the New York Mortgage and Security Co. as well as director of several other firms.

[29] James Hampden Robb, prominent New York Democrat, state senator and assemblyman in the 1880s, and retired banker and cotton merchant.

[30] The enclosure listing the amounts is missing.

[31] Lindley Miller Garrison, Vice-Chancellor of New Jersey since 1904 and Secretary of War during Wilson's first administration.

[32] Both documents are missing.

somewhere and give your mind and body at least half a chance to "react" gently. You have a man's job ahead of you and, however little you may feel the need now, you should seize the first opportunity to store up strength for the future. *So much depends!*

Don't mind please, my saying in closing as I do say from the bottom of my heart, the good old words: "God bless and keep and help you." As ever, faithfully yours, George Harvey

TLS (WP, DLC).

From Edward Seymour Wilde[1]

My dear Sir: Dover, New Jersey, Nov. 14. 1910.

In the interview with *Mr. James Smith Jr.* published today in the New York Herald and other newspapers as news, *Mr Smith*, while claiming that, "During the last fifteen years of democratic losses and struggles in this State I have worked constantly, sometimes quite alone among the leaders, to maintain the party organization and keep it in condition to grasp the opportunity when it came"[2]—fails to realize that his very prominence has contributed in as great degree as any other factor to maintain democratic State losses during the last fifteen years.

Is there any one so ignorant of political conditions here, or, is it possible that any one should have become so infatuated with the claims of this mediocre aspirant to, for a moment, suppose that had Mr. Smith been a candidate for Governor in the late election instead of Woodrow Wilson there would have been a ghost of a chance of the success that has come to us? Mr. Smith could not succeed to any preferment in the politics of the State should his candidature come directly before the people. His name has never been prominent in the ranks of the New Jersey democracy save in connection with the use of money, and, like John R. McPherson,[3] who purchased the caucus and who was for eighteen years the disgraced representative of New Jersey in the United States Senate, the colorless terms of both have tended progressively to maintain the "losses and struggles" so benevolently claimed as a party condition.

Indirectly Mr. Smith's success now would be felt two years hence in our utter defeat. The margin is very narrow. Taking into account the number of polling districts in the State small change in each becomes effective.

I am a graduate of the class of '61. During a period of more than forty years I have, with a single exception, voted for every

Democratic candidate for the Presidency but, should the clouds of McPherson and Smith again darken our horizon pure disgust would rather welcome the aftermath. The latent democratic leaven of the State does not become sensible under McPherson and Smith conditions.

The writer does not feel that an excuse should be offered for this letter as it comes from one who has taken great pride in supporting the ticket in the late election and he feels that your emphatic challenge to boss rule during the campaign was earnest of a legitimate influence to really better our representation in the Senate of the United States.

Believe me, my dear Governor,

yours very truly,   Edward S. Wilde.

Personal, not confidential.

P.S. I cannot and do not entertain the belief that there was a preelection understanding between yourself and Mr Smith of intersupport. This to my mind is to be taken as the height of absurdity, yet the fact remains that such is being asserted to be true and can be disproved only by your subsequent action as leader of the party.

My motive in this writing is a sincere desire to be of service to the party and to you.   W.

ALS (WP, DLC).
¹ Princeton 1861, an attorney who practiced law until 1873 and then retired to supervise his family's extensive real estate holdings.
² This interview does not appear in extant editions of the *New York Herald* of November 14, but it did appear in the *Newark Sunday Call*, Nov. 13, 1910. In the interview, Smith hedged only slightly on whether he would become an active candidate for the United States Senate. "I have not yet decided whether I will enter the race or not," Smith declared, "and I shall not decide until I have had consultations with my friends upon a conclusion, and act accordingly." He said that the Democratic senatorial primary had little meaning and claimed that the office had few attractions for him; but, as Wilde's quotation indicates, he also pointed out his service to the New Jersey Democratic party. "If I find that my friends think I should make the fight, I will enter the race and I will win it," Smith predicted, adding, "The majority of the caucus would give me the nomination, and there would be no further question of the result."
³ James Rhoderic McPherson (1833-97) of Jersey City, Democratic senator from New Jersey, 1877-95.

From John Wesley Wescott

My dear Doctor Wilson: Camden, N. J., November 14th, 1910.

Yours of the 11th instant¹ is in hand. The terms of your letter are a greater reward to me than all the offices at your command compounded in one and given me on a golden platter. It is the mutual confidence of earnest men, engaged in great work, that explains progress. It is enough for me to share such confidence and remain in the ranks.

Just before reading your letter, I had dictated the following to you: "My duty to you, to good government and Democratic achievement require me to say that the United States Senatorship presents grave possibilities. From scores of people I have gathered an argument that runs this wise: if Mr. Smith is chosen, these results are certain: (1) his election will prove a bargain and sale, the office going to the highest bidder; (2) Doctor Wilson is controlled by the same interests and methods that control Mr. Smith; (3) Dr. Wilson, so far as his usefulness in American regeneration is concerned, would be a negative quality and quantity; (4) the Democratic party in New Jersey would be put out of power at the next election and its restoration thereto would be postponed another twenty years. Without doubt, the matter is of vast consequence. My opinion is that, during the next two years, the nation at large will recognize the great difference between you and Governor Harmon as to capacity and personal power, and will, therefore, put you at the head of the Presidential ticket. I say this because I know the two men and their respective abilities to effect progress in proper directions. The conscience and intelligence of the public believe in you to a degree never before witnessed by me.

"It is my conviction that a few words from you to the proper parties will avoid the calamity sure to follow the choice of Mr. Smith. The people of this state, as well as the country generally, are familiar with Senator Smith's course in the Senate[2] and they are opposed to him.

"Enclosed you will find a clipping, by a careful observer and thinker, from the North American.[3] It is very near the truth. I believe that you will take these suggestions as founded upon my belief in your destiny to do more for our common country than any man in public life. My language is strong, but so is the truth."

Your sense of "responsibility rather than elation" is inevitable. So far as my ability to comprehend serious and historic movement and consequence permits, I understand your feelings. It is the surest evidence of your fitness and the assurance of your future achievements for humanity. Your faith in the common desire to advance is my faith. You can depend upon me to contribute my utmost service upon this principle.

Sincerely and, I may add, affectionately yours,

John W. Wescott.

TLS (WP, DLC).
[1] It is missing in the J. W. Wescott Coll., NjP.

2 About this subject, see E. A. Stevens to WW, Nov. 29, 1910, n. 2.

3 It is missing, but it was probably an editorial, "Who Won and Who Lost," Philadelphia *North American*, Nov. 14, 1910. The piece was unsigned, but it was undoubtedly written by the strongly pro-Roosevelt editor and publisher of the *North American*, Edwin Augustus Van Valkenburg. The editorial argued that the elections of 1910 did not demonstrate any massive switch to the Democratic party; rather, they indicated a repudiation of standpat Republicans and President William Howard Taft and an endorsement of Roosevelt and the principles of insurgency.

From Melancthon Williams Jacobus

My dear Dr. Wilson: Hartford, Conn., November 14th, 1910

You will remember the short conference which some of your friends on the Board had with you immediately after the last meeting of the Trustees, in regard to your agreement to the Board's desire that you should allow the President's salary to be continued up to the middle of next January, and its invitation to you to remain in residence at Prospect, and its earnest request that you should continue the professorship in Jurisprudence and Politics.[1]

This last item, affecting as it does the University's curriculum, was handed over to the Curriculum Committee for such further conference with you as might be necessary.

I understand that you are planning to go away for a needed rest, and perhaps will have already gone by the time this reaches you; but I am anxious, if there is anything remaining in your mind to hinder a favorable response to this urgency regarding the professorship, that you will give me an opportunity to see you and talk things over with you.

Frankly, if there is any possible way by which you can arrange to give the lectures, I know of no greater opportunity to bring upon the thoughtful minds of the present generation of students the serious facts which confront the people of this land today than that which is possessed by you in your present official position and your now accepted leadership in a sane and constitutional development of politics.[2]

I can be in Princeton any Monday, Wednesday or Friday, or if Tuesday, Thursday or Saturday evenings would suit you better, I could go to Princeton late enough on those days to see you by 8:30.

With kindest regards and best wishes,

Yours very sincerely,   M. W. Jacobus

TLS (WP, DLC).

1 For the resolutions adopted by the board, see C. W. McAlpin to WW, Nov. 3, 1910, Vol. 21.

2 Wilson never reconsidered his resignation from the McCormick chair, and

at the trustees' meeting on January 12, 1911, his resignation was accepted, effective October 20, 1910. At this same meeting, the Committee on the Curriculum reported that Wilson had been urged to retain the McCormick professorship but declined to do so. However, the report also indicated that Wilson left open the possibility of delivering a series of lectures in the future. "Minutes of the Trustees of Princeton University, April 1908-June 1913," Jan. 12, 1911, bound minute book (UA, NjP).

From Robert Alexander Falconer[1]

Dear Mr. Woodrow Wilson: [Toronto] November 14th, 1910.

I have been intending for the last few days to send you my congratulations on the result of the political campaign which you have waged so successfully. Your election to the Governorship has given many in Canada a great deal of pleasure, and I need hardly say that I am among the number.

It means I am aware your abandonment for the present of academic work. Indeed, I hope that before you resume academic work you may be advanced to a still higher position in your country's service. From your courage, your knowledge of the United States and its history, and your ability, not only the State of New Jersey will benefit from your occupancy of the office of Governor, but the effect will, I am sure, be felt in other States of the Union.

I suppose it will not be possible for you to come to Toronto and give us an address in the University before your installation into office? If you could do so, you would have a warm welcome from us all.[2]

Please give my congratulations to Mrs. Wilson, and believe me, with kind regards,

Yours very sincerely,   Robt. A. Falconer.

TLS (WP, DLC).
[1] The Rev. Dr. Robert Alexander Falconer, President of the University of Toronto since 1907.
[2] Wilson was unable to accept this invitation.

From Dudley Field Malone[1]

My dear Doctor Wilson: New York November 14th, 1910.

I beg to congratulate you most heartily on your great victory which has reached such magnificent proportions.

My delay in sending you this little letter is due to the fact that it has taken me a week to recover from the very active campaign in this State for John A. Dix,[2] but from which I was able to tear myself away on four or five occasions to take part in the great fight which your friends made throughout the entire State of New Jersey.

Trusting and believing that the success of your administration of office will be as highly successful as was the result of the election,

Believe me to be,

Yours most respectfully,   Dudley Field Malone.

TLS (WP, DLC).
  1 City Attorney of the City of New York, who had been active in the campaign for Wilson.
  2 John Alden Dix, Democratic Governor-elect of New York.

To George Brinton McClellan Harvey

PARSONAL and CONFIDENTIAL.

My dear Colonel,   Princeton, N. J. 15 November, 1910.

Your letter is characteristically frank and generous, and I thank you for it with all my heart. As you say, its information and assurances were unnecessary, so far as I am concerned; but it was wise, as well as interesting, matter of record, and I shall value the letter as one of my treasured documents: as at once an evidence of your thoughtful friendship and of your admirable judgment, which I learn to value more and more.

There are many names on the list which it pleased me deeply to see there, but the ones which pleased me most were those of Alma P. Harvey, Dorothy Harvey, and the gentlemen connected with the House.[1] I am particularly touched by these evidences of generous friendship.

You are very kind to advise rest. I had really intended to seek it. But two thousand letters and telegrams needing answers, and the press of things to learn that I as yet know nothing about make me fear that I shall get it only by taking railway journeys to fulfil the engagements which are going to take me hither and thither between now and the twenty-fourth of January. I can make that suffice. I am pretty tough and elastic!

I am very anxious about the question of the senatorship. If not handled right, it will destroy every fortunate impression of the campaign and open my administration with a split party. I have learned to have a very high opinion of Senator Smith. I have very little doubt that, if he were sent to the Senate he would acquit himself with honour and do a great deal to correct the impressions of his former term. But his election would be intolerable to the very people who elected me and gave us a majority in the legislature. They would never give it to us again: that I think I can say I know, from what has been said to me in every quarter during the campaign. They count upon me to prevent it. I shall forfeit their confidence if I do not. All their ugliest suspicions, dispelled by my campaign assurances, will be confirmed.

It was no Democratic victory. It was a victory of the "progressives" of both parties, who are determined to live no longer under either of the political organizations that have controlled the two parties of the State. The Democrats who left us in 1896 came back, with enthusiasm, but will again draw off in disgust if we disappoint their expectations. For myself, I simply cannot. It is grossly unjust that they should regard Senator Smith as the impersonation of all that they hate and fear; but they do, and there's an end of the matter. If he should become a candidate, I would have to fight him; and there is nothing I would more sincerely deplore. It would offend every instinct in me,—except the instinct as to what was right and necessary from the point of view of the public service. I have had to do similar things in the University.

By the same token,—ridiculous though it undoubtedly is,—I think we shall have to stand by Mr. Martine. After all that has been said and done, we shall be stultified if we do not. There is no man who stands out in the party as conspicuously the man whom the entire body of public opinion in the State would accept as of course the man to send. Moreover, if we do not send Martine, apparently it may be Katzenbach; and in my opinion a worse choice could not be made. Through sheer weakness and lack of virile intelligence and principle, he would serve the interests of which the State is most jealous much more directly and readily than a man like Senator Smith would, who has wide-eyed political intelligence and knows what he is about. I had several talks with men who have dealt with K. at short range and who saw him close at hand during the campaign three years ago (men whom we would both trust), and they thanked God that he was not elected. They believed that his administration would have put the party out of credit for the rest of our lives,— as mine will unless there is an absolutely and obviously new deal.

I have stripped my whole thought, and my whole resolution, naked for you to see just as it is. Senator Smith can make himself the biggest man in the State by a dignified refusal to let his name be considered. I hope, as I hope for the rejuvenation of our party, that he may see it and may be persuaded to do so.

It is a national as well as a State question. If the independent Republicans who in this State voted for me are not to be attracted to us they will assuredly turn again, in desperation, to Mr. Roosevelt, and the chance of a generation will be lost to the Democracy: the chance to draw all the liberal elements of the country to it, through new leaders, the chance that Mr. Roosevelt missed in his folly, and to constitute the ruling party of the country for the next generation.

I know that I write to an understanding and sympathizing mind, and that I need make no apology. It is another way of expressing my confidence and my close and affectionate friendship.

Always, with warmest messages to those at Deal, and my cordial regard to the gentlemen of the House who are such generous friends of mine,   Faithfully Yours,   Woodrow Wilson[2]

WWTLS (WP, DLC).
   [1] That is, Harper and Bros.
   [2] There is a WWsh draft of this letter, dated Nov. 15, 1910, in WP, DLC.

To Thomas Davies Jones

My dear Mr. Jones: Princeton, N. J. Nov. 15th, 1910.

Thank you most warmly for your generous message of congratulation.[1] I find that my predominant feeling is one of deep responsibility.

It will be delightful to have a chance to talk with you this week when I am in Chicago[2] and get my thoughts settled in many things.

In haste,

Cordially and faithfully yours,   Woodrow Wilson

TLS (Mineral Point, Wisc., Public Library).
   [1] T. D. Jones to WW, Nov. 9, 1910, Vol. 21.
   [2] When he was to speak to the Business Service Lecture League on November 18. A news report of his speech is printed at Nov. 19, 1910.

To William Goodell Frost

My dear Dr. Frost: Princeton, N. J. November 15, 1910

It is a genuine delight to know that you are well again and in the harness you love to pull in.[1] I congratulate you and the rest of the country that you are fit again to continue the great work you have been doing.

You may be sure that I am ready to serve Berea whenever I can. The dates ahead of me are so miscellaneous and exacting that I cannot be at all sure that I will be there in January, but if you will let me know as the dates approach, I will certainly try to be at at least one of the meetings, the one nearest at hand. I cannot promise but I shall certainly try.[2]

In haste, with warmest regard,
         Cordially and sincerely yours,   Woodrow Wilson

TLS (W. G. Frost Papers, KyBB).
  [1] Frost's letter, to which this was a reply, is printed at Nov. 7, 1910, Vol. 21.
  [2] Wilson's address on behalf of Berea College is printed at Feb. 10, 1911.

To James Ford Rhodes

My dear Mr. Rhodes,   Princeton, N. J. 15 November, 1910.

You are very generous, and I thank you with all my heart for your letter of the eleventh. It made me glad that I had made my little excursion into politics. I shall try hard not to let my colleagues of the Academy and of the Historical Association feel ashamed of the part I play.

With warm regard and appreciation, and the hope that you are feeling quite yourself again,
                    Faithfully Yours,   Woodrow Wilson

WWTLS (J. F. Rhodes Papers, MHi).

From James Richard Nugent

My dear Sir,   Newark, N. J. November 15 1910.

I wish to thank you kindly for the hearty appreciation expressed in your letter of the fourteenth instant[1] of my efforts in the late campaign, and I hasten to assure you, that I am ready to help to the best of my ability the carrying on of your good work only just begun.

I believe you are going away for a short vacation, and I would be pleased on your return, or before you go if you so desire, to talk over with you the preparation of the necessary legislation intended to be enacted at the next session of the legislature— that is, the bills to be introduced and the drafting of them; I would also like to talk with you some other matters connected with the future welfare of the Party. There is no immediate hurry for this, so I leave it to your convenience.

I am going to Atlantic City the latter part of this week to make arrangements to carry on the work there against false registration and false voting and look for good results.

We are still carrying on the same line of work in Camden County and have the powerful aid of the Bar Association, irrespective of politics.

I am gratified to know that you intend to publish your campaign speeches[2]—they will command wide circulation. The chief stenographer is Clarence Sackett of 658 Mount Prospect Avenue Newark.

Wishing you good health and a pleasant vacation,

I remain,   Yours very truly,   James R. Nugent

ALS (WP, DLC).
[1] It is missing.
[2] Wilson never did publish his speeches; however, Charles Reade Bacon, a reporter for the Philadelphia *Record* who accompanied Wilson throughout the campaign, published his news reports as *A People Awakened: The Story of Woodrow Wilson's First Campaign* (Garden City, N. Y., 1912).

From William Monroe Trotter

Dear Sir: Boston, Mass., November 15, 1910.

I congratulate you on your election with such a magnificent majority as Governor of New Jersey. I congratulate you also on your declaration that you will treat all citizens alike.[1] This justifies the independent Colored men of the country in the stand taken by the campaign committee of the National Political League at its public meeting October 6, 1910 at the National capital. At that time you were endorsed by the League.[2] We trust that no word or action of yours on the great question of equal rights will ever cause us to regret our stand.

I ardently wish that you would tomorrow speak out against the threat of lynching an untried Colored man in the state of New Jersey.[3]   Yours for freedom,   Wm. Monroe Trotter.
                    Sec. of the National Independent
                              Political League.

TLS (WP, DLC).
[1] That is, Wilson's repeated campaign assurances that he would be governor of all the people of New Jersey. There is no record of any statements by Wilson addressed specifically to blacks.
[2] See W. T. Ferguson to WW, Oct. 7, 1910, n. 2, Vol. 21.
[3] Trotter's concern was prompted by news reports of an impending lynching in Asbury Park, N. J. On November 13, Marie Smith, a ten-year-old white school girl who had been missing for four days, was found dead with her skull crushed. Immediately after the discovery of her body in woods near Asbury Park, the police began searching the Negro community in the town for Thomas Williams, who was seized late on the evening of November 13. Williams was suspected, according to the news reports, because he was employed by Marie's great-aunt. A mob, which gathered around the police station on the night of November 13, was beaten back by the police, but the mob returned again on the next day. At 1:30 A.M. on November 15, Williams was secretly taken to the Monmouth County jail at Freehold. Williams con-

sistently proclaimed his innocence, and when the National Association for the Advancement of Colored People challenged the evidence against him with a writ of *habeas corpus*, the charge was changed from murder to violation of the election laws. In January 1911, Williams was still incarcerated. *New York Herald*, Nov. 14 and 15, 1910; *The Crisis*, I (Jan. 1911), 20.

From William Gibbs McAdoo

Dear Doctor Wilson: New York November 15th, 1910.

I sent you a telegram[1] this afternoon urging you to accept the invitation of the New York Southern Society to be its guest of honor at the forthcoming annual dinner on the 14th of December, at the Waldorf-Astoria. I can thoroughly apprecaite [appreciate] the pressure which is being brought upon you from all sorts of directions to accept invitations of like character, but we Southerners feel that we have a peculiar claim upon you, and take an especial pride in your distinguished career and your recent great achievement, and want an opportunity of expressing it.

I hope sincerely that you may be able to accept the invitation and honor us with your presence.

Very sincerely yours,   W G McAdoo
President,
New York Southern Society.

TLS (WP, DLC).
[1] W. G. McAdoo to WW, Nov. 15, 1910, T telegram (WP, DLC).

To William Gibbs McAdoo

[Princeton, N. J., c. Nov. 15, 1910]

Am planning with great pleasure to be present Dec. 14th.[1]

WW

Typed on W. G. McAdoo to WW, Nov. 15, 1910, T telegram (WP, DLC).
[1] Wilson's address to the New York Southern Society is printed at Dec. 14, 1910.

From Charles Scribner

Dear Dr. Wilson: New-York Nov. 15, 1910.

An invitation has been sent asking you to attend and speak at the Dinner to be given by the Periodical Publishers' Association on January 6th. I write to express my personal interest in having you there and my hope that you will find it possible to attend.[1] The Association includes among its members many very active and rather influential men and it seems to me it would be a suitable place for you to appear in this provincial metropolis. By this mail I am sending the list of speakers at the last dinner which was held in Washington, and on this occasion we expect Colonel Roosevelt to be present.

It would give me great pleasure to have you spend the night with me at my house (12 East 38th Street).

Yours sincerely   Charles Scribner

TLS (WP, DLC).
[1] Wilson declined the invitation.

From James Edgar Martine

My dear Governor Wilson,   Plainfield [N. J.] Nov. 16th 1910

Your very kind note is much appreciated and I thank you for it. I never felt more earnest in my life. We had so much to contend for, and so grand a candidate to lead our cause, that we were just invincible. Yes the result was splendid and it will be most healthful to the whole country. Hoping to see you soon, I am

Sincerely yours   James E Martine

ALS (WP, DLC).

From Charles Richard Williams[1]

My dear Mr. Wilson,   [Indianapolis, Ind.] November 16 [1910].

I was deeply grieved at first that you should give up your great work at Princeton. But I am satisfied now that you had a clear call to a greater work and to more important responsibilities. I gloried in the kind of campaign you made, and my heart leaped joyously at the response it received and the triumph that followed. It was all the more satisfying to me, because your appeal to the "intelligence and judgment" of the voters was a justification of the ideal I have always tried to follow in the conduct of this paper.

I have serene confidence that if your health and strength are spared, and you are able measurably to carry out your high purposes for the purification of New Jersey politics that an insistent call from the nation will come to you.

I am taking the liberty of mailing you a volume of verse[2] that I have somewhat vainly printed for my friends. Perhaps you will care to have it, at least for the Princeton verses. No acknowledgement is necessary.

Yours with great admiration and regard,

Chas R. Williams

TLS (WP, DLC).
  [1] Princeton 1875, editor-in-chief of the *Indianapolis News* since 1892.
  [2] *In Many Moods* (Indianapolis, Ind., 1910).

From Charles Franklin Thwing[1]

My dear Mr. Wilson: New York November 16, 1910.

Your letter of the 11th November, addressed to the Board of Trustees of the Carnegie Foundation for the Advancement of Teaching, resigning your membership in the Board, was read at the meeting of the Foundation held to-day. The members saw no other method open to them than to heed your request and to accept your resignation.

But the Board could not bring itself to this conclusion without instructing me to convey to you the assurance of the great respect and regard of its members and to bid you godspeed in the great career upon which you are entering. The Board feels itself honored that one of its members, greatly beloved, is able to give himself to a great service for the people as an officer of the state.

I beg to remain, with respect and regard,

Very truly yours,   Charles F. Thwing

TLS (WP, DLC).
  [1] President of Western Reserve University and secretary of the Carnegie Foundation for the Advancement of Teaching.

From John Franklin Fort

[Trenton, N. J.]

My dear Doctor Wilson: November sixteenth 1910.

The matter of your Inauguration is already being considered here[1] and it is essential that we know your views about it. If it is your wish to be inaugurated as all the other Governors have been, in the Taylor Opera House, where you were nominated, it will be necessary for us to engage the building at once. Senator Leavitt of this County[2] has already spoken to me about it and is holding it against other engagements.

If you desire any military demonstration in connection with your Inauguration, it is also a matter which we shall soon desire to know.

I spoke to you on Saturday last when at your home, suggesting that you visit me at the Capitol on Tuesday next and lunch with me at one o'clock and meet the heads of the various departments of the State. We all lunch down stairs in the Capitol on Tuesdays, and I will be very glad if I may have you for a guest upon that day.

I fear that my statement that I should probably consult you with relation to the vacancy in the Court of Errors and Appeals, caused by the death of Judge Gray,[3] is giving you some trouble. I know that I am getting letters here which purport to be copies of letters being sent to you. I should be very sorry if this gives you any annoyance, and when we meet on Tuesday, if it is doing so, you can turn the whole matter over to me, and of course I will confer with you about it. I do not want to put any work on you, because I know what labors you have had and must have in getting ready for your Inauguration.

As to our going to Frankfort,[4] I should like also to confer with you about that on Tuesday. Adjutant-General [Wilbur Fisk] Sadler will arrange for our tickets and I will cover the cost of them here and have them for us both. If we can know our train, we can travel together. Mrs. Fort[5] was intending to accompany me but has decided not to do so, so it would be pleasant for me, if agreeable to you, that we should go together.

I trust that you have fully recovered from your campaign exertions, and awaiting your reply, I am, with kind regards,

Yours very sincerely,   John Franklin Fort

TLS (WP, DLC).
    [1] Wilson was to be inaugurated on January 17, 1911.
    [2] Harry D. Leavitt, state senator from Mercer County and assistant cashier of the Mechanics National Bank of Trenton.
    [3] George R. Gray of Newark, who died on November 4, 1910, of a stroke.
    [4] For the third annual meeting of the Governors' Conference, November 29-December 1, 1910, in Frankfort and Louisville, Ky. Wilson's speech to the conference is printed at Nov. 29, 1910.
    [5] Charlotte Stainsby Fort.

From Benjamin Ide Wheeler[1]

My dear President Wilson: Berkeley [Cal.], November 16, 1910.

I want to congratulate you very heartily on your election, but still more on the manner in which you conducted your campaign. You set a new standard. It cheers me to think of you as running on the Democratic ticket and it arouses my old enthusiasm for the Democracy. I am patiently waiting for an opportunity to vote the Democratic ticket. I do it every time I have even half a chance.

Very faithfully yours,   Benj. Ide Wheeler.

TLS (WP, DLC).
    [1] President of the University of California.

From Hopson Owen Murfee[1]

My dear Mr. Wilson: Marion, Alabama 16 November 1910

The Executive Committee of the Alabama Educational Association has unanimously voted to extend to you the invitation to deliver the chief address before the Association on Friday night of the 13th of April—Jefferson's Birthday. The Chairman of the Committee should extend the formal invitation this week.

I sincerely hope that it will be possible for you to accept. The session of the Association will be held in Birmingham, and there will be present probably over three thousand teachers. Education is rapidly becoming Jefferson's "holy cause" in Alabama, and you can render the work a great service by bringing our teachers and our people a message next April.[2]

I have been requested to lay before you in person this invitation on my visit North within the next ten days; but as I may be delayed in reaching Princeton, I hasten to write you before your plans are made for next April.

Our people rejoice in your election, and look to you to lead them in 1912.

With cordial regards, I am
                    Very sincerely yours   H. O. Murfee

TLS (WP, DLC).
  [1] Superintendent of the Marion Institute, Marion, Ala., and an old friend and correspondent.
  [2] Wilson had to decline.

To Robert Randolph Henderson

My dear Bob: Princeton, N. J. November 17, 1910

Your letter touched me deeply.[1] God bless you for it.
                    Affectionately yours,   Woodrow Wilson

TLS (WC, NjP).
  [1] R. R. Henderson to WW, Nov. 9, 1910, Vol. 21.

A News Report About Wilson's Arrival in Milwaukee

[Nov. 17, 1910]

"I AM UNDER OBLIGATION TO STOP TALKING," SAYS
WOODROW WILSON, NEW JERSEY'S NEW DEMOCRATIC
GOVERNOR, AS HE STEPS FROM TRAIN IN MILWAUKEE

Woodrow Wilson, governor-elect of New Jersey, arrived in Milwaukee at 11:30 a.m. Thursday fatigued after his long and strenuous campaign in New Jersey, and disinclined to submit to interviews.

"I expressed my opinions very fully about matters during the campaign, and before it," said Dr. Wilson, "and now that the election is over, I think I am under obligations, as it were, to stop talking and think about what I ought to do—what my duties demand of me. I want to keep as quiet as possible.

"I hate men who fire off their opinions on general subjects: and I think I have done all the talking that I ought to do. I had over 2,000 letters and telegrams last week which I have tried to answer, and that made it impos[s]ible for me to do anything else."

The governor's declination to be interviewed was not made brusquely, and it was apparent that he was fatigued, as he said. He asked that an automobile trip arranged for him immediately after the luncheon at noon be eliminated, so that he might have an opportunity to go to his hotel and rest.

"I appreciate the idea of the committee in desiring to give me an opportunity to be refreshed after the luncheon by the drive," he said; "but I have been through quite a strenuous campaign, you know."

Dr. Wilson's democratic manner and courtesy are his striking characteristics. He speaks frankly and openly, and his sincerity is apparent. He is of medium height, wears glasses, and clothes modest in cut. He is neither overdressed, nor badly dressed, and his carriage is that of a man sure of himself, while his statements are positive and explicit. He has an open and smiling countenance, and an alert eye, and one who did not know his history would at once stamp him as a student or a man of affairs.

Dr. Wilson was met at the depot by a delegation of Milwaukee citizens headed by Judge W. D. Tarrant,[1] and was taken to his hotel and then to the luncheon at the Palm Garden arranged in his honor by the City club. Later in the day he visited the Press club, and in the evening will be given a supper at the University club, preceding his lecture at the Pabst theater.

Printed in the *Milwaukee Journal*, Nov. 17, 1910.

[1] Warren Downes Tarrant, judge of the state circuit court for Milwaukee County.

A News Report of a Luncheon Address in Milwaukee

[Nov. 17, 1910]

WILSON SCORES VOTING SYSTEM AT PALM GARDEN

New Jersey's Governor-Elect Says Our System Is World's Most Complicated.

. . . It took the unintended joke of the photographer in the Palm garden to first enthuse the large and representative crowd who had gathered there to hear Dr. Woodrow Wilson, Democratic governor-elect of New Jersey and president of Princeton university, speak at the City club's luncheon Thursday noon.

"Look pleasant," said the picture maker, "the flashlight will only make a noise like a toy pistol."

The report that followed sounded like a cannon.

Everybody laughed. This was after the first course.

Mr. Wilson himself came early and his appearance was entirely unannounced. He took his place at the speakers' table, with Fred Morehouse,[1] toastmaster, at his left, and Chief Justice John B[radley]. Winslow of the Wisconsin supreme court, at his right.

Next to them respectively came A[dolph]. J[ohn]. Schmitz, Democratic candidate for Governor, and Francis E[dward]. McGovern, governor-elect.

Mr. Schmitz and Mr. McGovern shook hands warmly when they met.

There was a large number of women among the diners, and a surprisingly large number of clergymen.

"We came here to pay our respects to the next president," said a friend to John I. Beggs,[2] who arrived late.

"He would make a very good one, I know," returned the street railway head.

After being introduced by A. J. Schmitz, Mr. Wilson, speaking at the City club banquet in the Schlitz palm garden at 1:30 p.m., said:

"It is a great privilege to address an audience like this, and I am sincerely obliged to the distinguished guest who has introduced me. I never hear myself being introduced in laudatory terms without feeling my sense of identity, for I don't always recognize myself when placed on such a high level.

[1] Frederic Cook Morehouse, editor and publisher of *The Living Church*, an Episcopalian weekly, and a lay reader.

[2] John Irvin Beggs, financier and president of the Milwaukee Electric Railway & Light Co., manager and director of the North American Co., and president of the Laclede Gas Light Co., Union Electric Light and Power Co., and of the United Railways Company of St. Louis.

"I have looked around and seen one or two Princeton men here. Whenever there are a great many of them present, I feel like the old lady who found herself inside the circus. She was horrified to see one of the performers informing his audience that he could see through a two inch board. She arose and hurriedly made an exit with the remark that if there was any one present who could see through a two inch board why that certainly was no place for her. I usually feel the same way when Princeton men are about—the disguise may be too transparent.

"I was told before I came here that this was to be a very informal function. It shows the abundance of hospitality shown here. After a man has gone through a campaign, and has made all and more than all the speeches he ever knew, it is a very formidable matter to be compelled to get up and make another speech to persons who can understand what he is saying. If I could deceive you I would not be so embarras[s]ed. Fortunately one of your members gave me an intimation of a subject which might interest you.

"I was approached by a representative of one of your newspapers at a station several miles from here. He had just stalked into the train to interview me. He had a series of typewritten questions which he wished to submit to me.

"I told him that I had done more than enough talking at the present time, and that I was of the opinion that the next thing for me to do was to find out what troubles were ahead of me, and that silence was more becoming to me now.

"But there are certain things which we are all thinking about. Indeed, there is one all comprehensive thing that we are thinking about, and that is the best way we can serve the people of this country.

"So largely is this true that if you have witnessed the consequences of this campaign you have found that party labels count for very little.

"Men are makikngk [making] their choices of candidates on the basis of no particular party program, but from a program which is in the people's mind. People of this country realize that we are facing some of the most complicated political questions that have ever been before us.

["]They want people who will serve them in a disinterested, frank and candid way. It makes no difference whether they choose from the Republicans or Democrats.

"They are going to have men who will lead them in the direction of the common need. Those who they have chosen may disappoint them, but then they will simply go on and choose again until the thing is done.

"One of the most interesting things is this. You know that the American has invented the most complicated system of government in the world. Think of the extraordinary intelligence he must have. He is supposed to pick out everybody who is to serve him.

"I belong to an organization recently formed in New York, called the Short Ballot organization. When we were conferring about the organization of this society, we had sample ballots of every description lying before us.

"One of these was red in color, and contained 700 names. It was larger than a newspaper. It was printed in columns like a newspaper. It was printed in what is called our latest reformed methods, that is, without the mention of those who had nominated the men named, without any party symbols, or any explanatory paragraphs signifying who had named the men. Every voter was supposed to pick out the whole official make-up of the city —something absolutely impossible for any man to do.

"I include men who have been making a practice of conducting political machines. I doubt if they could pick out their own nominees among all the multitude of nominees. Now the American people have become awake. They are insisting upon methods in which there is absolutely no ambush.

"You remember the cartoon by Thomas Nash [Nast] in which he represents the Tweed ring in New York as a circle of men on a platform each one with his platform [hand] on his neighbor and saying 'Twant me.'

"Our system is so complicated that each man in it can say 'Twant me.' We want an arrangement by which it can be said 'You are the one and we can hold you responsible.['] What else does the commission form of government for cities mean? Our system now is so complicated that people can't find out where the trouble is. The commission form picks out a few men to govern and holds them responsible.

"It means the shortening of the ballot, so that the men responsible will be known throughout the community and can't escape responsibility.

"Another interesting thing is going on in this country. We forget that there are all sorts of services to be rendered to the people in this country. A few years ago somebody arose to cry us awake.[3] We were asleep. There was a movement that had dis-

---

[3] Undoubtedly a reference to Theodore Roosevelt.

connected business from morality and had connected it with politics. We didn't see where we were driving. It was necessary for somebody to talk loud enough to attract our attention. It doesn't matter much what he said. We were awake.

"Members of legislatures and members of congress represent distinct neighborhoods. Nowhere else in the state is there a spokesman for the people beside the governor.

"I had an interesting conference during the last presidential election on a train with a senator of New Jersey.

"I said to him, 'What is the matetr [matter]?'

"He said, 'I wish the constitution hadn't given the president the right to send messages to congress.'

" 'I think you are barking up the wrong tree,' said I. 'It isn't wrong for the president to send messages to congress; it is wrong to have them printed in the newspapers.'

"The only person in this country whose views are printed in full is the president of the United States. His is the only national voice. How eagerly they ask him to lead.

"The same thing is coming to be expected of the governor.

"People want politics brought out into the open. They feel that in this complicated thing they are on the outside and they don't know what is going on.

"You know how legislative matters go on in Washington. Most of the bills that die die because they never come out of committee. They don't die because they are brought out on the floor. They are smothered in committee when it is not thought advisable to have them brought out by the party in power. People are tired of that. They have made up their minds that by proxy they are going to get inside and know what is going on.

"They want to know, if a bill is smothered, who smothered it. They are longing to have masks, veils and concealments torn absolutely away and have everything brought out into pitiless publicity.

"This can be done by having those talk who know what is going on. I am under public pledge to tell the people of New Jersey everything I know when I am governor. I hope I will tell it politely and like a gentleman, but I will tell it without fear or favor.

"The old regime is gone. What is the old regime? We have inveighed against political machines and with a profundity of ignorance. If there is a long slate to be made up you know you won't take time to make it up. Somebody must make a business of the mere matter of making nominations. That's the machine. In making the nominations, the machine got hold of the power to punish. It can deprive you of all chance of election. Most machines are run by men whom nobody has selected for any office. Look over the country and put your finger on the bosses. They hold no office or only inconspicuous ones. They were picked by no one."

Printed in the *Milwaukee Journal*, Nov. 17, 1910; some editorial headings omitted.

A Public Lecture in Milwaukee[1]

[[Nov. 17, 1910]]

Mr. Chairman,[2] Mr. McGovern, ladies and gentlemen: I was invited to deliver this lecture many months ago, before I knew I was going to get into trouble. I could not say no after Mr. Hanson[3] had explained to me the character of the organization before which I was going to speak. Nothing struck me more than the spirit of community, nothing struck me more than the effort toward an enlightened point of view in public affairs, of an enlightened public conscience, one behind which we all ought to stand. We are in an age when this kind of service is absolutely indispensible. It is a truism, I suppose, to say that this age is an age of transition, for all ages are ages of transition. Age follows age, and there is a constant modification of affairs. It is true in some peculiar degree that this age is an age of readjustment. Many new and unprecedented things have happened.

One reason why politics is of interest is that men are casting about for party connection. Party labels now stand for little. Nobody can define a Republican or a Democrat. I have heard of Insurgent Republicans. There are other Republicans besides Insurgents. There are some called Standpatters, men who hadn't moved for generations and who had forgotten how to move.

There are very many brands of Democrats but that's a family matter and I will not discuss it. Obviously the bonds of party set very lightly upon the voter. Now-a-days he is casting about to find a leader who will lead him in some particular direction. That's what I mean by readjustment, when we are reaccommodating ourselves to conditions.

This is an age of danger, an age of peculiar danger because what we are trying to readjust is the relation of powerful interests to each other. And the moment you try to readjust relations you excite jealousies of interests, you excite their rivalry, their an-

[1] Delivered under the auspices of the Milwaukee Lecture Service League in the Pabst Theater.
[2] Judge Warren Downes Tarrant.
[3] Charles A. Hanson, secretary of the Milwaukee Lecture Service League.

tagonism, you bring into the arena of affairs hostilities which the majority feel against the minority and no one interest is a minority. That is the interesting thing. The business of politics is to safeguard those who are not in a majority and to accom[m]odate the impulses of the majority to that safeguarding.

Thomas Carlyle once said the problem of society was how out of a multitude of knaves to make an honest people. I don't accept that as a just statement of the problem for I do not think any body of people constitute a multitude of knaves. But even on these terms I might suggest how the miracle might be wrought. Imagine to yourselves, but it is not difficult for you to imagine[,] a body of 40,000 people collected around a football field. The game has not begun. Suppose two men, dressed in ordinary citizens' clothes, appeared on the field. They may come as officials. No one knows who they are. Suddenly they fall to blows. Nobody knows what has happened; nobody knows what has been said. Everybody is outraged. The cry is, "Stop them; put them out!" Everybody disapproves of their behavior. Now, it does not follow that there is a single man on those seats, who, if another man had said the same thing would not have hit him. The probability is any man there would have done just the same thing if the intolerable thing had been said.

But it happens it was not. It happens so far as this particular quarrel is concerned it is none of his business and he is impartial because he is a disinterested witness. He knows not what these men have done. He knows that it is a matter of shame that these men should in that public place have so far forgotten themselves. That is his solution of the Carlyle problem. Take a great nation. So far as the interest of one group of men is concerned, most of them are disinterested and therefore in a normal, moral attitude toward the affair. They are not concerned and therefore are able to judge. And so a whole nation can get a large restraint upon themselves and deal with those who would push their own affairs and forget the public interest. Of course the premises are false. It is not a multitude of knaves we are dealing with.

They are not necessar[i]ly knaves. They have forgotten themselves. They have not taken a broad view and they cannot advance their interests in any direction unless they regard common interest. We are dealing with a readjustment that means a community of points of view.

The one thing that is most dangerous is to play with fire in the presence of inflammable material. Public opinion in America is inflammable, and the man who casts fire abroad as he speaks is a public enemy.

What he should try to do is to project into the minds of men the calm dictates of reason, and reason does underlie the body politic. So my first suggestion is that this age more than any other one that we have been concerned in requires careful, moderate thought and that we apply reason to the great and difficult and complicated questions.

There has been in our day a very extraordinary civic awakening. But when we say there has been civic awakening, what do we mean men have awakened to find out? It seems to me that we have awakened to the fact that there has been evidence on every hand of organized, unenlightened selfishness.

We have witnessed an exaggeration of irresponsible power. That's what we have awakened to. I believe it is unjust to indict the business men of this country for the things that have been detrimental to the public interest. I think most of these things have happened without consciousness; without deliberation, but we must, nevertheless, face the facts very frankly; face them and discuss them like men who would do justice, but not men who would avoid coming face to face with naked facts.

You know one of the obvious things is that the individual has been submerged. The fact that business is done and necessarily done has made it necessary to do a very interesting—a momentous, thing. Modern business can not be undertaken by individual capital. It must be undertaken by accumulated capital—the capital of a large number of persons put together in a single fund and administered by men who did not accumulate it. That's what a joint stock company is—the administration of the money of thousands of persons by a small number of persons—a board of directors who did not accumulate it; who have borrowed in a very wide sense of the word but who are acting as trustees in their administration. The result is, most men who work, work for a corporation.

Now, if you work for a corporation you are a mere fraction; you are not an integer. You are a subordinate, a submerged part of the great organization. In nine cases out of ten you do not deal with, you have not access to the men who direct the business. Your attitude is to obey orders. You can't decline without losing your place. You can't criticise the orders either from a legal or moral point of view. You must take them or leave the occupation. That's what I mean by the submergence—the taking away of a man's moral choice with regard to his daily conduct in business.

While most individuals are submerged, some individuals are left with the most extraordinary power that individuals have ever exercised in an economic world. They make all the business

choice and by consequence all the moral choice of our daily conduct as members of society. There then you have a society in
which the power and the consciences of vast numbers of men
are constructed and controlled by small groups of men.

That, it seems, is not an unfair statement of organizations of
economic societies. Very well, then, that's what I mean by the
exaggeration of irresistible power. And this exaggeration has run
along lines which have shown that these men in many instances
do not understand because they would not, or could not, or because their attention had never been directed. They have not
understood the common interest, and therefore their selfishness
has been unenlightened selfishness.

That is what we have got awake to. That is what we see we
have got to handle. As Mr. McGovern says, we know that we
have got to settle this question whether great business interests
are to be masters of the body politic or its servants in the community. It is a very difficult thing in which to keep from getting
hot. It is very hard not to take up a big club and get after somebody. But that is to conduct a Donnybrook fair and not a state,
because states are not conducted by hostilities but by argument,
by reconciliation and not divorcement or hostility.

The chief damage is not to our fortunes, for we are not materially worse except as to the higher cost of living—but that would
be a long story. The chief damage is in our minds. The damage
is chiefly psychological. Everybody is excited. Something is going
to happen but nobody knows what. Others are resentful because
they think it is going to happen to them. We are resentful because we don't like to be submerged and don't like to be ridden.
We are all up in the air, fighting a shadow. Nobody can tell us
what we are going to fight. Of course we are going to fight, but
show us where we are going to hit.

It is one of those interesting acts where it is more or less easy
to diagnose the situation. What are you going to do?

Then there is another thing. We have discovered what this
civic awakening has made us aware of, and that is there is
something more fundamental than we had ever dreamed of
about the common interest. Whether we will or not we are going
to get into trouble unless private interests are squared with public interest. Some gentlemen have not discovered it yet but they
are in process of being shown one method or another because
the weather is thickening and they can't help observing the signs
of the skies.

But generally speaking the communities of this country are
awake to the fact that there is such a thing as business con-

science, else why was this organization formed I am lecturing for. Why talk about the civic conscience unless there is some point of standardization for the business conscience. That point of standardization is public interest. It is now beginning to dawn upon us that man can't put forth his own private interest without regard to the public interest, without in the long run damaging his private interest as much as he damages the public interest. We are all under a great solidarity of interest which we cannot disentangle. The public interest is the best basis for every man to accommodate himself to. That's what we have awakened to and it's a great advance that we are aware of these fundamental things. Don't let us ever be so unjust as to forget the man who woke us up. I remember hearing it objected to by a certain public man that he was generally in the right but that it was no use going around with a brass band to tell about it. The reply was made that unless the brass band was there it wouldn't be known. And it was a very pertinent reply.

We have been so sound asleep nothing less than a brass band would wake us up. And I think it was perfectly just. It was necessary to talk loud; to talk very excited and to have as many brass bands as possible in order that we might sit up and take notice.

There are two different programs, ladies and gentlemen. The first is a general one and the second is proper organization and support and direction of the army. The second is the task, the infinitely varied and difficult task of constructing statesmen, which is a very different matter. We have now come to the threshold of a time when shouting has become unnecessary and impolite. It is not necessary to raise your voice any more above the proper point of etiquette, but it is necessary that when you talk you should have something to say.

Now don't let us ever forget the one man who had the courage and pertinacity to shout long enough and loud enough to make sure everybody was paying attention.

But don't let us forget there is a difference of functions and that those gentlemen are not the gentlemen to settle the matters to which they called our attention.

We do not need our attention called to the moral situation. We must have something suggested to us that we can all unite on. It is now a case, to use the vulgar expression, of put up or shut up. It is a case that requires the application of general principles in a concrete measure. That is the reason why party bonds have gone to pieces. Time was when it was easy for a man to know what party he belonged to. But now it has come to action, and men are looking around for the party that fits them. The situation reminds me of the story of an Englishman, who, when he was asked what party he belonged to, said: "I am rather between sizes in politics," and that is the case with a great many of us. We are between sizes and we have not found what party fitted us. We have looked askance at their programs. It has made our heads go round. We have been going round after a will o' the wisp when we follow these programs which we can't put down into business terms.

I have an interesting method of getting rid of a reformer if you happen to be pestered with one here. Say to him, "Why, my dear fellow, if you will bring round a statute which will work, I will subscribe to your reform." The reformer knows that he can't draw up a statute that will work. For how are you going to arrest the man against whom your law is directed, and after you have arrested him, what are you going to do with him? You want certain things done by the railroads, which they fail to do; how are you going to have them do those things under the law?

And you can dispose of your reforming friends in that way. And it is good for them as well as a relief to you. Just as one of the best methods in which to treat a loquacious friend is to advise him to hire a hall so a larger number of persons may hear him. Nothing so exploits folly as exposure to open air. If you can get a fool to talk long enough everybody will know he is a fool. So with our program now. Of course, I haven't meant to apply anything I have said here, even by implication, to modern men of affairs, but I have tried to illustrate this point.

Differences in many senses are as uninteresting and unentertaining as the task of getting down to business; the task of constructing statesmen. Now it is in that connection that it seems to me most vital to discuss the public obligation of business. I haven't any program that I care to lay before this audience. I have for New Jersey, but that is another matter, but I haven't any program here. I am trying in this discussion to lay the basis of a program, trying to contribute my little mite to the awakening of the business conscience.

What are the public obligations to [of] business? Well, in the first place it ought to be obvious to us the primary obligation of business is to abide by the law; to act in accordance, not only with the letter of the law, but with the spirit and not try to get around [it]. That's the first public obligation to [of] business. The second obligation is contributing to the general enlightenment and the general guidance in some active way. You don't need to have me tell you what has been the practice of only too many business

men. The minute statutes have been drawn which interfered
with the process they had been using, they call in lawyers to see
how they can keep on with the process and keep out of jail; how
they can avoid the obligation of the law. There seems to have
been in the past generation in this country insistent effort on the
part of many business men to avoid obeying the law in its obvious
meaning and intent. I do not wonder at this.

Everybody has an instinct to disobey the law; particularly
when he thinks it has not been determined as meant for them.
They reason that it is interference with what they are pleased
to call private affairs by public regulation, forgetting in no community in the world is there anything that affects anybody but
yourself, which is a private affair. So far as I myself am concerned, if there is anything that concerns me absolutely and
nobody else, I dare say I may do as I please. I may clarify my judgment, purify my character or obscure my judgment. I may be-
smirch my character, I may abuse it and if I go and die in shame
alone I dare say it is nobody's business but my own. I can't imagine a circumstance where I could so separate myself, but theoreti-
cally I am willing to admit that's a private affair. There isn't
anything that doesn't affect some of the great masses of business.

And will you look me in the eye and say that is a private affair? That it is nobody's business but your own when in the conduct of your business you are drawing thousands of men into
relations with yourself? Do you mean that you can conduct your
business as a purely private affair? There is no such thing as
private business unless you want to conduct it without customers.

I dare say I can run a political party with only myself in it
as a private affair and I would be in no danger of governing anything.

So that the first thing is to abide by the law in letter and
spirit. When a statute is passed, put about and see that you
conform with the new trade winds. You are a servant of the
community. That is a fundamental and most neglected obligation of business. I can give you an interesting illustration. You
know most states have passed inheritance and succession taxes.
After they were passed persons of large fortunes consulted their
lawyers as to how they could evade the statutes and escape paying these taxes. It was suggested that they incorporate the family, so that there wouldn't be any succession. I haven't asked
any judge how that would work but perhaps it is a feasible
suggestion. Under it the head of the family is the head of the
corporation, and as soon as he dies another is elected to take his
place. And so the law would be set at naught. It is just as much

nullification as the action of the state of South Carolina years ago, when the state said that because the people of South Carolina did not believe congress had the right to pass such laws as had been passed with respect to the tariff, South Carolina would refuse to pay duty, standing on its rights as a sovereign state. It didn't work.

You do not believe they are just, therefore you will get around them; you will not obey them. You set at defiance the rulings of society. It is impossible, ladies and gentlemen, for a self governed state to be conducted on such terms. Business men have the choice now—a choice which I almost envy them—of lending their hearty co-operation to the enforcement of the law and so make other legislation absolutely unnecessary.

If the business interests of this country had the enlightenment to see the opportunity they could prove themselves governed by statesmen and could make unnecessary difficult work of statesmenship in party affairs. I used to be a lawyer. I repented early and stopped. I was saying to a body of lawyers the other day[4] that I could quite agree with them that most of the legislation directed against the corporations had been ill advised, but, I said, the reason is you men who advise the corporations do not advise the legislatures. You know what things are going on and you know how they could be settled. When you tell the legislators how we shall have the right sort of legislation and not before, and if you want to preserve your corporations, you will volunteer this advice just as soon as possible.

If you don't think the laws are right, make them right. The minute people see you are doing it in the spirit of those who would reform the body politic and the body economic, you will have destroyed the whole air of hostility and bring about a condition of affairs in which business can prosper. And when I hear men say with respect to legislative programs, "Let business alone. Give it time to take a breath and it will recover," I always reply, "Put business upon a footing where we can afford to let it alone and we will do so with the greatest of pleasure, but no business can prosper or ought not to prosper that is not right."

Don't you realize, gentlemen, that most of the attacks made upon business are made upon a false body of information? Don't you know that the trouble in politics now is the number of impressions widespread throughout the country which are not founded upon fact? Don't you know that the way to purify the

---

[4] In his speech, "The Lawyer and the Community," delivered in Chattanooga before the American Bar Association and printed at Aug. 31, 1910, Vol. 21.

air is to clarify it; that the way to check wrong courses is to supply the information? It is the obligation of business men to inform the public in detail concerning conditions upon which business is transacted.

For example: It is believed that a great many corporations have a very large proportion of watered stock. Is it so? Is it so? Just suppose—it would be like a fairy tale to suppose—just suppose that certain corporations would come out and say, "Yes, such and such a proportion of our stock is fictitious, is watered stock. Some has been sold to bona fide purchasers. We are sorry, but we don't know what to do about it. The rest is distributed among persons whom we can name because they are on our books. Will it do to sponge that off and stop paying dividends on it?"

How the public would be electrified. How business would look up. I say up, because sometimes business is so flat on its back that it can't look any other way. Now by one process or another we have got a lot of watered stock because high prices pay for the watered stock.

It is robbery to make people pay prices so high as to pay for the dividends on watered stock. Just as soon as the business conscience grasps that fundamental fact it will become active and begin to do things.

You can't long conduct business in an atmosphere of public suspicion. Moral: Remove the suspicion. How? By coming out and removing the things upon which suspicion is based. Let us know what the facts are from the books and from the men themselves.

It is a big thing. It is a moral regeneration but I am among those who are hopeful it is coming. Now the part of it all that lies nearest my conscience is the third public obligation to [of] business. It is to take hands off politics. The corporate connection of business with politics; politics being corporate also, is the most fundamental evil of our day. That's the reason that every corrupt practices act that our legislatures pass has to contain the statement there shall be no contribution from corporations or business houses of any kind to campaign funds. You know what happens. Individuals connected with great business houses contribute as individuals, obeying neither the letter nor the spirit of the law. As a matter of fact they contribute as members of the business association. The most manifest obligation that rests upon business now is to get that connection absolute [dissolved] and put politics again upon an open footing, getting the campaign funds contributed be [by] genuine individuals.

Why do great corporations in states where parties are very

nearly divided in the power they exercise, why do they contribute to the funds of both parties. Because they want to stand in with whichever party is in power, not thinking of the program of reform. Why, it has come to such a pass as, I need not tell you[,] that in some states certain legislators introduce bills for the purpose of being bought off. They call them strike bills, striking for money and holding the threat of passage over the head of certain business interests which they will injure in order to be bought not to pass them.

I am happy to say that this practice is not general, but you will find it sporadically here, there and elsewhere. And that is because private business is behind the move to buy immunity from legislation. Now if legislation is such as to be detrimental to business with the likelihood that it will be detrimental to others as well, there is a better way, and that is to come out in the open with argument and persuasion, which is better than to buy votes.

Shaping political manhood and political capacity, therefore, it goes without saying, is an obligation of business, to lead public opinion and by honorable methods to control legislation and the opinion that lies back of it. One trouble is that we discuss these matters only [at] election time, just as if the main business is to put men into office. That is not the main business at all. There should be discussion between elections so that opinion can be made.

All that I am pleading for is a revival in some sense of the true spirit of America. America was born to serve the common interest. America came into existence as a place where institutions were to be set up to serve mankind. That is the basis of every honorable thing that has characterized American history. The interest of the people is something that ought not to have to be recovered in America. We should see to it that we serve nobody in particular, that we are not friends of capital as against labor or anybody else.

But we are friends of that universal operation of justice which will unite those interests in a common cause with the common understanding of what the interest of mankind demands. Why, America will have forgotten her reason for existence when she has forgotten these things! America is not the first to be wealthy, to have the support, the moral strength. Other nations have rivaled her in that. They have been just as great proportionately as we and have gone down to oblivion and shame upon the wreckage of power. America has as her one distinction that she has sought to use power for service, for progress, for enlightenment, for life.

Men should not be debauched, but should be liberated, given free air to breathe not only the way nature vouchsafed but the air of just opinion, the air of just laws, the support of broad courts and maintenance which can be got only by the rectifying judgment of instructed public opinion. This was the standard of America. I wonder if you remember certain lines of Tennyson which seem to embody this:

> A nation yet, the rulers and the ruled—
> Some sense of duty, something of a faith,
> Some reverence for the laws ourselves have made,
> Some patient force to change them when we will,
> Some civic manhood firm against the crowd.[5]

Can you find anywhere in the perfect sentences of literature a better summary of what is the spirit of America and does it need that we should make journeys to commend the youth of what we would fain have our nation be?[6]

Printed in the *Milwaukee Journal*, Nov. 18, 1910.
  [5] From "The Princess, Conclusion."
  [6] There is a WWT outline of this address, with the composition date of Nov. 15, 1910, and an undated WWhw and WWsh outline in WP, DLC.

From Cyrus Hall McCormick

My dear Woodrow: Chicago 17 November 1910.

David Jones and I went to the station to meet you this morning, but thinking, you were coming by the "Special" which was an hour late, we did not get to the Pennsylvania Station until you had come and gone; but I am glad to learn that William L. Wilson[1] met you, as he tells me he did.

David Jones wishes to know when you are arriving tomorrow. I understand from William L. Wilson that you will lunch with the Princeton men at the University Club, and I will be there to meet you.

The matter that I especially wished to talk with you about is whether it is advisable for you to return on December twelfth to speak to the Manufacturers' Association. It is quite possible that you have made such promises now that you cannot change this appointment; but on the merits of the case, it is hard for me to see how it could help you, and it might be embar[r]assing for you: so that before I see you, you might be thinking, over the circumstances of the case to see whether this appointment can be changed for you. David Jones agrees with me in this.[2]

I am,   Very sincerely yours,   Cyrus H. McCormick.

S.

TLS (WP, DLC).
¹ William Lawrence Wilson, Princeton 1903, salesman for the Aluminum Company of America.
² He did speak, despite McCormick's advice; a news report of his address is printed at Dec. 13, 1910.

From James Alphonsus Hamill¹

Dear Governor Wilson: Jersey City [N.J.], November 17, 1910.

I am very thankful for your kind letter congratulating me upon my re-election to Congress. In returning my deepest congratulations to you on your own sweeping triumph, I want to take occasion to remark that it is over your election that all Jersey Democrats are justly highly elated. The Democratic party is now on top again and I know that, under your administration, its conduct during the next three years will do credit to its best traditions.

I am, with warmest assurances,

Very sincerely yours,   James A. Hamill

TLS (WP, DLC).
¹ Democratic representative from the 10th congressional district of New Jersey.

From Cleveland Hoadley Dodge

Dear Woodrow,   New York Nov. 18th, 1910

Without using your name or mine [George W.] Perkins has had several talks with Harvey who has seen Smith, but without any satisfactory result, & it is evident that Smith proposes to go to the Senate. I hear from a reliable source that all the Democratic Assemblymen, but six, are under such financial obligations to him that he owns them absolutely.

In this connection, Frank Speir¹ came to see me Thursday & I had a long talk with him. He is very close to Jim Bathgate '94,² & though they are both Republicans, they are warm supporters of your's & very anxious about the present situation as it affects you. Bathgate is evidently in touch with those high in Democratic counsels, for he told Speir of Smith's conversation with you, & repeated almost verbatim what was said, in the very language which you used in describing it to me.³

Both Speir & Bathgate have very decided views as to the best policy for you to pursue, & whilst I do not *entirely* agree with them, & whilst moreover, you are the doctor, & cannot blindly follow anyone, nevertheless, they have considerable valuable information & understand the situation so well that I think it would be well for you to see them. They have no axes to grind & are not seeking anything for themselves, but are only interested in your future. They are willing to take a day off & go down to see you if you are willing & I have suggested to Speir, that when you are home, he communicate with you & endeavor to make an appointment. I thought, though, that it would be well to post you first. You will probably hear from him next week

   Trusting that you have had a pleasant trip

   With warm regards   Y'rs aff'ly   C H Dodge

ALS (WP, DLC).

[1] Francis Speir, Jr., Princeton 1877, a Wall Street lawyer who resided in South Orange, N. J.

[2] James Edward Bathgate, Jr., Princeton 1894, associated with Bimbler Van Wagenen & Co., pork dealers of Newark. His home was in Basking Ridge, N. J.

[3] Dodge referred to Wilson's first conference, in Princeton on November 11, 1910, with Smith to discuss the election of a United States senator. Wilson and Smith gave two different versions of what transpired at this meeting; for Wilson's account, see his statement printed at December 23, 1910; for Smith's recollection, see the portions of his statement quoted in the news report printed at December 28, 1910, and Smith's full statement, printed in the *Newark Evening News* and the Trenton *True American*, Dec. 27, 1910, and not reproduced in this volume.

In his statement of December 23, 1910, Wilson claimed that, before he consented to become a gubernatorial candidate, a spokesman for Smith had assured him that Smith would not be a candidate for the Senate, that he, Smith, was in poor health, and that he did not desire the office. However, according to Wilson's account, at their meeting on November 11, Smith said that he was now "feeling stronger" and hoped that the legislature would offer him the seat. Wilson said that he told Smith that his candidacy "would confirm all the ugliest suspicions of the campaign concerning him, and urged him very strongly not to allow his name to be used at all." Wilson added that his arguments had no effect on Smith.

In contrast, Smith insisted that he had not decided to seek the senatorship when he visited Wilson in November. He said that Wilson professed a high regard for him but warned that his candidacy would meet with some opposition from the people. According to Smith, Wilson said that the people wanted someone who had not previously been involved in politics. Smith also stated that Wilson told him that he considered the senatorial primary "a farce" and Martine's possible election "a disgrace" to the state. Smith further claimed that Wilson suggested that he and Smith look for a compromise candidate (*Newark Evening News*, Dec. 28, 1910). Although Wilson later claimed that he was suggesting only that Smith himself consider proposing a compromise candidate and that he, Wilson, was not making the proposal for himself (news report printed at Dec. 28, 1910), he admitted in one interview (printed at Dec. 21, 1910) that he did make such a suggestion to Smith at a subsequent meeting on December 6. Although Wilson at once categorically and vehemently denied saying this (*Newark Evening News*, Dec. 22, 1910), there seems no reason to doubt the accuracy of any portion of this interview. It is very probable that Wilson initiated the proposal at the first meeting on November 11, as Smith remembered, and not at the second meeting.

After the conference with Wilson, Smith conferred with Harvey at Deal, N. J., and while both men agreed that Wilson would probably defeat him, Smith concluded, "Well, by God, I guess I'll let him beat me." Harvey told Smith that his sole interest was making Wilson President and promised to stay out of the entire fight. William O. Inglis, "Helping to Make a President," *Collier's Weekly*, LVIII (Oct. 21, 1916), 14.

Dodge's letter of November 18 was only one of a series of signs that Smith was determined to run. Two days after his meeting with Wilson on November 11, Smith for the first time hinted publicly that he might become a candidate (E. S. Wilde to WW, Nov. 14, 1910, n. 2). In a letter dated November 19,

Essex County's eleven Democratic assemblymen-elect wrote to Smith urging him to be a candidate (*Newark Evening News*, Nov. 21, 1910). On November 23, Smith's lieutenant, James R. Nugent, allegedly boasted that Robert Davis, Hudson County Democratic boss, had promised to deliver the votes of the entire Hudson county legislative delegation to Smith (*Trenton Evening Times*, Nov. 23, 1910). On November 25, Nugent denied having made any such statement (*ibid.*, Nov. 26, 1910). However, as W. W. St. John to WW, Nov. 22, 1910, n. 1, reveals, Davis had pledged at least his personal support to Smith.

A News Report of a Public Lecture in Chicago

[Nov. 19, 1910]

WILSON APOSTLE OF LAW'S REIGN

Schoolman, Who Is Governor Elect of New Jersey, Urges Business to Bow to Government.

"Let us never be so forgetful of our debts as to forget the men who have awakened us to the social and civic conditions of our day," said Woodrow Wilson, historian, president of Princeton university, and Democratic governor-elect of New Jersey, in an address before the Business Service Lecture league in Chicago last night.

"But," he added, "let us beware of the agitator. It has been truly said that the people of the country were so fast asleep that it took a brass band to wake them up. But we can't solve the problems of the day by getting in behind the brass band. The solution will come in quiet conferences, where men get down to brass tacks."

Dr. Wilson came to Chicago to deliver a lecture upon the "Development of the Business Conscience" at Association hall.[1] It was not a large audience—some sixty odd persons being present—but an enthusiastic one. Some men prominent in local politics were noticed, among them Roger Sullivan, John Maynard Harlan, and Congressman Foss.[2]

The gist of Dr. Wilson's advice, his panacea for the correction of the evils against which the ardor of the people has been aroused, is contained in these three categorical statements which he made:

"The fundamental obligation of business is to comply with the law in letter and in spirit, and if the law is bad, we are going to find it out and correct it with less poison than through the processes of chicanery.

"The second obligation of business is to co-operate in the extension of such parts of the law which are found to be just and equitable.

"The third obligation of business is to withdraw from politics."

Dr. Wilson led up to the crisis of his argument by a general declaration that novel and complicated conditions have arisen in American life during the last twenty years, which make this an age beset with peculiar dangers. He contended the difficulty of solving the problems was enhanced because the people do not view them "with the calmness of noonday, for we are just awake, and are in the excitement of the morning."

He described the great interests—"spelled with a capital I"— when arrayed against each other as "painfully resembling warfare, and disturbing the whole equilibrium of society." Continuing on this thought, he said:

"The problem of today is whether the interests shall be the masters of society, or whether society shall control the interests and make them servants of the people."

He declared that today there is no such thing as "private business," and said: "In our day we have witnessed in America the submergence of the individual into the organization, particularly into that economic organization known as the corporation. The small group of men who manage these corporations have the power of thousands, and some of them have risen so high that they are easily picked out as the men who control the economic organization and energy of the whole nation and whose power extends into foreign lands so as to make their operations the subject of international politics.

"Some of the irresponsible men use this power in a hazardous way, and there are no means to hold them responsible except their own conscience."

Dr. Wilson said he believed in the heroic exercises from the platform and the magnificent oratory that had stirred up the conscience of the people and brought about the civic awakening, but he contended that these forensics did not create an atmosphere in which things can be settled.

"When I hear men say, 'Let business alone, let us go back to prosperous times,' I answer them, 'If business will conduct itself as we are trying to make it do by pressure of the law, then we will stop the pressure of the law.' If you expect men to make progress, then the progress must come from within the community and not through the law. The main object of good business should be to make the law unnecessary.

"So many of the big business corporations are trying to circumvent the law that the impression has gone out that lawyers are employed by all business men to find out how the law can be evaded rather than to show them how to keep within its bounds."

He remarked that one of the greatest troubles in modern times came from the "conspiracy for silence and concealment" on the part of the corporations. He said if the people could only find out the basis for making rates or for the prices fixed on commodities they could easily tell whether they were too high or too low.

He declared emphatically for government regulation of rates, and stated as his belief that the people of the country were so fair that if an honest attempt was made by corporations to show that rates are too low the people would be willing to see them increased.

"American communities are not bent upon the destruction of business," he said. "The corporations should coöperate in the enlightenment of the people and the spread of knowledge. The American public wants to know with what it is dealing, and when it knows you can depend upon it to deal justly."

He asserted the political organization is a necessity, and said the country cannot be run without it. "But when the people find that organization is not run for the advancement of political policies, but for the advancement of the private fortunes of the men who constitute the machine, when they find a corrupt alliance between the corrupt political machine and the corrupt business, it must be broken up at any cost. That is why the people prefer the amateur in politics, to the professional politician, who is in the game for what it brings him. If there isn't money in politics, there isn't going to be any corrupt politics.

"Where does the money come from?" he concluded.[3]

Printed in the *Chicago Daily Tribune*, Nov. 19, 1910; some editorial headings omitted.

[1] He was speaking in the Young Men's Christian Association Hall.

[2] Sullivan and Harlan are identified in Vol. 21. George Edmund Foss was a Republican representative from the 10th congressional district of Illinois and a brother of Eugene Noble Foss of Massachusetts.

[3] For this address, Wilson used the outlines described in n. 6 to the public lecture printed at Nov. 17, 1910.

From William W. St. John

Dear Mr. Wilson: Trenton, N. J. Nov. 19, 1910.

Within the last few days I have collected column upon column of news articles and editorial comment from papers in all parts of the State dealing with the Senatorial situation. But I will not burden you with it all, as I am tempted to. However, the enclosed clippings are from today's Jersey City Journal and the Trenton Times,[1] and I submit them as showing the importance and drift of the situation at this time.

With best wishes, I am

Sincerely Yours   W W St John.

ALS (WP, DLC).
[1] The enclosures are missing. The Jersey City *Jersey Journal* Nov. 19, 1910, included several articles dealing with the senatorial situation. A front-page news report contained the announcement by Frank S. Katzenbach, Jr., that he would not be a candidate for the Senate seat, and it further indicated growing support for Martine among incoming Democratic members of the legislature. An editorial urged Martine's election, calling his possible defeat "the most flagrant exhibition of bad faith ever given by any political party in this State." "The public," it continued, "could place only one interpretation upon it, and that would be that the votes of a majority of the Democrats in the Legislature had been bought outright. No one would mince matters in passing judgment upon such an act of perfidy." Similarly, George Lawrence Record warned in his column that "powerful financial interests, which we term 'Wall Street,' " were "keenly interested" in the outcome of the senatorial election. He praised Martine as "a man of unquestioned probity of character," whose sympathies were with the people and who could not be reached by money. If Martine did not receive sufficient support, Record wrote, Republican and Democratic conservatives would unite behind the candidacy of James Smith, Jr., who would be "a power in the Senate for the protection of every corporate interest." Record also maintained that Smith's election would seriously damage Wilson's ability to achieve the reforms which he had pledged in his campaign.

The *Trenton Evening Times*, Nov. 19, 1910, reprinted editorials from the *Newark Evening News*, Hoboken *Observer*, *New York Tribune*, Jersey City *Jersey Journal*, *Paterson Guardian*, and *Elizabeth Evening Times*, all emphasizing the significance of the coming senatorial election, some warning that the Democrats would be betraying faith with the voters if they turned their backs on Martine and elected Smith, and some denouncing Smith as the prototype of the corrupt political boss, able to purchase a seat in the Senate. The *Trenton Evening Times* in the same issue also featured Katzenbach's announcement that he was not a candidate.

From John Grier Hibben

My dear Woodrow   Princeton, New Jersey. November 21, 1910

I had hoped to express to you in person what I am about to write; but as we have not chanced to meet since your election as Governor, I am now sending this letter. As you know, I always had an intimate part in your joys and successes, and in all that related to your welfare. And although these experiences are in that past which time and circumstance have put behind us both, nevertheless, in memory of those old days you will allow me the privilege, I am sure, of presenting to you my congratulations upon the splendid victory and distinguished honour which you have won in the recent election.

Ever faithfully yours   John Grier Hibben

ALS (WP, DLC).

From Charles William Eliot[1]

My dear Doctor Wilson: New York November 21, 1910

I have just heard from Mr. [Elliot Hersey] Goodwin, the Secretary of the National Civil Service Reform League, that he is inviting you to speak at the forthcoming annual meeting of the League at Baltimore.[2] I hope very much that you will accept this invitation. Your influence will be peculiarly valuable at this moment, when you are about to enter on an important public office, after a campaign remarkable for its admirable methods and its effective results. I feel sure that you are in entire sympathy with the objects of the League and that you will make a very effective statement on its behalf. To my thinking, civil service reform lies at the foundation of all other governmental reforms. Some people have supposed that it was a reform accomplished, but as you doubtless know, it is only a good beginning that has been made. All the higher offices in the public service are still under the spoils system, the merit system applying with very few exceptions only to subordinate places.

The National government can never have efficient, businesslike, honest service until the merit system is applied not only to new appointments but to promotions, and the higher places are visibly within reach of competent young men who go in at the bottom.

With hearty congratulations on your primary success and with strong hope that the service of the Nation will next claim you, I am   Sincerely yours,   Charles W. Eliot

TLS (WP, DLC).
¹ Who was writing in his capacity as president of the National Civil Service Reform League.
² Goodwin's letter of invitation is missing.

To Charles William Eliot

My dear Doctor Eliot: Princeton, N. J. November 22, 1910

I warmly appreciate your letter of November 21st.

There is no one whose approval and good wishes I more sincerely desire or appreciate than your own. It gives me courage and additional hope in the new career I have been drawn into.

I wish with all my heart I could attend the Annual Meeting of the National Civil Service Reform League. Like yourself I regard the reforms set by that League as fundamental to all good government. I shall always hold myself ready to do anything possible to promote the realizations of its members, but unhappily I have bound myself to engagements at the time of the meeting, from which I cannot honorably withdraw.

With warm regard and appreciation,

Sincerely yours,   Woodrow Wilson

TLS (C. W. Eliot Papers, MH-Ar).

From William Francis Magie, with Enclosure

Dear Sir: Princeton, N. J. November 22, 1910.

The enclosed resolutions were adopted by the University Faculty at their meeting held November 21, 1910 and were ordered sent to you and published in the Alumni Weekly.

I am,   Yours truly,   W. F. Magie

TLS (WP, DLC).

E N C L O S U R E

A Resolution

Nov. 22, 1910.

MINUTE OF THE FACULTY OF PRINCETON UNIVERSITY ON THE RESIGNATION OF DR. WOODROW WILSON FROM THE PRESIDENCY

In view of the resignation of Dr. Woodrow Wilson from the Presidency of Princeton University, the Faculty wish hereby to put on record their sense of the great loss the University has suffered. As a student, as our colleague in the Faculty and as President, Dr. Wilson has been for many years an esteemed and distinguished member of this academic body. Coming to the Presidency at a critical period in the history of Princeton and of higher education in this country, he found himself confronted with some of the most vital questions of University policy. The demand which had arisen for a revision of the course of study was met during the first year of his administration by the institution of the Departmental System in the election of studies which led not only to a more effective organization of the curriculum as a whole, but also supplied a happy solution to the question of the relation of requirement and free election in the choice of studies. The demand for more efficient methods of instruction which was due in great measure to increased numbers of students here as well as in other colleges and universities, was met by the introduction of the Preceptorial System which resulted in a substantial enlargement of the Faculty by the addition of a body of carefully selected men and made it possible to give individual instruction by dividing classes into smaller groups, thereby bringing the student into closer and less formal relations with his instructors.

The social conditions prevailing in the undergraduate life of the University was another subject to which Dr. Wilson devoted much anxious thought and attention. He was convinced that forces were at work which were inconsistent with that spirit of equality on which Princeton has always laid so much stress, and though the only measure that was proposed as a remedy gave rise to violent controversy, it will be readily acknowledged that Dr. Wilson has by his powerful appeals aroused the attention of the academic world to the existence of certain tendencies in the social life of our colleges and universities which demand the most serious consideration.

The administration of Dr. Wilson has been signalized by the enlargement and strengthening of all the great departments of study, through the addition of professors who had won eminence in their special fields; by the great development of the scientific departments of the university in the building and equipment of great laboratories for study and research; by the splendid material growth of the university made possible by the unstinted generosity of its friends; by the notable increase of endowments and of other sources of income in which the liberality of Princeton's alumni has been one of the largest factors. In material prosperity Dr. Wilson's administration stands as one of the most notable in the history of Princeton or of any other university; while this record of material progress has been paralleled by one of intellectual growth no less marked, in the development of the courses of study, in practically doubling the size of the Faculty, and in the reforms which have been effected in methods of instruction. To this must be added a corresponding increase of Graduate courses of study, the development of the Graduate School and the liberal endowment, through the generosity of several donors, of the Graduate College.

Continuing the noble tradition followed by his predecessors, Dr. Wilson has not failed to magnify the public side of his great office. Throughout his administration it has been his practice to devote his extraordinary powers of speech and debate to the public discussion of leading questions of educational and national interest. It is not too much to say that in the exercise of this function he has won a national reputation and has brought fame to Princeton and secured for her a position of leadership in the educational movements of the country.

In connection with the internal life of the University we wish to recognize as no unimportant part of his service the constant efforts he has put forth to raise the intellectual standards of the student body by holding them true to the highest ideals of scholarship and in pursuance of this aim, his abiding sense of the importance of keeping Princeton in close touch and sympathy with the broader life of the nation and with the federation of universities[1] of which Princeton is a part.

With a deep sense of our loss in Dr. Wilson's resignation, it is yet with feelings of pride that we spare him to the wider service of the state to which he has been called. Princeton has ever been the mother of statesmen and of men who have responded to the call to public service and she takes pride in this opportunity of affording a notable proof that the spirit of older Princeton still lives in her sons. We wish to assure Dr. Wilson that he bears with him in his great work for the state, our pride as well as our affectionate remembrance. The laurels that he wins will be ours also, and we shall claim a share in the great service which he renders to the state and nation.

Attest   W. F. Magie   Clerk

T MS (WP, DLC).
[1] The Association of American Universities.

From William W. St. John

Dear Mr. Wilson: [Trenton, N. J.] Nov. 22, 1910.

As your telephone was reported out of order tonight, I am sending Mr. Davis' address[1] by letter. It is:

Robert Davis,
City Collector's Office,
City Hall, Jersey City N. J.
L. D. Telephone 6 Jersey City

Today's Newark News contains the enclosed paragraph about Mr. Davis.[2] As you will note, a conference with the legislative delegation is scheduled for tomorrow (Wednesday.)

Sincerely,   W W St John

ALS (WP, DLC).
[1] Wilson wanted to dissolve the alliance between Hudson County Democratic boss Robert Davis and Smith and to win Davis's support for Martine. In a conference at Princeton on November 20, he had asked Matthias C. Ely, editor of the Hoboken *Observer*, to arrange for an early conference between himself and Davis (see J. A. Dear, Jr., to WW, Nov. 26, 1910).
Wilson made the unannounced trip to Jersey City on November 25, but before he saw Davis, he met with Joseph P. Tumulty, former progressive Democratic assemblyman from Hudson County and James E. Martine's manager in the senatorial fight. According to Tumulty's recollection in 1916, Wil-

son was not altogether certain that he could prevent Smith's election and pointed out that some of his friends had advised him to permit the matter to drift, that Martine was incompetent, and that the state would resent his interference. Tumulty allegedly replied that New Jersey was yearning for leadership, that the decent people who needed to be aroused were in favor of Martine, and that if Wilson did not lead, someone else would take the leadership much to his injury and loss of prestige. J. P. Tumulty to WW, Jan. 17, 1916, TLS (WP, DLC). Tumulty's account of this conversation in his *Woodrow Wilson as I Know Him* (Garden City, N. Y., and Toronto, 1921), pp. 51-55, seems to the Editors highly imaginative.

Tumulty escorted Wilson from his law office to Davis's modest brick home at 230 Grove Street, but Tumulty did not participate in the conference (*Newark Evening News*, Nov. 26, 1910). Davis, who was terminally ill, had recently returned from New York after treatment at a sanitarium. Wilson presented the case for Martine's election to Davis, arguing that failure to elect him would be a violation of party pledges. However, Wilson reportedly coupled this appeal with a tougher political approach. He told Davis that he was determined to be the leader of both the party and the state, and that failure to support Martine would be an act of party disloyalty. "Dissident" Democrats could expect to be treated as Republicans, and Wilson implied that he would use his powers of patronage accordingly (*ibid.*; Trenton *True American*, Nov. 28, 1910). As reported in a later account, Davis urged Wilson to stay out of the senatorial fight and promised in return to support his entire legislative program. Wilson replied, "How do I know you will? If you beat me in this the first fight, how do I know you won't be able to beat me in everything?" Thereupon Davis affectionately placed his hand on Wilson's shoulder and told him that he could not violate his agreement with Smith. Burton J. Hendrick, "Woodrow Wilson: Political Leader," *McClure's Magazine*, xxxviii (Dec. 1911), 225. Davis also expressed the hope that he and Wilson would not become enemies because of his pledge to Smith (*Newark Evening News*, Nov. 26, 1910).

Wilson's visit to Davis and the amicable tone of the meeting played an important role in securing additional support for Martine. Even before Wilson's conference with Davis, the Hudson County legislative delegation was in open revolt over Davis's alleged promise to deliver its votes to Smith, and the *Newark Evening News* reported on November 25 that ten of the twelve Hudson County assemblymen-elect were opposed to Smith. In the face of such disagreement within his own ranks, even Davis began to waver and wonder if there was a possible way out of his commitment to Smith. He quietly let it be known that he would not be "hurt" if the Hudson County delegation disobeyed his orders and voted against Smith (J. P. Tumulty to WW, Nov. 30, 1910; J. M. Noonan to WW, Dec. 4, 1910). Since the Hudson delegation held the key block of votes in the senatorial fight, Wilson conferred with most of the Hudson members on December 5 at his home in Princeton. About this meeting, see WW to O. G. Villard, Dec. 5, 1910, n. 1.

² The enclosure is missing, but it was a brief news report of Robert Davis' return to Jersey City after treatment for stomach trouble at a sanitarium in New York. The article stated that Davis would be meeting with the Hudson County assemblymen-elect on November 23 to discuss the senatorial question and that the outcome of this and similar conferences throughout the state would determine whether Smith became a declared candidate. *Newark Evening News*, Nov. 22, 1910.

From George Mason La Monte

Bound Brook New Jersey
My dear Dr. Wilson: November 22, 1910.

I was very glad to have the talk I did with you yesterday, and the more I think of it the more I am convinced that we must stand out against the senatorial aspirations of Mr. Smith.

If we were committed to his side, it would create a condition which we could not possibly explain. Besides this, I really believe that if we stand firm, he will, eventually, withdraw. It is a trial, and if he should succeed something might come up later on that would appear to him just as important as the senatorship, and he would be quite likely to again make demands. If he does withdraw, he is not likely to make any demands which you, and your friends, would not be quite glad to concede.

I think if he could be assured, in some way, that Martine could be eliminated, he would be quite likely to withdraw promptly. The difficulty ahead is that if he does persist, we have to apply to the Martine men for help to defeat the Smith aspitations [aspirations]; and then would have to immediately apply to the Smith men to help select someone in the place of Martine.

I find it hard to believe that we can be blocked at the very outset of the administration. We must find some way to escape from the dilemna [dilemma].

Please give my best regards to the members of your family, and believe me   Yours very truly,   Geo. M. La Monte

TLS (WP, DLC).

From Oswald Garrison Villard

Dear Dr. Wilson: New York November 22, 1910.

Would it be possible for me to see you either next Saturday morning or some afternoon next week? I would like very much to keep in personal touch with you in order that the Evening Post may assist you to the greatest advantage, and also because there is a New Jersey matter which will be of considerable interest to you about which I have just received some information and on which the editors would like your advice.

With kind regards,
                Sincerely yours,   Oswald Garrison Villard.

TLS (WP, DLC).

From Thomas Nesbitt McCarter[1]

My Dear Dr. Wilson: Newark, N. J. November 22nd, 1910.

I congratulate you heartily upon the result of the election and wish for you a most successful and useful administration as Governor of the State.

The campaign conducted by you was altogether the most effective ever carried on in the State.

So far as the performance of our respective spheres of duty brings us in contact during your administration I assure you of my desire to co-operate with you and not to embarrass you.

Prior to your inauguration, or before you take any definite step by way of inaugural address or otherwise, I desire the opportunity of convincing you that the existing public utilities law[2] is not a meaningless make-shift, as you seemed to indicate during your campaign, but that on the other hand it contains all the essential provisions of supervision that such a measure should have, except rate-making. And furthermore, I would like to present to you my views on the kind of rate-making provision that should be adopted. For this purpose I will come to Princeton or elsewhere, as you may elect, at any time other than Mondays and Tuesdays, when my time is occupied by meetings at home.

With kind regards, I am,

Very truly yours,   Thos. N. McCarter.

TLS (WP, DLC).
 [1] Princeton 1888, president of the Public Service Corporation of New Jersey.
 [2] For a description, see n. 2 to the speech printed at Sept. 30, 1910, Vol. 21.

To Robert Garrett

My dear Mr. Garrett: Princeton, N. J. Nov. 23, 1910.

I need not tell you how deeply I appreciated your generous message,[1] but I must give myself the pleasure of doing so, if only to send in return my own warm regards and greetings along with my heartfelt thanks.

Gratefully yours,   Woodrow Wilson

TLS (Selected Corr. of R. Garrett, NjP).
 [1] R. Garrett to WW, Nov. 9, 1910, Vol. 21.

From Henry Jones Ford

Dear Governor: Princeton, New Jersey Nov. 23, 1910

I desire to add to what I said yesterday that whatever you decide to do prompt and positive action is extremely important. To allow the situation to drift would mean steady leakage of your influence. As matters now stand Smith will be compelled to make every effort to control the organization of the legislature, for as he approaches members he will be met by requests for his aid in getting the committee appointments they desire. There are already distinct signs that the situation is hardening and to mould it you cannot begin too soon.

"There is a tide in the affairs of men—"

Most Cordially Yours   Henry J. Ford

ALS (WP, DLC).

From Samuel Sidney McClure[1]

My dear Dr. Wilson: New York. November twenty-third, 1910.

In August McClure's Magazine published an article dealing with the reforms which Governor Hughes had been able to effect in the Republican party, and the handicaps under which he labored in making these reforms.[2] We hoped originally to have this article from Governor Hughes' own pen, and he would have written the article himself but for the fact that he was very much pressed for time in preparations for his new duties at Washington.[3] But he consented to give a morning to Mr. Burton J. Hendrick of our staff, and the article referred to in the August McClure's was prepared by Mr. Hendrick from the facts the Governor gave him at that interview.

Now that the Republican party has gone down to defeat, it seems an opportune time for a broad-gauged expression of opinion in regard to the meaning and probable outcome of the recent great Democratic victories. No one is better equipped to express such an opinion than yourself, and I should be glad to publish in McClure's an article, or a series of articles, dealing with the question. If the time at your disposal, and if your inclination are such that you can place your views before our readers, I shall indeed be glad. Would it be possible for Mr. Hendrick to have a talk with you in regard to it?[4]

Faithfully yours,   S S M Clure.

TLS (WP, DLC).
[1] Publisher and editor of McClure's Magazine.
[2] Burton J. Hendrick, "Governor Hughes and the Albany Gang," McClure's Magazine, XXXV (Sept. 1910), 495-512.
[3] He had just been appointed Associate Justice of the Supreme Court by President Taft.
[4] Wilson did not write the article, nor was one written by Hendrick on the basis of an interview on this subject with Wilson.

From Matthias Cowell Ely

Dear Sir: Hoboken, N. J. November 23, 1910

So far as I have been able, I have secured the co-operation of newspapers in carrying out your wishes as expressed last Sun-

day,[1] but I fear it will be impossible to make a thoroughly successful job of it. Mr. Smith seems to be moving forward with all his
energy toward his goal. This end of the State is thoroughly
aroused, and were it not for the belief that you could be relied
upon to prevent a great misfortune, it is difficult to say to what
extreme decent citizens would go. I am told that preparations
are being made for mass meetings in several Counties and if
necessary the uprising will be formidable. I dare say however,
that you are aware of most of these facts.

We are all convinced that the sole reliance of the Party at this
time is yourself. If there is anything you want me to do at any
time or anything you want the paper to do, you need only ask
it. We are heart and soul for the new Democratic leader.

Yours very respectfully   Matt C Ely.

TLS (WP, DLC).

[1] November 20, in a conference at Prospect attended by Wilson, Ely, and
James Kerney. Wilson had obviously asked Ely to rally Democratic editors
in the state in a campaign to discourage Smith from entering the senatorial
race. As has already been noted, Wilson had also asked Ely to arrange an early
meeting between himself and Robert Davis.

Kerney, *The Political Education of Woodrow Wilson* (New York and London,
1926), pp. 80-83, is the only account of this conference by a participant. He
says that Wilson expressed the belief that Smith would not run and that
Martine was not qualified for the senatorship. "He gave voice to the thought
that the Democrats should pick a man of the exceptional type of John R.
Hardin, a Princeton '80 man, who had first-class ability and would represent
New Jersey with both intelligence and credit. . . . Wilson had known Hardin
since their student days. To our suggestion that the Democrats had already
definitely decided on Martine he gave little weight."

Kerney's account runs contrary to contemporary evidence in one important
particular: Wilson had already decided that he had to support Martine, distasteful though the idea was to him. His letter to Harvey of November 15,
1910, makes this clear. However, we know that Wilson would have preferred
a compromise candidate. It is quite possible that he did say at the Prospect
conference that the best outcome would be Martine's withdrawal and Smith's
announcement not to run, followed by the choice of a candidate acceptable
to all Democratic factions. However, he might also have added that it was
obvious that this solution was not possible and he had no alternative but to go
all out for Martine. In any event, as we know, he asked Ely to rally Democratic
editors against Smith and to arrange for his meeting with Davis five days later,
when he, Wilson, came out openly and strongly for Martine.

In the light of what we know about Wilson's activities during the week
following the Prospect conference of December 20, the balance of Kerney's
account—to the effect that Wilson read no New Jersey newspapers, knew nothing
about the political situation in the state, and had to be spurred to come out
for Martine by William St. John's reports in the New York *Evening Post*—seems
far-fetched.

From Dan Fellows Platt

New Englewood, N. J. November 23, 1910.

The article in the Hoboken Observer tonight as to your fore
knowledge and approval of the action of the Bergen County
Democratic Committee endorsing Martine is unwarranted by

anything that occurred at the meeting or elsewhere. If you wish me to publicly deny your knowledge of the matter command me.
Dan Fellows Platt.

T telegram (WP, DLC).

To Dan Fellows Platt

[Princeton, N. J., Nov. 24, 1910]

Would be very much obliged if you would deny it. Could you arrange to have Senator-elect Johnson[1] meet me Collingwood Hotel New York, 45 W. 35 St. tomorrow afternoon about 5.[2] Do not know his address. If not then would like to know when he could see me there.   [Woodrow Wilson]

Transcript of WWsh telegram written on D. F. Platt to WW, Nov. 23, 1910.
  [1] James A. Courvoisier Johnson, lawyer and Mayor of Englewood and state senator-elect from Bergen County.
  [2] After Wilson concluded his conference with Robert Davis on November 25, he rejoined Tumulty and went into New York where they met for approximately two hours with Mark A. Sullivan. Wilson then left Sullivan and Tumulty to meet Johnson and Bergen County's assemblymen-elect, Garrabrant R. Alyea and William Henry Hinners. The Bergen County Democratic Committee had already declared in favor of Martine, and Wilson's conference with the three men was presumably designed to make sure of their votes. *Newark Evening News*, Nov. 26, 1910.

A Thanksgiving Day Address[1]

[[Nov. 24, 1910]]

After I had chosen the theme for this morning, "The Spirit of America," I marvelled at my own temerity. There is no man who can put into words the "Spirit of America." That spirit is made up alike of things that dwell in the heart; that linger in the imagination; that constitute the visions of individuals and of peoples. I suppose that every serious person, when a Thanksgiving Day comes, thinks first of all not of what things there are to be grateful for, but of the things that are in his life and in the life of the nation of which we ought to be ashamed. I suppose that it is impossible for any one to shake off the burden of the sense of sin and of wrong that there is in all life. And I am sorry to observe that, as my friends grow older, they grow less hopeful. They grow more thoughtful of the things that are burdensome and make less of the things that speak out confidence for the future. I find that the tendency of years is to bring pessimism, is to depress the expectations rather than exalt them.

  [1] Delivered in Har Sinai Temple in Trenton, N. J.

And so, every Thanksgiving Day ought to be a day in which we put aside these things and remind ourselves that it is a very common fact, shown through all the courses of history, that all life is a struggle against evil. All the evil in the world is antique; it is hoary with age. All the new things, or the good things, I would say, are new things. They have come into existence in a long, I am happy to believe, unbroken series with the progress of the ages. Each in the fullness of the time; each comes driven by the struggles of men; driven by that persistent heart-beat of hope that is behind all life, particularly of human life.

What we ought to remember on this Thanksgiving Day is that the grade is upward, and just because we feel the struggle of the muscle it is because we are pulling uphill. We would not do justice if we let ourselves go downhill. There is no exertion in that. If the decline be imperceptible, there is no struggle in it. We would not be depressed if we were going downhill. We feel the stream because we are going uphill. The heart is put to its utmost to sustain the struggle, and just because we know that the heart must resist, we should be impelled forward, for we know that there is something that is adventurous, something that is worth it; something that challenges our strength in the whole process.

The proclamation of the President, which you have just heard, speaks of the abundance of our material resources; their increasing abundance and abundance of our crops; and the growth of our population as an evidence of our increasing prosperity. That is true undoubtedly, but it would not be true if we didn't believe that in these increasing forces there resides a spirit which was meant for the service of mankind. There is no assurance in the increase of numbers if those numbers mean the spirit of the mob. There is no assurance in the increase of our material resources if our strength is going to be used for things that are wrong and unrighteous. Mere growth don't mean progress. It all depends upon the use that is made of these things; of the spirit that is in this multiplying people; for the purposes to which these multiplying resources are applied. There is no basis of hope unless there be in America a spirit which will make these things great by the uses to which they are put.

And so, when we ask ourselves what spirit is there in these people? What is it we are doing with our lives, our individual lives not only but our national lives, we must look that we don't deceive ourselves. There are two ways in which we may deceive ourselves. Every one knows the strength of evil that is in him. We are not to deceive ourselves by supposing that by the turn of the hand we can right all the wrong that is in us. But there is another way by which we may deceive ourselves. We may be so conscious of the power of evil that we may think we are well prepared to combat it. We must meet it. No matter how many times a man feels the force of the evil that is in him, if he comes out and conquers it he is just that much stronger. So that we are not battling ourselves to think meanly of America if the spirit that is in her doesn't rapidly accomplish the reforms we think desirable.

I suppose that any one who would undertake to put into words the spirit of America would choose first of all the word "toler-ance," the catholic spirit of the country, her welcome to all the world, her welcome to all races, to all creeds, to all undertakings, to all those things that constitute the hopes and aspirations and inspirations of life.

You know that a quaint old writer in the colonial times said of the population of New England that "God had sifted a whole nation to plant this seed in America."[2] When we grow anxious about the great streams of immigration that pour into our bor-ders, we must remember that during the greater part of the time of this process of increase or renewal or change that is exactly what has been going on. Other nations have been sifted in order to settle ours with the most vigorous portion of their population. If you are in any community and want to pick out the most promising lads, it will be those whom you expect to be aggressive and accomplished men.

You remember Kipling spoke of the difficulty of satisfying the feet of the young man.[3] Well, that is what America has been for the whole world. It has been to satisfy the feet of the young man. And for the most part the world is sending us her vigorous men.

I belong to a society[4] which is not intended for the purpose

2 Wilson was paraphrasing that famous classic of American homiletical litera-ture by William Stoughton, *New Englands True Interest; Not to Lie: Or, A Treatise declaring from the Word of Truth the Terms on which we stand, and the Tenure by which we hold our hitherto-continued Precious and Pleasant Things. Shewing What the blessed God expecteth from his People, and what they may rationally look for from him* (Cambridge, Mass., 1670). In this sermon preached in Boston on April 29, 1668, Stoughton actually said: "God sifted a whole Nation that he might send choice Grain over into this Wilder-ness."

3 Wilson referred to Rudyard Kipling's poem, "The Feet of the Young Men," which reads in part:
Who hath smelt wood-smoke at twilight? Who hath heard the birch-log burning?
Who is quick to read the noises of the night?
Let him follow with the others, for the Young Men's feet are turning
To the camps of proved desire and known delight!

4 Wilson had been a member since 1906 of the general committee of the

of encouraging immigration but instead of helping immigrants to place themselves to advantage after they get here. For instance, to guide those who come from agricultural countries to the sections of this country where they will receive the most benefit. And this society receives from time to time very full reports from agents in foreign countries whose business it is to watch the tendencies of immigration from these countries and let us know what elements of the population are coming. I remember in one of these reports reading one of the most interesting things I remember to have read in that connection.

It gave a picture of a town in one of the southern countries of Europe that had once held thirty thousand people, a well-built, solidly constructed town with good houses, a good town which, when there were thirty thousand people in it, was overcrowded and pinched for food for its people. Out of this town had come to America twenty thousand people, the twenty thousand fittest people of the town. Those who were left were the old men, the old women, the young people who were not physically fit for transportation. And the town, now spread broad at ease in houses built for thirty thousand, was living very comfortably and prosperously and happily on money sent back home from America. That may be an extreme instance, but it is an instance of what is happening. The men who work, the brains that originate, the brains that plan and conceive new things come from there.

And so, apparently God is sifting the nations yet to plant seed in America. But see what that means. That means that while the spirit of America is the spirit of welcome, while it welcomes the people of all creeds or purposes that are consistent with orderly life, it is a conglomerate people. It is made up of bloods of all kinds. You have to make a homogeneous thing out of a heterogeneous thing when you are dealing with America. But think of the benefits we receive. I like to think on a day of thanksgiving of the extraordinary multiplicity of gifts that have come to America in this way. It happens, historically speaking, that all the great nations in the world have been conglomerate. And America disturbs us now by this mixture, sometimes. But look at what we get. Look at the enriching national gifts we have received.

I said once in a public address that the American, the original American, stock, by which I meant the English, Irish and Scotch-Irish stock, has not given us any music, and I was once chided

---

National Liberal Immigration League, the headquarters of which were in New York.

by a friend of mine, who pointed out a few American masters.[5]
One half a dozen composers don't make a musical nation. And
what ever may be the exceptions to the rule the truth is that we
have got our music other than from America. We have got it out
of the German stock, the Scandinavian stock, the Italian stock.
American life is, therefore, enriched and beautified by the strain
of music that comes, I will not say, out of alien stocks, for these
stocks are bound by adoption, by mixture and by union. I don't
regard these national elements, that is, race elements, that make
up American life as something outside America for they have
come in and been identified with her. They are all instantly
recognizable as Americans and America is enriched with the
variety of their gifts and the variety of their national characterization.

And so, this thing that we call tolerance is perhaps misnamed
as tolerance. If I keep open house and am glad to see everybody
that comes, that is not tolerance if I am very glad to see them.
If I grudgingly open the doors and say that I don't care to see
them, but they can stay now that they are here and I won't interfere, that is tolerance. The spirit of America is more than tolerant. It is the spirit of the open mind and of opportunity. If I
should attempt to pick out the chief characteristic of America,
and the thing to be proudest of, it is that there isn't any difference
between us. Then if I should pick out a second characteristic, I
would say that it is the spirit of progress, and yet I never use the
word progress without feeling the necessity of defining it. It is
very difficult to say what progress is. If I intend to accomplish
certain things, then by moving towards those things I know I
am making progress, but if I don't know what my objects are I
don't know whether I am making progress or not. If I don't know
where I am going, of course I don't know whether I am going
there or not. You have got to have your direction, your standards,
your aspirations before you know whether you are making progress or not. There is an old adage, "Everything comes to the
man who waits." A wise friend of mine added, "provided he
knows what he is waiting for." If he doesn't know what he is
waiting for, he doesn't know whether he is getting it or not.

If the object of America was to accumulate such physical
power that it could get the rest of the world in its relentless heel
and govern it for its own benefit, there would be no progress in
moving in that direction. There would simply be calamity and

[5] Felix Adler. See Wilson's remarks at the opening exercises of the Institute
of Musical Art in New York, printed at Oct. 31, 1905, and the news report
printed at Nov. 1, 1905, both in Vol. 16.

distress. But if America wishes to pile up her wealth and increase her powers in order to serve the world there is progress provided she knows what services the world needs.

The pathetic circumstance in the case of many wealthy men is that they want to give their money away for things that are serviceable and that [they] cannot be sure that the things proposed to them are serviceable. They are afraid of pauperizing; they are afraid of spoiling this whole fine struggle of life. It isn't easy, I understand, to give money away. It isn't easy for those who want to give it away because they are not sure they would not do more harm than good. I think we can understand it even if we haven't the money.

Now, there is the power of America with unlimited resources of wealth. What are we going to do with it? This involves the principle of conservation. Until we make up our minds we don't know whether we are making progress or not.

So that progress, if I may venture to define it in words, is an adaptation of means to ends, the successful adaptation and application of means to ends. It is going somewhere in particular. I believe that America has that desire. She has not always the vision very clear, but she has unmistakably in her the great desire to move in the better direction of mankind. Americans would not recognize the spirit of their own country if they felt that that spirit was selfish; that it was aggressive; that its object was the aggrandizement of America regardless of the consequences. So that if the spirit of progress that is in it is a spirit of helpfulness and of improvement we will advance. That is the reason we are interested in the question of conservation.

I don't always realize it, but another characteristic of the spirit of America is a consciousness of law and the desire for it. Those of you who have paid any attention to this matter can realize how instinctive is the desire of the American for a statute. There is something pathetic on [about] the reliance of the American on the statute to save him from some one or some thing. This appetite for legislation is a consuming appetite in the American mind. The real way to have good government is to put it in the hands of good men.

I suppose that our faith in law goes back to the thing which seems to me to be the most characteristic party [part] of the spirit of America. Her faith in ideals. America believes that in her original constitutions and in her original bodies of law she did express in tolerably clear terms the ideals of men in respect of politics and social structure. She believes that she did put in her bills of rights in fall [full] those usual phrases which she was repeating from the Magna Charta and bills of rights which she got from across the water, that governments should be based upon the general conceptions of welfare and not those particular conceptions conceived by privileged classes. She meant to strip off everything that had laid in the way of a realization of those ideals that had lain so long in the bill of rights and for which the English speaking races and others had been steadily fighting their way through a thicket of opponents. So that she believes now that in her laws lie her moral judgments, that in her laws are contained all the visions expressed as nearly as they may be in words, and she goes forward with a faith that is almost childlike in its sincerity, that by the virtue of her words, by the virtue of her mandates, by the virtue of her spoken standards, she can achieve happiness.

I believe that law is not a dynamic force. Its object is to hold things where they are. It makes fast what has been achieved. True progress must be in the lives and hearts of the people rather than in a slavish dependence upon laws.

There is no mistaking the fact that every American who stops to think of his country or to feel the impulses of her life, knows that he is seeking a vision of perfection, a vision of liberty, a vision of perfected human justice. America was dedicated to it at the first, and with many an error, many a flagrant blunder, has nevertheless gained the right path, sometimes a feeling for it in the darkness, but recognizing it when its feet touched it, and so struggling onward.[6]

Printed in the Trenton *True American*, Nov. 25, 1910, with additions and corrections from the partial text in the *Newark Evening News*, Nov. 25, 1910.
[6] There is a WWhw outline of this address, with the composition date of Nov. 23, 1910, in WP, DLC.

From John Sharp Williams, with Enclosure

Benton, Miss., Nov. 24 1910

Yours 15th received on time though I was away when it came. Like you I have fears that our fellows may not act wisely. A new Congressman always regards himself a national, if not a world factor, & so many of next Congress are new. Let us hope for the best. I feel as glad of your victory in N. J. as if [it] had been some striking success of my own. I enclose a telegram from Jim Martine. It speaks for itself. He has devoted his energy, strength & substance always to the party—in season & out of seasons. Is one of nature's own noblemen—enthusiastic & optimistic as a child or a poet. It would be a shame after his victory at primary especially if he were defeated—especially if defeated by monied influence.

Yours truly   John Sharp Williams

ALS (WP, DLC).

E N C L O S U R E

James Edgar Martine to John Sharp Williams

Trenton, N. J. No[v]. 13th-14th, 1910.

Kindly write or wire A good word as to my character and capacity to Woodrow Wilson our new democratic governor   at direct primaries I was endorsed for United States Senator getting 48000 votes but now that legislature is elected James Smith Jr. is seeking to defeat popular expression   in this crisis it is essential that I have Wilson's support and a favorable word from you will be of greatest value.

James E. Martin[e]

T telegram (WP, DLC).

From Cleveland Hoadley Dodge

Dear Woodrow: New York November 25, 1910.

Frank Speeir [Speir] has told me of his interview with you, and I am very glad that you were able to see him. I do not propose to give any advice, as you are much better able to judge on this important matter than I am, and I know that you will be guided right to do the wisest and best thing.

I see by the papers that you are going to the Governors' Conference next week, but write now to let you know that Mr. Austen Fox[1] spoke to me the other day and asked me to let you know that he was anxious to see you when you came to New York, regarding the movement in which he is interested, for securing concerted action on the part of the Democrats throughout the country in reference to the Income Tax Amendment. I do not suppose there is any immediate hurry about it, but if you are coming to New York in the not distant future and care to meet Mr. Fox, I shall be very glad to arrange an interview for you.

Trusting that you have become well rested after your arduous work, with best wishes,

Yours affectionately,   C. H. Dodge

TLS (WP, DLC).

[1] Austen George Fox, New York attorney involved in various reform causes.

From Oscar Wilder Underwood[1]

My dear Sir: Birmingham, Alabama, November 25, 1910.

I am advised that the Alabama Educational Association has invited you to make an address before that Association either at Birmingham or Mobile in the near future, and I wish to join with them in their request that you accept the invitation.[2]

Our people here regard you as one of the South's standard bearers in the Nation and will receive you with open arms if you will come to our State.

Very truly yours,   O W Underwood

TLS (WP, DLC).
[1] Democratic representative from the 9th congressional district of Alabama since 1895.
[2] As has been previously noted, Wilson was unable to accept this invitation.

From Joseph R. Wilson, Jr.

My dear brother: Nashville, Tenn. Nov. 25, 1910.

I have been receiving innumerable congratulations over your remarkable victory in New Jersey. Scores of people have stopped me on the street, others have written and still others telephoned to me on the subject. As a result I almost feel that I have myself won a political contest. The nice things being said about you on all sides are sufficient to please the most exacting. They are certainly very pleasing to me. The press of the state, too, has been kind enough to couple our names together in making very complementary notices of us both. Friends have been kind enough to nominate me for nearly everything from Governor of Tennessee down. In some way they seem [to] expect that your success will mean something for me, but I explain that I do not consider myself in line for any position within the gift of the Governor of a state of which I am not a citizen.

I notice from the dispatches that you expect to attend the coming conference of governors and governors-elect to be held in Louisville. I sincerely hope you will find it possible to come a little further South and be with us for at least a few days. Cant you do this? You would find a good sized presidential boom for you in Tennessee and it is evidently sincere, too.[1] Please come if at all possible.[2] Could you not bring sister Ellie with you? We are so anxious for her to visit us.

When you can, write me more in detail about your campaign. When will you be inaugurated? Had the Interstate Commerce Commission not been so unkind as to cut off all newspaper passes outside of the state, I would certainly make a great effort to be present when you assume the official duties of New Jersey's Chief Executive. Under the circumstances, however, it will not be possible for me to be present.

With the exception of severe colds, which one must have just now in order to be in style, we are all reasonably well and send unbounded love to you and the other dear Princeton folks. Write soon and tell us we may look for you when you come South early in December.

Your affectionate brother,   Joseph.

TLS (WP, DLC).
¹ About this subject, see Arthur S. Link, "Democratic Politics and the Presidential Campaign of 1912 in Tennessee," *The East Tennessee Historical Society's Publications*, No. 18 (1946), pp. 107-130.
² Wilson was unable to visit his brother.

From Thomas Dixon, Jr.[1]

My Dear Wilson: New York City, Nov. 25 1910

You will see from the enclosed clipping from the Montgomery Advertizer of Wednesday[2] that I've been rooting for you on my recent tour of the South launching my new play.[3] Let me know if I can help you to the White House. Id like to see you there.

Sincerely,   Thomas Dixon

ALS (WP, DLC).
¹ Baptist clergyman, novelist, playwright, old friend of Wilson's from the Johns Hopkins, and at this time vice-president of the Southern Amusement Co., a touring theatrical company based in New York.
² It is missing.
³ "Sins of the Father: A Drama of the New South" (1910).

From Peyton Cochran and Charles MaCaulay East[1]

Staunton, Va. Nov. 26, 1910

At the call of Hon. Hampton H. Wait [Wayt], Mayor of Staunton, a large meeting of representative Democrats was held to-night and formed the Woodrow Wilson Democratic Club with Peyton Cochran, President and Charles M. East, Secretary. The object of the Club is to promote your election as President of the United States, strong resolutions offered by Judge H. W. Holt, Hon. Joseph A. Glasgow Rev. A. M. Fraier D.D.,[2] were adopted warm speeches delivered and a large enrollment of membership

Peyton Cochran, President,
Charles M. East, Secretary.

T telegram (WP, DLC).

1 Cochran, Princeton A.M. 1902, lawyer of Staunton, Va. East was also a Staunton lawyer.

2 Henry Winston Holt, judge of the Corporation Court of Staunton; Joseph Anderson Glasgow, a Staunton attorney; the Rev. Dr. Abel McIver Fraser, pastor of the First Presbyterian Church of Staunton since 1893 and a fellow student of Wilson's at Davidson College.

From Edward Field Goltra

Dear Governor Wilson: St. Louis. November 26, 1910.

This to advise that I was unable to get in touch with Mr. James Smith at Newark, Wednesday. I expect to be in New York, however, Thursday of next week, and shall endeavor to have a meeting with him then; whereupon, I will report.

                    Yours very truly,   Edward F. Goltra

TLS (WP, DLC).

From Joseph Albert Dear, Jr.

My dear Doctor: Jersey City, N. J. November 26, 1910.

Enclosed is from yesterday's Hoboken Observer,[1] and it makes me feel that we have some just cause for criticism. I am given to understand that your visit to Jersey City was arranged by yourself and Mr. Ely of the Observer during an interview last Sunday.[2] Now, we have no criticism to make of any course you may take in such matters, but that you should arrange for such a visit and leave us entirely out of the reckoning, thus enabling the Observer to print the story, and us to be beaten on it, is not at all to our liking.

We are asking for no favors, yet you surely must realize that some of the most effective assistance you received from any newspaper during your campaign was rendered by the Jersey Journal. Furthermore, you cannot be ignorant of the fact that the Observer did all it possibly could to prevent your nomination. Under these circumstances, we might at least look for sufficient consideration from you to prevent us from being beaten by a story like this in our own county.

I know the running of a newspaper is not your business, and you cannot be expected to keep the interests of the various newspapers always in mind; still, I do not think that we should have been placed in a position of such disadvantage.

                    Yours sincerely,   Joseph A. Dear

TLS (WP, DLC).

1 The enclosure was a front-page news report from the Hoboken, N. J.,

Observer, Nov. 25, 1910, highlighting Wilson's visit to Jersey City to consult with Robert Davis and Joseph P. Tumulty about Smith's candidacy. The article also speculated that Wilson would inform the Hudson County organization of his opposition to Smith.

[2] For a description of this meeting, see M. C. Ely to WW, Nov. 23, 1910, n. 1.

From Robert Underwood Johnson

My dear Dr. Woodrow: New York, Nov. 26, 1910.

I wish very much that I might have the chance of seeing you when you next come to New York, as I have something in mind which I think may interest you to write about.

Altogether, politics seems to be in a pretty healthy condition, and if the Democrats can only pull together to good purpose, all will be well, but there are a great many people in this country who are engaged, at the present moment, in trying to make dissensions in your ranks.

                    Sincerely yours,   R. U. Johnson

If you have something in your line of compact and cogent writing that needs to be said, do let me know.

TLS (WP, DLC).

From James Edward Shepard[1]

Dear Sir: Durham, North Carolina, November 26, 1910.

I desire to call your attention to the work of the National Religious Training School for the Colored People located at Durham, N. C. We believe that this is the most far reaching movement ever attempted for the uplift of the race because we are striving to reach the leaders and through them the masses.

By means of extension courses, literary and industrial centers, settlement work, and Institutes we hope to carry the School to the people.

I am sending you under separate cover and attaching also to this letter full information concerning this work,[2] and I beg for it your careful consideration. You are in position to render us great good, and we believe that it will be a service that you will be proud of in the years to come.

I know that your hands are full of multitudinous cares, but I believe that you are never too busy to step aside to lend a hand of help or speak a word of cheer to those less fortunate than you are. It is for this reason that I have the honor to extend to you an invitation in behalf of the Board of Trustees to deliver the commencement address at the National Religious Training School on May 25, 1911. A welcome awaits you from all classes of the citizens of Durham, both white and black, and I know nothing that will help the cause of the colored people more than a visit by yourself.[3]

Invitations will be showered upon you, but I am quite sure that none will be extended where you could do more good or where the influence would be more far reaching.

With sentiments of warm personal esteem, I am

Yours very sincerely,   James E. Shepard   President.

TLS (WP, DLC).
1 Identified in J. E. Shepard to WW, Oct. 2, 1909, n. 1, Vol. 19.
2 The enclosures are three printed circulars.
3 He was unable to accept.

From Robert W. Shultice[1]

[Norfolk, Va., Nov. 26, 1910]

A number of your admirers have this night organized a club in the city of Norfolk, Va., under the name of the Woodrow Wilson Club to advocate you as the nominee of the Democratic party for President of the United States for 1912.

Robert W. Shultice.
President Woodrow Wilson Club.

Printed in the Norfolk, Va., *Ledger-Dispatch*, Nov. 28, 1910.
1 An attorney and commissioner in chancery of Norfolk.

To Robert W. Shultice

My Dear Mr. Shultice: [Princeton, N. J., Nov. 27, 1910]

The news brought by your kind telegram of yesterday has given me the greatest pleasure. I do not feel that I have at all proven my fitness to be the nominee of the Democratic party for the Presidency; but it is very delightful that you and your associates in the new club should entertain such confidence in me, and I want to express my very deep appreciation and gratitude.

With warmest regards,

[Sincerely yours,   Woodrow Wilson]

Printed in the *Trenton Evening Times*, Dec. 1, 1910.

From Mary Allen Hulbert Peck

Dearest Friend:

Glencove, Paget West, Bermuda.
Nov. 27th [1910]

Alas for the journal letter! I am tired, I am *rushed*, and I can not speak aloud; not that it is necessary to shriek on paper.

I had a comfortable trip, but that does not seem to be the universal description of our voyage. We did not get in until five o'clock, and I am told the ship dropped a sea anchor during the night it was so rough. Mother is better, but very feeble. Bermuda has not *seized* me yet although today was wonderful, and the Islands are fresher and greener, and many more of the deciduous trees in leaf, than I've ever known here at this time of year. The hibiscus is in full glory, and the poinsettia is flaunting its crimson every where. Mrs. Russell[1] is with us until Friday, and I think it tires her in this small house, to have so many people in it. Poor Mrs. R.'s trunks have not come, and she is in motley— very gay for a *real* widow. I will have—*so* sorry: I was interrupted to kill a mouse, Mrs. R. being afraid.

I will write tomorrow and have a longer if not better letter to post next mail. *Will* you let Mr. Herman Sobel[2] come to tell you about an explosive that lessens danger to life & limb. It will take 15 min. If so write & give him an appointment, addressing 39 E. 27th. I do not wish to *use* my friends, but he is a decent little Jew, & it may help if you at least give him a hearing. He has seen you once or twice when you called & was apologetic when he asked me.   Goodnight dearest friend   M. A.

ALS (WP, DLC).
    [1] May Pomeroy Russell of Pittsfield, Mass., widow of Frank Russell.
    [2] Who ran a dry goods store on First Avenue in New York and presumably was an amateur inventor.

From Elmer Hendrickson Geran

Dear Doctor: Jersey City [N. J.], Nov. 28, 1910

I have been talking with Charles Egan and Thomas Griffin, two of the Assemblymen-elect from Hudson County, concerning senatorial matters. They are among those from Hudson County who have come out in favor of Martine and against Smith. They expressed regret at not having seen you personally when you were in this County.

Should affairs develope so that Senator Smith continues in the race as a Candidate, considerable pressure might be brought to bear upon these men, as well as the other Candidates in Hudson County who declared for Martine.

My thought is, that if you could see these men now and talk with them, they having the effect of your personality and assuring you personally that they are against Smith and for Martine, might help to make them steadfast at some future crisis.[1]

If you wrote each of them, or wrote one of them and asked him to request the others to call at Princeton, I believe that most of them would come.

I am also interested in A. C. Strietwolf, of New Brunswick.[2] I have talked with him personally, and he is against Mr Smith, but through Mr Ross of New Brunswick,[3] I fear that considerable pressure might be brought to bear upon him. I know that Mr Strietwolf will be pleased to see you, and I think an interview would help to make him steadfast.

You will pardon my suggestions in this letter, but I take this liberty knowing that our purpose is in common.

Very respectfully yours,   Elmer H. Geran

TLS (WP, DLC).

[1] Wilson did meet with the Hudson County delegation on December 5, 1910. For a description of this conference, see WW to O. G. Villard, Dec. 5, 1910, n. 1.

[2] August C. Streitwolf, Jr., lawyer of New Brunswick and New York and assemblyman-elect from Middlesex County.

[3] Millard Fillmore Ross, Democratic boss of Middlesex County and one of Smith's chief lieutenants.

From William Cavanagh Gebhardt

My dear Doctor Wilson: Jersey City [N. J.], November 28, 1910.

I have just had a talk with our mutual friend, Assemblyman-elect Geran, and I am most happy to learn from him of your position on the United States Senator election. It is not necessary for me to give you my views for I presume that you have already seen them published in the daily papers. Please don't fail to call on me if I can be of service to you.

Very sincerely yours,   Wm. C. Gebhardt

TLS (WP, DLC).

From Oswald Garrison Villard

New York, N. Y. Nov 28-10.

Believe I have found a very promising man[1] for you[2]   experienced newspaper man, College graduate resident of New Jersey

for some years on the staff of the Sun and now one of our trusted
sub editors   please let me know on your return when you can
see him.   O. G. Villard

T telegram (WP, DLC).
  1 Charles Albert Selden, reporter for the New York *Evening Post*.
  2 To serve as Wilson's secretary when he became governor.

An Address to the Conference of Governors in Frankfort, Kentucky

[[Nov. 29, 1910]]

We are met together to take counsel. No doubt there is much
else that we gain by coming together besides a knowledge of each
other's views with regard to large public questions. We take stimulation from one another. We are drawn together by friendliness
and sympathy and the common interests of similar tasks. We
learn to know one another, not only, but also to know better the
great country which we serve—to know it in its variety and with
a touch of intimacy and reality which would not otherwise be
easily possible. But our main object is counsel, sober and deliberate conference upon great questions and problems of State
upon which we would, if possible, be guided by full knowledge
and by clear principles of action.

Why should we organize such a council upon such matters of
common concern? Do we draw together simply as friends, or has
there arisen in our minds the thought that we have some quasi-
constitutional function? Are we seeking, in this voluntary fashion, to supplement the Congress of the United States? Is there
in our minds something that the Congress does not or cannot
do which we, perhaps, can do? Clearly we have neither the right
nor the wish to invade the sphere of any regularly constituted
organ of government. What, then, is our purpose? What do we
seek?

Certainly our institutional life need not confine itself to the
processes explicitly defined in our constitutions. It cannot. Life
has proceeded out of those constitutions. Our life as a nation
has waxed strong and abounded; it rises limitless to the eye and
to the comprehension. It outruns constitutions. I do not mean
that it runs counter to them or that it threatens to set them at
naught. I mean simply that it transcends all forms and definitions; presses on from age to age its own will, without asking how
it is to adjust itself to formulas or to lawyers' conceptions; is
fuller of mere energy than of careful thought for law. It is as
various as it is boundless. It is impatient of the restraints of law.

It displays itself in ever new and varying fashion. It often eludes classification and order. It is in this sense that it outruns our constitutions and must ever do so so long as it thus abounds with an irresistible vitality.

And so it is plain to be seen by any, even the most casual looker on that our constitutional life is constantly changing; I mean the uses to which we put the powers of our Legislatures, of our executives, and of our courts. Not only is the series of constitutional decisions of any one of our supreme courts a history of change and constant, though related, variation, but there is a whole sphere of experiment, of influence, of varied action which the courts never touch, where forces play which never settle to any such form as can afford the courts subject matter for decision—the rules of legislative bodies, the personal relations of executives and Legislatures, the action and organization of parties, the interplay of all those intangible forces of agitation and quiet opinion which affect legislation and the public thought in communities great and small, States, cities, homogeneous regions that span whole groups of States, climatic or social or economic units which have a consciousness and a movement of their own and whose life springs into forms native, natural, distinctive.

The thing we are here trying to do is to co-ordinate and form some of these otherwise vagrant forces. It is an extra-constitutional enterprise, but natural, spontaneous, imperative, perhaps creative. If it is not constitutional in kind, according to the strict uses of that word in America, it is at least institutional. If these conferences become fixed annual events, planned for and carried forward from year to year as an habitual means of working towards common ends of counsel and co-operation, this council will at least become an institution. I do not know how better to define an institution than by saying that it is an habitual and systematic way of doing something which calls for co-operation and a certain union in action.

If it grows into a dignified and permanent institution, it will be because we have found it necessary to supply some vital means of co-operation in matters which lie outside the sphere of the Federal Government, matters which the States must regulate but which they find it to their interest, and to the interest of the country as a whole, to regulate according to common principles and a very careful adaptation of conditions which no one State can control—matters in regard to which they ought to act, not necessarily alike, but with a careful regard to imperative consideration of general policy which can be differently applied but cannot safely or wisely be differently conceived. In brief, we are setting up, outside the sphere of the Federal Congress, a new instrument of political life, national in its character, scope, and intention; an instrument, not of legislation, but of opinion, exercising the authority of influence, not of law.

It is odd how every process of our national development has sooner or later swung our thought back to the Federal structure and action of our Government. After all, the main fact about our national life whenever we come to speak of politics is, that its action is dual, that the power of government has been parcelled out between a central government and nearly half a hundred States, to which is assigned almost the whole body of the ordinary business of legislation, of economic and social readjustment from age to age. We are not likely again, in considering this complex arrangement, to use the terms of the old states-right controversies. The embers of old passions which once set a whole nation aflame still glow warm at the heart of the ashes which lie piled high upon them, the ashes of bitter conflict. It would not only be imprudent, it would be very misleading, and would give our thought about matters now to be handled an artificial and antique setting. We are speaking now of the matters of another day, a day of peace and concord and accommodation. But we are speaking of the same old subject.

It is interesting to note, however, how different, how altogether new our specific trouble is. We are now disturbed to find, not that the interests of the States are so different and apparently so antagonistic in respect of the matters in which they are authorized to act separately and in virtual independence of each other that they wish to draw apart and are watching each other with jealous differences of purpose, but that their interests are similar, in many things almost indentical; that they recognize that a wise co-operation is desirable not only but imperative in the common interest and for their own safety and prosperity, but they lack the means, the instrumentalities that would serve them in their new community of action. They are seeking a common policy and lack the means of common counsel. They are looking for common ground, but must look for it separately and in isolation. They are in the same case, but not in the same boat. They must seek the same course under different captains and with different crews. They should act together, but inevitably find co-operation more difficult than action under a common authority.

Their variety and their autonomy are, in my opinion, worth all they cost. If our system of States had not come to us by historical necessity, I think it would have been worth while to invent it. Our people are spread abroad upon a vast continent; they live in many latitudes, under many skies, amidst hills and plains and valleys which would in another age have been the seats of as many kingdoms, the homes of independent peoples; every sort of soil under their feet, every varied resource of mine and forest and watercourse, of lake and sea and mountain covert, at their hand, to multiply their undertakings and complete the tale of their unbounded variety. Uniform laws would intolerably embarrass them. Their affairs are not alike, and cannot be made so by compulsion of law.

Moreover, by their free self-government they are put upon their mettle. They are bound together into communities; they are compelled to study and comprehend their own particular interests, and to depend upon themselves to work them out. They are forced to contrive their own salvation, to depend upon their own sagacity and initiative, to develop their own lives by their own means. Nothing moves faster with them than it can move by the force of their own convictions, by means of what their own sense and experience suggest. They grow in institutions and in material force by compulsion of their own necessities, their own characters, their own circumstances. They must rely upon themselves. Not even imitation will serve their necessities, for they must adapt everything that they touch to their own case. We are a vital and a living people because over every mile of our territory we have been obliged to build with our own hands out of material that was of the time and place. Every commonwealth has been a nursery of new strength; and out of these nurseries have come men and communities which no other process could have produced. Self-government has here had its richest harvest.

Democracy has had amongst us, therefore, its freest possible field. Every State has been free to make itself at will an experiment station in the varying work of reform and readjustment. We have not had to wait upon the slow and cumbrous movement of a great national body, embarrassed in all its processes of change by the fact that it served a various people, a multitude of communities which differed with an infinite variety in the character and accompaniments of their affairs and of their settled interests. Each State could follow its own fresh and native impulses and try its own vital experiments at its own time and choice, boast its own successes, repair its own mistakes. There is no overestimating the vivid interest and importance of the multifarious process. Communities old and young were united in a common life and yet lived after their own fashion, followed their own characteristic ways of action, without friction or interference. One would not have wished to impair the quickening variety. No single congress could have guided or determined the life of such a people.

But meanwhile common influences spread themselves throughout the multiform body politic. The last sixty years have seen the great continent knit together by systems of railways and telegraph and telephone. More and more completely has the network spread over every region and quarter of the great area. With the perfecting of the means of intercommunication with the swifter and swifter movement of trains, the more and more rapid growth of traffic, business has spread itself with a new organization and volume. As it has spread it has been interwoven, in actual organization as well as in the rapid interchange of goods. The organization of business has become more centralized, vastly more centralized than the political organization of the country itself. Corporations have come to cover greater areas than States, have come to live under a greater variety of laws than the citizen himself, have excelled States in their budgets and loomed bigger than whole commonwealths in their influence over the lives and fortunes of entire communities of men. Centralized business has built up vast structures of organization and equipment which overtop all States and seem to have no match or competitor except the Federal Government itself, which was not intended for such competitions. Amidst a confused variety of States and statutes stands now the colossus of business, uniform, concentrated, poised upon a single plan, governed, not by votes, but by commands, seeking, not service, but profits.

No wonder we began to turn to the National Government, to cope with it, to regulate, in the name of the sovereign nation itself, what had become a force as great as the nation in its scope and consequence. The influence to be dealt with extended from one end of the country to the other. The great organizations of business seemed to play with the States, to take advantage of the variety of the laws, to make terms of their own with one State at a time, and by one device of control or another to dominate wherever they chose, because too big to be dominated by the small processes of local legislation. No machinery seemed to stretch to the size of the task of regulation except the machinery of national legislation at Washington, the long arm of the executive that could be stretched forth from a national capital to every remotest nook and corner of the land. No wonder the instinct and inclination were to resort to Washington for relief and protection. The need was great and the Government was powerful.

But this intimate task of regulation was not one for which its constitution had furnished it with actually suitable or entirely adequate powers and authority. Only the States were fully equipped with the legislative and executive power to handle at will and as they pleased this new organization of business and manufacture. A new problem was presented to us. We still did not desire rigid uniformity of law, even in these matters of common concern. It was still desirable that the States should adapt their regulation and restraint of the new forces to their own conditions of life and circumstance. To put Federal law back of the great corporations would have been to give them the right to dominate and override local conditions, to equip them with the majesty and supremacy of the law which created and regulated them, and to level the variety of communities before them. No absolute, uniform set of rules are likely to fit the infinitely various circumstances of the States and their people. Hence this conference. We have no foolish or pedantic jealousy of Federal power. We believe in the exercise of the Federal powers to the utmost extent wherever it is necessary that they should be brought into action for the common benefit. But we do not believe the invention of Federal powers either necessary or desirable. We are not attempting a task of mediation; neither are we trying to fend off revolution. We are striving neither to defend the States nor to resist the development of the Federal Government as the instrument of the common life of the country. Our function is one of leadership. Leadership, I take it, is a task of suggestion, of adaptation, of the quickening of thought and the devising of means. It is our privilege and duty to study the problems common to all the States, and to suggest the means by which the States, without loss of their natural variety or of their opportunities of local adaptation, may yet freely throw their energies into a common task of protection and development, as if in the spirit of a single commonwealth, their measures varied but their purpose the same. Our effort to render this service may result in the setting up of one of those voluntary institutions of counsel by which the life of free countries is enriched, both in action and in opinion. We shall be all the more sober, I believe, because we speak by no authority but that of reasonableness and good sense. Where we go astray we bind no one; where we are right we shall prevail.

For the country awaits sober, disinterested counsel, and will follow it. It desires it in nothing so much as in those affairs in which the States have power and can control, but do not. And this is the body of men who are expected to lead. The people of our commonwealths, as well as the people of our nation, desire leadership—are calling for it with some impatience. They cannot find it in their legislatures amidst the confused medley of committees. There is no one in any legislature who represents the whole commonwealth—no one connected with legislation who does, except the Governor. Everyone else represents some section or locality, except, indeed, the lieutenant governor, who is expected to be as discreetly quiescent as the Vice President himself. Legislative procedure is full of ambushes and coverts. It is hide-and-seek to follow a measure through its passage. Only those upon the spot can ascertain or comprehend what is going on. Debate upon the floor of our assemblies has gone out of fashion; it is now closeted with committees and caucuses. Opinion, consequently, is turning, for information and guidance to the few men who are representatives at large, to the President and the governors of the States, men chosen, by however whimsical or haphazard a process, for leadership by the whole electorate.

We ought not to allow ourselves to be pedants, stickling at words and phrases. We ought to deal with realities, and deal with them very frankly. Let us distinguish legal power from personal influence; the two things ought to be easily distinguishable. A certain amount of legal power every Governor has. Every Governor of a State is by the terms of the Constitution a part of the legislature. No bill can become law without his assent and signature. It can be passed over his veto, but only by deliberate process and generally only by more than the vote of a majority. His legislative vote, so to say, is never less than that of half of the legislature. He has the right of initiative in legislation, too, though he has so far, singularly enough, made little use of it. It is the popular notion that the governor has, in respect to legislation, only the message power; but the language of most of our constitutions is the same, is the language of the federal constitution also. It gives him the right to recommend "measures," and it does not limit him in respect of the form in which he shall make the recommendation. He can make it in the form of bills if he pleases.

Of course his recommendations may be treated as the Houses please. Like private members' bills they may be given the decent burial of reference to a committee. They may be considered or left unconsidered. He has no place on the floor and must get his recommendations considered by such means as he may honorably use outside the chambers. There begins the sphere of his personal influence, as distinguished from his legal power. His personal influence is the power of his character and of his ability to convince and persuade. Coercion is out of the question. It is absurd to speak of it. We are not children; we are speaking of grown up people and of realities.

Governors have a means of coercion. They can use their power of appointment to get votes and offset opposition. But they are only fools for their pains when they do. They lose credit with the very people from whom their power came. They lose respect and standing with honest men; and it is the respect of honest men, the support and faith of honest men, that is their source of might. Their real power over a legislature is their ability to convince the people. If they can carry an opinion through the constituencies, they can carry it through the legislature. No legislature need be jealous of that, unless it be jealous of putting public questions upon a footing of open and frank debate. The field is free—as free for those who oppose the governor as for the governor himself. The best arguments, the handsomest motives, the most valid and straightforward purpose, the most defensible programme wins. It is too late, moreover, to be jealous of that method of control. The people are ready for it, wait for it, demand it, expect all who hope to serve them to accept the ordeal. No real man who speaks his real convictions need be afraid of it. The jury is not packed, cannot be "fixed." It is the people themselves.

I am sure that I am not mistaken when I say that the people are calling for open leadership, and that they wish their leaders to be men who represent them all. They are tired of the hide-and-seek of legislation as it has generally been conducted. We shall not bring clear action out of confusion until we supply the need, until we assist at the simplification which will inevitably come when some one man undertakes in each State to keep the people informed as to every chief step of their business, particularly of the business of legislation, and to challenge all who are engaged in it to submit to the frank and clarifying processes of debate. There is no executive usurpation in a governor's undertaking to do that. He usurps nothing which does not belong to him of right, uses no power which would not belong to him whether he were governor or not. He employs nothing but his own personal force and the prevailing power of his opinions. He who cries usurpation against him is afraid of debate, wishes to keep legislation safe against scrutiny, behind closed doors and within the covert of partisan consultations. We are consulting here because the leadership of half a hundred commonwealths calls for consultation among the leaders wherever many weighty matters must in the common interest be managed to a common end.

This, as well as our individual leadership in our several commonwealths, is, by intention at least, a simplifying process. Consultation always is a simplifying process, when it is frank and is intended for the common interest. We wish to simplify our tasks of leadership by making ourselves acquainted with all the elements of the complex problems we are called upon to deal with. That we can do by informing ourselves and by informing one another. We shall by our leadership under such influences bind our States together more truly than ever before into a nation, whose standard and aims are the same, however different may be their forms of action, however various their several measures may be in their adaptation to time and place and circumstance. Co-operation amidst variety is what we seek. If we find it we shall in a new age of energy illustrate once more the American genius for affairs, for the making and use of institutions.

I have already stated our problem in general terms. It is how to make our States efficient instruments wisely used in the regulation of economic conditions which have been organized upon a scale, and must continue to exhibit themselves upon a scale, that is nation wide, no State being more than a part, and generally a small part, of the territory which they cover. It is the problem of railway regulation and of the regulation of the many other vast corporations whose business spreads like a network over every part of the country. We speak of public service corporations and of those which are not public service corporations, and there is of course a difference, a clearly marked difference, between them; but when we speak of modern business is it speaking of reality in any case to speak of a modern corporation as a private corporation, of its business as private business? It acts only upon license. Its transactions are interlaced with the whole of modern life and set up the conditions under which that life goes forward. This is in no sense a private matter. Our corporations are not dealing with individuals so much as with communities. If those who conduct them would look at their business from that point of view and conduct themselves in the temper and spirit of public servants there would be no need of regulation. So long as they do not, so long as they transact their business in the spirit of those who manage private affairs, for private gain and not for public service, regulation will be necessary. Individual affairs and public interests must be accommodated, and the public interests, not the private advantage, must be the standard of regulation and accommodation.

Here then, in more particular terms, are the large items of our tasks, as we must view them in counsel together. There is, first, the task of regulation; for that we seek common principles, common ideas and aims, at the same time that we recognize that these common principles must be put into effect in our several States in somewhat different ways, in order to serve local needs and conditions. We seek co-operation but can wear no straight-jacket. The task of right regulation, for example, in the case of common carriers, in particular, whose business spans a score of States, is a task in which we must co-operate, with one another and with the federal authorities, though it may be that local regulation may without injustice or serious breach of common practice be based upon different calculations and different elements of business in different commonwealths. Variety will not impair energy if there be genuine co-operation and a real common understanding such as we ought to be able to bring about.

For our problem, looked at from another angle, is one of co-ordination. I am not now referring to the important matter we are so much concerned with in regard to uniformity of laws; the laws of marriage and divorce, for example, the laws of commercial transaction, and those many other matters which so vitally affect the morals or the convenience of our scattered communities. I am thinking of the matter of forests and water-sheds and mines, of the great tasks of sanitation, of the treatment of epidemics, the care of the poor and the restraint of the vagrant, of the safeguarding of labor, and all that long list of vital interests with regard to which we can do so much more if we act together and upon the same common plan.

Conservation is a very much bigger subject than would appear from many of our discussions of it, and it is a much more difficult and intricate subject for the States than for the Federal government. The greater part of the resources of the country are outside the bounds of the federal domain and there is much more to conserve than what we generally include under the term natural resources. The vitality of the country lies chiefly in its people, in their moral wholesomeness and their physical strength and soundness. The purification of our life and of our politics is a central matter of conservation, fundamental to all the rest. We cannot make men moral or make them well by statute, but we can lend the aid of the community in many powerful ways in the safeguarding of health and the purification of life; and our moral and physical contagions are interstate. We give and take in these matters throughout the Union.

But of course the more tangible things are our physical resources, their protection and renewal; and these can seldom be effectually accomplished without the co-operation of State with State. We must safeguard and renew our forests; we must renew our soils and improve our methods of agriculture; we must preserve our great streams—not only preserve them in their undiminished volume in order that they may continue to be the highways of intercourse, but also preserve them from contamination in order that they may be wholesome and serviceable for all uses; and so treat them that they may furnish cheap power to drive our industries; we must guard against exhaustion by selfish private use of our great mineral resources—particularly those which, like coal, furnish the necessities of life to whole communities. We must develop as well as preserve. We must dig canals where they will be serviceable and see to it that they are not monopolized by private interests. In all things we must quicken as well as conserve.

We must equalize, too; I mean that we must seek common means by which to open opportunities of all kinds as freely as possible to the choice of individuals, so that our lives may not be too much tied up in organization, may be as open as possible to honest competition and individual initiative. Many of our laws of business need reconsideration from top to bottom. They were made in one economic age and are being used, clumsily enough, in another. Their adaptation may well be a matter of common counsel along with the other matters of general adjustment of which I have spoken.

But the list is not of consequence. No one man, no one conference, can make the programme. I have not spoken of political questions, like the popular selection of United States Senators, or the extension of the powers of the federal government to the taxation of incomes, because these are not matters of necessity, they are matters of expediency. They are not questions raised by the irresistible circumstances of a new age like the economic questions that press upon us. Moreover, I have sought to use every question I have alluded to only as an illustration. It is the theme that holds my attention and enlists my enthusiasm; the institutional life of the country, the gathering together of the infinitely varied threads of our national experience, the mediation of vital processes, the hope here held out in these quiet conferences that the economic life of the nation may be eased and facilitated, its political life purified and quickened by our counsels and purpose. This has ever been the way in which America has proved her fertility of political capacity. Voluntary conferences of men who have nothing to offer but service and sober counsel have at every stage of our development furnished the subject matter of our reforms. We are doing what each generation of public men before us have done; we are seeking to find out by counsel a way of life.[1]

Printed in *Proceedings of the Third Meeting of the Governors of the States of the Union Held at Frankfort and Louisville, Kentucky, November 29, 30, December 1, 1910* (Lakewood, N. J., n.d.), pp. 42-54, with minor corrections from the T MS in WP, DLC.
[1] There are WWsh, WWT, and T drafts of this address in WP, DLC.

From Edwin Augustus Stevens

My dear Tommy: Hoboken, N. J. November 29th, 1910.

I am delighted to see by the papers this morning that you have taken positive ground against the election of Senator Smith to the United States Senate to fill the vacancy caused by the expiration of the term of Senator John Kean.[1] To be perfectly frank with you, I feel that Martine is hardly of Senatorial timber, but the party having committed themselves to him in the Primaries he should not be thrust aside. If he makes up his mind to withdraw, another contingency would be created. Even in that contingency I do not feel that Senator Smith could adequately represent the party in this State. His record on the Wilson bill, and the scandal attached to his first election,[2] would seem to me to make his success equivalent to stultification of the party.

If you want a backing of some earnest Democrats of good position on this matter, I will be very glad to get you a number of names of men of some prominence in their respective lines who feel as I do in the matter. You are, of course, at liberty to use my name, if you wish to do so.

Congratulating you on this good beginning, I am

Sincerely yours,   E. A. Stevens

TLS (WP, DLC).
[1] Stevens referred to a news report saying that Wilson had written a letter notifying Smith of his opposition to his contemplated candidacy. Both Smith and an unidentified "confidential friend" of Wilson denied that Wilson had written such a letter. *Newark Evening News*, Nov. 29, 1910.
[2] By 1892, Smith, through his alliance with railroads and business interests, had become the dominant force in state Democratic politics. He switched the New Jersey delegation from David Bennett Hill to Grover Cleveland at the Democratic national convention in 1892; and, after Cleveland's victory and the election of a Democratic state legislature, Smith sought the Senate seat from New Jersey. "With a crowd of railroad lobbyists besieging the Capitol, and with money as plentiful as ugly rumors," James Kerney wrote, "Smith was elected by the Legislature." *The Political Education of Woodrow Wilson*, p. 20.
In the Senate, Smith immediately allied himself with Calvin Stewart Brice of Ohio and Arthur Pue Gorman of Maryland in an attempt to raise dramatically the schedules of the Wilson tariff bill of 1894. Smith was also alleged to have joined other senators in speculating in sugar stocks while the tariff was pending before Congress. In testimony before a Senate investigating committee in 1894, he at one point said that he might have bought 1,000 shares of sugar

stock but later flatly denied that he had bought or sold any at all. The scandal surrounding the allegation continued to plague him after he left office. During the senatorial fight in 1910, Smith's alleged involvement with the sugar trust was raised again by hostile newspapers; see, for example, the Hoboken *Observer*, Nov. 19, 1910.

From John Moody[1]

Dear Dr. Wilson,   New York Nov. 29, 1910

As one who was for many years actively interested in politics on the Democratic side in the State of New Jersey, I am constrained to write you a few lines in reference to the contest which now seems underway regarding the candidate for the United States Senatorship.

For about seven years prior to 1908, I was very active in the Democratic party in Union County, N. J., where Mr. Martine lives and for about half of this time, was chairman of the Democratic County Committee. As chairman of that Committee, I had some unusual experience with Mr. Jas. Smith, Jr., which proved to me that he was by far the most undesirable man in the party in New Jersey, and for several years, I was active with many others in efforts to force him and his crowd out of power. My antagonism to Smith was, at the beginning, the result of an interview I had with him in the fall of 1903, when, as chairman of the Union County Committe[e], I was sent to him to appeal for campaign funds from the State Committee. Up to that time, I had never met Smith and knew very little about him. He apparently assumed that as I was a Wall Street man, I was naturally interested in politics "for revenue only" and he was very frank in his conversation with me regarding his precise relationship to the Democratic organization and to corporation interests generally. He told me in so many words that for many years he had been the dispenser of money received from the Pennsylvania Railroad and other corporations to influence legislation in the State of New Jersey. He explained that any men we might send to the legislature should surely "behave themselves" and not introduce any anti-corporation bills, for, as he said, if we sent men to Trenton who annoy the railroads by raising such issues as railroad taxation and corporation regulation, then his source of income from the railroads would be cut off. He told me that this whole matter had been discussed by him with Mr. [Alexander Johnston] Cassatt, President of the Pennsylvania Railroad and that Mr. Cassatt was even then threatening to cut out all contributions unless Democrats were sent to the legislature who would "behave themselves."

He further said that he had threatened Mr. Cassatt, if the contributions were cut off or cut down, by telling him that unless the proper funds were forthcoming, then the Democratic members of the legislature would deliberately and systematically introduce anti-corporation legislation and all kinds of strike bills.[2] Finally, in answer to my own request for a contribution from the State Committee, he explained that the State Committee never had any money, but that he personally supplied all the money and at this particular time could not promise me anything until he had seen Mr. Cassatt.

I give you this incident in detail in order that you may see how I came to view Mr. Jas. Smith, Jr. as a political grafter of the largest kind. Many other incidents in the following few years still further confirmed this opinion and I believe today that Smith holds practically the same position as an intermediary between corporate interests and the Democratic party.

I am not one of those who take the extreme and fanatical view that corporations are unmixed evils and that they should be legislated out of existence. But I do believe very strongly that they should be kept out of politics and I think that you are entirely in accord with this view. Now there could be no more disastrous act, in my opinion, than the election of Jas. Smith, Jr. to the United States Senate at this time. It would certainly set the Democratic party back all over the United States and would bring their sincerity in question from Maine to California.

I am thoroughly familiar with Jas. Smith, Jr's. method in politics in the State of New Jersey. I know that time and again he has lined up the political leaders in different counties through the dispensing of liberal [a]mounts of money; this money coming into his hands through his methods of holding up and threatening corporations. There is no real Smith following outside of that which is based on dollars and cents. I have seen more than one young man in the State of New Jersey enter politics with clean hands and in the course of five or six years, under the tutelage of Smith, become a cheap political grafter.

Probably you are yourself more or less familiar with this situation, but while I am not actively in politics at the present time, I feel very strongly that it is the duty of every man who is interested in the cause of good government, to help save the present dangerous situation, if possible.

Now I wish to say a word or two in reference to Mr. Martine. I have known Mr. Martine intimately for a good many years. I have not always agreed with him on political questions and in 1896, when he supported Bryan, I was directly opposed to his position.

But while I think he was wrong in his stand at that time, just as a vast number of others of great intelligence and ability were wrong, I hardly know of any one in the State of New Jersey who measures up to the United States Senatorship so well as Mr. Martine does at this time. First of all, he is an absolutely honest man and all of his political enemies will freely admit this. Furthermore, he is a fundamental Democrat; he has been a careful student of public questions for many years and on the broad and vital issues such as the tariff, his convictions are absolutely sound. He is also a man of genuine ability and his whole career has been characterized by a close adherence to political ideals. It is true that he has often gone down to defeat in running for office, but this has been due to the fact that he has never hesitated to lead a forlorn hope and has accepted nominations again and again without hope of success when every other available man had taken to the woods.

If any man in the State of New Jersey is entitled to the United States Senatorship, that man is Jas. E. Martine.

Very truly yours,   John Moody.

TLS (WP, DLC).
  ¹ Resident of Cranford, N. J.; senior partner of Moody & Co., bond dealers of New York; founder in 1900 of *Moody's Manual of Railroad and Corporation Securities*; best known as author of *The Truth About the Trusts: A Description and Analysis of the American Trust Movement* (New York and Chicago, 1904).
  ² Wilson described them in his address printed at Nov. 17, 1910.

From Leroy J. Ellis

Dear Sir: Plainfield, N. J., November 29th, 1910

May I not without the risk of seeming officious, advise you of a circumstance which you ought to know about, if you do not already know about?

. Mr. James Martine has been personally approached on the subject of his withdrawing from the Senatorical race, with the assurance, and seemingly with quasi authority, that if he would withdraw he would be given a position in your official family which would pay him handsomly, and the position guaranteed to him for a period of eight or ten years.

Of course I know that this does not come directly or indirectly from you. And of this Mr. Martine also is confident. It goes without saying that he has indignantly rejected all propositions looking to his voluntary retirement. In this connection may i add that it is very gratifying to note from newspaper comments, the influence your private talks are having on the Senatorial situation. The belief is growing that you can and will shape events so that the vote at the primary will be the guide of the legislature. Unless it is, the party in New Jersey will be greatly discredited and demoralized whether deservedly so or not.

I am going to take occasion to enclose copy of a speech I delivered during the campaign which may or may not have escaped your attention.[1] I believe the sentiment and expectations expressed therein are those of many thousands of people all over the country. In the rush of the campaign I failed to enclose the copy of your first speech at Plainfield which this Club printed and distributed liberally. I enclose one now under separate cover.[2]

With renewed assurances of the highest esteem, I am,

Very cordially yours,   L. J. Ellis.

TLS (WP, DLC).
    [1] The enclosure was a news article in the *Elizabeth*, N. J., *Evening Times*, Nov. 5, 1910, reporting Ellis' speech to the Plainfield Democratic Club. In it, Ellis likened Wilson to Wordsworth's "Happy Warrior" and argued that his nomination was not the result of political manipulation by party bosses but a response to popular sentiment. Ellis further suggested that Wilson's victory in the gubernatorial election would be a prelude to a presidential bid in 1912.
    [2] It is missing. A news report of this speech is printed at Oct. 30, 1909, Vol. 19.

From Frederick K. Pulsifer[1]

Dear Sir: New York November 29th, 1910.

As a Republican who wished earnestly for your success at the polls, even to the extent of voting for the whole Essex Democratic Assembly delegation in the hope that this might "hold up your hands" as you yourself suggested, I feel that I have a right to protest against the betrayal of my confidence and my vote involved in the tendering of the Essex votes to James Smith, Jr., for United States Senator,[2] (in common with many other Republicans who voted as I did, and for identical reasons).

I am looking to you for an infinitely higher course of conduct than that of the Assemblymen who begged our votes and betrayed us: I look to you to oppose to the utmost the selection of Smith, or any man of his type, perhaps of any other man than the one already designated by the ballots as U. S. Senator from New Jersey.

Am I not well within my rights in so doing?

Yours respectfully,   F. K. Pulsifer.

TLS (WP, DLC).
    [1] Banker of New York, who lived in Glen Ridge, N. J.
    [2] See C. H. Dodge to WW, Nov. 18, 1910, n. 3.

From Peyton Cochran

My dear Dr. Wilson: Staunton, Virginia November 29th 1910.

Please accept my heartiest congratulations upon your recent splendid victory in New Jersey. May this victory be the forerunner of a national sentiment, which will make you, as the leader of Democracy, our next President.

In the years that have passed since my graduation from Princeton, in nineteen hundred and two, you have perhaps forgotten me; but your inspiration as a teacher, your advice and friendliness to me made the year that I studied under you one of the pleasantest and most profitable of my life. After leaving Princeton I graduated in law at the University of Virginia and then located in my home town, Staunton, where I have succeeded in establishing myself in the practice of my profession.

The people of Staunton have followed with great interest your successful career, and are particularly pleased at your most recent triumph in being elected Governor of New Jersey.

On Saturday evening a large meeting of Democrats was held, at which meeting addresses were made by a former college mate of yours, Dr A. M. Fraser, pastor of the First Presbyterian Church, and myself. The Woodrow Wilson Democratic Club of Staunton, Va., was organised with the purpose of aiding in the upbuilding and success of the Democratic party, and in assisting your election to the Presidency in 1912.

We, as citizens of this your native town wish to be among the first to show our appreciation of your high ability and eminent fitness for the position of President.

Trusting that you are well and with sincere good wishes for a successful administration as Governor,

I remain sir,   Sincerely yours,   Peyton Cochran.

ALS (WP, DLC).

From Joseph Patrick Tumulty

My dear Governor: Jersey City [N. J.] November 30, 1910.

Since conferring with you last Friday[1] I have had several very earnest talks with Mr. Davis and have urged upon him the necessity of supporting your attitude on the United States Senatorial problem. While at first he manifested disapproval of your proposed course, he now seems to be of the opinion that the situation that confronts him *in his own County* is rather threatening and one that calls for some quick, effective action on his part to check the impending storm. A messenger direct from Mr. Davis called at my home on Sunday evening, and informed me that it was Mr. Davis' desire that I confer with Judge [Robert Stephen] Hudspeth the following day regarding the situation and to request Judge Hudspeth *in his name* to confer with Senator Smith and to suggest to the Senator the advisability of declining longer to remain a candidate. I was of the opinion that this idea would not be effective, and I insisted upon a committee of prominent Democratic citizens, but my efforts in this respect were unavailing. Judge Hudspeth agreed to see Mr. Smith immediately upon his return from Old Point Comfort, and suggested that I write to you and ask that you refrain from making any statement on the Senatorial situation until you hear further from him as to the result of his conference with Senator Smith. Whether this would be advisable under the circumstances, I do not feel free to say, for this may be another method that is being invoked for the purpose of "sparring for time" and thus give Senator Smith and his friends a more ample opportunity to influence weak and vacillating legislators.

That your visit to Jersey City has helped the cause, no one can doubt, for even the closest friends and advisors of Mr. Davis have counseled him to go slowly and to repudiate Senator Smith. The sentiment in our County is daily growing and the people await your announcement with patience and great expectation, and evidence their willingness to follow "the true and courageous."

Today, after talking with Mr. Davis, I learned from a most reliable source that Mr. Davis would not feel "hurt" if the Hudson Delegation would refuse to take his orders on the Senatorial proposition.

From present indications, I firmly believe that Mr. Davis cannot count on the support of more than three members of the Hudson Delegation. I have conferred with many of them, at your suggestion, and have quietly informed them of what I believe your attitude will be in this crisis in our party's affairs.

Mr. [Mark A.] Sullivan and I are agreed, however, that more effective work could be done if you could find time to confer with the whole Delegation from Hudson County, and are firmly convinced that a conference with them would result in your having the united Hudson Delegation to support you and to follow your leadership.

I have tried to force a conference of the Hudson Delegation, so that Mr. Davis might be immediately apprised of the number of those in the Delegation who will refuse to support Mr. Smith in his Senatorial aspirations, but my efforts have failed of success.

Will you kindly let me know what you think of the advisability of meeting the Hudson Delegation, and if you so desire, I will arrange it subject to your wishes as to time and place.

With kindest and best wishes, I am,

Sincerely,   Joseph P. Tumulty.

TLS (WP, DLC).

¹ That is, November 25, when Wilson went to Jersey City to confer with Tumulty and Robert Davis, about which see W. W. St. John to WW, Nov. 22, 1910, n. 1.

From Ralph Waldo Emerson Donges

My dear Doctor Wilson: Camden, N. J., November 30, 1910.

The question of the United States Senatorship has been in my mind a great deal since election. I have very pronounced views on the subject, and have been tempted many times to write to you about it. I have not done so, because I felt sure that you had the matter in mind, and would, at the proper time, do what you could to prevent the Legislature from making the mistake of electing Mr. Smith.

Today's papers contain an account of a letter sent by you to Mr. Smith defining your position on the question, and advising him that you do not favor his selection. I cannot refrain from expressing my appreciation of the stand you have taken. To send him to the Senate without a protest, would, in my judgment, discredit your Administration at the outset, create a suspicion as to the bona fides of your declarations, and set the party back fifteen years. It would be a confirmation of the statement that the party is engaged in a barter of the office. It would put in this position of great power and responsibility a man whose record in the office is not such as to commend him to the people of the State, and, especially, to the members of our party who are striving for the re-establishment of Democratic principles in the State and Nation,—a man who, by his unwillingness to submit his candidacy to the people for approval, manifested his consciousness that he neither deserves nor commands the confidence of those whom he would represent.

Whatever may be the outcome of the contest, I am glad you have put yourself squarely on record. You have kept faith. It is now for all of us to do our utmost to bring about the proper result. If there is anything you think I can do, please let me know.

It will not be necessary for you to acknowledge receipt of this letter.   Yours very sincerely,   Ralph W. E. Donges

TLS (WP, DLC).

From Josephus Daniels

My dear Mr. Wilson: Raleigh, N. C. Nov. 30th. 1910.

I am enclosing you an extract from the News & Observer to-day, which I think might interest you.[1] I know Hon. James Smith well and like him very much, but I feel that under the circumstances his election would embarrass you and the party.

I hope to see you during the winter or early spring and talk to you about public matters. My wife[2] sends best regards.

Sincerely yours,   Josephus Daniels

TLS (WP, DLC).
    [1] It is missing. There is no extant copy of the Raleigh *News and Observer* of Nov. 30, 1910.
    [2] Addie Worth Bagley Daniels.

From Frederick Todd[1]

Dear Sir: New York, December 1, 1910.

We would very much like to print in the Annual Financial Review of the New York Times a telling discussion of the question of Federal or State regulation of corporations. The Review, you may not know, gets a wide, careful reading by bankers and students of business and economics in America and in Europe and its leading articles are probably read casually by thousands of others, a quarter of a million copies being the print of this edition. We mention this matter of wide publicity because we know that men who are engaged earnestly upon public problems do seriously appreciate the advantages of a wide, serious audience for their views. We would like to have you give us in as definite form as your time will permit, your opinion how the separate States may be able to regulate corporations. We will ask Mr. Francis Lynde Stetson, or some other one of the gentlemen who favor Federal incorporation laws, to state his views of the advantage of Federal control.

As we understand it, those who believe in Federal regulation do not admit that an individual State is able, even within its own borders, to regulate the business of corporations chartered in other States, or even its own corporations, when the business can be consid[e]red interstate commerce. In the Minnesota Rate case,[2] for instance, the Master's report, if confirmed by the United States Court, will establish the rule that a State cannot enforce railroad rates within its borders, regardless of the reasonableness of the state-named rate, if the State thereby causes derangement of interstate schedules. On the other hand the advocates of a Federal incorporation act, (who are not necessarily in favor of any kind of regulation), want it because they think it will free corporations doing an in[t]erstate business from annoying actions on the part of States. The question is, how, remembering the United States Courts, the States can practically meet the corporations at necessary points. We are confident that many readers would be deeply interested in knowing definitely and in detail, the ways in which the States may solve this problem, if they will, without recourse to Federal control. These modern political problems are financial problems too, and in a publication devoted to the discussion of broad economic information such a statement, if you will consent to make it, is of particular appropriateness.[3]

Yours very sincerely,   Frederick Todd
for the Annual Financial Review

TLS (WP, DLC).
[1] Financial editor of the *New York Times*.
[2] A case pending at this time in the United States Circuit Court, District of Minnesota, involving action by the Minnesota Railroad and Warehouse Commission which litigants claimed was detrimental to interstate commerce. The Supreme Court, in 1913, upheld the Minnesota commission's particular action, but ruled that Congress had control over intrastate rates when they affected interstate commerce. In the following year, in the Shreveport Rate Cases, the court carried this doctrine a step further by saying that Congress's creature, the Interstate Commerce Commission, also had control over intrastate rates when they adversely affected interstate commerce.
[3] See F. Todd to WW, Dec. 13, 1910, n. 1.

From Thomas Bell Love

My dear Mr. Wilson: Dallas, Texas December 1st, 1910.

I am writing to thank you very much for your kind note of November 11th., in response to my telegram sent you the night of the election.[1]

If I may do so without immodesty, in order that you may properly understand my motives, I wish to say, that I represented this county in the Legislature of Texas in the Sessions of 1903, 1905 and 1907, being Speaker of the House during the latter Session, and that I have written a great many of the present statutes of this State intended to carry into effect the spirit of the platform upon which you made your campaign.

In the summer of 1907 I was induced by the present Governor of this State[2] to accept, at a sacrifice, the post of Commissioner of Insurance and Banking for the State, with the end in view of revamping and rehabilitating these departments, and re-writing the Insurance and Banking laws of the State. I think that I may say, that it is considered by the majority of the people of the State, that I rendered them some service in this capacity. At any rate, the department was completely reformed and re-established, and the Insurance and Banking laws of the State were almost completely re-written in obedience to my recommendation, and by the enactment of my bills, in the face of the most stren[u]ous opposition from special interests.

On February 1st, of this year, being unable to longer make the financial sacrifice entailed by continuing in the public service in view of the necessities of my family, I voluntarily retired, and became Vice-president and Counsel of the Southwestern Life Insurance Company, which, though a young and small institution, is the oldest and largest Life Insurance Company in the Southwest.

Now, this much by way of self-introduction, as a preface to what I really wish to say, which is, that I very much desire to be of service in any way possible, in promoting your nomination for the Presidency, and I can say that I have already ascertained that in such a movement many of the strongest and most influential Democrats in Texas, scattered throughout the State, are willing to co-operate.[3] Therefore, I am desirous of obtaining at once, if I can conveniently, copies of your platform, and campaign speeches made during the late campaign, and also, to be put in communication with your Committee Chairman, Secretary, or some discreet person with whom I can correspond concerning the matters I have in mind.

I fully understand the possible impropriety of my writing you at this time along these lines, but I know no one else to write, and I am sure, that it is desirable that lines of communication should be opened with as little delay as possible.

With best wishes, believe me,

Yours very truly,　Thos B Love

TLS (WP, DLC).
[1] T. B. Love to WW, Nov. 8, 1910, Vol. 21.
[2] Thomas Mitchell Campbell, Governor of Texas, 1907-11.
[3] For accounts of the Wilson movement in Texas, see Arthur S. Link, "The Wilson Movement in Texas, 1910-1912," *Southwestern Historical Quarterly*, XLVIII (Oct. 1944), 169-85, and Lewis L. Gould, *Progressives and Prohibitionists: Texas Democrats in the Wilson Era* (Austin, Tex., and London, 1973), pp. 58-84.

From Charles O'Connor Hennessy[1]

Dear Sir: New York Dec. 1, 1910.

As a New Jersey Democrat (a resident of Bergen County) and one who was made happy by your election to Governorship, I beg permission to express my support of the position you are reported to be taking in the Senatorship matter. My acquaintance with Mr. Martine is slight, although I know him to be a man of large experience, upright character and broad Democratic instincts. Men with these characteristics are more needed, I believe, in the United States Senate at this time than men of astuteness in the ways of business, or profundity in learning.

You have no doubt learned that there are many men like myself, interested in politics in the larger way, and seeking no office, who feel very intensely about this Senatorship question, and who believe that it will provoke a party scandal of most destructive consequences if the referendum vote in the September primaries is to be disregarded by the Democratic members of the Legislature.

I rejoice in the hope that you will permit no one to construe the proper limits of the opportunities that have recently been opened to you, in such manner as to exclude you from the exercise of the great power and prestige that now is yours for the benefit of your party and your State.

The question, it seems to me, is much larger than any consideration of whether or not Mr. Martine is the best man for the Senatorship. Indeed, I think that all questions of individual claims, or even of party expediency, are transcended by the obligation to recognize the result of the appeal to the popular vote as decisive, and to recognize that a repudiation of the primary result would completely discredit the party professions.

I trust this unsolicited advice will not offend. I would not offer it but for my feeling of great respect for your character, the knowledge that you are being offered advice of a different kind from many sources, and a belief that the outcome of this matter will determine largely whether our party is to remain in power in the State of New Jersey.

Yours very truly,   C. O'Connor Hennessy.

TLS (WP, DLC).
  [1] Manager of the Franklin Society for Home Building and Savings in New York, a resident of Haworth, New Jersey, and a writer and speaker on cooperative financing.

From Job Herbert Lippincott

My dear Dr. Wilson: Jersey City [N. J.], December 1, 1910.

If the stories in the press are correct, you are about to enter upon a campaign to force our party [to] redeem its campaign pledges and to choose a United States Senator, who has been endorsed by the popular vote. If this is your intention, I believe you are entirely right, and should like to be of some assistance to you in the matter.

I believe [the] United States Senatorship is not a question of men but purely a question of principle on which the sincerity of our party will be decided.

If any knowledge or experience that I may have in campaigns in New Jersey will be of the slightest service to you, I trust you will feel at liberty to command me. If it is your intention to organize meetings in different parts of the State and to conduct a[n] aggressive campaign, I believe I might be able to assist you in reaching men who are in sympathy with this movement.

Trusting I may hear from you in this matter, I am,

Very truly yours,   Job H Lippincott

TLS (WP, DLC).

From Frederick H. Levey[1]

Dear Sir: New York December 1st, 1910.

I hesitate to address you on a subject which it is well known is occupying your attention to a considerable degree at the present time, but as a citizen of New Jersey I feel you will pardon my perhaps intrusion on your time. I had the privilege of voting this year the entire Democratic ticket for the first time in twenty years, and feel that the Democratic party has the greatest opportunity presented to it to reinstate itself with the voters of the country, provided it shows that it is determined to put into office only the best equipped, and most intelligent men in its ranks. It has already in the case of Governors elected in Maine, Connecticut, New Jersey, Ohio and New York selected the most eminent members of the Democratic party; men whose character for intelligence and statesmanship cannot be questioned. In New York state there is a strong movement in support of Mr. Shepherd for Senator[2] who is most eminently fitted for the position. I feel that the Republican voters who supported you by the thousands would feel most gratified if you would use your influence in the favor of the *most eminently qualified* member of the Democratic party for United States Senator, regardless either of a primary suggestion, or of a past political influence. I have no suggestion to make of any name, but feel that a strong man sent from the State of New Jersey to the United States Senate would have a very great influence to retain in the ranks of the Democratic party men, like myself, who have become dissatisfied with the measures of the Republican party. Perhaps the earliest action of the New Jersey Democrats will be the election of a Senator, and first impressions of the purposes of a party are most important to those who are looking for a sign of its future action.

I had the pleasure of dining with you last June at the Rev. Dr. Glazebrook's[3] house and trust to have the pleasure of again meeting you.   Very truly yours,   Fredk H Levey

TLS (WP, DLC).
  [1] President of the Frederick H. Levey Co., manufacturers of printing inks, and a resident of Elizabeth, N. J.
  [2] Edward Morse Shepard, the anti-Tammany candidate. For a description of the Democratic senatorial fight in New York, see W. Hughes to WW, Dec. 9, 1910, n. 1.
  [3] The Rev. Dr. Otis Allan Glazebrook, rector of St. John's Protestant Episcopal Church in Elizabeth, N. J.

From Thomas Davies Jones

My dear Mr. Wilson: Chicago December 1st, 1910.

Sometime before the 12th I wish you would advise me on what date, by what road and train you will arrive in Chicago on your approaching visit. I will meet you at the train. My brother will be away but I shall be at home, and I understand that you will be our guest while in Chicago.

I was sorry to see that you have been compelled to come out into the open in the matter of Smith's election to the Senate. We were in hopes here that you might prevail on the Senator to withdraw without a fight. It is very unfortunate, but now that you are in the fight, there is nothing to do but to fight for all there is in it.
                    Faithfully yours,   Thomas D. Jones.
TLS (WP, DLC).

To Robert Underwood Johnson

My dear Mr. Johnson: Princeton, N. J. December 3, 1910

Your message to me at Frankfort[1] reached me promptly but I found that it was the policy of the Governors' Conference not to adopt resolutions on any public subject.

Their only function, and I must say I think it is wise for them to confine themselves to it, they considered to be that of discussion and and [sic] interchange of opinion. They feel that any attempt to pass resolutions would seem to be a combined attempt on their part to influence legislation and they are not ready for that.

It is very kind of you to say[2] that you would like to have a talk with me about something that might interest me to write about but alas! I know that it is absolutely impossible for me to write about anything, the most I hope to do is to find time to put my speeches together in a way that will not be wholly flimsy and offhand.

I shall hope to have many opportunities in the near future to see you but just at this time my movements are so uncertain that I dare not predict where it will be.

In haste,

Cordially and faithfully yours,   Woodrow Wilson

TLS (Berg Coll., NN).
  [1] It is missing.
  [2] In R. U. Johnson to WW, Nov. 26, 1910.

From Oswald Garrison Villard

Dear Dr. Wilson: New York December 3, 1910.

I telegraphed you to Frankfort that I believed I had found the man for you. I do not know why I did not think of him at the very moment you spoke; he naturally suggested himself as soon as I came to talk the matter over in the office. I think very highly of him indeed as a solid, hard-working, reliable man, quick to take an idea and an excellent writer. I would not, naturally, give you the impression that he is a man of transcendent ability, and you will, of course, decide whether he has sufficient personality to meet with your needs. He is, as you will see by his letter enclosed,[1] a resident of New Jersey.

I am most anxious to hear of your next move in the Smith matter. I am sure that from a personal point of view you could do nothing better than to come our [out] publicly against him, and when you do so your action will have a wonderfully stimulating effect upon our own senatorial situation, which is a most uncomfortable one. Would you be good enough to send me just a word as to how the situation now stands with you? I should greatly appreciate it.

Sincerely yours,   Oswald Garrison Villard.

TLS (WP, DLC).
  [1] It is missing.

From Martin Patrick Devlin

Dear Sir: Trenton, N. J., December 3, 1910.

I want to congratulate you on your election and your having assumed the leadership of our party, and to tell you how general and genuinely hearty are the words of praise to be heard on all sides because of your stand on the senatorship. I have heard, directly and indirectly, from all walks of life, and from those sources come strong, unanimous approval of your courage and your attitude.

Men had come to regard the utterances of aspirants for public office as expressed merely for the purpose of expediency. It is most refreshingly gratifying to have a successful candidate stand boldly up on the right side for a right and a vital principle, regardless of its effect upon his own political fortunes.

The official who is ready to play the public with the same fairness and frankness as you are doing is certain to find himself more lastingly honored and respected by his fellow men, regardless of party.

I have had an intimate knowledge of the doings of the Democratic party during the last twenty years. I can fairly say that it will be just as impossible to serve the people and men of the type of Senator James Smith and Robert Davis, as it has ever been to serve both God and mammon. There is nothing personal in my objection to Senator Smith or Robert Davis. In fact, I have done some law business for Senator Smith within the last year, but this does not blind me to the fact that his politics are wrong and dangerous to the success of the Democratic party. As for Robert Davis, I class him in politics as a man who would sell the government of a state for the offices of a city. I consider that the acts of both men in the past have been a detriment instead of a help to the Democratic party.

In some ways Mr. Martine may not measure up to the ideal statesman, but this is not the question at stake. The primary election for Senator has left our party with a solemn, binding contract with the people, and no matter what comes that contract should be kept.

Your position on this question makes me feel that the citizens of this State will have a novel experience of having New Jersey represented in the United States Senate by Mr. Martine, whom I know to be a perfectly honest man, and who can be counted upon to vote for a reduction of the tariff on an honest basis, together with other national reforms so badly needed. Martine can be relied upon to look to the Democratic leaders of integrity for guidance, and how much better this is for the people than to have in the Senate a representative of privilege masquerading as a Democrat.

It is a great pleasure and privilege for an earnest Democrat to see your administration opened with the support of all the great forces that seek only righteousness in public life. Every insurgent and every independent citizen glories in your stand. The fact that you have won such widely read and fearless newspapers as the Hudson Observer and the Trenton Times—in my humble judgment, because of their absolute fearlessness and honesty of purpose, the greatest agencies for public good in New Jersey— means that you will have the hearty cooperation of every free journal in this State. And that is mighty in the battle for better things.

This is all very fine and I must sincerely congratulate the Democracy of this State on such a splendid beginning.

I was opposed to your nomination, but let me assure you that there is no one in this State more pleased than I am to find that you have been an agreeable disappointment to my expectations. You can count on my help in this good work at any time you may think I am needed.

Yours respectfully,   Martin P Devlin

TLS (WP, DLC).

From John Henry Eastwood[1]

My dear Mr. Wilson: Belleville, New Jersey, Dec. 3, [19]10.

As I have not had the pleasure of meeting you and also am on the opposite side in politics, you may consider it a liberty on my part to address you on the subject of the United States Senatorship. I notice by the papers that there is considerable controversy and some opposition to the election of the Hon. James Smith, Jr. I sincerely regret this as having known Mr. Smith for some twenty-five years I feel as a business man with considerable interest in this portion of the State, that if we are to have a Democratic Senator, that no one could so ably represent the State in the Senate as Mr. Smith. The business community know him and know that his only object will be for the interest of the people at large.

I am writing this letter merely to show what one of the business men of the City of Newark and its suburbs think of Mr. Smith, and I trust that he will secure the election and that the leaders of the party will assist him.

Again apologizing for having intruded and occupied your time to the extent of this letter, I remain with sincere respect,

Very truly yours,   John H. Eastwood.

TLS (WP, DLC).
[1] Treasurer and general manager of the Eastwood Wire Manufacturing Co. of Belleville, N. J.

From Henry Smith Pritchett, with Enclosure

Personal

My dear Wilson,   New York December 3, 1910

In the places of yourself and Provost Harrison[1] on the executive committee,[2] the trustees elected Hadley and Schurman. The first meeting of the new committee will be on the eighth of December. At that time I shall bring up for consideration the matter of the retiring allowance in your own case and also in the case of President Jordan, who contemplates retiring from the presidency of Leland Stanford Junior University to undertake another piece of work, a matter which he wishes to keep for the present out of public knowledge.[3]

My colleagues will, like myself, want to go to the furthest possible limit to show their recognition of what you have done in education. I find myself, however, as the executive officer most heavily charged with responsibility in the matter, in some doubt whether the Foundation ought in any case to pay a retiring allowance to a man, however distinguished, who retires from educational service to undertake other work on salary. Mr. Jordan in his change would expect also to receive about the same salary as he is receiving now. I have tried pretty hard to make myself see that an out and out vote of a retiring allowance in these cases is justifiable; but the more I have thought over it, the more doubtful I feel as to the proposition that the Foundation should pay a retired salary to a man who leaves an educational post to take up work in another field on salary. I do not know what my colleagues on the committee would feel like doing; but I am telling you frankly what has been passing through my mind.

I have tried also to ask myself what is a fair recognition of educational service for the Foundation to make in the case of one who has served education in a distinguished way and who goes into another field as you and Jordan are about to do? I am disposed to feel that the continuance of the retiring allowance privilege is such a recognition. If, for example, we say to you and Jordan: Go ahead in your new fields. We will continue to you in these fields the retiring allowance privilege so that in case of disability you can avail yourself of it, or on coming to the right age; and your wife shall have the protection which she would have had in case you had remained in service in an accepted institution. Such action as this I feel ready to recommend. I do not know, however, whether this would be agreeable to you or not.

I hope you will understand that I have tried to look at the whole matter in the most sympathetic and friendly way, while at the same time trying to carry out what seems to me the right line of action for the Foundation.

I read with keen interest your speech at the Conference of Governors. It seems to me one of the most timely and admirable utterances which has been made by a public man in years. It has commanded universal attention and respect.

Always faithfully yours, Henry S. Pritchett

Under this newly adopted rule the trustees of Princeton could by paying your retiring allowance in the interval make you regularly eligible to a retiring allowance at sixty-five.[4]

H.S.P

TLS (WP, DLC).

[1] Charles Custis Harrison, retiring Provost of the University of Pennsylvania.

[2] That is, of the Carnegie Foundation for the Advancement of Teaching.

[3] David Starr Jordan had been appointed director of the World Peace Foundation in 1909 (he was appointed "Chief Director" the following year), and he took two half-year sabbaticals from the presidency of Stanford University in 1909 and 1910 to work and speak in behalf of the foundation in Europe, Japan, Korea, and elsewhere. He was considering resigning as president of Stanford to pursue full-time work for the organization but remained as president until 1913 and as chancellor until 1916. Orrin Leslie Elliott, *Stanford University: The First Twenty-five Years* (Stanford, Cal., and London, 1937), pp. 557-58.

[4] Wilson did not withdraw his application. The executive committee considered the application but never took action on it. As Pritchett explained: "The Executive Committee felt that the objections which I had voiced were too grave to be put aside. At the same time they were all personal friends of Wilson; they knew his financial situation, and they desired to give him a pension if it could be done in any way consistent with sound practice. The committee finally decided to leave the application on the table and to ask the Board of Trustees at the annual meeting of November last [1911] to construe the resolution passed two years before and make clear to the Executive Committee whether the trustees had in mind to make exceptions of such cases as that of President Wilson. Mr. Wilson's application was not considered at this meeting at all. Such details are left to the Executive Committee. After discussion of the general question the Trustees decided that the action of the Trustees two years before could not apply to such cases, and in view of the difficulties of administering such a provision, they voted to rescind the resolution altogether. . . . Technically Mr. Wilson's application has never been declined. It is still pending, but the action of the Trustees was to give practical refusal to such request, and I have so informed Gov. Wilson." H. S. Pritchett to N. Hapgood, Jan. 20, 1912, printed in the *New York Times*, June 25, 1912.

Rule 4. In addition to the provisions for retiring allowances made in Rules 1, 2, and 3, the Foundation will coöperate with institutions on the accepted list in the retirement of teachers who have had twenty-five years of service as professor, or thirty years of service as professor and instructor, but who, not being sixty-five years of age, are not eligible for retirement under Rule 1, upon the following basis:

If the institution grants to such a teacher a retiring allowance at its own cost, the Foundation will consider such teacher eligible to a retiring allowance on reaching the age of sixty-five under the rules in force at that time, and at the same rate which the institution has paid in the interval, provided the retiring allowance so paid shall not be less than that to which the teacher would be entitled if he retired under Rule 2 on the ground of disability, and provided further that under no circumstances will the Foundation pay a higher retiring allowance to such a teacher than that to which he would have been entitled had he remained in service until the age of sixty-five and retired under Rule 1. Should a teacher so retired by an institution die before reaching the age of sixty-five, his widow would be eligible under the rules to receive a pension from the Foundation equal to one-half of that which her husband had been receiving, provided that under no circumstances would such widow be entitled to a higher allowance than that which she would have received had her husband been eligible to retirement under the rules of the Foundation.

T MS (WP, DLC).

From James Smith, Jr.

My dear Governor Wilson: Newark, N. J. December 3rd, 1910

Permit me, please, to express my appreciation of your speech before the Governors' convention at Frankfort. Your views on corporations should receive general approval. Their legal control is one of the vital problems of the hour, but it is a problem which should be approached in a spirit of fairness. From so much ill-considered matter that has been urged in this behalf, it is pleasing to turn to your treatment of the subject. Some people in high places may not agree with you, but the best judgment of the country will accord with your view that the solving of this problem is a state, not a national, duty. I was especially interested in the way you safe-guarded New Jersey's position. While you advocated co-operation on the part of the several states, you would have no such fixed and uniform laws as would destroy the advantages which one state now holds over another. New Jersey's pre-eminence in the creation of corporations is well known. My earnest hope is that under your administration we may attain equal eminence in their control.

The press credit you with giving encouragement to the presidential aspirations of men outside our state.[1] That is an act of magnanimity, but is it not a little unfair to us? New Jersey may wish to have something to say in that regard when the time comes.

With best wishes for your good health and success, I am
Very truly yours,   James Smith Jr.

TLS (WP, DLC).
[1] According to the *Newark Evening News*, Dec. 1, 1910, Wilson briefly discussed the presidential race in 1912 during his trip to the Governors' Conference in Kentucky and said, "If the people of the United States elect Governor Harmon President they will make no mistake."

From Joseph M. Noonan

My dear Governor: Jersey City, N. J. Dec 4th 1910

During your triumphal campaign in Old Kentucky, of which I have read with great pleasure, things have been developing here in the Senatorial situation. As matters now stand I think you have won your fight and won it without making a single enemy or leaving the slightest trace of bad feeling in this county.

A few days ago I called on Mr Davis to inquire about his health and he asked me to tell him frankly what I thought about the Senatorship. He knew my opinion at the time but I think he asked me for the benefit of those who were present on this occassion. So I gave him my opinion with perfect candor and as forcibly as I could put it. Then he told us of his promise to Smith, of which I already knew, and asked me if I knew of any way in which he could honorably default on it. I said that, while I recognized the delicacy of his position, he had already done all that could be legitimately exacted from him under his promise by giving the members of the Hudson legislative delegation to understand that he would like to have them vote for Smith. [Charles Henry] Gallagher of Trenton was present but took no part in the discussion while I was there. A day or two afterward I met Assemblyman-elect Eagan[1] who said he had told Davis the day before that he was going to vote for Martine and that Davis made no attempt to dissuade him[.] On the same day that I met Eagan Senator Fielder called on me at my office and said, to use his own words, that he didn't see there was anything else to do but to vote for Martine. I advised him to see you or communicate with you but he thought that it would be more becoming for him to wait until you should send for him and then, he said, he would gladly answer your summons and acquaint you with his purpose to fall into line for Martine.

Mr Tumulty has told me of your intention to meet our Hudson legislators-elect tomorrow. It is, I think, a very good idea. You will not be likely to have any difficulty in managing any of them.

I am very glad you have come to know and appreciate Tumulty. He is an able and an honorable young man and his views on all public questions are in entire accord with your own. He has been very earnest in trying to make our delegation solid for Martine but has acted always with great prudence and restraint.

My impression of the situation here is that Davis is very sorry that he finds himself in his present predicament, that he is anxious to please you in all things but that he will adhere formally, perfunctorily, to his promise to Smith. I am quite convinced that he will not attempt to exert any "pressure" on any of our legislative delegation. If tomorrow they should declare publicly for Martine I think it would be a great relief to Davis.

Excuse this scrawl and believe me to be

Very Sincerely Yours   Jos. M. Noonan

ALS (WP, DLC).
¹ Charles Michael Egan, lawyer of Jersey City.

To St. Clair McKelway

Personal and Private.

My dear Mr. McKelway: Princeton, N. J. December 5, 1910

I am sure that you were not yourself responsible for the editorial entitled "Woodrow Wilson attracts attention," which appeared in the Eagle on the evening of November 30th,¹ but I am wondering if you would honor me with your confidence as to how it originated. Its statements as to what I urged in my address at Frankfort were so far from the truth that I must believe that the writer had not read my address, and the whole animous of the article is so evident to do me personal damage that I am entirely at a loss to understand how it could possibly have appeared in the Eagle.

If I am presuming too far on your cordial friendship I hope that you will properly rebuke me and tell me that it is none of my business, but if you would be kind enough to give me some light in this matter, which has distressed me, I feel that it would guide me not a little in treading a very difficult path.

With warmest regards and with great desire to see you sometime soon and talk many important matters over with you,

Cordially and faithfully,   Woodrow Wilson

TLS (WP, DLC).
1 "If," went the editorial in summarizing Wilson's speech at the Governors' Conference, "we understand Mr. Wilson, he contends that the Governor should claim from the people the admission of his political mastery and have it conceded to him, requiring the Legislature to take and heed notice thereof. That is what his careful but bold words at Frankfort signify. It is a demand for larger gubernatorial power and fuller popular and legislative recognition of it. Mr. Wilson would magnify his office. He would be not only the head of the State, but the head of the party in the fullest sense." The editorial, noting that any increase in executive power had to come through constitutional means, continued: "Of course, Mr. Wilson knows this, but he talks as if he did not. The novelty of his position, the pleasure and activity of his mind in the study of his new office, his desire to arouse attention account for his words. The effect of them is dramatically startling. The substance of them is not a discovery, so much as an excavation. . . . He will bring forth things old out of the Constitution in a way to make them seem to be things new." The editorial then described the divisions Wilson had created during his presidency of Princeton University, and, while leaving open the question of Wilson's political skill, the editorial expressed doubts about his ability to win political support for his legislative program. In conclusion, it pointedly remarked, "The experienced politician to whom he [Wilson] owed his nomination did not engage to relinquish his own ambition or to efface himself as the price or the penalty of Mr. Wilson's success." *Brooklyn Daily Eagle*, Nov. 30, 1910.

To Oswald Garrison Villard

My dear Mr. Villard: Princeton, N. J. December 5, 1910

I am back from Kentucky to find your kind letter of December 3rd. I also received your telegram at Frankfort and greatly appreciated it. I am so busy just now with this Senatorial business that I cannot even give the matter of the appointment of my secretary the least thought at present, but I assure you I shall certainly consider the man you mention with the greatest care when I can turn to it, and I am warmly obliged to you for your thoughtful kindness in the matter.

It looks as if we had Smith safely beaten for the Senatorship. It is equally clear that we have sufficient majority to elect Mr. Martine.

The present transactions are these: I am to see the Hudson County Delegation here at Princeton this afternoon.[1] After I see them I shall know much better than I do now how I stand. I hope tomorrow to see Senator Smith, and tell him very plainly what my position is in order to induce him, if possible, to decline the candidacy. If he will not do that I will come out openly against him.

I will try to keep you informed of each step of this tiresome but important matter

With warmest regards,

Cordially and sincerely yours   Woodrow Wilson

TLS (O. G. Villard Papers, MH).

¹ Wilson conferred with ten of the thirteen members of the Hudson County delegation on December 5 in the library of Prospect in Princeton. Those missing were Edward Kenny, James J. McGrath, and Thomas M. Donnelly, but Donnelly had already issued a public statement in support of Martine. Wilson stressed the necessity of adhering to the principle of the senatorial primary and electing Martine. *Newark Evening News*, Dec. 6, 1910; *Trenton Evening Times*, Dec. 6, 1910. However, one participant, Thomas Francis Martin, later charged that Wilson said that the Democratic party "played a joke upon itself by nominating James E. Martine." Wilson replied: "I never made that statement to any one, and it seems ridiculous that I should even take the trouble to deny it." *Trenton Evening Times*, Jan. 12, 1911. As J. P. Tumulty to WW, Dec. 7, 1910, indicates, the conference did succeed in obtaining some firmer commitments from the Hudson County assemblymen-elect, and it paved the way for Wilson's summit meeting with Smith on December 6, about which see WW to Mary A. H. Peck, Dec. 7, 1910, n. 1.

To Frederick H. Levey

My dear Mr. Levey: Princeton, N. J. December 5, 1910

I warmly appreciate the personal confidence in me as evidenced by your kind letter of December 1st, which I have read with greatest interest and attention.

It goes without saying that it is impossible without betraying the whole party and wrecking its prospects to send James Smith back to the United States Senate, and I again assure you that I am doing everything in my power to prevent that, but in view of the fact that the Democratic party of the State introduced and pressed to enactment the present primary law, I feel that it would be a very grave breach of faith on its part to ignore the vote in favor of Mr. Martine at the recent primary.

If the field were clear for our choice I should subscribe to every part of your letter, but I am sure that you will appreciate why I feel bound in honor to take the position I do.

Recalling with genuine pleasure our meeting at Doctor Glaze-brook's,

Cordially and sincerely yours,   Woodrow Wilson

TLS (WC, NjP).

From Lucius Thompson Russell

My dear Mr. Wilson: Elizabeth, N. J., Dec. 5th, 1910.

I enclose you about the only comment I have made on the senatorial matter.[1] On only one other occasion have I mentioned the subject. I hope my statement of your attitude is a fair one. It is my purpose to aid you and not embarrass you in the conduct of the state affairs. I feel fully justified in awaiting your lead, in view of your campaign utterances to the effect that the people would be electing you their party leader as well as Governor of the state.

The table of votes cast, which I carried in the paper for several days, is enough to make any sane man understand that the people of New Jersey were not giving the senatorial contest any more consideration during the late campaign than if it had not been before them. The few votes cast, in my opinion, were almost accidental. Eliminating Mr. Martine's home county and Hudson County the remainder of the state does not seem to have remembered there was a senatorial contest on. It seems to me preposterous that the democratic party is obligated to disfranchise nearly ninety per cent of the voters of this state on the senatorial question on the very flimsy ground that an habitual office-seeker's name was placed on the ticket, and marked ballots sent out by a space-filling newspaper correspondent.[2]

If you finally decide to take no further part in this matter than to insist upon the elimination of ex-Sen. Smith, I will then lead a fight for a justification and indorsement of your conduct that will not make you feel ashamed.

I also enclose you a letter received from a fellow townsman, a personal friend of Mr. Martine, and a loyal democrat, Mr. Edward C. Pearson.[3]

As stated over the 'phone, I will try to run down in a purely informal way for only a few minutes some time during this week.

Very Sincerely   L T Russell

TLS (WP, DLC).

[1] This was a front-page article from the *Elizabeth*, N. J., *Evening Times*, c. Dec. 3, 1910, stating that Wilson opposed Smith but not because of any personal animosity toward him or his political views. "Mr. Wilson," the article said, "does not, however, propose to set up his personal opinions against a state-wide prejudice and a general understanding that Mr. Smith should not succeed John Kean." Accordingly, it continued, Wilson had frankly stated his opinion of the senatorial situation to Smith and any other party leader who asked for it but would not "boss" the legislature in this or any other matter.

[2] William W. St. John.

[3] The letter from Edward Clarence Pearson, a lawyer of Plainfield, N. J., was printed in the *Elizabeth*, N. J., *Evening Times*, Dec. 3, 1910. Pearson argued that neither Smith nor Martine was qualified for the Senate and that the primary vote was scarcely a true measure of popular sentiment. While stopping short

of suggesting a compromise candidate, Pearson maintained that the old issues which had divided the Democratic party in New Jersey should be abandoned, and that new men should provide leadership to solve pressing contemporary problems.

From Gamaliel Bradford

My dear Gov. Wilson: Boston Dec 5. 1910

I was sorry not to see more of you at Louisville[1] but besides that you were very busy. I was somewhat diffident

You will remember the enthusiasm with which I greeted your book on Congressional Government,[2] which I still hold in undiminished estimation. But if you remember also the long walk and talk which we held later in Cambridge,[3] you may recall that we differed on the subject of executive responsibility which has been my hobby ever since the war, & I had not seen anything in your recent speeches to indicate a change of view.

The passage from your speech[4] in the enclosed slip[5] makes me more hopeful. There does not seem to be any other clear issue, (barring the abstract one of state rights) except the tariff and that is a boomerang. I believe the democrats will make such a mess of it in their first session as almost to insure the election of a Republican president in 1812 [1912], unless some powerfully divergent topic can be brought forward. Now the disgust & despair of the country with state & city government, and at the same time the dread of federal encroachment is furnishing a golden opportunity. The public mind is all ripe for turning to the state governors, and if the subject is taken hold of gently & gradually—and tentatively—I do not believe there is any such direct road to the presidency. I am looking round for some governor who is ready for it, and would much rather work with you. I have no wish for anything for myself. My age of 80 years and the loss of an only and beloved grandson[6] have crushed all personal ambition. But the one earthly passion left is to see my country get out of the mire in which she is floundering and start on a fresh career of greatness and honor.

Yours sincerely in past remembrance   Gam'l Bradford

ALS (WP, DLC).
  [1] Some sessions of the Governors' Conference were held in Frankfort, some in Louisville.
  [2] His review is printed at Feb. 12, 1885, Vol. 4.
  [3] See WW to ELA, April 26, 1886, Vol. 5.
  [4] To the Governors' Conference on November 29.
  [5] It is missing.
  [6] Gamaliel Bradford III, who died on August 8, 1910, shortly after receiving the A.B. degree from Harvard. He was the son of Helen Hubbard Ford Bradford and Gamaliel Bradford, Jr.

To Mary Allen Hulbert Peck

Dearest Friend,   Princeton, New Jersey 6 December, '10.

I was away a whole week, attending the conference of governors in Kentucky, and now that I am back at home I find that there is no list of the sailings for B[ermuda]. in the house. For fear there is a steamer to-morrow, I send this hasty line to thank you for your sweet letter and to send all possible messages to my dear friend from

Your devoted friend   Woodrow Wilson

Quite well

WWT and WWhwLS (WP, DLC).

From Shosuke Sato[1]

My dear Sir: Sapporo, Japan Dec. 6, 1910.

I was greatly pleased to hear of your being elected the Governor of the state of New Jersey and now send you my hearty congratulation for your success. Sometime ago, I received a kind letter from Dr [Davis Rich] Dewey of the Institute of Technology, Boston, and to-day I happened to read the November number of the Review of Reviews, in which I was glad to find a brief sketch of your life.[2] I sincerely hope that this will be only a step to your higher career in the national politics of the United States. Ever since my return here from Baltimore in 1886, I have been faithfully serving my Alma-Mater and was fortunate enough to have it raised to the standard of a university, but many things still remain undone, and I now find out that life is only too short for any single individual to undertake such a work as the founding of a university in its truest sense. May Providence guide you to success in your new life.

With all my best wishes to you,

I remain,   Yours sincerely,   Shosuke Sato

TLS (WP, DLC).
[1] A friend from the Johns Hopkins, Acting President of Tohoku (Northeastern) Imperial University at Sendai.
[2] "Woodrow Wilson and the New Jersey Governorship," New York *Review of Reviews*, XLII (Nov. 1910), 555-62.

From Hollis Burke Frissell[1]

Hampton, Virginia

My dear President Wilson: December 6, 1910

For a number of years we have had meetings in Carnegie Hall in the interest of industrial education in the South. On these occasions President Taft, Mr. Roosevelt, Governor Hughes, Mr. Henry Watterson, and various other men of prominence, have spoken. Our object is not so much an appeal for funds, as an endeavor to present to a New York audience conditions in the South, especially as regards the Negro race, and what seems, to us, the solution of the problems involved.

There is no one who understands the whole situation better than you do, or who can express more forcibly his opinions. I know how crowded you are with work, but if [it] would be possible for you to speak at such a meeting in New York, similar to the one that you addressed in Philadelphia about two years ago,[2] I feel that you would help the whole Southern cause. The latter part of January or the first of February would probably be the best time for such a meeting.

We held a meeting in Washington last winter, at the house of Miss Helen Boardman,[3] at which Thomas Nelson Page, President Taft, President [Samuel Chiles] Mitchell of the University of South Carolina, President [William Wilson] Finlay of the Southern Road, Dr. [Edwin Anderson] Alderman of the University of Virginia, and Dr. James H[ardy]. Dillard,[4] pleaded the cause of industrial education for the Negro as it is carried on at Hampton. Last month we had here between seventy and eighty of the County School Superintendents, and also twelve of the Southern State Superintendents of Education. I feel that we are each year getting into closer touch with the Southern people and are therefore able to render more efficient service.

We rejoice in the honors which have come to you and the opportunities which you have for the best sort of public service.

Hoping that we may hear that it will be possible for you to speak for the cause of Hampton this winter,[5]

Very truly yours,   H. B. Frissell

TLS (WP, DLC).

[1] Principal of the Hampton Normal and Agricultural Institute.

[2] Wilson's notes for this address are printed at Feb. 26, 1909, Vol. 19.

[3] The Editors have been unable to identify her. It is possible that Frissell meant Mabel Thorp Boardman of Washington, who was involved in various charitable activities, especially the Red Cross.

[4] Prominent southern educator, at this time president of the Jeanes Foundation for Negro rural schools, and director of the John F. Slater Fund for Negro education in the South.

[5] Wilson was unable to accept this invitation.

To Mary Allen Hulbert Peck

Dearest Friend,   Hotel Collingwood New York 7 Dec., 1910

I can at least *begin* a letter here,—though some more politicians will be in within ten minutes. This little hotel is my New York 'headquarters' to which I summon my henchmen for conference!

I find that no boat went yesterday, after all,—so that this will catch up with the tiny note I wrote in such frantic haste yesterday. I had *thought* myself busy at previous times in my life,—but I now find that I never before knew what I was capable of in the line of busy-ness. Since I got back from Kentucky,—whither I went the day after you sailed,—I have not till this moment had leisure for a thought of my own. And now I find that the minute I have, and look out on the snow covered housetops of the city, I am desperately lonely,—as lonely as I was when I walked away from Pier 47 the day you sailed,—and evidently for the same reason. My dear friend is not here, and the great city is *empty*! Alas that Bermuda should be so far away, so inaccessible, and yet so delectable and the home of so sweet a lady!

I am glad you have Glencove. I always liked it, within and without. I suppose you have the upper floor. It seems to me a charming place, and I am *so* glad that you are where I can visualize your surroundings. I can see everything—and every foot of ground outside your gate, to and from Salt Kettle ferry is as familiar to me as the front drive at "Prospect" (Princeton "Prospect").

With me everything centres upon the question, who shall be Senator from New Jersey

Continued in Princeton, 9 December, '10.

I tried my best to bring about a peaceful settlement,[1] but Jim Smith was bent on having the place whether it ruined the party or not and I have (this morning) come out in a statement against him, which means war, and perhaps another stumping tour of the State for me. It is hard sledding, but a fellow must fight at every step who means to clean up the dirty politics of this machine-ridden State, and I shall enjoy doing the thing as much like a gentleman as the circumstances permit.

I have not been able to write more than a sentence of this letter at a time without interruption, but it has been a deep pleasure to write it nevertheless. The delight of writing to a dear friend is that she can read what is not written, can supply the passages left out and understand that more would have been written had it been possible to find the time to write it.

I am sorry that the charm of dear Bermuda should be slow to come back over you again, but I feel sure that when you once get settled again in your little corner of a peninsula at Glencove the old love and delight of the place will creep back upon you, and that the nerves which New York has so stretched and racked will be quieted and soothed, and you will have the old happiness.

Give my warmest love to Mrs. Allen and to your son; think of me often and pity me for being so far away from your paradise; and remember me always as, amidst whatever distractions,

Your devoted friend,   Woodrow Wilson

ALS and WWTLS (WP, DLC).

[1] Wilson visited James Smith, Jr., in Newark on the afternoon of December 6 to make one last attempt to persuade Smith to stay out of the senatorial race. Wilson was met at the train station by Smith's son, George Doane Smith, Princeton 1908, and escorted to Smith's home, arriving at approximately 5:30 P.M. *Newark Evening News*, Dec. 7, 1910.

Afterwards, neither Smith nor Wilson would describe what happened in the meeting. According to later accounts, the Governor-elect pleaded with Smith to withdraw for the sake of party unity and fidelity to campaign pledges and told him, "You have a chance to be the biggest man in the state by not running for the Senate." S. Axson to R. S. Baker, Aug. 29, 1928, ALS (RSB Coll., DLC). Smith told Wilson that he wanted to return to the Senate to remove the cloud of suspicion that hung over his first term and to redeem his political reputation. He reminded Wilson of his long service and financial contributions to the Democratic party of New Jersey. Wilson responded that this was beside the point. The main issue was the senatorial primary and Martine's selection by the people. When Smith ridiculed Martine's qualifications, Wilson answered that the great majority of the 55,000 Democrats who had voted in the primary had endorsed Martine. Burton J. Hendrick, "Woodrow Wilson: Political Leader," *McClure's Magazine*, XXXVIII (Dec. 1911), 225; Tumulty, *Woodrow Wilson As I Know Him*, pp. 58-59.

According to William Bayard Hale, who based his narrative of Wilson's life largely on information which he received from Wilson himself, Wilson warned Smith that he would have to oppose him publicly if he did not withdraw. "Will you be content in having thus publicly announced your opposition?" Smith inquired. "No," Wilson answered. "I shall actively oppose you with every honorable means in my power." Smith then asked, "Does that mean that you will employ the state patronage against me?" Wilson responded, "No. I should not regard that as an honorable means. Besides, that will not be necessary." William Bayard Hale, *Woodrow Wilson: The Story of His Life* (Garden City, N. Y., 1912), pp. 181-82; see also Hendrick, "Woodrow Wilson: Political Leader," p. 225. Smith reportedly told Wilson that he controlled thirty-four of the fifty Democratic votes in the legislature and that he would run. *Trenton Evening Times*, Dec. 7, 1910.

Wilson asked Smith to reconsider his candidacy and informed him that, unless he heard from him by the last mail of December 8, he would issue a statement opposing him. Wilson received no word from Smith on December 8; the next day he made public his statement, printed at December 8. One-half hour after the release was given to the press, Wilson received a special delivery letter from Smith, asking for more time. Hale, *Woodrow Wilson*, p. 182; J. Smith, Jr., to WW, Dec. 8, 1910. The publication of Wilson's statement prompted Smith's reply, printed at December 9.

Subsequently, as has been noted, Smith claimed that Wilson had proposed a compromise candidate at their meeting in November, and Wilson, in the interview printed at December 21, 1910, admitted doing so at the meeting of December 6, although he later significantly qualified this admission in the news report printed at December 28, 1910.

It is difficult to determine the accuracy of any of the accounts of Wilson's conferences with Smith, for as James Kerney noted, the senatorial fight was "full of bitterness," and "in that campaign, truth, which of old was said to hide in a well, was more often to be found in a twilight zone between the opposing propagandas." *The Political Education of Woodrow Wilson*, pp. 90, 92.

From Henry Watterson

My Dear Governor: New York. Dec 7th 1910

Smith did not show as much heat as I expected. After getting fuller and better knowledge of the situation from you I was able to talk to him with greater confidence and intelligence. I took occasion out of abundant experience to impress the wisdom of accepting the inevitable with good grace, and, if he was not especially sympathetic, he was nowise irascible. I rather think he has been seeing light—a little light—since last week. I am just off for Washington where I expect to meet Col Harvey and run over matters with him. Between high-minded and honest men there can not be two opinions about your attitude. My homage to Mrs Wilson, along with the regret that I could not see more of those dear girls. Sincerely Your Friend Henry Watterson

ALS (WP, DLC).

From Isaac Wayne MacVeagh

Personal

Dear Mr. Wilson, Palm Beach Florida December 7: 1910.

If you will read the article enclosed called "Neville of Kensington"[1] you can rest assured this note is the last with which I am likely to trouble you for some time

As I am sure you are too appreciative of the confidence New Jersey has shown in you to wish to use it *at once* as a stepping stone to a higher office, I trust you will think over "The New Statehood" rather than "The New Nationalism" not in opposition to this latter but as just now calling for *your* best efforts in doing what you can to re-make the honorable and most useful office of governor of an important and rich commonwealth what it ought to be.

The powers of the State, atrophied by disuse, are of far-reaching beneficence, and in many instances the benefits they can confer can only be conferred by the State—old age pensions—and if Great Britain importing even her bread can afford them surely New Jersey whose treasury is overflowing can care for her small number of aged and deserving poor. So with State Insurance for the working classes. You can furnish it to them at 30 per cent of what the "Prudential" charges them counting "lapses" from recurring poverty. So with labor exchanges and insurance against unemployment. The State *only* can confer these blessings. So as to child labor.

There are others the State has the *undoubted* right to confer, while the action of the National Government is, to say the least, of *doubtful* jurisdiction. Take the cases of the Ag. Dep't. You have at New Brunswick a far more useful institution,[2] and I have made many trials of both. So as to the Bureau of Roads. Surely there is enough intelligence in New Jersey to decide on the best methods for New Jersey's Roads, while you can do the work at 1/10 the cost.

So too with the conservation of any natural resources New Jersey possesses. Gifford Pinchot—if asked by *you*—would doubtless make a survey of New Jersey and a report in that matter at a very modest expense. He inherits from his father an admirable "school of forestry"[3] just over your border in Pike County in our State.

So too with graduated—to my mind they ought to be *heavily* graduated—taxes on incomes and inheritances. The State is right to lay such taxes as nobody disputes and whenever the U. S. lays them it is sure to allow a reduction for any such taxes paid to any State, so as to make the burden equal in each State when those payable to State and Nation are added together.

Ungrudging recognition of all rights possessed by U. S. for National objects, but a new life and dignity in the work of each state in the matters within its rights[.] Think of the millions which would be saved!

Sincerely Yours,   Wayne MacVeagh.

When read please return *without comment*. I send the other pages because I wish to re-read the other articles and to seperate them wou[l]d require their mutilation. You might enjoy running your eye [—] over them (so far away from politics!) if not too busy.   W. Mc.

ALS (WP, DLC).

1 Wilson returned the enclosure. It was "Neville of Kensington," London *Nation*, VIII (Oct. 29, 1910), 190-191, by an anonymous author. It recounted the tale of a middle-aged laborer from Kensington, John T. Neville, who, unable to find employment and unwilling to go to the poor house, cut the throats of his two young sons and then his own. The incident, the article maintained, demonstrated the alienation of workers from a society in which the division between rich and poor was becoming increasingly severe. Workers in England, it asserted, had less employment security than "that of a Bechuana or a South Sea Islander," and the result was not the setting of class against class but class against society. The necessary reform was the institution of greater taxation to

create more jobs and stable employment. The great need, the article said, was a social order in which the case of John T. Neville was not exceptional but impossible.

2 The New Jersey State Agricultural Experiment Station.

3 The Pinchot family donated $150,000 in 1900 to Yale University to establish the Yale Forestry School. In addition, Pinchot's father, James Wallace Pinchot, gave space at his estate, Grey Towers, in Milford, Pa., for the school's field work and a summer school of forestry.

From Elmer Hendrickson Geran

Dear Doctor Wilson: Jersey City [N. J.], December 7th, 1910

Mr Ross of New Brunswick has been to see me in behalf of Mr Smith and against Mr Martine. He has arranged for an interview with Mr Strietwolf for to-morrow. Strong pressure will be brought to bear, but believe he will stand for Martine.

I think it would be well for you to see Strietwolf within the course of a few days if possible. Are you sure of Newman[1] from Ocean?   Yours very respectfully,   Elmer H Geran

TLS (WP, DLC).
1 Harry Ellsworth Newman, Princeton 1904, lawyer of Lakewood, N. J., and assemblyman-elect from Ocean County.

From Joseph Patrick Tumulty

My dear Governor: Jersey City [N. J.] December 7, 1910.

Mr. Elmer Geran called on me yesterday and we had a long talk regarding the Senatorial situation. In the talk I had with him he informed me that Mr. Streitwolf, an Assemblyman from Middlesex County, was rather inclined to be opposed to Senator Smith, and that Mr. Neuman, an Assemblyman from Ocean County, was quite decided in his opposition to sending Mr. Smith to the Senate. I would suggest, therefore, that you confer as soon as possible with these two gentlemen in an endeavor to induce them to support the popular nominee.

Since your conference with the Hudson Delegation some of those who constitute it have been rather reluctant to speak about the result of it, but I am convinced from their attitude that your talk with them has had rather a chastening influence on those who have been reluctant to state just what their position will be.

Mr. Nugent just called to see me and gave abundant evidence of his disapproval of my course, and he felt deeply aggri[e]ved at the attitude which you have taken in the matter. From what he told me, I am convinced that Senator Smith intends to remain in the fight, and that his friends count upon substantial support in our own County, which I am convinced from certain happenings they will not receive.

If I can be of any aid to you, please call upon me.

Sincerely yours,   J. P. Tumulty

TLS (WP, DLC).

From Frederick Wallace Kelsey[1]

My dear Mr. Wilson,   New York December 7th, 1910.

This morning by appointment as requested by Mr. Smith, I had a long talk with him regarding the Senatorial situation.

My acquaintance with him is such that I had a very frank talk with him and I emphasized the seriousness, as it seemed to me, of his making an issue by his candidacy, as will naturally result should you declare for Mr. Martine and he announce that he is to be a candidate.

The seriousness of this situation impresses me more and more and, while many of your friends like myself will stand by you, it looks to me as though a real contest along the lines—as between yourself and Martine and friends on the one side and Mr. Smith and his followers on the other side—may so imperil the future for better things in our State by diverting principles to a factional contest that, if there is any way by which this contest may be avoided, it seems to me in every way desirable that it should be avoided.

Mr. Smith referred to his recent conversation with you and I presume he has fully explained to you, as he did to me, the reasons why he has felt he should be accorded the honor; and, from his standpoint, his friends will be likely to elaborate indefinitely should the contest occur.

I cannot explain now in writing you hurriedly my view as to the desirability of avoiding, if possible, this contest as I could personally.

In a word, however, it looks to me that it may be one of those instances where an avoidance of trouble can be far better anticipated before than after the trouble begins, and, so far as Mr. Martine is concerned, I—knowing him but slightly—do not feel that he or any individual is strong enough or of sufficient importance to precipitate a condition which I am inclined to look upon with some apprehension as to results for the future.

I say this without the slightest change in my own conviction as to the undesirability of Mr. Smith's return to the Senate and so informed him, or of my loyalty to you and the principles for which you stand, but the possibilities reaching far beyond the lines of our own State in such a contest may, as it seems to me—should the Senatorship get into an aggressive fight—be of serious import.

With best wishes and fully appreciating the spirit indicated in your letter received at Orange yesterday, believe me

Sincerely yours,   Fred'k W. Kelsey

TLS (WP, DLC).
[1] President of E. W. Kelsey Nursery Co. of New York and a resident of Orange, N. J.

From John J. Lane[1]

My dear Governor: Summit, N. J., Dec. 7, 1910

As one of your first supporters for the nomination as Governor, you will pardon me for taking the liberty of expressing my personal views on the United States Senatorial question.

I have known Martine since 1876, and so far as his being a primary choice for that office is concerned, it is ridiculous. He was not endorsed by any Convention or party and I am at a loss to understand by what right his friends claim he should be chosen because a principal is involved. Would the same noise be made if McDermot[2] by an accident should have received more votes than Martine? Not a candidate for the Legislature signed the necessary papers endorsing either. His candidacy was considered as a joke by the voters because he had not been endorsed by the party, and the fact that he had been defeated for every office he ever ran for made it appear more of a joke.

The fact that he has been defeated in each case is sufficient evidence that the voters in his home district do not trust him. He has advocated every "ism" that has come up, and it would certainly make New Jersey look foolish to elect such a man to the United States Senate. For the good of your administration I hope you will let this matter be decided by the members of the Legislature without interference. I have taken personal interest in campaigns and elections for thirty years and am therefore in a position to speak intelligently.

We have not had a Democratic Governor for fifteen years, and if Martine is elected I believe it will be twenty years before we elect another Democratic Governor.

With best wishes for your Administration, I remain,

Very truly yours,   J J Lane

TLS (WP, DLC).
[1] Freight agent in Summit, N. J., for the Delaware, Lackawanna, and Western Railroad.
[2] Frank M. McDermit, a Newark lawyer and Martine's only rival in the Democratic senatorial preferential primary in September.

From Henry Smith Pritchett

Personal

My dear Wilson,   New York Dec. 7 1910

Yesterday afternoon I sent you a message to enquire when I could see you either at N. Y. or Princeton. This was in consequence of a talk I had with one of the Executive Committee. He made a suggestion of such importance that I will do nothing in the matter of the retiring allowance till I see you. I am unfortunately suffering much at the hands of the dentist from a serious difficulty likely to last some time and find it difficult to get through the business of the day or keep up with correspondence.

Yours Cordially   Henry S Pritchett

ALS (WP, DLC).

A News Report of a Message to the Sons of Delaware of Philadelphia

[Dec. 8, 1910]

PUBLIC WIDEAWAKE, IS DR. WILSON'S MESSAGE
TO SONS OF DELAWARE

The blue hen, frozen solid and nestled upon a groundwork of spun sugar, would last night have lifted up its head at the Bellevue-Stratford and cackled most joyously, if it had not been frozen. This rarely colored bird signified the nearest and dearest thing to the hearts of some 300 diners who sat at table for the annual feast making of the Sons of Delaware, and what cackling about home nest the frozen foul could not give vent to the diners did very cheerfully and to the heartiest content of the most pugnacious and jealous-minded son of Delaware there present.

Although Governor-elect Woodrow Wilson, from the next-door small state which is just now doing such large things, was down on the card but did not come, sending a graceful and significant letter in his stead, there were speakers in abundance to sound the glories of the little Blue Hen state and of the nation at large. The guinea hen, dear to the Delawarean, spread its lusc[i]ous meats upon the dinner plate. Kent county sorbet helped some to think of the old homestead and New Castle county roast turkey tasted as it "ust to" long ago. . . .

Governor-elect Wilson's letter of regret contained some significant reference to the recent political upheaval as indicating a new and changed condition in the political life of the nation. He wrote:

"It is with the most genuine regret that I find myself obliged by public duty to be absent from the dinner of the Sons of Delaware. I had looked forward with the greatest pleasure to meeting the distinguished company which was to assemble.

"I hope you will convey to them my congratulations and warm good wishes, and that you will say to them that such occasions seem to me fraught with possibilities of the highest service to the country.

"It has impressed me more and more in recent years that the tone of our public dinners has grown more and more serious and elevated; that those who come together on such occasions have seemed more and more inclined to turn after dinner to the important questions of the state and of the communities in which they live.

"Perhaps this change of tone and purpose has had something to do with the very remarkable change in our whole political temper and action. Public opinion is wide awake from one end of the country to the other. Its energy is bound not toward the exaltation of parties, but toward the choice of responsible leaders and well-considered policies. It is, therefore, a day of political reconstruction and a day of ardent hope, in which, if thoughtful men bind themselves together, great things can be accomplished for the welfare of the union.

"I am sure that the Sons of Delaware feel the opportunity they enjoy when they gather together to contribute to this great process of good counsel. I should have considered it a privilege to take part with them in a public function that I am sure will be touched with the spirit of patriotism and of service.

"If it could have been my privilege to have been present, of course, I would not have ventured to discuss politics, but I should have considered it a privilege to join in the consideration of the public welfare.["]

Printed in the Philadelphia *North American*, Dec. 8, 1910; some editorial headings omitted.

Two News Reports of a Farewell Address
to the Senior Class

[Dec. 8, 1910]

DR. WOODROW WILSON THE GUEST OF SENIOR CLASS

A farewell dinner was tendered to Dr. Woodrow Wilson '79 at the Princeton Inn last night by the members of the Senior Class, as a mark of appreciation for the distinguished services which he rendered the University during the eight brief years of his presidency.

As a token of esteem, a silver cup was presented to Dr. Wilson bearing the inscription: "Presented to Woodrow Wilson by the Class of 1911 in Memory of Four Years Spent under his Inspiring Influence." On the second side the initials "W.W." were set in gold, while on the third side were the dates of Dr. Wilson's term— "September 1902-October 1910." . . .

Maitland Dwight, President of the Senior Class[,] spoke briefly of the mingled feelings entertained by those present: of esteem and honor for their distinguished guest, and regret in the realization that the intimate and inspiring relations with him, by which we have all benefitted, are not to exist in the future. On the other hand, he said, "all of us rejoice, when we realize that New Jersey is entering upon a new political era, and that it is to assume a more prominent position under the guiding hand of a master statesman." In al[l]uding to Dr. Wilson's achievements here he said that the inauguration of the preceptorial system had placed Princeton in the front rank of American Universities.

Then in presenting the cup to Dr. Wilson he continued: "It is needless to try to express in words the estimation in which 1911 holds you. We will be satisfied if you remember us as the last class that has graduated under your regime. We feel proud to present this cup to the greatest president Princeton has ever had."

Dr. Wilson responded in part as follows:

"It would be impossible for me to thank you in adequate terms for this thing so beautiful in itself, but so much more beautiful in what it represents. It represents, I take it, the regard and I hope the affection of a body of men to whom I have felt very close, and whose confidence and affection I would rather have than the confidence and affection of any other men in the world. You fellows have lived here and seen me at close range. I have never been on dress parade in your presence, and no man who has lived in an academic community can fail to see that the eyes of undergraduates are seeing eyes.

"There have been many classes in Princeton. I have had the privilege of being closely associated with a long series of them, but in this culminating time, this class seems to me to represent the whole body of Princeton men. It represents it very worthily indeed, in spirit, in aims, in conceptions of what college life means, and of what the responsibilities of college men really are.

"My thoughts run back to the time when I, like you, was a college student. And as I look back the thing that I chiefly remember is not the fun of it all, but the serious part of undergraduate life. The danger of college life is that it may seem to you as a thing apart from the life of the world.

"During the recent political campaign I always felt more at home before an audience composed of humble working men than in the presence of audiences in highly cultured communities. When I came before an audience of the latter type, I felt that I had to explain to them some of the rudiments of life. They were just enough removed from the stern pressure of life not to know what was really going on in the world.

"The danger of college communities is that they will seem like a recess from life. We must make college students forget how the world looks from the point of view of some particular industry, and let them look at it like citizens of the world. It is our duty to regeneralize each generation.

"Does this general view of life that you are getting here mean something to you? Are you getting something out of it? Are you going to go home and tackle your fathers, to tell them that there are certain things they have forgotten.

"What is going to be the future of this country? We hope that the day is coming when men of the type that are produced in our best colleges will occupy the chief places in our political world. Will they understand what they are about? The majority of college men are looking at life through the spectacles of theory. If you want college men to govern our communities, then let college men think in the terms of our communities. Let them think in the relations of life, and ascertain what are the real tragedies of life itself.

"And so as I turn away from this place that I have loved so dearly I find that what I most desire for Princeton is that she should not concentrate her thoughts upon herself. In proportion as the University concentrates her affection on herself, she loses force instead of gaining it. It has been characteristic of Princeton in many generations to spend her force for the country, to spend it in altroistic [altruistic] ways.

"The characteristic of our age is the amount of good sane sense that is going to be necessary within the next generation. If the college men are not going to supply it, we must look to the mother wit of the country. If we are to be guided by thoughtful men, we must first produce thoughtful men.

"Do not let the misleading idea get into your heads, that you are under a double duty, to society and to yourself. It is easy to see how to contribute to the general progress of society, but it is almost impossible to separate yourself from the general movement, and to serve yourself.

"I shall always look back upon this evening as one of the evenings which has strengthened me for everything that I shall try to do. I feel as I face you that it would be impossible to excite the confidence of a body of men like this and then go back on it. You may think of this cup as something that you have contributed not only to my happiness but to my strength."

Printed in the *Daily Princetonian*, Dec. 8, 1910; some editorial headings omitted.

✧

WILSON GUEST OF SENIOR CLASS

Princeton, New Jersey, Dec. 7.—Governor-elect Woodrow Wilson was the guest of honor tonight at a banquet given by the Senior class of the University. He was the recipient of a silver loving cup. As president of the class, President M. Dwight of Morristown, N. J., spoke about higher honors than the governorship.

Dr. Wilson said:

"Your gift is a token to a Princettonian [Princetonian] embarking on a voyage, for what port I do not know. Nor do I care. I am making it for the fun of navigating well, whatever the destination.

"This gift is infinitely more valuable to me because there is no conceivable way in which there can be anything in this for me. (Laughter.) Since I've become a politician I have become suspicious of gifts.

"You seniors are soon to go out into the world, and if you have not secured more in your college course than you would be able to secure during four years in your father's business it were probably better if you had not come to college.

"Your course here is a preparation for your entrance into a sphere of greater activities, and do not allow yourselves to look at things from the viewpoint of a college student only. A prominent man asked me today if I were interested in a child labor law. I certainly am, and all public men should be interested in laws of this nature.

"A law of this kind is of more importance than laws regulating corporations, since they directly affect ninety-eight per cent. of the people—the working people, while the other law only affects two per cent of the capitalists."

Printed in the Trenton *True American*, Dec. 8, 1910; some editorial headings omitted.

A Statement on the Senatorship

[*Dec. 8, 1910*]

The question, Who should be chosen by the incoming Legislature of the State to occupy the seat in the Senate of the United States, which will presently be made vacant by the expiration of the term of Mr. Kean, is of such vital importance to the people of the State, both as a question of political good faith and as a question of genuine representation in the Senate, that I feel constrained to express my own opinion with regard to it in terms which cannot be misunderstood. I had hoped that it would not be necessary for me to speak, but it is.

I realize the delicacy of taking any part in the discussion of the matter. As Governor of New Jersey I shall have no part in the choice of a Senator. Legally speaking, it is not my duty even to give advice with regard to the choice. But there are other duties besides legal duties. The recent campaign has put me in an unusual position. I offered, if elected, to be the political spokesman and adviser of the people. I even asked those who did not care to make their choice of Governor upon that understanding not to vote for me. I believe that the choice was made upon that understanding; and I cannot escape the responsibility involved. I have no desire to escape it. It is my duty to say, with a full sense of the peculiar responsibility of my position, what I deem it to be the obligation of the Legislature to do in this gravely important matter.

I know that the people of New Jersey do not desire Mr. James Smith, Jr., to be sent again to the Senate. If he should be, he will not go as their representative. The only means I have of knowing whom they do desire to represent them is the vote at the recent primaries, where forty-eight thousand Democratic voters, a majority of the whole number who voted at the primaries, declared their preference for Mr. Martine, of Union County. For me, that vote is conclusive. I think it should be for every member of the Legislature. Absolute good faith in dealing with the people, an unhesitating fidelity to every principle avowed, is the highest law of political morality under a constitutional government. The Democratic party has been given a majority in the Legislature; the Democratic voters of the State have expressed their preference under a law advocated and supported by the opinion of their party, declared alike in platforms and in enacted law. It is clearly the duty of every Democratic legislator, who would keep faith with the law of the State and with the avowed principles of his party, to vote for Mr. Martine. It is my duty to advocate his election—to urge it by every honorable means at my command.   Woodrow Wilson.[1]

Printed in the Trenton *True American*, Dec. 9, 1910; with one correction from the text in the *Trenton Evening Times*, Dec. 9, 1910.
[1] There is a WWT draft with WWhw emendations of this statement in WP, DLC.

To Thomas Davies Jones

My dear Mr. Jones: Princeton, N. J. December 8th 1910

Thank you sincerely for your letter of December 1st. I am planning to leave here for Chicago on Sunday afternoon by the Pennsylvania Special, which should get me to Chicago on Monday morning. It will be very delightful to see you again.

Ex-Senator Smith proves to be the tough customer he is reputed to be and there is nothing for it but to fight him openly and to a finish. It is a hard necessity but I think that the public opinion of the State is eager for an opportunity to express itself openly, and with empathis [emphasis] on my part.

With warmest regard,
                    Faithfully yours,   Woodrow Wilson

TLS (Mineral Point, Wisc., Public Library).

From James Smith, Jr.

My dear Governor: Newark, N. J. December 8, 1910.

I promised to write to you to-day concerning the United States senatorship. In compliance with that promise, I beg to advise you that I am not prepared as yet to make announcement of my purpose with regard to that office. When I am prepared to make such announcement, I shall notify you at once. The position is a high one, but the duties are burdensome and exacting. If I should be induced ultimately to aspire to the office, and should be chosen by the legislature, it will be my purpose to mark the closing days of a long and active public life with such devotion to duty that the interest of all the people may be well served, and the welfare of my party be fostered.

With kind regards, believe me
                    Very truly yours,   James Smith Jr.

TLS (WP, DLC).

From William W. St. John

Dear Mr. Wilson: Trenton, N. J., December 8, 1910.

Your statement on the Senatorial situation is splendid. Of course, it will be easy for you to understand how intensely pleased I am over the firm manner in which you have come out in public on the proposition. Personally, I have never had a serious doubt about the successful outcome of the struggle for those who are demanding that the Legislature shall pursue an honorable course. Your declaration, in my opinion, will have the effect of focusing the question in such a manner as will relieve it of features that otherwise might have been not only distressing but disgraceful to civic virtue and good citizenship.

Permit me to thank you for your kindness in having your secretary notify me by telephone last night of the fact that you had given out the statement. I received a copy of it promptly by courtesy of the True American and was able to take care of all my papers in good shape.

I take it that it is hardly necessary for me to say that I am at your command for any service that you might think I would be able to perform further in connection with this subject, or any other that you are interested in.

With best wishes, I am,

Sincerely yours,   W W St John

TLS (WP, DLC).

From Richard Cole Newton[1]

Montclair, New Jersey

My dear President Wilson: December 8th, 1910

The question of who shall succeed Senator Kean in the next Congress is so vitally important to the future of the democratic party in the State of New Jersey that I daresay that you will pardon the liberty I take in addressing you a letter in regard to the matter.

I have followed carefully the newspaper accounts of the affair and their prognostications of the probable outcome. From these I infer that you are diametrically opposed to the election of Ex Senator Smith and in favor of the election of Mr. Martine.

These are precisely my own sentiments and I sincerely hope that the event may be in accordance with my wishes.

My opinion is that if Mr Smith shall be elected U. S. Senator the large independent vote in New Jersey will probably be cast for the republican candidates at the next election. It was largely Senator Smith's conduct while in the Senate that drove many independent democrats, myself included, into the republican ranks. The democratic party in New Jersey has, so far as I can recollect, been unfortunate in its leaders and perhaps in no way have we suffered from the leadership of sordid and short sighted men more seriously than in the style of men that we have sent to the U. S. Senate. That remark is also true of the republicans.

However I understand from the public prints that your attitude is an entirely impersonal one & that you believe that the awarding of the Senatorship should no longer like the awarding of the county registrarship in Essex County be a return for past political services but that the primary vote must be respected. In this I also most heartily agree.

I write this letter hoping that it may encourage you a little in the noble but difficult task you have undertaken of purifying and elevating New Jersey State politics. The republicans do not seem in any way equal to this task, nor the so called old line democrats. But you, sir, with your unprecedented majority & with the assurance that the best men of both parties are back of you, have been afforded an opportunity so splendid and far reaching that it fills the mind with wonder & delight. To be instrumental in giving the government of this State back to the people is indeed a glorious task worthy of anyone's ambition.

If I can be of any help in my humble way I should esteem it the greatest privilege & would thank you very much if you could make any use of me to further the good work.

Personally I have not been able to see where I could do any good & have so far done nothing except talk to a few friends.

Please believe me with sincere wishes for the success of your administration.

Faithfully yours   Richard Cole Newton

ALS (WP, DLC).
  [1] Physician of Montclair, N. J., unsuccessful Democratic candidate for mayor of that city in the recent election.

From Juliet Clannon Cushing[1]

Dear Mr. Wilson: East Orange [N. J.] December 8, 1910

It was with feelings of the liveliest satisfaction that I read in this morning's paper an account of a dinner given to you last evening at which you expressed your interest in the subject of child labor.

The committee of which I have the honor to be chairman will be greatly strengthened by your endorsement of its program, and I am hoping that you will be willing to include in your message the recommendation of some laws which we hope to have introduced during the session of the Legislature this winter. After ten years of effort on the part, first of The Consumers' League and later of The Child Labor Committee[2] which grew out of The Consumers' League, a law was passed last year prohibiting night work for children, in factories only.[3]

So much still remains to be done. Will you appoint some time when I, in company with Mr. [Owen Reed] Lovejoy, the Secretary of the National Child Labor Committee may confer with you regarding matters of which we hope you will approve and which we hope you will recommend in your message?

Will you kindly appoint two dates upon either one of which we may call upon you?

Senators Osborne and Fielder were of the greatest assistance last year, and I am confident that we may count upon them, as well as upon many of the Republican Senators.

The universal expression of those interested in reform work, so far as I have heard, is that of congratulation to the State of New Jersey upon your election, in which I very earnestly join.

Yours respectfully   (Mrs. G. W. B.) J. C. Cushing.

ALS (WP, DLC).

[1] Mrs. George W. B. Cushing, chairman of the New Jersey Child Labor Committee, organized in 1904 by the Consumers' League of New Jersey. She had served as president of the latter since its inception in 1900.

The Consumers' League of New Jersey was affiliated with the National Consumers' League, organized in 1899 by Josephine Shaw Lowell, with John Graham Brooks as president and Florence Kelley as general secretary. Its original purpose was to organize consumers to patronize only those stores which dealt humanely with their employees. However, under the leadership of Miss Kelley and Josephine Clara Goldmark, the organization broadened its concerns to the working conditions of women and children in manufacturing. It conducted several studies and attempted to educate public opinion about the effect of long hours and night work on women and children. It also lobbied for effective regulation of working conditions.

The New Jersey Child Labor Committee was affiliated with the National Child Labor Committee, organized in April 1904 to promote the amelioration and eventually the prohibition of child labor. Prominent among its founders were Edgar Gardner Murphy, Episcopal clergyman of Alabama and founder of the first state organization to work against child labor; Felix Adler of the New York Ethical Culture Society; Edward T. Devine, editor of *Charities*; Robert Weeks de Forest, New York lawyer involved in various charitable enterprises; and settlement house workers Florence Kelley, Jane Addams, and especially Lillian D. Wald, who became the committee's most influential advocate.

[2] She was here referring to the state organizations.

[3] Actually, the law was enacted on April 12, 1910. See *Laws of New Jersey, 1910*, Chap. 277.

From Hiram Woods

Dear Tommy: Baltimore. Dec. 8 1910.

This morning The [Baltimore] Sun called me up and wanted
to know if I knew you. Honesty compelled an affirmative reply.
"Isn't Governor Wilson an intimate friend of yours?" When assured that this intimacy was as close as circumstances permitted,
and told of its foundation, The Sun asked that I write you a personal letter, and here it is.

The Maryland Democracy is to have a "Love Feast" here on
January 17th. A mass-meeting is scheduled for the afternoon
and a banquet at night. To both of these you are to have an invitation, and they "want you bad." The Sun and the Politicians
seem to think that a little personal force from John [Miller Tur-
pin] Finney and myself will be all that is needed to secure your
presence and elicit a speech. So, old man, this is to say that if
you can come, a hearty welcome awaits you and I hope my home
will be yours while you are here. I believe that Democratic Lumi-
naries of various shades of brilliancy will be on hand. I don't
know who they are, but you will have no trouble in finding out
when you receive your formal invitation. The evening paper says
that you may be here on the 15th to address the Civil Service
League. Will this interfere with the visit in January? On either
day we will be delighted to see you, and I feel that you need no
assurance on this score.

And now for another matter. I am President of our Alunmni
[Alumni] Association this year, and we had a meeting of the Executive Committee on Tuesday. It was decided to have the banquet during the first two weeks of March, and to ask you to fix
the date. The first Friday is preferred: but if some other day suits
you better, it will be all the same to us. Anyway, to a man, the
Committee wants you, and personally I should rather have you
at this event than either of the others. Of course, your time is in
demand, and there is no doubt that new circumstances will tie
you up more and more. However, the Maryland Alumni Association is practically a unit in supporting your administration of the
University Presidency, and they are letting you know early so
that you can arrange matters if such a thing is possible. Write
me as soon as you are in position to do so.[1] With love to the
family,   Affectionately Yours: Hiram Woods.

TLS (WP, DLC).
[1] Wilson was unable to accept the invitation.

From John E. Lathrop[1]

My dear Sir: Washington, D. C., Dec. 8, 1910.

Acknowledging the receipt of your letter dated December 6, I will hold myself in readiness to go to Princeton at such a time as you will find convenient, and trust that you will be able to arrange it in a short time. I thank you very much for the courtesy you have shown me in promising the interview, and shall regard it as a distinguished honor to be permitted to discuss with you the Oregon system of popular government laws. Permit me to suggest that you appoint the meeting some days before Christmas, as I would like to hang my stocking Christmas Eve by the fireplace in my home.

Yours very truly,   John E Lathrop

TLS (WP, DLC).
[1] An editor of News, Inc., an agency serving newspapers in far western states.

A News Report of a Religious Meeting at Princeton University

[Dec. 9, 1910]

FIRST PEKING DAY A MARKED SUCCESS

A mass meeting under the auspices of the Philadelphian Society filled Alexander Hall last evening in celebration of the Princeton work in Peking. Remarkable addresses were delivered by John R. Mott LL.D. one of the most prominent religious leaders of the present day, and by Dr. Woodrow Wilson '79, Governor-elect of New Jersey. . . .

Dr. Wilson, taking the floor after an enthusiastic reception on the part of the audience, then paid a fitting tribute to the speech and life of Dr. Mott, disclosing many facts in his life-work, which had not been as yet presented. He laid especial emphasis on the power and force which is being brought to bear by Western nations on the plastic Chinese conditions, saying that the changes should be made upon firm foundations and by strong and capable men such as Dr. Mott.

"How are we going to make good," was the theme which constituted the bulk of Dr. Wilson's address. In loving Princeton, he said, we should not love her too intensively but love her so that our love may go out in power into the whole world. In these words he sums up the general and main line of thought, which has run through so many of his best speeches, namely, those on "Princeton for the Nation's Service."

He discussed the unselfish spirit of America which has been so prevalent wherever Americans have colonized or taught, saying that the ignorant races know that the United States has not sought to aggrandize herself at their expense. "The Spirit of Princeton," he continued, "when properly understood is the Spirit of America."

"Our Universities," he said, "are not intended to enjoy their own fraternity, but to make the torches which light men's paths through the world."

Printed in the *Daily Princetonian*, Dec. 9, 1910; some editorial headings omitted.

From Henry Watterson

My Dear Governor: Washington, D.C. Dec 9th 1910

The enclosed clipping from the Washington Herald of this morning shows the cloven foot very clearly.[1] It is the report of what is known as the Laffan Press, being the News Service of the New York Sun. The reduction of Martine's vote to "4000" was intentional. Of course it was inspired by Smith, and illustrates the Smith tactics.

I have had a talk over the telephone with George Harvey, who is down at Oak Ridge with Ryan.[2] As a result I am going down there tomorrow, Saturday, night for a conference. Just why Ryan wants to see me I do not know; but I shall know more before I get back. If we are to organize a movement for 1912, we must start right, must understand precisely one another and where we are "at," and *what* we expect and *how*. We need to avoid if possible the mistakes of 1904. In that year Ryan shot a good many arrows in the air—very bravely and with the best intentions as I thought, [August] Belmont the fly in the ointment. . . .

I will write you on my return here on Monday. With regards to your lovely household, I am

Sincerely Your Friend Henry Watterson

ALS (WP, DLC).

[1] The article was from the Washington *Herald*, Dec. 9, 1910, and reported on Wilson's statement of December 8 on the senatorial question. After quoting the statement in full, the article expressed surprise that Wilson had gone so far as to say that the people of New Jersey preferred Martine to Smith. It called the senatorial primary "a farce" and noted that Wilson's statement constituted an open break with Smith, in which Wilson would have the powers of the governor while Smith had political debts in local organizations throughout the state which he could collect. As Watterson indicates, the article also misquoted Wilson's statement by printing "4,000" instead of "forty-eight thousand" as it was in Wilson's text.

[2] Thomas Fortune Ryan's estate near Lovingston, the county seat of Nelson County, Va.

From William Hughes

My dear Governor: Washington December 9th, 1910.

I wish to extend to you my heartiest congratulations on the stands you have taken in the matter of the election of the United States Senator from New Jersey. When I say that your attitude in this matter accords fully with the estimate that was formed of you during the campaign I am saying everything that can possibly be said in the way of praise and appreciation.

The Senatorial situations in New York, New Jersey and Ohio are exciting the most intense interest among the members of the House.[1] Owing to the peculiar circumstances there is more interest taken, I think, in the situation in New Jersey than in either of the other two states. One very cautious and conservative member of Congress said to me yesterday that he had never been a fervent admirer of Mr. Bryan, and was somewhat rejoiced at the fact that the Democracy seemed to be getting from under his sway, but that if freedom from Bryan's domination could only be purchased by the exaltation of these gentlemen, he was inclined to think that we made a very bad bargain after all.

I imagine that you cannot possibly help being gratified to know that the members of Congress have taken the keenest sort of an interest in you, and in your campaign. They take a personal satisfaction in your victory. I think I am safe in saying that at the present time they pay far more attention to you as a presidential possibility than any man in the country. In fact, I have stated, and I believe it to be true, that a poll of the House at the present time would show that you are an overwhelming favorite for the presidential nomination in 1912. In saying this I do not mean to create the impression that it will be an easy thing for New Jersey to secure this high honor, because I feel that a state like Ohio will present claims that will demand attention. Nevertheless, the fact that we have within our party a man who, I am morally certain would carry the states of New York and New Jersey, ought to be, and is, a great source of comfort to men who are sincerely interested in the success of Democracy.

I would like very much to have a talk with you when it is convenient as there are a number of matters I would be very glad indeed to discuss with you. I know that your time is almost entirely taken up and I hesitate very much about inflicting myself upon you. I leave this entirely to you, but will try to arrange my affairs so as to see you at any time that you care to have me do so.

                    Very truly yours,   Wm. Hughes

TLS (WP, DLC).

1 In both New York and Ohio, as in New Jersey, Democratic schisms were developing over the election of United States senators. In New York, the lines were drawn between the Tammany forces controlled by Charles Francis Murphy and an anti-Tammany coalition led by a newly-elected state senator from Hyde Park, Franklin Delano Roosevelt. The Tammany candidate was William Francis ("Blue-eyed Billy") Sheehan, Speaker of the New York Assembly, 1891, lieutenant governor, 1892-95, and a lawyer and utilities magnate of New York City. The anti-Tammany choice was Edward Morse Shepard, also a New York lawyer, who had been active in good government movements in the metropolis. Soon after the New York legislature convened in early January 1911, the minority of insurgent Democrats led by Roosevelt prevented Sheehan's selection by the Democratic caucus for ten weeks and, simultaneously, his election by the joint session of the legislature. When Murphy realized that Sheehan could not be elected, he proposed a series of compromise candidates. Roosevelt and the insurgent Democrats, on the sixty-fourth legislative ballot on March 31, 1911, finally acquiesced in the election of State Supreme Court Justice James Aloysius O'Gorman, who had earned a reputation for independence on the bench, but who earlier had been closely associated with Tammany. Throughout the long struggle, Governor John Alden Dix remained largely aloof. Frank Freidel, *Franklin D. Roosevelt: The Apprenticeship* (Boston, 1952), pp. 98-116.

In Ohio, the Democratic senatorial fight divided progressives and conservatives. The candidate of the latter was Dayton boss Edward W. Hanley, a major figure in the Democratic state committee, who was considered a representative of the traction interests. Although the progressives, who were allied with ex-Mayor Tom Loftin Johnson of Cleveland, preferred Mayor Brand Whitlock of Toledo, they united with other reform Democrats behind Atlee Pomerene, Princeton 1884, a Canton lawyer and newly-elected lieutenant governor. After a series of public debates between Hanley and Pomerene during December and an intensive editorial campaign by progressive newspapers, public opinion turned strongly in Pomerene's favor, and he was elected in January 1911. Hoyt Landon Warner, *Progressivism in Ohio, 1897-1917* (Columbus, Ohio, 1964), pp. 262-65.

From William Cavanagh Gebhardt

My dear Dr. Wilson: Jersey City [N. J.], December 9, 1910.

I congratulate you upon your signed statement in this morning's newspapers. While your statement will give the enemies of Martine a chance to say that you are trying to dictate to the legislature, the people will see plainly that it is not a matter of dictation, but a matter of trying to lead your party in the direction in which the people wish the party to go.

I am sending you, by separate cover, today, three copies of the [Flemington, N. J.] "Hunterdon County Democrat,"[1] containing articles which reflect the very strongly prevailing opinion in my county. I am with you in this fight with all my heart, and I am in a position, if the fight becomes very desperate, to make it almost impossible for Mr. Smith to be elected. When I see you I will explain what I mean.

With kindest regards and wishing you the greatest of success, I am,   Very sincerely yours,   Wm. C. Gebhardt

TLS (WP, DLC).
1 They are missing.

From John Joseph Treacy[1]

Dear Sir: Jersey City, N. J. December 9, 1910.

I have read your statement on the United States Senatorship matter. While I do not consider Mr. Martine the type of man who should represent New Jersey in the United States Senate, I believe that the Democratic Party should stand by its principles. When it was a minority party it professed to favor the idea of a popular vote for the United States Senatorship. Now that it is a majority party it should live up to its professions.

But in the light of your letter, it seems to me that Mr. Martine can be lost sight of altogether. The issue now is between yourself and the bosses who have controlled the Democratic Machine in this State for years. My humble service may not be of great value to you in the contest that seems inevitable, but whatever it may be worth, I desire to inform you that it is at your command.

Very truly yours,   John J. Treacy

TLS (WP, DLC).
 [1] A lawyer of Jersey City, assemblyman from Hudson County, 1902-1903, and leader of the Democratic minority in the Assembly during the latter year. Wilson appointed him to the Court of Errors and Appeals in December 1911.

From Thomas H. Dillow[1]

My Dear Mr Wilson   Orange, N. J Dec 9th/10

You may remember that I addressed you last September concerning your attitude toward Organized Labor,[2] and received from you in reply a letter that I prize very much, and shall keep as a memento of the late campaign. I presume to once more address you for the purpose of *Thanking* you from my *soul* for the stand you are taking in respect to the choice of a United States Senator. I feel that you are the right man in the right place, there has been to much of the kind of work in our party, that is now being propogated by the same coterie of people. I do not *hesitate* to *bluntly say* that had it not been for these very people, our party would not have been in the slough of discord and out of touch with the people so long. We fought in the late campaign for the very principles these people now wish to abrogate, and with a gaurdian like you at the Helm I feel that we are going to get a square deal and no favoritism.

The argument of the supporters of a certain gentleman is that he found the sinews of war, and should be handed the price thereof, little doubting after the master stroke they ackomplished in corrupting the Essex Eleven[3] that you in your flush of triumph would keep your hands off.

I worked hard in this campaign through these counties and as far south as Gloucester county, and I feel proud of your magnificent victory, for you are the Elect of the state, not a section, and I believe you will so govern, that our party will once more be respected, and the state offices purified.

Very faithfully   Thos. H. Dillow

ALS (WP, DLC).
  [1] A carpenter of Orange, N. J.
  [2] T. H. Dillow to WW, Sept. 1, 1910, Vol. 21.
  [3] That is, the Essex assemblymen-elect who had asked Smith to run.

From Anthony Killgore[1]

My dear Sir   Flemington, New Jersey Dec 9/10

I read today, in the daily press, your statement.

It does not disappoint me. It is as direct to the point as any statement ever made. It represents the kind of party politics I want to fight for, and indicates the advent of a leader I shall take pride in fighting under.

Being one, of the few perhaps, who ask for no public office, I can, without fear of being misunderstood or accused of any selfish object, offer you the support of my paper and and [sic] myself, in any effort to uphold the honor and integrity of our party.

Such a statement as you have made today looks like the dawn of a better condition in the public life and of party politics.

The very method and circumstances of Mr Smiths candidacy, though I have always held the kindest feeling toward him, is abhorrent to any man with a spark of political integrity.

Thanking you for the stand you have taken, I am

Yours very truly   Anthony Killgore

ALS (WP, DLC).
  [1] Editor of the Flemington, N. J., *Hunterdon County Democrat*.

From Charles F. Sleeper[1]

Dear Sir: Palmyra, N. J., Dec 9th, 1910

I am a Roosevelt Republican but voted and worked for your election, and this town made a notable change—from an usual Republican majority of 235 we gave you 115 majority! But I want to commend your action in this Smith-Martine matter. We, and I think the majority of sensible people, are tired of Bosses & if you allow, as we do not think you will, them to beguile you, all this election will go for nought. We admire your frankness to the people. Keep it up.

Yours for good government,   C. F. Sleeper

ALS (WP, DLC).
[1] Editor and proprietor of *The Weekly News* of Palmyra, N. J.

From Edward Wright Sheldon

My dear Dr. Wilson: New York. December 9, 1910.

The Treasurer of the University reports to me that you have not yet accepted any salary as President or Professor of the University subsequent to October 20th last. By resolution of the Board of Trustees adopted November 3rd, your salary in both capacities was continued until the end of the current academic term, which closes, I believe, February 9th. This action of the Board was not only unanimously, but most cordially and earnestly, taken. In addition, it followed a well established custom in such matters, of continuing the salary of a retiring officer until the conclusion of the current period of service. I trust, therefore, that you will feel able to yield to our wish in this regard and that I may instruct the Treasurer to make proper remittances to you.

Believe me, with warmest regards,

Yours sincerely,   Edward W. Sheldon,
Chairman, Finance Committee.

TLS (WP, DLC).

From Charles Howard McIlwain[1]

My Dear Dr. Wilson,   Brunswick, Maine Dec. 9, 1910.

I am taking the liberty of having the publishers send you a copy of my book, "The High Court of Parliament."[2] When it comes I beg that you will receive it as a small testimony of my personal regard for you as well as an indication of my feeling as an alumnus and a member of your faculty, regarding your services to the University.

I regarded and I still regard those services as indispensable to the best interests of the University, and as a Princeton man I feel that we have sustained a terrible loss and one that can never be made good. This may be unpatriotic I know, and you understand I do not begrudge the State and the nation those services whose value I know so well. I am glad for their sake, but I am sorry for Princeton.

Very sincerely yours,   C. H. McIlwain.

TLS (WP, DLC).

¹ Princeton 1894, Preceptor in History at Princeton, 1905-10, at this time Thomas Brackett Reed Professor of History and Political Science at Bowdoin College.

² *The High Court of Parliament and Its Supremacy* . . . (New Haven, Conn., 1910).

A Statement by James Smith, Jr.

[Dec. 9, 1910]

I have read Governor-elect Wilson's statement on the United States Senatorial situation. The statement is a remarkable one for two reasons. It is a gratuitous attack upon one who has befriended him, but whose candidacy has not been announced, and it is an unwarranted attempt to coerce the Legislature.

The Governor-elect knew that I had not reached a decision in this important matter. That he saw fit to make an uncalled-for reference to me deprives his act of that fine courtesy which should control not only Southern gentlemen, but the conduct of all gentlemen.

Dr. Wilson will attempt, probably, to defend his statement on the ground that it is not the utterance of a Governor-elect, but the voice of a new leader. It will be difficult for the people to mark the line which separates the two. In either view his act lacks commendatory quality.

Its unfairness is so manifest that it will come as a shock to the great body of the people. Above all things, the American public loves fair play. The Governor-elect has given striking evidence of his aptitude in the art of foul play.

Gratitude was not expected of him, but fairness was, and his act denies it.

The statement purports to give the views of the people. Mr. Wilson claims to be their spokesman. He is apparently too modest as yet to claim leadership.

He says he has no means of knowing what the people want except as they expressed themselves at the primary.

Three times as many voters cast their ballots for the legislative candidates as expressed a preference for United States Senator. This great body of voters asked no pledge of the candidates. They received none. The legislators go into office as the representatives of all the people.

Three-fourths of the legislative supporters expressed no will. Dr. Wilson would have the men thus elected recognize a law which seeks to evade the Constitution. He would have them disregard the interest of the vast body of voters because one-fourth have expressed a preference.

He overlooks the fact that only one member of the incoming Legislature agreed to be bound by the primary vote. He gives no thought to the refusal of the legislators to deal with the matter other than in a spirit of fairness and justice to all. He evidently believes that the practises he once condemned of dangling patronage before a hungry constituency may give to his position a support which fairness denies it.

His reasons, when analyzed, ceased to be reasons. They are merely excuses for an act which marks his initial step as Governor-elect with worse than a blunder—with an assault that is neither fair nor honorable.

Printed in the *Newark Evening News*, Dec. 9, 1910.

To John Fox[1]

My dear Mr. Fox: Princeton, N. J., December 10th 1910.

It is with most genuine regret that I find it impossible to accept the invitation of the National Democratic Club, and be present with it on the evening of December 15th. Nothing but imperative public duties has prevented my accepting an invitation that was so attractive and so important.

May I not beg that you will convey my very cordial and respectful greetings to the Club and to its distinguished guests. I congratulate them and all those who have won the confidence of the people on their opportunity to serve it and to give the great Democratic party a role of constructive power in an age which awaits nothing less than a reorganization of the forces of society, and in which a statesmanship is demanded which will be not only progressive, but infinitely thoughtful, scrupulously moderate, fearlessly fair.

So far it would seem as if we had tried only stimulation and development in our effort to serve the Union. We have tried the building up of great interests through fostering them by favoring processes of policy and of legislation. We have seemed to let all the great forces of the nation loose upon a disordered field. It remains to attempt readjustment, reaccommodation, the creation of a common interest both in our consciousness and in our legislation.

It is partly a task of comprehension; of sympathy; of insight. The programme must follow the lines of real need and of genuine accommodation.

Some part of what we must do is clear, and though it must be stated in very general terms, it is none the less definite on that account. In the first place we must insist at every stage upon discovering what the facts are and what inference can be justly based upon them. We must do this by thorough debate in our legislative bodies and out of them; public debate; debate extended to all classes of society; the complete uncovering of the elements we have to deal with.

When that process has gone far enough to create public opinion every step we take must be grounded upon that opinion, not upon what special interests urge, but upon what the common thought comprehends and approves. It is no small matter to create public opinion of the genuine sort, and when it is created it should govern absolutely.

It can govern only if we see to it that it is genuinely represented by some direct and simple process in every legislative assembly, and in every office where the power of guidance and determination is exercised. A frank, genuine, responsible representation of the people is the basis of every just government. This is the problem which not only our people themselves and our parties have to solve, in the electoral machinery which they construct and use, but it is the problem which our State Legislatures have also to solve in the choice of Senators of the United States, and they should solve it with a very sensitive regard for their obvious duty as spokesmen, not masters, of the people they represent.

There must be added, if the common interest is to be served, fearless leadership. Not leadership whose object is the aggrandizement of parties, or the aggrandizement of the leaders themselves, but leadership which is elevated to a new level and with a genuine desire to personify a common impulse rather than seek a private end.

With much respect and consideration,

Sincerely yours,   [Woodrow Wilson][2]

CCL (WP, DLC), with corrections from the text in the *New York Times*, Dec. 16, 1910.
[1] Intimate associate of the former Tammany boss, Richard Croker, and influential Democrat in New York, who had served as president of the National Democratic Club of New York since 1894. An iron merchant of New York City, Fox had served in Congress from 1867 to 1871.
[2] There is a WWhw outline of this letter, dated Dec. 9, 1910, in WP, DLC, and a carbon copy dated Dec. 10, 1910, in *ibid*.

From Charles Clarke Black[1]

My Dear Governor,   Jersey City [N. J.] Nov. [Dec.] 10 1910

I want you to know that your open letter, of yesterday, on the United States Senatorship, has infused new hope and courage to those who believe in better things, in the politics of New Jersey. It has been received with commendation from all sides. The man on the street has heard the voice of a new leader whom he is willing to trust and follow. You will need strength and courage as you proceed[.] This is but the expression of one in the crowd who whishes [wishes] you success

I am sincerely   Chas. C Black

ALS (WP, DLC).
   1 Princeton 1878, Democratic candidate for governor in 1904, and state circuit court judge since 1908, with responsibility for Bergen, Morris, Passaic, Sussex, and Warren counties.

From John Wesley Wescott

My dear Doctor Wilson: Camden, N. J. Dec. 10, 1910.

You may be sailing on an unknown sea, but it is one of human interest and welfare. The safest chart is downright political morality. With such a guide you cannot go wrong. The people of New Jersey and of the country generally, while reposing confidence in you heretofore, have to-day, by reason of the senatorial situation in our state and your attitude thereto, have vastly more confidence in you and your future work as a public man. Of course, it was inevitable that you would run against the prevalent political notion of bargain and sale, of the balance of one favor against another. You will have still further trouble, but the powers of decency and patriotism, directed by your commanding faculty, will do more than triumph; they will result in a new political organization founded upon honest public service. In this part of the state, and, for the same reasons, I assume in every part of the state, your words and conduct not only receive well nigh universal approbation, but stir the hearts and minds of everyone I meet.

If Senator Smith, and those interested in his personal fortunes, reduce politics to the principle of gratitude, and quid pro quo, I would like to know how the disinterested and noble services of ordinary men are to be rewarded? I know one case in Camden of a man making ten dollars a week, having a family, who gave me ten dollars to aid your election. Many others, equally poor, made similar contributions of money and personal services for the same purpose. I saw poor men take their lives in their hands to promote your election, by brave defense of the ballot box. Poor as I am, I donated $2000 to aid in achieving your success. Similar facts, in all probability, arose throughout the state. These were innumerable expressions of an intense desire to promote a better public life, to install decency and morality in public affairs. I would like to know how such efforts are to be compensated, how the principle of gratitude would operate in respect to them? The very object of your election was to forever do away with, if possible, the notion that every man who did a political duty must expect to have some official reward. I do not know what Senator Smith contributed, but I do know that the ten dollars contributed by the poor man, measured by the ability to give, would probably out-weigh the pound of Mr. Smith's morality by tons of a vastly purer morality. While I regret to burden you with a letter so lengthy, I am unable to restrain my admiration for your courageous, moral and consistent conduct. If regeneracy in politics is possible, it can be achieved solely and only by such men as you. The people who want decent and efficient government are with you to a man, body and soul.

Affectionately yours,   John W. Wescott

TLS (WP, DLC).

From St. Clair McKelway

Dear Dr. Wilson: Brooklyn-New York December tenth [1910]

Your letter lingered here, while I was away. On my return this morning, I lost no time in causing the paper to retract a course that should not have been taken.[1] The offender will not have the power again so to offend here. Let that suffice. "The rest is silence." I beg to return your letter to me, though thanking you heartily for it. It should not lie around loose here, possibly to be thumbed over by others in my absence.

Accept my congratulations on your latest manifesto. In it are heart and hope; also prophecy which will become history and that soon.

Yours for manifest duty and manifest destiny,

St Clair McKelway

HwLS (WP, DLC).
[1] He did so with an editorial in the *Brooklyn Daily Eagle* on that same day entitled, "Woodrow Wilson's 'New and Novel' Departure." It discussed the senatorial contest and contained several observations that were clearly intended to negate the critical implications in the editorial of November 30, 1910 (about

which see WW to St. C. McKelway, Dec. 5, 1910, n. 1). "When Woodrow Wilson lately stumped New Jersey," read the editorial of December 10, "he frankly said he would take his election as a warrant to be the leader of the party as well as the Governor of the State. His enormous majority was the State's response to that notice. He has now shown how he respects and interprets it. To him the vote for Mr. Martine signifies the Democratic desire on the Senatorship. The great majority for Mr. Wilson himself signifies the order to him to be the leader of the party as well as the Governor of the State. The fitness of Mr. Martine enforces support of him on Mr. Wilson. This requires Mr. Wilson to refuse the role of being made a stalking horse for Mr. Smith for Senator. The party vote for Mr. Martine coincided with the State vote for Mr. Wilson and for the State's acceptance of Mr. Wilson as the Democratic leader. He will do his best to influence the Legislature to elect Mr. Martine. It is believed he will succeed." The editorial then noted that Wilson admitted that he was a political novice and reckoned that the voters of New Jersey no doubt preferred such to experts like Smith, under whom the party had been "beaten so often as to suggest to the people it was only a trading annex to the Republican machine." Wilson, continued the editorial, "will use argument, discussion and his legitimate power of veto and of patronage to establish for the party a long tenure of power by merit, and he will take his chances on Democracy, on manhood and on the future, as against machinehood and threats of revenge now." The editorial praised Wilson's "political prescience and the moral courage" in supporting Martine and concluded that this act revealed Wilson's "determination to be the State leader as well as the Governor of the State as a fact or force that carries in it the open secret of Democratic rehabilitation for New Jersey and a demonstration of exemplary value to the party in the nation."

From James Richard Nugent

My dear Sir,   Newark New Jersey December 10 1910.

I received your letter of the ninth instant.

I received a similar letter from you two or three days before your Kentucky trip. I replied immediately and personally dropped the letter in the proper box at the main office in Newark. I see from the requests made in your present letter, that you did not receive my answer to your former one.

Clarence Sackett 738 Broad Street Newark, is the name and office address of the stenographer in charge during the campaign.

It will give me great pleasure to meet you at any place or at any time you suggest that will suit your engagements.

I am very anxious to have proper bills ready for introduction into the Legislature, so that the session may be a short businesslike one. These bills should cover every platform pledge made in the late campaign and be submitted before introduction to our best Democratic lawyers, so that no unconstitutional bills be passed. This and several other important matters I wish to discuss with you and so requested in my answer that you did not receive.

I am very well thank you and am engaged on the new charter for Newark and other important matters relating to City and County affairs.

I sincerely hope that you are enjoying good health, and that you will be in good shape at the big send-off we are going to give you at your inauguration and with my kindest personal regards,

I remain   Yours very truly,   James R. Nugent

ALS (WP, DLC).

From William Goodell Frost

My dear Dr. Wilson: New York, December 11, 1910.

One of Berea's most precious assets is your letter of November 15th, in reference to speaking for Berea and the Southern mountains, in New York, and possibly also in Philadelphia or Boston, the coming January.

You said: "The dates ahead of me are so miscellaneous and exacting that I cannot be at all sure that I will be there in January, but if you will let me know as the dates approach I will certainly try to be at at least one of the meetings. You may be sure I am ready to serve Berea whenever I can."

The time has come when we must engage hall, chairman, etc. I am expecting either Hamilton W[right]. Mabie or Hon. Seth Low[1] to preside, and have good prospect of a speech at the same time from Governor [Augustus Everett] Willson, of Kentucky. Won't that make an irresistible combination?

You can't well be far from your own state in January. Please select from the following dates, or name one more convenient to yourself. *Let us meet your convenience*, but don't by any means fail us. We slightly prefer for New York Tuesday, January 24th, but could use the 19th, the 23d, or the 26th.

Kindly let me hear from you at once. I should be glad to come to Princeton for a conference if I could be sure of finding you there, or to talk with you over the long distance 'phone, any time you set. This matter must be tied up before I can start home for Christmas![2]

Yours for the Southern Mountaineers,

Wm Goodell Frost.

TLS (WP, DLC).
  [1] Mabie was associate editor of the New York *Outlook*. Seth Low, President of Columbia University, 1890-1901, and Mayor of New York, 1902-1903, was at this time president of the National Civic Federation and active in several reform organizations.
  [2] As has been noted, Wilson's address is printed at Feb. 10, 1911.

From Edwin Augustus Stevens

My dear "Tommy,"   Hoboken, N. J. December 12th, 1910.

I enclose you a couple of letters[1] received in answer to my circular letter with reference to the Senatorial question. I have been away several days, and during my absence noticed your very courageous stand. If you had kept quiet there is no doubt in my mind but what Smith would have turned up with the goods.

I do not know whether you recall the manner of his previous election. I do—as I was very much interested in politics at that time on account of my friendship for Leon Abbett[2] (in spite of the fact that I could not stand for all of his actions). Abbett was very anxious to secure the Senatorship; in fact, it was the ambition of his life. He had practically directed his second administration to that end. At the State Convention which nominated George Werts[3] for the Governorship, it was tacitly understood that Abbett was the Party candidate for Senator. This was urged against us on the stump by the Republicans. You will remember that the election in that year, 1892, resulted in an overwhelming Democratic victory, in spite of the troubles in which the Democratic State machine had then become involved.

As I recall matters now, and my memory is quite vivid, little or nothing was heard of Mr. Smith as a candidate until the caucus, at which time a majority of the Democratic members at that conference suddenly discovered he had a remarkable aptitude for a Senatorial career. Mr. Smith's previous qualifications had been holding the office of Alderman in Newark, and the ability he had even then developed, of raising campaign funds. If therefore, it had not been for your stand, I think history would have repeated itself.

I feel, as do a good many others, that however kindly my personal feelings may be toward Martine, he is not personally qualified to represent the State in the United States Senate. The question of choice, however, between him and Smith, has come to be one of principle, in which the personal qualifications of men are of secondary importance.

Within my memory, and I have taken a lively interest in politics during the past thirty years, there has never been a Senatorial election in which one could not help but feel that the result of it was influenced, if not caused, by the use of money—if not by direct bribery. Mr. Smith has stood for the use of money in politics, and however his election might be brought about he could not but be regarded as a representative of that interest. His connection with the Sugar schedules of the Wilson Bill would not assist in dispelling this idea.

It would seem to me, therefore, best that both the men heretofore mentioned be, if possible, eliminated; Mr. Smith by the voice of the people, and Mr. Martine of his own accord. I think he is unselfish and patriotic enough to do this if the case is properly put to him. As my name has been mentioned in the past in connection with the job, I cannot help but feel a certain delicacy in the matter, in spite of the fact that I am not a candidate and do not want the place. I feel, however, that I can write to you with perfect frankness.

I will endeavor to stir up as many public expressions of opinions as possible with regard to your stand.

Can I do anything more?

Sincerely yours,   E. A. Stevens

TLS (WP, DLC).

1 There are twelve, all in WP, DLC, and all addressed to Stevens. The senders and the dates are as follows: R. V. Lawrence, Dec. 6, 1910, TLS; J. R. Salmon, Dec. 7, 1910, TLS; W. Hughes (two letters), Dec. 7, 1910, TLS; J. A. Burgan, Dec. 7, 1910, TLS; D. Harvey, Jr., Dec. 8, 1910, TLS; H. C. Bartlett, Dec. 8, 1910, TLS; F. C. Sutro, Dec. 8, 1910, ALS; A. T. Holley, Dec. 8, 1910, TLS; H. O. Wittpenn, Dec. 9, 1910, TLS; S. S. Swackhamer, Dec. 10, 1910, TLS; and W. Linbarger, Dec. 14, 1910, TLS. In his circular, Stevens had asked the recipients whether they thought that the party was obligated to support Martine. Of the eleven writers, eight said that it was, two that it was not, and one equivocated. Stevens had also asked them if they had other objections to Smith. Seven replied that they did, three said that they did not, and one gave a mixed answer.

2 Governor of New Jersey, 1884-87, 1890-1893.

3 George Theodore Werts, Governor of New Jersey, 1893-96.

From George Mason La Monte

My dear Dr. Wilson: Bound Brook New Jersey Dec. 12, 1910.

I have your notes of the 9th and 11th inst, both of which were received this morning. I will be glad to come to see you on Saturday afternoon, the 17th, to discuss several matters.

You may be interested to know that Senator Smith came over to New York to see me last week, and that I have a letter from him to-day asking for my support should he become a candidate. I have of course, replied that under the circumstances it will be impossible for me to give him my support.

Very truly yours,   Geo. M. La Monte

TLS (WP, DLC).

From George Earle Chamberlain[1]

My dear Mr. Wilson: Washington, D. C. December 12, 1910.

I want to congratulate you on the stand taken by you with reference to the election of a United States Senator. I am not acquainted with either Mr. Smith or Mr. Martine, but I am one of those who believe firmly in the right of the people (even in the absence of a constitutional provision) to participate in the election of United States Senators. This can only be done, under present conditions, by an expression of choice at the primary elections, ratified possibly later at the general elections, as is the case in Oregon. I am sure that your course will be commended by the people of the whole country who believe in getting the Government back to the people and away from the representatives of special interests.

In this connection, I do hope you may be able to take a decided stand in favor of progressiveism in the Democratic Party. The time is not far distant when both parties must stand for the Initiative and Referendum, a real Direct Primary law, a Corrupt Practices act, and possibly the Recall, and would it not be possible for you to recommend these measures to the New Jersey Legislature? Six or seven states have already followed in the footsteps of Oregon in adopting these measures, copied from the Oregon system or slightly in modification thereof, and the people of other states are endeavoring as rapidly as may be to adopt the same system. It is the only instrumentality through which the corrupt convention system can be abolished and the political boss put out of commission.

Mr. [John E.] Lathrop, correspondent here of a number of Western papers and a personal friend of mine, tells me he is going over to see you shortly, and I want to commend him to you as a thoroughly capable and reliable gentleman. He is an Oregonian by adoption, is familiar with the system there and will explain to you its operations. You can rely on his statements.

Again congratulating you upon the position you have taken on the side of the people, I have the honor to remain,

Yours very respectfully,   Geo. E. Chamberlain

TLS (WP, DLC).
[1] Democratic Governor of Oregon, 1903-1909; senator from Oregon since 1909.

From Hiram Woods

Dear Tommy: Baltimore. Dec. 12 1910.

Your note came this morning. Maybe you can catch time on the fly and look at the enclosed. The Sun seems pretty fond of cartooning you these days. It's a pretty fair picture, all the same. I have been asked what you meant by the word "fun" in that loving cup speech.[1] Some non-college fellows seemed to think it

"HE DON'T KNOW WHERE HE'S GOING, BUT HE'S ON HIS WAY"

"I am a Princetonian embarking on a voyage, for what port, I don't know, nor do I care. I am making it for the fun of navigating well whatever the destination." —*Woodrow Wilson*

was a queer word to use in connection with a Governorship. I have tried to explain that different people had different ideas of "fun," and that it is at least conceivable that a conflict between peanut politics and intelligent conception of Right, as applied to politics, could afford a lot of fun to one who could recognize it when it came his way. I guess this isn't far from your "idee."

I don't blame you for not coming to Balto. for the Civil Service Hot Air or the buncombe of the Maryland Democratic Love Feast. But you forgot the main thing—the Princeton dinner. I will fall eternally from Princeton Grace down here if I fail to land you. That's what I'm President for. Review things, when you get time, and tell me the MOST LIKELY day in the first *fortnight of March.* Then I shall fix the date, and if a Sugar Trust Senator or a hanging keeps you in Trenton, it won't be my fault.

Thanks for your invitation to "run up." I'm going to New York Saturday to an Eye conference at the Sage Foundation. There's just a possibility of my stopping in Princeton over Sunday if you are to be there: but don't look on this as a certainty. With love to the family, in which Mrs. Woods[2] joins,

Affectionately Yours: Hiram Woods.

TLS (WP, DLC).
  [1] See the second news report of the address printed at Dec. 8, 1910.
  [2] Laura Hall Woods.

Edward Wright Sheldon to Henry Green Duffield

My dear Sir: New York. December 12, 1910.

Referring to your letter of December 7th, I have communicated with Dr. Wilson upon the subject of his salary which, by vote of the Board on November 3rd, was directed to be paid to him until the end of the first term. In view of the financial needs of the University and the ending of his own active services on October 20th, Dr. Wilson feels unable to alter the decision already announced by him. It seems, therefore, that we have no other course open than to acquiesce in his conclusion, and I suggest that you do not send him the check for the instalment which would otherwise have been paid him on January 1st.

Yours very truly,   Edward W. Sheldon,
Chairman, Finance Committee.

TCL (WP, DLC).

An Advance Text of an Address in Chicago
to the Illinois Manufacturers' Association

[[Dec. 12, 1910]]

Looked at from the point of view of a student of public affairs, business is the economic service of society for profit. There are two partners in it, the business concern itself and the public. The most enlightened men of business, as well as the most serious servants of the State, have always looked on business in this light. Politics is the adjustment of all affairs to the common interest; it therefore must concern itself with the forces of business in order that the forces enlisted there, as well as elsewhere, may conform to the common principle of the public welfare. There can be no disputing these genuine conceptions, but it is much easier to state them than to apply them, particularly in this age of the complicated interplay of innumerable interests.

Extraordinary things are exacted of the business man if he would be successful. It is necessary not only that he should master his own business, but also that he should have the broad vision of the man of affairs. Modern business is not done on the modest scale of a generation ago; it is massed in great organizations. These organizations cover continents and effect trade between nations. The connections are therefore universal, not local. Their control is a sort of minor statesmanship. When criticism has been directed against business in our day it has really been because of the fear that the men who control it had not the spirit of statesmanship, but rather the spirit of private selfishness. Whenever they have shown this disposition to look upon business as a thing with two sides to it, namely, the interests of the public as well as the profits of the organization, they have invariably reaped not only success, but honor and the support of public opinion.

Undoubtedly the trouble with business in this recent period of extraordinary expansion has been too much exploitation, too little regard for the permanent interests of society and of all concerned. Good business rests on a community of interest. We have been too apt to set our conception of prosperity in a very nearsighted way. We have supposed that profitable business meant a prosperous nation, whereas profits obtained against the general interest may be piled high, but cannot contribute to the general prosperity. There is a genuine reciprocity here which even business must depend upon for its ultimate and permanent success. It will not do to exploit the public. It will not do to dominate markets and prices.

It will not do, either, to make of the workingman a mere instrument instead of a partner. The conditions which determine the relations of employer and employe have radically changed within a generation. Workingmen are no longer dealt with individual by individual in their employment. They are martialed in gangs and masses. Their dealings with their employers are impersonal for the most part. There is no true or conscious sympathetic relationship involved except in the rarest instances.

Since workingmen are being dealt with in bodies they must be dealt with on principles of reciprocity and partnership, which did not have to be considered in an age of smaller organizations. Wherever they are so dealt with the business prospers in an unusual degree and the usual antagonisms between labor and capital do not occur. There must be a very real partnership between capital and labor if modern business is to be put upon its right footing, just as there must be beyond that a vague, but nevertheless thoughtful, partnership between business and the general public. The business of exploiting anybody or anything for private profit must be abandoned for the larger, more wholesome principle of profitable service, the more profitable as it is genuine and faithful.

The trouble with politics, in so far as it has concerned itself with an effort to regulate business, has been that the problems of readjustment between private and public interests have not been fully comprehended. We are only slowly approaching a full understanding of the elements of the legislation we are trying to effect. In the field of legislation, which is the field of adjustment, we have experimented first in one direction and then in another. First, legislation has tried to hold one set of interests and check another set; then it has tried to shift its barriers and transfer its bounties and favors. It has been a game of alliance, first with one set of forces and then with another. They have been set off against one another and their rivalries emphasized and enhanced.

No one can speak with confidence as to how the accommodation is to be brought about, but certainly we can say that it is accommodation we seek and not mere offsetting of force against force. What we lack is knowledge of all the conditions involved. What we need is very frank inquiry and a thorough public consideration, without fear or favor, of everything involved; well-served communities make prosperous business. Merely profitable business may in many cases mean not only ill-served communities, but communities that have been crushed under a competition which destroys the very substance business ought to rest upon. Vital people must be the support of all successful economic enterprises.

We are working in the interest of business, not against it, when we oblige all to regard its action as a process of service, not exploitation. Every great business man knows this to be true and makes the interest of those he serves the centre of all his plans.

In order to carry out such purposes in the field of legislation, it is necessary that it should be universally understood that our purpose is not war, but peace and accommodation; not destruction, but the building together, as well as the building up, of the forces that constitute our strength.

For this enterprise we need the will and candor to see and to accept the facts as we see them, courage in action, justice in judgment, and throughout all the process the purpose not to destroy but to rectify and make safe every undertaking of our life. This is a counsel of perfection, but it is only by seeing our goal that we can move toward it.

Printed in the *Newark Evening News*, Dec. 13, 1910.

A News Report of Remarks in Chicago
to the Illinois Manufacturers' Association

[Dec. 13, 1910]

PUNISH OFFICERS OF ERRING ROADS, DEMANDS STUBBS

Railroads of the United States faced a triple fire at the annual banquet of the Illinois Manufacturers' association at the Congress hotel last night. Gov. W. R. Stubbs of Kansas, La Verne W. Noyes, president of the association,[1] and Woodrow Wilson, governor elect of New Jersey, followed one another in rapid succession in attacks upon various features of business as conducted by the big systems. . . .

Gov. Elect Wilson said politics is the adjustment of all affairs to the common interest, and therefore must concern itself with the forces of business.

From a discussion of the dangers of exploitation of the public and business, he took a rap at the hypocritical methods of some business interests.

"Why, what are some men doing?" he asked. "They attend peace congresses and sit on the platform in order to sustain the speakers and give them their moral support and applause, and these very men, engaged in business, are exploiting the orient in such fashion as will inevitably bring on war, because they are ignoring every national prejudice of the people they are dealing with, and they are sowing the seed of passion which some day will spring up in a great crop of absolutely irrepressible bloody strife. They had better think, while they sit upon these platforms, what they are doing to foment the fundamental passions of mankind.

"Do you not know, gentlemen, that we have come to a day of reckoning? Parties are dissolving in America. Can you find the frontiers of the Republican party? I can find the hinterland of the Republican party; I don't know where the frontiers are. Can you find the frontiers of the Democratic party? Can you draw a line that will define the place of division between the Democratic party and the Republican party? I cannot. When I talk with progressive Republicans I can only say to them that I regret that they are in the wrong camp; I think they ought to be Democrats. If somebody could draw together the liberal elements of both parties in this country he could build up a party which could not be beaten in a generation, for the very reason that we would all join it.

"Now, what does a progressive Republican mean? What does a liberal and progressive Democrat mean? It means a man who, to the best of his ability, is trying to find the best way to serve the country. That is all it means. Those men are daily increasing in number, and they are the bosses of America. America isn't governed by the standpatters of either party for they are in the minority. It is governed by the men whose votes you cannot predict."[2]

Printed in the *Chicago Daily Tribune*, Dec. 13, 1910; some editorial headings omitted.

[1] Walter Roscoe Stubbs, Governor of Kansas since 1909; Noyes was an inventor and industrialist, active in many civic organizations, and a generous philanthropist.

[2] There is a brief WWhw and WWsh outline of this address, with the composition date of Dec. 9, 1910, in WP, DLC.

From Harry Vliet Osborne

My dear Governor: Newark [N. J] December 13, 1910.

Confirming my suggestion to you over the telephone on Saturday regarding the Senatorial situation, I would urge, if I may do so, that, in the event of your making a further public statement, you make it clear that you consented to become a candidate upon the express understanding that Mr. Smith would not be a candidate for United States Senator.[1]

Yours very sincerely,   H V Osborne

TLS (WP, DLC).

¹ As early as November 26, 1910, the *Newark Evening News* had reported: "It is understood that last summer, when Mr. Wilson consented to become a candidate for Governor, the impression was given to him that Mr. Smith would not be a candidate for Senator." Two days later, the *Trenton Evening Times* had reported that Wilson had been worried about Smith's possible candidacy for the Senate and had been "unqualifiedly" assured at the Lawyers' Club conference on July 12, 1910 (about which see the Editorial Note, "The Lawyers' Club Conference," Vol. 20), that Smith would not be a candidate should the Democrats control the joint session of the legislature in 1911. This story was repeated in the New York *Evening Post*, Dec. 13, 1910, and in the *Newark Evening News*, Dec. 14, 1910.

Wilson, in his telephonic conversation with Osborne on December 10, must have added the important detail that he had consented to run for governor upon the "express understanding" that Smith would not be a candidate for the Senate. Wilson repeated this allegation in a modified form in his statement printed at December 23, 1910, as follows: "Before I consented to allow my name to be put before the State Democratic Convention for the nomination as Governor, I asked the gentleman who was acting as Mr. Smith's spokesman if Mr. Smith would desire to return to the Senate, in case the Democrats should win a majority in the State Legislature. I was assured that he would not. I was told that the state of his health would not permit it and that he did not desire it." Smith at once denied that either he or anyone representing him ever gave any such assurance to Wilson at any time and challenged Wilson to name the man. Wilson refused. See the news report printed at Dec. 28, 1910. It should perhaps be added that Wilson never said that the assurance was given at the Lawyers' Club conference. It is impossible on a basis of reliable evidence definitively to resolve this issue. Harvey might have given Wilson the assurance at some time during their early discussions about Wilson's gubernatorial candidacy, but there is no evidence to support this surmise.

It also seems virtually certain that the assurance was *not* given at the Lawyers' Club conference. Richard Vliet Lindabury, who was present and can be deemed a very reliable witness, on December 24, 1910, categorically denied that Smith's name was mentioned at all during this conference. New York *Evening Post*, Dec. 24, 1910. And none of the participants who gave any testimony concerning it years later mentioned any discussion of the senatorial situation except Nugent, Smith's spokesman at the conference, who claimed that Wilson pledged his support to Smith if he should run (again, see the Editorial Note, "The Lawyers' Club Conference").

One piece of evidence about the matter relating to the period before Wilson's nomination on September 15, 1910, comes from Henry Watterson's statement that Smith told Wilson, at the conference at Harvey's home in Deal, N. J., on June 26, 1910, that "he wanted nothing for himself; only to see the State redeemed; that no one but Dr. Wilson could redeem it and the like." "To the Democrats of the United States," New York *World*, Jan. 30, 1912. Another bit of evidence comes from William O. Inglis, "Helping to Make a President," *Collier's Weekly*, LVIII (Oct. 14, 1916), 12. Inglis writes that Wilson, in a conference with Colonel Harvey on about August 19, expressed concern over rumors that Smith would be a candidate in the event of a Democratic victory in New Jersey. According to Inglis, Harvey said: "You must make up your mind for more of that, for it cannot be avoided. I have the senator's authority to withdraw him absolutely whenever, if at all, I should consider it necessary, but I don't dare do it before the [state Democratic] convention. That is a purely party matter, and the senator is going to need all the help he can get from the workers who want him but are not enthusiastic over you. It may become necessary to ask him to stand aside after the nomination, but not before. There is nothing to do but grin and bear it."

In addition, once the senatorial controversy had erupted, Smith told a New York reporter: "I do not mind saying . . . that assurance was given to Dr. Wilson during the campaign that if he thought the prominence given to my candidacy through the State was hurting his chances I would announce that I was not in the field." New York *Evening World*, Dec. 19, 1910.

It is possible—perhaps likely is the more accurate word—that by late 1910 Wilson had in his own mind converted Harvey's statement and Smith's later assurance of his willingness to withdraw into an assurance given on or before July 12, 1910, indeed, not only into an assurance but into an "express understanding" that Smith would not be a candidate. Refusing Smith's challenge to name the man who had given the assurance, Wilson said that he was a person whom he very highly esteemed and did not want to mortify him by drawing him into a public discussion. He must have meant Harvey; surely he would not have spoken thus about Nugent.

The question of course also arises as to the sources of the newspaper reports, cited at the beginning of this note, saying that the assurance was given at the Lawyers' Club conference. Evidence on this important matter does not exist.

From Solomon Foster[1]

My dear Doctor Wilson: Newark, N. J., Dec. 13 1910.

I handed your esteemed favor of the 9th inst., to the committee arranging for our Golden Jubilee celebration,[2] and I was requested to inform you, in the name of the committee, that your intimation that you would, if possible, accept our invitation to be present and to speak at our meeting aroused genuine pleasure on all sides. I can assure you that you will be most heartily welcomed in the midst of a host of your ardent admirers and supporters.

On Sunday evening January 8th, we shall have a meeting in Temple B'nai Jeshurun to which the representative Jews of this city will be invited, to commemorate in fitting manner the completion of 50 years of service of our organization. We hope to have the honor to welcome you and Judge Rosalsky[3] of New York on this occasion. It was thought that if you knew how eager the Jewish citizens of Newark are to be enrolled under your banner of good government, that you would consent to address them on some of your lofty ideals of citizenship. I am sure that you will meet with a hearty response.

Will you permit us to announce your acceptance of our invitation for the evening of January 8th? We would be most happy to have you come to Newark on Sunday as our guest.[4]

With hearty greetings and best wishes for your health,
Yours sincerely   Solomon Foster.

ALS (WP, DLC).
[1] Rabbi of Congregation B'nai Jeshurun of Newark, N. J.
[2] Of the Hebrew Benevolent and Orphan Asylum Society and United Hebrew Charities of Newark.
[3] Otto A. Rosalsky, judge of the General Sessions Court of New York City.
[4] Wilson accepted; his address is printed at Jan. 8, 1911.

From Arthur Twining Hadley

New Haven, Connecticut.

My dear Mr. Wilson: December 13th, 1910.

Some years ago Mr. William Earl Dodge gave Yale a fund for a series of lectures on the Responsibilities of Citizenship. We have had each year a course of from four to seven lectures to the students and friends of Yale, on a topic which can be brought under this head. The lectures are afterwards published at the expense of the University in a little volume which forms part of a connected series. The copyright belongs to the University. Our lecturer for the present year was Dr. Lyman Abbott, last year Governor Hughes. In previous years we have had lectures from Mr. Taft, Mr. Bryce, Mr. Root, and other men of public distinction.

I write, at the request of the University Council, to invite you to be the Yale Lecturer on The Responsibilities of Citizenship for the academic year 1911-1912. The exact dates of the lectures can be left largely to your convenience. We regard it as on the whole preferable that your lectures should come in the autumn—say the latter part of October or early part of November—but this is not a point of cardinal importance.

The honorarium for the delivery and copyright of the lectures is twelve hundred dollars.

We appreciate how much we are asking of you, at a time when you are so busy taking the responsibilities of citizenship that you may find little time to talk about them. But this very condition of things will make the boys care all the more for what you say.

I was sorry to be in Europe during your remarkable and triumphant campaign. I congratulate you on the result, and I congratulate you particularly on the courage and squareness with which you are meeting the issue now before you in New Jersey. I have no question that the course you have chosen is the politic one as well as the right one.

Faithfully yours,   Arthur T Hadley

TLS (WP, DLC).

From Henry Watterson

My Dear Governor: Washington, D. C. Dec 13th 1910

I quite agree with you about Ryan, with the addition that there is a strong community of interest between the professional capitalists. I found him "away off." After a night to think it over he accepted my insistance, and seemed to acquiesce in it, that

he should "wait for developements." George Harvey, who returned with me to Washington, appeared to be both worried and
distressed. He left me last night for home. His idea is that Smith
and Martine will be forced to give way to some one to be named
hereafter. I dare say he will see you at once. I write from the
midst of a rush of work merely to make this brief report.
Sincerely Your Friend   Henry Watterson

ALS (WP, DLC).

From Frederick Todd

Dear Sir,   New York, December 13, 1910.

Since the interview that you were so kind as to give last Thursday evening, I have read closely the address before the Convention of Governors and the Bar Association address; and these addresses, in connection with the remarks about State action in
regulation of corporations that you made during our talk, have
so impressed us with the definiteness with which you have
thought out the comprehensive and constructive scheme of re-
born State sovereignty adapted to the present time of progress—
a conception which, as it shows out in your different speeches,
is very attractive—that I am writing again to ask if you will not
give us just a terse, round outilne [outline] of the whole plan,
that we may use in introduction, followed by the parts of the two
addresses that have to do with corporation control.

As I understand it, you plan a revival of the old feeling about
the sovereignty of the States. You hold that there is no need of
inventing new Federal powers or of building up a system for
Federal regulation, for if the States will only use thair [their]
full powers, which they have let become atrophied during the
sweep of the centralization idea, they may, severally or in concert, develop a more effective system than the Federal Government's could be. I gathered from what you said last Thursday,
that the difficulties which some eminent corporation lawyers see
in State regulation are generally technical, and can be overcome
if the States, ably represented in court, assert their Constitutional standing, and particularly, if there is a determined and
intelligent popular demand for a return to the old ideas. You
hold, too, that Federal incorporation law might endanger State
rights and create embar[r]assing vested rights. You concede, I
believe, the need of Federal law wherever interstate commerce is
involved, and even say that experience may show other cases
where Federal law might be more effective.

An especially engaging part of the new doctrine is this, that a surer and better-founded development of methods of controlling industrial organizations and of solving the problems involved will come out of the experience of the separate States, after some of them have worked out methods adapted to their peculiar conditions, have had the benefit of each others' experience, and have conferred; as compared with the attempt, all at once, and guided by opinion only, to construct a law for the whole Nation. This idea of regulation coming out of a dozen melting pots is attractive. It gives even a minority of progressive States a chance to work out the very best law, in spite of obstacles. It is a new idea of progressive popular representative government, this working out of public policies in the communities, close to the people. Your aggressive Governor as the representative of the State, doing things; the "House of Governors" as a pureply [purely] parliamentary body; the good effect upon the people of having their national affairs brought close to them, make your plan attractive.

If you, yourself, would outline the plan in a few words, the things you have to say in the addresses, on several phases of it, would follow very naturally in a statement of the "New Stateism" (Do you call it that?) and some who, like myself, had read fragmentary bits of it, would catch its full significance. As I said in my other letter, our Financial Review is not only a part of a regular issue of the New York Times, but is widely distributed among careful readers, and is something like a professional financial publication.

If you will give us half an hour, at a time convenient, I will come to Princeton, get a stenographer, and make the work of putting together this introductory statement[1] as light as possible for you   Yours very truly,   Fred'k Todd

TLS (WP, DLC).
[1] The interview is printed at Jan. 8, 1911.

From Henry Green Duffield

Dear Dr. Wilson: Princeton, N. J., Dec. 13, 1910.

I have just received from Mr. Sheldon a letter, relative to the action of the Board of Trustees authorizing me to pay your salary for the first half year, in which he requests me to follow your wishes that you should be paid only until the date of your resignation, viz: Oct. 20th last.

As I explained to Prof. Axson the amount due you to Oct. 20th is $3,037.63, of which amount you have received $3000.00[.] I therefore beg to hand you, herewith, check for $37.63 in accordance with Mr. Sheldon's letter and in compliance with your wishes. Will you kindly sign and return the enclosed receipts.

Very respectfully,   H G Duffield
Treasurer

TLS (WP, DLC).

To Frederic Yates

My dear Yates: Princeton, N. J. December 14, 1910

It is a shame that the girls have not written to you.[1] We are all right. We have kept track of you as well as we could and are perfectly delighted at the great success you are having and the powerful friends you are making. Vanderlip is true studd down to the bottom.[2] A splendid man.

We are all right except Stockton Axson is down with another attack of nervous prostration and we are all very anxious about him and it has quite upset Mrs. Wilson. My own affairs go very strenuously but you may be sure that again and again throughout the days my thought turns, with the thought of the rest, to our dear friend.   Always faithfully,   Woodrow Wilson

TLS (F. Yates Coll., NjP).
[1] The letter to which Wilson was replying was F. Yates to WW, Dec. 10, 1910, ALS (WP, DLC).
[2] Yates was at Frank Arthur Vanderlip's estate, Beechwood, at Scarborough-on-Hudson, N. Y., painting portraits of members of the Vanderlip family.

To Arthur Twining Hadley

My dear Mr. Hadley: Princeton, N. J. December 14, 1910

Your letter of yesterday is very kind and tempts me very much but I am finding the responsibilities of the Governorship so difficult to master and every consideration so absorbing that I really dare not promise to lecture on ["]The Responsibilities of Citizenship." I am very much complimented that you should desire me to do so and feel that I am denying myself a real privilege, but I feel in duty bound to devote at least the first year of my Governorship to a thorough mastery of the tasks assigned me, which promises to be various and many.

Allow me to thank you very warmly for your kind congratulations. I sincerely hope that your trip abroad brought not only pleasure but invigoration.

With warmest regards,
Cordially and faithfully yours,   Woodrow Wilson

TLS (A. T. Hadley Papers, Archives, CtY).

An Address to the New York Southern Society

[[Dec. 14, 1910]]

Mr. President, ladies and gentlemen: The very kind introduction[1] I have just heard destroys my sense of identity. I am told by psychologists, that our memories are the seat of our sense of identity, and that if I did not remember who I was yesterday, I could not for the life of me tell you who I am to-day. In view of the confused and unexpected happenings of the recent past, I find it difficult to remember who I was yesterday. I find myself in one respect (I hope in only one respect), resembling certain individuals I heard of in a story that was repeated to me the other day. A friend of mine was in Canada with a fishing party, and one member of the party was imprudent enough to sample some whiskey that was called "Squirrel" whiskey. It was understood that it was called "Squirrel" whiskey because it made those who drank it inclined to climb a tree. This gentleman imbibed too much of this dangerous liquid and the consequence was that when he went to the train to go with the rest of the company, he took a train bound South instead of a train bound North. Wishing to recover him, his companions telegraphed the conductor of the south-bound train: "Send short man named Johnson back for the north-bound train. He is intoxicated." Presently, they got a reply from the conductor, "Further particulars needed; there are thirteen men on the train who don't know either their name or their destination."

Now, I am sure that I know my name, but I am not as sure as Mr. McAdoo that I know my destination, and I have at the present so much to do, that I don't think I am very much concerned where I land, provided I land on some people's necks.

Mr. McAdoo said I was one of those rare specimens that have backbone. If that is true, and I have reason to suspect that it is, I deserve no credit for it, for I come of about as pure fighting stock as can be found on this continent, with a dash of that excellent fighting element known as "the Irish" in me. I have no documentary proof of that fact, but only internal evidence. There is something in me that takes the strain off my Scotch conscience occasionally, and gives me delightful irresponsible moments.

I was thinking, as I looked over this company of fellow-Southerners that we were about to lose one of our distinctions. During the recent campaign in New Jersey, I was driving to the place of meeting where I was condemned to speak, and the gentleman who was accompanying me said: "I am feeling very

[1] By William Gibbs McAdoo, president of the society.

uneasy. Here I have been working in a hopeless minority for twenty years, and now I am afraid it is becoming fashionable to be a Democrat." If it should become fashionable to be a Democrat, we would lose one of our distinctions. We have prided ourselves upon being Democrats, but if it becomes common, at least it will not be a matter of pride; and it looks very much as though it were becoming common. Then there will be some distinction that we will have to recover out of our past, so as not to mix with the common herd.

After all, gentlemen, when we look back upon the past there are more things to be glad about than to be sad about. As I look back upon the past of the South, it seems to me to contain that best of all dynamic forces, the force of emotion. We talk a great deal about being governed by mind, by intellect, by intelligence, in this boastful day of ours; but as a matter of fact, I don't believe that one man out of a thousand is governed by his mind.

Men, no matter what their training, are governed by their passions, and the most we can hope to accomplish is to keep the handsome passions in the majority.

One of the handsomest passions is that sort of love which binds us to the communities in which we live; and as I look back to my life in the South, and recall all the things that we have said and read and written about that region to which our affection clings, it seems to me that the most conspicuous thing of all is the sense of solidarity among Southerners, the sense of a common origin, a common set of ideals, a common set of purposes; a union which cannot be severed with the neighborhoods to which they once belonged. The peril of a man is detachment from the compulsions of a neighborhood, and what saves him is the integrity of his attachment to a neighborhood. If you have made a career which makes you hesitate, because of a touch of shame, to go back and see your old neighbors in the South, then, if it is not too late, reform. Turn right about face, and do something that will make you willing and proud to go back and see the old neighbors, because after all, those are the rootages of patriotism. A man cannot love a country in the abstract, a man cannot love a country that he has not seen and touched and been part of, and the real rootages of your patriotism are the rootages of your youth, those wells from which you drew all the first inspirations of your life and of your action.

It pays to have gone through the fire, as the South has gone through the fire, because it means a body of chastened emotion. It means men who have submitted to the inevitable, and then, recalling those broader motives of the earlier day of the South, they turn again to the common love of country, and are devoting to the country the great impulses which have sprung out of neighborly men and loving women.

There is another thing that Southerners have got out of the South which is a great capital to bank upon in the conduct of public affairs. There was a strange contradiction in the old South, and it is to be found lingering as a characteristic in the modern Southerner. The old Southerner was a great individualist; nothing was so marked in him as his sense of his individual dignity. He resented nothing so much as having people impose their opinions upon him. And yet, at the same time, there went with that the compulsion, the absolute compulsion, of common ideals. He was an individual, but he said to himself also that he was a Southerner, that he belonged to a Society, a Society in which there were definite rules of conduct from which even he, if he wished, did not dare to depart. There was in him a strange combination of individualism, plus submission to common ideals; and yet, when you think of it, that is the very analysis of a vital nation—men of initiative, men who follow the impulses of their own characters, men who will not be put upon, men who will not be put into a common mould of opinion and obliged to conform to it, and yet men who do not wish to fling free from the understandings of communities, from the standards of nations, from the historic memories which constitute the compulsions for the present and for the future. That is the way you combine a free and a vigorous and united people.

There went along with that, in the old South, something which, after all, is the essence of all movement together, namely, loyalty to leaders. Many of the things that I am saying can also be said with equal truth of some other parts of the country. They can be said of old New England, as well as of the old South. I am not now discriminating by way of disparaging other communities, I am simply recalling to you what was characteristic of ourselves in the past; and one of the chief of those characteristics was loyalty to leaders. And that for a very interesting reason, it seems to me. The old leaders in the South may be said to have been embodiments of the South itself. Do you remember the very interesting analysis that the historian [John Richard] Green gives of the power of Queen Elizabeth over her subjects? She was a sort of generalized Englishwoman; the impulses that she had were the impulses that were common to English men and women throughout her kingdom, so that her judgments they instinctively recognized as their judgments; her purposes for the country they at once accepted as their purposes. There was England embodied in an imperious woman, which makes her one of the great figures and one of the great forces of history. Whenever you get a person who is an essential leader, you will find that he or she embodies a people. A leader may embody the worst part or the best part for the time being, but people must find their own selves expressed in those whom they follow.

You remember that Elizabeth had the very interesting instinct always to lie to foreign governments, but she never lied to her English subjects. In the vulgar they were on to her. If she had lied to them they would have known it, whereas she could lie to foreign ministers, and they didn't know it. She was the most consummate liar, and yet the most honest impersonation of England that English history has produced. I won't apologize to the English people for that statement, because I take it from an Englishman.

But, that will illustrate for you what I am thinking of when I am speaking of the relation of the old Southerner to his leader. His leader did not have to explain things to him, he knew what was in his mind; he could go anywhere, for example to Congress, and could say anything he pleased for the impression that it would make upon Northern audiences; he didn't have to tell the people at home what he really meant or why he was saying it. He was their spokesman and embodiment. There were things that he said for others, but they understood. Do you remember that story that Polk Miller[2] tells so admirably, and which I wish I could tell as well? An old darkey went into a drug store in Richmond and said, "Boss, will you call the Colonel on the telephone?" "Yes." And he called the Colonel. The old darkey said, "Colonel, dat'ar mule dun stall right in the main street right out here in front of the store." "Yassah, I dun tied strings round his ears, but he didn't budge." "What's that? What's that? Yes, sir, I build a fire under him, but it didn't do nuthin' but scorch the harness." "Yassah, yassah, I took the things out, but he wouldn't budge." "Yassah, yassah; what's that? No sah, no sah, Colonel, I didn't twist his tail." "Yassah, yassah, another gentleman twist his tail, he looked like a Northern gentleman." "What's dat, Colonel? Yassah; dey dun take him to the hospital." "No sah, no sah, I ain't heerd yet."

Now, you see that doesn't need any explanation to you. You ain't gwine twist his tail, you don't need to have the habits of the animal explained to you; but the Northern gentleman did, in that case.

2 (1844-1914), Virginia merchant, best known for his humorous lectures and talks on southern plantation life.

All these things, gentlemen, though we may give them a whimsical turn, have a very serious import, because, look at the analysis we are now trying to make of our national life and of our national government. Mr. Littleton[3] has referred to it. We hear a great deal nowadays about the contest of opinion between the powers which should be exercised by the federal government and the powers which should be exercised by the state. I must say I don't know how to debate the question in its latest terms, because its latest terms are elusive; they vary from utterance to utterance, and I don't think there ought to be any sense of controversy about this thing. No sane man that I know is jealous of the power of the federal government. We wish the federal government to exercise to the utmost its legitimate powers in the protection of our common interests and we want it to find ways in which it may protect us within the field naturally and properly assigned to the action of the common government. There is no jealousy there, and there ought to be no contest or opposition there. But, don't you see that that is only one side of our character, this compulsion of common purposes, common ideals, common standards, and that, on the other hand, there is our instinct of individualism. We believe that as Southerners, and we believe it as Americans—for I believe that in these respects the Southerner expresses in some unusually vivid way what belongs to all Americans. We do not wish individual initiative to be choked by the common action; and what we are really striving for is the utmost variety of initiative, the utmost variety of energy, in the midst of action towards common purposes. That is the reason we are jealous to see the powers of the states wisely and energetically exercised; not because they are in competition with the powers of the federal government, but because they are in themselves the seat in which resides so much of the energy and initiative and common sense of our own people. We want to see every center of vitality exercise its energy to the utmost, and with the utmost intelligence; just as the individual must not be crushed by the community, so the state must not be crushed by the common action, not because of theoretical jealousies, but because of the nature of energy in human action. Crush the individual and the body declines in energy; crush the initiative of the locality, of the community, of the state, and there begins the decline of the common energy which lies back of the federal government itself. That is the reason it is no joke to be elected the Governor of a state.

---

[3] Democratic Congressman-elect Martin Wiley Littleton of the 1st congressional district of New York. He was the other principal speaker at the dinner.

Now, all of that means that you must not look in any one place for your leader, you must raise up your leaders wherever you are. That is the price of energy and of action. You must multiply your leaders by the number of instrumentalities there are to lead, and you must insist upon it that wherever leadership is necessary, you will find a leader who will embody the community—not simply somebody who is grinding his own axe, or who represents a small group of persons, but somebody who really represents the community and can be its spokesman and leader.

That is the only real leadership; but you must demand a particular kind of leadership, which is more necessary at this time than it has ever been before in the history of this country. It will be difficult to find; you can get it only by disciplining your leaders, not by throwing the reins upon their necks and allowing them to have their own way. You must insist that your leaders combine self-assertion with self-sacrifice. You must demand of them that they take the lead fearlessly, and that the particular thing that they shall not fear shall be the consequences.

I remember the story of a Mississippi steamboat captain who had to tie up, because a fog lay low on the river. The upper decks of the boat were left above the fog. If you stood on the upper deck you could see the clear heaven above you, but all the river bottom lay shrouded in mist, and one of the passengers, impatient to get on, said, "Captain, why don't you go ahead?" The captain replied, "I can't see the way." "Well," said the passenger, "you can see the north star." "Yes," said the captain, "but we are not going that way."

Now, it is all very well to see ulterior objects, it is all very well to have your eye upon distant goals, but don't steer by them; steer by the channel of the river, steer by the thing near at hand, steer by the immediate task, and duty, and oblige your men to combine with self-assertion, self-forgetfulness and self-sacrifice.

I believe that that was the spirit of the old leadership in the South, that men were willing to sacrifice themselves for what they believed to be a cause, knowing that political preferment and political success did not lie in any personal ambition for them. Every man must have a vision of what the people are being lifted to; for, it is not individuals who are to seek political advance, it is communities that are to seek political advance, and the only real leaders are the leaders that lift them up, by never so little, to the new levels, that advance communities from achievement to achievement.

There is another combination that they must make, and an equally difficult combination; they must combine energy with moderation.

We talk about progressives and reactionaries, radicals and conservatives, and I think we use the words rather recklessly. Nothing is progress which does not progress, and some of the most radical courses perhaps are not progressive, because they are not feasible, and therefore progress does not lie in that direction. That is not the way in which the channel of the river curves, and you cannot steer that way. You must have energy, therefore, combined with moderation.

An English writer once defined a constitutional statesman, by which he meant a statesman under a government controlled by public opinion, as a man of ordinary opinions and extraordinary abilities.[4] That is a very good working idea. We do not want his opinions to be too extraordinary; it won't make any difference how extraordinary his abilities are, provided he shares in some way the general opinion, shares it, perhaps, with a clearer vision as to what it is, but nevertheless sees in terms of the common life, and moves with moderation towards feasible ends.

What we are really after in our day is adjustment, accommodation. We do not want a warfare of interests. We have tried too long to accomplish movement by the mere correlation of hostile forces, by setting one set of interests against another, by siding with capital against labor, or with labor against capital, as if they were not, deep down underneath the whole superficial view of the question, essential partners in the thing to be accomplished. Until you get rid of the idea that business is the exploitation of somebody or of some thing, you will not have come even to the frame of mind which makes progress possible. You may pile profits mountain high by crushing out the communities, the energies upon which future profits depend; but, a well-served community is the only possible permanent basis for prosperous business. Well considered working men, working men dealt with fairly, dealt with generously, are the only men who will produce you the stuff that will yield you future profit.

I have read in the textbooks of political economy about enlightened selfishness. I have never seen any selfishness that was

---

4 He referred to Walter Bagehot's comment about Sir Robert Peel. "No man," Bagehot wrote, "has come so near our definition of a constitutional statesman,—the powers of a first-rate man and the creed of a second-rate man. . . . Of almost all the great measures with which his name is associated, he attained great eminence as an opponent before he attained even greater eminence as their advocate. . . . So soon as these same measures, by the progress of time, the striving of understanding, the conversion of receptive minds, became the property of second-class intellects, Sir Robert Peel became possessed of them also. He was converted at the conversion of the average man. His creed was, as it had ever been, ordinary; but his extraordinary abilities never showed themselves so much." Norman St. John-Stevas (ed.), The Collected Works of Walter Bagehot (4 vols. to date, Cambridge, Mass., 1965-   ), III, 245-46.

enlightened. Selfishness is a state of utter darkness, it is a state of utter blindness, and if men could only see that generosity and public service are profitable, then the millenium would come along faster than it is coming. What we are seeking, as I just now said, is a programme, but not a programme of warfare, not a programme of hostilities, not a programme of the accommodation of hostilities even; we are not seeking that poor, negative, pale, colorless thing called a truce; we are not seeking a peace which is a mere holding off of the action of passion. We are seeking the kind of peace which brings co-operation, which brings independence, which brings sympathies, which brings the release of all the handsomer motives of humanity. We are seeking accommodation. Every act, therefore, of public men and of private men, should have as its object to withdraw the veil from men's eyes, so that they can see their own affairs in the terms of the neighborhood, in the terms of the community, in the terms of the life of the nation itself. When we see things in that vision, we shall have begun to see our way amidst the perplexities of modern business, and we shall then have not only a programme of action, but a programme of adjustment.

Did you ever think of what you mean by liberty, by freedom? I have pictured it to myself in this way: What is a perfectly free engine, a perfectly free locomotive? It is a locomotive whose forces are applied with the least friction, it is a locomotive whose parts are so assembled that they will least interfere with each other; and when the great machine runs free, you mean nothing else than that she is running with perfect adjustment. That to my mind is an image of the freedom of the body politic. When you are sailing a boat, and you say she is sailing free, what do you mean? If you throw her up into the wind, if you are defying the forces of nature, try it and see every stick and inch of canvas in her tremble, and hear the sailors say "She is in irons," because she is not obedient to the forces of nature; but let her fall off a point or two, let her yield to the great forces of nature, let them be her servant and not her antagonist, and see her run, see how then she skims over the water like a thing of freedom and a thing of beauty.

There again it is a matter of adjustment, a matter of accommodation, not a matter of resistance. I am free to go to the top of this building, in a false sense of freedom, and jump off; but if I do, there won't be much freedom to boast of afterwards. Nature will say to me "You fool, didn't you know the terms of your freedom? Didn't you know you would break your neck?" Well, I have got to know that under certain circumstances I will break my

neck, before I am free. In other words, I cannot be free and a
fool.

Now, business wishes to be free of restraint. Very well, it cannot be free of restraint until it has found its perfect adjustment
to the common welfare. How are you going to get this spirit that
I have been speaking of expressed in action? Only by finding
leaders—if you can—I cannot point them out to you—by searching for leaders and finding them if you can, who embody the
people they are trying to serve; by understanding them, by having a catholic sympathy, by not being ready to take up the claim
of any class against any other class, but by being ready, so far
as in their power lies, to combine the interests of classes in a
search for the common adjustment. When you find somebody
like that great woman who presided in the spacious times of
great Elizabeth, who will embody for you the just and common
spirit of America, then you will have found the way in which to
express the forces of America.

Now, I have said to you that I do not know where to point
such a leader out, but I have this to suggest: you cannot find him
until you know what you are looking for. If you are looking for a
leader to express the interests of your class, you are looking in the
wrong direction. That is not a leader, that is somebody to stir
up antagonism; that is not a leader. Look for somebody who
does not represent your class any more than he represents some
other class. A friend of mine said of the old adage that everything comes to the man who waits, "Yes, that is all very well if
you add the proviso 'provided he knows what he is waiting for.'"
You cannot stand at the corner and find the man you are looking
for unless you know what he looks like, unless you know whom
you are seeking; then, if you know whom you are looking for,
when he comes down the road you will know that you have got
your man; therefore, our point of view, our object, our vision,
is the first thing and the fundamental thing in the future of the
nation. When you have had a vision of what you want, when
you have fallen in love with that vision; when it has seemed
to you the vision of a perfected nation, a nation perfected by
common purposes and love of what is just, then it will not be
difficult to recognize the man who, in his character and purposes
and ideals fits that position, who seems to have the light of it
upon his face, seems to follow the trail of its glory along the
path that leads to genuine national achievement.[5]

Printed in *Year Book of the New York Southern Society For the Year 1911-1912*
(New York, 1911), pp. 29-43.

[5] There is a WWhw outline of this address, with the composition date of
Dec. 9, 1910, in WP, DLC, and a typed press release, dated Dec. 14, 1910,
in *ibid.*

From William Simon U'Ren[1]

My dear Governor: Oregon City, Ore., December 14, 1910.

This is just a line to congratulate the people of New Jersey on your election for your fighting qualities, and yourself on the opportunity you have. It hurts the politicians to play your game and their squeals are audible through the Associated Press even so far away as Oregon. Smith's whine that you are ungrateful is a very old story in Oregon, though we have not heard it since our Direct Primary Law was adopted.

I have a copy of the "Optional Third Class Law" for cities,[2] I like it very much in the main, and have got some good ideas from it for my own use. I am enclosing one of our sample ballots at the recent election that may interest you.[3] Don't tax your time to write a reply to this. Wishing you all success, I am

Sincerely yours,   W. S. U'Ren

TLS (WP, DLC).

[1] Lawyer and progressive leader of Oregon, one of the pioneers in the movement for the direct primary, the initiative, referendum, and recall and other progressive measures, with whom Wilson was associated in the Short Ballot Organization.

[2] A draft of a model bill, prepared by Richard Spencer Childs of the Short Ballot Organization, permitting cities of the second and third class of New York to adopt the commission form of government. See Richard S. Childs, *Civic Victories: The Story of an Unfinished Revolution* (New York, 1952), pp. 144-45.

[3] It is missing.

From John Sharp Williams

My dear Sir   Benton, Miss., Dec 14 1910

Don't take up office time answering this. It is only to acknowledge receipt of yours of Dec 5th and to express my gratification. I see Smith thinks you are not "polite." Polite! Heavens! when the question is about balking the publicly expressed will of a Party & furthermore of preventing the return to the Senate of one of the four men who in '93 & '94 as members of that august body converted tariff revision & reformation into a *fiasco* that made the very gods on Olympus hold their sides with piteous laughter —so piteous that in the end it became strangely like tears. You did exactly right.   Yours truly   John S Williams

ALS (WP, DLC).

From Edward Field Goltra

Dear Governor: En Route, Dec. 14th, 1910.

After sounding several parties in New York and Newark I decided that it would be far better not to approach Senator Smith.

It was plain to me that it might be dangerous to do so, and I found the consensus of opinion to be that you had in no way harmed yourself in the position you had taken on the Senatorship.

The people of the state expressed their choice in this Senatorial matter, and they having given you such over whelming support, you naturally should not thwart their will.

Sorry I missed you in Princeton yesterday. Will communicate with you about the St. Louis dinner early next week.[1] It is my intention to ask Champ Clark, Ex-Governor Stephens, Governor Francis, Attorney General Major and possibly Joseph W. Folk.[2]   Yours very sincerely,   Edward F. Goltra

TLS (WP, DLC).
[1] He referred to a dinner to be given by the City Club of St. Louis on December 28, 1910. A news report of Wilson's address on this occasion is printed at Dec. 29, 1910.
[2] Champ [James Beauchamp] Clark of Missouri, at this time Democratic minority leader in the House of Representatives; Lawrence Vest Stephens, St. Louis banker, Governor of Missouri, 1897-1901; David Rowland Francis, St. Louis grain merchant, Governor of Missouri, 1889-93, and Secretary of the Interior, 1896-97; Elliott Woolfolk Major, Attorney General of Missouri since 1908; and Joseph Wingate Folk, lawyer and progressive leader of St. Louis, Governor of Missouri, 1905-1909.

From Calvin Easton Brodhead

#140 Cedar St., New York.
My Dear Sir: Plainfield, N. J., Dec. 14, 1910.

If it is convenient to you I should like very much to see you during the next week or ten days. I have refrained from writing you heretofore, realizing how very busy you have been; but now the Senatorial question has come to a stage where I feel like getting in the fight and seeing whether there is anything that I can do to further Mr. Martine's interests. He has not asked me to do anything for him, but as the Assemblyman elect from his home town I think it is incumbent on me to do whatever I can.

I am in a fortunate position in having no strings on me and being under no obligations to any of the politicians. You can therefore count on me to do what I can in carrying out the Party's promises and supporting you. I have been very much disgusted over Mr. Smith's attitude on this question of the Senatorship. He is about the last man in the State in my judgment that ought to be elected. People seem to be supporting your side of this controversy almost to a man in our County.

With kind regards I am,
Yours very truly,   Calvin E. Brodhead

P.S. If you will let me know either at my Plainfield or New York address when it will be convenient to see me I will come to Princeton, or anywhere you suggest.

TLS (WP, DLC).

To Edward Field Goltra

My dear Mr. Goltra: Princeton, N. J. December 15, 1910

I am sincerely sorry that I missed you in Princeton. Better luck next time.

I dare say it would have been useless to see Ex-Senator Smith. The battle is now on and the people of the State are absolutely behind me. There is a set of interests centering in Newark which have had this State by the throat and have controlled its legislation for years past. It is our local branch of Wall Street. It is to be beaten or else the State will be forever helpless. I have gone into this matter pretty deeply and I know that Senator Smith is no more a Democrat than John Kean, whom he desires to succeed, is a republican. They have played into each other's hands constantly and have a perfectly non-partisan arrangement by which to control the legislation of the State. I have at last joined issue and now the battle must be to a finish.

It will be very delightful to see you in St. Louis.

In haste,

    Cordially and faithfully yours,   Woodrow Wilson

TLS (received from David W. Steck).

To Calvin Easton Brodhead

My dear Mr. Brodhead: Princeton, N. J. December 15, 1910

Your letter of yesterday has gratified me very much and I shall look forward with real pleasure to seeing you in Princeton. Would it be possible for you to come over to Princeton on the afternoon of Monday the 19th? I am to be in Trenton during the forenoon of that day but expect to get back to Princeton before four o'clock in the afternoon.

In haste, with warm regard,

                Sincerely yours,   Woodrow Wilson

TLS (received from W. M. Brodhead).

To Clarence Sackett

My dear Mr. Sackett: Princeton, N. J. December 15, 1910

I am wondering if you kept copies of my campaign speeches? There have been a great many demands for their publication in pamphlet form, and if you have kept copies I would like to know whether it would be possible for you to let me have them in pretty good shape.

I remember your constant courtesy throughout the campaign with the greatest pleasure and owe you my sincere thanks for the careful way in which the reporting was done.

          Cordially and sincerely yours,   Woodrow Wilson

TLS (received from David Flanzman).

From Joseph Patrick Tumulty

My dear Governor: Jersey City [N. J.] December 15, 1910.

Several of your friends including Messrs. Ely, Kearny [Kerney], Deer [Dear] and St. John met a few evenings ago in New York, and discussed at great length the Senatorial problem, with the result that we decided to suggest to you the advisability of addressing public meetings in Hudson, Essex, Middlesex and Monmouth Counties at an early date.

We sincerely feel that certain legislators cannot be made to fully realize the vital importance of this question in any other way than by such a forcible presentment as would be effectuated by this method.

Your courageous stand has won for you the sincere affection of our people including, those members of the Hudson County Democratic organization, who look with disapproval upon the avowed course of Mr. Davis.

I learned today that two members of the Hudson delegation, who openly declared a few weeks ago that they would support Mr. Martine, have since that time been influenced to withdraw their support from him.

I have been urged to institute a movement in this County, that would have for its object the holding of meetings here, but I am reluctant to do anything until I hear from you just what you think ought to be done. I will appreciate a word from you in this matter.   Sincerely,   Joseph P. Tumulty.

TLS (WP, DLC).

From James Kerney

Dear Dr. Wilson: Trenton, New Jersey December 15, 1910

The Smith forces are counting with so much confidence upon the Morris [County] delegation as to lead to the belief that there is basis for their hopes. They have some pretty influential agencies at work, circulating, with considerable effect, the story that your reference to Smith was uncalled for, and this is creating some sympathy. I hope that at an early date the authentic view of the representations that were made that he was not to be a candidate for the Senatorship, prior to your consenting to accept the nomination, may be given to the public. This information has been published, but I find it is not generally credited.

Mr. Ely says the Hudson situation remains good, but some hard work will have to be done there, as well as in Morris, Middlesex and Essex. The opposition is at it night and day and strong pressure of all kinds is being employed. Smith's winning now, despite any promises of Nugent and Davis, would give their style of politics such an impetus that it would not be possible to get any reform legislation this winter.

It may interest you to know with what eagerness and enthusiasm your course is being watched by the country at large. I spent two days this week at the conference of the National Civil Service Association, at Baltimore, and was quite astonished at the keen attention that your program has attracted. Senator Smith, by his personal attack on you, has rendered the valuable service of more sharply fastening the eyes of the nation on the battle. But, because of his resourcefulness and ability at manipulation, some of the southern newspapers think you are up against an impossible job. It surely is'nt any snap, and there is a very earnest army ready to help; but to be effective this effort must be properly organized and directed at an early date.
                    Yours very sincerely,   James Kerney

An acknowledgment of this is unnecessary. I simply wanted to get the information before you

TLS (WP, DLC).

From Marion Jackson Verdery[1]

My very dear Doctor Wilson: New York, Dec. 15, 1910.

I have been richly blessed in my life through a more or less intimate acquaintance with many of the truly great men of my day and my privileged friendship with you enriches that experience.

Without the slightest trace of lingering champagne exhilaration from last night's feast, in the dead calm of the next day's reflection I want to tell you about it. It was to my mind the very greatest of the many great speeches I have heard you make. Thinking over it now, it seems to me to have been the most splendid condensation of the philosophy of politics and patriotism that has been uttered since the Civil War. Of course, we had a stenographer present, who was presumed to take the speech word for word; but I am afraid that he may not have thoroughly succeeded in his task. The result of his effort will be submitted to you for correction and editing. After it has had that treatment, I am in hopes it will be practically a faithful reproduction of your utterances. I know you must have had innumerable congratulations from men and women last night, and yet I cannot resist repeating to you this consummate praise that I heard. Mr. Starling W. Childs, Mr. William P. Bonbright,[2] Doctor John A. Wyeth, Mr. George W. Perkins and, most enthusiastic of all, my dear friend Mr. Ernest Groesbeck,[3]—each one told me that he thought it was positively the very best speech he had ever heard.

You no doubt remember Groesbeck as that friend of mine who came with me to see you at Princeton the first Sunday afternoon following your nomination. He has never recovered from your infatuation of him that day.

I have just been to lunch with him. He is a manly man, full of the highest sense of honor and the noblest impulses. He compelled me to promise him that I would give thought to the very best method of putting the speech you made last night before the whole people. He said he would himself be willing to subscribe to the cost of such an undertaking, and he felt confident of being able to raise among his friends whatever amount was necessary to carry out the plan. Of course, he does not know that I am writing you this letter. If he did, his shrinking modesty in all things, which is a dominant characteristic in his nature, would make him object to my having mentioned his name in such connection. Now, I want to ask your opinion and advice on the subject. Do you think, if the speech was printed on a separate newspaper sheet, that several of the leading papers of the country would agree to use it as a filler in a Sunday's edition? If such an arrangement as that could be made, I believe the speech could be put before a greater number of people than by any other method that occurs to me. I do not believe that you yourself realize how great the speech was. I sincerely believe that if its doctrine could be made the corner-stone of our faith and practice, that it would result in an actual uplift of the republic and would give to the people of our country a clearer vision of political obligation than anything that has ever been spoken to them. I am writing under the influence of a profound impression, which makes me almost, if not altogether, as enthusiastic as my friend Groesbeck. Please send me a line of wise counsel and friendly suggestion out of your good judgment as to whether the plan I suggest would probably accomplish the desired end, and if such an undertaking could be made with your entire approval.[4]

With best wishes, I remain

Very sincerely your friend,   M. J. Verdery

TLS (WP, DLC).

[1] Secretary and superintendent of the New York Stock Exchange Building Co., prominent in the affairs of the New York Southern Society.

[2] Starling Winston Childs, member of the New York banking firm of William P. Bonbright and Co., Inc., of which William Prescott Bonbright was president.

[3] Ernest Groesbeck, New York broker.

[4] Insofar as the Editors know, this plan was never carried out.

From James Richard Nugent

My dear Sir: Newark New Jersey December 15, 1910.

I received your very kind letter of the fourteenth instant.

I will call upon you at Princeton tomorrow (Friday) afternoon at two o'clock.[1]

Yours very truly,   James R. Nugent

TLS (WP, DLC).

[1] The brief news account of this meeting (*Newark Evening News*, Dec. 16, 1910) said that Nugent and Wilson met for "some time" about legislative matters. Nugent told the reporter that "the Senatorship was not discussed or even hinted at."

From Evans Griffiths Slaughter[1]

My Dear Sir,   Philadelphia, Pa. Dec 15th 1910.

When, and where, will it be convenient for you to hold a little conference with me, as I am anxious to formulate a policy for the future of our Party in Cape May County.

I would very much like to talk matters over with you this comming week.

With kind regards, I remain

Sincerely Yours   Evans G. Slaughter

ALS (WP, DLC).
  ¹ Owner and proprietor of the Hotel Aldine Apartments in Wildwood, N. J., and chairman of the Cape May County Democratic Executive Committee.

To Mary Allen Hulbert Peck

Dearest Friend,   Princeton, New Jersey 16 December, 1910

It *hurts* me to have to squeeze my letters to you into little corners of time which others (to whom I am perfectly indifferent) have not cared to appropriate. The result is that I am *always* tired when I write,—too tired to be able to express either thoughts or feelings,—too tired to do anything but say in commonplace phrase how constantly I think of you and how ardently I desire your happiness. It is delightful to hear that Glencove begins to take on the look and comfort of a home.¹ I know that you will be happy there and that you will love the place presently as your first real haven of rest in all the weary years since you began to *need* Bermuda. Alas! I shall not see the dear place! I am driven every minute of the day, and it is my present duty to allow myself to be driven,—to be at the service of practically any and every body that wishes to consult me on public business. Smith has at last come openly out and defied me to defeat him:² and defeated he must be if it takes every ounce of strength out of me. I feel pretty confident it can be done; but a nasty enough fight is ahead, and I shall have to do some rather heartless things which I had hoped might be avoided. They are against all the instincts of kindliness in me. But you cannot fight the unscrupulous without using very brutal weapons. I only hope I shall use them like a gentleman and a man of honour. Probably I shall have to go out on the stump again and conduct something like a systematic campaign against the whole gang: for Smith is only one of a gang that has had its grip upon the throat of the State for a generation. He is no Democrat. He has been in close alliance with men calling themselves Republicans and their purposes have been wholly non-partisan, as non-partisan as those of the plain (and much more picturesque) highwayman.

I cannot say whether I relish the new job or not. It is grim and forbidding in many ways, and there is a certain indomitable something in me that gets satisfaction out of it all; and, for the rest, I have not time to think whether I like it or not. It does not matter. It has to be faced and carried through. If I could only escape long enough at a time from interviewers of all kinds and get a little rest and refreshment, it would go easier. The only refreshment I get is an occasional gleam of delightful thought about dear distant friends whose sympathy I know I have and who are themselves dear and delightful to think about. It is splendid to be believed in and sustained by the faith of people worth having for friends. And so my thought seeks strength very, very often by turning to Bermuda, and thinking of all the kind things that are being thought about me in the ship-like house that stands by Salt Kettle Ferry. How I wish I could tell the dear people there all I think about them! But, after all, they know, do they not? A short letter can carry as much affection as a long one, when a short letter is *meant* for a long one, and overflows with all the warm feelings of

Your devoted friend, Woodrow Wilson

All join me in affectionate messages.

WWTLS (WP, DLC).

1 Mrs. Peck's letter, to which this was a reply, is missing.

2 Smith's announcement of his candidacy had just appeared in the press. It was in the form of a reply to the eleven Essex County assemblymen-elect who, in the public letter cited earlier (C. H. Dodge to WW, Nov. 18, 1910, n. 3), had requested him to run. "Your request," Smith wrote (*Newark Evening News*, Dec. 16, 1910), "that I permit the use of my name as a candidate for the office of United States Senator has deeply impressed me, and your promise to support such candidacy has caused me much gratification. I have received so many assurances of like nature from other members-elect that I am convinced the majority view of the Democratic members who will compose the next Legislature coincide with your views. Under such circumstances, while in no sense eager to assume the great responsibility involved, I feel that my duty to our party requires that I give assent to your request." Smith then went on to list a number of measures he would support if elected. They included downward revision of the tariff, an amendment for popular election of senators, economy in government, revival of the merchant marine, an adequate army and navy, fortification of the Panama Canal, and conservation of natural resources. There was no mention in the letter of Wilson's opposition or of Martine's candidacy.

To Isaac Wayne MacVeagh

My dear Mr. McVeagh: Princeton, N. J. December 16, 1910

I have read your letter of December 7th with a great deal of interest. I need not tell you that I subscribe to its principles without any hesitation. It will give me pleasurable pride to study the matters to which it calls my attention with the utmost care so that I may partly assure New Jersey playing a great part among her states [sister] states in meeting the needs of our people.

It was very generous of you to write as you did and I am taking the liberty of returning the extract from "The Nation" which you were kind enough to send.

Sincerely yours, Woodrow Wilson

TLS (I. W. MacVeagh Papers, PHi).

To John Wesley Wescott

My dear Judge Wescott: Princeton, N. J. December 16, 1910

Your letters cheer and strengthen me always and I am particularly obliged to you for your letter of December 10th. It is like having had a cheering talk with you. I certainly need all the cheer I can get in the present perplexing and exasperating circumstances.

In haste,

Cordially and faithfully yours,   Woodrow Wilson

TLS (J. W. Wescott Coll., NjP).

From Calvin Easton Brodhead

My Dear Sir: New York. Dec. 16, 1910.

I have your letter of yesterday, and shall come to Princeton next Monday afternoon leaving here at ten minutes after two. I understand this will get me to Princeton at 4.14.

I was not surprised to see the contents of Senator Smith's letter as given out this morning, as it has been his purpose all along to go after this position, without regard to anything but his personal and selfish interests. It now remains to be seen how many members of the Legislature are going to vote for him. It is clear that their constituents do not want him. Had these men during the campaign indicated their purpose to vote for Smith we could not have mustered a Corporals Guard among the Democratic Legislators next year.

Yours very sincerely,   Calvin E. Brodhead

TLS (WP, DLC).

From Alexander Jeffrey McKelway[1]

Dear Dr. Wilson: Washington, D. C., December 16, 1910.

I have just been informed by the Secretary of the Southern Commercial Congress that you are expected to be with them in Atlanta about the 10th of March.[2] The meeting of our National Child Labor Committee, of which I spoke to you in New York the other day, is to be held just after the Atlanta meeting. So I hope it will be even more probable than it was that you can preside at one of our meetings in Birmingham. I am sending you a few of my own pamphlets on the subject of Child Labor in the South,[3] which I hope you will have time to glance at, and, of course, no man born in the South can preside at a meeting and not make a speech! I am anxious for a clear note from you on the subject of this reform, not only for the sake of the cause, but for the sake of the Democratic party. I am tolerably familiar with the Democracy as it is now represented in Congress, having been in Washington during several sessions of Congress, and having an acquaintance with nearly every member of each house.

For reasons that are obvious enough, the main one being that the Democratic party has been limited to the Southern states, in recent years, where sociological problems are somewhat new, I have found it much more difficult to interest the *Democratic* members of Congress in such a project, for example, as that of the Children's Bureau, which is simply to investigate and report on the various problems of childhood, having special reference to the unfortunate children of the country.[4] I have been with a committee, this week, trying to secure an appropriation of $75,-ooo for ten additional educational experts for the Bureau of Education, such as an Expert on School Hygiene, one on School Architecture, one on Industrial Education, etc. I have found the same difficulty in getting the attention of our Democratic friends, although this project is endorsed by practically the whole teaching force in the country, having been officially endorsed by the National Educational Association, which met in Boston in July.

Now, if I interpret aright the recent revolution in the country, there has been enough resentment at the attitude of the Republican reactionaries in such matters alone to cause the Republican reverses in a number of states. Such bodies as the National Conference of Charities and Corrections, the American Prison Association, the various organizations interested in the welfare of children, resent the stand-pat attitude of rigid economy in all matters pertaining to human welfare, while there is extravagance enough where there is a political or a commercial interest involved. These people have considerably more influence than is generally credited to them. Their demands upon the National government are, of necessity, moderate, and yet, what I fear is that if Mr. Burleson, of Texas,[5] for example, shall succeed Mr. Tawney[6] as Chairman of the Committee on Appropriations, the same hostile attitude will be maintained towards all such matters. I use Mr. Burleson as an example because he takes sides with Mr. Tawney on this very question of providing the educational experts for the Bureau of Education. We must look to the new blood in the Democratic party that has come in with the recent elections, and, I hope, will be increased in 1912, to invigorate the whole body, and thus to win and maintain the favor of the country.

With high regards, I remain,

Cordially yours,   A. J. McKelway.

TLS (WP, DLC).

[1] Southern Presbyterian minister, social worker and, since 1904, secretary for the southern states of the National Child Labor Committee.

[2] Wilson spoke to the Southern Commercial Congress on March 10, 1911. A news report of his address is printed at that date.

[3] They are missing.

[4] McKelway had been leading the publicity campaign for the creation of a children's bureau from the Washington offices of the National Child Labor Committee. The idea for such a bureau had originated about 1905 with Lillian D. Wald, head of Henry Street settlement, in New York, and with Samuel McCune Lindsay, then Professor of Sociology at the University of Pennsylvania and executive secretary of the National Child Labor Committee. In an interview in 1905, they won the support of President Theodore Roosevelt, and a bill to establish the bureau was introduced in every session of Congress from 1905 to 1912. In the latter year, Congress finally created the Children's Bureau in the Department of Commerce and Labor.

[5] Albert Sidney Burleson, Democratic congressman from Texas since 1899; Postmaster General, 1913-21.

[6] James Albertus Tawney, Republican standpat congressman from Minnesota, who had been defeated for re-nomination by a progressive in the Republican primary earlier in 1910. John Joseph Fitzgerald, New York Democrat, succeeded him as chairman of the House Appropriations Committee.

From Robert Latham Owen[1]

My Dear Dr. Wilson: Washington, D. C. December 16, 1910.

I was greatly interested in your letter to the National Democratic Club.[2]

You know, of course, that your name is now being considered by many of the Democrats of the Nation, as a possible Presidential Candidate in 1912. Your letter indicates that you stand for a genuine representation of the people, and of public opinion, but I have understood that you were opposed to the Initiative and Referendum.

I hope, sincerely, that this is not true, or that, upon examination you may give your adherence to the doctrine of direct legislation by the People. At all events, I wish to ask you the plain question, as to whether or not you approve the Initiative and Referendum, in any form, or would be willing to give it your support?   Yours very respectfully,   Robt L. Owen

TLS (WP, DLC).

[1] Progressive Democratic senator from Oklahoma since 1907.

[2] WW to J. Fox, Dec. 10, 1910.

From George Arthur Plimpton[1]

My dear Governor: New York December 16, 1910

I suppose it is perfectly safe to call you "Governor" even though you have not yet been inaugurated!

Mr. Francis W. Hirst, Editor of the London Economist, is going to dine with a few of his friends at the Century Club on next Monday evening at seven-thirty. We hope to get Theodore Roosevelt, President Nicholas Murray Butler, and perhaps a dozen or so more men, and I wonder if you would not like to come in and be one of the party? We want to get Mr. Hirst to talk on the situation in English politics.

I want to take this opportunity, even at this late date, to congratulate you everlastingly on the good work which you have done for Princeton. I think that Princeton University, for many years to come, is going to feel the good effect of your administration. Personally I am mighty sorry to have you give it up, but I believe that you are going to have the same good influence on the country by going into politics that you had at Princeton. You certainly have my very best wishes and congratulations.

I hope we shall have the pleasure of seeing you on Monday night, and I shall appreciate your telegraphing me on receipt of this letter whether or not it will be possible for you to come.

Sincerely yours,   Geo. A. Plimpton.

TLS (WP, DLC).
[1] A.B., Amherst 1876, book and manuscript collector, and member of the publishing firm of Ginn and Co.

To Mary Allen Hulbert Peck

Dearest Friend,   Princeton, New Jersey 17 December, '10

Perhaps, if I begin now and add sentence by sentence as a moment falls free from day to day, I may be able to write you a less meagre and disappointing letter than the hasty fragments I have so far sent you. I was heartily ashamed of them, and would not have sent them if I had not known that you would understand. It was more my loss than yours. It is such a comfort, these strenuous days, filled with anxiety and a sort of silent struggle against almost unseen forces, to turn aside to thoughts of you and serene Bermuda, with its peace and gaiety. You are yourself so cheerful a person to think of, and it is stimulating to talk to you, even at a distance—for you have so vivid an individuality that it carries across any reach of time or space, and I can fancy that I see and hear you as I write. I know so well what you would say,—what your comment would be, and laugh aloud as if at some whimsical sally or audacious quip that you had actually uttered! By the way, will you not draw me a rough ground play [plan] of your rooms at Glencove? Have you taken the whole house, upstairs and down, or only the upper part, as the Garrisons[1] did, and the Chamberlains[2] before them? It is odd that that particular house should be the one, aside from Inwood and Shoreby,[3] with which I have the most definite associations, is it not? And then I passed it so often in going and coming from the ferry that its exterior is as familiar to my thought, at least on the side it presents to the road and to the little bay, as if I had lived in it myself.

Things go as usual with me: it is Smith, Smith, Smith all the days through. My statement, which I sent you, smoked him out. He has now declared himself openly as a candidate, with hypocritical protestations of doing it in response to the urgency of friends, and with a desire to serve the country; and so the war is definitely on and the challengers in the field. My plan of campaign is not yet fixed upon; but of course, as I said in my last letter, it will be chiefly an affair of terribly plain spoken speechmaking. I will keep you informed of what happens.

And so I am soon to issue another book, am I? When do you suppose I wrote it? I cannot imagine what your informant can have been thinking of. I have been urged to print my campaign speeches, and they would make quite a pamphlet, no doubt; but that is the only offence of the kind I have even thought of; and that seems hardly worth while. They were so entirely local in their subject and purpose,—except for the stories and jibes they contained. You probably read scraps of them in the papers, as they were delivered. I went down to Kentucky the last week of November to the Governors' Conference; on Monday last I dined with the Illinois Manufacturers' Association in Chicago; and on Wednesday evening I dined with the Southern Society in New York. In the Christmas vacation I must be in St. Louis at the meeting of the American Political Science Association, of which I am president, and to which I must deliver an address.[4] It is precious hard work to find time to prepare a speech or an address nowadays: I can do it, indeed, only by callously neglecting [neglecting] something else, and shutting myself off from all callers in the tower;[5] but it is a relief to attempt it. To get that old, faithful hack, my mind, back to systematic use and studious contact with the English language again is infinitely restful, refreshing, calming and serviceable in every way. It saves my life: for it restores my poise. I used to think such things the hardest part of the day's work. Now they seem the most refreshing and rewarding. All else is confusion and weariness! What will happen to me next?

25 December, 1910.

This is heartbreaking! I literally have not been able to turn away from work for so much as ten minutes since I wrote what is on the other sheet. Now I am about to start for St. Louis, and can only tell you how the Christmas season has filled my mind more than ever with thoughts of you. Will you not send me sailing lists of all the steamers that go from New York to you? I simply have not a chance to get them. I suppose I let a boat slip away yesterday without a letter, and that you will be disappointed! At any rate, you will know that I did not neglect or forget you. I am caught in the toils of fate and am a bit distracted. It will be at least a rest to get away on a long journey.

All the most affectionate greetings of the season, and of all seasons, from us all. I am well and hearty. I enclose my second bolt.[6]　　　Your devoted friend,　Woodrow Wilson

WWTLS (WP, DLC).

[1] Probably Lindley Miller Garrison and Margaret Hildeburn Garrison of Jersey City.

[2] The Editors have been unable to identify them.

[3] Shoreby was the house she rented in Bermuda in 1907-1908. For a description of Inwood, which she had rented in 1906-1907, see Mary A. H. Peck to WW, Feb. 25, 1907, n. 1, Vol. 17.

[4] It is printed at Dec. 27, 1910.

[5] That is, the tower room of Prospect.

[6] The enclosure was a clipping from the Jersey City *Jersey Journal*, Dec. 23, 1910, with Wilson's statement on the senatorship printed at Dec. 23, 1910.

To James Bryce

My dear Mr. Bryce:　　　Princeton, N. J. December 17, 1910

I do not know just where to send this letter but suppose that if I send it to Washington it will reach you sooner than if I tried to catch you elsewhere.

I want to express my very deep appreciation of your kindness.[1] There is no one whose approval I would rather deserve than your own, and I shall hope, if my public career should last, I may have the benefit of your advice and friendship for my guidance.

Mrs. Wilson joins me in warmest regards to Mrs. Bryce[2] and yourself, and I am as always,

Cordially and faithfully yours,　Woodrow Wilson

TLS (J. Bryce Papers, Bodleian Library).

[1] J. Bryce to WW, Nov. 12, 1910.

[2] Elizabeth Marion Ashton Bryce.

To William Pierce Macksey[1]

My dear Mr. Macksey: Princeton, N. J. December 17, 1910

I think that it is imperative in the common interest that we should fully understand each other with regard to the question of the United States Senatorship, and I should be very much assisted by a personal interview with you. May I not ask that you will make it possible to see me at Princeton next Wednesday the 21st in the late afternoon or evening? I would esteem it a real favor if you would do this.[2]

Cordially and sincerely yours,   Woodrow Wilson

TCL (RSB Coll., DLC).
[1] Assemblyman-elect from Essex County and owner of W. P. Macksey and Co., real estate and insurance brokers of Newark, N. J.
[2] A news report of this conference is printed at Dec. 21, 1910.

From Henry Watterson

My dear Governor: Washington, D. C. Dec 17th 1910

As I am taking a train for home just this word. You have everything to gain, and nothing to lose, by taking up the gauge Smith has thrown down and anticipating the Legislature by an appeal to the people. These two clippings[1] show the lay of the land. If Smith can win by a coalition with the Republicans, you are vindicated; but the issue should be made so clear that the whole country will understand. It is indeed here that your opportunity comes to you and that you must stand, or fall. Smith is a wolf and the rest are of the same species. Publicity, publicity, and again publicity, is the killing dose to such predatories. By taking the field, and making aggressive war, you still further take yourself out of the academic class and signalize the puisance shown in the campaign of last fall, proclaiming the moral issue and reasserting the personality that won you the election. The "Old Guard" crowd are doing their uttermost to befog the one and misrepresent the other. Win this fight in the open—so that all men may see and know—and the rest will follow: complete possession of the local machinery and a place of vantage in the national field.   Your Friend   Henry Watterson

ALS (WP, DLC).
[1] They are missing.

From Henry Skillman Breckinridge

My dear Governor Wilson: Baltimore, Md. Dec. 17. 1910.

You cannot know with what gratification and applause we have witnessed your ascendancy in the world of practical politics. In the theory of politics you have been long preeminent, and recent events seem to have justified the remark of the late Dean [James Barr] Ames of the Harvard Law School that "good theory is good practice."

You may remember receiving from me a letter some weeks before your election[1] suggesting the promotion of a nation wide "Woodrow Wilson Democratic Association," and a subsidiary "Young Men's Woodrow Wilson Democratic Association." At the time of receiving that letter it seemed to you premature for such an undertaking, as I believe.[2] Is it possible now that you would see fit to sanction such an organization? Of course it should not be undertaken unless it recommends itself to you as expedient and wise.

Your election, in a sense, was a triumph over organization of a machine nature, but this seems not to be a reason against crystallizing the sentiment in your favor into an organization, just as it is not improper to organize charitable and other worthy movements into effective working bodies

One year from next summer is the time for the national conventions. Primarily, your noteworthy utterances upon important subjects bring you to the notice of the people. Secondarily, I would urge this scheme to show tangibly to the public the effect those utterances are having in summoning men to your standard, and to bring into mutual contact and cooperation the uncoordinated forces desiring your elevation to the Presidency. Eighteen months is not too long a time in which to convince ninety-three millions of people of what is good for them, and for them in turn to show their leaders they must be given what they want. Conventions nominate. We cannot. But we can use every honorable effort to send men to conventions to do what we hope and believe to be the will of the people, i.e., to nominate Your Excellency the standard bearer of the Democratic party in the next Presidential campaign.

The great State of Ohio has an able and just son[3] who well may bid high for this honor. I would seek to forestall him in his natural and worthy ambition only because I am convinced that there is one more fitted for the place by reason of his great comprehension and understanding of the structure and needs of our body politic, and by reason of his ability to devise means to meet those needs.

Would not Col. Geo. Harvey be the man eminently fitted to start this organization?

Gordon Rentschler, '07, of Hamilton, Ohio, a "Progressive Republican" delegate to the last Ohio Republican State convention, is in favor of this plan and willing to participate in its execution. I had intended to send this to him to seek his signature to make this a joint letter, but decided to avoid the delay involved.

With great respect,

Faithfully yours,   Henry S. Breckinridge.

ALS (WP, DLC).
[1] H. S. Breckinridge to WW, Aug. 8, 1910, ALS (WP, DLC).
[2] WW to H. S. Breckinridge, Sept. 16, 1910, TLS (H. S. Breckinridge Papers, DLC).
[3] That is, Judson Harmon.

From William Hunter Maxwell[1]

Honorable Sir: Newark, N. J., Dec. 17, 1910.

As a believer in you and your policies and an interested citizen I am not simply watching the Senatorial controversy, but I am doing my utmost to arouse the people with whom I happen to come in contact, to your standard.

You are to be highly thanked, respected and appreciated for your courage and uprightness in the stand you take in the Senatorship matter. Certainly a principle is involved. I am trying to get the people to send protests and demands to all of our Assemblymen-elect.

Work and not talk wins now. The people should be made to realize that they are the masters and not the servants.

I am with you and will do all in my power to help, as a citizen, hold up your hands.

Very Truly Your's,   Wm. H. Maxwell.

TLS (WP, DLC).
[1] Jeweler of Newark and president of the Newark Negro Council.

From William Goodell Frost

My dear Dr. Wilson: Berea, Kentucky December 17, 1910.

This is to acknowledge the receipt of your telegram accepting Friday night, February tenth, as the date in which you will speak for Berea and the Southern mountains, in Carnegie Hall.

As I have already informed you, Mr. Seth Low can preside on that occasion, and I am negotiating with Governor Willson, of

Kentucky. Will communicate with you further as the time draws near.

You have a right to a Merry Christmas, and the good wishes of thousands are with you.

Gratefully and faithfully yours,   Wm Goodell Frost

TLS (WP, DLC).

From Clarence Sackett

My dear Governor: Newark, N. J. Dec. 17th, 1910

Replying to your favor of the 15th inst., which was not answered upon its receipt, yesterday, because I was hurrying on my way to the United States Court at Trenton, where I am very busily engaged just now, I beg to say that I have kept copies of your campaign speeches and I have them all except two or three, which I believe I can also furnish, and of course, I would be very glad to furnish you with the same.

I have some plans on foot, with Mr. Bacon,[1] looking toward the publication of a book containing these speeches,[2] and if I would not be encrotching [encroaching] on your very valuable time these days, may I not come to Princeton some evening next week, to be designated by you, and talk over the matter? And I will be guided by whatever your views are.

I take this opportunity also, in my humble way, to congratulate you upon the stand that you have taken in the matter of the senatorship, which is so thoroughly consistent with your attitude throughout the campaign. To my mind, if you will pardon me for the suggestion, to have done less would have been to place yourself in a false light before the people of the state. God speed you in the good work that you have so auspicially [auspiciously] commenced.

Thanking you for the kind sentiments expressed in your letter, I am   Very sincerely yours,   Clarence Sackett

TLS (WP, DLC).
    [1] Charles Reade Bacon, reporter for the Philadelphia *Record*.
    [2] Bacon's book is cited in J. R. Nugent to WW, Nov. 15, 1910, n. 2. Sackett apparently played no role in the publication of this volume.

From George Frederick Baer[1]

My dear Mr. Wilson: Philadelphia. 17 December 1910.

A committee of "old-time" Democrats[2] will call upon you this afternoon to ask you to come to Philadelphia for their "Jackson's Day Dinner."

I think there is more need of missionary effort in the City of Philadelphia to revive the Democratic party than in any other place in the United States; and if you can, without too much inconvenience to yourself, grant the request of these gentlemen you will be doing a very good work.[3]

Personally, I am handicapped from taking any active part in this effort to revive true Democracy because of my official position. Railroad Presidents are not in great favor with the public; and it is possible that their efforts to help any such situation would do more harm than good.

Yours very truly,   Geo. F. Baer

TLS (WP, DLC).

[1] President of the Philadelphia and Reading Railway Co., the Philadelphia and Reading Coal and Iron Co., and the Central Railroad Co. of New Jersey, who, during the anthracite coal strike of 1902, had won nationwide notoriety upon the publication of a letter attributed to him, saying: "The rights and interests of the laboring man will be protected and cared for—not by the labor agitators, but by the Christian men to whom God in his infinite wisdom has given the control of the property interests of the country, and upon the successful management of which so much depends."

[2] Representing the Democratic Club of Philadelphia.

[3] Wilson and other Democratic leaders invited were unable to speak in Philadelphia on January 8, 1911, because of previous engagements. The dinner was postponed to February 21, 1911. See F. F. Kane to WW, Dec. 22, 1910, printed below, and the *Trenton Evening Times*, Feb. 22, 1910.

An Interview

[Dec. 18, 1910]

DEMOCRATS MUST REDUCE TARIFF TAXES AND CURB
CORPORATIONS—WOODROW WILSON, The Fighting Gov. Elect
of New Jersey.

By James Creelman.

In spite of his cool, passionless voice and shy insistence that he was without authority to speak for the future of the Democratic party in the nation, there was a ring to the words of Governor-elect Woodrow Wilson, of New Jersey, that revealed a new leadership as he sat in his private library at Princeton University and talked of the smashing defeat inflicted upon the Republicans by the voters of the country.

"The people did not endorse any particular programme of the Democratic party," he said, "but turned away in despair from the Republican party. The Democrats have not so much won a victory as they have obtained an opportunity. That is the present political situation as I see it."

Not only is Dr. Wilson the freshest and most interesting personality among the Democratic Presidential probabilities emerging from the chaos of the recent political struggle, but his utterance carries a marked importance because his vote shows such an extraordinary gain over the vote of Mr. Bryan. The great victory in Ohio, due to non-voting Republicans, shows no such sensational change in Democratic strength since the thrice-defeated Nebraskan made his supreme test at the polls.

For many years the Virginia-born president of Princeton University has been teaching political science and writing books on statecraft full of the idea that society is greater than government and that government must not dominate society, but must serve it; yet his declaration of war on ex-Senator James R. Smith and the corrupt Democratic leaders who have made New Jersey a Republican State for so many years, and his bold announcement that the next United States Senator from New Jersey must be the man endorsed by the popular vote, and not the man chosen by political bosses and the unspeakable secret league of private corporations, has done more to put heart and strength and meaning into his victory than all the splendid abstractions of his books and speeches.

While Dr. Wilson spoke of the real significance of the Democratic success in the nation, his political friends were waiting in the next room to devise means to prevent the plundering and traitorous elements of Democracy from again appearing in the United States Senate in the portly person of Mr. Smith.

The new Democratic master of New Jersey is a man of singular appearance. He is tall, thin and straight. He has the head and visage of a mediaeval scholar. The face is long and narrow and of a melancholy lean[n]ess. The eyes are grey and honest. The jaws are very long and thin and bend inward in a startling way as they approach the flat, perpendicular ears, which stand out with some abruptness from the slim line of the head. The forehead is neither broad nor high nor is there any massiveness in the shape or size of the head.

Such a face would indicate a mere scholar in search of knowledge for its own sake, a narrow, ascetic pedant, were it not for the fine curving nose of command, the remarkably long and protruding chin and the full lips, all eloquent of courage, initiative, humor and generosity. Yet, notwithstanding the almost forbidding solemnity of the long, bony countenance, when Dr. Wilson talks a rare smile comes to his gray eyes and mobile mouth and he shows not only a light-darting, playful humor, but an almost boyish simplicity and eagerness. The forlorn, severe appearance, which makes one think of dead and gone generations of doctrinaires pictured in ancient engravings, is a mere mask for an up-to-date, fearless gentleman whose moral nerve is not only alive, but tingling with energy, a man of vision and with a decent personal sense of proportion; one who has not only taught, but has led, and who recognizes and hates a crook both by instinct and reason; a man of sweet temper and good sense.

"What seems to me to be the real case," said Dr. Wilson, "is that certain progressive, but not radical, elements in the country that tried to make their impulses effective through the Republican party—I speak, of course, of the people and not of the leaders—found that, for one reason or another, their wishes had been thwarted, and, in a moment of disappointment and confusion as to which way they should turn, the Democratic party seemed to offer a means of relief under men whom, for the time being, they were willing to try.

"The mere calling of a convention and the selection of a candidate by that convention is a very uncertain way of choosing a leader, but it is the only way we have under our existing elective system, and the people had to take a sporting chance.

"Those who had failed to find a serviceable instrumentality of Government in the Republican party took the risk of turning to the Democratic party. I think that was it; I am sure of it."

The tall scholar leaned on his big library table and looked out of the window across the snow-covered lawn through the evergreen trees and wilted clumps of rhododendrons shaking in the winter wind. Around him were the signs of a busy life in the large light room—crowded bookcases, a desk cluttered with papers, a telephone, a typewriter, a filing case with a little statue of Narcissus on top of it, and on the walls portraits of James Madison, once a student at Princeton; Gladstone and Daniel Webster; plaster casts of Homer, Raphael and the sandalled Nike, with a white figure of Cupid standing tiptoe on the mantel.

In that quiet room Grover Cleveland had many a time discussed the sorrows of Democracy in his retirement, and it is only a short walk to the little Princeton cemetery where, under the snow, lie the graves of Cleveland and Aaron Burr, between whose lives stretch such long years of Democratic glory and shame.

"It seems to me," continued Mr. Wilson, placing his hands palm to palm and speaking very slowly, "that just at the moment when the free element of the country was seeking an outlet the Democratic party appeared to offer it a chance. The result of the election is not so much of a permanent Republican defeat as a turning of the free element of the people in the direction which holds out most hope of action favorable to the common interests.

It is a Republican defeat in this sense: that it seemed as if the Republicans were unable to act in the common interest because of their too great implication in special interests. The free element had been trying and trying for years along Republican lines, and finally they found that they were absolutely blocked. Now they have turned to the Democrats."

"Which do you think was the decisive issue in the election, Dr. Wilson, the tariff question or the desire for an effective control and regulation of private business corporations and combinations?"

"It was both; they are closely related. I believe that the free element turned to the Democratic party not because they particularly wanted any Democratic tariff programme, but because they felt, as I do, that the tariff as a whole is a mass of favors granted to special interests, and experience has shown that the Republican party cannot extricate itself enough to serve the whole people. They chose the party which was the freer of the two along that line."

"What should the Democratic party now do to retain its success?"

"Well, this period distinctly disconnects the Democratic party with any of the unfortunate factional differences existing in its ranks in earlier times, and therefore Democrats are fortunate in being able now to act without reviving old differences or even remembering them."

"Do you really think that is possible?"

"I do, indeed. I feel confident of it. The present is not a turning back to this, that or the other wing of the party, because the old differences are forgotten in the presence of the new situation. It is a new party to-day. I see no good in mentioning the names of this leader or that—it would merely wound susceptibilities— but it would be as absurd and senseless to return to the party divisions of 1896 as to go back to the dissensions of any former generation."

"Why do you think that the Democratic party can address itself with a new heart to the problems of the country?"

"The situation of the country has been shifting constantly and rapidly since the party differences of 1896."

"But it is the same party, Mr. Wilson."

"The new elements which have come into the Democratic party, making it in one sense a new party, bring with them the question of what we propose to do with the tariff question as well as other great pending questions. They have turned to the Democratic party, not so much because it has offered a remedy for existing evils, but because they have seen that it is free to act. My own idea is that the tariff should be dealt with schedule by schedule. I have announced my position publicly and definitely. I think it should be the policy of the Democratic party. But President Taft has also declared in favor of a revision of the tariff schedule by schedule. Why then did the people turn to the Democratic party? Because they thought we were likely to do it, were freer to do it."

"What, in your opinion, will happen if the Democratic party should now become conservative, rather than progressive?"

"There is not the least danger of the Democratic party becoming conservative in the reactionary sense in dealing with the question of corporations. The Republican insurgents—again I mean the people and not the leaders—have come to the Democratic party. They have failed to accomplish what they seek through the Republican party and they are not a big enough party themselves to do anything independently. This is the thing I recognize in the result of the last campaign. To-day I can see no great difference between a sincere insurgent Republican and a sincere Democrat."

"Doesn't the defeat of the standpat element and the popular endorsement of the leading Republican insurgents in the last Congress mean that the country is now ready for and expects progressive legislation for the control of corporations?"

Dr. Wilson gently evaded all attempts to drift him into a discussion of definite solutions for tariff or corporation problems. His mind appeared to be concentrated on the fact that with the union of Democrats and insurgent Republicans at the polls last November a practically new Democratic party had come into existence. That seemed to make him hesitate about obtruding advice or views on the party at large.

It will be remembered that in 1896 Mr. Bryan took a somewhat similar view with respect to the alliance of the free-silver Republicans with the Democratic party, and that he refused to continue the fight for tariff reform lest he might lose the sympathy and support of the protectionists among his roaring Republican followers. Again and again prominent Democrats appealed to him not to abandon the issue of tariff reform, which had been the main theme of Democratic appeal and which had given the party its only national victories since the Civil War, but he was governed, not by the Democracy, but by the free-silver Republicans and Populists.

The rush of what Dr. Wilson calls the "free element" of the people to the support of Democratic candidates in the last election has deeply impressed him with the idea that there is a new alignment in national politics and that the Democratic party, having absorbed for the time being the mass of those who followed the insurgent Republican leaders, has become a new party and that it does not have to consider the bitter quarrels of the Bryanites and Clevelandites, but is free to work out a new programme for the relief and advancement of the country.

In dealing with the question of corporate lawlessness Dr. Wilson has put himself on record in favor of the theory of personal guilt and has declared that society in enforcing the laws must always find the individual and refuse to allow him to be lost under any cover of corporate disguise. "Government supervision there must be," he has said, "but of the kind that has always been in district attorneys' offices; not the kind that seeks to determine the processes of business, but the kind that brings home to individuals the obligations of the law," to which he added: "Government must regulate, not as a superintendent does, but as a judge does; it must safeguard, it must not direct."

It was odd to find the university president suddenly turned political leader showing such reluctance in sounding keynotes for his party, especially after he had shown such reckless bravery and dashing methods in his attack upon the powerful Democratic bosses of New Jersey. Yet no one could look into those sincere, intelligent gray eyes and mark the frank, open expression of that thin, pale face, without feeling that Dr. Wilson's reserve was due to a desire for Democratic party harmony along the lines of a new alliance rather than to timidity or craftiness.

"But, Dr. Wilson, you have not yet made it quite plain whether you think now, and as the result of the last election, that the Democratic party should follow a progressive policy respecting the regulation and control of corporations?"

A smile came into the gray eyes. Dr. Wilson hesitated for a moment and shifted in his seat.

"It is not easy to make a direct and compact answer to so broad a question," he said. "I think that the position of the Democratic party ought to be, as I know my own position is, that in touching capital and labor, producer and consumer, and other similar apparently competitive interests or classes, we should seek not to set interest against interest, but to find and serve the common interest, with a capital C and a capital L. We should not array ourselves on one side or the other, but should act for the benefit of both. It would be a great mistake for the Democratic party to make itself the representative of any special interest or to encourage warfare between interests in the country. The scale of modern business is so enormous at the present time that to settle such questions as trouble capital and labor, for instance, requires a touch of actual statesmanship.

"The success of business cannot be judged by the mere profits of one interest. It is always a mistake to look at the thing that way. My formula is this: You can't produce prosperity by exploitation, because the prosperity is only that of the exploiter, and a well-served people make prosperous business. Business may be prosperous while the people are miserable. That is undeniable. The statesmanship of business consists in seeing that the prosperity of the community is an indispensable basis for the permanent success of big business."

Dr. Wilson's long arm moved out impressively and he seemed to take aim with his forefinger. The whole man came into the strong angular countenance.

"The sympathetic service of the people is the only permanently profitable thing. The more you think of it, the more experience you have, the more you see of the clash of interest with interest, the plainer these ideas appear. Such conceptions are the true basis of progressive legislation. The Democratic party is bound by every principle and every sympathy it has ever had to serve the people in the most intelligent and progressive manner possible. This is an age of readjustment. Reaction is impossible, and progress, not only imperative, but hopeful, if you know what you are after.["]

"What is the meaning of the doubling of the Socialist vote in the recent elections?"

"I think it means an increasing dissatisfaction with the vague and unfulfilled programmes of the other parties. If the conservatives do not do things, the radicals will."

"Can you not indicate more explicitly what you think ought to be done about the tariff and about the control of corporations?"

"I believe that the country is determined to have the tariff reformed and business corporations regulated intelligently and effectively, and the Democratic party must be its servant in effecting these purposes.

"If the Democratic party should now be conservative in that sense it will undoubtedly become a permanent minority. There can be no doubt about it. That will be the certain result."

"Would that mean the rise of a new party, with the Democratic and Republican progressives as a nucleus?"

"No, certainly not. I can hardly see anything around which a new party could crystallize. But we shall not come to that. I believe that the Democratic party in its new situation will be able to find new and effective remedies."

"But what should the Democratic party now do?"

"It must show that it knows how to revise the tariff and to attack the corporation problem. The people have not ratified any Democratic plans, but have authorized it to make plans."

"Which of the two is the most important?"

"They are equally important. The tariff system and the great corporations are closely connected; you cannot separate them in considering a remedy. The truth is that the present tariff is not a system of protection, but a system of favors and, in its present form, it does not deserve the support even of those who believe in the principle of protection."

Printed in the *New York American*, Dec. 18, 1910; several editorial headings omitted.

To Winifred Jones[1]

My dear Miss Jones,   Princeton, New Jersey 18 Dec., 1910.

It was delightful to be with you when I was in Chicago, and I owe you and your uncle[2] a real debt of gratitude for your kindness. You make me feel like a familiar friend, and it is a real privilege.

Please give my warm regards to your uncle and to all your household,—which I hope is by this time reunited. I reached home well, and committed the indiscretion of another speech, at the dinner of the Southern Society in New York on Wednesday evening.

With warmest regard,
                    Sincerely Yours,   Woodrow Wilson

ALS (Mineral Point, Wisc., Public Library).
    [1] Daughter of David Benton Jones.
    [2] Thomas Davies Jones, with whom Wilson had stayed during his recent trip to Chicago.

From Joseph M. Noonan

My dear Governor: Jersey City, N. J. Dec. 18th 1910

The "statement," which I read to you over the 'phone a week ago last Friday, I took to Mr Davis the next day and, on reading it, he said it was entirely satisfactory in its main features and that he would issue it about the middle of last week. The amendments which he suggested were two in number and quite trivial—one pointing out explicitly that his promise to Smith was made three months before the primaries, the other declaring that he always held his word sacred. His failure to publish it is, I am told, due to Smith's assertion, which appeared in the newspapers last Tuesday, that Davis had not made any promise to him, or said any thing at all to him, in reference to the Senatorship. I suppose Smith made that assertion in order to lend some sort of color to the fiction that he was in doubt up to last Thursday as to whether or not he would be a candidate. His assertion, if he really made it, is quite as false as his pretended doubt about his own candidacy.

But of one thing you may be absolutely certain; and that is that the position which you have taken, in reference to the great political principle involved in the Senatorial situation, has the practically unanimous approval of public opinion in this community. Even the most uncompromising politicians of the old regime are agreed that, however honorably binding on Mr Davis his engagements to Smith may be, the sole hope of the people and of the Democracy, in this crisis, lies in the success of the wise, patriotic and courageous policy to which you are committed and for which you are contending. I wish I could be of some real service to you in the struggle in which you are engaged.

If you should be able to anticipate a possible half hour of leisure sometime between now and the opening of the legislative session I should like very much to have a talk with you about some matters which, I think, may prove of some interest respecting legislation.

With best wishes I am

Very respectfully and cordially Yours   Jos. M. Noonan

ALS (WP, DLC).

From Thomas Bell Love

My dear Mr. Wilson: Dallas, Texas December 19, 1910.

I have received your favor of December 9th.,[1] and thank you for it very much.

I shall be very glad to have such documents and literature as you may be able to have sent me conveniently from time to time.

In my own way I have been endeavoring to ascertain the attitude of Hon. W. J. Bryan, who is now sojourning in this State, towards the end I have in view, and to-day was apprised by a mutual friend with whom Mr. Bryan has recently communicated on the subject, that he (Bryan) made the statement that "Governor-Elect Wilson is covering himself with glory by his course in the matter of the election of a United States Senator from New Jersey."

I think it well that you should be informed of this manifestation of his feeling at this time.

Knowing how thoroughly your time must be taken up, I shall not presume to burden you with communications calling for a reply, but from time to time I may take the liberty of keeping you informed as to the course of affairs in which I think you are likely to be interested in this section, without expecting any reply to my letters.

I am,   Very cordially yours,   Thos B Love

TLS (WP, DLC).
¹ It is missing.

From Wallace McIlvaine Scudder

Newark, New Jersey
My dear Doctor Wilson: December 19, 1910.

In accordance with your wish expressed in yours of the 17th, I have asked to see Mr. Gregory[1] and I heard from him that he would be at my office tomorrow morning, when I shall be glad to give him any suggestions that I may think of, to help.

I have also thought of speaking to Senator Osborne. These younger men are in the fighting line and it seems hard to drag out older men, who may be more or less sympathetic, but for business reasons, do not care to be prominent in any disturbance.

Mr. Fordyce,[2] the Vice-President of the Bipartizan Direct Primary League, was in my office the other morning. I suggested to him the same line of action as far as possible. Of course, I had to do it rather delicately and suggested that he consult with Mr. Frank Sommer,[3] for his Progressive Republicans.

I had a little talk with Mr. Lindabury on the same subject, the other morning. He saw me before election and urged me to do all I could for your success, and also assured me that it was impossible for Mr. Smith to reach the Senatorship. I told him I thought it was up to men like himself, now that the election was over, to give you what support they could. He said he had never been approached for advice and felt delicate about offering any. I do not know how enthusiastic Mr. Lindabury is over the so-called Progressive movement of today. Of course in my work I avoid taking any active party position, but I should be glad at any time if I could be of service to you in the cause of good government.

Very sincerely yours,   Wallace M. Scudder

TLS (WP, DLC).

¹ Julian Arthur Gregory, Princeton 1897, Democrat and lawyer of New York, who had recently been elected Mayor of East Orange, N. J. He was one of a group of Essex County progressives who had organized the Direct Primary League to oppose James Smith, Jr.

² Alexander Robert Fordyce, Jr., Princeton 1896, who practiced law in New York and lived in Dayton, N. J.; Republican assemblyman, 1904-1905.

³ Frank Henry Sommer, prominent lawyer, member of the firm of Sommer, Colby and Whiting of Newark, Sheriff of Essex County, 1905-1908, progressive Republican and associate of Everett Colby in the New Idea movement in New Jersey, about which see n. 1 to the news report printed at Nov. 10, 1905, n. 1, Vol. 16.

From Alexander Jeffrey McKelway

Dear Dr. Wilson: Washington, D. C., Dec. 19, 1910.

Your letter of December 17th just received. I hope indeed that you can be with us at the meeting of the National Child Labor Committee in Birmingham in March. Apropos of Speaker Cannon's attack upon you, last week,¹ which was one of the best things that could have happened, you may be interested to know that Senator Purcell² told me that Senators Keen and Briggs, of New Jersey, were greatly interested in the candidacy of Ex-Senator Smith. While I am not partisan enough to believe that no Republican has anything to do with the election of a Democratic Senator, this is not the kind of Republicans whose interference is desired. I presume that the time will come when Senator Smith will have to be attacked on his record during the tariff controversy of 1893 and 94.

Following the Catchings letter, written by Mr. Celveland [Cleveland],³ you will find an excellent editorial in the Brooklyn Eagle excoriating the Big Four in the Senate,⁴ who had been denounced for their treachery by Mr. Cleveland.⁵ I should be glad to look that up for you, and other editorials of the same nature, in the Library [of Congress] here, if you care to have me do so.   Cordially yours,   A. J. McKelway.

TLS (WP, DLC).

¹ Joseph Gurney Cannon, Speaker of the House of Representatives, had delivered a "vitriolic" attack on Wilson at a banquet of the New Jersey Society of Pennsylvania in Philadelphia on December 17, 1910, according to a news account in the Newark Evening News, Dec. 19, 1910. Cannon's objective, the story said, was to help his friend, James Smith, Jr., "to squirm back" into the Senate. The Speaker was particularly incensed, the report continued, by Wilson's "assumption of the leadership of his party, and of the Legislature, in opposing the return of former Senator Smith," and he "deplored the undue activity of these new-risen leaders, who would usurp, without constitutional authority, the rights of the Legislature to choose whom they saw fit to represent the State

in the National Congress." Cannon was then quoted as follows: "Here we have a man who declares in a public statement to the electors that he would oppose to the extent of his power and influence the election of a former United States Senator to the same office this year, and would insist (mark the word) upon the election of a man who, practically alone, submitted his claim to the members of his party at the primary, and who received less than one-fourth the votes of the party as recorded at the next election. Remember that he says this, in spite of the fact that only one member of the Legislature is pledged to follow the result of that primary, which in itself is not compulsory, but only optional with the Legislature."

2 William Edward Purcell, Democrat of North Dakota.

3 In his letter to Representative Thomas Clendinen Catchings of Mississippi, Aug. 27, 1894, Cleveland had explained his decision to permit the Wilson-Gorman tariff bill to become law without his signature. The letter was printed widely in the press at the time and may be found in Allan Nevins (ed.), *Letters of Grover Cleveland, 1850-1908* (Boston and New York, 1933), pp. 364-66.

4 No issue of the *Brooklyn Daily Eagle* with this editorial is extant.

5 For a discussion of Cleveland's denunciation of the senators who had succeeded in amending the Wilson tariff bill, see G. L. Record to WW, Oct. 17, 1910, n. 13, Vol. 21.

From George Brinton McClellan Harvey

Dear Mr. Wilson: New York December 19, 1910.

Is there not an opportunity to do a master-stroke in your inaugural by aiming at something concrete in the way of rectifying the abuses that have grown up in connection with cold storage warehouses? As you are doubtless aware, the law of supply and demand has been wholly subverted by the united action of the big trusts through their control of these warehouses. Take eggs alone—I understand that there are now in the warehouses in New Jersey something like 600,000,000 dozen. They are kept without regard to loss of nutrition or any other consideration for any length of time necessary to keep the market price artificially high. The same iniquitous policy is pursued in regard to beef, mutton and poultry; heedless of the fact that it has been scientifically demonstrated that food-stuffs kept beyond a certain period lose much of their efficiency and indeed become positively unwholesome.

Now it seems to me that here is a very vital matter whose rectification by the State through legislation providing for inspection and regulation as to time, etc. would not only be in itself a notable reform but would stand out in a most striking manner as an illustration of your determination to see that the State does its whole duty in order that the Federal government may be relieved of the necessity of constant interference. Also the plan is practical if statutes could be enacted forbidding the storage of such products beyond the period demonstrated to be fit and proper. The products would be put upon the market while they were still wholesome and the prices would follow the law of supply and demand. It is needless, of course, for me to point out to you that the most urgent and popular cry at the present time is for some definite and concrete method of placing the cost of living upon a natural basis in place of the artificial standard now maintained, under which these greedy and conscienceless men do not merely hesitate to filch excessive sums from the pockets of the people but even go so far as to imperil the health of the community. All New Jersey and all New York, to say nothing of the rest of the country, would, in my judgment, rise up in glad acclaim at such an instance of your putting your finger on the root of the evil and pointing the simple way to eradicate it. Of course, the scoundrels who profit from such outrageous treatment of the public would raise a howl against attacking a State industry and would threaten to transfer their plants to New York. This would have no effect whatever. New Jersey would, at any rate, be doing her full duty; New York would have to follow suit, and as it happens, these great warehouses have to be located near the great markets. There have been many spasmodic investigations of these conditions, but they have all come to nothing. I think Kincaid[1] has a bill now pending in Congress; but that is the very kind of a thing that ought to be averted as unnecessary. These various inquiries, however, have doubtless brought out all of the bitter facts that would be required for your preliminary purpose.

I should think it probable that Tumulty or Sullivan would have them at their fingers' ends. If not, or if you should prefer, I will put Inglis[2] on the job and have him dig out the data. It really impresses me as being a most rare opportunity for a masterstroke at the psychological moment. I hope you will think so, too.

As ever,   Faithfully yours,   George Harvey

TLS (WP, DLC).
   [1] Eugene Francis Kinkead, Democratic congressman from New Jersey.
   [2] That is, William Otto Inglis.

From John Jacob Lentz[1]

My dear Sir,   Columbus, Ohio December 19, 1910.

It has been my intention for several days to write you expressing my most cordial appreciation of the progressive spirit and Jacksonian courage shown in your endorsement of the Honorable James E. Martine for United States Senator, inasmuch as the people had so declared when the matter was before them.

I am going to take the liberty of sending an editorial from the Detroit Times with reference to my own candidacy for the senatorship in Ohio and a leaflet issued in connection with my work as National President of the American Insurance Union.[2] I might send you many others from our local papers, but I know you have no time for reading these. Hence shall not burden you with them. All I want to do is show that I belong and have belonged to that class of progressive Democrats, who have been fighting for the last fourteen years for honest government.

I looked with a trifle of suspicion upon your nomination for governor and have watched you most carefully and I know that I express what is substantially the opinion of the leading thinking Democrats of this state, and they are the progressive Democrats of this state and of these, as you know, Ohio has many.

I do not agree with George Washington that "Honesty is the best policy." I have modified the expression and say that "Honesty is the greatest ability," and my one hope is that we may have more of it among our executives and legislators.

I have had the pleasure of a call from our mutual friend Al Dulin[3] of the Tammany Times. I recently spent a good part of a day with Henry George, Jr.,[4] and they are certainly as well pleased as I am with the evidence you give of that high moral and political purpose, which lifts one so far above the level of that other class, who are spoken of as the catering and cringing politician.

May the good work go on and may your shadow never gros [grow] less is the wish of,

                    Yours faithfully,   John J. Lentz

TLS (WP, DLC).
    [1] Congressman from Ohio, 1897-1901, and a leader of the progressive faction in the Democratic party in Ohio. At this time he was practicing law in Columbus in the firm of Lentz, Karns and Linton.
    [2] They are missing.
    [3] The Editors have been unable to identify him further.
    [4] Unsuccessful mayoral candidate of "The Democracy of Thomas Jefferson" in New York in 1897, nominated to replace his father, who had died suddenly during the campaign; at this time a newspaper correspondent; Democratic congressman from New York, 1911-15.

A News Report

                                        [Dec. 20, 1910]

DR. WILSON REPLIES TO HIS PRIMARY CRITICS

PRINCETON, Dec. 20.—Upon his return to his home last night,[1] Governor-elect Wilson reiterated that there will be no extensive stumping tour on his part against James Smith Jr.

"It isn't necessary to rouse public opinion against Smith, because public opinion is already against him," he declared.

"How are you going to get the legislators to vote for Mr. Martine, even though public opinion is against Smith?" was asked.

"I suppose that some of them will hold out to the end," said Dr. Wilson, "but before January 24 most of them will know where they stand and what their constituents want them to do. The party is committed to the principle of a popular expression of opinion concerning the Senatorship election, and I do not see how there is reason for even a caucus on the subject."

Dr. Wilson was asked about the stock objections to his stand —the fact that a small part of the Democratic electorate had preferred Martine and the allegations about Martine's qualifications.

"Mr. Martine is the party's primary choice, and if the voters did not express an opinion it is their own fault," said Dr. Wilson. "Mr. Martine is an able and honest man, and he has served the party faithfully for many years. If you argue on the basis that men did not vote for him you can as well say that Harmon was not elected in Ohio, because hundreds of Republicans stayed away from the polls on election day."

Dr. Wilson requested that note be made of the fact that the ball scheduled for January 17, following his inaugural reception at the State House, was to be given by the Second Regiment at its armory and that he will be the guest of the regiment. The ball is not to be an expense to the State and is to be given by the regiment as a regiment and not for the Governor alone.

Printed in the *Newark Evening News*, Dec. 20, 1910; one editorial heading omitted.

1 He had been in Trenton conferring with certain Democratic leaders, including Harry V. Osborne, Joseph P. Tumulty, and Mark A. Sullivan. According to newspaper accounts (*Trenton Evening Times*, Dec. 19 and 20, 1910; *Newark Evening News*, Dec. 19 and 20, 1910), the conferees agreed that Wilson would launch his campaign against Smith with speeches in Jersey City and Newark and, if deemed necessary, would also speak in Morris, Middlesex, and Monmouth counties.

To John Joseph Bracken[1]

My dear Mr. Bracken: Princeton, N. J. December 20th, 1910

I expect to spend Thursday afternoon, the 22nd, in New York at the Collingwood Hotel, 45 West 35th St. It would gratify me very much if you could make it convenient to call on me there some time between the hours of two and five.[2]

Cordially and sincerely yours,   Woodrow Wilson

TLS (received from John J. Bracken, Jr.)
 1 Democratic assemblyman-elect from Essex County and a civil engineer in the landscape gardening business in Newark.
 2 A news report of this conference is printed at Dec. 23, 1910.

From Henry Eckert Alexander

Dear Mr. Wilson: Trenton, N. J. December 20, 1910.

The thought that I had in mind for your "manifesto" was that the legislators who stand by Martine and against any senatorial caucus are the *regulars* and *regularity* is the pretended life and breath of organization men.

I shall have for your own personal inspection a copy of Mr. Bryan's letter to Mr. Birch[1] which will come to me through General Grubb.[2] He is pleased with your Record letter and with your endorsement of Martine and repudiation of Smith. He will print your Record letter in the Commoner and also an editorial on the Martine endorsement.[3] All of which is interesting and significant.   Sincerely yours,   H. E. Alexander.

I thought that Mr. Van Valkenburg's editorial[4] was fine.

ALS (WP, DLC).
 1 William Jennings Bryan's friend, Thomas Howard Birch of Burlington, N. J., prominent in state Democratic politics, colonel in the New Jersey militia, and head of a carriage business founded by his father, who had also been a close friend of Bryan. Wilson appointed Birch as his military aide in 1911 and as Minister to Portugal in 1913.
 2 Edward Burd Grubb, breveted brigadier general by Congress in 1865 for "gallant and meritorious conduct" during many battles; unsuccessful Republican candidate for Governor of New Jersey in 1889; head of his family's iron manufacturing concern in Burlington, N. J.; at this time a member of the board of managers of the Disabled Soldiers' Home in Kearny, N. J. Wilson appointed him superintendent of the home in 1911.
 3 Wilson's letter to George Lawrence Record, printed at Oct. 24, 1910, Vol. 21, was never reproduced in Bryan's weekly, *The Commoner*, of Lincoln, Neb. However, Bryan did print Wilson's statement of December 8, 1910, opposing Smith's candidacy, together with a brief editorial entitled "Good for Governor Wilson." It praised Wilson for having served notice on Smith that he would not "stand for any candidate for the United States senate other than James E. Martine who was nominated at the primary last October." *The Commoner*, x (Dec. 23, 1910), 2.
 4 An editorial entitled "Woodrow Wilson Will Win," Philadelphia *North American*, Dec. 20, 1910, strongly supporting Wilson in the senatorial controversy and saying, among other things: "Out of the American political Nazareth, New Jersey, has come 1910's best boon to this nation—the sight of Woodrow Wilson fighting a good fight of patriotism and civic purification—a man of peace appealing to the sword because he disdains peace that is not honorable; the man of the hour of epochal exigency, abandoning the easy road of self-advancement because it is not in his nature to be false to himself or to the people of whom he is a born leader because he trusts them so implicitly. That splendid fight just beginning by Woodrow Wilson to save his state from the shame of sending James Smith to the United States senate is far and away above being any mere party matter. . . . Willingly or unwillingly, consciously or unwittingly, New Jersey is destined to political regeneration by the gift that has come to the country of this one pure patriot and first-rate fighting man."

From Cleveland Hoadley Dodge

My dear Woodrow: New York December 20, 1910.

I do not want to bother you with too many gushing letters, but I cannot help expressing to you my great joy and delight that you have taken the splendid stand which you have in the Senatorial fight. I have thought very often lately, in connection with what you are doing, of the truest words that were ever spoken, that "he who loseth his life shall save it." You are doing a perfectly splendid and courageous act in standing out the way you are, and although you are doing it from the highest principle, it seems to be proving the best kind of politics. The saddest regret which I have in your new political work is the fact that I do not seem to have a chance of seeing you.

Please do not bother to answer this letter, but if you are ever coming to town for the day, and can take lunch with me, or if you will spend the night with us at 90 Park Avenue, I shall be perfectly delighted if it is even to catch a glimpse of you.

With warm regards to Mrs. Wilson and the girls, wishing you all the compliments of the season, and with best wishes for the success of your glorious fight,

Yours affectionately,   C H Dodge

TLS (WP, DLC).

From William Pierce Macksey

My dear Mr. Wilson: Newark, N. J. December 20, 1910.

I have your letter of December 17, asking for a personal interview on the afternoon of December 21st. and will say that I will be very glad to see you and talk over the sityation [situation].

Together with several of the other Essex Assemblymen elect we will leave Newark about 4.30 P.M. and arrive at Princeton about 5.30 P.M.

Very Sincerely yours,   Wm. P. Macksey

TLS (WP, DLC).

From Calvin Easton Brodhead

My Dear Governor: [New York] Dec. 20, 1910.

Since seeing you yesterday I have had three different men, all exercising considerable influence in various spheres, call on me in the interest of Senator Smith. I only refer to this to illustrate the efforts that are being put forth to line up the legislators for him. I suppose every other Assemblyman is experiencing the same thing. I hope everybody will stand firm. Your suggestion about our having a meeting and lining up our forces seems most necessary.

I could not get hold of Streitwolf today but will get him tomorrow sure. I am told that while he has said he would not vote for Smith, he has not committed himself to Martine. This much at least is encouraging.   Sincerely,   Calvin E. Brodhead

TLS (WP, DLC).

From Joseph Patrick Tumulty

My dear Governor: Jersey City [N. J.] Dec. 20, 1910.

We conferred last night regarding a meeting in Jersey City, and concluded that the most effective meeting could be held between January 3rd and January 7th, and that January 9th, which, I understand, is an open date for you, is too late a day to begin the campaign.

Will you kindly let me know at once whether you can speak here on any of the following dates: January 3rd, 4th, 5th, or 6th.[1]
                    Sincerely yours,   J. P Tumulty

TLS (WP, DLC).
[1] Wilson spoke on the senatorial situation in Jersey City on January 5, 1911. His address is printed at that date.

From James Lafferty[1]

Dear Governor: Sewell, N. J., Dec. 20 1910

I have informed Jas Smith Jr that I can not support him for U. S. Senator. After making a careful canvass of Gloucester Co. I find 90 per ct of the voters opposed to his candidacy. Hoping you win your Senatorial fight, and that we may be able to carry out our pre election promises to the letter, I remain
                    Yours truly   James Lafferty.

ALS (WP, DLC).
[1] Assemblyman-elect of Gloucester County, in the lumber business in Sewell, N. J.

From Edward Wallace Scudder

Dear Governor: Newark, New Jersey December 20, 1910.

Enclosed you will find the clippings you spoke about the other night, also what we have since said on the Senatorial issue.[1]

I enclose my check for the telephone call that you were so kind as to allow me to use.

Many thanks for your kindness in granting me an interview, and I regret my belated arrival and rather unceremonious departure.   Sincerely yours,   Edward W Scudder

TLS (WP, DLC).
    ¹ They are all missing. The *Newark Evening News* had been in the vanguard of the fight against Smith's election.

From Francis Wrigley Hirst

Dear Sir   New York Dec 20. 1910

I fancy from the newspapers that you may be too busy to see strangers. But if you have five or ten minutes available on Friday morning I should like to pay a brief visit to Princeton returning here in time for lunch.

There is much (and legitimate) curiosity among English free traders about the policy which you are formulating; and after having had the privilege of a talk with Senator La Follette I should very much like to supplement it by hearing however briefly the opinions of the Governor Elect of New Jersey
                         Yours very sincerely   F W Hirst

ALS (WP, DLC).

Ellen Axson Wilson to Frederic Yates

My Dear Mr. Yates,   Princeton, New Jersey Dec. 20, 1910

Just a hurried line to *beg* that you will come to us for Christmas! I am ashamed not to have written before, for of course we have been *counting* upon you at that time. But we have been so absorbed in politics and the wedding (which is on the 31st)¹ that Christmas has leaped upon us unawares. In fact we do not propose to make any "fuss" over it at all this year, we havn't either the time or the money. But that only makes us want *you* all the more. Yet since I know you will have a jollier time at Beechwood I feel constrained to add that we will not feel "hurt" if you elect to stay there and come to us some other day. In any case we must see you soon.

Our warmest congratulations on the Vanderlip portrait. How eager I am to see them all!

Please excuse this scrawl—*so busy*! My brother has been and is still seriously ill;—so that my load has been pretty heavy of late. He is a little better now. It is another nervous breakdown.

We had a charming letter from Mrs. Yates.[2] Please thank her for us.

Hoping to see you soon, I am

Sincerely your friend,   Ellen A. Wilson.

ALS (photostat in RSB Coll., DLC).
  [1] Wilson's niece, Annie Wilson Howe, was to be married in the First Presbyterian Church of Princeton to Perrin Chiles Cothran of Greenwood, S. C. Wilson gave the bride away.
  [2] This letter from Emily Chapman Martin Yates is missing.

An Interview

[Dec. 21, 1910]

The Evening World to-day presents the views of the three principals in the Senatorial fight now at its height in New Jersey —a contest that is attracting national interest. It is the purpose of The Evening World to give to the public an insight into the character of these men and an accurate and authoritative statement of their motives and the principles which actuate them. . . .

It was Gov.-elect Wilson who fired the opening gun in the war by his declaration, two days before former Senator Smith openly announced his candidacy, that the people of New Jersey did not want Smith for Senator and that Martine must be chosen by the Legislature. As the basis of this manifesto, the Governor-elect cited the result of the primary in which Martine, the "farmer orator" of Plainfield, received 48,000 votes and his only opponent, a lawyer who only a few years ago was disbarred,[1] received 15,000.

Though Dr. Wilson now declares that he stands unwaveringly by the result of that primary, he admits that two days before he declared himself and before former Senator Smith formally entered the field, he proposed a compromise candidate to Mr. Smith.

When a reporter called on Dr. Wilson at his Princeton home the Governor-elect expressed a willingness to discuss the senatorial situation freely.

"My only restriction," he said, "is that you do not use quotation marks. You are at liberty to use the facts I give you in the form of a third person intereview. I shall be glad to answer any questions, but this matter is of such importance that I am afraid some misconstruction might be applied to my words if they appeared coldly within quotation marks."

"What is the ground for your declaration that Mr. Martine must be elected United States Senator?" the reporter asked.

Dr. Wilson replied that it was an absolute moral obligation which the Democratic party was bound to carry out if it kept faith with the people.

"Do you consider that obligation binding to such an extent that you would have insisted upon the selection of McDermitt if he had received a majority of the votes cast at the primary?"

The reply was that there could be no such supposition. The people of the State of New Jersey would never have made such a mistake, Dr. Wilson declared.

"Would you accept a compromise candidate in place of Mr. Martine?"

No compromise could be entertained, the Governor-elect said.

"But did you not go to Mr. Smith two days before you announced your opposition to him and suggest a compromise candidate?"

Dr. Wilson frankly admitted that he had made such an offer, but said that it was before he had a full knowledge of his duty or of the men.[2]

When asked if he intended to take the stump and appeal to the people in the interest of the "farmer orator," Dr. Wilson said that he should not organize any meetings, but that he stood ready to accept invitations to speak.

"Are you exerting your influence as a private citizen or as Governor?" was asked.

The Governor-elect replied, "Both." He said he felt that he was qualified to speak for the Democratic party, as the people had elected him the party leader.

Printed in the New York *Evening World*, Dec. 21, 1910; some editorial headings omitted.

[1] That is, Frank M. McDermit of Newark.

[2] In a statement issued the following day, Wilson said:

"I authorize you to deny emphatically and most positively the statements published in a New York and a Newark evening paper yesterday, and in some other papers this morning, that I ever offered a compromise candidate for United States Senator, in any interview with James Smith Jr."

"Mr. Wilson," the report embodying the statement said, "asserted that he had plainly denied to the reporter who came to see him that he had proposed a compromise candidate. The statement to the opposite was regarded by Mr. Wilson as a perversion of what he told the interviewer." *Newark Evening News*, Dec. 22, 1910.

To Henry Skillman Breckinridge

My dear Breckinridge: Princeton, N. J. December 21, 1910

You are very generous and your letter of December 17th has given me a great deal of pleasure.

I feel a most unaffected modesty about the plan you suggest of forming a young men's club all over the country but undoubtedly you are right that it is none too early to begin and I wish that I were not such an amateur in matters of this kind as to be the last to offer advice as to method and effective proceedure.

No doubt Colonel Harvey could give you useful advice in the matter but my own judgment, if I may speak confidently [confidentially], is that it would not do to have Colonel Harvey himself direct the plans. He is universally associated in the minds of Democrats throughout the country with the particular Wall Street influence of which they are most jealous. He is known as concerned with my entrance into public life as I find cases of real suspicion upon my methods and connections among those whose confidence it would be most necessary to win if a movement for my nomination in 1912 were to be undertaken. Of course the mere performance of my duty here in fighting Ex-Senator Smith, who has the same Wall Street label upon him, is doing a great deal to remove the impression so far as I am concerned, but you will see that it would not be wise to have Colonel Harvey as a public sponsor.

There is in Washington a Mr. John E. Lathrop (c/o The News Incorporated) whose acquaintance I have just made, who seems to be one of the most wide-awake and well informed men I have known. If you could run down and have a talk with him I am sure that he perhaps better than any other man I now know, could put you in the way of plans that would be a "go."

I advise in this matter with genuine diffidence but I cannot turn away from your generous kindness, and nothing would make me brighter or happier than to have you interest yourself in this matter, or to have my candidacy suggested by bodies of young men throughout the Union. They are my actual colleagues and friends.

With warmest regards and real affection,

                    Sincerely yours,   Woodrow Wilson

TLS (H. S. Breckinridge Papers, DLC).

To Cleveland Hoadley Dodge

My dear Cleve: Princeton, N. J. December 21, 1910

God bless you for your letter of December 20th. You do not know what warmth it brought to the corkles [cockles] of my heart or how I blessed you for it. The fight is a tough one and I must say some rough things before it is over but it is positively the right thing to do and it is delightful to know that you are thinking of me.

Always affectionately yours,   Woodrow Wilson

TLS (WC, NjP).

To Calvin Easton Brodhead

My dear Mr. Brodhead: Princeton, N. J. December 21, 1910

I was greatly strengthened by my conversation with you the other day and want to thank you for your kind letter of yesterday. It is certainly extraordinary the efforts the Smith forces are making. Your statement in the papers[1] as I saw it seemed to me admirable in every respect. We must certainly stand together in this good cause and I shall certainly lend my counsels to that end.

With warmest appreciation,

Sincerely yours,   Woodrow Wilson

TLS (received from William M. Brodhead).
[1] A statement, written by Brodhead and signed by more than one hundred of the business and professional men of Plainfield, N. J., strongly endorsing the candidacy of their fellow-townsman, Martine. It was published in the Trenton *True American*, Dec. 21, 1910.

To Thomas McKinsey[1]

Dear Sir: Princeton, N. J. December 21, 1910.

I have read your letter[2] with genuine interest and sympathy. I wish with all my heart there were something I could do for you but it is impossible for anyone outside of your state to assist you and I beg that you will look at life from another point of view. It is not right to desire to have your life taken. Surely you can make it worth while by seeking to keep up the spirits and better the life of those about you.[3]

Sincerely yours,   Woodrow Wilson.

Printed in the *Battle Creek*, Mich., *Journal*, Dec. 27, 1910.
[1] A blind itinerant minister, singer, and street vendor of Battle Creek, Mich., who had written to the governors of Ohio, New Jersey, New York, and West Virginia on December 15, 1910, requesting the use of an electric chair to end his life.
[2] It was printed in the *Battle Creek*, Mich., *Enquirer*, Dec. 16, 1910.
[3] McKinsey was killed on July 30, 1912, by an automobile while he was crossing a street in Battle Creek. *Battle Creek*, Mich., *Evening News*, July 31, 1912.

A Proposed Public Statement[1]

Newark, New Jersey, 21 December, 1910.

We, the undersigned, Assemblymen-elect from the County of Essex, were among those who some weeks ago signed a letter to Mr. James Smith, Jr., asking him to become a candidate for the Senate of the United States. At the time we signed that letter it had been made to appear to us by personal friends of Mr. Smith that it would be to the advantage of the party to have Mr. Smith again in the Senate. Since that time it has become so evident to us that his candidacy is most unwelcome to our constituents and to a large majority of the people of the State that we deem it our duty as representatives to withdraw our support from him and to declare that, as members of the Assembly, we cannot vote for him. It is our painful duty, in view of our present conviction with regard to public policy in this matter, to make this statement, in order that those who elected and trusted us may know our true position.

We deem it our further duty to say that, in view of the sincere advocacy by our party of the principle of the direct primary, we are convinced that it is best for the interest of the party and of the State to cast our votes for James E. Martine, who was the choice of a large majority of the Democratic voters who expressed their preference with regard to the senatorship at the primaries which preceded the recent elections.[2]

WWT MS (WP, DLC).

[1] Prepared by Wilson in the hope that the assemblymen-elect from Essex County would sign it after his conferences with them on December 21 and 22, 1910. Presumably none agreed to sign; in any event, the statement was never issued.

[2] There is a WWsh draft of this statement in WP, DLC.

A News Report

[Dec. 21, 1910]

WILSON NOW SURE OF DEFEATING SMITH

PRINCETON, N. J., Dec. 21.—After a three hours' conference this evening with five members of the Essex County Democratic delegation to the House of Assembly,[1] Governor-elect Woodrow Wilson declared that he was certain James E. Martine would be the next United States Senator from New Jersey.

"Smith will be defeated, and Martine will win. There is not the slightest doubt about that," said Dr. Wilson.

[1] They are identified later in this report.

"There has been some talk of a compromise candidate," suggested THE TIMES correspondent.

"No, Sir; there will be no compromise," said the Governor-elect with a snap.

"Why, I should not be able to sleep soundly a single night were I to recede from the position I have taken in accordance with solemn pledges to the people and later upon any compromise."

"Can Mr. Martine be elected without the Essex County delegation?" Dr. Wilson was asked.

"Yes, he replied emphatically, "even without the Essex County delegation.["]

It was suggested to Dr. Wilson that one reason advanced against the carrying out of the direct primary mandate was that only one-quarter of the Democratic vote came out at the primaries, and that for these reasons the primary verdict on the Senatorship did not really represent the party sentiment.

"I think I know what the people of this States [State] want," he replied. "I have not traveled up and down the State for nothing. I know what the popular feeling on this question is just as plainly as though I had it in writing."

In reply to a question bearing on the suggestion that the Smith-Martine fight and the attitude taken by him might endanger his legislature [legislative] programme, the Governor-elect said:

"I have no fear that the Legislature will go back on our platform pledges. If anything of the kind is attempted, I guess I can make more trouble for them than they can make for me. I will go out and tell the people all about it and let them judge."

There will be fifty-one Democrats—nine Senators and forty-two Assemblymen in the next Legislature. Altogether there are eighty-one members in both houses. Forty-one votes is a majority on a joint ballot. The opinion expressed by Democrats who have called on the Governor-elect to-day is that the best James Smith, Jr., can muster is twenty-five votes.

The five men from Essex, who listened to the pleas of Dr. Wilson in favor of James E. Martine, the primary chosen candidate for the seat in the United States Senate now occupied by John Kean, are pledged in common with the other Assemblymen-elect from Essex, the home county of James Smith, Jr., to support the ex-Senator when the question comes to a vote in the Legislature on Jan. 24. For some time there have been rumors that there might be a break in the Essex delegation, and it is significant that Gov.-elect Wilson, in inviting the prospective members from former Senator Smith's home county, asked the five members, with whom rumor has been busy as men who possibly might flop to Martine, to meet him at his home in Princeton to-night, and that he had made an appointment to meet the remaining six in New York to-morrow afternoon.

The five Assemblymen-elect who called on the Governor-elect are James P. Mylod of Glen Ridge, Charles W. Brown of East Orange, and Frank A. Boettner, William P. Macksey, and Edward D. Ballantine of Newark.

They arrived in Princeton on the 5:37 train and went at once to the residence of Dr. Wilson in the university grounds. He escorted them into his library, where he remained with them behind closed doors until 9 o'clock. Both the Governor-elect and the Assemblymen-elect missed their dinner over the conference.

"It should be understood that I have made no attempt to have these gentlemen or any other Democratic member of the next Legislature pledge themselves to Mr. Martine or any other candidate," said Dr. Wilson after the conference. "My only purpose in inviting prospective members of the Legislature to call on me is to give me an opportunity to make my attitude on the Senatorship and my grounds for taking the position I have perfectly clear."

The Governor-elect added that he had already conferred with all but eight members of the next Legislature, and that he expected to have a talk with these before the Legislature votes on the Senatorship.

The five men from Essex County, before they conferred with the Governor-elect, declared that they were just as firm for ex-Senator Smith as ever and intimated that they might reaffirm their action in asking Smith to become a candidate for United States Senator at a caucus of all the Assemblymen-elect from Essex, which is scheduled for Friday night in Newark. Some of the visitors even expressed annoyance that they should have been asked to attend a conference which they declared could not possibly lead to any result.

James P. Mylod, who acted as spokesman for the little delegation, said after the conference:

"The Governor-elect did not ask us to make any pledges and we did not make any. Dr. Wilson explained his attitude very fully. He took the ground that James E. Martine should be sent to the United States Senate because the voters had expressed a preference for him at the primaries. We had our say also. The conference was very amicable."

"Have the reasons advanced by the Governor-elect convinced you or any of the other members of the next Legislature who called on the Governor-elect this evening that Mr. Martine should have your support?"

"We were not asked to make any pledges and we made none," Mr. Mylod repeated.[2]

---

[2] It is difficult to gauge the impression that Wilson made on this group, for, although three of them—Mylod, Boettner, and Balentine—eventually did withdraw their support from Smith, each claimed to have done so for various reasons.

Mylod, in a statement printed in the *Newark Evening News*, Dec. 23, 1910, announced that he would not vote for Smith and insisted that in changing his mind he had acted "absolutely of his own volition, and independently of the arguments of Governor-elect Woodrow Wilson." He then explained why he had signed the petition asking Smith to become a candidate and why he had altered his position. "The general public," he said, "may believe that I am committed to Mr. Smith in a letter which had been signed by my ten Assembly colleagues on Sunday night, November 20, and brought to me at my home in Glen Ridge about midnight for my signature, which I refused at that time, but which I gave subsequently after going to Newark and conferring with the State chairman and three of the previous signers. Although I signed the letter I stated most emphatically that I believed the invitation to Mr. Smith was the biggest mistake the party could make; that the sentiment of the people was decidedly against Mr. Smith, and that I did so only because I deferred my individual judgment as to the effect of Mr. Smith's candidacy upon the future success of the party, to the combined judgments of the ten other Assemblymen-elect who had hours before signed the letter after what was represented to me as a full, fair, open and frank discussion of the wisdom of the indorsement, but which I now have very good reason to believe was anything but as represented." Becoming convinced that he had been deceived by the arguments in Smith's favor and that the invitation should not have been sent, Mylod went to Smith and told him of the circumstances under which the letter had been signed and made it plain to him that he could no longer support his candidacy. "I feel, therefore," Mylod continued, "that I am in no way pledged to Mr. Smith, and that it is only fair to the people, and a matter of justice to myself, that I should make public announcement of my attitude, for public opinion, after all, is the umpire of a man's character." He concluded by saying that he saw no reason to ignore the results of the senatorial primary, and that he now felt committed to Martine.

Boettner and Balentine did not defect from the Smith ranks until early January 1911. Their reasons for doing so stemmed from a falling out with the former Senator over a municipal appointment in Newark. According to the *Newark Evening News*, Jan. 4, 1911, the two assemblymen-elect had backed John V. Diefenthaler, a Newark businessman, for a position on the Newark Board of Works and understood that they had Smith's promise to support their candidate. However, Smith had failed to do so, and Mayor Jacob Haussling had appointed another man.

Boettner and Balentine lost no time in accusing Smith of bad faith. "I regard Mr. Smith's promise to see the Mayor," Balentine was quoted as saying, "just as sacred as any we made. The question now occupying my attention is as to whether a promise made by me is any weightier than one made by Mr. Smith." "There is no question," Boettner added, "that Diefenthaler is the victim of bad faith. I was with him when the Mayor told him that he intended to leave the filling of the appointment to the Democratic organization. I was with Mr. Balentine also when Senator Smith promised that he would see Mayor Haussling and use his influence with him to bring about the appointment of Diefenthaler. Just who worked the 'doublecross' I don't know, but some one has broken faith."

Boettner, in a brief letter to Smith printed in the *Newark Evening News*, Jan. 10, 1911, informed Smith that he wished to rescind his earlier endorsement of him because, after conferring with a large number of his constituents, he had come to believe that they did not approve his action in signing the letter to Smith. Balentine followed with a letter printed in the *Newark Evening News*, Jan. 12, 1911, in which he offered the same reasons as Boettner for deciding to withdraw his support, adding that he now believed that the

The conference in New York will be held to-morrow afternoon at the Collingwood Hotel, 43 West 53d Street.

Printed in the *New York Times*, Dec. 22, 1910; some editorial headings omitted.

"representations" made in Smith's behalf at the meeting of the Essex assembly-men-elect on November 20 "were not true."
On the crucial first ballot in the legislature on January 24, 1911, Mylod, Balentine, and Boettner voted for Martine.

From George Sebastian Silzer

My dear Doctor: New Brunswick, N. J. December 21, 1910.

I have been thinking over the statement which you read to me yesterday and would suggest revision in one particular.

The strength of your position on all questions has been your absolute frankness, and the fact that your statements are truthful. It is also true that the people have confidence in and admire Mr. Martine.

I have not your statement before me and must rely on my memory. The impression that I received was that you were very fulsome in your praise of Mr. Martine, from which I fear that your statement might lose some of its force. The people are not enthusiastic about Mr. Martine's ability. You could do him justice, and at the same time your statement[,] if more conservative on this point, would have more effect.

I am making this suggestion because I want to see every part of your statement not only truthful but effective, and one which the people will immediately approve.

I have taken the liberty of making this suggestion because you asked me yesterday to do so.[1]

I want also to talk with you about your message, referring particularly to whether ballots should be retained in the polling place or not, as I feel very strongly that it is better not to distribute them. In other words, we lose less by having an honest ballot, than by securing the "vest pocket vote," plus dishonest ballots.   Yours very truly,   Geo. S. Silzer.

TLS (WP, DLC).
[1] Wilson's comments about Martine in his statement printed at Dec. 23, 1910, would indicate that he did not take Silzer's advice.

From August C. Streitwolf, Jr.

My Dear Governor: New Brunswick, N. J., Dec. 21, 1910.

I had luncheon to-day with Mr. Calvin E. Brodhead, Assembly-man-elect of Union County. I want to reassure you that at no time have I regretted the declaration of my position to you, nor need you entertain any fear of a change of my decision.

Mr. Brodhead's remark of surprise at my position is accounted for by my refusal heretofore to commit myself definitely to anyone, except to those with whom I am intimately associated. While the organization is familiar with my views, they are not inclined to accept them as decisive, but continually resort to heavy pressure upon me from every conceivable source in the hope that I might take a change of position.

Respectfully yours,   A. C. Streitwolf Jr

TLS (WP, DLC).

From Leroy J. Ellis

Dear Sir: Plainfield, N. J., December 21, 1910.

I attach hereto copy of resolution passed by this club at its regular meeting last Monday evening. You will note that one of the propositions is that the mass meetings about to be held all over the state, should elect one or more delegates to go before the legislature as soon as it assembles, and demand that they be guided by the voice of the people, as shown at the primaries, in the election of a Senator.[1]

We believe that the mass meetings in themselves will have little effect on the legislature, and that some of them will be failures, and that the most effective way of reaching the legislature will be through appeal to it in person by representative men coming direct from the people.

In the event that the mass meeting should elect delegates for this purpose, do you think there would be any difficulty in their securing a hearing from the legislature, and could we count on your supporting our demand for such hearing?

Before attempting to promote this proposition, I would be glad to know if it meets with your approval. If so, I would like to say that it does meet with your approval in attempting to further the ends sought. If it does not meet with your approval, of course we will drop the proposition.[2]

Yours truly,   L. J. Ellis.

TLS (WP, DLC).

[1] The enclosure, an unidentified newspaper clipping, described the resolution adopted on December 19, 1910, by the Plainfield Democratic Club, of which Ellis was president. In addition to the recommendation mentioned by Ellis, it included an endorsement of Wilson's stand on the senatorial issue and stated that the "failure to elect Mr. Martine would be a specific violation of party pledges and party policy and result in lasting injury to the cause of Democracy."

[2] Wilson's reply is missing, but he probably vetoed the suggestion, as it was never implemented.

From Julian Arthur Gregory

My dear Dr. Wilson: New York December 21, 1910.

I was very pleased to receive your letter of the 17th inst. I note carefully your impressions of Col. [James C.] Sprigg, which are in accord with my own.

Yesterday morning I had a long interview with Mr. Wallace M. Scudder, of the Newark Evening News, relative to the Direct Primary League in Essex County. The conditions in Essex County are peculiar to themselves. I question whether you fully comprehend [comprehend] how many men of standing are afraid to openly oppose James Smith, Jr., though privately ninety per cent. of them have no hesitancy in decrying his candidacy for U. S. Senator. It is difficult therefore to get the men whom we would prefer to act in any public manner.

Senator Osborne and myself are working in the closest harmony, and I think are in accord with what each other is doing. Mr. Scudder I think, approves of what has been done to date. At any rate he had no suggestions to make, to me, [a]long lines different from those we are working on. I shall make it a point to confer with him, and other men in the county in whom I have implicit confidence.

I feel that your chances for success in this fight are very bright, especially if you will tell the public all the facts. The impression is being given in Essex that you considered all during the campaign that James Smith, Jr., was a candidate for U.S. Senate. When the facts are authoritatively published, by you, there will be few left in my judgment in support of Mr. Smith.

Assuring you of my willingness to do all in my power in aid of your fight in the peoples' interest, I remain,

Very respectfully yours,   Julian A. Gregory.

TLS (WP, DLC).

From Joseph M. Noonan

My dear Governor: Jersey City, N. J. December 22nd, 1910.

I enclose original manuscript draft of the statement drawn by me for Mr. Davis[1] and newspaper clipping of his statement actually issued.[2] About the latter I knew nothing, until I saw it in the newspaper. He would have done better, I think, by adhering to the original. In speaking to Mr. Tumulty in reference to the meetings which you may decide to hold for the purpose of bringing the Senatorial situation directly before the people, I ventured to suggest that the formality of selecting a lot of Vice-presidents and Secretaries to sit, in solemn grandeur, on the stage should be dispensed with;—first because the selection of these honorary officers, however comprehensive, must necessarily omit some who would be apt to feel slighted because they were not included; and, secondly, because the practice of having such ornaments at all is a mere piece of antiquated political mechanism designed to lend respectibality to an occasion which otherwise might be suspected of being sadly in need of that quality. You and a local man to introduce you would amply fill the stage; and the departure from the conventional way of doing this business would be sure to impress your audiences with your straight-forwardness, your deep earnestness and your entire and justifiable confidence in them, in yourself and in their and your common cause. But here I am giving advice where none may be needed.

With best wishes for your happiness and success I am,

Yours very sincerely,   Jos. M. Noonan

TLS (WP, DLC).

[1] It is missing, but see J. M. Noonan to WW, Dec. 18, 1910.

[2] The clipping was from the Jersey City *Jersey Journal*, Dec. 21, 1910. "I am sorry," Davis's statement read, "that Governor-elect Wilson and myself are not in accord on the Senatorial question. I understand his position, and I would like others to understand mine. We are both actuated by honest motives, however divergent our views may be." He was supporting Smith, he explained, because he thought that Smith was better qualified for the senatorship than Martine, and also because he had promised Smith to do so. Davis added that he strongly supported an amendment for the direct election of United States senators. However, he went on, the vote for Martine in the senatorial preferential primary had been too small to say that he was the choice of New Jersey Democrats, and none of the Hudson County legislative candidates had pledged that they would be bound by the results of that canvass. For these reasons, the outcome of the senatorial primary had no "weight" with him. The statement concluded with a tribute to Smith's service to the party and the assertion that it was his "influence and efforts" which had made the Democratic victory in 1910 possible.

From Francis Fisher Kane

Dear Doctor Wilson: Philadelphia, December 22nd [1910].

We could not get our rather large committee together until yesterday, but we then had a meeting at which I reported the result of our visit to Princeton last Saturday. I need hardly say that the report gave great satisfaction; that the men were delighted to hear of your promise to come to us on the 21st of February, and that a motion was immediately made and unanimously carried to postpone our banquet until then. As President of the Club I want to thank you again for accepting our invitation, and I desire also in behalf of the Club to assure you of the warm welcome you will receive. Your splendid fight against

Smith is being watched with the keenest interest here in Philadelphia, and it is making friends for you by the thousand.
Whether you succeed or not in preventing his election, you will
have on your side all honest, independent people, and the war
for a free, democratic government will go on, no matter what
may be the result of this first battle.

I can promise you that our dinner as an event will justify, or
at least that we shall try in every way to make it justify, your
acceptance of our invitation.[1] Personally, my pride and joy know
no bounds when I reflect that if I act as toastmaster I shall have
Dr. Wilson on my right hand.

Yours faithfully,   F. F. Kane.

ALS (WP, DLC).
  [1] Wilson's address is printed at Feb. 21, 1911.

From John E. Lathrop

Dear Doctor Wilson: Washington, D. C., Dec. 22, 1910.

I send herewith copy of Senate Document No. 624, Sixty-first
Congress, 2nd Session,[1] printing of which was procured by
Senator Owen and to whom I told your message. The Senator
suggests that I call your attention to a part of the Oklahoma law
which gives the legislature the right to propose a competing
measure, to be submitted under the initiative along with that
measure which has been initiated by petition, and that it gives
the legislature the right also to amend an initiative law. Senator
Owen declares that it works successfully.

Out in Oregon, practically the same arrangement is in effect,
and the legislature has the right to amend any law passed under
the initiative.

I am acknowledging the courtesy shown to me in Princeton
by you, and have many times gone over the delightful interview.
I came away from Princeton distinctly understanding that your
aims are precisely the same as those of the truly progressive men
of the country in both parties. The discussion centers, then,
around the methods to be pursued. Predicating the proposition
upon an absolute faith in the wisdom and conservatism of the
collective electorate, and venturing the opinion that such collective electorate is organic, according to every principle of evolution, my own method would be to step out with sufficient boldness to make the issue distinct. At this juncture in our political
development, to make the government truly representative is the
first desideratum. We must do that first. I believe the initiative

and referendum supply the means of bringing the government back to the people, and I hope very much that in your Inaugural address you will take decided stand in favor of it.

I had an extended conversation with Senator Owen, Senator Chamberlain, Senator Bourne, and several others, and I am glad to say that some impressions, which I frankly told you had been created, were removed by my statements to them.

Your plan, to conduct a referendum of your own, to take the people into your confidence, and to maintain honest and full publicity that the people may know what transpires at Trenton, appeals to them and to me. No man can make up his own political issues. They are forced on him by the evolution of events. In this fight now on, the progressive forces are for the initiative and referendum, and the reactionary forces are for the defeat of those measures. So that, probably, many good men will find themselves in reactionary company, although honestly objecting to these measures and not designing to be reactionary.

I give you good cheer and renew my expression of faith that your position on the pending popular government issues, as set forth in your Inaugural, will instantly constitute you the inevitable leader for 1912. Just as certainly as can be, an advanced stand such as I indicate will, first, be to forward a mighty movement for political salvation and, second, make Woodrow Wilson President, to succeed William H. Taft.[2]

Very truly yours,   John E. Lathrop.

TLS (WP, DLC).

[1] *Representative Government. Circulars of the "Direct Legislation League" of Massachusetts and the State of Washington Relative to "Representative Government," or Initiative, Referendum, and Recall* (Washington, 1910).

[2] For whatever reason, Wilson, in his inaugural address printed at Jan. 17, 1911, did commend to the New Jersey legislature's "careful consideration" the "laws in recent years adopted in the State of Oregon, whose effect has been to bring government back to the people and to protect it from the control of the representatives of selfish and special interests."

A Statement

Princeton, New Jersey, December 23, 1910.

In view of Mr. James Smith, Jr.'s, public avowal of his candidacy for the seat in the Senate of the United States presently to be vacated by the Hon. John Kean, it becomes my duty to lay before the voters of the State the facts as I know them, and the reasons why it seems to me imperative that Mr. Martine and not Mr. Smith should be sent to the Senate.

Before I consented to allow my name to be put before the State Democratic Convention for the nomination as Governor, I asked the gentleman who was acting as Mr. Smith's spokesman if Mr. Smith would desire to return to the Senate, in case the Democrats should win a majority in the State Legislature. I was assured that he would not, I was told that the state of his health would not permit it and that he did not desire it.

Immediately after the election Mr. Smith came to me and said that that had been his feeling before the election, but that he was feeling stronger and hoped that the Legislature would offer him the seat. I pointed out to him that this action on his part would confirm all the ugliest suspicions of the campaign concerning him, and urged him very strongly not to allow his name to be used at all; but my arguments had no effect upon him.

I subsequently learned that before my nomination and at the very time I was told that he would not desire the seat, he had made an agreement with the leader of the Hudson County organization that the votes of the Hudson County members in the Legislature would be cast for him as Senator in case the Legislature should be Democratic. The gentlemen who were to be nominated for the Assembly from Hudson were not consulted; it was an agreement between leaders. The vote was to be turned over to Mr. Smith by the organization in case of a Democratic victory.

Mr. Smith has at last publicly announced his candidacy, but he has been a candidate from the first. Ever since the election he has been using every means at his disposal to obtain the pledges of Democratic members of the Legislature to vote for him as Senator. He has assumed, in dealing with them, that the State organization would be in control of the Legislature; that its offices would be distributed as he should suggest; that members would be assigned to committees and the committees made up as he wished them to be. He has offered to assist members in obtaining membership on such committees as they might prefer. In brief, he has assumed that he and other gentlemen not elected to the Legislature by the people would have the same control over the action of the houses that is understood to have been exercised by the so-called Board of Guardians of the Republican party in recent years.

I said in my former statement regarding this matter that if Mr. Smith should be sent to the United States Senate he would not go as the representative of the people. I meant that he would go as the representative of particular interests in the State, with which it is well known he has always been identified. It is significant that his candidacy is supported by the Camden paper known to be owned or controlled by Mr. David Baird.[1] Mr. John W. Griggs, in a letter recently published,[2] has condemned me for taking any part in this matter and has thereby confirmed the impression that he also has clients who are interested in being represented in the Senate by Mr. Smith. So far as the voters of the State are concerned and the State's essential interests, there is no reason why a change should be made from Mr. John Kean to Mr. James Smith, Jr. They are believed to stand for the same influences and to represent the same group of selfish interests. It should be a matter of indifference to both Republicans and Democrats which of the two represents the State at Washington.

I say these things with genuine regret. I made every possible effort, consistent with dignity and self-respect, to induce Mr. Smith to withdraw from his candidacy. It was my sincere desire that he should earn the credit which is due him for the undoubted service of the Democratic State organization in the recent campaign. By withdrawing he would have won respect and applause and I should have been very glad to join in according him all just praise. I had hoped that it would be possible for me to assume office and enter on the performance of my duties without giving utterance to anything about individuals that would give them pain, or draw me away from the attitude of entire respect which I had tried to maintain. But I have been left without a choice in the matter.

The issue is plain. If Mr. Smith is sent back to the United States Senate, the Democratic party and the State itself is once more delivered into the hands of the very influences from which it had struggled to set itself free. Nothing could have been more unfortunate than Mr. Smith's candidacy. It revives the alarms and prejudices which make fair and just legislation so difficult

[1] The *Camden, N. J., Courier.*

[2] Griggs's letter, which appeared in the press on December 17, 1910, was in fact a message to a Theta Delta Chi fraternity dinner held at the Hotel Astor in New York on December 16. The guest of honor was John Alden Dix, Governor-elect of New York. The *Newark Evening News*, Dec. 17, 1910, quoted large portions of Griggs's letter, adding that it was apparently intended as a "boost for his Democratic friend, James Smith, Jr." Griggs did not mention Smith but compared Wilson and Dix, observing that Dix understood that he would be "only a Governor, not the Legislature and the Governor combined." While Wilson, Griggs continued, would be "spending nights and days and Sundays during his term as Governor of New Jersey in keeping the Legislature of the same mind with himself on all questions, and is stumping the State against the stubborn and perverse members, in order to have people apply to them the compelling lash of public sentiment," Dix would be expending his "high business ability, patient consideration, and sweet reasonableness" in the administration of his office. "It is refreshing," Griggs concluded, "to find a Governor-elect like Brother Dix, who appreciates the limitations of his office, and finds the voice of the people in the established order of government, rather than in transitory and ever-changing ideas given out in political discussion."

and doubtful. It renews and intensifies the struggle between the people and selfish interests, between popular rights and property rights, between privilege and opportunity, which ought to be accommodated by laws which will be fair to all parties. It is a sad circumstance that the conflict must be fought out through this last unfortunate stage. But of course it must be. Mr. Smith and those whom he represents have made it inevitable.

The people must now speak their minds in unmistakable terms to those whom they have chosen to represent them. It must now be determined whether the present members of the Legislature are representatives of the people or puppets of a bi-partisan machine. I believe in organization. I desire to co-operate with Democrats of every affiliation in carrying the party forward by union and harmony of action towards the great service which it can render the country, if it will but be true to its principles. But when organization is used for the elevation and benefit of individuals who do not represent the people, whose interests are opposed to those of the people, I must resist it by every means at my disposal.

Over against all this selfish effort to use a machine, over against all this sinister pressure to put a man into the United States Senate who by common consent will not represent the people, stands the candidacy of Mr. Martine, supported by the votes of a very large majority of the Democrats who chose to express their preference at the primaries. It is my earnest and deliberate judgment that it is the duty of the Democratic members of the Legislature to ratify that expression of preference by electing Mr. Martine a member of the Senate.

The last time a Senator from New Jersey was chosen the party caucus formally indorsed Mr. Martine as its candidate.[3] Three years ago Mr. Smith proposed Mr. Martine for the Governorship. Throughout the Union the Democratic party has turned with greater and greater enthusiasm to the practice of following the preference of the people expressed at the primaries in the choice of Senators. The Democratic party in New Jersey has again and again endorsed the principle and favored the practice. It cannot turn from its duty in this instance without completely discrediting itself and all its professions of faith in this popular and admirable reform.

Mr. Martine is a man of sterling character, of fine fidelity to his party and to its principles, and is considered by those who know him best to be undoubtedly qualified to serve the State well

[3] In 1907. See WW to C. C. Black, Jan. 11, 1907, n. 1, printed as an Enclosure with WW to C. C. Black of the same date, Vol. 16.

and honorably in the Senate. His election will definitely and finally commit the State to the practice of elevating to the Senate men endorsed at the polls by the people. This is the opportunity, the significant and critical opportunity, for the Democratic party to prove its good faith in this cardinal matter of self-government. Confirm the vote of Mr. Martine and the principle of the people's choice is established—will live vitally in practice; ignore it and the people will distrust both primaries and parties. If the present members of the Legislature turn away from the people now they will never again have or deserve another opportunity to enjoy their support and confidence.

The issue is, therefore, not merely an issue between choosing a representative of the people or a representative of the business machine, but an issue between sustaining or rejecting a great principle to which the party is unequivocally committed. I do not see how any true Democrat can in the circumstances doubt his duty or turn away from it to hazard shame and utter discredit.

Woodrow Wilson.[4]

Printed in the *Trenton Evening Times*, Dec. 23, 1910, with a few corrections from the T MS of this statement in WP, DLC.

[4] There is also a TS draft, dated Dec. 23, 1910, of this statement with many WWhw additions and emendations in WP, DLC.

To Various Correspondents

Dear Sir: Princeton, N. J. [c. Dec. 23, 1910]

I know that you will understand why I have not sent a personal reply to your kind letter. Letters have come in to me so much faster than they could be answered by a single secretary that it has been impossible to reply separately to each.

I am taking the liberty of sending you this because I am unwilling that the many friends who have expressed their generous approval and support in the critical matter of the election of a United States Senator from New Jersey, should not know how deeply grateful I am for their generous support, and how proud I am that I should be so sustained and kept in heart.

Sincerely yours,   Woodrow Wilson

Printed letter (WP, DLC).

A News Report

[Dec. 23, 1910]

SUSSEX MAN IS LIKELY WITH WILSON

NEW YORK, Dec. 23.—Governor-elect Woodrow Wilson, of New Jersey, held an all-afternoon conference at a New York hotel yesterday with several newly elected Democratic Assemblymen trying to bring them over to his viewpoint that James E. Martine and not James Smith, Jr., would be the most satisfactory man to represent New Jersey as United States Senator.

Five of the men he labored with were Assemblymen from Essex County, all of whom are said to be strong Smith adherents. Neither Mr. Wilson nor any of his conferees would give any indication, when the meeting was over, as to what the outcome was.

It was the general opinion, however, that not one of the five gave Mr. Wilson any hope that he would support Martine. The Governor-elect had a long talk with two other New Jersey legislators-to-be, Charles H. Meyer,[1] of Sussex County, and Eugene Burke,[2] of Morris. Mr. Meyer after the conference said Mr. Wilson had used many excellent arguments, and that he had come to the conclusion that the Democratic party of New Jersey could not afford to make any misstep in the matter of choosing the right kind of public servants. This was taken to mean that Mr. Meyer had been brought around to take Mr. Wilson's view of the situation.[3]

The five Essex Assemblymen with whom the Governor-elect argued yesterday were Harry F. Bac[k]us, Michael Loveen, John J. Bracken, M. A. Phillips and Frank P. Shalvoy.[4] M. J. McGowan, Jr.,[5] had been asked to attend, but he did not put in an appearance. He is looked upon as a stalwart Smith supporter with his mind too much made up to be changed.[6]

There are 11 Assemblymen from Essex County all told, and Mr. Wilson talked with five of them, Mylod, of Glen Ridge; Brown, of East Orange, and Boethener [Boettner], Macksey and Ballantine [Balentine] of Newark, for three hours on Wednesday at Princeton.

Printed in the *Trenton Evening Times*, Dec. 23, 1910.
  [1] Charles Anthony Meyer of Andover, N. J.
  [2] Eugene S. Burke of Morristown, N. J.
  [3] Meyer and Burke voted for Martine.
  [4] Harry F. Backus of Caldwell, N. J.; Michael Leveen of Newark; John J. Bracken of Orange, N. J.; Mark F. Phillips of Newark; and Frank P. Shalvoy of Newark.
  [5] Michael J. McGowan, Jr., of Newark.
  [6] Backus, Bracken, Phillips, Shalvoy, Leveen, and McGowan voted for Smith.

From Philip Alexander Bruce[1]

Dear Dr. Wilson,   Norfolk, Virginia, December 23d 1910.

I enclose you a notice which appeared in our morning papers touching the action of our local Democratic Club,[2] and I write as a private citizen to express the hope that it will be in your power to accept the invitation. There is a rapidly growing feeling here, which simply reflects the feeling throughout the State, so far as I have observed, that the weight of the State's influence should be cast in your favor from the very start in the next Democratic Convention for the Presidential nomination. We have organized here in Norfolk already, as you know.[3] I think you would be highly gratified by the character of the support which you are receiving,—not only the regular party rank and file, but men who are attracted towards you by the instinct of culture, and by their admiration for those lofty standards of public fitness which prevailed in the earlier years of the Republic, which they think you more nearly fulfil than any public man who has appeared in many decades. Indeed, for many of us whose lives are far removed from active politics, the prominence in political life which a great Scholar like yourself has assumed,—the honor in which you are everywhere held in this country,—has revived that confidence in our institutions which the events of recent years had so sadly dashed. With tens of thousands of others, I feel that a new era will open with your advent to office, and that a more hopeful outlook upon the political future will be fully justified from this time on. There is no State where you would receive a warmer welcome than in Virginia,—no place where your reception would be heartier than in Norfolk; and I voice the wishes of all our citizens that you will find it convenient in March to speak in this city in response to the general invitation. It would give Mrs Bruce[4] and myself very great pleasure to have you as our guest during your stay, should you decide to come.[5]

Yours Truly,   Philip Alexander Bruce

ALS (WP, DLC).

[1] Author of many works on the history of Virginia and of the South.

[2] It is missing, but it was probably an item in the Norfolk *Ledger-Dispatch*, Dec. 23, 1910, entitled "Dr. Woodrow Wilson May Speak in Norfolk." It read: "The newly organized Woodrow Wilson Presidential Club, of Norfolk, organized for the purpose of advancing the interest of the governor-elect of New Jersey for the next Democratic Presidential nomination will seek to have Dr. Wilson come to Norfolk and make an address on 'Good Citizenship' under the auspices of the club, and the Commission Form of Government League. Dr. Wilson will go to Atlanta, Ga., next March to address the Southern Commercial Congress and the idea is to have him stop here either on his way to Atlanta or en route back to New Jersey from that city."

[3] See R. W. Shultice to WW, Nov. 26, 1910.

[4] Elizabeth Tunstall Taylor Newton Bruce.

5 Wilson did not speak in Norfolk in March, but he did address the Pewter Platter Club of that city on April 29, 1911. Two news reports of his address are printed at April 30, 1911.

From John E. Lathrop

My dear Doctor Wilson: Washington, D. C., Dec. 23, 1910.

I enclose herewith copy of a letter I sent today to Mr. Bryan,[1] and also three enclosures, respectively, marked No. 1, a blank which is being circulated extensively among Granges and the Labor Union;[2] No. 2, blank supplied voters to send to members of their legislature;[3] and No. 3, a form of a resolution for a constitutional amendment for the initiative and referendum.[4] These are prepared by the non-partisan league,[5] and are merely suggestions to you.   Very truly yours,   John E. Lathrop.

TLS (WP, DLC).

1 J. E. Lathrop to W. J. Bryan, Dec. 23, 1910, CCL (WP, DLC). It was prompted by an editorial in *The Commoner*, x (Dec. 23, 1910), 1, in which Bryan had listed four possible candidates for the Democratic presidential nomination in 1912—Joseph Wingate Folk of Missouri, William Jay Gaynor of New York, Judson Harmon of Ohio, and Wilson. Lathrop, eager that Bryan should give precedence to Wilson over Harmon, informed him: "We, who do not write for the interests here in Washington, think we know that Governor Harmon is supported by the J. Pierpont Morgan financial coterie in New York." Then Lathrop continued: "I spent last Monday [December 19] with Woodrow Wilson in Princeton, and talked frankly with him regarding his attitude on public questions. He is absolutely independent, has no entangling alliances of a business nature, which is not true of Governor Harmon, and is, I think, the brightest hope of the Democratic party for 1912. He is devoting himself to the duties which devolve upon him as Governor of New Jersey, has faith in the people, and, although a few months ago the interests regarded his advent into politics complacently, today they understand that they misjudged their man. I trust that you will take pains to thoroughly investigate Doctor Wilson, and that in due time you may be able to differentiate between him and Governor Harmon." Lathrop criticized Harmon for defeating the plan for a senatorial preferential primary in Ohio because he wished to "bolster up in secret" the candidacy of a powerful supporter, John Roll McLean, owner of the *Washington Post* and *Cincinnati Enquirer*. It was only after Wilson had taken a positive stand in favor of the primary candidate in New Jersey that Harmon recognized Wilson as a "dangerous opponent" and subsequently forced McLean to withdraw. "I find the sentiment dividing," Lathrop concluded, "with reactionaries for Harmon, and the progressives for Wilson, and my personal investigation in New York, conducted at various times since last June, demonstrated to me that that is the correct line of division. I know your intense desire to wield your enormous influence in a way that will insure a nominee in 1912 who will lead the Democratic party in the paths of political righteousness and, knowing that, I am confident that you will find that your action will be consonant with the statements herein."

2 It was a typed form, with appropriate blanks, embodying a resolution endorsing the Oregon "system of Popular Government," which comprised the "Initiative and Referendum, Direct Primary, Corrupt Practices Act and Recall." It further stated that the signatory organization endorsed the introduction of a concurrent resolution in the state legislature and warned that, "regardless of party lines," the signatory would "never support for any office any member of the Legislature who fails or refuses to vote for the submission of the Initiative and Referendum amendment in the Oregon form."

3 This, too, was a typed form expressing the same positions as the enclosure

just described and, as Lathrop indicates, was designed to be sent by individual voters to their representatives.

[4] It was a typed draft of a joint resolution proposing an amendment to a state constitution and stated that, although the legislative power of a commonwealth was vested in its legislature, the "people reserve to themselves power to propose laws and amendments to the Constitution and to enact or reject the same at the polls, independent of the General Assembly, and also reserve power at their own option to approve or reject at the polls any act of the General Assembly." It then described the initiative and referendum and defined the percentage of signatures necessary to set their machinery in motion.

[5] He undoubtedly meant the People's Power League, organized by William S. U'Ren in 1906 to promote the initiative, referendum, and recall.

From Elliot Hersey Goodwin[1]

Dear Sir: New York December 23, 1910

I have the honor to inform you that at the annual meeting of the League held in Baltimore, Md., on December 15th and 16th, 1910, you were unanimously elected a Vice-President of the National Civil Service Reform League for the coming year.

Trusting that you will be willing to serve, I remain

Respectfully yours,   Elliot H. Goodwin

TLS (WP, DLC).
[1] Secretary of the National Civil Service Reform League.

From Charles Williston McAlpin

My dear Dr. Wilson: New York December 23, 1910

A week or more ago I was asked by my brother, Dr. McAlpin,[1] to hand you the enclosed,[2] but have neglected to do so until now. I know nothing about the contents but trust that they are harmless.

I have been wanting to talk with you in order that I might express my strong approval of your course in connection with the Senatorship, but I think you know by this time that I believe in you so thoroughly that whatever you may do seems right to me.

With kindest regards and best wishes for a Merry Christmas and a very happy and successful New Year, believe me as ever

Faithfully and sincerely yours,   C W McAlpin

TLS (WP, DLC).
[1] David Hunter McAlpin, M.D., Princeton, 1885, of New York.
[2] The enclosure is missing.

To Marion Jackson Verdery

My dear Mr. Verdery: Princeton, N. J. December 24, 1910

Your letter of the 15th has given me a great deal of pleasure. I do not feel that the speech at the Southern Dinner at all deserves the praise you bestow upon it but I am delighted that it was approved by good judges and you may be sure I am perfectly willing you should do anything with it that you think best. I shall be glad, of course, to revise the stenographer's notes and make the best out of them that I can, though, I never have been lucky enough to get a perfect verbatim report of anything I have said. I thank you with all my heart and wish that I could send more than this hasty note in reply.

Cordially and faithfully yours,   Woodrow Wilson

TLS (de Coppet Coll., NjP).

From William Cavanagh Gebhardt

Clinton N. J. Dec 24 1910

Can hardly find words to express my unbounded admiration of your last splendid statement   hearty congratulations   how can I help.   M C Gebhart.

T telegram (WP, DLC).

From Daniel Kiefer[1]

Dear Sir: Cincinnati, Ohio, December 24, 1910.

The position you have taken in the New Jersey senatorial contest is one that should have the support of every democrat to whom democracy means something more than the wearing of a party label and mechanically voting a party ticket. The state of New Jersey is fortunate indeed and so is the Democratic party of the State that the new Governor-elect has the courage and energy to oppose the designs of plutocratic corruptionists masquerading as democrats. In expressing my admiration of your course I can not avoid adding thereto regret that such conduct on the part of governors elected on the Democratic ticket is only too rare. Situations similar to the New Jersey one exist elsewhere but unfortunately they are not being dealt with in the same way.

I must confess I have not always thought so well of you. Last summer I had quite an extended correspondence with Mr. Richard Childs of the Short Ballot League in the course of which reference was made to your connection with that organization and I took occasion to express the opinion I then firmly held that you were the favorite candidate of plutocracy for the democratic presidential nomination. Since then I have come to feel that in all probability I was mistaken. While your reported opposition to such true democratic measures as the Initiative and referendum leave something lacking in your democracy it is clear that the predatory interests will not consider you the candidate for them. The party and the country need more men like you in places of power.

Respectfully yours,   Daniel Kiefer

TLS (WP, DLC).

¹ Retired Cincinnati businessman and Democrat; active in various political and economic reform movements; and chairman of the Joseph Fels Fund of America, devoted to promoting the single tax.

From Adolph Lankering

My dear Sir!   Hoboken, New Jersey December 24/1910.

Christmas is on hand. Kindly permit me to extend to you my best wishes.

The people of this State, especially the german speaking citizen, glory in the election of a man as their governor, who is going to endear himself to every right-thinking man and woman; who will elevate not only the standard of political life, but also awaken the moral good in everyone's heart and encourage the good will among all to help and assist in the re-establishment of a government by and for the people.

The courag[e]ous, progressive and firm stand you have taken for uprightness and honesty in politics, particularly in the present contest for the selection of a representative to the Senate of the United States has aroused a feeling, which upon call will bring all well meaning people to the front to defend the principals, without which no popular government can exist and pro[s]per.

To me personally this struggle is more than I can express, because I have been preaching your doctrines ever since the German-American Alliance has been brought into existence and when tested last year in Hudson County by me I found that the people are willing to follow an honest and sincere leader.

Once more my hearty and best wishes and a happy new year.

At your service, I remain

Very respectfully yours   A. Lankering.

ALS (WP, DLC).

From Samuel Colgate Hodge[1]

Dear Mr. Wilson,   Trenton, N. J. Dec. 24, 1910.

As an alumnus of Princeton, and as a friend, I want to express to you my appreciation of the stand you are taking in New Jersey politics. Yours is of course a difficult position, and one which, from time to time, may be opened to misunderstandings, but I want to assure you for one of my cordial sympathy, and willingness to cooperate in any way that I can.

I am pastor of a workingman's church here in the city, the Fifth Presbyterian. I am also Fraternal Delegate of the Interchurch Federation to the Central Labor Union, where I meet weekly with the Labor Union Men.

I want further to assure you that as a Princeton man I heartily sympathize with your position in the Princeton affair[.] Indeed you had the great majority of the alumni with you, as far as I can judge. Every man that I have talked to, with the exception of one who lived too near to Princeton to have a proper perspective, was on your side. May the principles of true Democracy win out both in Princeton and in the State. I represent the many who are standing behind you and wishing you godspeed in your administration.

Trusting that I am not imposing upon your time

I am   Sincerely Yours   Samuel C Hodge.

TLS (WP, DLC).
[1] Princeton 1888, pastor of the Fifth Presbyterian Church of Trenton, N. J.

To John Grier Hibben

My dear Jack,   Princeton, N. J. 25 December, 1910.

Not until to-day have I been left with leisure enough to turn to my own private matters and take up the letters which came, not out of the general rush, but from old friends.

I warmly appreciated your kind note of congratulations, and thank you for it very warmly. I find that I have undertaken a very difficult task; but there are many men of courage and honour who are ready to stand by me, and I think that it is feasible.

A Merry Chrsitmas [Christmas] and a Happy New Year to you all!   Faithfully Yours,   Woodrow Wilson

WWTLS (photostat in WC, NjP).

To George Brinton McClellan Harvey

My dear Colonel Harvey,   Princeton, N. J. 25 December, 1910.

Thank you most sincerely for your suggestion about the cold storage. It seems to me an admirable one. I am obliged to be off to-morrow for St. Louis, to preside over the meeting of the American Political Science Association, and shall not be back before the end of the week. If Mr. Inglis could put his hands on the facts while I am away, it would be of great service to me. The composition of my inaugural must necessarily be a hurried matter for me when I get back, and I should be hard put to it to get the material then. You are very kind and I appreciate all this very deeply.

With the most cordial messages of the season to Mrs. Harvey and yourself,

Faithfully and sincerely Yours,   Woodrow Wilson

WWTLS (WP, DLC).

From Solomon Foster

Dear Doctor Wilson: Newark, N. J., December 25th 1910

I wish to inform you that your letter of the 16th inst., expressing your intention to be present at our celebration on January 8th, greatly pleased our committee. In appreciation of the honor of your anticipated visit, but without any attempt to compensate you for your kind acceptance of our invitation, the committee is having made for you a gold medallion in commemoration of the event. We sincerely trust that your many duties will at last not interfere with your presence at our celebration.

At your leisure, please let me know when we may expect you here. If it will prove of any convenience to you, I can arrange to have an automobile call for you at Trenton on the afternoon of January the eighth.

May I take this opportunity heartily to commend your brave and enlightened position in the Senatorial situation in our State. I wish you success in your stand for principle, because your victory will give the people heart again and will make more solid the growing foundation of true Democracy.

With holiday greetings and best wishes for your health and happiness, I remain,   Yours sincerely,   Solomon Foster

TLS (WP, DLC).

To Daniel Kiefer

My Dear Mr. Kiefer: [Princeton, N. J., c. Dec. 26, 1910]

Your kind letter of December 24th has given me a great deal of pleasure. It makes me smile to think that I should ever have been regarded as the Wall Street candidate for the Presidency. I am sure that though I have many friends in Wall Street they never supposed for a moment that I would be serviceable to any interest that would be opposed to the interest of the people and to the country at large. I am not surprising them; I am only surprising those who do not understand me.

The duty of public men in our time is so clear that I do not see how any one can miss his way.

[Sincerely yours]   Woodrow Wilson.

Printed in the *New York Times*, Feb. 9, 1911.

From John Wesley Wescott

My dear Dr. Wilson: Camden, N. J. Dec. 26th, 1910.

I have purposely refrained from either writing to you or interviewing you, because I know the constant draft upon your time and, what is more important, your vital forces. I have a deep anxiety concerning your physical powers. My brother, Dr. Westcott,[1] and myself have several times discussed the advisability of interviewing you in respect to the economy of your strength. The labor before you is, in every respect, Herculean. In your anxiety to compass properly the immense task before you, you might possibly fail, in some measure, from lack of adequate attention to the expenditure of strength. In no other particular have I the slightest concern about the outcome of the revolution, which you are directing. You are the Napolean of the Revolution, the Luther of the Reformation. You cannot fail, for the reason that you are right and intend to be right. Situations, provocative of great exasperation, will frequently arise; but, behind you are the conscience and intelligence, not only of New Jersey, but of the entire country. It is inevitably characteristic of Democracy that cunning and base men will succeed in foisting upon the people commercial and legal conditions destructive of the fundamental principles of a democratic form of government, particularly, conditions destructive of the principle of equal opportunity and equal privilege. Such is the actual condition in the United States. Hence the Revolution, hence the Reformation, and hence the Napolean and the Luther. Your statement in regard to the

Senatorial embroglio was so masterful that it confounds the forces which the statement was aimed at, on the one hand, and, on the other, evokes a measure of trust by the people in you that marks an era in the development of our country.

I will, as soon as you are inaugurated, wish to briefly confer with you in respect to some appointments. My sole purpose will be, according to my very best judgment, to aid you in naming the right persons to hold office in our end of the state.² Together with the compliments of the season, I take this occasion to express to you my personal gratitude for what you have already done for the common good, and to assure you of my personal affection. The hearts of earnest men know with unerring certainty when a leader is kindly, patriotic and true.

Sincerely yours,   John W. Wescott

TLS (WP, DLC).
¹ William Augustus Westcott, M.D., of Berlin, N. J., southeast of Camden.
² Except for a small collection in the New Jersey State Library, Wilson's official papers as governor are missing, and the correspondence and other documents in this and following volumes will shed only partial light on his patronage policies. The only detailed discussion of this subject is in Link, *Wilson: The Road to the White House*, pp. 269-71, 299-301.

A News Report About Wilson's Arrival in St. Louis

[Dec. 27, 1910]

NEW GOVERNOR OF NEW JERSEY HERE TO SPEAK

Gov.-elect Woodrow Wilson of New Jersey, former president of Princeton University, arrived in St. Louis Tuesday afternoon, to address the joint session of the American Economic Association and the American Political Science Association at the Southern Hotel Tuesday evening.

He was met at Union Station by John D. Davis, representing the St. Louis Princeton alumni, and went to the Davis home in his host's automobile. He will leave St. Louis Wednesday afternoon, hurrying to his home in Princeton to attend the wedding of a niece.

President Wilson wore a dark business suit and a broad-brimmed felt hat of light hue. He said to a Post-Dispatch reporter at Union Station that the subject of his Southern Hotel address would be "The Law and the Facts."

Regarding his fight on James Smith Jr., Democratic boss of New Jersey, in the latter's effort to be elected to the United States Senate, Dr. Wilson said he intended to carry out his program of speeches at various places in New Jersey, at the homes of members of the Legislature, to urge their constituents to elect James E. Martine, the Democratic primary nominee.

"Any statement that I discussed with Mr. Smith, since the primary, the election of any other person than Mr. Martine to the senatorship is a falsehood," said the Governor-elect.

Printed in the *St. Louis Post-Dispatch*, Dec. 27, 1910; some editorial headings omitted.

A Presidential Address to the American
Political Science Association

[[Dec. 27, 1910]]

THE LAW AND THE FACTS

The life of society is a struggle for law. Where life is fixed in unalterable grooves, where it moves from day to day without change or thought of change, law is also, of course, stationary, permanent, graven upon the face of affairs as if upon tables of stone. But where life changes law changes, changes under the impulse and fingering of life itself. For it records life; it does not contain it; it does not originate it. It is subsequent to fact; it takes its origin and energy from the actual circumstances of social experience. Law is an effort to fix in definite practice what has been found to be convenient, expedient, adapted to the circumstances of the actual world. Law in a moving, vital society grows old, obsolete, impossible, item by item. It is not necessary to repeal it or to set it formally aside. It will die of itself,—for lack of breath,—because it is no longer sustained by the facts or by the moral or practical judgments of the community whose life it has attempted to embody.

There is, indeed, a sort of law which pushes ahead of fact, or seems to. I mean the law, so common in our day, which attempts to correct the habits or to guide the tendencies of society. Take our sanitary laws, for example. They do not record habit; they try to alter it. They are not a reduction to rule, merely, of practices into which society has naturally or instinctively settled. They seek to impose upon us, rather, habits and practices which we would not without their duress have adopted. They are based oftentimes upon scientific facts and principles which are not of common observation. We are very obedient to our men of science. We accept the conclusions of their laboratories without question or criticism and embody them in our rules of life, in our laws, with great benefit to our health, but in obedience to authority, not to experience,—at any rate not to experience which is of our own development or discovery.

But even this is only an apparent exception. Law is still subsequent to the facts. Though they be not of our own discovery and we receive them on faith, they are none the less facts. Law follows them; it does not precede or predict or invent them. It is obedient to experience. It accepts the ascertained, the accomplished, the proved and established circumstance, and frames it into an imperative rule of conduct under the compulsion of what men have found to be true.

I take the science of politics to be the accurate and detailed observation of these processes by which the lessons of experience are brought into the field of consciousness, transmuted into active purposes, put under the scrutiny of discussion, sifted, and at last given determinate form in law. Nothing that forms or affects human life seems to me to be properly foreign to the student of politics.

I do not know how some students of politics get along without literature, as some of them make shift to do,—without the interpretations of poetry or of any of the other imaginative illuminations of life,—or without art, or any of the means by which men have sought to picture to themselves what their days mean or to represent to themselves the voices that are forever in their ears as they go their doubtful journey. They read history, indeed, in search of the "facts"; but if they miss the deepest facts of all, the spiritual experiences, the visions of the mind, the aspirations of the spirit that are the pulse of life, I do not see how they can understand the facts or know what really moves the world. Very often they do not.

Politics is of the very stuff of life. Its motives are interlaced with the whole fibre of experience, private and public. Its relations are intensely human, and generally intimately personal. It is very dangerous to reason with regard to it on principles that are fancied to be universal; for it is local. Its items are of the time and place. What happens in its field is shot through with a thousand accidental elements which you will not find again upon another occasion, because occasions are not similar. And yet there is a large movement in it all which is independent in some strange way of time and place and accidental elements. There are big facts and tendencies to be picked out. There are circumstances which link whole communities together, make them feel their common interest, reveal to them their common relations, and push them forward into the field of law. They must seek a common order, whether they will or not; they must shape institutions to suit their lives and give vent to their common purposes; they must drive a strong, steadfast peg of law in at each step of their struggle forward to hold them where they are.

This study becomes more and more complex because society changes under our very eyes. I suppose there never was a time when things were actually simple. They look so to us in very ancient times of which we have scant record, no doubt, because we know very little about them. They were complex enough, even then, it may be; but we see them only in bulk, and the mass looks simple and easy of description. But manifestly affairs have grown more and more complex as civilization has deployed upon the modern stage.

There was a time, for example, when societies, when nations, seemed to move forward in mass, all together, their internal interests, at any rate, linked and interrelated in some reasonably manifest fashion. Their law was all of one weaving. The classes of which they were made up were formed in one common mould,—were at least continuously conscious of one another and united in a single nexus of forces. In our day, on the contrary, there is an extraordinary, an unprecedented differentiation. There is a perceptible movement in distinct economic and therefore distinct social sections. Society is too various to see itself as a whole, and the vision of those who study it is confused. Interests have their own separate and complicated development, and must, it has seemed, be made separately and individually the subject of legal regulation and adjustment. The relations which have come to rule in our day in the field of law seem to be the relations of interests, of vast and powerful economic sections of society, rather than of individuals. Laws intended to affect one set of interests directly and vitally are not only not meant to affect other interests directly but other interests are often ignorant of them, wholly indifferent to them. They do not touch their comprehension, do not enter into their calculations, are not permitted to affect their development.

For these sections and interests are powerfully organized, for the management, defence, and expansion of their own enterprises, personnel, and properties. Their power and their resources are concentrated, their management centered in definite and active agencies. They are equipped to take care of themselves, and are alert for every advantage.

Take the case of the United States. The development of its law in the generations with which we are most familiar has not been a development which yielded to or expressed a movement all along the line, an impulse of mass, a correlation of forces of which the whole social body was conscious. It has, on the contrary, been a rapid development of individual forces in a crowded field upon which interests did not move together but asserted themselves separately and in confused rivalry. Our national growth has been rapid not only but prodigious, alike in respect of population and of material wealth, of physical and of financial power. We were dealing with resources which we deemed inexhaustible. Hope and energy in a free field wrought marvels, as they must always do when untrammelled and with tools and materials at their hand. It has been a great spectacle of splendid force released and challenged by every circumstance to work its will. It has, too, been a regime of utter individualism. The forces as well as the men have acted independently, of their own initiative, at their own choice, in their own way. And law has not drawn them together,—it does not appear that it was its object to draw them together. Our national policy has been a policy of stimulation, but of miscellaneous stimulation. Any one who clamoured for legislative aid and brought the proper persuasive influences to bear could get assistance and encouragement. It was everybody for everything upon a disordered field. There was no attempt to coördinate. Our legislation has been atomistic, miscellaneous, piecemeal, makeshift.

And so individual interests without number have been built up. They have not been harnessed to a common cause; the common cause was supposed to be individual development and the right of those who could to use the country and its resources for the release of their private energy and the piling up of their own wealth. Separate opportunities were studied, not common obligations, variety, not community, of interest. A free field and all the favour the law could show was our rule of life, our standard of policy. Interests of this, that, or the other sort grew so big that they necessarily touched and interlaced. Their contacts made them conscious of one another. Each sought the whole field and met the others in it, made rivals of them, or allies. But there was no common guiding spirit or purpose; there was no mandate of law to mould them into one another, to unite, reconcile, harmonize, direct them. The courts mediated between them, but had no means or standard by which they could accommodate their activities to the interest of communities and of men of every kind outside directors' rooms and offices and banks.

And so the field, almost the subject-matter, of our study has changed. It is still the object of political science to see how the forces move, to note how experience develops into law. But experience does not move with an even front, and law responds to it after its own variety, in sections, in special channels, in segments fitted to special interests. Our search is for the common interest, but where shall we find it? It is displayed in no common phenomena,—at any rate in none that can be easily discerned. If we would discover it, we must compound it for ourselves out of scattered and disparate elements. We must look away from the piecemeal law books, the miscellaneous and disconnected statutes and legal maxims, the court decisions, to the life of men, in which there is always, of necessity, an essential unity, which, whether it will or no, whether it is conscious of it or not, *must* be of a piece, *must* have a pattern which can be traced. Here are the fragments: the laws, the separate forces, the eager competing interests, the disordered *disjecta membra* of a system which is no system, which does not even suggest system, but which must somehow be built together into a whole which shall be something more than a mere sum of the parts.

This is the task, the difficult, elusive, complex, and yet imperative task of political science. It is also the task of the new statesmanship, which must be, not a mere task of compromise and makeshift accommodation, but a task of genuine and lasting adjustment, synthesis, coordination, harmony, and union of parts.

It is first of all, I take it, a task of elucidation, not to say of discovery,—of discovery through thorough elucidation. We have heard a great deal of hopeful talk in recent months about the need of a non-partisan, expert commission to get the facts about the incidence and actual operation and effect of the protective tariff which Congress has built up into so wonderful and fearful a structure, about the cost of production and the proper basis for duties, about the condition of industry in its various branches and the precise result of this, that, or the other legislative stimulation by means of taxation. It is expected that such a commission would, by investigation of a dispassionate and disinterested sort, afford us what is optimistically spoken of as a "scientific" basis for a revision of the system,—by which, I suppose, it is meant that it would afford us light without heat, elucidation that would not be *ex parte* argument, an exposition of things that would not have the requisite tilt and surface for logrolling. I trust that such hopes are not ill-founded; but I refer to them here only for the sake of illustration, not to give myself the opportunity to express an opinion. Such a commission would be in fact a commission to discover, amidst our present economic chaos, a common interest, so that we might legislate for the whole country instead of for this, that, or the other interest, one by one. Students of political science are a self-constituted commission in the broader political field for a similar purpose.

They must discover, amidst the confusion of modern elements the common term, the common interest,—or, rather, they must discover the *missing* term. For, as I have said, the whole is not the mere sum of the parts. These scattered pieces, these separately developed elements of modern economic society, do not disclose, when put together, a whole and consistent pattern. The letters they contain do not make a complete word. The words they contain do not make a complete sentence. Express them all at their best and you still have not found a voice for the common interest, for the forces that must harmonize and round out the life of modern society.

Perhaps we can find a starting point for the new synthesis which this latest enterprize of our thinking must seek to accomplish in two definitions which I have recently ventured to suggest in another place. We are dealing, in our present discussion, with business and we are dealing with life as an organic whole, and modern politics is an accommodation of these two. Suppose we define business as the economic service of society for private profit, and suppose we define politics as the accommodation of all social forces, the forces of business of course included, to the common interest. We may thus perceive our task in all its magnitude and extraordinary significance. Business must be looked upon, not as the exploitation of society, not as its use for private ends, but as its sober service; and private profit must be regarded as legitimate only when it is in fact a reward for what is veritably serviceable,—serviceable to interests which are not single but common, as far as they go; and politics must be the discovery of this common interest, in order that the service may be tested and exacted.

In this conception society is the senior partner in all business. It must be first considered,—society as a whole, in its permanent and essential, not merely in its temporary and superficial, interests. If private profits are to be legitimatized, private fortunes made honourable, these great forces which play upon the modern field must, both individually and collectively, be accommodated to a common purpose. Politics has to deal with and harmonize many other forces besides those of business merely. Business serves our material needs, but not often our spiritual. But the business forces are nowadays the most powerful (perhaps they have always been the most powerful) with which politics has to deal. They are the hardest to correlate, tame, and harness; and for the time being our anxious interest centres upon them. Let us extract from them, if we can, the new term of peace and prosperity which will be found in their genuine and successful synthesis.

The economists cannot help us, I fear. They must segregate these great phenomena of which I have spoken, I suppose, and study them in their pure and separate force, as they are; whereas segregation is just what we, as students of political science, are seeking to offset and correct. We wish to study them, not separately, nor even in combination only with one another, but in combination with the influences, the interests, the aspects of life which are not economic, but stuff of fortune, of peace of mind, of fair and generous dealing, of good will and enlightenment and public service.

There is the statesmanship of thought and there is the statesmanship of action. The student of political science must furnish the first, out of his full store of truth, discovered by patient inquiry, dispassionate exposition, fearless analysis, and frank inference. He must spread a dragnet for all the facts, and must then look upon them steadily and look upon them whole. It is only thus that he can enrich the thinking and clarify the vision of the statesman of action, who has no time for patient inquiry, who must be found in his facts before he can apply them in law and policy, who must have stuff of truth for his conscience and his resolution to rely on.

I know that the statesman and the student of political science have not hitherto often been partners. The statesman has looked askance upon the student,—at any rate in America, and has too often been justified because the student did not perceive the real scope and importance of what he was set to do and overlooked much of the great field from which he should have drawn his facts,—was not a student of thought and of affairs but merely a reader of books and documents. But the partnership is feasible, with a change in the point of view; and the common interest must somehow be elucidated and made clear, if the field of action is not to be as confused as the field of thought.

I do not mean that the statesman must have a body of experts at his elbow. He cannot have. There is no body of experts. There is no such thing as an expert in human relationships. I mean merely that the man who has the time, the discrimination, and the sagacity to collect and comprehend the principal facts and the man who must act upon them must draw near to one another and feel that they are engaged in a common enterprise. The student must look upon his studies more like a human being and man of action, and the man of action must approach his conclusions more like a student.

Business is no longer in any proper sense a private matter. It is not in our day usually conducted by independent individuals, each acting upon his own initiative in the natural pursuit of his own economic wants. It is pursued by great companies, great corporations, which exist only by express license of law and for the convenience of society, and which are themselves, as it were, little segments of society. Law is not accommodating itself, therefore, to the impulses and enterprises of individuals, as experience pushes it forward from change to change; but is accommodating itself, rather, to the impulses of bodies of men, to the aggregate use of money drawn from a myriad of sources as if from the common savings of society at large. The processes of change will be organic only in proportion as they are guided and framed along self-consistent lines of general policy. As experience becomes more and more aggregate law must be more and more organic, institutional, constructive. It is a study in the correlation of forces.

After all, it is not a purely intellectual process, this interpretation of experience, this translation of experience into law. I said just now that I did not see how the student of political science could make shift to know what he was about without the lamps of literature to light his way,—those flames, those lambent spirits of men, that burn in the pages of books that some of you are apt to put away from you as having no significance as of science and of fact in them. Nothing interprets but vision, and ours is a function of interpretation. Nothing perceives but the spirit when you are dealing with the intricate life of men, shot through with passion and tragedy and ardour and great hope. That is the reason that I said that there were no experts in human relationships. Sympathy is your real key to the riddle of life. If you can put yourself in men's places, if you can see the same facts from the points of view of many scores of men of as many different temperaments, fortunes, environments, if you have Shakespearian range and vision, then things fall into their places as you look upon them and are no longer confused, disordered, scattered abroad without plan or relation. You must not classify men too symetrically; you must not gaze dispassionately upon them with scientific eye. You must yield to their passion and feel the pulse of their life when you are studying them no less than when you are acting for them. Organic processes of thought will bring you organic processes of law. Nothing else will.

Let us break with our formulas, therefore. It will not do to look at men congregated in bodies politic through the medium of the constitutions and traditions of the states they live in, as if that were the glass of interpretation. Constitutions are vehicles of life, but not sources of it. Look at all men everywhere first of all as at human beings struggling for existence, for a little comfort and ease of heart, for happiness amidst the things that bind and limit them. Such and such are the conditions of law and effort and rivalry amidst which they live, such and such are their impediments, their sympathies, their understandings with one another. See them in their habits as they live and perhaps you will discern their errors of method, their errors of motive, their confusions of purpose, and the assistance the wise legislator might afford them.

I do not like the term political science. Human relationships, whether in the family or in the state, in the counting house or in the factory, are not in any proper sense the subject-matter of science. They are stuff of insight and sympathy and spiritual comprehension. I prefer the term Politics, therefore, to include both the statesmanship of thinking and the statesmanship of action. Your real statesman is first of all, and chief of all, a great human being, with an eye for all the great field upon which men like himself struggle, with unflagging pathetic hope, towards better things. He is a man big enough to think in the terms of what others than himself are striving for and living for and seeking steadfastly to keep in heart till they get. He is a guide, a comrade, a mentor, a servant, a friend of mankind. May not the student of politics be the same? May not his eye, too, follow the dusty roads, scan the scattered mass, observe the crowded homes, heed the cry of the children as well as the silent play of the busy fingers that toil that they may be fed, follow the lines of strain, of power, of suffering, get a vision of all the things that tell; and then, with no precise talk of phenomena or of laws of action, interpret what he feels no less than what he sees to the man of action, too much engrossed, it may be, to see so much or over so wide a field, too much immersed to hear any but the nearby cries and clamours, too eagerly bent upon his immediate task to scan the distant view?

Know your people and you can lead them; study your people and you may know them. But study them, not as congeries of interests, but as a body of human souls, the least as significant as the greatest,—not as you would calculate forces, but as you would comprehend life. In such an atmosphere of thought and association even corporations may seem instrumentalities, not objects in themselves, and the means may presently appear whereby they may be made the servants, not the masters, of the people. The facts are precedent to all remedies; and the facts in this field are spiritually perceived. Law is subsequent to the facts, but the law and the facts stand related, not as cause and effect, but, rather, as life and its interpretation.[1]

Printed in the *American Political Science Review*, v (Feb. 1911), 1-11; with a few corrections of typographical errors from the T MS in WP, DLC.

[1] There is a WWhw outline, dated Dec. 17, 1910; a WWsh draft, dated Dec. 23, 1910; a WWT draft, dated Dec. 27, 1910; and an undated T draft of this address, all in WP, DLC.

A News Report of a Reply to James Smith, Jr.

[Dec. 28, 1910]

GOVERNOR-ELECT ADDS TO HIS EXPOSITION
OF JAMES SMITH'S TACTICS

With amplifications that lend added emphasis to his exposition of the course of James Smith, Jr. in the Senatorial struggle, Governor-elect Wilson has replied to the essentials in the statement made Monday by the former Senator. . . .

Smith's statement of Monday having been issued following the departure of Dr. Wilson for St. Louis, a telegram quoting portions of it was sent by the News to the Governor-elect, en route. In returning his answer last night he specifically stated that it was only in reply to the parts of Smith's statement quoted in the dispatch sent him.

These were as follows:

"Dr. Wilson says that he was assured by my spokesman before his nomination that I would not be a candidate for the Senatorial office. I never made such a statement. No one was ever authorized by me to make such statement, and no one representing me made such statement to Dr. Wilson.

"Let him name the man or men coming from me who so informed him. Let there be no hiding behind the seal of confidence. If he were my spokesman, I remove the seal. Let Dr. Wilson speak out, or by his silence stand convicted before the public of attempted trickery and deceit.

"I called upon Dr. Wilson shortly after election. The Senatorial matter was discussed. I told him that I had not yet reached a decision as to my candidacy. Professing a high regard for me, Dr. Wilson said that my candidacy would meet with some opposition from the people; that in his judgment they wanted a man who had not previously appeared in the political arena;

some untried man. Stating that the recent primary was a farce, and that it 'would be a disgrace' to the State to send James E. Martine to the Senate, he asked me to sit down with him, and agree upon a candidate who would be acceptable to him and to me."

Dr. Wilson's answer follows:

"I certainly would not have allowed my name to go before the convention that nominated me if I had not thought that the gentleman who told me that Mr. Smith would not be a candidate for the Senate spoke for Mr. Smith. I had every reason to think that he did.

"I will not name him because he is a man whom I very highly esteem, and upon whom I do not care to bring the mortification of being drawn into this now very public matter.

"I am quite willing to go with Mr. Smith before the court of public opinion on the charge of attempted trickery and deceit.

"If the gentleman of whom I have spoken did not speak for Mr. Smith, in what he told me, why did Mr. Smith corroborate what he had said? He himself told me exactly the same thing when he came to my home a few days after the election. He told me in the plainest terms that before the election he had not desired to go to Washington, had not felt equal to seeking or occupying the office; but that he was now feeling stronger and did desire it. He was evidently referring to something he knew I had known.

"Mr. Smith has a singularly distorted recollection of that conversation. I did speak as his friend. I felt very friendly toward him indeed, and wish that I might have been permitted to serve his real interest in this final decision of his public career.

"I pointed out to him the deep discredit that would fall upon him if he were himself to seek the Senatorship. Finding him utterly contemptuous of the primary and toward Mr. Martine; finding that he insisted that the State would be disgraced should Mr. Martine, rather than he, represent it in the Senate, I tried to point out to him in all kindness the only course that lay open to him in the circumstances, if he would win the respect of thoughtful men.

"I told him that feeling as he did the only honorable course open to him was to come out and say that he was not himself a candidate and would co-operate in the choice of any man whom general opinion might agree upon as representing not special interests, but the opinion and the character of the State.

"I was suggesting a course for him, not choosing one for myself. My own duty has been plain from the first. He told me that he did not know of any such man in the State who had any 'claim' on the party comparable to his own.

"I hope that I need not say again that I proposed no compromise candidate and no compromise of any kind for myself. I was foolishly trying to advise him; I was not making a choice for myself.   Woodrow Wilson."

Printed in the *Newark Evening News*, Dec. 28, 1910.

From Henry Watterson

My dear Governor: Louisville, Ky., Dec. 28, 1910.

The tornado has made such havoc with my winter home on the west coast of Florida that Mrs. Watterson and I shall go to the south of France instead, sailing on the "Amerika" next Thursday, the 5th of January, to return early in May. We shall be at the Waldorf-Astoria from next Tuesday afternoon until the hour of our departure for the steamer. Call me up if there be anything to say. I shall see George Harvey and perhaps Mr. Ryan whilst I am in town.

I wish I were in Jersey, or you in Kentucky. It would do me a world of good to help you directly with your fight. You have nothing to do but fight it out—to the bitter end, if need be.

Remember me to Mrs. Wilson and the young ladies, and believe me,   Your Friend   Henry Watterson

TLS (WP, DLC).

From Benjamin Barr Lindsey[1]

My dear Sir: Denver, Colo. December 28, 1910.

I want to congratulate you upon your courageous stand in the contest over the next United States Senator from New Jersey.

It was my pleasure to visit Trenton sometime the latter part of November, and I regret it very much that I was unable to meet you.

While I have always been a Democrat, my political experiences for the past few years have been of such a character that I was compelled to be more or less independent. Here in the West I have found the Insurgent Republicans offered a much more attractive home than did the Democratic organization which is the chief asset of the big business interests of this state and has been if anything a more servic[e]able tool for the great privilege grabbers than the Republican party. In fact it has grown quite absured [absurd] for either party to claim to be the only Simon pure champion of popular rights and popular government. There is, somehow,—whether justified or not—a feeling in the West that the great law-breaking privilege interests of the country are moving from the Republican party over to the Democratic party, and quietly taking possession for 1912, when they expect to get someone who is "safe and sane" to head the Democratic ticket for President of the United States.

During my recent trip East I heard only two or three men seriously discussed for national Democratic leadership. There is Governor Harmon, yourself and Governor Folk. It was very surprising to me how completely settled is the conviction everywhere that Governor Harmon—while an estimable gentleman who belongs to the old school—is already picked by the vested interests to head the Democratic ticket in 1912. This may be altogether unjust but I simply state the fact. I also heard the very common remark that if the vested interests of the country failed in their plan to champion Governor Harmon that they expected to turn to you as being "safe and sane"—which expression I suppose you in the East understand as well as we in the West understand. As one man very familiar with Wall Street said to me in New York: "If it isn't Harmon, and Wilson can be convinced to be equally conservative, it will of course be Wilson—he would be quite as servicable to the cause of conservatism," as against that insurgency—radicalism—progressive democracy, or whatever you may term the present demand for political and economic justice.

The test proposed to me by one man was your attitude in the New Jersey Senatorial contest. If you kept your mouth shut, you were of course safe and sane. If you took the action that you have taken, you were of course of a "dangerous" type. With the proper understanding of the new definitions for these terms, I am delighted that you are not safe and sane, but are a "dangerous" man.

If the Democratic party is going to be the conservative party of this country, and the Republican, the radical or progressive party, there is likely to be a change in the party affiliations of unnumbered thousands.

I am taking the liberty to send you, under separate cover, a copy of our story "The Beast."[2] It has been a very interesting, and, at times, a very strenuous experience, and I think all of the leading politicians in this state will tell you privately that it is not only an experience without serious contradiction, but the chief criticism I have had from all of these people is that I did not go far enough or tell it as strongly as I ought to have told it.

I am sure if I had, the story may have been so incredible it might have failed of effect altogether.

With kindest regards and best wishes, I am

Sincerely yours,   Ben B Lindsey

TLS (WP, DLC).

1 Political and social reformer; pioneer in dealing with juvenile delinquency as judge of the County Court of Denver since 1901.

2 Ben B. Lindsey and Harvey Jerrold O'Higgins, *The Beast* (New York, 1910). Written by O'Higgins from a series of autobiographical articles dictated by Lindsey, *The Beast* is a graphic account of Lindsey's fight against political and economic corruption in Denver.

A News Report of a Speech to the City Club of St. Louis

[*Dec. 29, 1910*]

Wilson Would Clear Away the Brush

St. Louis, Dec. 29.—Governor-elect Woodrow Wilson, of New Jersey, delighted nearly 1,000 members and guests of the City Club yesterday with a snappy discussion on the "Wilson Creed," which at the recent election swept New Jersey out of the Republican column and placed the former president of the Princeton University in the national limelight.

"All my life," he said, "I have been preaching to the students, as some Princeton men here can attest, that it is the duty of educated men to go into politics when called on to do so. When I was called on I had to take my own medicine, and I may frankly say that, so far as physical condition goes, I have thrived on it."

Governor Wilson likes to see everything done "out in the open," as he expressed it. He condemned star chamber sessions of all kinds, and advised his hearers to remove the underbrush wherever they found it, that they might see what was concealed from them.

"The practical politician least understands practical politics of 1910," he said. "He is in the game for what he can get out of it. This is the day of the amateur politician—not amateur in the sense that you can pull his leg, but amateur in the sense that he is not seeking personal gain.

"The independent voter is so numerous that no politician can cast a horoscope of the future. That is an ideal condition, because the best thing possible is to have the professional politician guessing."

In the course of his speech, Doctor Wilson used these epigrams:

"Mind your public business all the year round, not only at election time.

"Force public officials to report often, and watch their eyes to see if they are telling you all they know.

"The people are coming into their own.

"I have been an ardent Democrat all my life, with a big D and a little d.

"Common counsel is the purifying, rectifying process.

"Concentrate responsibility and hold it accountable.

"You can trust the people, providing you serve them.

"You cannot fool the people and trust them not to find you out.

"Reveal everything and the people will be just; conceal anything and make them jealous.

"The whole process of popular government must be a process of publicity.

"We are impatient with government that does not represent.

"Legislators blindly follow leaders. Sometimes the bellwether is trustworthy; sometimes he is an old goat.

"Cure politics as you would tuberculosis—with open air.

"The practical politician should sleep in the open; it will purify him."

"The Roman Catholic Church," said Dr. Wilson, "saved the Middle Ages from dry rot, because it was democratic. This open door to the common man was the door of elevation that kept Europe progressing. The aristocracy cannot be counted on, although there have been special instances where the aristocrat has proved helpful."

The speaker said that during the recent New Jersey campaign his enemies attacked him as a schoolmaster. "I accepted the charge," he declared, "and told the people that a schoolmaster is trained to find out things, to tell of his discoveries. And that is what I promised to do. It is exactly the thing the professional politician will not tell."

He included in his criticism secret sessions in legislatures, in Congress and in State boards. He held up the Railroad Commission of Wisconsin as a shining example of what may be accomplished by publicity.

"My personal ambition," he continued, "is to try and keep from getting behind anybody or to conceal anything. When you hear a bullet singing through the air you ought to think the next may hit you. Be ready for your judgment. It is risky business, but one is always safer in the open."

Printed in the Trenton *True American*, Dec. 30, 1910; some editorial headings omitted.

From Joseph Fels[1]

My Dear Sir: Philadelphia Dec. 29, 1910.

I was much interested in a statement from you quoted in the Public[2] of Chicago, December 16th, as follows:

"I know that the people of New Jersey do not desire James Smith, Jr., to be sent again to the Senate. If he should be, he will not go as their representative. The only means I have of knowing whom they desire to represent them is the vote at the recent primaries, where 48,000 Democratic voters, a majority, declared their preference for Mr. Martine of Union county. For me, that vote is conclusive. I think it should be for every member of the Legislature."

I am delighted, Dr. Wilson, to find that you are more progressive that [than] I thought you were. I am glad to see that you believe a United States Senator should represent the people, rather than the organization known as "the State," as was intended by the framers of the Constitution. While believing that the majority of the voters of the State should elect Senators, rather than a majority of the voters of one party, and that a popular election rather than a party primary should determine the election, regardless of the political complexion of the Legislature, as is done in the progressive State of Oregon, even an election by party voters is better than the common auction-block method of election by a Legislature.

The Public says your declaration puts you "farther to the front in the democracy of the Democratic party than ever before, on what is coming to be the test question—the principle and practice of people's rule." I sincerely hope that you will soon see, if you do not now see, the necessity for "People's Rule" in this country, and that control of legislation by the people is even of greater importance than control of Senatorial elections. To mention one example, Ex-Senator W. A. Clark[3] was elected by the Legislature of Montana in 1901. He could have won the election easily at Democratic primaries; he could have won easily that year at the general election. But even before he took his seat in the Senate he surrendered to the Interests that are trying to suppress "People's Rule" by sitting upon the safety valve of an almost red-hot boiler.

The State Senators and Representatives in the New Jersey Legislature are elected by popular vote; but even if the Democratic majority shall represent the party vote in electing a United States Senator, are not the people of New Jersey helpless as far as legislation is concerned—except as you will stand between the people and unwise or vicious laws? Are they not as helpless in that respect as the people of New York, Pennsylvania and some forty other States? And while you have the veto power—I believe the Governor of New Jersey has that power—over vicious and unwise legislation, you have absolutely no power to veto the failure or refusal of the Legislature to enact good and wise laws or to submit needed amendments to the State Constitution. And in those States in which the people have not the political power of Direct Legislation there is no power on the part of the Governors or of the people to repair the negligence, or worse, of the legislative servants of the people. On the contrary, all legislative power is in the hands of men who, when they enter the State House, may fail or refuse to "represent" the will of the people. Is that "popular government"? It is the form, but is it the substance of republican or representative government?

Have you voted [noted] the steady growth of the demand for the Initiative and Referendum? Have you read Lobinger's "The People's Law"?[4] Did you note the recent advisory vote in Illinois on the question of having an Initiative and Referendum amendment submitted—an almost four to one vote? The movement is growing. The people wwnt [want] power because they feel that "the rights of the people are safe with the people." The people must be trusted or they must be mastered with an iron hand; which shall it be?

The whole world is growing into democracy and outgrowing the old constitution and statutory clothes that no more fit the world than the clothes that fit you as a boy will fit you now; no more than the mental habits of boyhood and youth fit the mature man.

Political revolutions are not necessarily dangerous, but suppression of the people's will is dangerous. If this is to be a "government of the people, by the people and for the people," the people must control. The auction-block method of enacting laws and of refusing to enact needed legislation is even more vicious than the auction-block method of electing United States Senators. There would be no private ownership of Legislators and Congressmen if the people controlled legislation through Direct Legislation, because such private ownership would be unprofitable. The people of this country are awakening to that fact: in several States they have awakened to it. Fine words about the intent of the "fathers" will not deceive them, because they know thay [they] have a right not to be governed by the "fathers." The government clothes that fit the fathers of 125 years ago will not fit the people of this generation.

Jefferson did not fear to trust the people; Lincoln did not fear to trust them. If the people need guardians then they are unfit for a republican form of government. If they do not need guardians, why insist upon legislative guardianship. If they must be held in check by legislative masters, why speak of those masters as "representatives"?

It is a fact that the plain people, who cast many votes, distrust their Legislatures, their Executives and their Judiciary, because almost everywhere they see themselves blocked and suppressed by those public servants. That condition cannot last; it should not last; hence the growth of Socialism in this country. The votes in favor of the Initiative and Referendum show that the people demand "People's Rule."

Yours very truly,   Joseph Fels.

TLS (WP, DLC).

[1] Wealthy soap manufacturer, owner of Fels and Co. of Philadelphia; advocate of the single tax and founder of the Joseph Fels Fund of America and similar funds in other countries to promote the single tax; founder of labor and agricultural colonies for the unemployed in England and single tax communities in Mobile Bay, Ala., and Arden, Del.

[2] Progressive, single tax journal, edited by Louis Freeland Post.

[3] William Andrews Clark, Democratic senator from Montana, 1901-1907, with extensive copper mining, banking, and railroad interests in Montana.

[4] Charles Sumner Lobingier, *The People's Law; or, Popular Participation in Law-Making From Ancient Folk-Moot to Modern Referendum; A Study in the Evolution of Democracy and Direct Legislation* (New York, 1909).

From Elmer Hendrickson Geran

Dear Doctor Wilson: Jersey City [N. J.], December 29th, 1910

I can scar[c]ely refrain from dropping you a refreshing note this morning. I feel sort of tickled after having come in contact with the Assemblymen-elect at Newark.[1] Smith has and will retain unquestionably a number of men, but as I mingled among the Assemblymen yesterday and talked Martine enthusiastically, I was pleased to find a number of like notion, and zealously so.

I have been fearful that some of the Hudson delegation would consider that they had kept their promises for Martine, when they had voted for him once or twice and then switch to Smith, then persuade themselves and attempt to persuade others, that they had kept their promises, but that there was a deadlock and there was nothing for them to do, but vote for Mr Smith.

Thomas Griffin of the Hudson delegation assured me that he would vote for Martine until Smith was whipped. I think that was fine, and if we can get the Hudson delegation to take a similar stand a great deal will be accomplished.

Mr Boettner at the ninth hour became a Candidate for leader. The Essex delegation had promised him their support. Upon the vote it was divided. After the caucus adjourned he was open in his denunciation of those who deserted him and made the remark to one of them, that—"you fellows had better keep your eyes on me in Trenton."

In a conversation with me, he suggested that he would give anything if he could be in a position like myself. I suggested to him that he was twenty-one years of age, sane, and while he might be surrounded by influences and unfortunate conditions, he could break them and rise above them if he had the mind. I also tried to get him to publicly tell the facts in connection with the notorious Smith letter.[2] I believe that at a proper time, suggested by you, Mr Boettner will declare for Martine and lay bear [bare] the facts concerning the letter. Mr Balantine I hope will also join the ranks.

You may have had an inkling or suggestion of these matters before, and if so the re-assurance of them, at any rate, will tend to keep up courage for all of us in this fight. Smith is working by dastardly means and both he and his methods ought to be condemned and overthrown.

Yours very truly,   Elmer H. Geran

TLS (WP, DLC).
    [1] Geran had attended a caucus of Democratic members of the incoming House of Assembly held the day before at Democratic state headquarters in Newark.
    [2] See n. 2 to the news report printed at Dec. 21, 1910.

From Leon Abbett, Jr.[1]

Dear Doctor,   Hoboken, N. J. Dec. 29, 1910.

I wish to express my admiration for the stand you have taken for the good of the Democracy of our state, and of its people.

We have needed a leader of your standing and determination for some time, and it will be a pleasure to follow such leadership.

If I can be of any assistance at all in the fight you are making, I will be only too glad to help.

Very truly   Leon Abbett

ALS (WP, DLC).
    [1] Lawyer of Hoboken, assemblyman from Hudson County, 1899-1901, and son of Leon Abbett, Democratic Governor of New Jersey, 1884-87 and 1890-1893.

From Henry St. George Tucker[1]

My dear Mr. Wilson: Lexington, Va. Dec. 29, 1910.

I have been much interested in the contest which has been thrust upon you with ex-senator Smith, and am writing to express my sympathy with you and hope that the contest will result in favor of the people.

I was in congress with Smith at the time that he and Gorman did the work with the Wilson Bill, and if we are going to win the fight for the people in the next few years, that class of men can not be depended upon to help us out. He was probably the most conspicuous Senator, (not less so than Gorman himself) in destroying the Wilson Bill. He represents also in the State a type of ring politics that the people of the country are sorely tired of.

We are hoping in Virginia to get rid of it next summer and have just induced Wm. A. Jones to make the race against Martin for the Senate.[2] Of course the question of the effect of one's position on his future can not be considered where the path of duty lies, but it will be at least gratifying to you to know that the path of duty which leads you to fight Smith will greatly popularize you throughout the country among those who know Smith and know what he stands for.

I bid you God speed in the fight. I believe the people are in the saddle and here in Virginia no less than in New Jersey are we striving to purify the public morals and elevate the public sentiment.

With best wishes for the New Year for you.

Yours very truly,   H. S. G. Tucker

TLS (WP, DLC).

[1] Congressman from Virginia, 1889-97, 1922-32; Professor of Equity and Corporation Law and of Constitutional and International Law, 1897-1902, Washington and Lee University, Dean of the School of Law, 1899-1902, Acting President, 1900-1901; Dean of the Departments of Law and Jurisprudence, Columbian University (now George Washington University), 1903-1905; president of the American Bar Association, 1904-1905; president of the Jamestown Exposition Co., 1905-1907; unsuccessful candidate for the Democratic gubernatorial nomination in Virginia, 1909 and 1921; at this time practicing law in Lexington, Va. Tucker had long been a leader of the progressive wing of the Democratic party in Virginia opposed to the conservative organization headed by Senator Thomas Staples Martin, one of whose chief allies was Thomas Fortune Ryan. Tucker was also one of the early and most important Wilson leaders in the preconvention campaign in Virginia in 1911 and 1912. This subject is discussed in some detail in Arthur S. Link, "The South and the Democratic Campaign of 1910-1912," Ph.D. dissertation, University of North Carolina, 1945.

[2] Supported by the progressive faction, Representative William Atkinson Jones of Warsaw, Va., opposed Senator Martin in a bitter campaign during the summer of 1911 but was decisively defeated in the primary in September. Elected to Congress in 1891, Jones retained his seat until his death in 1918. Martin, elected in 1893, served in the Senate from 1895 until his death in 1919.

From Henry Smith Pritchett

Personal

My dear Wilson,   [New York] Dec 29 [1910]

A Mr. D. G. Slattery who claimed to be a news paper man[1] called at my office today and asked the details concerning the matter of a retiring allowance for you. I declined any talk with him & merely send you this line because I suspect he was trying to work up a story in the interest of those who are fighting you.[2] Where he got such information as he seemed to have I do not know. I think he is a Trenton man.

Yours faithfully,   Henry S. Pritchett

P.S. He asking [asked] me as he was leaving if I was "friendly" to you & got of course an unequiv[oc]al reply in this matter

ALS (WP, DLC).
[1] Daniel G. Slattery, reporter for the New York *Sun.*
[2] The story appeared on the front page of the New York *Sun* on December 5, 1911. There are many documents relating to this matter in Vol. 23.

A News Report of a Speech to the Princeton Club of St. Louis

[Dec. 30, 1910]

DR. WILSON TO STAY IN OPEN

ST. LOUIS, Dec. 30.—The American Political Science Association closed its sessions last night after electing Simeon E. Baldwin, Governor-elect of Connecticut, president to succeed Dr. Woodrow Wilson, Governor-elect of New Jersey. The latter presided at the closing session. He left for home yesterday afternoon.

Speaking of his transfer from the ranks of amateur politics to high office before the Princeton Club of St. Louis yesterday afternoon, Dr. Wilson said:

"I said openly that if I were elected Governor I would be the leader of the Democratic party in New Jersey. I didn't say I would be a good leader, because I did not know. But the convention took a sporting chance on me. A convention has to take that sort of a chance with any candidate."

He said he was determined to act in the open with reference to the duties of his new office and to take the people into his confidence, whether or not be [he] succeeded in carrying out his plans.

Dr. Wilson quoted a conversation between a Westerner and an Easterner in which the Westerner said: "You Easterners were so sound asleep that it took a brass band to wake you up," and added: "But now that the awakening has taken place, it would seem to be fit that the brass band should be retired and reform considered deliberately."

Dr. Wilson spoke of the difficulty of running business and politics together in the State of New Jersey, saying that neither the Republican nor the Democrat in politics as a profession in that State was true to either party.

"The politicians," he said, "belong to a party that wins, and they do not put up campaign funds and help men who may not win." He continued by saying they did not elect a man or party when it would in any way hurt their own business interests.

"This ought to be done away with," he continued. "What chance has a man in either party when he is playing a game with a man who has stacked the cards? When a man comes to you to play a game make him put the cards out on the table and play fair. Do not let him trick you, or he is likely to try it again.

"The obligation of men is to advance their community and not to lower it. I have made my rules and will follow them. Most men do not understand the elements in life they are dealing with, which causes them a great deal of worry and loss of sleep. The majority of them have more to do than they can attend to.

"When I was offered the nomination for Governor of New Jersey it was understood by the Democratic party that I was to become its leader. If I could not have been its leader I would have withdrawn from the race. I told them that in giving me this chance the leadership would not be dull, and there would be plenty of sport in it.

"I think the most pathetic feature of the political game so far is the many letters I have received from the people of the State of New Jersey congratulating me for the work I have done in trying to make the game a clean one. Men can't go on in the presence of wrong and serve the people and satisfy the hope of the American citizen."

Printed in the *Newark Evening News*, Dec. 30, 1910; some editorial headings omitted.

From Ryerson W. Jennings[1]

My dear Mr Wilson: Philadelphia 12 30. 1910

I do not know whether you have seen the within, or not.[2] It is the first time I have said anything against Mr Bryan. I came in the Democrat party when he was nominated, voting with it ever since, excepting in the Parker campaign, when I supported Mr Roosevelt. The last time Mr Bryan was here, was when he addressed the Pierce School.[3] Miss Pierce,[4] Roland S Morris and myself had breakfast with him. Mr Bryan asked Miss Pierce who was going to speak beside himself. She replied "O! I have had a lot of trouble, I tried to get Woodrow Wilson, but he told me that he would not speak on the same platform with you."

I noticed Mr Bryan felt hurt, and after breakfast, I told him I was certain Miss Pierce had reported you wrongly as she is a woman of very little tact, and [s]he's hardly conscious of what she is saying when she is once started.

Yours faithfully   Ryerson W. Jennings.

ALS (WP, DLC).

[1] Proprietor of the Little Hotel Wilmot and several restaurants in Philadelphia.

[2] The enclosure was a clipping of a letter dated December 26, 1910, which Jennings had sent to the editor of the Philadelphia *Public Ledger*. In it, Jennings referred to the issue of *The Commoner*, already cited, in which William Jennings Bryan had listed four Democrats who he thought were qualified to be presidential candidates. Jennings said that Wilson's name should have come first instead of last on the list since he stood "head and shoulders above the three others named." Jennings also noted that Champ Clark's name was missing. Praising Clark's record on the tariff, he said that it was the Missourian's "great defense against the forces of monopolistic greed . . . which gave his party the incentive and spirit that elected Wilson, Harmon, Foss and Dix and the decisive majority in Congress." Clark, he added, "has well earned the reward of being the leader of his party, even to the seat of the great men who have preceded him in the White House."

[3] A business and secretarial school, the Peirce School was located at 917-19 Chestnut Street in Philadelphia and had been founded by Thomas May Peirce in 1865. The last time that Bryan had spoken at the Peirce School was December 23, 1908.

[4] Mary Bisbing Peirce, principal of the Peirce School and daughter of Thomas May Peirce.

From Harry Vliet Osborne

My dear Doctor Wilson: Newark [N. J.] December 30, 1910.

We can secure Krueger's Auditorium for Friday, the 13th of January, or the New Auditorium for Saturday, the 14th. There may be some objection to holding a meeting on Saturday night on account of the difficulty of getting people out on that night. The New Auditorium has the advantage of being near the D.L. & W.R.R. depot, which would make it convenient for persons coming from Montclair and the Oranges, although that hall is not quite as large as Kruegers. I shall be pleased to have your views on this point.[1]

I am engaged in making up a committee of representative Democrats to take charge of the arrangements for the meeting should you desire to speak in Essex County.

Such opinions as I have been able to obtain as to the advisability of holding a meeting here at all have been divided, but I think if any other meetings are held than the Jersey City meeting, one should be held in Newark. I do not believe there is any danger of a "packed" meeting or any unfriendly demonstration.

Dr. R. C. Newton, a prominent physician of Montclair who ran for Mayor there on the Democratic ticket during the recent campaign, called to see me yesterday regarding a movement there to offer you such assistance as they could in the present crisis. They want to do something.

It was proposed to give a dinner to Mylod,[2] which, however, he refused to attend. Now they want to give the dinner anyway, or have their demonstration take some other form. They would hold a meeting in the school hall if you would go there, but I told him I did not think you would speak at more than one Essex County meeting and that probably in Newark. I asked him to let me submit the matter to you before he perfected any arrangements for a dinner or other demonstration. Do you see any objection to their taking some action, or do you desire to suggest any particular method by which they should proceed?

I shall be glad to discuss these matters with you on Sunday or Monday next if you desire it, and will let me know when it will be convenient for me to meet you at Princeton for that purpose.   Very truly yours,   H. V. Osborne.

TLS (WP, DLC).
  [1] Wilson spoke on the senatorial situation in the New Auditorium in Newark on January 14, 1911. A news report of his address is printed at Jan. 16, 1911.
  [2] To honor him for revoking his earlier support of Smith and for coming out for Martine. See n. 2 to the news report printed at Dec. 21, 1910.

To Henry Watterson

Princeton, N. J.
My dear Colonel Watterson: December 31, 1910

It is generous of you to let me know when you are to be in New York and I shall certainly make a special effort to see you, or at least call you up while you are there. I do not know anything that has heartened me more than your friendship and counsel. I want to express my genuine gratitude and my very warm friendship.

Cordially and faithfully yours,   Woodrow Wilson

TLS (H. Watterson Papers, DLC).

To Henry St. George Tucker

My dear Mr. Tucker: Princeton, N. J. December 31, 1910

Thank you most warmly for your kind letter of the 29th. It has given me a great deal of pleasure and encouragement. I am delighted to hear of what is afloat in Virginia. My thought constantly dwells with the greatest affection upon the affairs of the old State.

Cordially and faithfully yours,   Woodrow Wilson

TLS (Tucker Family Papers, NcU).

From Oswald Garrison Villard

My dear Mr. Wilson,   New York Dec 31st 1910

I do not wish to bother you about the secretaryship matter, but am wondering if you would care to have Mr. Selden report to you at Princeton some day since the inaugural approaches so rapidly. If so we shall be glad to give Mr Selden as much time off as you desire.

The Smith defeat bids fair to be a rout soon and Dix is working hard if quietly for Shepard.

With best New Year's wishes,

Sincerely yours,   Oswald Garrison Villard.

ALS (WP, DLC).

To Robert Bridges

My dear Bobby,   Princeton, N. J. 2 January, 1911.

A happy New Year! May it bring you everything you most hope for! I wish that I could convey the greeting in person and as heartily as I feel it. It is delightful that we should go the pilgrimage together and should be near enough to exchange frequent greetings as we fare along.

I have been thinking a great deal about that delightful thing you told me about the other night at the Club.[1] I think you must have seen how deeply it touched me. As I have thought of it, and talked it over with Mrs. Wilson, I have been unable to see any flaw in it. It seems to me the most beautiful thing I ever knew of; and it makes me very happy. I do not see how I can refuse it. I can accept it with perfect honour and with deep happiness that the fine men[2] involved should have deemed me worthy of it. If you can send me the four thousand which they said was now at my disposal, I can relieve my present anxieties and feel that I am under an obligation which increases my dignity rather than diminishes it.

I wish I knew how to frame a message that would be worthy of your conveying to the gentlemen concerned, but I cannot. I can only say that I feel that this thing, done in this perfect and noble way, is the honour of which I shall always feel proudest, and for which I shall always feel most deeply and peculiarly grateful.

With warm affection,

Always,   Your devoted friend,   Woodrow Wilson

WWTLS (WC, NjP).

¹ Either the Princeton Club or the University Club, both of New York.

² A group of Wilson's friends had conferred and agreed to subsidize at least his gubernatorial career, and Bridges was to be their liaison with Wilson. The names of the contributors, aside from Bridges, who of course may not have been one of them, is unknown. Only the amount donated in 1911—$4,000—is known; presumably the same sum was given in 1912. It is interesting that this was the sum that Wilson had hoped to receive annually from a Carnegie retirement allowance. For information about the payments, see R. Bridges to WW, Jan. 13, 1911, and WW to R. Bridges, Jan. 14, 1911, both in this volume, and WW to R. Bridges, Jan. 24, 27, and 31, 1912 all in Vol 24.

To Oswald Garrison Villard

My dear Mr. Villard: Princeton, N. J. Jan. 2nd 1911

I know that you will understand why I have not written you sooner about the secretaryship and Mr. Selden, but I want to apologize nevertheless and to explain that I have never been so robbed of time of my own in my life.

Everything that you tell me about Mr. Selden attracted me and interested me and my little interview with Mr. Selden at the Southern Society Dinner gave me a most favorable impression of him. I may yet turn to him and if I do I shall do so with pleasure.

But the plot thickens about me here; the Smith forces are trying to coil me about with plans of their own which it will take more knowledge of past transactions here than I now have to checkmate and defeat. I am therefore going to ask one of the ablest of the young Democratic politicians of the State if he will not act as my secretary in order that I may have a guide at my elbow in matters of which I know almost nothing.¹ If he declines the field will be open again.

I know that you will recognize the prudence of doing this in the circumstances, and I sincerely hope that it will not be a serious disappointment to Mr. Selden.

It is delightful to have you say that you think the Smith defeat "bids fair to be a rout soon" and it is equally cheering to hear that Dix is working for Shepard. If we could win in both States it would put us in great heart and certainly the Post has been doing tremendous service on both sides of the State border.

Cordially and gratefully yours,   Woodrow Wilson

TLS (O. G. Villard Papers, MH).
   1 Wilson's announcement of his appointment of Joseph Patrick Tumulty and of Tumulty's acceptance is printed at Jan. 13, 1911.

To John Wesley Wescott

My dear Judge Wescott: Princeton, N. J. January 2, 1911

Your letter of the 26th was most generous and I appreciate it very warmly. It would be delightful to see you as you suggest after my inauguration and I shall welcome your views upon appointments or anything else.

As for my physical strength, so far as I can judge, [it] is standing the strain excellently. The trouble is I do not get time enough for exercise but I think that can be remedied after I get down to some sort of system after my inauguration.

With warmest regards and appreciation of your kindness,
        Cordially and faithfully yours,   Woodrow Wilson

TLS (J. W. Wescott Coll., NjP).

From Clara Schlee Laddey and Mary Loring Colvin[1]

Sir: Arlington, N. J. January 2nd 1911

The New Jersey Woman Suffrage Association extends to you a sincere New Year's Greeting.

You are facing big problems as the New Year opens and we congratulate you upon the fearless and courageous manner in which you are handling them.

In the press of present issues the cause this Association represents may not seem to you either big or vital. But we assure you, when we think of the noble army of women who for the past sixty years have given their strength and their lives that the cause might triumph, we, who are endeavoring to carry on the work do feel it to be both big and vital.

This Association firmly believes you accept the definition of Democracy as being a government "of and by the *people*." It further believes your logical mind must draw from this definition the conclusion that we are not living in a real democracy or that women are not people.

In asking that the suffrage be extended to women we do not ask it as a panacea for all existing evils. We ask it simply in the name of right and justice.

This Association appreciates the magnitude of the work to which you have set your hand and would gladly be of service to you.

Most respectfully,   Clara S. Laddey,   Mary L. Colvin

TLS (WP, DLC).
[1] Mrs. Victor H. G. Laddey of Arlington, N. J., president of the New Jersey Woman's Suffrage Association, and Mrs. Fred H. Colvin of East Orange, N. J., corresponding secretary.

From William Hunter Maxwell

Honorable Sir: Newark, N. J., Jan. 2, 1911.

In what I am about to say I do not wish to appear as audacious or insolent in the least, and I honestly hope that you will not take it in that light.

To my personal knowledge a number of colored people here-about and in New Jersey seem always to be a little scrupulous as to their rights etc. when a southern man and a democrat holds office which administers over them. As for myself I am not one of those colored persons. As for yourself, I have believed in you since I first learned of you and I voted for you.

What I wish to suggest is this, since this feeling prevails to some extent, do you not think that it would be well to make some statement in your inaugural address, that will tend to assure the colored people of New Jersey of your utter and entire friendliness towards them.[1]

I regret very deeply to have to even hint of any separateness in the matter of human beings and their relations the one with the other. But the fact remains and has to be met.

I know that you intend to use all persons right, according to the standard of the true spirit of America. But of course that is a bit too general for some of our people of this day and time who have suffered from various and un-American discriminations, and that more than many of the other races. I hope that what I have said will appear to you as it does to me, I am not intimating anything special for one more than the other. Justice and un-selfish purpose in life is what all men should strive to. A life of pure and unselfish service is the only life worth living.

Very Truly Your's,   Wm. H. Maxwell.

TLS (WP, DLC).
  1 Wilson did not follow Maxwell's suggestion in his inaugural address printed
at Jan. 17, 1911.

From George Wylie Paul Hunt[1]

Dear Sir: Globe, Arizona, Jan 2rd 1911

I am taking the liberty to send you under seperate cover, the proposed CONSTITUTION FOR THE STATE OF ARIZONA,[2] I would respectfully request if you have the time at your disposal and feel enclined to give your views on this document. The election for its adoption by the people of this Terr. comes off on the 9th of Feb.

We feel that this Constitution as we have adopted represents the views of the vast majority of the people of Arizona, it is progressive, and from the stand point of some of the older Commonwealths it may be too advanced. I feel assured that after you have perused it and can say a good word for our work it will be greatly appreciated, not only by Arizonans, but it would be of vast benefit to us in the East.

As one of the great leaders of our party, whose advice is surely to be heeded, I feel that a word from you would be worth a kings ransom.   Yours Respectfully,   Geo. W. P. Hunt

TLS (WP, DLC).
  1 President of the Old Dominion Commercial Co. of Globe, Ariz.; president of the constitutional convention of the Territory of Arizona; first Governor of Arizona.
  2 The constitution had been adopted on December 9, 1910, by the constitutional convention in Phoenix. Democrats had dominated the convention in which organized labor was heavily represented. The result was a constitution with provisions for an eight-hour day for public employees, an employers' liability act and compulsory compensation for workers injured in hazardous occupations, child-labor regulations, and prohibition of the use of blacklists by employers. The most controversial provisions were those incorporating the initiative, referendum, and recall of elected officials, including judges, into the organic law. Arizona conservatives, led by Republicans, were opposed to these measures mainly on the ground that President Taft, known to be against the recall of judges, would veto a statehood bill. Supporters of the constitution formed the Arizona Statehood League with Hunt as president and launched a campaign for approval by an impressive vote. The league obtained a letter of endorsement from Judge Ben B. Lindsey which was printed widely in territorial newspapers, while Bryan spoke for the constitution in Phoenix. Wilson's response to Hunt's appeal, if he made one, is not extant.
  Arizonans approved the constitution by an overwhelming margin on February 9, 1911. Congress's joint resolution approving statehood was vetoed by Taft on August 15, 1911. However, on August 21, 1911, Taft signed another bill providing for statehood on the condition that judges be exempted by popular vote from the recall provision in the constitution. The constitution was so amended by Arizona voters at a general election on December 12, 1911, and Taft signed the proclamation admitting Arizona as the forty-eighth state on February 14, 1912. In the general election on November 5, 1912, the voters approved an amendment to the constitution providing for the recall of judges. The foregoing is based upon Jay J. Wagoner, *Arizona Territory, 1863-1912: A Political History* (Tuscon, Ariz., 1970), pp. 460-485, and Rufus Kay Wyllys, *Arizona, the History of a Frontier State* (Phoenix, Ariz., 1950), pp. 305-13.

To Mary Allen Hulbert Peck

Dearest Friend,   Princeton, New Jersey 3 January, 1911.

My trip to St. Louis cut a whole week out, and I am sure that some steamer for Bermuda got away without a letter for you from the friend whose thoughts are as constant as the seasons, but are not permitted to find their way to paper one day in ten. If it refreshes you to hear from me as much as it refreshes me to hear from you, I am ssrry [sorry] any steamer should go without at least a little note. It shall not happen when I can help it.

I believe I am making progress in my fight. It is made all the more exciting and dramatic because of the fact that all the country seems to be watching it with such eager interest, as *the* fight in the inter[e]st of the people as against the bosses. An editor told me the other day that in looking over his exchanges you could pick out a paper from any section of the country and be sure to find any where some space devoted to me,—from a single paragraph to a couple of columns. It ought to be an anxious business to be thus the centre of all eyes from one end of the country to the other; but, strangely enough, I do not find that it is. I take the reason to be that my course is so plain before me. No fool could miss it. I do not have to sit down and reason it out. It has no intricacies or doubtful places in it. I have only to state plainly and without any concealment of any kind at each stage of the fight where I stand and what I intend to do, and never budge or waver, to satisfy all expectations and win. For at that pace I shall win in all essentials even if I lose in the actual thing striven for,—as I shall not: for Smith is beaten, I feel confident. A well informed newspaper man from Washingtonn[1] told me an interesting thing the other day. He said that when I was first nominated they thought 'Oh yes, a fine man, unimpeachable character, no end of brains, but an academic person whom they will fool to the top of their bent.' My campaign disabused them of that idea; but they still looked askance at me because they found the Wall Street crowd so complacent about my candidacy. When I went straightway for Smith and began to show that I meant nothing less than to put him out of business, they were finally converted and threw their hats in air; and now they are waiting for me to be President. "You have the Wall Street crowd scared stiff," he said. But that is neither here nor there. I can say that to you, to whom I always say exactly what is really in my thought, and it is delightful to know that you will believe me. Undoubtedly I am just at this moment the most observed and the most talked of man in the country; and I am reassured to find that it does not have the least effect upon me. It is as it has been with me all my life. I feel detached from what is going on about me, and am like a man looking on. My thoughts are as apt to turn and play about some boyish recollection or some childish fancy as to dwell on the news and the problems of the day and of my own situation. I care for the game, the immediate object, immensely, but very little for what lies beyond. Thought of the presidency annoys me in a way. I do not *want* to be President. There is too little play in it, too little time for one's friends, too much distasteful publicity and fuss and frills. I dote on going my own way. I am an inveterate *simple* (if I may coin a noun): I hate to have what I do issue in complex things in only some of which I am interested. I love the affairs of the world and want to handle them, but I do not want to wear their harness and trappings.

But here I am talking about myself and all the while really *thinking* about *you*. I hope you realize how constantly I do, and with what deep admiration and affection,—with what eager hope that all goes happily with you. All join me in affectionate messages. I am perfectly well.

Your devoted friend,   Woodrow Wilson

The wedding went off famously, and the little bride seems very happy indeed; but the mother is dreadfully lonely.

WWTLS (WP, DLC).
[1] John E. Lathrop. The "Washingtonn" is Wilson's typographical error.

To Charles Williston McAlpin

My dear McAlpin: Princeton, N. J. January 3, 1911

Your letter of the 23rd has remained unanswered simply because I was away from home. Thank you for it with all my heart. It is delightful to know that I have the support of your judgment in the course I am now pursuing as I was fortunate enough to have it in the old days of the college troubles.

Mrs. Wilson joins me in most cordial greetings of the season to Mrs. McAlpin[1] and yourself, and I am,

Always affectionately and gratefully   Woodrow Wilson

TLS (photostat in RSB Coll., DLC).
[1] Sara Carter Pyle McAlpin.

From Calvin Easton Brodhead

My Dear Governor: Plainfield, N. J. Jan. 4, 1911.

I learned indirectly today that very strong pressure is being brought to bear on you to get you to appoint a Democrat to succeed Judge Adrain [Adrian] Lyon,[1] of Middlesex County. No one has asked me to say anything to you about this matter, but as I lived in Perth Amboy for twenty years and know Mr. Lyon I feel constrained to tell you what I think about the effort to replace him. Judge Lyon is one of the most upright and honorable gentlemen in the State, a first class lawyer and pos[s]esses the judicial temparment to a high degree. He has the confidence and respect of all good people in Middlesex County and I believe has made a splendid Judge. I have thought that it would be your policy to disregard political considerations in so far as possible in making judicial appointments. Therefore I think the reappointment of Judge Lyon would commend itself to most Democrats and Republicans. I believe the liquor interests do not take kindly to Judge Lyon, but I am sure no reasonable and fair minded man will question his character and fitness.

I have no desire to "butt in" to a matter that is outside my county. I realize that there may be very important considerations that may prompt you to appoint somebody in Judge Lyon's place.[2] I only do so because of my knowledge of the man and for your information.

Yours very sincerely,   Calvin E. Brodhead.

TLS (WP, DLC).
 [1] Progressive Republican of Perth Amboy, who had been appointed judge of the Court of Common Pleas of Middlesex County by Governor Fort in 1909 to fill an unexpired term.
 [2] Wilson did not reappoint Lyon. Instead, he named Peter Francis Daly in March 1911.

To Mary Allen Hulbert Peck

Dearest Friend,   University Club [New York] 5 Jan'y, '11

What a lovely letter that was you wrote me on the twenty-ninth of Dec.,[1] the day after my (fifty-fourth!) birthday (I suppose you did not mention it out of delicacy!) It stilled some of my anxiety about you—for it showed the old charm beginning to work again—the charm of dear Bermuda, its water, its sky, its almost personal moods of wind and weather, and it showed you at peace, at leisure, looking with calmness on the petty storms of the little social world,—and again wandering abroad in search of old furniture—best sign of all! Bermuda has not changed—the physical Bermuda which you love and which draws out all the sweet poetry that is in you—but you *have* changed—changed very much since I first met you. Do you realize it? Or, rather, you have come into your own. You were a great creature stunted, cabined, shut in—*now* you are coming, by some happy influence, into your own,—are realizing how big your real world of mind and heart is,—the world you were intended for, had longed for, had had glimpses into, but had never entered. *Bermuda* is not your world, nor any round of fashion and amusement; you were meant for a *big* stage of sympathy and insight and action, and Bermuda is only your *setting.* Your heart expands in it. There, where you are free and where that fine air fills your lungs, you are at peace, and the peace brings you knowledge of yourself—of your real longings, your real capacities, your real loves and ambitions! And what deep joy it gives me to think of those sweet, wholesome, self-revealing influences about you,—the dear friend I discovered—perhaps discovered to herself! Letters written in a distracting rush, when you are wasting your strength and your big, sweet nature on things that tire you out and give you no joy or lasting satisfaction. I am uneasy—I go about my tasks with a haunting anxiety and disappointment,—but a letter like this last one puts me in heart again and makes my thought of you happy, serene, content. God bless you! You can be as big, as satisfying, as true a source of inspiration as you choose to be —in Bermuda as well as in New York, and you will be if you give yourself leave under the charm.

I address a big meeting in Jersey City to-night about the Senatorial question. I will tell you about it next time.

I am well and in all things

Your devoted friend,   Woodrow Wilson

Warmest regards to Mrs. Allen. I have not had time yet to look up A[llen]. H[ulbert].

ALS (WP, DLC).
1 It is missing.

An Address in Jersey City, New Jersey[1]

[[Jan. 5, 1911]]

Mr. Chairman[2] and Fellow Citizens: Let me assure you that the reception you have just given me touches me very deeply, indeed. There is only one way in which a man can acquire great-

1 Delivered in St. Patrick's Hall.
2 Joseph P. Tumulty.

ness in a country like this, and that is by putting himself at the service of a great people to accomplish great objects; and it seems to me that one of the most interesting circumstances of my life is that in this town, in which I began my campaign for Governor, in this hall, where I addressed an interesting audience on the first evening of the campaign, I should again meet a great body of my fellow citizens; but not in order to convince them of anything, not in order to ask for their suffrages, but merely in my own person, to fulfill one of the promises that I made upon this stage at that time, that I would humbly offer myself as their spokesman in the declaration of their own principles. (Applause.)

I have not come here to argue anything; I have not come here to initiate any movement among you. I have come in response to your invitation in order to allow you to give vent to the principles which you entertain without any teaching from any man —the principles which have inspired American democracy from the first until now. For it is a very inspiring circumstance, ladies and gentlemen, that we should gather here to-night to give support to a great cause. I do not have to tell you what the cause is— it is the cause of the people. (Applause.) The people have for many a weary year been excluded from any efficient and effectual part in their own affairs. In this State and in some of the States they have come into their own, and in meetings like this they gather together to declare that they have come into possession and that their will is to be the will of the State.

I do not feel that this is an occasion when we will do anything except agree to the terms of the cause in which we are enlisted. It is a common cause; it is a cause to which many expressions are given; but it is a cause upon which we may all agree in terms which will satisfy every man, I venture to say, in this presence; for when we ask ourselves, "What is all this fight about?" it is easy to answer the question.

I have heard a great deal said in recent weeks about a split in the Democratic party. There is no split in the Democratic party. (Applause and voice, "That's it.") The circumstance which is now being brought to the attention of some politicians is that there is a united Democratic party, whose service they must obey. It is not, let me say, a capital process to cut off a wart. (Applause.) You do not have to go to a hospital or take an anaesthetic; the thing can be done while you wait. (Applause.) And it is being done. The clinic is open and every man can witness the operation. (Applause.)

Does the Democratic party consist of a little group of gentlemen in Essex County? (A voice, "No!") Of whom does the Democratic party consist? The Democratic party does not consist in any portion of any organization; it consists of the men who vote the Democratic ticket. Organizations are instruments—instruments to serve the people or take the consequences. They are instruments which govern the people in a patriotic way—in a general cause and object—and when any organization sets itself above the party which it undertakes to serve, or would have you believe that it pretends to serve, then it is time for the operation; the wart must be removed.

There is no split in the Democratic party. You can hear the processes of solidification. Men are coming together, shoulder to shoulder. They are looking into each other's eyes and saying for the first time: "We constitute an unbossed, undictated party which intends to have its way in the government of this State." Do you think that there would be any future life for the Democratic party if it could split it to do violence to a dying organization? Why, what is happening to the Democratic party? Gentlemen, it is plain what is happening to the Democratic party, provided the Democratic party prove worthy to serve the people. Young men are flocking into the Democratic party now—young men who, happily for themselves, do not entertain any very vivid recollection of some of the traditions of a portion of the Democratic organizations. (Applause.) These men will not have anything to do with the Democratic party if it is to be dominated by the influences which in some quarters have dominated it in past years. Have you not had pointed out to you again and again during the recent campaign, until you must have become familiar with it, the picture of what is going on in America? Do you know that the Republican party is a split party, not a split organization?

And for this reason some of the most public spirited, some of the wisest and most progressive men in the Republican party, discovered by slow degrees what it made their hearts very heavy to discover, that the party was being dominated by certain special interests. They therefore turned their faces away from those members of their party who represented that domination. They said, "We will no longer consent to this partnership"; they said, "We will no longer consent to serve some of the people when we ought to be serving all of the people." (Applause.) And therefore these gentlemen that in this State we call the New Idea Republicans (loud applause), these gentlemen that are in some quarters called Progressives and in others Insurgents, have this idea, which we ought to be ashamed to call a new idea, that their obligations are to the people, to the whole country, to the great mass of men whose fortunes make up for ill or for good the prosperity of America. (Loud applause.) That is the new, the ancient, the majestic idea that has always beckoned men to their highest duty in America.

Now these gentlemen by the score, by the thousand, in the last election—if we are to confine our views to our own commonwealth which we understand, flocked, temporarily it may be, permanently it may be if we have the wisdom to satisfy them, flocked to our standard because they thought that we were free from that domination. Only because they thought we were free from that domination. Now, what is to be the choice of the Democratic party? Is it to continue to grow up and be made strong and solid by these free elements of conscientious America, or is it to do the other thing?

Do you know what is true of the special interests at this moment, ladies and gentlemen? They have got all their baggage packed, and they are ready to strike camp over night (renewed laughter), provided they think it is profitable to them to come over to the Democratic party. They are waiting to come over bag and baggage and take possession of the Democratic party. Will they be welcome? Do you want them? (Cries of "No, no, no.") Very well, then; see that you do not want those who represent them. (Loud applause and laughter.) There is no question of the Democratic party in this business, gentlemen. There is no question of any party. I often think in this connection of the song in "Iolanthe," the comic opera, "The party I belong to is the party I sing this song to."

Business interests are involved in this matter and not political principles. These business interests intend, if they can, to own any organization—that is, the governing organization in the affairs of America. They cannot own it if the business is done in the open. They can own it if it is done under cover. They won't strike their camps and move over in the daytime; they will move over in the nighttime. (Laughter and applause.) I pray God we may never wake up some fine morning and find them in camp on our side. (Loud applause and laughter.)

If I understand my own heart, ladies and gentlemen, I do not entertain personal animosities in this matter. It is not a question of persons and their faults; it is a question of the records of some persons, because the records show the tendency. How do I know which way a man is heading unless I look up his record? How do I know who are his friends, his associates, what his connections have been, what his determinations have been, unless I look up his record?

And I want to point out to you that Mr. James Smith, Jr., (Hisses)—No, gentlemen, wait a minute—Mr. Smith represents not a party but a system, a system of political control which does not belong to either party and which, so far as it can be successfully managed, must belong to both parties. (Applause.)

Under this system it is just as necessary to maintain and subsidize, if possible, a faithful and subservient minority as a faithful and subservient majority; it is just as important to see that nobody in the minority jumps the track as it is to see that nobody in the majority jumps the track.

It is a matter of indifference to the people of New Jersey, as I have already said in public, which representative of this system is sent to the United States Senate, for it is the system that we are fighting and not the representatives. There are some representatives of that system who have, and I believe deserve, our respect for their candor, their honesty and their characters. There are men in this country who believe—conscientiously believe— that the prosperity of America is tied up with and identical with the prosperity of certain great financial interests in America. If a man believes that I must differ with him very emphatically in opinion, but I am not at liberty to say anything in derogation of his character or of his honesty. He may be just as honest a man as any of us, but he cannot think in the terms of America; he thinks in the terms of the influences with which he is connected; and a man who cannot think in the terms of America cannot represent any portion of America. (Applause.) You know what the system is. The system—it has been expounded so often that perhaps we do not notice it until we get excited—it is an old story. It is a stale story, but all true stories are old; all true stories are, in a sense, stale, because the truth is as old as creation.

This system consists in an alliance—a systematic, but covert alliance—between business and politics. Politics under this system is considered the means of securing and promoting certain financial and business interests. Wherever the greatest power is brought to bear, the greatest power of money, the greatest power of individual influence, there politics is made to yield to the influence, yield to the impulse. I want to call your attention to Mr. Smith's alliances. You know with whom Mr. Smith is allied. What Democratic papers are supporting the candidacy of Mr. James Smith, Jr., for the Senate? Two papers, which, it is said—of course, I know nothing personally about it—it is said that he owns himself.[3] Where does the rest of the support come from? I believe I overlooked the Long Branch Record. Where does his support come from? It comes from the papers which are understood to be the mouthpieces of the very members of the Republican Board of Guardians, who we had supposed that we had put out of business.

You know who Mr. Kuehnle is, do you not, of Atlantic City?[4] You know who Mr. Baird of Camden is, do you not? Mr. Smith has recently been in conference with Mr. Kuehnle and with Mr. Baird in Philadelphia; Mr. Smith has been in conference with Mr. Baird in New York. His conferences have all chiefly been with the gentlemen who are his allies on what we regard as their side, because there is a community of interests which nobody who has any power of vision at all can overlook, for these gentlemen openly support the candidacy of Mr. Smith and openly oppose those who oppose Mr. Smith; they know that Mr. Smith will safeguard the interests they are most concerned with if he should go to the United States Senate. I am not suggesting in this any corrupt influence; I am not suggesting anything except the fact that those are the interests he would represent. There are no surmises in this matter; we know what is going on; it is no longer underground; the whole thing has been smoked out.

These gentlemen have a perfect right, as American citizens, to support the candidacy of Mr. James Smith, but it is very interesting to us that they should be supporting it, and very significant of the things we are trying to do, and they are trying to cheat us out of, for we supposed, on that memorable evening of November 8th last, that we had thrashed that particular crowd. Well, we had, and they are going to stay thrashed. (Applause.) But I admire their complacency. There is something to be said of men who never know when they are licked, and they apparently do not.

But there is a very serious side to it all, gentlemen. You know that there is a reign of terror in certain parts of the State. Some gentlemen seem to have supposed, before I was elected, that I was simply using words for the sake of obtaining votes, and that I did not mean what I said; they also seemed to have supposed that I studied politics entirely out of books. (Applause and a voice, "They fooled themselves.") Now there isn't any politics worth talking about in books; in books everything looks very obvious, very symmetrical, very systematic and very complete; but

---

[3] The Newark *Morning Star* and the *Newark Evening Star and Newark Advertiser.*

[4] Louis Kuehnle, Republican boss of Atlantic County.

it is not the picture of life, and it is only in the picture of life that all of us are interested.

Now, there has been going on before my eyes for the last twenty years just what has been going on before your eyes. God gave me my eyes, and I do not use my eyelids except at night (applause), and I know that the same thing has been going on these last twenty years that is going on right now.

You know, very much to our discredit, that we pay members of the Assembly in New Jersey only five hundred dollars a year; no man, for five hundred dollars a year, without some independent means, can afford to represent you, and to pay them but five hundred dollars a year is to put them under direct temptation. I do not mean the temptation to accept money, but a temptation to be acquiescent on the side where business interests are involved. Now, some members of our Legislatures are employes of large business concerns; these business concerns put the screws on those men whenever there is any danger of any pending legislation being against their interests.

They do it to these men, for example, and say: "Why, don't you see that our direct interest is in the present schedules of the tariff? Don't you see that it is imperative that we have the right man to represent us in the United States Senate to see that that tariff is not too freely tampered with? Do you expect us to retain you in our service or to pay you the same salary if you act contrary to our interests as if you act in accordance with our interests?"

I am not hazarding a guess, gentlemen; I am speaking whereof I know, and I tell you that I have very high admiration for the splendid fidelity of some of these men upon whom this pressure has been brought to bear; they will not submit to it; you must see to it that they are requited for their fidelity to you.

It is easy to pick these men out; it is easy to find out the men who in recent years have grown reckless; there has been too little concealment for their health. These things are common talk. It is common talk in South Jersey that Mr. Smith can have as many Republican votes as he needs to elect him Senator. I don't believe it. I don't believe that the Republican members of the Senate and Assembly would so disgrace themselves and their party as to enter into a contract of that kind.

But the point that I call your attention to is that some leaders do believe it; some leaders do believe that they can deliver the votes to Smith. There is a chance to single out the right men and give them your co-operation and support. There has come a time when this reign of terror is being carried to the very verge of desperation on the part of the men engaged in it. But don't concern yourselves; sit serenely in your seats and only look on, and it will not happen. (Applause.) It fills one's lungs as if with a fresh and revivifying air to feel the winds of opinion that are clarifying everything in our day. This irresistible purifying operation that resides in the human spirit, that cannot look upon false and corrupt things without their disappearing as if under the genial rays of a wholesome sun. And this is what is happening in our time and putting heart into men everywhere.

A gentleman was talking to me only last night—a gentleman who has been prominent in the public service of this State—and he said to me: "This is a fight that is going on all over the country, but New Jersey is the bloody angle." You know what he was referring to when he said that New Jersey was the bloody angle: he was referring to the battle field of Gettysburg, where, at a certain angle of a stone wall the principle slaughter of the day centered. That has always been known since as the bloody angle, and he said that this campaign in New Jersey is the bloody angle of national fights. But our fight is not like the fight at Gettysburg, where gallant heroes were engaged on both sides, where the fight was open, where the fight was in the open, for in this battle one party is supplying the ammunition and keeping under cover, dodging from tree to tree and from ambush to ambush, while the other party stands in the open and challenges them to the contest. (Long and continued applause.) The bloody angle indeed! But it will not be our bodies that are in the breach.

You remember the story of the poor old Confederate soldier who was coming home after everything was over, who said: "Well, I killed as many of them as they did of me, anyway." (Applause.) And I think we all can go home after this fight feeling just that way, that we killed as many of them as they did of us.

Now, gentlemen, what is the other side of the picture? Mere negation don't count for anything in accomplishment. You can defeat as many special interests as you please, they always have their representatives; you cannot reach the end of the waiting list. (Applause.) You can induce, possibly, conceivably—I tried it, but did not succeed—you might induce James Smith, Jr., to retire, but if Mr. Smith did retire somebody else would take his place. The interests are not of a retiring nature. (Applause.) And they have a great many presentable persons whom they could put forward, and if you looked them over hastily you would not recognize them. For my part, I would rather have somebody that I knew as their representative than somebody that I did not know and who has not disclosed himself, because it is very hard in some parts of this commonwealth to pick conspicuous gentlemen who are not in some way connected with the special interests. Some of them are capital men, but most of them have the fatal prepossession so far as the public interests are concerned, men who cannot think in terms of the people's interests, because they do not know what these terms mean; they believe that the destinies of America are tied up with the prosperity of their particular business.

Mr. Martine (applause) has the great good fortune to represent this critical juncture in the affairs of New Jersey's great popular cause; he represents an opportunity for the people of New Jersey to say whether they believe in the popular choice of United States Senators, or do not believe in it.

There has been a great deal of sophistication about this question. Men have said that the primary vote was small and they do not see how it can be claimed that they are morally bound to acquiesce in that relatively small vote as compared with the total Democratic vote in New Jersey. Very well, I can see how they are morally bound by it. But if they cannot see, can they see this, that there is a tremendous moral compulsion put upon them by the opportunity? (Applause.) The opportunity to show that, from this time on, this is going to be the method by which Senators are chosen by New Jersey. (Loud applause.) Turn for one instant from Mr. Martine and see what you have done. You have said that what you have so far done in this direction you did not mean. You have said that in 1907 you were deliberately throwing a sop to Cerberus;[5] you were deliberately deceiving, misleading public opinion; giving them the impression that you were offering them bread when you were deliberately and of your own knowledge offering them a stone. You are saying that whereas you once professed that you believed in following the popular expression of preference for Senator, you did not believe it then, but you are going to believe it next time. (Applause.) You will fill everybody with loathing and contempt by such a course, whereas by standing steadfast to the moral obligation of this great principle, and insisting that your representatives make Mr. Martine the Senator from New Jersey (loud applause), you will have achieved, in view of the whole country, one of the most important and decisive triumphs for popular government that has been achieved in our day.

Shall men turn away from this opportunity and say that they do not observe the moral obligation of it? Shall any man go

[5] That is, when the legislature provided for the holding of senatorial preferential primaries.

about amongst you and continue to enjoy your respect for political discrimination, to say nothing of political honesty, who will
turn away from such an opportunity with such a blindness and
obtuseness? Men who cannot see this opportunity cannot in
other matters see how they are morally bound to serve the State
and the interests of the people.

I have heard a great many men hope for compromise. God
defend us against compromise! (Applause.) All weak men want
compromise. (Applause.) Every man who is afraid to stand to
his guns wants compromise. Every man who finds a duty difficult to perform wants the form of the duty changed; but change
it for him, and you simply confirm his weakness. I appeal to Mr.
Martine[6] never under any circumstances to withdraw. (Applause
and cheers.)

We are not in this fight to find the easy way, the complacent
way. We are in it to find and pursue the right way (applause)
and any man who turns away from the right way will be marked
and labeled. (Applause.)

I would not have you believe that there are many weak parts
in this struggle among the men actually involved, for I do not
believe there are. There are some weak hearts, and I am sorry for
them. I would rather be a knave than a coward. (Applause.) It is
no temptation to be a coward—it is so ridiculous. One would wish
to go off the stage with erect figure at any rate and not running.
(Laughter.) There is nothing dignified in the running, that is
retreat.

There are plenty of brave souls in this contest and I have come
into contact with them, and it would hearten any man to be surrounded by men of the determination of the men I know are to
be counted, not by the handful, but by large proportions in the
ranks of the men who are to help us in the Legislature of New
Jersey. Look, what an honor it is. The whole State knows the
roll of the names of men who have stood by the people in
the past sessions of the Legislature. Hudson County has had the
honor of producing many of them. (Applause.) I am going to
take the liberty of mentioning three because they are no longer
in the Legislature, and I would not be drawing comparisons.
Take the instances of Mr. Tracey [Treacy] and Judge Sullivan
and Mr. Tumulty. (Applause and cheers.) Mr. Tracey, Judge
Sullivan and Mr. Tumulty. (Applause.) The whole State knows
that that is a roll of honor (applause), and the whole State is
heartened by this further circumstance that here is a group of
men who illustrate in their lives and conduct not only public

[6] Martine was in the audience and spoke briefly after Wilson.

morality but the teachings of the great Church of which they are members. (Applause.) Men sometimes forget, ladies and gentlemen, that religious principle is the one solid and remaining and abiding foundation. (Applause.) Find a man whose conscience is buttressed by that intimate principle and you will find a man into whose hands you can safely entrust your affairs. (Applause.) For the man who steers by expediency, the man who trims his course by what he thinks will be the political consequence, the man who always has his eye upon the weather, is a man whom you cannot trust.

We are sailing, whenever it is necessary, directly into the teeth of the wind. We know how to sail close to the wind in honest fashion and not dishonest fashion. We know how all the forces that pulse in this world are moral forces. Why, gentlemen, one of the things that makes this one of the most interesting crises in the history of New Jersey is that there is nothing selfish in this battle. You are not fighting for some favorite person whom you wish to elevate into the Senate of the United States, because he is a favorite son of your county, because he is a favorite and beloved personal friend, because he represents some interest with which you are connected. You have the honor—you have the excitement—you have the delight—of fighting for a man because he embodies a principle that you believe in, and there is nothing more honorable than that, and I tell you there is nothing more irresistible than that.

Once let unselfish passion get into the hearts of great bodies of men and no living man can resist them; for the interesting difference between selfish and unselfish passion is this: Selfish passion makes a mob of men, and mobs never know how to cooperate; but unselfish passion brings reason into the field, puts counsel in the saddle; yokes men together with generous impulse so that they do not look askance at each other, but look forward in the common cause; they are not a mob but an army, disciplined for triumph, battling is [in] an age of achievement, when every man shall say: "That was a renewal of the great age of American politics, when men first turned again to look upon the State as a whole," when they did not discuss their private interests, when they did not ask: "What effect will it have upon me? How will my neighbors treat me? How will my employers treat me? How will my associates look upon me?" but when they said: "I hear a voice calling out of all America, saying a new day has come, old mists have rolled away." We see. We hear this great host of free people coming on, not to destroy anything, not to wreak their vengeance upon anything as if they were a mob, but achieving that thing upon which all human happiness is based —namely, justice and equity among men, for I cannot end this address to you, gentlemen, without saying this about the interests of which I have been speaking.

I am sorry that they should make it so hard to come to a just arrangement. By insisting upon their selfish advantage they do make it hard to withhold our hearts from hostile passion, and we ought not to entertain hostile passion. We ought not to wreak our vengeance upon anything. We wish to do justice to the great interests of this country. We wish to be their comrades in a common enterprise of fairness and equity and wretchedness [righteousness]; and we cannot allow ourselves to be put upon by them, by any unjust and unholy alliance. Our attitude is that of just men; but we have terms to propose. The terms are that they dissolve their political partnership. (Applause.) We are going to put their partner out of business. (Applause.) If they know anything of the law of safety and of justice, they will not involve themselves in his downfall.

These are our terms: War, if you are allied with the enemy. Peace if you are on the other side of justice. (Applause.) It is not a truce, but it is honest, fair, equitable peace, but implacable war, if any alliance—though never so slender—remains with the men who are our enemies, and who do not know their welfare.

I would not excite a company like this to any sort of hostility. We are not met to work our will in any unselfish fashion. We are met to see that the purposes to which our hearts are devoted are carried out, and that the men who have mistakenly opposed us shall be induced by reason, by the excellence of our cause to turn about and go with us. The camp that may be removed in the night has many a gallant fellow in it. Let him show that he is willing to come over in the daytime upon terms of honorable alliance with the people, and he will be welcomed; but let him beware of transferring his connections from those whom we fear and shall fight on one side, to those whom we fear and shall fight on the other.

That is the intolerable thing against which this meeting is a protest, and this protest will be heard, gentlemen, not only through the State of New Jersey, but through the length of America, and men will say: "That great old State that we have lightly spoken of as the refuge of predatory corporations, turns out to be the place where men will study justice and do right." (Applause.) There will come out of this contest no advantage of which any man need to be ashamed—no personal advantage—no selfish advantage, but honor, credit, the respect of the abiding glory of the dear old State of New Jersey.[7]

Printed in the Jersey City *Jersey Journal*, Jan. 6, 1911, with minor corrections and additions from the text in the Trenton *True American*, Jan. 6, 1911.
   [7] There are WWhw and WWT outlines of this address, both dated Jan. 5, 1911, in WP, DLC.

From William Jennings Bryan

My Dear Mr Wilson,   Mission, Texas, Jany 5 [1911]

I am expecting to come East early in March and would like to see you for an hour or so on political matters. The fact that you were against us in 1896 raised a question in my mind in regard to your views on public questions but your attitude in the Senatorial case has tended to reassure me. I could call at Trenton or if you think better to avoid publicity, I can meet you at Burlington.[1] I have a good friend there Mr T. H. Birch whom I expect to visit at that time. In the mean time I would like to have your opinion of the various planks of the Denver platform. Many of the planks you could endorse or condemn on the margin—others you could discuss more at length.

                    Yours truly   W. J. Bryan

ALS (WP, DLC).
   [1] About Wilson's first meeting with Bryan, see WW to Mary A. H. Peck, March 12, 1911, and the news report printed at March 13, 1911.

From Oswald Garrison Villard

Dear Dr. Wilson,   [New York] Jan 5, 1911

Selden is much disappointed, and not unnaturally, for he is as keen as the rest of us for your great fight. But your decision for a political lieutenant or, better, one with political knowledge, appeals to all of us—to him, too. He will be available later should you want him.

So great is our interest in your contest that we shall, a little later, send another reporter into New Jersey. You will, I am sure, be kind enough to give him your confidence, that we may be of the greatest possible assistance to you.

                    Faithfully yours,   Oswald Garrison Villard.

ALS (WP, DLC).

To Calvin Easton Brodhead

My dear Mr. Brodhead: Princeton, N. J. January 6th 1911

Thank you sincerely for your letter of January 4th. I have heard Judge Lyon very highly spoken of, but I must say I am very much puzzled what to do about the appointments in Middlesex. Your letter will serve me very greatly in enabling me to form a judgment at any rate of Judge Lyon's claims, and I am most sincerely obliged to you for writing it.

Cordially yours,   Woodrow Wilson

TLS (received from W. M. Brodhead).

To Oswald Garrison Villard

My dear Mr. Villard: Princeton, N. J. January 6, 1911

Thank you sincerely for your characteristically kind note of January 5th. You may be sure that if you should send someone over to see me I will take him fully into my confidence because I know that you will send me a man who can be trusted. Certainly nothing has done greater service that [than] the splendid support of the Evening Post in our fight on this side of the River.

In haste,

Cordially and gratefully yours,   Woodrow Wilson

TLS (O. G. Villard Papers, MH).

From George Mason La Monte

Dear Dr. Wilson: New York January 6/1911.

I meant to have written you before in regard to Judge Adrian Lyon.

I have made inquires in regard to him from a number of personal friends, and everything that I can hear confirms what has been said as regards his personal character and sterling integrity. He certainly seems to be very highly regarded by his neighbors and the people who know him throughout the County.

Mr. Streitwolf, one of the Members of the Assembly from Middlesex County, did say that he would be "put in wrong" should the Republican Judge be appointed there, instead of the Democratic. He is the only one who has made any such suggestion to me.

I am inclined to think that it would be a very good idea to have a talk with Mr. Streitwolf some time, as I believe he is inclined to be strongly influenced by what you say.

In the Senatorial matter, it is a fact that a good deal of pressure is going to be brought to bear upon him not to stand against Mr. Smith. I think, however, that he will keep his word.

I have arranged with Mr. Broadhead from Union, and Mr. Geran from Monmouth, to meet with me and Mr. Streitwolf at luncheon next Monday, with the special intent of keeping Mr. Streitwolf up to the mark. This, of course, is confidential.

I think we are gaining in our position every day.

Very truly yours,   Geo. M. La Monte

TLS (WP, DLC).

From Harvey Thomas[1]

Atlantic City, N. J.

My Dear Governor Wilson: January 6, 1910 [1911].

It is with some little reluctance that I write you knowing, as I feel I do, how you may view communications on a subject such as I would write about. However this is a matter in which I am greatly interested and I feel I must say what I have to say, anyhow.

Of Atlantic City's political history there is little need to tell you as you have heard a lot, no doubt, and your speech in Jersey City last night is proof convincing you know of what you speak. The "machine" here has owned Atlantic City and does own it. It has owned the city's newspapers up to Sept. 1 last. I came here then and bought the Review. I have fought the "machine" since, if I may be pardoned for saying a word personally. I have fought the "machine" in every possible way as Mr. Clarence L. Cole or others can tell you. It is the first time any paper in Atlantic City has ever spoken against the "machine." I have taken a stand for clean, honest government. I have opposed every dishonest official in power. I have damned Kuehnle and his associates and damned them, as I think, with vigor. I opposed Lewis for Governor and supported Wilson. I did that for two reasons —because I believed and do believe Wilson would and will give a more independent and honest administration to the state, and because it meant a change for Atlantic City and Atlantic County. I argued both of these possibilities in every way I could. I took the position editorially that Atlantic City should have a thorough cleansing officially, and I insisted this could only be accomplished by your election. I said we need a different set of officials than the ones in power. I meant particularly a different set of judges, a different prosecutor. Atlantic City will be as it is always if it does not get a different set of these officials. I am, as I said, deeply interested in all this. I have paid the penalty for this interest and am willing to pay it. Grand juries have been asked to indict me for criminal libel. Advertisers controlled through notes in "machine" banks have quit us. And in other ways am I feeling the effect of the "machine." But that is my fight and I am getting along all right.

What I wish this letter to tell you is this—I would like to see you before you make your first appointment here—that of a district court judge. I do not and will not advocate anyone. I have no favorites. I am for no one. I am against certain ones. I would like to tell you why I am against certain ones. I do not want to suggest a name to you. For instance I am opposed to H. R. Coulomb[2] for district court judge. I am inclined to think the Democratic organization is for him. The enclosed news item and enclosed editorial may give you an idea why I am against Mr. Coulomb.[3] There have been other editorials and other stories on the same subject by me and the fact remains Mr. Coulomb quit his association with Judge Higbee[4] last Monday on the recommendation of Mr. Kuehnle's personal counsel, so as to make himself more eligible in your eyes as a candidate for this judgeship. I have insisted that this disassociation from Judge Higbee on the eve of the appointment is not a sincere one.

However I will tire you no longer. I would like you to pardon my impertinence, if you view it as such, and grant me an interview before this appointment is made. I want you to believe me when I say I will have no candidate for this or any other office to present to you. I simply wish to be given a chance to prove my opposition to Mr. Coulomb. Can I?[5]

With very best wishes, believe me,
Sincerely,   Harvey Thomas.

TLS (WP, DLC).
  [1] President and editor of the Atlantic City, N. J., *Atlantic Review*.
  [2] Harry R. Coulomb, lawyer of Atlantic City.
  [3] They are missing.
  [4] Enoch A. Higbee, judge of the Court of Common Pleas of Atlantic County.
  [5] Wilson appointed Frank Smathers, an ex-North Carolinian, to be district judge for the city of Atlantic City in February 1911.

From Harry Vliet Osborne

My dear Mr. Wilson: Newark [N. J.] January 7th, 1911.

I enclose herewith a draft of a proposed public utility bill upon which Mr. Sommer and myself have been working.[1]

If there are any suggestion[s] which you may desire to make I thought it would be well for you to look this over before putting it into final shape, so that we could incorporate your suggestions in it.

We have had before us the Wisconsin, New York and New Jersey statutes on this subject as well as the various bills that have been introduced in the New Jersey legislature during the past two years.

We hope to have this bill in shape for introduction in the very near future.   Yours very truly,   Harry V Osborne

TLS (WP, DLC).
1 It is missing.

From Henry Collin Minton[1]

Dear Dr. Wilson: Trenton [N. J.]. January 7, 1911

I have read your Thursday night speech with unstinted admiration. For fine self-restraint and for a calm and clear setting out of the whole situation in the large, I think it was simply splendid.

It's both "magnificent" and "war." But you are bound to win in either event. For if you lose in the battle, you will have succeeded in showing how strongly entrenched is the evil you are resisting and that will surely lead to winning in the war.

Be sure that hosts of good people are standing by you.
                Very truly yours   Henry Collin Minton

ALS (WP, DLC).
1 Pastor of the First Presbyterian Church of Trenton.

From George Sebastian Silzer

My dear Doctor Wilson: New Brunswick [N. J.] January 7, 1911.

I have your letter of January 6th, and too have felt that we ought to keep in closer touch with each other, for we are now working in rather a disorganized way. Of course, after your inauguration this will not be so. I have had in mind some suggestions to make to you which I will do at the first opportunity after our Tuesday session.

You are right about compromise. We are not fighting for Mr. Martine, but the establishment of the principle, and if we compromise the fight is lost.

I was much amused by the latest "reply" in this morning's Star.[1] This to me is a strong sign of weakness. Whenever a "Boss" begins to talk and is forced out into the light he is having his death struggle. So long as he can maintain silence he is not in danger.

This was so with Croker, and in every case that has come to my observation.

I believe it would be advantageous to have a meeting after Tuesday, at which Mr. Tumulty, Senator Osborne, Senator Hinchliffe,[2] and such others as you think best could be present to go over the entire situation. There may be many things that we can do and which will suggest themselves at a conference of this kind. At any rate the situation could be thoroughly canvassed and our further plans developed.

Sincerely yours,   Geo. S. Silzer.

TLS (WP, DLC).

[1] He referred to a long statement released by Smith on the day before. In it, Smith described Wilson's address in Jersey City on January 5 as "rather disappointing." Denying that he had "recently" conferred with Kuehnle and Baird, Smith said that Wilson left unanswered his, Smith's, assertion that Wilson had spoken of the senatorial primary as "a farce" and of Martine's election as a "disgrace" to the state. "My challenge to name the man who informed him that I would not be a candidate is also still to be answered," Smith continued. "He was brave enough when dispensing false words, but when confronted by a public challenge he lacked the courage to go forward or backward. In a 'partial reply,' he steps to one side and takes refuge behind a fabricated incident of friendly loyalty. He has had ten days in which to answer that challenge. Having failed to do so I now regretfully charge him publicly with resorting to the trick of attempting to deceive the people that he might strike down one who had befriended him and upbuild an ambition that has mastered him." Charging Wilson with hypocrisy for standing on both sides of the question of the senatorial primary, Smith added: "He talks of principle to some and of his power to others. Now his conscience is at work; later he puts aside conscience and tries the arts of untruthfulness and deceit. In private he laughs at the primary law and scowls at its 'preference.' In public he treats both as holy. In theory he is swayed by lofty impulses. In practice he is using the baser emotions to accomplish his purpose. In the annals of political history there is no such example of insincerity as is here presented." New York *Sun,* Jan. 7, 1911.

[2] John Hinchliffe of Paterson, Democratic state senator, 1907-1910.

An Interview

[Jan. 8, 1911]

TO SOLVE CORPORATION PROBLEMS THROUGH STATE LAWS.

Why Governor Wilson of New Jersey Believes
the States Can Regulate Trusts
More Effectually Than the Federal Government.

A few weeks after his election as Governor of the State of New Jersey Woodrow Wilson was asked[1] to outline for THE NEW YORK TIMES ANNUAL FINANCIAL REVIEW his plan for the regulation of corporations and other business enterprises by means

[1] See F. Todd to WW, Dec. 1 and 13, 1910.

of State laws and powers, as against the rapidly growing system of Federal control by bureau and commission. In a number of recent public addresses he had spoken confidently of the feasibility of State control. Other men of prominence had expressed themselves just as confidently that the only possible way of effectively meeting the extensively ramified growth of corporation activities is to meet it with homogeneous Federal power, that can move quickly and evenly and act at once in a dozen places over the country; also that Federal incorporation is the only escape for business enterprise from irresponsible interference, here and there, among the States.

In particular, the rapid trend of corporation law in the United States courts toward the suppression of State power whenever it interferes with Federal control had been pointed out by foremost lawyers. Gov. Wilson was asked if he would not show with definiteness the ways in which the States may act effectively in the case of corporation activities extending over State lines.

The Governor was then right in the midst of the New Jersey Senatorial controversy, and he replied that the subject was entirely too important and too difficult for him to attempt to formulate the statement asked for and do justice to it without more time and hard thinking than he could then spare. But he discussed the subject informally and turned over to THE REVIEW the full text of what he has recently written or spoken that has to do with the particular matter. Because Gov. Wilson is without doubt the foremost exponent of the movement for the utilization and development of State powers that has appeared independently in a number of places, and because the political influence that is conceded to a man who achieves a clean success like Dr. Wilson's in New Jersey means that his beliefs are very likely to be pushed forward to the place of a National issue in the next two years, what he says here of the possibilities of future corporation control by the States will be recognized as having much practical significance for those interested in large business affairs and investments.

The Minnesota rate case, in which a Master in Chancery appointed by a United States Circuit Court has recently outlined a new principle of inter-State commerce law, which, if confirmed by the Supreme Court, will make unconstitutional any regulation of railroad rates by State Commissions, even of purely State rates, if they render necessary inter-State rate adjustments, (as all State ratemaking does,) was called to Dr. Wilson's attention as a particular instance of the Federal Court decisions that lawyers point out are every day taking away State powers of regulation.[2]

"That is an interesting case," said Dr. Wilson, "but the Master's recommendation is not yet the law of the land." He went on to say, regarding this and other specific court decisions that lawyers commonly regard as fixing the boundaries of corporation law, that, while he was himself a lawyer, he did not look at these decisions just from the point of view of practicing lawyers. Dr. Wilson has on a number of occasions declared that in a constitutional Government the courts are the final interpreters of law and the Constitution, and he stands for an orderly course of legal procedure. But most lawyers, he said, entirely lose sight of the political side of the great questions involved in great cases affecting public policy that come before the courts for determination.

"I do not regard any decision as finally establishing a matter of law," he said. "Capable lawyers can find ways to bring almost any question before the courts for reconsideration." He said that judicial interpretation was a constant development. The courts are ready to change their attitude toward public questions if they can be convinced. They change their opinions, slowly but surely, under the influence of persistent, well-informed public sentiment. Court-made law bends and becomes representative.

The trend in favor of Federal power had followed public sentiment. The powers of the States had been allowed to go by default. Once let the States go into court with determined and able counsel, Gov. Wilson said, and make a fight, and there was no doubt that the courts would respect their rights. He thought that the Supreme Court had already shown a disposition to bend the line of interpretation in the direction of State powers in particular leading cases. It was natural for lawyers representing corporations with inter-State activities, he said, to think first of the Federal courts as the place to go when threatened by some action of State authority. The decisions and everything were handy. It was just as handy for those acting for the public to take the short cut by invoking Federal power. But this did not prove that this was the only way or the best way in either case.

To begin at once in the courts the contest for State authority whenever the occasion presents itself, Gov. Wilson made plain to be part of his plan. It is only part of a well thought out and constructive scheme the political features of which command his enthusiasm. He spoke briefly in talking about further law-

2 About this case, see F. Todd to WW, Dec. 1, 1910, n. 2.

making that may be necessary to solve the problems of business regulation, of the possibilities of working out good practical laws in the States. He repeated what he has said in many speeches about the separateness of the States; that if the States were not already made it would have been a good thing to invent them, to give us the advantage of separate communities, each with its own peculiar conditions, each working out, close to the people, its own problems, finding its best way of doing things, then talking it over with other communities and agreeing upon some good common rule for handling common problems.

Of the problem of regulation of the activities of great business aggregations that stretch over many States, Gov. Wilson says in one of his recent speeches:[3] . . .

Dr. Wilson expressly disavows any desire to revive the old-time issue of State rights. His new political issue, he said, in a recent letter,[4] "is not an effort for a revival of the conception of the State sovereignty; it is an effort of State vitality and versatility in our attack upon the problems of present-day lawmaking." . . .

One feature of Gov. Wilson's scheme of community lawmaking is that it substitutes for the more radical propositions that have been put forward for the furtherance of popular participation in government—the initiative and the referendum in particular—what may be called popular representative government. One of the things that he is most enthusiastic about in it is the fact that the states provide the means by which government may be molded in communities, close to the people, along home-rule lines. His idea of what the Governor of a State should be, the active representative of the people, leading them, finding out what they want, directing their opinion, using his influence and skill to get what they want in the Legislatures, (and probably in the courts,) he told to the Convention of Governors, and he has put directly into practice in New Jersey.

Gov. Wilson's attitude toward corporation enterprise is liberal. But he speaks for an orderly plan of strict control over them. He calls for the personal punishment of officers who are guilty of violation of law, rather than anything directed against the corporation itself. In one of the pamphlets given to THE REVIEW he says:[5] . . .

Gov. Wilson was asked if he did not think that in the end

---

[3] This and the following elisions are long extracts from Wilson's address to the Governors' Conference printed at Nov. 29, 1910.

[4] Undoubtedly in a letter to Frederick Todd, which is missing.

[5] This elision is three paragraphs from Wilson's address to the American Bar Association printed at Aug. 31, 1910, Vol. 21.

it would be found that Federal law would have to govern inter-State commerce and some collateral activities. He replied that the Federal Congress was empowered constitutionally to make laws for commerce between the States and that those who believe in the fostering of State authority and in developing its possibilities must admit that inter-State commerce will probably have to be left largely to the Federal Government. He added that it might also be found after trial that the States would better concede to the Federal Government control in other lines. He was not opposed to the Federal Government or jealous of it. Wherever Federal authority is well-founded or needed for the common good, he believed in upholding it to the utmost. He said that he recognized the difficulties directly confronting the attempt to build up a system based on State authority. There was the fact that some States were bidding against each other in selling favors to corporations. He had acknowledged that New Jersey was at fault in giving away lavishly powers and privileges that embarrass other States. But he said he was confident that the separate States can, if they will, control activities within their own borders and enforce laws they may make for themselves. The people of a State that will not fight for its authority to enforce just laws within its borders, deserve no sympathy.

Printed in the *New York Times Annual Financial Review*, Jan. 8, 1911.

An Address in Newark, New Jersey, at Temple B'nai Jeshurun

[Jan. 8, 1911]

Ladies and Gentlemen: Your greeting is very cordial and I thank you for it most heartily. I can only say that it gives me peculiar pleasure to be here and to take part in this interesting celebration.[1] There is a certain thing which distinguishes a free country like America, and that thing is illustrated in gatherings like this and in institutions such as gatherings like this come together to celebrate—I mean the voluntary association of men together to do good. There is something very fine that underlies an institution like this. It is not singular when men are pitiful and sympathetic towards those whom they love, towards those whom they know, towards those with whom they are daily brought into contact, but there is something that deserves remark when men associate themselves together to be pitiful and gener-

[1] The golden jubilee of the Hebrew Benevolent and Orphan Asylum Society of Newark.

ous towards those whom they have never seen, towards those whose conditions are merely reported to them, whose names are upon the benevolent list and whose names spring into their imagination as something really that touches and makes vibrate one of the deepest chords in the human spirit, and I think the Hebrew people have always enjoyed a very honorable distinction in this sort of benevolence. They have always been the first to associate themselves together for purposes of this kind, purposes for which we are in the habit of calling philanthropic, but which that big word does not exactly adapt to our imagination. Philanthropy—the abstract love of our fellowmen, it is a very pretty thing to talk about, but the real love of our fellowmen is something simpler and deeper than that—the depth of the heart, attitude of the mind and expression of the character. When a great race like the Hebrew race can express itself spontaneously and naturally in a matter of this sort, it shows the whole depth and soundness of its nature.

It sometimes seems to me that the thing we ought to safeguard above everything else in developing human life is the power of free association, the free co-ordination of forces, not only of individual forces but of associated forces. A foreign statesman said long ago that it would do a foreign army no good to occupy the city of Washington, that the seats of government in America were not where the men lived who had been temporarily elected to conduct the government. The seat of government in a free country is in the capacity of the people to take care of themselves whether there is any government or not, and whether it is conceivable or not. If our Federal or State governments should be swallowed up over night, we would not be at a loss in the morning what to do. Those men are not indispensable—we can make another government when we please, but not unless we have practice with respect to those matters all the time, not unless we are in the habit of associating ourselves together to do what we please by concerted action, and the nation which has the best self government does not need to resort to its Capitol to be taken care of; does not need to ask for protection, but can by any informal gathering together start an association which from little beginnings grows to great expansion as this Society has done. It is this voluntary, free, spontaneous association that makes the involuntary association vital; I mean the associations of government, because they are largely voluntary, not involuntary. We do not re-conceive our laws in each generation; much of our law is old and proceeds from generation to generation. We take it by habit under authority because we must, not because we will; not because we choose it, but are born under it and are subject to it. That is the involuntary part of our life. We have institutions governing us, institutions which we do not think of changing and they have made it very difficult to change. These things would be empty shells, they would be merely perfunctory if they did not assert within them this constant association of voluntary forces by which we make institutions, change institutions and develop all sorts of qualities and capacities within ourselves in a sort of corporate fashion. They used to tell about the people of the self-governed race that sprang from the people who had learned to govern themselves in the early days of the gold fever of California, "the golden prime of '49," as some one has called it jocularly, when they met a vein of gold they would not try to work it one man at a time; they would form an association and begin to work the vein. Men who had not sprung from races accustomed to self government would hide their find and each one would try to work his claim by himself. Nothing can spring out of that. The present government sprang out of the association of miners together; it could not have been born out of men who did not know how to associate. It was because these men, thrown upon an unsettled part of the country, torn away from settled civilization, knew how to take care of themselves. Certain bodies of settlers gathered together in a part of the country where there was no provisional government even, where territorial government had not been set up, and in the day of Andrew Jackson sent a petition to Washington to ask that a territorial government be sent to them, and Jackson sent back the message, "Are you Americans and don't know how to take care of yourselves? Set up a government of your own. If men don't behave themselves, hang them; we won't interfere with you."[2] We don't have to refer to Washington. We know how to take care of ourselves. This is the vital blood, the red blood that courses in our veins; we take care of our own, and so there is a pulse in all our forces, which is the pulse of life and excessive vitality.

The interesting thing about associations of this sort is that they have a very distinct significance for the growth of the whole community. There is something more than that which lies upon the surface of an undertaking of an institution of this kind. It is not merely that you find those that need your benevolence, that you organize yourselves to take care of orphans, to take care of them in the best way for their mental and physical growth, but by the very reason of associating yourselves in this

[2] The Editors have not been able to find any such statement by Jackson.

way, you develop in yourselves and put in the community in which you live a social spirit which you would not otherwise have; your eyes travel beyond that faint and narrow line of your own self-interest and your own immediate forces. There is nothing more fatal to communities than to draw the limit of your own sympathies to the limit of the work which you meet every day. If you are not interested in anybody, you cannot understand; if you do not associate with others daily, you are a very unreasonable member of society. You must think and think with deep sympathy of the conditions of lives you do not share. Sometimes I think the greatest barrier to democratic government is taste. There are so many things we refrain from doing because they are not to our taste. Many persons keep away from the slums of cities because their sensibilities are affected by what they see. It is that abominable barrier of taste. It is at the bottom of aristocracy. You don't like to associate with persons not of your own intellectual outlook, and taste is at the bottom of it all. You have no stomach for the things you have not been accustomed to eat. It was said that one person asked another if they did not think Miss So-and-So had a great deal of taste, and he said "Yes, and some of it good." Because you have intense taste it is not necessarily good taste. Taste that shows the quality of your nature—because if you would have the fine quality, you must have the cosmopolitan feeling, the impulse to touch those things you know not of. One of the great services of society is to extend the boundary of taste, sympathy and insight, so that you are not looking always in upon yourself or your own family, but have your eyes lifted to see the movements of men and the means of knowing how men fare beyond your own circle and your own narrow interests. You can govern your own lives better by understanding the forces at work in society, the forces that are pulling men down as well as the forces that are building men up. There are a great many forces that are pulling men down that seem to be lifting them up. Many a successful man of business has been elevated to a point where every one of his fellow beings sees him because of his material success, but sometimes he has climbed to those heights by methods which have sunk him to the levels of immorality, which are infinitely demoralizing to society. It may be some of the men you are trying to succor are some of those whom he has trodden underfoot in order to climb to his pinnacle. You discover the processes of success as well as of failure, and sometimes they are a commentary upon the whole institution of society. So that when a man enters into work of this kind he

becomes a better citizen and he sees more things and understands more of things that are universal, and presently he feels
his brotherhood and union with mankind. In studying the individual, you are revealing society, because no two individuals
are alike and no two individual fortunes are alike. There is no
way to study mankind except specimen by specimen, and by
having a few good specimens you begin to form a generaliza-
tion of the kind of men you are dealing with. A hermit always
supposes that all of his characteristics are peculiar to himself,
but that is simply because he knows only himself and sees
nobody but himself. We find other people have exactly the same
fault.

Then there is another element very useful, and that is the
knowledge it affords us of the racial elements in a great nation
like ours and to know how people fare, both those who prosper
and those who do not; that is to study one of the most important
needs in America, because America is extraordinary in this respect, there is what one might call a great combination of people.

The reason America grows more and more vigorous and more
and more various in its vigor is because it has more and more
elements of power, because of the new infusion that is constantly taking place in its blood and thinking. Each race contributes
its own quota. You can pick out the influences that Englishmen
have contributed to America and that Irishmen have contributed, and also the Germans. The American is not naturally a
philosophical nation—I mean the original American coming from
the English and Scottish; he gets his music from the German
element, and his philosophical power of thought is largely from
the German element and so you can pick out race by race, and
you can see, if you look upon America, particularly New York,
how the great Hebrew element has enriched the composite people, how the force of the Orient has begun to play its part
far and wide in our society and has infused a great passionate
movement of feeling, that tide of feeling which is so characteristic of the original people. All of this is enriching America, and
the study of this enables you to understand America, the racial,
the economical, social and political make-up of this country, and
so it seems to me a celebration like this has more than a local
significance.

You remember with deserved veneration the names of the
men who founded this society, and it enhances them to know
that they proved themselves great Americans as well as great
human souls, worthy representative citizens in a country where
free associated effort carries the great processes of life. It is this

that we look forward to; the freedom of America is the strength of America, the power of men to act for themselves and associ-ate themselves for what purposes they please. It is the promise of society, promise of politics and everything that has been lift-ing, and lifting, and lifting America from generation to gener-ation, and has so lifted it until it has shaken itself free from everything of which we have reason to be ashamed. It is with the deepest feeling of privilege therefore that I join in congratu-lating you on the fiftieth anniversary of this great Association.[3]

TC (received from the Jewish Community Council, Newark, N. J.)
   [3] There is a WWhw outline of this address, with the composition date of Jan. 7, 1911, in WP, DLC.

From William Cavanagh Gebhardt

Jersey City [N. J.],
My dear Governor-elect Wilson: January 9, 1911.

I received both of your letters of recent dates, and am very glad indeed to know that you appreciate my help. I am going to Trenton tonight for the express purpose of seeing any of the new members-elect of the Legislature to learn just how they stand, as nearly as possible. My opinion is that Mr. Smith is not, and has not been, a real candidate for the past three weeks. I think he knows as well as you and I do, that he is hopelessly beaten and I believe he is staying in the race for the express purpose of beating Mr. Martine. I have acted upon this theory for sometime, and have been trying to show my friends, both in and out of the Legislature, that the thing now to do is to bend our efforts toward making sure of Mr. Martine's election. After tomorrow I will write you telling you just what I have been able to learn. I would just as soon see Mr. Smith elected as to see one of his tools elected, and I fully agree with you that Mr. Martine's defeat means a most decided defeat for us.

With kindest regards, I am,
               Very sincerely yours,   Wm. C. Gebhardt

TLS (WP, DLC).

From Robert Stephen Hudspeth

Dear Dr. Wilson: Jersey City, N. J. January 9, 1911.

As a member of the New Jersey Democratic State Committee, I write you on behalf of Mr. Edward E. Grosscup, also a mem-ber of that committee, from Gloucester County, this State. Mr.

Grosscup is one of the most active and respected members of the Democratic State Committee. He has always given the ticket his loyal and influential support and aided very materially in the success of our ticket at the last election, particularly in his own County.

He has for many years been engaged in the real estate business in his county, having an office in Philadelphia. He is a man of wide experience in business affairs and particularly expert concerning real estate and real estate values. He is an applicant for appointment to the State Board of Equalization of Taxes.[1]

I think I can safely say that I know no man better fitted or equipped to discharge the duties of that important position than Mr. Grosscup. I am,   Very truly yours,   R S Hudspeth

TLS (Governors' Files, Nj).
[1] Wilson appointed Grosscup, who was in the real estate business in Wenonah, N. J., to the State Board for the Equalization of Taxes in April 1911. He was elected chairman of the Democratic State Committee in August 1911.

A News Report

[Jan. 9, 1911]

WILSON TESTIMONIAL

An Expression of Esteem Presented To Former President by the Undergraduates.

A representative committee, consisting of the presidents of the four classes, called upon former President Woodrow Wilson '79, at his home Saturday noon. As a token of the love and respect in which he is held by Princeton men, they presented to Dr. Wilson a testimonial volume, bound in olive morocco leather, with the initials "W.W.," in gold on the cover. The book contains the following expression of esteem:

"To Dr. Woodrow Wilson, from the undergraduates of Princeton University, on the occasion of his resignation from the Presidency of the University, October, nineteen hundred and ten:

"Dear Dr. Wilson—In view of your resignation from the Presidency of Princeton University, in order to assume your new duties as Governor of New Jersey, we wish to take this opportunity to express to you our profound regret at your departure.

"We deeply appreciate your earnest work during the last eight years in behalf of the undergraduates of the University, and as members of the University we thank you for all that you have done by your untiring efforts to advance Princeton.

"We are truly sorry that you will not be more closely connected with Princeton in the future, and we wish to add that your loss

Wilson reviewing the Inaugural Parade

Wilson at his desk in the New Jersey State House

Henry Watterson

James Edgar Martine

Samuel Kalisch

John Wesley Wescott

Walter Evans Edge

Elmer Hendrickson Geran

Joseph Albert Dear, Jr.

Henry Smith Pritchett

will be keenly felt throughout the undergraduate body. Princeton, under your guidance and leadership, has developed to a remarkable degree, and it is largely due to you that it occupies the position which it now holds among American institutions of learning.

"We heartily congratulate you on your recent election to the Governorship of New Jersey and we sincerely offer to you our best wishes for success in the future, such as you have achieved in the past.

(Signed)

Maitland Dwight,
President of the Senior Class.

Joseph Neff Ewing,
President of the Junior Class.

Maxwell Chaplin,
President of the Sophomore Class.

Alwyn Ball, III,
President of the Freshman Class.

"For the undergraduates of Princeton University."

Printed in the *Daily Princetonian*, Jan. 9, 1911.

To Mary Allen Hulbert Peck

My dearest Friend,   Princeton, N. J. 10 Jan'y, 1911.[1]

I have just had a great, great treat: your letter of the sixth,[1] which came this morning,—a perfectly delightful letter, breathing the sweetest airs—as if of a singularly delightful person in an adorable mood, writing out of her heart! And how am I requiting her? By sending her no letter by the steamer that sails tomorrow. I am writing this after dinner, and there is no post that leaves here in time in the morning to catch the boat. I really could not help it! The day has been full to overflowing with engagements over which I had no control at all, as it turned out. Hour after hour slipped away, each task seemed imperative, and now the day is over, and I am giving my dear friend only what is left of me. It is not fair; and it is none the less mean because She will understand and be generously patient.

I am really dead tired. It is not fair to impose myself upon you. I never imagined such a various strain and so constant an engrossment of attention as this new life (so far) imposes on me. I do not feel that it is a killing pace, but certainly is a deadening one, and night often finds me unfit for anything but bed.

Perhaps the pleasure of writing to you will revive me. It revives me only to think of you, for no one can be dull in your presence, and thinking of you always seems to mean a consciousness of your presence. How delightful it is to think of you and turn away from myself! The life I am leading seems to make it almost necessary to think of myself all day long: everybody looking to me to do something, everybody talking of what I have been doing and wanting to know what I am going to do next,—an interminable round of comment and planning and speculation and consultation and advice—the press of the whole country discussing me; Senators of the United States sending me word that I have the greatest opportunity that any one in the country has,—to do just what they do not specify,—and I, meanwhile, toiling on in my thought, feeling singularly lonely, feeling as if I were only looking on at a career that was not mine, but a sort of inevitable, detached thing, my humility, not my pride, enhanced, and entirely unable to take any active interest in my presidential "boom." When men write to me, all alive with interest in it, and ask me to supply them with material and suggest to them what they can do, not an idea comes into my head: I do not in the least know what to say; and it all seems so silly, so premature, when I have not even *begun* to be governor and still have all my record to make. "A poor politician," you will say, "and a very stupid fellow," but only the work in hand seems important or possible. Nobody but you would believe all this, but it is true.

I am enclosing a poor copy of a speech I made the other night. I have not read it all. I dare say it is an imperfect enough report (it was taken stenographically); but it will give you some idea of what I said. I enclose also a comment upon it. Shall I have one of the Jersey papers sent you? I fear you would hate the criticism as much as you would like the appreciation heaped upon me.

Why *did* you remind me of Mrs. Moncure Robinson!² I had entirely forgotten her, and I do not know of any woman who ever left a more unpleasant impression upon me! What you repeat from her is as deliciously funny as it is evidently malicious; but she ought really to invent credible things. It happens that Mrs. Borden Harriman³ did not attract me enoogh [enough] to make me call as often as courtesy and her own kindness made it proper I should. I felt rather ashamed of myself about it, because she was a fine, uninteresting person; and her interest in me was as perfunctory as my interest in her.

I resent the talk about you and the Governor.⁴ What Town Talk⁵ started that? Are there enemies of the old sort about you?

I wish that you liked the Colonial Secretary and his wife[6] better than you do. I had some delicious hours in that dear little house with the bougainvillia (?) on the road to the South Shore,—hours when I lost all of the abominable self-consciousness that has been my bane all my life, and felt perfectly at ease, happily myself, released from bonds to enjoy the real freedom of my mind. And they were so interesting, so full of the good things that are in books and in the better sort of talk about people. It was a place where, if I had but known them long enough, I could have learned to loaf and invite my soul. Why not sample them again, and give them a chance to enjoy you as keenly as I am sure they would?

Do not be anxious about me. I am well and all right. The new work ii [is] immensely interesting, and cannot in the nature of things grow dull or monotonous. It will keep me on the qui vive, and, if I can really accomplish something for the patient people of the State, it will be full of stimulation and reward. Your letters are a perfect boon to me. They come with all the dear air of Bermuda in them, at once stimulating and soothing and restful,—the air in which I first knew you, and must, I believe always think of you when I am not actually with you elsewhere. All join me in most affectionate messages, and I am, as always,

Your devoted friend,   Woodrow Wilson

WWhw and WWTLS (WP, DLC).

[1] It is missing.

[2] Lydia Biddle (Mrs. Moncure) Robinson of Philadelphia.

[3] Florence Jaffray Hurst (Mrs. Jefferson Borden) Harriman of New York.

[4] Lieutenant General Sir Frederick Walter Kitchener, Governor of Bermuda since 1908. There were rumors that they were engaged.

[5] He meant *Town Topics*, a New York weekly filled with society news and gossip and some criticism of the arts.

[6] Reginald Popham Lobb, Colonial Secretary and Registrar-General of Bermuda since 1908, and Mary Beatrice Jackson Lobb.

From Jacob Cole Price[1]

My Dear Dr Wilson   Branchville [N. J., c. Jan. 10, 1911]

An absence from home for a few days past has prevented an answer to your favor of Jan 6th. I realize full well how how [sic] deeply you feel the importance of carrying out the wishes of the voters as expressed at the primary election. I have said very little about the choice of a Senator, but I have kept my ear close to the ground and I am satisfied that there is a strong sentiment in this county against the election of Senator Smith. This feeling prevails throughout the state. That should be sufficient to guide every fair minded member of the legislature. I shall so inform my old friend[2] for I want to be honest and frank with him   Very sincerely yours   J. C. Price

ALS (WP, DLC).
    [1] A physician of Branchville, N. J., Democratic member of the New Jersey Senate since 1904.
    [2] That is, James Smith, Jr.

From Charles William Kent

My dear Woodrow,   [Charlottesville, Va.] Jan 10th 1911

I can not permit myself to send you an official note[1] without at least accompanying it with a personal expression of my keenest interest in you under your new conditions. I have delayed my congratulations so that they would mean more for, in the flood of those that must have overwhelmed you at the time, they would have counted for little. I need not assure you that no one of your many friends rejoiced more ardently in your triumphant success than I did and no one felt more impelled to tell you so. I note with absorbing attention every mention of your present problem and I wish you all success in your first battle with bossism. Your friends and admirers here are very proud of you and anxious to show at any time their sympathy and support.   Cordially   Charles W. Kent

ALS (WP, DLC).
    [1] The "official note," which is missing, was an invitation to speak to the Y.M.C.A. of the University of Virginia.

To George Brinton McClellan Harvey

My dear Colonel Harvey: Princeton, N. J. Jan. 11, 1911

Thank you very cordially for the material which you supplied me.[1] It enabled me to insert in my inauguration address something which I hope will have real significance. I am returning to you the papers you were kind enough to lend me under another cover.

I am sincerely obliged to you for having called my attention to this important matter which seems to me of vital significance from every point of view.

I have not said anything about the Income Tax because I wanted to make my inaugural very brief and wished to confine it to matters which had been prominent in the campaign. I want to enter office with as simple a manifesto as possible.

Always cordially and faithfully yours

Woodrow Wilson

TLS (WP, DLC).
[1] Harvey's letter, to which this was a reply, is missing. Harvey's memorandum on the cold storage problem is in WP, DLC.

From Robert Brodnax Glenn[1]

My dear Governor: Winston-Salem, N. C. January 11, 1911.

Doubtless you have forgotten Bob Glenn of Davidson College days, and I am frank to confess that until I saw W. S. Plummer Bryan,[2] who was our mutual friend, I did not know that you were the same boy that we used to call "Tom Wilson" at college.

I was very much interested in your campaign, and while doing some temperance work in New Jersey, on the quiet did everything I could to help your cause, and I am now thoroughly with you in all that you are undertaking to do for the upbuilding of your state. Having been Governor of North Carolina for four years, I know something of the weighty responsibilities that will rest upon you as New Jersey's Chief Executive, but I have faith in your ability and your patriotic love for your State, and know that your courage and conscientious convictions of right will cause you to win in the end.

This is but the beginning of your political career, and both your friends of the past and present will be greatly disappointed if you are not untimately [ultimately] elevated to a still higher position.

Please accept my best wishes for your success, with the hope that when I come to New Jersey in the near future I may have the pleasure of seeing you in the Executive Office, and rest assured if there is any way in which I can aid you, I will most cheerfully do so, as not only our college relations, but present interest in your great work make me hope for your success in all that you may undertake.

With kind regards, I am,

Sincerely your friend,   R. B. Glenn.

TLS (WP, DLC).
[1] Fellow-student of Wilson at Davidson College, lawyer, Governor of North Carolina, 1905-1909, and lecturer for the Anti-Saloon League and the Chautauqua and Lyceum bureaus.
[2] William Swan Plumer Bryan, A.B., Davidson College, 1875, at this time pastor of the Presbyterian Church of the Covenant in Chicago.

From George Sebastian Silzer

My dear Doctor: New Brunswick, N. J. January 12, 1911.

I have your letter of January 11th and regret very much that I cannot be with you on Monday.[1] On that day I have a matter before the U. S. Circuit Court at Trenton in the morning, and in the afternoon I am subpoenaed to appear here as a witness against an attorney charged with embezzlement.

I am very sorry indeed, because I am a strong believer in conferences. Furthermore, we ought to go over not only the bills but the Senatorship and decide on a plan of action.

I have been working on the Senatorship, but do not think it will be possible to change Ramsay.[2] I had a long talk yesterday with Streitwolf, who assures me that he is against Smith. He had an engagement, however, with Mr. Ross last night which he seemed to fear a great deal, the result of which I have not yet ascertained. I stiffened his backbone, however, as much as I could.

I have also had a talk by phone with Booraem,[3] who is ill, and I believe he will eventually follow the directions given at the primary.

So far as I can learn there is practically no one but Mr. Ross in this county favorable to Mr. Smith, but of course, his power is feared.

I believe you have not yet seen Mr. Booraem on account of his illness, and would therefore suggest that you write him again as well as Streitwolf, and before seeing them I would like to make a suggestion or two.

Of future conferences I wish you would give me as much notice as possible.   Yours very truly,   Geo. S. Silzer.

TLS (WP, DLC).
  [1] Wilson planned to hold a conference with his legislative leaders at the Hotel Martinique in New York on January 16. About this meeting, see the news report and statement printed at Jan. 19, 1911.
  [2] William E. Ramsay, physician of Perth Amboy and assemblyman from Middlesex County.
  [3] John Van Liew Booraem, contractor and farmer of New Brunswick, also an assemblyman from Middlesex County.

An Announcement

[Jan. 13, 1911]

I regard the office of secretary to the Governor as one of the most important in the administration of the State, requiring unusual knowledge of affairs, great tact and ability, high character and a quick understanding of the demands and needs of the public. It is, therefore, with peculiar pleasure that I announce that Mr. Joseph P. Tumulty has consented at my earnest request, to undertake the duties of the position.

I feel sure that he will give distinction to the office because of his universally recognized qualifications for faithful and disinterested public service.

Printed in the Jersey City *Jersey Journal*, Jan. 13, 1911.

To Mary Allen Hulbert Peck

Dearest Friend, Princeton, N. J. 13 Jan'y, 1911

I shall have some ink in a few minutes, meanwhile, will you forgive pencil? As usual, I have only a little interspace of a few moments in which to write. We have just left "Prospect" and I am writing from a little den, quite strange to me, in the Princeton Inn. Mrs. Wilson, Nellie, and I are to live here till early summer; Jessie, who spends Monday–Thursday in settlement work in Philadelphia, will be with us over week ends; and Margaret is established in two pleasant rooms in New York, as a full fledged independent student of music,—just a city block away from her teacher. Nellie will go and come, to and from Philadelphia every day, to study at the Academy of Fine Arts, as before. Alas! it is *not* pleasant: My heart aches at the break-up of the old life, interesting and vital as the new life is. I did not realize it until it touched our home and sent us into lodgings at an inn. I feel like a nomad! The idea of a man of fifty-four (no less!) leaving a definite career and a settled way of life of a sudden and launching out into a vast sea of Ifs and Buts! It sounds like an account of a fool. At any rate, there is nothing in it of private advantage! Every private comfort and satisfaction (for example and chief of all, the freedom to go to Bermuda) is destroyed and broken up and one's life is made to turn upon public affairs altogether. What can be snatched from the public (from office seekers and reporters and an occasional serious discussion of something really interesting and important) one *can* devote to his family or his friends or some hastily enjoyed pleasure. Even his *thinking*, which used to be done deliberately and upon the independent impulse of his own mind, he must do as bidden, at any moment, upon expected or unexpected summons,—at the call of the casual acquaintance or the exaction of the newest correspondence! I shall get used to it, but at present I am in revolt, and wish I were—in Bermuda, sitting by my dear friend, for a long, intimate chat that would get my thoughts and my spirits into perfect fettle again.

Is dear old Mrs. Jones[1] living yet? If she is, *please* give her my love. My thoughts have recently run back at tired moments to that delicious half hour (or was it more?) I spent with her one afternoon, in real human talk—chiefly of you—and how you first flashed, a radiant vision, on Bermudan ken—and in sipping cordial and eating good cake, quite as if I were a lad again sitting, "on my manners,["] with some gracious dame of the old regime in our own dear, forgotten South. It is a balm to irritated nerves to think of it,—a rest to my spirit,—and "Inwood," with the very spirit of peace resting upon it,—and within the most delectable suggestions of *you* and of the first time I had a real glimpse of you as I was to know you from that time on! Ah, how delightful it all is! And how different from New Jersey politics,—which is full of the devil (as well as with promise of his defeat) and of war!

I am perfectly well. Next Tuesday (the 17th) I am to be sworn in as Governor—(which will not increase my troubles)—but we are still to be here. The fight makes good progress. All join me in most affectionate messages. Bless you for your letters—they delight me now that you are happy again and Bermuda has once more got hold on your spirits.

Your devoted friend   Woodrow Wilson

ALS (WP, DLC).

[1] Louisa Lightbourn Trimingham (Mrs. Eugenius) Jones, mother of Clarence Trimingham Jones, owner of Inwood, about which see Mary A. H. Peck to WW, Feb. 25, 1907, n. 1, Vol. 17. Mrs. Jones died on June 20, 1913.

To William Pierce Macksey

My dear Mr. Macksey: Princeton, N. J. Jan. 13, 1911

In these latter days when everything seems to be coming to a head and the whole matter of our controversy about to be settled I have more than once been about to seek another interview with you, but I have refrained simply because I thought it might be embarrassing to you. I do not want you to feel that I am in any way putting pressure upon you even the pressure of friendly advice. I know that you will pardon me, however, if I send you just this line to express the hope that you will see your way to coming out in support of the peoples' candidate. It would give added strength to the cause, and I take the liberty of believing that you, yourself, would feel better about the matter.[1]

Cordially and sincerely yours,   Woodrow Wilson

TLS (WP, DLC).
¹ Macksey voted for Smith in the Democratic caucus on January 23, 1911, and placed his name in nomination in the Assembly on the following day. At the final vote of the joint session on January 25, he supported Martine.

From Mary Allen Hulbert Peck

Dearest Friend,   Paget West, Bermuda. Jan. 13th [1911]

The days since the sailing of the boat Tuesday have been full of "such a number of things" I've had no time to write any of the thoughts of you ever in my mind. The getting in of a new and disappointing cook, and an elephantine and ignorant housemaid, has taken some of the joy of life out of me, but I'm a hopeful soul, and my untutored savage has turned out so well, my hope is justified. All the savage needed was a kind word. And after all she was not wholly untutored, for she wrote down every night all the pearls of household wisdom that had fallen from my lips during the day. She says I'm *perfect*—large praise that I like. I've spent one weary morning with Mr. Eells who has written a short story & come down to read it to me and have my assistance (?) in in [sic] correcting & improving it.¹ It took 2½ hrs. to read and the only way it can be improved is by using an ink eraser, or dropping it from my window (with a stone attached) to a watery grave. That was *one* wasted day, for although I had a little nap behind Mother's back, during one chapter, I was exhausted the rest of the day. Last night I went to a concert or operetta, given by the Girls High School class, and sat with royalty,² thus no doubt confirming the reported engagement. Today I went to Hamilton to buy supplies for the cook to spoil and in the afternoon drove with my antique friend Mr. Wayland,³ (whose wife⁴ died in October) who finds in me a congenial soul, so he says. He said today, I know Mrs Wayland got very tired of me, for she said at the wedding of a young girl, "How little that young thing knows what is before her." You know, as I told him, that *that* is a stock phrase of all married women, and means nothing much. He is egoist and egotist, but rather nice and original, and I love to drive behind his horses, and like the groom who with the asthmatic and rheumatic dog, chaperones us from the rumble. While Mr. W. was in the P.O. the groom fairly wept on my shoulder in telling me how lonely he was in his stable rooms with not a soul to speak to in nights. I meanly advised him to marry, at least matrimony would serve as David Harums⁵ dog's flea did. Did I tell you I found a "near" birthday ring for you? It is 1858-1859, and you will hate it, but

I rather like it. Is it possible I forgot to send my birthday greetings to you? I thought of it often, but I have so much to say to you always that the words may not have been written. *You know* what your coming into the world meant to me, and all you think I am, and the best of me that is to be, is because of you.

Do you know the Oceana leaves N. Y. on Saturdays, making a quick trip down here, stopping for a few hours, and returning directly to N. Y.? Would not the ocean trip and even a few hours here do you good? *Can't* you come? If only to see how *fat* I am. I can barely see over my cheeks. I must say Good night, dearest, best of friends. *Please* take great care of yourself. You *sound* well, but *are* you?

"Don't lie to the Doctor." Tell me *where* you are—the papers tell me *who* you are. I'm so proud of you, and so proud to be your friend, that I think after all it *isn't* fat, its just vanity puff.

      Goodnight, Goodnight,   M. A.

ALS (WP, DLC).
  [1] Stillman Witt Eells, businessman of New York who had retired to Bermuda in 1909. He apparently never published anything.
  [2] That is, with General Kitchener, a widower.
  [3] Chandler Norton Wayland of Stonington, Conn.
  [4] Lucy Elton Wayland.
  [5] Edward Noyes Westcott, *David Harum: A Story of American Life* (New York, 1898).

From Robert Bridges

Dear Tommy: New York. January 13, 1911.

I am very glad that you made the decision which you did in regard to the matter about which we talked. I know it will heartily please all those concerned, as it does me. It was a noble thing to do and you have crowned it by your decision.

I enclose you herewith my personal cheque for $4000 which I have every reason to believe will be good when it reaches the bank.

I understand that the Tigers[1] met with the approval of the students and most of the people who have seen them.

With best wishes for your term of office which is about to begin   Faithfully yours   Robert Bridges

TLS (WP, DLC).
  [1] The bronze tigers commissioned by the Class of 1879 for the steps of Nassau Hall, about which see the news report printed at Feb. 19, 1909, Vol. 19. The *Daily Princetonian*, Jan. 6, 1911, reported that they had recently been installed; the formal dedication took place on June 10, 1911 during a reunion of the class. For a description of this affair, see the *Princeton Alumni Weekly*, XI (June 14, 1911), 585.

To Robert Bridges

Dear Bobby,   Princeton, N. J. 14 Jan'y, 1911

Thank you heartily for the cheque, wh. came safely—and equally for the note wh. accompanied it. This generous arrangement will relieve me of much anxiety.

I am just off for a meeting in Newark.[1]

The tigers are great! and just the right size.

Affectionately,   Woodrow Wilson

ALS (WC, NjP).

[1] A news report of his address is printed at Jan. 16, 1911.

To Charles William Kent

My dear Charlie: Princeton, N. J. January 14, 1911

Your letters of Jan. 9th and 10th have both given me a great deal of pleasure. I particularly want to thank you for the personal note about my entrance into public life. You may be sure it went to the right spot. It is perfectly delightful to have my old friends believe in me and think as they do about my new venture. I wish with all my heart I could accept the YMCA invitation but it is literally impossible. I am so involved in engagements that it would be a positive derilection of manifest duty if I were to turn away from my tasks here during the first year of my administration.

I am denying myself of a pleasure but I really have no choice in the matter.

In haste,   Faithfully yours,   Woodrow Wilson

TLS (Tucker-Harrison-Smith Coll., ViU).

To Mary Allen Hulbert Peck

University Club [New York]

Dearest Friend,   Sunday, 15 Jan'y, 1911.

As I look forward into the week I see only too plainly that this is to be my only chance to catch the Wednesday boat. To-morrow I am to be in conference all day long with a group of about a dozen men concerning the programme of the legislative session —the bills to be drawn and presented, &c.—and on Tuesday I am to be inaugurated. I must be in Trenton by ten; at eleven I will review a parade (a civil parade); at noon I will be formally sworn in, at the opera house, and make my inaugural address; all afternoon and all evening I must stand and shake hands with all comers,—probably thousands, curious to see a *Democratic* governor once more. To-day, for a little while, I am free. Last night I spoke in Newark (his own home) against Smith again. There were some twenty-two hundred people in the hall, I was told, and as many more had been turned away at the doors,—and that notwithstanding the fact that it was a drenching night of rain and fog. I got back to the club here at about a quarter to eleven,—but not to sleep: there was a man lying in wait to talk to me for an hour more. This morning I went, by appointment, to the Belmont and spent about an hour and a half with Senator Bourne, of Oregon, a *very* progressive 'Republican' who is pleased to be interested in me as a possible leader of the people and President. It is all very amusing and very interesting,—and still I seem to look on, as if it were not myself that was involved!

It is interesting how you rouse interest and *enthusiasm* in others by being interested in *them*! Bryan made scores of hero worshippers out of men young and old by filling them with the conviction that he was their friend and tribune. It is the power of vivid sympathy,—or, to put it more truly,—the power of love. I was thinking of your young friend on the American man-of-war, whose letter you did *not* send me. It is not only your beauty, my dear lady, and your extraordinary vivacious charm, but your power of throwing yourself into their lives and your extraordinary power of womanly sympathy and real affection that links those youngsters to you with hooks of steel. Older men you capture, even without intending it, by other means, though there is the sympathy and the understanding there, too, of course. They see in you more than the youngsters *can* see,—the whole vivid power of a delightful *woman*,—I do not know how to put it into words; I only know, as every one does who approaches you, that it is in you,—that wonderful combination of qualities and charms and the means of giving them lively expression that from the beginning until now has made persons like yourself—pardon me!—adorable! I miss you dreadfully. How are my faculties to be at their best unless I can have you to chat with and let myself go—to listen to and get the most varied stimulation!

I am well, astonishingly well. We have moved out of "Prospect," as I told you, and just a little touch of the sense of 'home' is beginning to attach to the Inn. After all, home is not a place, so much as an atmosphere and association. All join me in the most affectionate messages. Please give my warmest regard to Mrs Allen and your son, and think of me always as

Your devoted friend   Woodrow Wilson

My hand has given out! My mind goes on. Please make up the rest to please yourself!

ALS (WP, DLC).

From Lamson Allen[1]

My Dear Sir: Worcester, Mass., Jan. 15th. 1911.

I want to most heartily endorse the sentiments of your speech at Newark, N. J., last night as reported by the Associated Press. They are just right and I am sure that the majority of honest thinking men of the country believe in them. I have been a life-long Republican, but always an *American citizen*, and a lover of truth.

I am glad, also, that you mentioned the *howl* of stand-pat politicians against the constitutionality of the governor's so-called interference in cases of the sort you & Gov. Foss of Mass., are fighting. May you both win.

I am constantly reminded in our present-day occurrences of that magnificent poem of J. Russell Lowell "The Present Crisis." It fits to a "T."

I shall hail with joy the day when the voters can cast their individual votes directly for senators. May it come soon.

God bless you in your noble efforts to improve the country.
                        Your fellow citizen   Lamson Allen.

ALS (WP, DLC).
[1] A physician whose office was at 20 Elm St., Worcester, Mass.

A News Report of an Address in Newark, New Jersey

[Jan. 16, 1911]

CHEERS STAND WILSON TAKES

Great Essex Audience Shows Approval of
Governor-elect's Fight on Senatorship.

If proof had previously been wanting regarding the sentiment of Essex County upon the United States Senatorship contest, it was shown, in the opinion of political observers, at the meeting in the New Auditorium Saturday night, at which Governor-elect Wilson spoke.

Had the hall been twice as large, it would not have accommodated the throng that sought to hear the Governor-elect speak for the maintenance of the direct primary principle. . . .

Mr. Wilson's talk was in part as follows:

Fellow-citizens of Essex, the feeling that is uppermost in my mind as I rise to address you to-night is one of genuine regret that the fighting out of a great cause like this should centre upon individuals. I am sorry that it is necessary for me to come to Essex and give reasons why I think an eminent citizen of Essex should not be sent to the United States Senate.

I wish very much that this contest might have taken some other form. I can say to you with absolute candor that I did everything that I honorably could to prevent its taking this form. It is never willingly that I oppose myself to persons, though I very willingly oppose myself to certain objects sought by certain persons.

I would wish never to bring a man's character into question. I might wish to bring his policy, the project that he is seeking, into question. This campaign has brought to me a very great surprise. You know, gentlemen, that I did not seek the nomination as Governor of New Jersey. I was sought, I was asked to allow myself to be nominated, and for a long time it was impossible for me to understand why I had been asked, and now it is more difficult for me than ever.

What did the gentlemen do who were seeking to put me in nomination? They deliberately went entirely outside of the ranks of recognized politics and picked out a man who they knew would be regarded as an absolutely independent person; and for a while at that time I tried to form a working theory in my mind as to why they should do it. I asked very impertinent and direct questions of some of the gentlemen as to why they wanted me to run; they did not give me any very satisfactory explanation; therefore I had to work out one myself, which proved to be a false theory.

I said that these gentlemen recognized the fact that a new day had come in American politics, and that they would have to conduct them henceforth after a new fashion. Then I discovered, just as soon as the election was over, that they had discovered nothing of the kind; and so my explanation was knocked into a cocked hat. There is only one other possible explanation, and that, I am afraid, is the true one.

They did not believe I meant what I said. And the fundamental mistake that I made was that I did believe that they meant what they said. If I had not believed it, I never would have stood upon this occasion upon this platform.

The fight, therefore, gentlemen, I call you to witness is not of my making, and I did everything in candor to make it unnecessary that it should occur. But it has occurred, and the Scotch-Irish blood in me does not object.

I supposed that Mr. Smith was going to give himself the privilege of showing that he knew how to represent the people of New Jersey and so confound his enemies by a display of genuine public spirit and statesmanship, thereby making himself the greatest political figure in New Jersey.

I supposed that he intended to represent the new public opinion of our day. But he did not, and so the question arises, whom does he represent?

"Special interests," shouted some one in the audience.

He does not represent a State-wide organization. I do not know how to guess how many persons he represents. Let us say at a liberal estimate, that he represents 1,000 persons. I can make a very extensive catalogue of a portion of the one thousand, but I cannot name them all and therefore I have to guess.

As against the one thousand he may represent stand the two hundred and more thousand Democrats of this State not represented by anything that he has proposed. He has declined to represent the wishes and purposes of the two hundred thousand and has made up his mind still to represent that little manageable group which heretofore has tried to run politics in the State of New Jersey.

It was what I least expected of Senator Smith; it was a colossal blunder in political judgment. I thought that he was at least an astute politician, but an astute politician would at least know that it was the year 1910 in which the campaign occurred, and that in 1911 the thing would not work.

I have been very much interested at the force of argument in this fight. The gentlemen who are opposed to carrying out the will of the people, as expressed at the primaries, have not been nearly as much opposed to that as they were opposed to the Governor expressing any opinion about it whatever.

I received a very interesting editorial just before leaving home to-day. There is a paper in the State of New York[1] which, when I first began this interesting business, compared me very unfavorably indeed with the newly elected Governor of New York, saying of him: "There is a man who knows how to mind his own business."[2] That same paper sent to me an editorial this morning which said that it would not do for Governor Dix not to

---

[1] The *New York Times*.
[2] A puzzling statement. The Editors have been unable to find any such editorial in the *New York Times* between the election of 1910 and the date of this speech. In fact, the *Times* consistently supported Wilson in the senatorial controversy.

say who he thought ought to be elected for Senator from New York.[3]

They have come around to the usurpation theory. They have come around to the theory that a Governor ought not to mind his own business. If I had been intended to mind my own business I would have been left to my own business, and would not have been asked to attend to the business of the people. They say that it is unconstitutional for a Governor-elect to do what I have been attempting to do, namely, to act merely as the spokesman and representative of the people who elected me.

Certain gentlemen have grown particularly scrupulous about the Constitution. A very eminent constitutional lawyer, John W. Griggs, has grown very uneasy about this matter, but Mr. Griggs is thinking about one Constitution and talking about another. The thing that I am violating is not the Constitution of the State, but the constitution of politics. Mr. Griggs knows that politics was not managed by the people when he was Governor.

I am, from the point of view of the old-fashioned, privately conducted tours in politics, an unconstitutional Governor, but not from the point of view of anybody else. You know how the Constitution of the State reads under the old order of politics. It is already old. If it were not, I don't know why it should be so offensive.

Under the old order of politics the Constitution of the State was to this effect: That legislation, as well as appointments, were to be managed by persons who had not been elected by the people. It is a very interesting thing that this is literally true. Legislation, and particularly the selection of Senators, has been managed by persons whom the people never invited to take charge of anything whatever. There are men in this audience who can recall that sad, that dispiriting, that disgraceful series of elections of United States Senators that marks the history of politics in this State.

But now a very interesting thing has happened. Did you ever hear more futile public attacks than are being put forth by the other side? They know how to manage, but they don't know how to talk. They remind me of a story that I was telling a friend of mine to-night.

There was a campaign down in Virginia, which, for a time, was very one-sided. There was there a man named Massey,[4] a

---

[3] An editorial in the *New York Times*, Jan. 14, 1911, emphasizing the importance to the state, the nation, and the Democratic party of the New York senatorial election and Governor Dix's duty as leader of his party to play an active role in the election of a senator.

[4] John Edward Massey, Baptist clergyman and Virginia politician who ran

very adroit stump speaker; he was a champion of the minority, of the side which at that time was in a very small minority in the State. There was one particular county in the State in which there was not a single adherent of his, but this did not dismay him at all, so he sent a challenge into that county. Though they didn't like to, his opponents got a debater, a great burly man with a great loud voice, while he himself was a little, wiry, springy man. He had the first speech of the debate, and had not used more than half of his time, when some of the local partizans began to be very anxious, and finally a man back in the hall said: "Tom, call him a liar and make it a fight."

That is what has happened. They have nothing to say in answer to arguments, so they call me a liar. It does not do a man who tells the truth the least harm to be called a liar. The only thing that makes a man mad is what is true, and I am afraid the other side have lost their temper a little bit.

They say a great deal about the primary at which Mr. Martine received, as they put it, only some 58,500 [48,500] votes, and they point out to you how many Democrats there were who did not vote, and they assume, apparently, that the Democrats who did not vote wanted Mr. Smith for Senator. It is a very convenient way of reckoning; but suppose for a moment that we leave all of that argument to them and ask ourselves this question: What has happened since the primaries? What is this? How do they think the primary has been supplemented since that vote was given?

What is going on everywhere in the State of New Jersey is an informal referendum, and do you doubt what the people of New Jersey are now saying about the return of Mr. Martine to the Senate? Do you wish to wipe the primary vote off? Wipe it off and let us begin right there and notice whath [what] has happened since. Why, there are certain gentlemen in the Legislature of New Jersey who know that they must vote for Mr. Martine because if they do not, they might as well move out of the county in which they live.

Do you know what has happened in your own county? Did you not read a letter which was addressed to Mr. Smith asking him to become a candidate for the Senate? I do not question the motives or the judgment of the men that signed that letter, but three of them, Mr. Mylod and Mr. Boettner and Mr. Balentine have substantially said this:

"When we signed that letter we did not understand the state

for many offices, one of the early leaders of the Readjuster movement in Virginia, about which see WW to R. Bridges, May 24, 1881, n. 1, Vol. 2.

of opinion in Essex County or in the State of New Jersey. eW [We] do now understand it and as representatives of the people we accept the present state of opinion as our mandate."

What is the answer to that argument? Can anybody misunderstand the present state of opinion in the State of New Jersey or in the county of Essex? No sane and sincere man questions for a moment what the mandate of that opinion is, and all honor to them for honorably yielding to that expression of opinion.

It takes bravery on a man's part to publicly change his position, but it is a very honorable bravery in a representative to declare that he will truly represent. Nothing else has moved these gentlemen. There has been no threatening, there has been no cajoling that I know of. They have seen what their constituents desired.

Why, except for a few individuals in New Jersey to-day nobody has missed it. The United States has taken notice of it. Take up almost any paper printed anywhere in the United States and you will see this question discussed, and you will see the editorials putting it this way—that it simply remains to be seen whether the Democratic members of the Legislature of New Jersey are responsive to the Democratic opinion of New Jersey.

There is a contrast which I wish you to think of very carefully, gentlemen. Those who are sustaining the side of the primary and of public opinion are not putting up any candidate of their own. They are making no private choice and urging you to put him into the United States Senate. Whereas on the other hand there is the old-fashioned, usual, habitual private choice of a machine. So that the men who are fighting for Mr. Martine are not fighting for personal power, but against personal power.

Am I fighting for my nominee for the United States Senate? I tell you this, gentlemen, I shall fight to the last ditch against any compromise whatever. And I want you to know why—not because I am constitutionally opposed to compromise, though I am, but because a compromise would mean that we were then undertaking to choose the individual instead of allowing the people to choose him.

If not Mr. Smith and not Mr. Martine, then who chooses, I would like to know? Some private coterie sitting somewhere alone chooses, and I don't care who the coterie is or where they are, they have no right to choose a Senator.

If neither of these gentlemen, who has been nominated? Does anybody know? Can anybody guess? Does not everybody know that it would be privately arranged somehow? I am opposed to compromise because I am absolutely and forever opposed to private arrangements.

Mr. Martine will be elected Senator from New Jersey. We shall see after that if anybody will have the audacity to choose a Senator for the people of New Jersey. We are out to establish not only a principle, but a cause. We are out to make and confirm history for the State of New Jersey.

I have no feeling as regards the various persons whom I am opposing in this fight except as they represent what I hate. Let us keep our minds concentrated upon that, not upon them. They are our neighbors, they are men who in many instances are acting as they think right, and, unhappily, according to the precedents of American politics.

We shall not judge them as individuals, but we must judge them as representatives of ideas and processes. But even there we must be fair.

Then the Governor-elect spoke of the other side, showing the relations existing between the political managers and the special interests and telling how in some instances the former are compensated for their services to the latter by a transaction in cash, and if not in that way by an understanding of certain advantages to accrue. Mr. Wilson continued:

I have heard a great many gentlemen connected with the so-called interests say that they had to do these things in order to protect themselves.

The only man who has to pay to be protected is a coward. Suppose some great, legitimate business interest in the State of New Jersey is threatened with legislation at Trenton that will be to its detriment and harm, what is it to do? Play the coward and see to it, by arrangement with political managers, that the legislation is killed? Or, let the legislation be passed to enactment, if they dare, and then let all the State know what the object was—that it was blackmail and not legislation?

Do you suppose that after the public opinion of the State became aware of that process there would be blackmailing legislation any more? These gentlemen foster by their business arrangement with political managers the very things that they are pretending to fight. They have debauched politics, and politics has debauched them.

This fight that we are fighting now is merely an incident in the emancipation of politics from secret processes. We are opposed to secret processes and private arrangements in the selection of United States Senators because we are opposed to secret understandings with regard to anything that concerns the public interest.

We are concentrating our attention upon this thing because this is the thing to be done now. When we get through with this we will attend to the rest, and we are getting through with it. Somebody asked me how long this campaign was going to be. I said, "About two meetings."

Just once give the citizens of any populous part of the State a chance to show how they feel and nobody will need any demonstration after that. The business will then be done not in vindictiveness, I hope, not with hard feelings, I trust, but in order to put men in heart again and make them feel that things have returned into their own hands again.

Gentlemen, what is it that we are fighting for? Does not your blood jump quicker in your veins when you think that this is part of the age-long struggle for human liberty? What do men feel curtails and destroys their liberty? Matters in which they have no voice. The control of little groups and cliques and bodies of special interests, the things that are managed without regard to the public welfare or general opinion—the things that are contrived without any referendum to the great mass of feelings and opinions and purposes that are abroad among free men in a free country.

Whenever things go to cover, then men stand up and know and say that liberty is in jeopardy, and so every time a fight of this sort occurs, we are simply setting up the standard again.

Why are you afraid of shadows? Why did prominent citizens of the city of Newark and other parts of Essex County send in their regrets when they were asked to serve on the committee of this meeting? Whom were they afraid of? It suffices to say—I am so[r]ry to say it of any man—that they were afraid of something. Let them reassure themselves. They have been in a dream. There is nothing to be afraid of. Let them once come out and stand on the people's side, and they will find that all the mists of fear are blown away.

There is no name that can be conjured with in any free community except the name of the man who serves the people and wins their confidence. Then you fear not him but the people themselves. There was something to be afraid of, but these gentlemen did not know what it was. They ought to have been afraid to say, "No." They have deceived themselves and have been afraid to say, "Yes." They will awake. They will find that things are not what they supposed them to be. I have had gentlemen say to me, "Why, if I take part in this thing, somebody"—

they do not ever specify whom—"will ruin my business." Why, with whom do you transact business? Don't you transact it with the people among whom you live? Once show them that you are free, courageous, honorable men and nobody can spoil your business; but once show them that you are a coward in politics, you are not free to fulfil your contracts. If these men want guaranties they better come out and get their certificates.

It was at this point that the Governor-elect was urged to go on after he had remarked that he was detaining his hearers. In proceeding he declared that in appearing before them on this occasion he was simply acting in fulfilment of the promise he made in the campaign to act as the representative of the people and as their spokesman in respect to opinion.

A little further along Mr. Wilson observed that there is a perfectly easy way for any man to be great. If he honestly joins in the common effort of honest government and veritable liberty he can rest assured, said the speaker, that some of the power and the greatness of the people will have gone into it. Concluding, the Governor-elect said:

You remember the two men who were talking together and one referred to a third man's head, and his friend said, 'Head! That is not a head; that is just a knot the Almighty put there to keep him from raveling out.' But if he has a head that contains something, well, then, the finest inflatus that can get into it and the most wholesome is the feeling that he is privileged, no matter how humble he is by the accident of position—by the accident of election—for so far as the managers were concerned I think my election was an accident. I ought not to have said that, even in jest, for I think that the men who managed the recent campaign did work most honestly and efficiently; I was tempted by the opportunity for a jest to say what was not so. But if by the accident of election or a choice of one kind or another a man stands in such a place of privilege his power consists not in himself, but in his privilege.

It is the privilege of the legislators who represent the Democratic party in the Legislature of New Jersey to enjoy the greatness of the people of New Jersey. It is their privilege once for all to put New Jersey on record as on the people's side, as determined, no matter who may suffer for their stand, to see to it that only the judgment of the people be registered in this State from this time on, and then we shall have established our connection with the records of liberty; then we shall have taken our place in those handsome annals of history which record how men have massed themselves, caught a single idea with generous enthusiasm, forgotten their differences, sunk their selfish interests and, united in irresistible force, have carried men to the next level of achievement, where they can look forward to still greater achievements, when not only the historians, but every future generation shall look back and bless them and say: "Those men saw the light and rescued us from those things which would have put us to shame, but made it possible for us as self-respecting communities to govern our own affairs."

Shall we not make this one of the years which shall always be marked in the annals of New Jersey as a year of regeneration?[5]

Printed in the *Newark Evening News*, Jan. 16, 1911; some editorial headings omitted.

[5] There is an undated WWhw and WWsh outline of this address and a WWT outline with the composition date of Jan. 13, 1911, in WP, DLC. There is also an undated typed press release in *ibid.*, from which the following paragraph, which Wilson apparently did not use in his speech, is taken:

"A peoples' government means a public government; an honest government; government by discussion and not by arrangement; government in which all parties play for the same things. There has been a great deal of thoughtless talk about 'muck-raking' and sensationalism in our magazines and journals and no doubt a great deal that is mysterious has been said and believed. But any sensation that we have called 'muck-raking' has only amounted to uncovering hidden things. The things hidden had to do with the methods by which the people were privately influenced and decieved [deceived]. But in most other cases the end of the process has been something that proved to be for the benefit of the people, a rectification of things that were wrong. We must not flinch at any kind of publicity; at any kind of inquiry; at any kind of discussion honestly undertaken. We must bring everything into the open and then in all fairness, all honor, all charity readjust and reorganize the elements of our political life."

From Charles Apffel Eypper

Dear Sir: Guttenberg, N. J. Jan. 16th, 1911.

I take great pleasure in enclosing herewith a resolution unanimously adopted at a Martine Mass Meeting of citizens, held Saturday the 14th inst.[1] At the adoption of the resolution, and since then, we have secured the signature of over 300 citizens of our town in support of this resolution, which, however, I do not care to burden you with.

I take this opportunity also, so that no selfish motive shall be imputed to me in my activity in this senatorial controversy, of asking to withdraw my application for appointment to the Hudson County Board of Taxation, recently sent you.[2] I have the honor to remain,   Very truly yours,   Chas A Eypper

TLS (WP, DLC).
[1] It is missing.
[2] It is also missing.

An Inaugural Address

TRENTON, 17 January, 1911.

GENTLEMEN OF THE LEGISLATURE: I assume the great office of Governor of the State with unaffected diffidence. Many great men have made this office illustrious. A long tradition of honorable public service connects each incumbent of it with the generation of men who set up our governments here in free America, to give men perpetual assurance of liberty and justice and opportunity. No one dare be sure that he is qualified to play the part expected of him by the people of the commonwealth in the execution of this high trust. It is best for him, as he sets out, to look away from himself and to concentrate his thought upon the people whom he serves, the sacred interests which are entrusted to his care, and the day in which he is to work, its challenge, its promise, its energies of opinion and of purpose, its sustaining hopes and exciting expectations. The scene will inspire him, not thought of himself.

The opportunity of our day in the field of politics no man can mistake who can read any, even the most superficial, signs of the times. We have never seen a day when duty was more plain, the task to be performed more obvious, the way in which to accomplish it more easy to determine. The air has in recent months cleared amazingly about us, and thousands, hundreds of thousands, have lifted their eyes to look about them, to see things they never saw before, to comprehend things that once seemed vague and elusive. The whole world has changed within the lifetime of men not yet in their thirties; the world of business, and therefore the world of society and the world of politics. The organization and movement of business are new and upon a novel scale. Business has changed so rapidly that for a long time we were confused, alarmed, bewildered, in a sort of terror of the things we had ourselves raised up. We talked about them either in sensational articles in the magazines which distorted every line of the picture, or in conservative editorials in our newspapers, which stoutly denied that anything at all had happened, or in grave discourses which tried to treat them as perfectly normal phenomena, or in legislative debates which sought to govern them with statutes which matched them neither in size nor shape.

But, if only by sheer dint of talking about them, either to frighten or to reassure one another, or to make ourselves out wiser or more knowing than our fellows, we have at last turned them about and looked at them from almost every angle and begin to see them whole, as they are. Corporations are no longer hobgoblins which have sprung at us out of some mysterious ambush, nor yet unholy inventions of rascally rich men, nor yet the puzzling devices by which ingenious lawyers build up huge rights out of a multitude of small wrongs; but merely organizations of a perfectly intelligible sort which the law has licensed for the convenience of extensive business; organizations which have proved very useful but which have for the time being slipped out of the control of the very law that gave them leave to be and that can make or unmake them at pleasure. We have now to set ourselves to control them, soberly but effectively, and to bring them thoroughly within the regulation of the law.

There is a great opportunity here; for wise regulation, wise adjustment, will mean the removal of half the difficulties that now beset us in our search for justice and equality and fair chances of fortune for the individuals who make up our modern society. And there is a great obligation as well as a great opportunity, an imperative obligation, from which we cannot escape if we would. Public opinion is at last wide awake. It begins to understand the problems to be dealt with; it begins to see very clearly indeed the objects to be sought. It knows what has been going on. It sees where resistance has come from whenever efforts at reform have been made, and knows also the means of resistance that have been resorted to. It is watchful, insistent, suspicious. No man who wishes to enjoy the public confidence dare hold back, and, if he is wise, he will not resort to subterfuge. A duty is exacted of him which he must perform simply, directly, immediately. The gate of opportunity stands wide open. If we are foolish enough to be unwilling to pass through it, the whip of opinion will drive us through.

No wise man will say, of course, that he sees the whole problem of reform lying plain before him, or knows how to frame the entire body of law that will be necessary to square business with the general interest, and put right and fairness and public spirit in the saddle again in all the transactions of our new society; but some things are plain enough, and upon these we can act.

In the first place, it is plain that our laws with regard to the relations of employer and employe are in many respects wholly antiquated and impossible.[1] They were framed for another age, which nobody now living remembers, which is, indeed, so remote from our life that it would be difficult for many of us to understand it if it were described to us. The employer is now generally a corporation or huge company of some kind; the em-

---

[1] See n. 9 to the speech printed at Oct. 5, 1910, Vol. 21.

ploye is one of hundreds or of thousands brought together, not by individual masters whom they know and with whom they have personal relations, but by agents of one sort or another. Workingmen are marshalled in great numbers for the performance of a multitude of particular tasks under a common discipline. They generally use dangerous and powerful machinery, over whose repair and renewal they have no control. New rules must be devised with regard to their obligations and their rights, their obligations to their employers and their responsibilities to one another. New rules must be devised for their protection, for their compensation when injured, for their support when disabled.

We call these questions of employers' liability, questions of workingmen's compensation, but those terms do not suggest quite the whole matter. There is something very new and very big and very complex about these new relations of capital and labor. A new economic society has sprung up, and we must effect a new set of adjustments. We must not pit power against weakness. The employer is generally in our day, as I have said, not an individual, but a powerful group of individuals, and yet the workingman is still, under our existing law, an individual when dealing with his employer, in case of accident, for example, or of loss or of illness, as well as in every contractual relationship. We must have a workingman's compensation act which will not put upon him the burden of fighting powerful composite employers to obtain his rights, but which will give him his rights without suit, directly, and without contest, by automatic operation of law, as if of a law of insurance.

This is the first adjustment needed, because it affects the rights, the happiness, the lives and fortunes of the largest number, and because it is the adjustment for which justice cries loudest and with the most direct appeal, to our hearts as well as to our consciences.

But there is regulation needed which lies back of that and is much more fundamental. The composite employer himself needs to have his character and powers overhauled, his constitution and rights reconsidered, readjusted to the fundamental and abiding interests of society. If I may speak very plainly, we are much too free with grants of charters to corporations in New Jersey. A corporation exists, not of natural right, but only by license of law, and the law, if we look at the matter in good conscience, is responsible for what it creates. It can never rightly authorize any kind of fraud or imposition. It cannot righteously allow the setting up of a business which has no sound basis, or which follows methods which in any way outrage justice or fair dealing or the principles of honest industry. The law cannot give its license to things of that kind. It thereby authenticates what it ought of right to forbid.

I would urge, therefore, the imperative obligation of public policy and of public honesty we are under to effect such changes in the law of the State as will henceforth effectually prevent the abuse of the privilege of incorporation which has in recent years brought so much discredit upon our State. In order to do this it will be necessary to regulate and restrict the issue of securities, to enforce regulations with regard to bona fide capital, examining very rigorously the basis of capitalization, and to prescribe methods by which the public shall be safeguarded against fraud, deception, extortion, and every abuse of its confidence.

And such scrutiny and regulation ought not to be confined to corporations seeking charters. They ought also to be extended to corporations already operating under the license and authority of the State. For the right to undertake such regulation is susceptible of easy and obvious justification. A modern corporation—that is, a modern joint stock company—is in no proper sense an intimate or private concern. It is not set up on the risk and adventure of a few persons, the persons who originated it, manage it, carry it to failure or success. On the contrary, it is set up at what may be called the common risk. It is a risk and adventure in which the public are invited to share, and the hundreds, perhaps thousands, who subscribe to the stock do in fact share in it, oftentimes without sharing also, in any effectual manner, in the control and development of the business in which their risk is taken. Moreover, these modern enterprises, with their exchequers replenished out of the common store of the savings of the nation, conduct business transactions whose scope and influence are as wide as whole regions of the Union, often as wide as the nation itself. They affect sometimes the lives and fortunes of whole communities, dominate prices, determine land values, make and unmake markets, develop or check the growth of city and of countryside. If law is at liberty to adjust the general conditions of society itself, it is at liberty to control these great instrumentalities which nowadays, in so large part, determine the character of society. Wherever we can find what the common interest is in respect of them we shall find a solid enough basis for law, for reform.

The matter is most obvious when we turn to what we have come to designate public service, or public utility, corporations—those which supply us with the means of transportation and with those common necessaries, water, light, heat, and power. Here are corporations exercising peculiar and extraordinary franchises, and bearing such a relation to society in respect of the services they render that it may be said that they are the very medium of its life. They render a public and common service of which it is necessary that practically everybody should avail himself.

We have a Public Utilities Commission in New Jersey, but it has hardly more than powers of inquiry and advice.[2] It could even as it stands, be made a powerful instrument of publicity and of opinion, but it may also modestly wait until it is asked before expressing a judgment, and in any case it will have the uncomfortable consciousness that its opinion is gratuitous, and carries no weight of effective authority. This will not do. It is understood by everybody who knows anything of the common interest that it must have complete regulative powers: the power to regulate rates, the power to learn and make public everything that should furnish a basis for the public judgment with regard to the soundness, the efficiency, the economy of the business— the power, in brief, to adjust such service at every point and in every respect, whether of equipment or charges or methods of financing or means of service, to the general interest of the communities affected. This can be done, as experience elsewhere has demonstrated, not only without destroying the profits of such business, but also with the effect of putting it upon a more satisfactory footing for those who conduct it no less than for those who make use of it day by day.

Such regulation, based on thorough and authoritative inquiry, will go far towards disclosing and establishing those debatable values upon which so many questions of taxation turn. There is an uneasy feeling throughout the State, in which, I dare say, we all share, that there are glaring inequalities in our system— or, at any rate, in our practice—of taxation. The most general complaint is, that there is great inequality as between individuals and corporations. I do not see how anyone can determine whether there are or not, for we have absolutely no uniform system of assessment. It would seem that in every locality there is some local variety of practice, in the rate, the ratio of assessment value to market value, and that every assessor is a law unto himself. Our whole system of taxation, which is no system at all, needs overhauling from top to bottom. There can be no system, no safety, no regulation in a multitude of boards. An efficient Public Utilities Commission will be a beginning towards

2 See n. 2 to the address printed at Sept. 30, 1910, *ibid.*

a system of taxation as well as towards a system of corporate control. We cannot fairly tax values until we have ascertained and established them.

And the great matter of conservation seems to me like a part of the same subject. The safeguarding of our water supply, the purification of our streams in order to maintain them as sources of life, and their protection against those who would divert them or diminish their volume for private profit, the maintenance of such woodlands as are left us and the reforestation of bare tracts more suited for forest than for field, the sanitation of great urban districts such as cover the northern portions of our State, by thorough systems of drainage and of refuse disposal; the protection of the public health and the facilitation of urban and suburban life—these are all public obligations which fall sooner or later upon you as the lawmakers of the commonwealth, and they are all parts of the one great task of adjustment which has fallen to our generation. Our business is to adjust right to right, interest to interest, and to systematize right and convenience, individual rights and corporate privileges, upon the single basis of the general good, the good of whole communities, the good which no one will look after or suffice to secure if the legislator does not, the common good for whose safeguarding and main-tenance government is intended.

This readjustment has not been going on very fast or very favorably in New Jersey. It has been observed that it limped, or was prevented, or neglected, in other States as well. Every-where there has been confusion of counsel and many a sad mis-carriage of plan. There have, consequently, been some very radi-cal criticisms of our methods of political action. There is widespread dissatisfaction with what our legislatures do, and still more serious dissatisfaction with what they do not do. Some persons have said that representative government has proved too indirect and clumsy an instrument, and has broken down as a means of popular control. Others, looking a little deeper, have said that it was not representative government that had broken down, but the effort to get it. They have pointed out that with our present methods of machine nomination and our present methods of elections, which were nothing more than a choice between one set of machine nominees and another, we did not get representative government at all—at least not government representative of the people, but government representative of political managers who served their own interests and the in-terests of those with whom they found it profitable to establish partnerships.

Obviously this is something that goes to the root of the whole matter. Back of all reform lies the method of getting it. Back of the question what you want lies the question, the fundamental question of all government, how are you going to get it? How are you going to get public servants who will obtain it for you? How are you going to get genuine representatives who will serve your real interests, and not their own or the interests of some special group or body of your fellow-citizens whose power is of the few and not of the many? These are the queries which have drawn the attention of the whole country to the subject of the direct primary, the direct choice of representatives by the people, without the intervention of the nominating machine, the nominating organization.

I earnestly commend to your careful consideration in this connection the laws in recent years adopted in the State of Oregon, whose effect has been to bring government back to the people and to protect it from the control of the representatives of selfish and special interests. They seem to me to point the direction which we must also take before we have completed our regeneration of a government which has suffered so seriously and so long as ours has here in New Jersey from private management and organized selfishness. Our primary laws, extended and perfected, will pave the way. They should be extended to every elective office, and to the selection of every party committee or official as well, in order that the people may once for all take charge of their own affairs, their own political organization and association; and the methods of primary selection should be so perfected that the primaries will be put upon the same free footing that the methods of election themselves are meant to rest upon.

We have here the undoubtedly sound chain and sequence of reforms: an actual direct choice by the people of the men who are to organize alike their parties and their government, and those measures which true representatives of the people will certainly favor and adopt—systematic compensation for injured workingmen; the careful regulation in the common interest of all corporations, both in respect of their organization and of their methods of business, and especially of public service corporations; the equalization of taxes; and the conservation of the natural resources of the State and of the health and safety of its people.

Another matter of the most vital consequence goes with all these: namely, systematic ballot reform and thorough and stringent provisions of law against corrupt practices in connection alike with primaries and with elections. We have lagged behind our sister States in these important matters, and should make haste to avail ourselves of their example and their experience. Here, again, Oregon may be our guide.

This is a big programme, but it is a perfectly consistent programme, and a perfectly feasible programme, and one upon whose details it ought to be possible to agree even within the limits of a single legislative session. You may count upon my co-operation at every step of the work.

I have not spoken of the broad question of economy in the administration of the State government, an economy which can probably be effected only through a thorough reorganization upon business principles, the familiar business principles so thoroughly understood and so intelligently practiced by Americans, but so seldom applied to their governments. We make offices for party purposes too often instead of conducting our public business by the organization best adapted to efficiency and economy. I have not dwelt upon the subject in this address because it is a very complicated one, hardly suited for brief exposition, and because so obvious a requirement of honest government needs hardly more than to be mentioned to be universally endorsed by the public. I shall try to point out to you from time to time the means by which reorganization and economy may be secured with benefit to the public service.

But there is a subject which lies a little off the beaten track to which I do wish to turn for a moment before I close. The whole country has remarked the extraordinary rise in the prices of food stuffs in recent years, and the fact that prices are successfully maintained at an intolerably high level at all seasons, whether they be the seasons of plenty or of scarcity. We have a partial remedy at our own hand—a remedy which was proposed to the Legislature last year by Mr. James, of Hudson county, but which is said to have been defeated in some questionable fashion in the last hours of the session.[3] It is estimated that most of the food supply of the people of northern New Jersey, and half the food supply for New York City, is kept in cold-storage warehouses in Hudson county, awaiting the desired state of the market. There is abundant reason to believe that it is the practice of dealers to

[3] He referred to Assembly bill No. 112, "An Act Relating to Cold Storage and Refrigerating Warehouses and Places, and the Sale or Disposition of the Food Kept or Preserved Therein," introduced in the Assembly on January 31, 1910, by Peter H. James of Jersey City. Referred to the Committee on Labor and Industries, the bill was not reported out and passed by the Assembly until April 16, 1910, the last day of the session. On the same day it was sent to the Senate where it was referred to the Committee on Public Health, there to expire as the session ended.

seclude immense quantities of beef and other meats, poultry, eggs, fish, etc., in cold-storage in times of abundance in order that the price of these indispensable foods may be kept high and the foods dealt out only when the market is satisfactory for that purpose, even if the meats and eggs have to be kept for years together before being sold. Figures, said to be actually of record, foot up almost incredible totals of the amounts thus held in waiting, running into millions of heads of cattle, of sheep and lambs, of hogs, millions of pounds of poultry, and hundreds of millions of eggs.

The result is not only to control prices but also to endanger health, because of the effect of too long storage upon the food stuffs themselves, and because of the deleterious effects of taking them out of cold-storage and exposing them to thaw in the markets. The least effect is loss of nutritious quality; the worst, the generation of actual poisons by decay and even putrefaction.

No limit at all is put upon this abuse by law, and strong influences are brought to bear by interested parties to prevent the enactment of remedial legislation. Indictments were brought in Hudson county, but there was no sufficient law to sustain them. A bill was introduced, as I have said, at the last session of the Legislature, but was, I am told, after lingering a very long time in the Assembly committee, mysteriously lost when called up for passage in the Senate during the last hours of the session. I earnestly urge that the Legislature take up this important matter at the earliest possible time, and push some effective law of inspection and limitation to enactment. It would give me great pleasure to sign a bill that would really accomplish the purpose.

I shall take the liberty from time to time to make detailed recommendations to you on the matters I have dwelt upon, and on others, sometimes in the form of bills if necessary.[4]

We are servants of the people, of the whole people. Their interest should be our constant study. We should pursue it without fear or favor. Our reward will be greater than that to be obtained in any other service: the satisfaction of furthering large ends, large purposes, of being an intimate part of that slow but constant and ever hopeful force of liberty and of enlightenment that is lifting mankind from age to age to new levels of progress and achievement, and of having been something greater than successful men. For we shall have been instruments of humanity, men whose thought was not for themselves, but for the true and lasting comfort and happiness of men everywhere.

[4] This paragraph is a WWhw addition.

It is not the foolish ardor of too sanguine or too radical reform that I urge upon you, but merely the tasks that are evident and pressing, the things we have knowledge and guidance enough to do; and to do with confidence and energy. I merely point out the present business of progressive and serviceable government, the next stage on the journey of duty. The path is as inviting as it is plain. Shall we hesitate to tread it? I look forward with genuine pleasure to the prospect of being your comrade upon it.[5]

Printed reading copy (WP, DLC).

[5] There is a WWhw outline, dated Jan. 17, 1911; a WWsh draft, with the composition date of Jan. 7, 1911; and an undated WWT draft of this address in WP, DLC.

An Interview

[Jan. 17, 1911]

WILSON TO ATTEMPT TO KILL LOBBY

By Virginia Tyler Hudson.

Governor Woodrow Wilson has been governor of the state of New Jersey just one day. But it did not take one day—it took only the first hour after his inauguration—to show that the people not only are proud of him, but love their governor and have faith in him.

That he cares for the regard of even the lowliest of his constituents the new governor evidenced in a simple way as he talked with me for a few moments after three hours of standing and shaking the hands of the thousands who were eager to do him honor. His room in the state house was banked with flowers, rare exotics, and costly blossoms. But as he talked, he lovingly fondled a single offering that lay in a place of honor on his desk —a bouquet of paper flowers, fashioned arduously by loving hands, and attached to which was a slip of paper with its message of well wishing scrawled by hands unfamiliar with writing.

Since his election—one who is familiar with the political situation in New Jersey might almost say "since the accident of his selection, campaign and election"—Governor Wilson has been many times spoken of as radical. With the conservatism of the true political economist, however, he qualifies this—as he is modest in admitting freely many of the plans he has made to make legislation in New Jersey approach the ideal.

"Don't use the word 'radical,'" he urged. "There are too many people who are afraid of it—who do not yet understand radicalism, and see in it only an approach to socialism."

"Then you do not approve of socialism?" I asked the point-blank question, but Governor Wilson did not answer yes or no. Again he weighed his words and qualified his remarks.

"The people of the east and the west see things differently," he said, "and what is considered radical here may be taken as a matter of course in the west as a step nearer ideal conditions."

In his inaugural address Governor Wilson several times made reference to the laws in the state of Oregon, urging them as examples which might well be followed.

"Do you then," I asked him, "consider Oregon an ideal state, legislatively considered?"

"I think they have many laws out there which have proven their worth, though I wouldn't care to go so far as to say they would apply equally well in New Jersey. I am particularly interested in their laws of initiative and referendum, their law of recall, and their preference law, and direct vote for United States senators, binding the legislators to choose a senator of the people's choice. I should like especially to call attention to the recall, which makes it imperative for the man elected to serve the people as they choose to be served, to be truly instruments of humanity, men whose thought is not for themselves, but for the true and lasting comfort of men everywhere, and, by the recall, if the man elected is not such, he can be made to be, or else step aside for a worthier man."

Among his campaign pledges Governor Wilson made one to bring questions which concerned the people directly before them —thus, in a measure, doing away with lobbying, which time-worn system he condemns. "Of course, I cannot do away with the lobbyist," he said, "that is for the legislators to do—but when a bill comes up which directly concerns the people, I intend to have their voice, which I shall do by going to their county court houses and calling them about me for a direct opinion."

Above all other things, the "reform governor," as Governor Wilson has come to be called, is modest about the reform he intends to bring about. Insistently he calls himself merely a comrade of the people in bringing about a progressive and serviceable government. Far different is he from the mere book-taught figurehead it is reported some of those who selected him believed he would prove to be.

"I believe and hope I am a practical politician," he says. "Where did I learn practical politics? Principally in the school of life and by keeping my eyes open and my wits alert. God gave me eyes, and I don't use the lids except at night.

"I earnestly commend to the careful consideration of the people of New Jersey, though, a study of the new laws of Oregon. That state may not yet have reached the ideal, but its laws point the direction we must take before we have completed the regeneration of a government which has suffered so seriously and so long from private management and organized selfishness."

In the mean time, while he had been speaking, several hundreds of those who had not been presented to the new governor by the gold-draped guard clamored for a chance to shake his limp and aching hand. There remained still one inevitable question.

"How about woman suffrage?" I asked.

The governor's eyes lighted up.

"Ah, there is my wife," he exclaimed. "I must speak to her a moment. Thank you so much for your interest and for not detaining me long."

So you know now, also, as much as I do about the educator-governor's attitude on the suffrage question. It may be, though, that that is to have a part in his curriculum in the campaign of education he is to wage in teaching radicalism and other things, however much he deprecates the idea and insists that to call his intentions by any such name would savor of condescension.

Printed in the New York *Globe and Commercial Advertiser*, Jan. 17, 1911.

Joseph Patrick Tumulty to James E. W. Cook[1]

Dear Mr. Cook: [Trenton, N. J.] January 18, 1911.

The Governor has requested me to acknowledge receipt of your letter of January sixteenth[2] with reference to the condition of the little cripple girl,[3] in which he is deeply interested. This case has appealed very strongly to the Governor and I have taken the matter up with one of the members of the Board of Managers of the New Jersey Tuberculosis Sanitorium.[4] He has suggested that I write you for the purpose of having you communicate with Dr. P[aul]. H[amilton]. Markley of 515 Cooper City, Camden, N. J. He is the examiner for the Sanitorium in your District.

Please advise me as to the result of the examination and let me have any other suggestions in this matter that you think will be helpful in any way.[5]

Very truly yours,   [J. P. Tumulty]

TCL (Governors' Files, Nj).
[1] Of Camden, N. J.

2 It is missing.
3 Barbara Scharnagle of Camden, fifteen, afflicted with various diseases, including advanced tuberculosis.
4 This letter is missing.
5 Dr. Markley advised in a typed report, Jan. 30, 1911 (Governors' Files, Nj), that the advanced condition of Barbara's tuberculosis and existing complications made her ineligible for admission to the state sanitarium.

A News Report and a Statement about the Hotel Martinique Conference

[Jan. 19, 1911]

NOT SECRET, SAYS WILSON

GOVERNOR TELLS ABOUT HOTEL MARTINIQUE CONFERENCE.

TRENTON, N. J., January 19.—Replying to an article in ex-Senator Smith's Newark newspaper, the *Star*, to the effect that, at a conference in the Hotel Martinique in New York on Monday night, he had chosen George L. Record of Jersey City, the "progressive" Republican leader, as his chief adviser,[1] Gov. Wilson to-day gave out the following statement:

"There was absolutely nothing secret about the conference held in the Hotel Martinique. It was simply a continuation of the policy I have followed ever since my election of consulting everyone who was interested in the reforms which concern the whole State.

"The conference was held for the convenience of consulting a large number of persons at the same time, and getting their various points of view with regard to matters which ought not to be decided from any one point of view. It was not a conference to fix upon a programme, or determine anything,[2] but merely to compare views from as wide a variety of sources as possible, and to discuss the real demands of the public opinion of the State, as well as the best and most straightforward and thorough means of meeting those demands.

"Those present were Senators Gebhardt, Fielder, and Osborne; Mr. John J. Matthews, the leader of the majority of the House; Mr. Matthew [Matthias] Ely, Mr. James Kerney, Messrs. Walter and Joseph Dear, Mr. Tumulty, Mr. Rider,[3] Mr. Tracey [Treacy], and Mr. Record. Speaker [Edward] Kenny was prevented by illness from attending. Senator Silzer and Judge Mark A. Sullivan were prevented from attending by reason of engagements in court, and Mr. Wallace N[M.]. Scudder of the Newark *Evening News* also found it impossible to attend.

"Mr. Record is well known to be one of the best informed men in this State with regard to the details involved in most of the reforms proposed. He is particularly versed in legislation else-where, as well as in New Jersey, with regard to ballot reform and corrupt practices, as well as with regard to the regulation of primaries. He generously consented to put his unusual store of information at the service of the conference, which was non-partisan in its purpose and meant in the public interest."[4]

Printed in the New York *Evening Post*, Jan. 19, 1911; some editorial headings omitted.

[1] Newark *Morning Star*, Jan. 19, 1911.

[2] According to Kerney, *The Political Education of Woodrow Wilson*, p. 101, Wilson had written in his letters of invitation to the conferees: "I think it would be to the common advantage to have a little conference of a few gentlemen particularly interested in formulating bills for consideration of the Legislature before my actual entrance upon my office as Governor."

[3] Frederic Rider of Jersey City, a political associate of Tumulty.

[4] Kerney has left the best account of the conference in general and of Record's role in particular. "At the Martinique Hotel conference in New York," he writes, "Record took command and presented the essentials of a primary and election law, and of a corrupt practices act, as well as recommendations for a public utility bill . . . and an employers' liability bill. . . . There was some protest that we were proceeding too fast and that the people of a conservative State like New Jersey were hardly ripe for all the Oregon theories. Wilson, however, sided with Record, and the conference headed for everything that Oregon offered. To Record was allotted the task of framing the primary bill as well as the blanket ballot and corrupt practices bill. The shaping up of the other bills was subdivided, and the meeting adjourned with the understanding that it was to be called together again when the bills were ready for discussion." *Ibid.*, pp. 103-104.

To Charles Williston McAlpin

My dear McAlpin: [Trenton, N. J.] January 19, 1911.

Thank you very much indeed for your thoughtfulness in sending me the Trustees' Calendar and the Catalogue and copy of the President's Report. I think probably it would be best to send everything of any bulk to my office here in Trenton. We have not found places to bestow them at the Inn in Princeton yet.

I wish I might have caught sight of you at the Inauguration exercises. It was delightful to feel that so many friends were there.

Do let me see you whenever you can at Princeton. I shall generally be there and free in the evening.

Always affectionately yours,   Woodrow Wilson

TLS (photostat in RSB Coll., DLC).

To William Royal Wilder

My dear Wilder: [Trenton, N. J.] January 19, 1911.

You may be sure I have no foolish delicacy about non-interference,[1] but it does seem to me that it would not be wise for me, the Governor of one State, to make suggestions to Osborne[2] with regard to the action of Dix, the Governor of another State. I feel there would be a very decided undelicacy about that, much as I dread the election of Sheehan, and much as I should like to assist in anything that would prevent it.[3]

Always faithfully yours,   Woodrow Wilson

TLS (W. R. Wilder Coll., NjP).
  [1] Wilder's letter to which this was a reply is missing.
  [2] William Church Osborn, Princeton 1883, legal adviser to Governor John Alden Dix of New York.
  [3] About the senatorial contest in New York and Sheehan, see W. Hughes to WW, Dec. 9, 1910, n. 1.

A News Report of the Annual Dinner of the Jersey City Board of Trade

[Jan. 20, 1911]

WILSON, M'CARTER AND SCHURMAN DISCUSS GRAFT AND GRAFTING

Bribery and the corruption of public officials by men interested in large business enterprises, was the chief topic discussed by the speakers at the annual dinner of the Jersey City Board of Trade, held last night at the Jersey City Club theatre.

President Jacob Gould Schurman, of Cornell University, thought the man who used bribery in any form was a traitor to his State; President Thomas N. McCarter, of the Public Service Corporation, made excuse for the man who yielded to blackmail, declaring that it was often necessary for his self-preservation, while Governor Wilson, who was the last speaker, flayed the grafters and the graft-givers alike and said that he wanted none of them. . . .

Governor Wilson was the last speaker. He said:

"I was interested in the remarks of President Schurman. They sounded like the voice of the opinion which I once held. I was once an expert and am now a politician. Dr. Schurman's argument is against the service of politicians and for the service of experts in public life. I have never met a man who could be called an expert on the tariff. There are experts upon economic questions, but the politicians are experts upon economic facts, and facts are different from questions. The politician acts upon the facts, and when he acts he can get the facts.

"The moment the facts are changed he throws out all the calculations of the experts. The politician deals with the every-day life of the people, and there is no such thing as an expert in friendship, an expert in pity, an expert in human sympathy or the responsibility of the individuals to each other in helpfulness.

"This world does not consist of business. Politics should deal with human relationships, and can only deal with them by insight and sympathy. Sympathy in politics must run over the whole field, wherever the human heart beats, and men are struggling for existence and a little bit of happiness.

"Shall any body of experts direct us as to the needs of our fellow men. No. If we take the veil from our own honest eyes, and our own honest hearts we don't ne[e]d any guide outside of our own insight and sympathy."

Speaking of the responsibility of the individual in all the affairs of the community, Dr. Wilson said: "Do you imagine that the reforms which you demand should be left to the Legislature and public men? We are partners in this enterprise. Statesmanship is a business in which it is your imperative duty to engage. There should reside in business the temper of statesmanship. No community is greater than the hearts and consciences of the men who compose it. You are the custodians of the standard of the community in which you serve.

"No business can possibly prosper that is touched with corruption. Don't you know that a man who will bribe a politician will cheat a competitor. You can't keep your morals in airtight compartments. Corruption is a taint that will spread itself. There is danger of it spreading until it taints the whole body.

"If a man who has a duty to perform is afraid of what he is going to do, or is governed in his act through fear, how do we know that he will keep his contract after he has made it? Once let that coward fear come in to your dealings, I don't want anything to do with you.

"The greatest asset a man can have is moral courage. Any shrewd creature can follow the line of self-preservation and stay alive a long while, but he must have a very bad taste in his mouth when he swallows. Every community is kept alive by moral courage. The English people admired Lord Palmerston, with all his faults, because of what they called his 'u[n]be-damn[e]dness.' We have our own salvation or our own corruption in our own hands.

"There is no political salvation but our own conscience. It is the duty of everyone in Americans [America] to serve all America. It is the duty of every citizen to be a public man, and a shame on him to be a private man."

Printed in the Hoboken, N. J., *Hudson Observer* (formerly the Hoboken *Observer*), Jan. 20, 1911; some editorial headings omitted.

To Harriet Hyde[1]

My dear Miss Hyde: Princeton, N. J. January 21, 1911

I have read your letter of the 17th with a great deal of interest and beg you to believe that I am no less interested in you because you are a girl and not a boy. I cannot feel as you do that girls are in any sense useless and I believe you will find, as you grow older, many ways in which to make your life and the lives of friends happy and useful.

Cordially and sincerely yours,   Woodrow Wilson

TLS (WP, DLC).
1 Of Ridgefield Park, N. J. Her letter is missing, and the Editors have been unable to find any information about her.

From William Royal Wilder

My dear Wilson: New York January 21st, 1911.

I am fairly in touch with the situation at Albany, and can assure you that Mr. Sheehan will not be elected Senator. It is also equally sure that Mr. Shepard will not be elected. From what Osborn and several members of the Legislature tell me, we are likely to have a fairly good representative at Washington.

My idea in having you write to Osborn '81, who is the Governor's legal advisor, was based on the fact that you might feel as though you could rely on his personal friendship and loyalty. You will see however, from a copy of his letter to me,[1] that he is doing his level best anyhow.

I was sorry that two cases in court prevented me from being present on Tuesday. Bob Bridges assures me that you were duly inaugurated and I probably was not missed.

Much strength to your muscles and red corpuscles in your fight with James Smith.

What do you think of the Royal Bengal Beasts? You must be present when they are consecrated.

Faithfully yours,   Wm R Wilder

TLS (Governors' Files, Nj).
1 W. C. Osborn to W. R. Wilder, Jan. 17, 1911, TCL (Governors' Files, Nj).

From Oren Britt Brown[1]

My Dear Governor: Dayton, Ohio, January 21, 1911.

Now that you are inaugurated Governor of New Jersey, it will not be out of place for a Republican who has had some experience in politics and who was a member of the class of '76 of Princeton to extend to you my sincere congratulations without appearing to be unfaithful to my Republican principles.

I have taken great interest in your canvas from the first and have talked among Princetonians as well as other people of both parties and I find nothing but the best of wishes for your success, because we believe that you will make good.

Personally I am very much delighted and politically I desire to say of all the men suggested for President on the Democratic ticket I prefer you; I also prefer you above most of the men who are liable to be named by the Republicans, outside of my personal friend, President Taft, to whom I have been devoted politically and personally.

As you remember my saying once before in Cincinnati, "the Freshman '79 is saluted by the Senior '76," and may success attend you.   Sincerely yours,   Oren Britt Brown

(How our old friend Harlan Cleveland[2] would have enjoyed your success!)

TLS (Governors' Files, Nj).
    [1] Princeton 1876, judge of the Court of Common Pleas of the Second Ohio District, Dayton, Ohio.
    [2] James Harlan Cleveland, Princeton 1885, United States attorney for the southern district of Ohio, 1894-98; until his death in 1906 a lawyer in Cincinnati and Professor of Law at the University of Cincinnati.

To Mary Allen Hulbert Peck

Dearest Friend,   Princeton, N. J. 22 January, 1911.

It looks as if Sunday were the only day when I can be sure, for the present at least, of a free hour in which to give myself the pleasure of a little talk with you. And what a pleasure it is! I am so sure of what I can count on in your mind as I talk and of what the answering thought will be; and to turn to you is to turn to associations so delightful, so removed from anxiety (when you are well) and from the petty worries and the doubtful sympathies of the rest of the day, when I must be thinking (except for the dear ones immediately around me) of the shifts and spites of politics! What an asset you are—what a resource—what a delight; and when once two persons are such friends as we are separation (whatever else of pain it involves) does not mean disconnection in the least, but only a slower flow of sympathy upon this, that, or the other point of common concern,—and all that affects either of us *is* a point of common concern!

I got into harness last Tuesday. The ceremony was simple enough: the exercises of the inauguration were over in an hour. Only the all-afternoon and all-evening receptions were fatiguing; and even in them there was variety enough to take at least monotony away and afford constant amusement, and, better than amusement, constant human interest. All sorts and conditions of people came, men, women, and children, and I felt very close to all of them, and very much touched by the thought that I was their representative and spokesman, and in a very real sense their help and hope, after year upon year of selfish machine domination when nothing at all had been done for them that could possibly be withheld! Since Tuesday I have been in Trenton every day, except yesterday, getting into harness and learning the daily routine of the office; and all the while deeply moved by the thought of my new responsibilities as the representative and champion of the common people against those who have been preying upon them. I have felt a sort of solemnity in it all that I feel sure will not wear off. I do not see how a man in such a position could possibly be afraid of anything except failing to do his honourable duty and set all temptations (if they were disguised enough to be temptations) contemptuously on one side. I shall make mistakes, but I do not think I shall sin against my knowledge of duty. May I not say that to you, who will know that I am not speaking with the least touch of pride of [or] of self-confidence, but only as one who is obliged to see and know his duty by mere plainness of circumstance and force of education?

To-morrow issue is finally joined on the senatorial election. The voting begins on Tuesday. Smith goes down to Trenton to-morrow to do everything that money and improper influence can do to obtain the seat. The town will swarm with his agents and partisans. We shall pass through trying days of deep mortification, in which it will be necessary to be vigilant day and night against subtile public enemies, who work in covert and with instruments we would not deign touch. I shall have to stay down there day and night, no doubt, until some issue is reached. It will be an awful strain upon my self-control and upon my judgment and good sense. But it will soon end, I believe. It can have but one outcome, unless I and all who advise with me are radically misled by the events of the past week or so. And, when once it is over, I believe that the State will be freed forever of these demoralizing and disgraceful struggles for seats in the Senate, for private, not for public use. After that the people will always choose their own Senators and the legislatures will be freed from one of the most dangerous influences that has worked upoo [upon] them. It is worth a few days of extraordinary effort and even of actual pain. No price is too great to pay for emancipation. I will let you know the outcome at the earliest poss[i]ble moment at which I can venture to take my eyes off the men I am fighting.

Meanwhile, I am perfectly well. Of course I am aware of the extraordinary strain on my nerves. My dreams are burdened with vague anxieties and I do not get up in the mornings quite as much refreshed as in less strenuous seasons; but it is doing me no harm. There is one interesting proof. Miss Green,[1] who is preserving (?) my remaining locks, says that I have not been so well for several years: my circulation is so good, so easy to stimulate in the scalp, and the skin is so much less often dry and feverish. That seems to me very good evidence; and Miss Green sees me in the midst of hurry and distraction, when I hardly find time enough to sit still long enough for her to do her work. I have to be deaf to telephones and deny myself to the most important callers in order to see her at all, and then rush back into the fray, so that she does not see me when I am at leisure or rested.

You cannot know what a delight your letters are![2] The pleasure I take in them is like the pleasure I take in you. When I open them, and while I read them, I am with a dear companion and chum. I can read between all the lines and know all the things that have not been said. My dear friend's atmosphere is about me and holds me. I am intensely conscious of her, and all that our friendship has meant is, as it were, renewed and refreshed. Make them as long as you can. Of course I can read them again and again; but presently I know them. If they could but always go on and on, the spell would be so delightfully prolonged. I would have just that much more of your companionship. I wonder if my letters contain as much of me as yours do of you? It would do you much less good, simply because you are more delightful than I am, but I should at least feel that I was really calling on you when I despatched a letter. I hope that the mail goes over by Salt Kettle Ferry as I used to!

Good night, and God bless you! All join me in affectionate messages, and I am always and altogether

Your devoted friend, Woodrow Wilson

WWTLS (WP, DLC).

[1] Kate or Katheryne Green, a woman's hairdresser, whose shop was located in her home at 683 Lamberton St. in Trenton.

[2] All of Mrs. Peck's letters between January 13 and July 22, 1911, are missing.

A Statement on James Edgar Martine's Impending Election

[Jan. 24, 1911]

What I have to say is very obvious. I can sincerely say that the outcome is what I expected.[1] I had not the slightest doubt that the Democratic members of the Legislature would act in a spirit of responsibility to their constituents. I think the gratification of the people of the State in the result will be chiefly based upon the knowledge that henceforth the selection of United States Senators will be on an entirely different basis. The people will know that henceforth they will make free choice of Senators on their own responsibility.

This is in line with the manifest movement of public opinion all over the country.

What has just been done is most convincing evidence of the sincerity of the Democratic party in New Jersey in respect to the principles of their party. Mr. Martine is to be congratulated on the privilege of representing this principle in the State, and I am sure the best wishes of the people of the State will follow him to Washington.

The Democratic members of the Legislature are also to be congratulated upon having the opportunity to institute this great and salutary change, and there is every evidence that they have done it with heartiness and satisfaction.

Printed in the *Newark Evening News*, Jan. 24, 1911.
[1] That is, the outcome of the first ballot on January 24 as each house voted separately, when Martine received forty votes, one less than necessary for election.

From Henry Smith Pritchett

CONFIDENTIAL

My dear Wilson: New York January 24, 1911.

At the meeting of the executive committee held on January 19 there was taken up the question of a retiring allowance in the case of several college presidents who had not reached sixty-five years of age, but whose service to education had been conspicuous.

The committee had a long discussion over the question as to what the trustees meant by the direction "to safeguard the interests" of such men. The committee decided at the end of the discussion to take no action in any of the cases under consideration, but to refer the whole question back to the trustees at their next meeting for a more definite interpretation as to what was understood and intended by this phrase.

We miss you greatly and watch your career with keenest interest.   Always faithfully yours,   Henry S. Pritchett

TLS (WP, DLC).

From Edmund Burke Osborne[1]

My dear Governor Wilson: Newark, N. J. Jan. 24, 1911

As a citizen, I want to express to you the great satisfaction that I think all good citizens of New Jersey are taking in the splendid fight you are making for clean politics and the rule of the majority; and as a Progressive Republican, I want to express my gratification that you are doing more than has ever been done by any other man in New Jersey to promote the principles for which this League[2] stands.

We were very anxious to have a Progressive Republican nominated and elected Governor, but "things equal to the same thing are equal to each other," and as you are doing the work we want done as effectually as we could have hoped any Progressive Republican would have done it, we consider you our Governor and are as anxious for your success as if we had procured your nomination and election. Knowing, as you must, that you will have to fight the "bi-partisan machine," as you have termed the two Republican organizations, it may be some satisfaction to you to feel assured, as you may, that you have the moral support of the Progressive Republicans of this State.

You frequently stated, before Election, that you would interpret your election to mean that you were to be the leader of your Party in New Jersey; that is obviously what the Democratic voters intended, but I want to go farther than that and say that you are more than the leader of the Democratic Party,—you are today the moral leader of the State of New Jersey, and you have behind you the best people in the State, regardless of their political affiliations.   Sincerely yours,   Edmund B Osborne

TLS (Governors' Files, Nj).
  [1] President of the Osborne Co., printers of art calendars, and of the American Colortype Co., both of Newark. Wilson appointed him to the state Board of Education in 1911.
  [2] The Progressive Republican League of New Jersey, of which he was president. Everett Colby was chairman of the executive committee.

A News Report of Comments on Martine's Election

[*Jan. 25, 1911*]

MARTINE ELECTION AN EPOCH IN JERSEY

Governor Is Modest

Trenton, Jan. 25.—It required less than an hour all told to-day to finish that interesting chapter of New Jersey history concerning the triumph of the people in the election of James E. Martine, modest hero of many a losing fight, United States Senator to succeed John Kean for six years from March 4 next. Of the 81 votes in the Legislature he received 47, only four of the 51 Democratic votes going astray. Three[1] of them insisted upon sticking to James Smith, Jr., disappointed and disheartened leader, and one[2] declined to vote at all for reasons which the people of Hudson county will probably seek an explanation. . . .

When, overwhelmed by delighted Democrats who had been in the forefront of the fight with him, Governor Wilson was warmly congratulated, he said: "Why congratulate me? It is the people who are to be congratulated. All you have to do is to tell them what is going on and they will respond." Later, when asked to make some comment upon the result, which marks him out as a leader of such power that none can gainsay his position before the party and the people, the Governor said: "I feel confident that it is the sincere purpose and desire of the Democratic members of the Legislature to carry out the program of the platform. It is a matter for sincere congratulation that the Senatorship is happily settled and they are now free to apply themselves to the business of the session. The whole State must admire the way in which the Democratic members have acted in this important matter."

Printed in the *Philadelphia Record*, Jan. 26, 1911; some editorial headings omitted.
[1] Michael J. McGowan, Jr., Mark F. Phillips, and Frank P. Shalvoy, all of Newark.
[2] James J. McGrath of Hoboken.

An Address to the Newark Board of Trade

[[Jan. 25, 1911]]

Mr. Toastmaster[1] and Gentlemen of the Board of Trade—I thank you sincerely for the very cordial and gracious greeting you have given me, and I congratulate myself that I have not

[1] Curtis R. Burnett, secretary of the American Oil and Supply Co. of Newark.

come to make a political speech. I have formed the habit recently of making political speeches, and I am very glad to revert to a character which temporarily I had left off.

Now, it has been my privilege to discuss before bodies like this those general aspects of our life which may be discussed without any touch of political feeling or political purpose. I must admit that Senator Heyburn[2] has tempted me exceedingly. But I am going to show my good Presbyterian training by resisting temptation. I find that as I get older I get less and less suited to after-dinner speaking, because I get more and more serious as I get older.

It is very difficult as you get older and responsibilities accumulate upon you, to take things in the lighter spirit in which it is sometimes expected you will take them after dinner; and as I sat here I have thought a great deal about what assemblies like this represent and stand for; particularly what assemblies like this ought to represent and stand for in our own beloved commonwealth of New Jersey.

New Jersey occupies a very singular position in the sisterhood of States; her position has from the very first, even from colony days, forced upon her a very peculiar function. If you reflect upon it, our outlet into the world of commerce is, whether you look to the north or to the south, an outlet afforded outside of our own borders for the most part.

We have always been inconvenienced by New York on the one hand and Philadelphia on the other. We have always seen the point of that rather theological remark that was once made about us that New Jersey is the intermediate State.[3] I do not know whether you will know the theological import of that or not.

New Jersey is what I may call a mediating State. Her life mediates in some degree the life of the surrounding portions of the country. Think of the circumstance, for example, that it is necessary that New Jersey affairs should get into the New York papers before a considerable part of the northern portion of New Jersey knows anything about them.

There are splendid papers in New Jersey, but the great body of commuters who occupy so much of the northern portion of the neighboring parts of New Jersey—I mean the part neighboring to this part—read in the morning almost invariably papers published in the city of New York. That means that their thought is for the most part outside of New Jersey, but some of their deepest con-

[2] Weldon Brinton Heyburn, Republican senator from Idaho.

[3] The condition of souls between death and the resurrection or the last judgment.

nections, some of the most important aspects of their lives, are rooted in New Jersey; New Jersey is their home; New Jersey is the place for the training of their children; New Jersey is the place of their love, because of their personal connections, and no matter how much their thoughts may be withdrawn, their interests, consciously or unconsciously, rest here.

Think how much we mediate the life of other portions of this country by supplying the homes of the men who are active in other portions of this country, and think what that means with regard to local government in New Jersey.

Our homes cannot be separately established, you cannot determine the character of your home in independence of the character of the homes about you, and the homes about you are going to have their character determined by considerations of community life rather than by considerations of individual life. Communities are made up not by mere physical juxtaposition. Communities are made up by common feeling, by the consciousness of common interests, by the arrangements of government, by the principles and motives which underlie the action of government.

There is an action and interaction among human beings which constitutes the most important part of human life. And this alembic of our life, this place where our minds are united, and this place that supplies all the subtle impulses of motive is found in New Jersey. As are the homes of New Jersey, so in a certain important sense will be the operations of life outside of New Jersey, in New York and in several of the great centres of Pennsylvania. These interlacings of the fibers of life are infinitely important to the welfare of New Jersey.

New Jersey, therefore, must be a sort of laboratory in which the best blood is prepared for other communities to thrive upon. Not only that, but when you turn to the trade of the country you will find that New Jersey's most interesting relations, many of her most interesting relations, are what I might describe as interminal relations.

There is a great deal of New Jersey that most of you gentlemen never think about at all. Most of you never think of South Jersey, those interesting regions in which one may find, perhaps, more that is characteristic of Jersey, if you take her history at large, than is to be found anywhere else in our borders.

Do you realize how far south New Jersey extends? It extends so far south that our guests had to leave in order to get that far south before morning. Cape May is as far south as Baltimore, and by the time these gentlemen get as far south as Cape May they will be within three-quarters of an hour of Washington. We do not think of these parts of New Jersey when we are thinking of New Jersey trade nearly so much as we should think of it.

And then those beautiful regions of the State which rise into the lovely mountains of Warren and Sussex. We do not often think of New Jersey problems as lying there among the mountains, and where those beautiful lakes spread themselves for our pleasure, for our pleasure in the summer time. We think of this little place where the string is around the bag. Did you ever look at a map of New Jersey and fancy that it looks like a bag with a string tied around the middle? The line of the Pennsylvania Railroad is a string. And sometimes it is pulled pretty tight. Now, this string tied around the centre of the bag is where most of the arteries of trade that carry the great traffic that runs through this State lie.

The reason, one of the reasons, why this great State has grown up was first of all that she touched the waters which are an outlet to the world, but, second, because this line of intercommunication on the land lay here and touched this centre of population and made it grow and grow more and more, because this is the place from which you can touch the rest of the continent, as well as the rest of the world, by water.

And all the congestions, all the great urban problems, all the great problems of water supply and of drainage, all the problems which are created by congestion of population lie here, right around us, where we are. Jersey has to solve the problem of the home and the problem of the city, and the problem of transportation under conditions which put her character and her sagacity to a greater test than the character and sagacity of any other equal population in the country is put. That is what is infinitely interesting about New Jersey. We have got the problems of the country in such a form that they are raised to their highest degree of difficulty and complexity.

Very well—what is the moral? That we in New Jersey have got to show the country how these problems are to be met and settled. We have been taking it very easy in New Jersey and I think I can tell you why. We have made the conditions under which we live pay our bills. Just because we are a mediating State, just because we serve the rest of the country, the surrounding country, at any rate, as a home, and as a foothold, so to say, for industry and population, so we have served a great many large corporations as a home, and we have drawn a large revenue from these corporations; and our revenue drawn not from direct taxation, but from these incidents of our life, so to say, has sufficed us for the most part for the expenses of the State government.

It is very easy to spend money that is not derived from direct taxation. There is no kick to be feared. And we have gone at our ease, spending money, spending money, spending money, always with the hope that the spending of the money is going to lead to something. Just think how often we have hopefully set up commissions with the expectation that when the commission reported we were going to do something. Well, a great many commissions have reported and we have not done much. It is time we began to act on the reports of the commissions; it is time we began to tackle the problems which are the problems of our own life and by example the problems of the country, with the certain knowledge that, if we do not solve them, we are going to disappoint all the expectations of our own life and deepen the complexity of our own problems.

I was going to refer to something that Senator Heyburn said, but I won't.[4]

(That the crowd was eager to have him go back at the Senator from Iowa was made very apparent. There were shouts of "Go ahead!" "Give it to him!" When quiet was restored Dr. Wilson continued:)

His intentional change of the word "conservation" into "conversation" reminded me of some lines that were written about the Spanish war. You remember that the controversy over the battle of Santiago[5] was very much longer than the war. And some newspaper man, I think it was, devised these lines:

"War is rude and impolite,
It quite upsets a nation;
It is made of several weeks of fight,
And years of conversation."[6]

Now, there have been several years of conversation about conservation, but there is a fight at the centre of that problem. I

[4] Senator Heyburn had just delivered an address on "Problems of Legislation." After speaking in favor of bills to subsidize the American merchant marine and against direct primaries and the popular election of United States senators, he moved on to the problem of conservation. " 'Conservation' was Senator Heyburn's next problem," the *Newark Evening News*, January 26, 1911, reported. "He pronounced it 'Conversation' the first time, as if by a slip of the tongue, and corrected himself when the laughter subsided. Conservation, he said, meant nothing or anything, as one chose to apply it. . . . The natural resources, the speaker urged, reproduced themselves as a result of wise provisions of nature, and the use of such resources by a living generation was not to be decried."

[5] About the Battle of Santiago Bay and the prolonged controversy over the actions of the various American commanders, see Margaret Leech, *In the Days of McKinley* (New York, 1959), pp. 241-77.

[6] The Editors have been unable to discover the author of this ditty.

have yet to find a problem at which there is not a fight in the centre, because what we call a fight when we speak of it soberly and not playfully, when we speak of it in the public interest, is this: All sorts of opinions are going to be formed, all sorts of opinions are going to contest, and slowly men will draw together men of like opinions, and then there is going to be a settlement as to which opinion is going to prevail, and that is the fight at the heart of it. Very well.

Opinion has been drifting rather aimlessly in New Jersey about the conservation of her resources, and men are slowly beginning to end the period of conversation and to take sides. And this is a matter of life and death; this is not a matter merely of the rights of certain corporations; this is not merely a question of the sacredness of private property; this is a question of the life and health of whole populations, and, therefore, there is going to be a fight and we are going to settle it.

Conservation has passed the period of conversation in New Jersey. Senator Heyburn said that the Lord had provided that things reproduced themselves—coal, for example. It does get made, but if you wait on the process you will go out of business in the mean time. The Lord did not provide that human life should be as long as a geological process. Why He omitted to do so I have never asked Him. And the Lord did not provide that streams should provide for their own purification, or that if you diverted them they would have the same volume that they had before you diverted them.

The Lord provided us with minds and purposes, and you have got to use your mind and carry out your purposes if life is going to be tolerable. So that the moral of my tale this evening is this: New Jersey is the fighting centre of the most important social questions of our time. The whole suburban question, the whole question of such transportation as will serve suburban communities, the whole question of the regulation of corporations and the right attitude of all trades, their formation and conduct; the whole question of those trade relationships which will put the States in the right relation to each other and yet keep commerce of the nation-wide sort free of unreasonable restraint, centre in New Jersey more than in any other single State of the Union. And I take it as one of the advantages of New Jersey that these questions have not in them anywhere, so far as I can find, a partizan quality.

I do not know of a Democratic way to settle these things, and nobody has apparently found a Republican way of settling them. It is absurd to apply party terms to questions of this sort that are questions of experience, questions of knowledge, questions of good sense. And they are also questions of public spirit.

A Board of Trade of the city of Newark ought never to think in the terms of the city of Newark only. It ought to think in the terms of the State of New Jersey. And it cannot think in the terms of the State of New Jersey without thinking in the terms of the United States of America.

It is our privilege, in short, gentlemen, to attack these difficult problems in that large spirit which is the spirit of statesmanship and the spirit of America, for I need not remind you what the spirit of America is. America was founded to benefit mankind; America was founded in order to establish new conditions of human life; America was founded in order that men might be happier here, freer here, safer here, and because happier and freer and safer, more prosperous here; more prosperous in the freedom of their thoughts, more prosperous, in their release from anxiety, more prosperous in their free and untrammeled access to the resources of nature; that they should be more prosperous in those imaginings which lead men on from one stage of progress to another, for the principal way of stopping progress is to stop hope.

No man presses on in whom the fire of hope does not glow continuously, like the fire upon the old altars which the vestal virgins kept aflame. That fire of hope is the life of the human spirit. That is the reason we are interested in not shutting the doors of hope; that is the reason we are interested in not allowing monopoly, or anything that concentrates privilege, to shut the door of hope against any man, or the door of opportunity, the opportunity of achievement, the opportunity of a larger life, the feeling that his life may reach to any level of success.

Here in New Jersey, therefore, we are privileged to be politicians without partizan purposes; we are privileged to be citizens who have a common purpose; we are privileged to put away the things that are selfish and to band ourselves together for that kind of prosperity which is the true prosperity of the human spirit. There is nothing else, gentlemen, that is worth fighting for. It is better to have a sweet sleep at night, such as love of your neighbors and devotion to your State will give you, than to prosper infinitely in respect of the mere rewards of commerce.

It is better to draw your counsels into the service of things out of which you can make no money than it is to confine your counsels to those things which will increase your bank account and give you, not in your purposes, a greater power to help, but a greater power to master your fellow-men. The mastery that is worth having is the mastery of our own spirits; the achievement that is worth having is the achievement which has always made America great, the achievement which rests upon a devotion to the rights of men, which rests upon conviction of the intelligence and capacity for self-government of men, which rests upon a reliance upon the general conscience and the general intelligence. When I lose that confidence and faith I shall lose all confidence and faith in the institutions of America.

We speak in these days of progressives and reactionaries. When we speak of progressives we do not mean men who believe in some particular program of reform, but we mean men who believe in the feasibility of reform itself. When we speak of reactionaries we mean the men who do not believe that their fellow-citizens are honest or hopeful enough to achieve the undertakings of reform. You can tell a reactionary from a progressive by inquiring his attitude toward the common people of the community and land in which he lives.

Find the man that does not believe in their unlimited capacity for development and you have found a reactionary. I have found a good many such persons, and just as soon as I find them I stop consulting them and I stop thinking about them at all. They are no more to be thought about than the dead wood in the forest in which there is no longer any more capacity of growth. They ought to be cleared out and put into the consuming fire which is made by the energies of moving peoples that consumes everything that is in its way.

The time of progress not only has not passed, but it has just begun. Men are just beginning to realize what the united intelligence of educated peoples can accomplish, and it is our privilege to take part in the realization of these expectations.

Shall we not band ourselves together to serve mankind with self negation, with all those energies of the mind which put self on one side and put the great processes of humanity in the centre? For, after all, every one of us, gentlemen, is ephemeral. We go quickly to our graves, but mankind does not go to its grave. Mankind persists, and the only human immortality of any man is to connect all the processes of his blood with the endless processes of human perfection.[7]

Printed in the *Newark Evening News*, Jan. 26, 1911.
[7] There is a WWhw outline of this address, dated Jan. 25, 1911, in WP, DLC.

From Frank Rose Austin[1]

Dear Governor   Tuckerton, New Jersey Jany 25th 1911

I became so interested in the Senatorial contest that I went to Trenton to see the ballot taken in the separate houses. I had allready ascertained that our Senator Low[2] would stand by you, and as soon as the result was known I started for home feeling certain the victory was ours. The joint ballot today clinches it and I now write, not only to congratulate you, but also to thank you for your splendid championship of the open primary, and the rights of the common people as against the "special interests." It was with great pleasure I listened to your address on "Inaugural day" and every *true* Jerseyman is proud of his Governor, and may God give you strength (equal to your courage and high ideals) to carry on the good work. You are right in saying the people called you as a *leader*, and they are gladly following you.

Sincerely Yours   F. R. Austin

ALS (Governors' Files, Nj).
  [1] President of the Tuckerton, N. J., Bank.
  [2] George Clark Low, who spent one year at Princeton in the Class of 1878, a lawyer of Toms River, Democratic state senator from Ocean County.

From Samuel Huston Thompson, Jr.

My dear Mr. Wilson,   Denver, Colorado January 25, 1911.

Last night the Rocky Mountain Princeton Club held its annual banquet which was a most delightful affair. Ralph Adams Cram was the principal speaker.

In a conversation with him before his speech, he said that, while he had differed radically from you on the architecture of Princeton, he considered you the greatest man in America to-day. At the close of his speech, which by the way was a splendid one, he said that Princeton had reached the fulfillment of its promise by giving us the man who would be the next President of the United States. The demonstration was such that you ought to have heard it back in Trenton.

Our Club was always for you in your trouble at Princeton; and, now that you are looked upon out here as the most likely candidate for President, I think it will support you regardless of party affiliations.

One of our evening papers is coming out this afternoon in an editorial declaring that either you or Roosevelt will be the next President.

In view of the fact that your position is firmly established now that you have won your glorious victory over Smith, I do hope that you can create a condition, either by an independent party or on some other line, so that those of us who are independent Republicans can take the field for you.

Ex-Governor [Charles Spalding] Thomas informed me the other day that he had written you[1] that he was going to do all he could to swing the Democratic delegation for you at the next convention.

I hope you can see your way clear to making a trip to this country in the next year. It might be only a "rest" trip and you could make a short trip in the mountains. We could then get up a demonstration here.

The subject of the initiative and referendum is a thing that is keeping a good many apart in the country who agree along all other lines. I have not been able to get over this obstacle thus far and the reason for it is laid at your door because you grounded us in a constitutional law which certainly did not contemplate any such radical change. If it were possible for you to express your views, without injuring yourself publicly, on this question, I would certainly like to know them.

                    Very truly yours,   S. H. Thompson Jr.

TLS (WP, DLC).
  [1] If he wrote, his letter is missing.

From Edward Bushrod Stahlman[1]

                                Nashville Tenn Jan 25 [1911]

Hearty congratulations. The country will applaude your victory our [over] machine methods and allied special interests
                                E Stahlman.

T telegram (WP, DLC).
  [1] Publisher of the *Nashville*, Tenn., *Banner*.

From George G. Feigl[1]

                                New York Jan 25th 1911.

Your victory is ma[r]velous. Your hard work for the people should be recognized at once and appreciated throughout the land. You have rendered a service to the democratic party never to be forgotten[.] I trust the almighty will keep you well and strong so that you may continue your good work in 1912. You will lead us on to a still greater victory. Always your[s] very truly.
                                George G. Feigl

T telegram (WP, DLC).
    1 Editor of the *Tammany Times* and treasurer of the Tammany Times Publishing Co. of New York.

To Thomas Nelson Page

My dear Mr. Page: [Trenton, N. J.] January 26, 1911.

Thank you sincerely for your kindness.[1] It will give me the greatest pleasure to be your guest the night of the thirty-first, and I am honored that you are to introduce me to the Club. I shall look forward to the evening with the greater pleasure because I am to be with you.

I shall expect to go to Washington on the Pennsylvania Railroad train which is scheduled to arrive there at 4:20 P.M.

          Cordially and faithfully yours,   Woodrow Wilson

TLS (T. N. Page Papers, NcD).
    1 Page had either written or telephoned to ask Wilson to be his guest when he was to speak to the National Press Club in Washington on January 31, 1911 (Wilson's address is printed at that date). If Page wrote, his letter is missing.

From Cleveland Hoadley Dodge

Dear Woodrow   New York. Jan 26th 1911

You poor dear scholar & amateur in politics! I feel so sorry for you. Why don't you get an expert like Smith to advise you? You are getting to be rather tiresome as one spends too much time congratulating you. If you keep on doing such impossible stunts I think I will hereafter write you an omnibus letter once every six months or else get a stereotyped form

Anyhow your latest is perfectly glorious and I rejoice with you

God bless you   Y'rs affly   C H Dodge

ALS (WP, DLC).

From Joseph M. Noonan

My dear Governor: Jersey City, N. J. Janry 26th 1911

Congratulations on your great victory. If epitaph be needed for Extinguished Statesman would suggest "procumbit humi bos(s)."   Yours sincerely   Jos. M. Noonan

ALS (WP, DLC).

From Jacob L. Bunnell[1]

Dear Governor Wilson: Newton, N. J., Jan. 26, 1911.

Thanks for your kind letter. Allow me to extend congratulation upon the election of James E. Martine. It is a great victory for the people of New Jersey. It marks an important epoch in the political history of our state, where in more recent years selfish interests have so largely controlled party nominations.

Conditions prevailing so widely in Essex County are true of Sussex County. If the interests cannot control a Democrat politically they seek to crush him socially and financially.

Martine petitions were issued in Newton. Parties consenting to circulate them were shadowed by former Senator Lewis J. Martin[2] and leaders of a wing of the Republican party.

Material pressure was brought to bear upon those consenting to circulate the Martine petitions, in some instances causing them to abandon the work they had voluntarily offered to perform.

Others were discovered pleased to have the opportunity of serving their party in a cause so agreeable to their wishes, with the result that Jan. 21, petitions were forwarded Senator [Jacob Cole] Price and Assemblyman Myers [Charles Anthony Meyer] containing the names of 242 representative residents of Newton requesting that they cast their votes for James E. Martine AND FOR NO OTHER CANDIDATE.

I give you these facts as the recognized leader of the Democracy of the State of New Jersey.

Further, I am of the belief that the more information a party leader has of the actual condition in the various counties of the State, the greater will be his power to faithfully serve his party.

Sincerely yours,   Jacob L Bunnell

Believing you should know the good feeling existing in Sussex County over the election of Mr. Martine, I am trespassing upon your busy moments by forwarding copy of the Herald printed to-day.[3]

TLS (Governors' Files, Nj).

[1] Part owner since 1888 and editor since 1892 of the Newton, N. J., *New Jersey Herald.*

[2] Democratic assemblyman (1879-81) and senator from Sussex County (1898-1903), at this time attorney for the Board of Freeholders of Sussex County. Wilson appointed him county judge in 1911. He also served in Congress from March 4, 1913, until his death on May 5, 1913.

[3] It is missing.

From Alexander Francis Chamberlain[1]

Sir: Worcester, Massachusetts Jan. 26. 1910 [1911].

Permit me to congratulate you on the victory you have just won. It is a convincing proof of the effectiveness of the individual in American democracy; one more evidence of a high order that the sympathetic alliance of great personalities with public opinion is both possible and ethically profitable in a Republic such as is the United States.

with best wishes   Alexander F. Chamberlain

ALS (Governors' Files, Nj).
1 Professor of Anthropology, Clark University.

A News Report of an Address in Trenton

[Jan. 27, 1911]

INACTIVE CITIZENS ROUNDLY CENSURED BY GOVERNOR WILSON

Know Your City Movement Endorsed by Chief Executive of State
Who Urges Trentonians to Make Most of It—
Other Strong Addresses Made

KNOW YOUR CITY WEEK, its aims, the people who made it possible and those who are participating in it, were unqualifiedly endorsed and unlimitedly encouraged by Governor Woodrow Wilson in an address last evening in the Y.M.C.A. auditorium and before an audience which filled the big hall. This meeting was one of the series of welfare conferences of the KNOW YOUR CITY movement.

Without solicitation and with a tone of sincerity that was unmistakable, Governor Wilson pledged himself to do all in his power to bring results from this discovery campaign intended to bring about many civic improvements. His words in this relation were:

"I congratulate Trenton that this systematic effort for civic improvement has been started, and I pledge my best endeavors to know Trenton and to do what I can to promote her best intere[s]ts."

Governor Wilson was introduced by John A. Campbell, president of the Trenton Potteries Company and former president of the Y.M.C.A., who was chairman of the meeting. When the chief executive of New Jersey appeared on the platform there was an outburst of enthusiasm which has seldom been surpassed in this city for any public man. The evening's program was opened with prayer by the Rev. Dr. John Dixon, former pastor of the First Presbyterian Church. A splendid program was furnished by Winkler's Orchestra.

Introducing Governor Wilson, Mr. Campbell said that the audience was honored by the presence of a man who, by the grace of the people of this state, has been elected Governor. "In view of the fact that Governor Wilson will be at least a temporary resident of Trenton for the next three years," said Mr. Campbell, "it is but natural that he should consent to have a part in this KNOW YOUR CITY movement. He is a man ever ready to lend his aid and voice to any cause for good morals and good citizenship."

This pretty expression by Mr. Campbell sent the audience into a whirlwind of applause, which increased when Governor Wilson proceeded to his address. The Governor was at his best as a public speaker. His address, though unprepared in advance, was a scholarly effort enlivened with much fine humor.

"I have recently made so many speeches that I feel that I have spoken about all the pieces I know," said the Governor in his opening. He then launched into a discussion of civic awakening which characterizes this day throughout the land.

"There is an awakened civic spirit," said Governor Wilson. "It is easy to do public spirited things now because the public spirit is awakened and there exists an atmosphere to support greater things in civic life.

"We are going back to the original spirit of America, a deepseated enthusiasm for its liberties and rights for all the people and not for classes. The populating and establishment of America and her institutions was prompted by a desire for religious freedom."

Governor Wilson then briefly discussed the process of population of America, showing that after 1890 the makers of maps were no longer to include a frontier in their drawings. He spoke of the epoch-making events in the history of this country and of England and defined the movements of men which led to the struggles for freedom. Then he took his hearers down to these days, when men will brook no trammel in their quest for proper civic liberties.

"Ever since 1890, when the frontier disappeared," said the Governor, "we have slowly developed our population. Now the free spirit of America is beginning to look at the unfinished sidewalks, the unswept streets, the slums and the unfinished condition of our hurriedly built cities." He then discussed the character of the hurriedly built cities, and concluded that the cities have been wonderfully built considering how fast they were made.

The speaker referred to the former attention of the American people to whole projects. "But now we are turning about to look after the details of life," he continued. "You cannot stop just any person on the streets and find out about Trenton. The only things many of the citizens of cities know is confined to those things they are obliged to know because of their daily life.

"The moment an American city begins to look at itself and to regard itself as a community, then begins what we call civic pride. We become ashamed of the things our hearts have neglected and a new life begins. Then comes common understanding among the people.

"A man who piles up millions of dollars and thinks only of himself is a very little man, and when he dies he is promptly and willingly forgotten. The man with a heart and who does things, though he has not a dollar, is a big man, and when he dies he is missed. When men of this spirit get together something must be accomplished. A man is just as big as the things he does and just as little as the things he does not do."

Dr. Wilson then discussed citizenship in a most happy mood. He referred to the origin of the word idiot among the Greeks as meaning a private citizen. He condemned private citizenship insofar as it relates to inactive citizenship and said that persistent privacy is a co[n]cealment of incapacity.

"We would not have room enough in our jails if we were to lock up all of our private citizens," said Governor Wilson. "The future of Trenton depends upon those who become active, talkative and insistent members of the community.

"Kick systematically and something will happen. I sometimes think that the price of liberty is to be always disagreeable. But you don't get anything unless you fight for it, except affection.

"Being odd means that you avail yourself of the privilege of being yourself. Know your neighbor and know him with some degree of tolerance. This neighborly knowledge will spread to knowledge of your ward, then to knowledge of your city, and its greatness and shortcomings."

As soon as Dr. Wilson concluded his address he left for Princeton, where he was called by a previous engagement. He was given a rousing ovation when he finished speaking and the great audience clearly showed that it had been urged on to better civic efforts through having heard and having been encouraged by the Governor of New Jersey.

Printed in the *Trenton Evening Times*, Jan. 27, 1911; some editorial headings omitted.

To Mary Allen Hulbert Peck

Dearest Friend, [Trenton, N. J.] 27 Jan'y, 1910 [1911]

I know you understand and that you make allowances, but it is a shame and a grief to me that I have to let the Saturday steamer go with only a little note. But you will forgive and will know that more was impossible.

We have triumphed *entirely*. Martine was elected *on the first ballot*,[1] and the Smith forces are (admittedly) routed horse, foot, and dragoons. Thank God! What lies before me is easier—and now there will be less resistance. The country is ringing with praises, but I know that the work has only just begun and rejoice constantly that I am

Your devoted friend, Woodrow Wilson

ALS (WP, DLC).
[1] That is, of the joint session of the legislature.

To Cleveland Hoadley Dodge

Personal.

My dear Cleve: [Trenton, N. J.] January 27, 1911.

I do not know anything that cheers me more than a letter from you. It brings with it such a delightful breath of affection and unselfish loyalty and makes my heart warm. God bless you for it and for all your generous thoughts about me.

Affectionately yours, Woodrow Wilson

TLS (WC, NjP).

To George Lawrence Record

My dear Mr. Record: [Trenton, N. J.] January 27, 1911.

Thank you sincerely for your letter of yesterday.[1] It does you honor. I am sure that I understand your position thoroughly and I have been very grateful to you for exercising the good taste you have exercised, in view of the unreasonable, but nevertheless, very mischievous representations recently made by the Star.[2]

I have been handed copies of the bills you drew up[3] and shall read them with greatest attention. My hope will be to get them introduced and to get them out as Committee reports, if that is possible. We are working for the same end, though along somewhat different lines which policy dictates and principle does not condemn.

In haste,

Cordially and sincerely yours,   Woodrow Wilson

TLS (A. R. E. Pinchot Papers, DLC).
  [1] It is missing.
  [2] That is, in the Newark *Morning Star*, Jan. 19, 1911.
  [3] According to James Kerney, Record drafted bills covering primary and election reforms, corrupt practices, and employers' liability and delivered them to Wilson. With the exception of the latter bill, Kerney says, all were introduced in the legislature exactly as Record had drawn them. *The Political Education of Woodrow Wilson*, p. 105.

To Henry Groves Connor[1]

My dear Judge Connor: [Trenton, N. J.] January 27, 1911.

Your letter of the twenty-third[2] has given me very great pleasure. Nothing gratifies me more than to have my friends in the South think as you think of my entrance into public life and of the things I am trying to do. It gives me additional incentive to keep on in the course I have laid out for myself.

Cordially and faithfully yours,   Woodrow Wilson

TLS (H. G. Connor Papers, NcU).
  [1] United States district judge of the eastern district of North Carolina since 1909.
  [2] It is missing.

From Alexander Barclay Guigon[1]

My dear Wilson: Richmond, Virginia January 27, 1911.

This may seem very informal and improper after the very formal address, but though I realize and rejoice in your new office and well-merited fame, I cannot bring myself to be formal to you in a personal letter. To me you will always be the dear old Wilson of the University of Virginia, the law class, the Jeff Society,[2] and above all, the Octette.[3]

I often laugh with Carter Scott, who is now Judge of our Circuit Court here,[4] over the near-quarrel we had in discussing my disgust at your receiving the orator's medal instead of the debater's medal, which absurdly enough went to Willie Bruce.[5]

My devotion to music has grown with the passing of the years, and I have had occasion a number of times to mention publicly and privately the careers of the different members of our Octette, in proof of my contention that a reasonable, sensible and moderate enjoyment of, and interest in music, lessens no man's usefulness or value in life, but, on the contrary, is in the way of a benefit as well as a pleasure.

I have been intending to write you ever since your name was first mentioned for the nomination, but waited for that, and then for the election, and then for the triumph which has just come to you in the defeat of Smith for the Senate, which, it seems to me, is the greatest triumph of all.

It was a great disappointment to me not to see you again at Atlantic City, but I felt it would not be fair to you and the political friends who were with you. I do want you, however, to feel that among the many personal friends who rejoice in your growing fame and popularity, as well as in your most unusual achievements, few, I believe, are more sincerely delighted than I am. As the years pass I realize more and more the value of the old college friendships and their permanency, and I would give a great deal to get together for instance the old Octette, or have a chat with you and dear old Mountjoy[6] and Brock Beckwith,[7] God rest his bones. As I think of the old University days, I feel almost as if that were the reality and the present the dream, though, as you may well imagine, there is no opportunity in a busy man's life for this mood to last long. In five minutes I shall be plunging into a mass of contracts, deeds and franchises, and be well into the stern realities once more, but the retrospect has been a pleasure.

I hope that when you come this way sometime you will let me know, and let me take you into my little family circle.

Sincerely your friend,   A B Guigon

The clipping which I enclose[8] is one of dozens which have appeared in our local papers in the last few months.

TLS (WP, DLC).

[1] Fellow-student of Wilson at the University of Virginia, prominent Virginia corporation lawyer who at this time was general counsel for the Virginia Railway and Power Co.

[2] The Jefferson Society of the University of Virginia.

[3] The University of Virginia Glee Club, for the membership of which see the second news item printed at Dec. 1, 1879, Vol. 1.

[4] Richard Carter Scott, who attended the University of Virginia from 1879 to 1881.

5 About which, see the Editorial Note, "Wilson's Debate with William Cabell Bruce," Vol. I.

6 Clifford Arnold Mountjoy, who attended the University of Virginia from 1871 to 1875 and received the M.A. degree in the latter year.

7 John F. B. Beckwith, who studied at the University of Virginia from 1878 to 1882 but did not receive a degree. He later lived in Alice and Houston, Texas; the Editors have been unable to discover the date of his death.

8 It is missing.

A News Report of an Address in Trenton
to the Inter-Church Federation of New Jersey

[Jan. 28, 1911]

GOVERNOR WILSON'S MESSAGE TO THE CHURCH FEDERATION

Governor Woodrow Wilson addressed the conference of the Inter-Church Federation of New Jersey yesterday afternoon in First Methodist Episcopal Church. The Governor brought a message to the Federation that was listened to with deep interest by the assemblage. He was accorded a most enthusiastic reception when he entered the auditorium, the people rising when he stepped onto the platform. President of the Federation, Dr. J. William Marshall,[1] of New Brunswick, formally presented the Governor, and the assemblage rose and applauded the State's executive. The Governor said:

"Ladies and Gentlemen: It is a privilege for me to be here to extend my great personal gratitude to this assemblage. I don't know whether I can meet the expectations of those here or not.

"This movement is an interesting part of what is going on all over the world, and of what is showing itself in very vital form in the United States. I think one of the most interesting conferences and one of the most significant was that which occurred in Edinburg, Scotland, last summer, when men from all parts of the world drew together in order to make plans.[2] There was absolutely no danominational concert [concern] in the promotion of this great work.

"I remember saying something at a dinner in New York City which,[3] I think, perhaps, was not altogether justified, but I have always been candid about saying the things which I think should be said (applause), and what I said was this: 'This is a very vital thing and a very beautiful thing, this drawing together of men and women of all beliefs, bound together by a common faith in Christ, working with a consistent effort in the field of foreign missions. It is very delightful to know that this is a common cause, but I hope that these heathen people won't look to us for their example, because we are infinitely divided. We are unreasonably divided. We are setting before them an example of Christianity which we are not apparently ready to copy in our own efforts toward the salvation of our people.' I believe I was not altogether justified.

"This is an extraordinary age in the awakening of the social conscience." In defining his use of social conscience he distinguished between it and doctrinal conscience, saying that the social conscience pooled all the great interests.

"Difference in worship is a difference in taste. Nothing so much stands in the way of effort as taste. You can march twice as far behind a brass band as you can to the tune of doctrinal teaching. The Salvation Army is not preaching ideas but great saving facts."

To further illustrate this idea, he took up Democracy as applied to government, saying—

"Democracy is founded upon a comprehension and a love of mankind. It is based upon the doctrine of the equality of the human soul. Government is thought of for everybody in general and not for somebody in particular. You can't imagine a religion based on privilege.

"I like to dwell upon the expression that Christ came to save the world. This idea is running out from these conferences and being projected by these gatherings. It is one of the delightful evidences that we are seeking the service of men in their present life.

"When I read the history of the middle ages it seems that men believed themselves shackled in this world that they might be free in the next. Christianity should be used to set things right here. It should be used to purify this world. We should rectify by social action backed by right motives.

"This purification should not be a segregated thing. If you cannot set forth a religion of which all can partake, then you have not Christianity. Denominational problems should not be in a place with a great many inner compartments, but an open place where all may find what they are seeking.

"I look upon this movement with great and unaffected joy, and I want to express my deep interest in and sympathy with movements of this kind."

The Rev. Dr. James L. Gardiner, pastor of the First M. E. Church, moved a rising vote of thanks to the Governor. This was given, accompanied by applause.

Printed in the Trenton *True American*, Jan. 28, 1911; some editorial headings omitted.

1 The Rev. Dr. James William Marshall, pastor of the First Methodist Episcopal Church of New Brunswick, N. J.

2 The World Missionary Conference which met in Edinburgh from June 14 to June 23, 1910. More than 1,200 delegates from approximately 160 missionary societies in the United States, Canada, Great Britain, Europe, South Africa, Australia and New Zealand met to plan ecumenical missionary strategy. John R. Mott was the primary organizer of the conference and presided at most of its sessions. The conference's chief significance was its ecumenical character, and, according to one historian, it was "the birthplace of the modern ecumenical movement." Kenneth Scott Latourette, "Ecumenical Bearings of the Missionary Movement and the International Missionary Council," in Ruth Rouse and Stephen Charles Neill (eds.), *A History of the Ecumenical Movement, 1517-1948* (London, second edn., 1967), pp. 355-62.

3 At a "China dinner" on January 14, 1909, about which see W. H. Grant to WW, Dec. 19, 1908, Vol. 18.

From Thomas Pryor Gore[1]

My dear Governor: Washington. Jan. 28, 1911.

I beg to assure you of the intense interest with which I have watched the senatorial contest in New Jersey, and also to assure you of the intense gratification which your success has afforded me. It was not merely a personal triumph either for yourself or for Mr. Martine. It was the right of self-government which had been put at hazard, and you have maintained that right without variableness or shadow of turning. The moral heroism which you have exhibited not only brings credit to your own name but the influence of your example will serve as an inspiration to others in a similiar situation. This is the substantial proof of your victory. The time-server would have shrunk from such a contest.

With assurances of the highest esteem and best wishes for a brilliant administration, I beg to remain

Truly your friend,   T. P. Gore

TLS (WP, DLC).
1 Blind Democratic senator from Oklahoma.

From Benjamin Barr Lindsey

My dear Governor: Denver, Colo. January 28, 1911.

I am just delighted over your victory and so proud of you. I wish sometime I had a chance to tell you of some of the things that I had heard before you came out for Martine and took the stand that you have taken—that has lined you up with the Progressives—I hope for all time, for there is certainly a big fight ahead, and it is so good to know *you* are on the right side. I am taking the liberty to send you an account of our senatorial fight here,[1] and many of us regret that Governor Shafroth has not taken a stronger stand, although he is a well meaning man, but we do so much need *strong* men in this struggle. Mayor Speer, the candidate of the "Interests," has through his power as boss made the Democratic party in Denver a mere asset to the crimes of Big Business, as I have detailed in "The Beast and the Jungle." I am sure that politicians here will tell you privately that we have under rather than over-stated all of our facts, especially those in the chapter on "A City Pillaged."

With kindest regards and best wishes for your administration, I am,   Sincerely yours,   Ben B Lindsey

TLS (WP, DLC).

    [1] It is missing, but it recounted the contest over the vacant Senate seat from Colorado. The incumbent, Charles James Hughes, Jr., had died on January 11, 1911, after serving only two years. Because his death occurred while the Colorado legislature was in session, Governor John Franklin Shafroth could not appoint a replacement to fill out his term; rather, a new senator had to be elected by the legislature. As Lindsey indicated, Mayor Robert Walter Speer of Denver was the leading machine candidate, but he was opposed by a number of candidates as well as by the Denver *Rocky Mountain News.* Neither Speer nor his opponents would capitulate, and the seat remained vacant until January 1913, when the legislature elected Charles Spalding Thomas, Democratic Governor of Colorado, 1899-1901. Thomas was elected to a full term in 1914.

From Cyrus Hall McCormick

My dear Woodrow: Chicago 28 January 1911.

Allow me to send you my most sincere congratulations over the tremendous victory which you have won.

Here is an editorial from the "Chicago Evening Post" of 25 January[1] which makes me proud that I am the friend of a man who can win such victories against large odds.

I am,   Very sincerely yours,   Cyrus H McCormick.

TLS (WP, DLC).

    [1] The enclosed editorial described Wilson's victory in the senatorial fight as "unusually inspiring" because it was "a plain issue of right and wrong." "What makes his victory most notable," it continued, "is the memory of his ringing refusal to compromise. Once more it has been proved to our conciliating, compromising politicians that the man who stands absolutely true to his convictions can and does win against the most overwhelming odds." *Chicago Evening Post,* Jan. 25, 1911.

A News Report of an After-Dinner Speech
to the Kansas Society of New York[1]

[Jan. 29, 1911]

GOV. WILSON TO KANSAS FOLKS

Defines "Progressive" And Classes Himself As One.

If there is anything the matter with Kansas that fault was overlooked by Gov. Woodrow Wilson of New Jersey and the other speakers who last night at the Waldorf addressed about one hundred and fifty Kansans, their wives and daughters, at the sixth annual dinner of the Kansas Society of New York. The occasion was the fiftieth anniversary of Kansas statehood.

Gov. Wilson told the diners how fortunate New York city is to have new blood such as might come in from Kansas infused into the Manhattan tissues. Also he defined some terms for his listeners.

A radical, according to Gov. Wilson, is one who is said to go too far. A conservative is one who doesn't go far enough. A reactionary is one who doesn't go at all. The Governor called attention to the fact that some people object to all of these terms and all the people object to some of them. Therefore, he said, a new term, a progressive, has been coined. Gov. Wilson hinted that he might be classed in the ranks of this new army.

The speaker who throughout his address argued for publicity in business because of the debt to society which in the Governor's opinion every big enterprise owes took time during his speech to tell the Kansans his idea of what the word business means.

"I should define business," said Gov. Wilson, "as an economic service of society for private profit, and a business is illegitimate unless society is served." . . .

Gov. Wilson was the first speaker of the evening. He was received with a Kansas tornado of applause which blew the diners to their feet that the Governor might the better see their waving napkins. When the toastmaster[2] worked from the crossing of the Delaware by Washington in order that the General might capture enemies and then on up to the recent captures made by the Governor, a victory which might soon be the cause of his "crossing the Potomac and capturing the White House," Kansas let loose again.

The Governor seemed to have a liking for Kansas. He was

---

[1] In the Waldorf-Astoria Hotel.

[2] Thomas H. Dinsmore, former President of the Kansas State Normal School of Emporia, Kan.; pioneer scientific rainmaker; president of the Kansas Society of New York.

glad that New York has captured so many Kansans (A voice, "I commute to New Jersey"), but thought that so fine a body of banqueters looked as they "might have remained in their own State."

"There's always something that quickens the blood," said Gov. Wilson, "in the word Kansas. The name suggests fighters. I've wondered as I sat here watching you to-night why you ever left your own State. (Laughter.) And I may tell you that you will never be good New Yorkers unless you remain good Kansans." .

The speaker said that there were political, social and in some cases fanatical reasons for settling Kansas fifty years and more ago during the slavery days.

"Rhode Island," the Governor continued, "was settled and is made up of people who found it unbearable to live anywhere else in New England. (Laughter.) They couldn't bear to be contradicted. I noticed when speaking one night at Providence, for instance, that something was going on all over the room. (Laughter.) At one table two men would be saying 'Nothing in what he says,' and at another two more would be agreeing. 'That's it; he's right.' (Laughter.)

"It's dramatic to speak in Providence, R. I.," continued Gov. Wilson. "Kansas must be much the same—though to-night I feared while looking over you comfortable diners—at least I couldn't help wondering—that perhaps you might be gradually succumbing to the seductive feeling of New York. (Laughter.)

"Kansas has a reputation of being a radical State. Labels now are important; we fight over labels. A radical is one of whom people say 'He goes too far.' A conservative, on the other hand, is one who 'doesn't go far enough.' Then there is the reactionary, 'one who doesn't go at all.' All these terms are more or less objectionable, wherefore we have coined the term progressive.

"I should say that a progressive is one who insists upon recognizing new facts as they present themselves—one who adjusts legislation to these new facts, a legislator who legislates for 1910, not for 1900. A progressive policy must be one of big plans, one that has living tissue. The progressive is not satisfied merely with patching things that have gone wrong. And so the progressive must not hold hostility toward new facts, nor should he base his actions on concession, because concession at best is but a compromise, a patched up peace.

"The progressive must make a new adjustment resting on universal frankness. There is nothing so hostile to progress as the reticence of men at the head of big business enterprises.

Business to-day is run on so big a scale that now there is nothing about it which is private.

"You begin an enterprise, say, and invite the United States (Some one, "And England.") and England, yes, to buy shares of the stock. Now in a room a small group of directors call this business private. But what is happening to the stocks all the time? Sometimes these people of the country who were invited to buy the stock don't know who some of the new officers are.

"All this is necessarily public business, and therefore publicity is one solution. I am arguing for a change in the point of view of those who conduct business. I should define business as an economic service of society for private profit and the business is illegi[ti]mate unless society is served.

"That is my argument in conducting public commissions which regulate public utilities. Americans always are ready to pay their fare; they are ready even to pay more than they are paying now if they are shown that they should pay more. Just now they want to pay less simply because they don't know.

"What I call progressiveness, therefore, is a revitalization of the tissues of society, which now are so interlaced that it is almost impossible to untangle them. About twenty-five years ago things were easily explained because things then were simple. They're not simple to-day.

"What you Kansans are going to stand for in these changes is what Kansas always stood for—you at least will be unafraid to open your hearts to the truth and then fight for the right. It will not do to get excited; just be tolerant. In this new country let us settle things as Kansas always settled them, by sending forth tolerant fighters to fight for the right. We should all say with Harry Hotspur, 'Fie upon this settled life! Let's go to Kansas!' "³ (Prolonged applause.)

Printed in the New York *Sun*, Jan. 29, 1911; some editorial headings omitted.
    ³ There is a WWT outline of this address, with the composition date of Jan. 28, 1911, in WP, DLC.

To Mary Allen Hulbert Peck

Dearest Friend,   University Club [New York] 29 Jan'y, 1911

Again Sunday finds me in New York. I think I shall always associate this writing room with the pleasure of talking to (how I wish I could say *with*!) you and trying to annihilate, in thought at any rate, the distance that separates us. I cannot tell you what a joy it is to me that you are in a house I *know*, where I can visualize you—where I can fancy I can *see* you. It makes it so easy *to go to see you*, in fancy—and that is so much better than nothing. God bless you! what a delight it is to think of you as resting, free and with a mind at ease! Of course you are for the time relaxed and uninterested in the things you used to waste your force upon. The reaction was bound to take that form. You used to seek all sorts of excitement and mere diversion in order to forget. Now your mind is at ease, you are relaxed from anxiety, repulsion, actual fear, and *rest*, comfort, cosy repose seem all that you want. Presently your real tastes will assert themselves and the zest for beautiful things and for books worth reading, persons worth knowing, will make a new life for you. Your heart has thrown off its burden not only but has found new objects, and it also has *found* itself. Am I not right?

How unfortunate that that vulgar Lord Frederick Hamilton[1] should have turned up again! My dislike of him was instinctive and deep seated. I do not like to think of his being near you!

My victory last week was overwhelmingly complete. The whole country is marvelling at it, and I am getting more credit than I deserve. I pittied [pitied] Smith at the last. It was so plain that he had few real friends,—that he held men by fear and power and the benefits he could bestow, not by love or loyalty or any genuine devotion. The minute it was seen that he was defeated his adherents began to desert him like rats leaving a sinking ship. He left Trenton (where his headquarters had at first been crowded) attended, I am told, only by his sons,[2] and looking old and broken. He wept, they say, as he admitted himself utterly beaten. Such is the end of political power—particularly when selfishly obtained and heartlessly used. It is a pitiless game, in which, it would seem, one takes one's life in one's hands,— and for me it has only begun! How unspeakably delightful it is to know that I have your generous confidence and affection and that your loyalty will always be steadfast, something to sustain and delight me to the end!

I attended a banquet of the Kansas Society last night at the Waldorf, got home a little after twelve, and slept until about a quarter to one this afternoon! I think I would have been asleep yet (four o'clock) if my telephone had not waked me!

Never apologize for your letters,—they always delight me, no matter what the mood in which they are written. The best thing about them,—as about what you say to me,—is that they contain what is really at the moment in your mind, and always, underneath what is said or written, if not through it, I see your real, splendid, admirable self,—the big, steadfast, lovely, *perceiving*, womanly self that makes your friendship so great a thing in the life of   Your devoted friend,   Woodrow Wilson

ALS (WP, DLC).

¹ Lord Frederick Spencer Hamilton, fourth surviving son of James Hamilton, 2nd Marquess and 1st Duke of Abercorn; M.P., 1885-86, 1892-95; former member of the British foreign service; sometime editor of the *Pall Mall Magazine* of London.

² James Smith III; John Henry Smith, Princeton 1907; George Doane Smith, Princeton 1908; and Joseph Lyndon Smith, Princeton 1913.

From Henry Watterson

My Dear Governor: Monte Carlo, le 29th de Jan'y, 1911

Hearty gratulation on your splendid triumph. I never doubted it. If you can clean house for Jersey the next fifteen months, we shall have a powerful, if not a resistless, issue for 1912. The advice I gave George Harvey and Thomas Fortune [Ryan] to "stand pat and wait for developements," they both agreed to follow. They must now begin to see that it was good counsel.

I have seen much of Mr Bennett,¹ as I always do when I am over here. He has a house at Beaulieu near by and with him [I have] gone over the situation and outlook without reserve. He is a life-long friend and since his residence abroad has relied upon me for some advisement both political and professional. I told him the whole story of last Summer and Fall—the nomination, the campaign, the victory—Smith's subsequent demand for his pound of flesh, and all about you, personally. He was deeply interested. I have no doubt that you will have the active sympathy of the Herald from now onward, and—when the time comes —its leadership toward the next National Convention. Your Southern birth, which I made the most of knowing his weakness in that direction—he has been running me for President the last twenty years solely on that idea—greatly appealed to him. He is an able and sincere, though an eccentric, man; all stories about him since his mad escapade thirty odd years ago being mainly if not wholly fictions.² At seventy he is as hale and hearty as most men of sixty and very concerned and alert in the character and management of his great journal.

Mrs Watterson and I had a pleasant crossing in the "Amerika," a week of unusual sunshine in Paris, and a leisurely journey Southward to this palace of a hotel and paradise of a climate. Monte Carlo is most known as the headquarters of gambling[.] It is really the headquarters of fashion and the most brilliant and interesting resort in the world. This is our fifth winter here and we are not "broke" yet! So, we shall remain till the middle of March.

Kind remembrance to Mrs Wilson and the young ladies. Mrs. Watterson so much desires to meet them and so greatly regretted missing you the day we sailed.

Sincerely Your Friend   Henry Watterson

ALS (WP, DLC).

[1] James Gordon Bennett, publisher of the New York, London, and Paris *Herald*, who lived in Paris.

[2] Bennett's "mad escapade" was his underwriting of an Arctic expedition led by George Washington De Long, 1879-81, in which De Long and most of his crew perished.

To John Wesley Wescott

My dear Judge Westcott: [Trenton, N. J.] January 30,1911.

You are a true helper and I thank you sincerely for the list you furnish.[1] I hope that you will not hesitate at any time to express your own opinions to me with the utmost frankness and freedom.

In haste,

Cordially and faitfhfully [faithfully] yours,

Woodrow Wilson

TLS (J. W. Wescott Coll., NjP).

[1] It is missing, as is Wescott's covering letter, if he sent one.

From Cook Conkling[1]

Sir: Rutherford, N. J. Jan. 30th, 1911.

I was in Trenton last Monday night and Tuesday lending what aid I could to the accomplishment of the purpose you had in view, never doubting seriously for a moment but that your triumph would be as great as it has subsequently proven to be.

As I passed your door and observed your serene composure and that you were being called upon by many persons, I refrained from calling, knowing that I could do more good by working rather than talking.

I congratulate you on your magnificent generalship but I feel also that the people of New Jersey are to be congratulated more perhaps than the people in any other State in the Union, because, through you, we have been able to set a precedent which not only cannot be disregarded in the future of this State but which has inspired the people of the entire Nation to take an active interest in questions of government seeing that they have tremendous power once a medium in sympathy with them is established between them and the governmental machinery.

I have yet to hear the first person, who supported you in the last election, express regret but, on the contrary, the profoundest gratification amounting almost to delight.

Wishing you every success and standing ready to the extent of my ability to help you achieve it, I am,

Very truly yours,   Cook Conkling

TLS (WP, DLC).
1 Lawyer of Rutherford, N. J., in the firm of Shafer & Conkling.

From Allan Benny[1]

Dear Governor Wilson: Washington, D. C., January 30, 1911.

Former Governor John Lind, of Minnesota,[2] with whom I had the honor to serve in the fifty eighth Congress, met me here to-day and immediately brought up the question of your nomination for the presidency. He said his people wanted to see you nominated and that if nominated he believed nothing could prevent your election. He admires you very greatly and said that if your speeches were to be published he wanted to be placed on the list for all of them. He asked me especially about a short speech you made to a young men's club, in which you defined Democracy,[3] and he wants one thousand copies of that speech, if it is to be printed, for distribution among his friends in Minnesota.

The former Governor's son[4] (a man about thirty years old, I judge) who resides in Everett, State of Washington, was with us at the interview and he reports a strong sentiment for you in his neighborhood.

I wish some concerted action were under way to get the people of the entire country as well acquainted with you as we in New Jersey are and to help the country to an early appreciation of the opportunity for progress presented by your entrance into politics.   Very truly yours,   Allan Benny.

TLS (WP, DLC).
1 United States representative, 1903-1905; at this time practicing law in Bayonne, N. J.
2 Governor of Minnesota, 1898-1900; United States representative, 1903-1905; at this time practicing law in Minneapolis and president of the Board of Regents of the University of Minnesota.
3 It is printed at Aug. 31, 1901, Vol. 12.
4 Norman Lind, secretary-treasurer of the Pacific Timber Co., the Nelson-Neal Lumber Co., and the Mukilteo Shingle Co. of Everett, Wash.

To Mary Allen Hulbert Peck

Dearest Friend,   Phila., 31 Jan'y, '11

I am on my way to Washington to speak at the National Press
Club dinner to-night and be looked over by the Washington correspondents of papers all over the country. Your *perfectly delightful* letter of the 25th and 28th came this morning and fills
my mind like a piece of sweet music—it is so full of all that is
best in Bermuda and sweetest and noblest, like noble poetry in
you. You are coming into your best and *will* do something worth
while if you will but give that noble, poetical self leave in your
new freedom, your new dignity of liberty and peace of spirit.

All goes well. I am in good form and nothing is quite so satisfactory as a friend whom I can enjoy down to the depths of my
admiration and affection.

No further news in Trenton. We have settled to the work of
the legislative session.

With affectionate messages from us all
                          Your devoted friend   W.W.

ALS (WP, DLC).

An Address in Washington to the National Press Club[1]

[[Jan. 31, 1911]]

What we are after in the field of politics is to drive everything
into the field of facts, drive everything into the open. The root
of all evil in politics is privacy and concealment. After all, when
you think of the things of which we have been complaining,
they are summed up in this, that the people do not know, and,
therefore, cannot control the processes of their own politics. It
is easy to speak of the standard of the public welfare; it is easy
to say that every one should work for the common interest, but
first of all you have got to establish the common interest, and
the common interest cannot be established upon theories. It
cannot be established upon views; it can be established only
upon facts.

Until you know how the various elements of our economic
life and of our social life are related to each other, you cannot

---

[1] Wilson was one of five speakers at the National Press Club's second annual
"hobby night," and each of them spoke for ten minutes on the subject which
most occupied their daily thoughts. The other speakers were Ambassador James
Bryce, Dr. William Henry Welch of the Johns Hopkins, Major-General Leonard
Wood, Army Chief of Staff, and Secretary of the Treasury Franklin MacVeagh.
Thomas Nelson Page was the toastmaster.

find the common term. Now, when half of them are in ambush, when half of them are making their plans behind closed doors, when half of them are basing their whole effort upon private rights, then there is no means of coming at the common term at all. I wonder if you ever reflected that we have passed through a series of transformations or changes without passing through any series of transformations of opinions or of doctrines. You know the last thing which a man, of an English-speaking race, at any rate, changes, is his opinion. He will change his life, but he will continue to live under the terms of his old opinions.

My very distinguished colleague, President Patten,[2] of Princeton, once said, that it is characteristic of men of our time that they will get along with perfectly inconsistent pieces of ideas, and go on, as he quaintly expressed it, all their lives wearing a coat they cannot button up the belly without splitting it down the back.

Now that is just about our present condition. The coat we are wearing is a coat which is based upon this old doctrine that a man may do what he will with his own; that he may build up his own private fortune in any manner that suits him, provided he does not do a direct criminal wrong to another, and it is no business of the public to intervene and determine in any degree how his private business is conducted—all that in the face of the fact that almost none of our private business can now properly be described as private business at all. The reach of it, the complexity of it, has come to be such that it affects whole communities, and you cannot segregate it, you cannot treat it as if it were the business of a few individuals, as if it were property rights when the effects of the property right are community charges, and therefore we cannot button this coat up the belly without splitting it down the back.

We need a new coat of doctrine, namely, that business on its present scale is the service of communities for private profit, and that it is legitimate only in proportion as it serves; that profit cannot be legitimately built upon considerations wholly private, because no business is in its contacts or effects wholly a private matter in our day.

The same is true of politics. Politics has in recent years been tied to this private arrangement of a board of directors sitting behind closed doors and administering everybody's business as if it were their business. That is exactly the way in which politics has been conducted in recent years, with this addition, that

[2] That is, Francis Landey Patton.

many of these gentlemen, sitting behind closed doors and administering the business of corporations, have also been administering the business of parties. There has been a very close relation between politics and business, and it has been impossible to separate them without vivisection.

We are after the facts. We are going to run the facts out in the open, no matter how long it takes. Then we are going to try to be fair about the facts.

Now I admit that business and politics are very closely related because politics is not something separated from our life. It has to handle the vital matter of our business and because our business is public, our politics must be public.

There is a very clear reason, in my mind, why so few newspaper men have universally influential views. It is because our newspapermen are connected with newspapers that are known not to be disengaged from private interests. If you can once establish the reputation that you are speaking, so far as your knowledge and capacity enable you to speak, from the view point of the common interest then your views will be influential, and in proportion as they are disinterested they will be influential.

That is the reason why my hobby, if I have any, is the hobby of publicity. I cannot imagine anything legitimate that a man is doing that he need be afraid to talk about. I cannot imagine any legitimate part of the management of a party or of the organization of a political movement that cannot be talked about to anybody at any time. I cannot imagine any portion of the public business which can be privately and confidentially dealt with. In other words, I cannot imagine any portion of the business with regard to which you can say to one of the partners, "It is none of your business."

That is the whole present purpose of what we call the popular movement. The popular movement in our country is to change the machinery of our government from privacy to publicity; it is to chase it out of committee rooms; it is to get at the nominating process by a widespread method which is called the primary. You cannot conduct a state-wide primary privately. You can conduct a caucus privately, but not a primary—not the present kind of primary.

Everything we are trying to do, though complicated, is worth doing, because it is sending out a summons to all the partners to take part in the business. That is what interests me, and that is what makes discussion the heart and center and basis of all our modern affairs.

That, if I have any, is my hobby. The only reason that I have
been thought to ride a high horse is that I was, during the greater
part of my life, trained to talk, and then took the liberty of talking about what I understood was everybody's business.[3]

Printed in the *Washington Post*, Feb. 1, 1911, with additions from the partial
texts in the *Newark Evening News*, Feb. 1, 1911, and the Trenton *True American*, Feb. 1, 1911.
[3] There is a WWT outline of this talk, with the composition date of Jan. 31,
1911, in WP, DLC.

From Jacob Gould Schurman

My dear Governor Wilson: Ithaca, New York January 31, 1911

I have now finished a careful reading, and indeed re-reading
of Ford's "Rise and Growth of American Politics,"[1] which you
called to my attention on the occasion of the Chamber of Commerce banquet in Jersey City. It seems to me an unusually able
book—a book abounding in knowledge and showing an admirable capacity of expression, and possessing also the mark of
considerable originality of thought. In the vigorous slang of the
day, it shows us "where we are at" politically and how we have
got there. Its forecast of the future seems to me less successful.
I cannot think that the executive officer (presidency or governorship) after having been made a vigorous organ of popular
opinion and volition should ultimately go the way of the English kingship. A *faineant* president seems to me an impossible
goal. Might not Ford have found a better point of comparison
in the Hohenzollern kingship?

I am deeply interested in the organic political developments
which are imminent or actually taking place. You have certainly
started one line of development in your successful insistence
on the right of a State governor to act as the leader of his party
and force his views upon a legislature which otherwise would
have been controlled by a boss. No other governor, so far as I
know, has ever taken such a stand, and I shall watch with great
interest your further steps in bringing together the executive and
legislative departments and eliminating the influence of the
machine which, as Ford truly says, has in this country made
itself a part of the apparatus of government, serving as a con-
nective tissue between the executive and legislative departments,
or indeed, occupying the place which in the parliamentary or
English type of government is filled by the ministry.

Perhaps sometime when I go to New York I may have an
opportunity to spend the week-end in Princeton, and I should

certainly very much desire to do so if I might have an opportunity of talking over this subject with you. We seem in the matter of State governments to be on the eve of a new era. And as both parties in New York have committed themselves to the direct primary important changes may take place in this State in the near future.[2]   Very sincerely yours,   J. G. Schurman

TLS (WP, DLC).

[1] Henry Jones Ford, *The Rise and Growth of American Politics: A Sketch of Constitutional Development* (New York, 1898).

[2] About the earlier fate of direct primary legislation in New York, see A. C. Ludington to WW, Feb. 4, 1909, n. 6, Vol. 19. Both major parties in New York supported the principle of the direct primary in their platforms in 1910, and a direct primary law was enacted in 1914, during the governorship of Martin Henry Glynn.

A Tribute to Mark Anthony Sullivan[1]

[[Feb. 1, 1911]]

I am sorry to postpone for you what is the real treat of the evening, hearing the principal and most distinguished guest, and yet I would not deny myself the pleasure of saying the few simple words that I have to say in appreciation of what he stands for and what this gathering this evening means.

I sometimes marvel that men should ever miss the point of such a career as that of Mark Sullivan, and yet many men do, singularly, miss it. Why should a man like Mr. Sullivan come so quickly and singularly to the recognition of public opinion throughout a great State as a man truly devoted to the public interest? Simply because he has proved that his service is disinterested, that it is fearless, and that it is honest. Judge Sullivan has great abilities, but other men of great abilities have missed the honor which he has received in the minds of his fellow countrymen. Judge Sullivan has devoted himself with a singular industry to the profession which he adorns, but other men have used the same industry and have not been honored as he is honored even by their fellow practitioners at the bar. Do men not see that selfish service never brings honor? Do men not see that when they make a mistake, in serving themselves, instead of serving their country, they have put a stain upon themselves which nothing afterwards can remove or redeem? Have we not in our lives again and again seen exemplification of the fact that when once a man betrays a public trust he never can regain the confidence of his fellow citizens? Nothing will ever re-establish

[1] Delivered at a banquet given in Sullivan's honor at the Columbian Club of Jersey City by the alumni association of St. Peter's College.

him in the confidence of the men with whom he deals. How easy is honor if you will but be honorable? I am not overlooking the training of the man or the individual gifts of the man, for those I recognize and honor. There is, gentlemen, a fine school, in which some men are bred.

When a man has the example, for instance, of a self-sacrificing and noble mother[2] who devotes all her days with absolute unselfishness to the interests and education of a numerous family, and knows that every pulse of her heart beats for an unselfish purpose, it is no mean school in which to prepare for life. When a man knows that he comes of a stock which has not been stained by any kind of dishonor, when a man is schooled by teachers who hold up to him the example of Christ and the history of the self-sacrifi[c]es of the church, these are no mean preparations for public life. I remember that when I was an undergraduate at college, I was kept from doing some of the things I was tempted to do not so much by any native virtue in myself, as by the knowledge that there were dear people at home who believed me incapable of those things, to whom I should never wish to go back, and into whose eyes I should never wish to look again, if I betrayed the confidence that they had in me. There is a steadiness with purpose bred by love and confidence that is not easily bred in any other way. And when you expand that idea to communities; when you know that whole bodies of men have trusted you, then will you go back and look them in the eyes and pretend that you did not betray them, if you were unworthy of the trust? Are we not all a great family? Are we not all beholden to one another by the principles of trust and of trustworthiness? And then there is the idea which, I suppose, lies at the heart of the toast which has been assigned me on the menu—the College.

The college has a direct relation to politics—at any rate, as I have always conceived the college. Learning, I take it, gentlemen, so far as human affairs are concerned, has this particular value: It establishes the long connections of thought; each one of us is an ephemerial item of the great account of history, and we cannot make our calculations, we cannot establish our relations, unless we have the long measurements of human affairs that lie behind us, so that we shall know what the standards of honor and progress have been in order that we may lift ourselves from stage to stage in the slow progress of humanity. You know it has sometimes been said of a library that it is like that lobe of the brain which contains the memory, though the library con-

2 Catherine Driscoll (Mrs. Mark) Sullivan.

tains the memory of humanity or mankind than of the individual, and there is stored up there all the means by which we are to standardize anything in our conduct.

Such is the function of learning so far as we are concerned. Now, what possible excuse can a college man have for not knowing whether he is going right or going wrong in the conduct of his life as it touches human affairs? Here are the records of history and of literature, the songs and the biographies of those records which tell us to the men who have won fame and the men who have won honor. Can a man, if he be not a fool, miss his opportunity when he knows these things? Will he deliberately devote himself to shame? Will he with his eyes open, repeat the innumerable mistakes of human conduct, and will he, above all, make the irredeemable mistakes of honor—for they are nothing else in the light of knowledge than stupid blunders.

I marvel, in the face of all this, that there should be so much moral cowardice. I marvel, above all, that men should suppose that they are not going to be found out. I marvel to see men act on both sides of questions. It amazes me that they should suppose that they are taking anybody in; and I will tell you frankly that it dismays me, as a student of human nature, to find out the number of my friends has increased since the Senatorial election. Do these gentlemen suppose that they are rectifying their record? They are confirming it; they are confirming it by mere tergiversation.

Now, there is no question of this sort that has ever attached to the honored guest of the evening. Everybody knows the beacons by which he has steered. He has steered in the open, so that men always could perceive whither he was bound and how he was holding his compass. That is the reason why his choice as a judge of the highest court of the State[3] is acclaimed as a suitable choice, in spite of his youth;[4] for a man is as old as his judgment and as mature as his honor. Those are the standards by which such preferment is earned, though it is not always received. And so, it seems to me, that though I have been called upon very frequently to appear in public of recent days—and have yielded, perhaps, too often—this is the particular kind of occasion from which I could not stay. I could not deny myself the pleasure of rendering tribute to qualities which I truly admire and honor.

[3] Sullivan was appointed to the Court of Errors and Appeals by Governor Fort in 1910 and reappointed by Governor Wilson on February 6, 1911.
[4] He was born November 23, 1878.

Gentlemen, I do not know whether it is a dream that we have entered upon more hopeful days in American public affairs. I hope that it is not a dream.

I hope that we are perceiving things that are real, when we say that opinion in this country has awakened to a new kind of vigor, not the vigor of a mere audience[,] and applauds when it is pleased, but the vigor of those who thrust aside with impatience the men who cannot serve them with public spirit, and will continue to thrust such men aside until a corps of men is picked out who can lead the country into new adventures of honor that will rival the adventures of an ea[r]lier day, for there is nothing that enthuses the ardor of America as to know that she is moving forward to new days of human liberty, to new leadership, to a new sense of justice, to a new reading of the book of fate, which is no other than the book of prophecy, the book of divine guidance. I believe that there is no country in the world that is more heartened, more quickly lifted to enthusiasm than is America by those things which are ideal, by those things which are altruistic, by those things which have had their beginnings in self-sacrifice.

I know that America is the place where, above all other virtues, the virtue of courage is honored. It used to be said, if you will pardon the language, that what Englishmen most admired about Lord Palmerston was his "you-be-damnedness," his attitude as a man who, perhaps because of his class, perhaps because of the people from whom he was sprung, moved forward from act to act with absolute indifference to anything except the standards of honor which he had set for himself.

I wish that young men everywhere could learn how easy honor is to get in America. You do not need high gifts, you do not need poses; the particular thing you need is to forget yourself and to think of your fellow man, to think of America, the beloved home which has nurtured us and which has nurtured liberty and which has given us the right to speak on occasions of this sort without reserve, the sentiments we utter, if we are true to ourselves, if we are true to America. And then every man will bow to us, though it be only a little circle that knows us, with that kind of support which makes a man strong.

For a man is strong in America in proportion to the number of hearts and consciences he draws unto himself. The most delightful thing on an occasion like this—for I can see it as well as hear it—is that you love the man whom you have met to honor. I have admired a great many men whom it would be impossible to love, but I have never loved a man whom it would be impossible to admire, and the beautiful character of this occasion is that you should admire, and that your admiration is enhanced by your affection. I know how naturally, among the younger men, at any rate, in this community, leadership falls to Judge Sullivan and I want to say that in Hudson County, as well as elsewhere, I am glad also to be reckoned in his following.

Printed in the *Newark Evening News*, Feb. 2, 1911.

From Francis Landey Patton

My dear Governor: Princeton New Jersey Feby 1. 1911

I thank you for the very kind way in which you introduced my name into your speech at Washington; but I hasten to say that you are in error in imputing to me the witticism regarding the "coat." It is not mine—I wish it were for it is a good one—but Mallock's;[1] & in quoting it I have always given Mallock credit for it.

Wishing you great & continued success in the administration of your high office & in your future political career I am

Very faithfully yours   Francis L. Patton.

ALS (WP, DLC).
[1] William Hurrell Mallock, English author of satires, novels, and philosophical and political writings.

From John E. Lathrop

My dear Doctor Wilson: Washington, D. C., February 1, 1911.

Just briefly—your hobby talk before the Press Club is the talk of the town, and I am not exaggerating when I say it was the chief topic of conversation in the press galleries today, which are the daily rendezvous of 180 correspondents. I heard extensive discussion of it, its literary quality, its political significance, and the moral force back of it, and there was not a dissenting note. I congratulate the Press Club upon the honor you paid it by delivering such a high-minded comment so timely and so valuable. I shall be in Trenton on my way to New York, and shall advise you so that I could suit the trip to your convenience and see you en route. My wife says, "Tell Doctor Wilson I think his speech was just splendid," and my wife is a pretty good judge of splendid things.   Cordially yours,   John E. Lathrop

TLS (WP, DLC).

To Benjamin Barr Lindsey

My dear Judge Lindsey: [Trenton, N. J.] February 3, 1911.

Your letter of January twenty-eighth has given me deep and peculiar pleasure. It is delightful to have won your friendship. I have never hesitated for a moment as to which side I was to take and I quite agree with you that a long and stubborn fight is ahead of us. I think, however, the victory is certain if we but deny ourselves self seeking of every kind and make the cause and not ourselves the object. If there are any rewards they will be incidental and not essential.

With warmest regards, in haste,
                    Cordially yours,   Woodrow Wilson

TLS (B. B. Lindsey Papers, DLC).

To Samuel Huston Thompson, Jr.

My dear Mr. Thompson: [Trenton, N. J.] February 3, 1911.

You do not realize how I value your kindness and friendship. You may be sure that if I can stretch my tether far enough I shall be delighted to go to Colorado, and I can say very frankly that it makes me very happy that the feeling in Colorado should be what you represent it to be about my modest political achievements.

I feel an unconquerable hesitation about myself doing anything to initiate a movement that would lead to anything further in the way of political preferment and I am afraid, if I were so inclined, I should not know how to go about it. It is not, therefore, because I do not deeply appreciate what you say, but only because I am non-plussed that I should make no reply to your suggestion that I might "create a condition" that those of you who are independent Republicans might take the field for me.

With warmest regard,
                    Cordially and faithfully yours,   Woodrow Wilson

TLS (S. H. Thompson, Jr., Papers, DLC).

To Cyrus Hall McCormick

My dear Cyrus: [Trenton, N. J.] February 4, 1911.

Your note of January twenty-eighth has given me a great deal of pleasure, and I thank you for it with all my heart. I cannot tell you how proud it makes me that you and the other men I most trust and love should think of me as you do.

Affectionately yours,   Woodrow Wilson

TLS (WP, DLC).

To Robert Underwood Johnson

My dear Mr. Johnson: [Trenton, N. J.] February 4, 1911.

I have not before had time to thank you as I do most cordially for your kind note of January thirtieth.[1] It was certainly most generous.

You are undoubtedly right in your statement that the party is daily losing ground in New York. Certainly the situation there is most deplorable.

In haste,

Cordially and faithfully yours,   Woodrow Wilson

TLS (WC, NjP).
[1] It is missing.

To William Henry Rideing

My dear Mr. Rideing: [Trenton, N. J.] February 4, 1911.

No persuasion would be necessary if it were possible for me to write, but I am speaking the literal truth when I say that it would be impossible, my days and evenings are so absorbed by my duties.[1]

I thank you most cordially for remembering me in this way.

Sincerely yours,   Woodrow Wilson

TLS (PP).
[1] Rideing's letter is missing. He had obviously asked Wilson for a contribution to *The Youth's Companion*, of which he was associate editor.

From Josephus Daniels

Dear Sir and Friend: Raleigh, N. C. Feb. 4th, 1911

We are all greatly pleased to know that you are going to deliver the Commencement Address at the University of North Carolina at the Commencement about the last of May.[1]

My wife joins me in requesting that you will come to Raleigh and be our guest going to and coming from Chapel Hill.

I expect to go to New York about April and if so, I wish to drop by and see you either going or coming.

I enclose and [an] editorial from yesterday's News and Observer.[2]   Sincerely,   Josephus Daniels

Your victory in the senatorial fight was the most glorious of this era.

TLS (WP, DLC).
  [1] Wilson's address is printed at May 30, 1911, Vol. 23.
  [2] It is missing, but it was an editorial, "Duty and Power of a Governor," which compared Governor Dix's and Wilson's conceptions of their office. Dix, the editorial asserted, saw the governorship in merely executive terms, while Wilson insisted that he was not only the state's chief executive but also his party's leader and therefore responsible for using all his influence to achieve his party's program. Specifically, the editorial commended Wilson for entering the New Jersey senatorial fight and for not remaining aloof, as Dix was doing in New York. "The mere power to veto or make appointments," the editorial concluded, "is nothing in comparison with the immense power that goes with it when the incumbent has the ability, courage and conscience of Woodrow Wilson." Raleigh, N. C., *News and Observer*, Feb. 3, 1911.

To Mary Allen Hulbert Peck

Dearest Friend,   Princeton, N. J. 5 Feb'y, 1911

For once, I am at home on Sunday, if one may speak of an inn a 'home.' Again I have played heathen, I am ashamed to say, and stayed away from church, to sleep till midday,—sleeping off the labours of the week. This afternoon I read bills and other papers for which it had proved impossible to find time during the week. It's a weary business being governor. I have literally *no* time to myself, am at everybody's disposal but my own,—and, like every other man in similar case, the question of appointments drives me nearly distracted, it is so nearly impossible to get true information or disinterested advice about persons—and so many persons are trying to impose upon me. I shall get used to it, but am not yet, and it goes hard.

How delightful it is, in intervals of business (and even when there are none), when I am left alone for a few moments, or withdraw my attention and let my thoughts go their own way, to take Salt Kettle Ferry, see the bright water, feel the cool, sweet air of the bay, pay my tuppence to the lazy, friendly captain (or whatever he may be), look at the nearing shore where Shoreby is perched, above the steering mask by which the *Bermudian* keeps to her narrow channel as she threads her way in, step ashore on the narrow dock which lies so remote and quiet there in dear Paget, hurry up the path to the corner and turn in to 'Glencove' where my dear friend is, it may be lying in her hammock and waiting and *wishing* to talk,—full of whimsical anecdote and comment upon the people and things amongst which she moves and of the (less interesting) folk who play a mimic game of high Society in and about Government House! How easy it is to get rid of Trenton and, even as I seem to listen to importunate office seekers, forget the great formal office in which I sit, and see out of its windows, instead of the city street on one side and the river with its uncouth banks on the other, the sights and sweet radiant spaces, the familiar houses and scenes, of dear Bermuda. It soothes and cheers and refreshes me like Wordsworth's vision of the daffodils. The mind is master of its own fate, of its own world and its own moods. It can take its pleasure as it will. And so I do not expect to grow old as fast as some men do, whose minds do not know where or whence to seek their renewal. My poor body must stay every day in Trenton, but my mind goes where it will.

I spend every day but Saturday and Sunday at my office. Monday I stay till bed-time and come back on a late train, because the legislature sits Monday evenings and Tuesday mornings. Other days I generally get away by four or five in the afternoon.

I am quite well. The work makes me very tired, but nothing worse, and keeps me out of mischief. I should get along very well if it were not for my incorrigible habit of making public speeches! I am trying to swear off.

Bless you for your letters: they are delightful. All unite with me in affectionate messages, and I am always

Your devoted friend   Woodrow Wilson

ALS (WP, DLC).

From Vance Criswell McCormick

Dear Governor: Harrisburg, Penn. February 6th, 1911

The Central Democratic Club of Harrisburg, of which I am a member, regretted very much that you could not accept their invitation to be the guest of honor at the Jefferson Day Banquet, owing to previous engagements.

Not only the State Capital but Central Pennsylvania is anxious to have an opportunity to make your acquaintance and would consider it a great honor, if you could accept an invitation from the club at such time as would be convenient for you. It would be especially opportune, if you could do so in the near future, as there is a strong movement in this State to re-organize our Democratic Party and restore it to the confidence of the voters of the State.[1] We are fighting for the same thing that you have so splendidly stood for in New Jersey, and your presence here would greatly strengthen the cause and help to redeem our party from the traitors who were so deservedly repudiated at our last election.[2]

This is a very important matter for Pennsylvania and, if it would not inconvenience you, I will be glad to call upon you to extend to you an invitation in person.

Hoping you will give this matter your very careful consideration and assuring you of a very hearty welcome, if you can accept the invitation,[3] I remain

Very truly yours,   Vance C McCormick

TLS (Governors' Files, Nj).

[1] The Democratic party in Pennsylvania was bitterly divided into two factions at this time. One, the regular organization, was headed by the wealthy oil producer of Pittsburgh, James McClurg Guffey, who had risen to power as a supporter of Bryan and free silver and was the Pennsylvania member of the Democratic National Committee from 1898 to 1908. By 1911, he had a reputation for dealing with the Republican leadership of the state and with the most conservative state leaders in national politics. The second was a group of progressives led, among others, by Roland S. Morris and Francis Fisher Kane of Philadelphia, Vance C. McCormick of Harrisburg, George W. Guthrie of Pittsburgh, and Warren Worth Bailey of Johnstown. At this very time, they were maturing plans to seize control of the state party machinery. See Stanley Coben, *A. Mitchell Palmer: Politician* (New York and London, 1963), pp. 29-35.

[2] The Guffey organization, which in agreement with Boies Penrose, Republican boss of Pennsylvania, in 1910 had nominated a weak gubernatorial candidate, Webster Grim, so that he would lose to his Republican opponent, John Kinley Tener. The progressive Democrats then joined insurgent Republicans to run a Democrat, William H. Berry, on a third-party ticket. Tener won a narrow plurality over Berry, 415,614 votes to 382,127. Grim received only 129,395 votes. *Ibid.*, pp. 31-34.

[3] Wilson did not speak to the Central Democratic Club of Harrisburg. However, he did address a state-wide rally of progressive Democrats in that city on June 15, 1911 (see the news reports printed at June 16, 1911), Vol. 23, and his address in Philadelphia on February 21, 1911, noted earlier, was to a meeting held by the progressive faction.

From Thomas Bell Love

My dear Governor Wilson: [Dallas, Tex.] February 7, 1911.

I have intended writing you for some weeks past, but have been so thoroughly engrossed with business matters that I have been unable to find time to do so earlier.

Some weeks ago I had a personal conference with Mr. Bryan at Austin and took advantage of the opportunity to very strongly urge upon him my views as to your availability as a candidate for the presidency next year, and while he did not in any wise avow his position in the matter, but insisted that it was his purpose to keep an open mind on the subject for some months to come, I was convinced that I made some impression upon him, and that there is a fair prospect of him taking definitely the position which I am very sincerely desirous of seeing him take.

I have not as yet received a copy of your campaign platform, and I should like very much to have one, and also copies of your inaugural address and messages to the Legislature.

I want to congratulate you most heartily upon your splendid victory in the Senatorship matter, in which I think you have rendered the Democratic party a national and signal benefit.

I am frequently asked now and then by Texas Democrats, what your position is on the subject of adoption by the Legislature of New Jersey of the Income Tax Amendment to the Constitution of the United States, and I will be glad to know what position you have taken in the premises.

I am more and more convinced as time passes, of the existence of a general sentiment in this State favorable to your nomination for the Presidency, which, by proper effort and organization, can be so developed as to assure the sending of a delegation to the next National Convention, favorable to your nomination.

I will be glad indeed if you will have someone send me the papers referred to above, as well as any others expressive of your views on public questions.

With best wishes, I am

Yours very truly,   Thomas B. Love.

TCL (T. B. Love Papers, Dallas Hist. Soc.).

A News Report of an After-Dinner Speech

[*Feb. 8, 1911*]

WILSON FELT AT HOME IN NOISE

The Governor So Declared Last Night at Alumni Dinner
of Stevens Institute.

New York, Feb. 8.—The alumni of Stevens Institute of Technology came over from Hoboken tonight to celebrate the 40th anniversary of "the opening of the college for regular instruction," and they brought New Jersey's Governor with them. There were 366 Stevens men in the banquet hall of the Hotel Astor and they made noise enough for twice that number. The cheers had no Princeton tiger at the end, but the noise gave Governor Wilson a homey feeling and he said as much.

"I don't know your faces," said he, "but your manners are familiar. I feel more at home in this boisterous company than I have for weeks."

He had to stop just there while Stevens cheered some more, and when he went on Governor Wilson praised the profession of engineering and drew a moral from it.

He told the engineers old and young that their profession found its real significance in the fact that upon it rested the comfort of the world. "You must work in form that will last," he said. "Your work must hold together and by the same token your work must be honest. In your work there is no denying the evidence, you can't be accidentally mistaken."

He went on to say that the profession of engineering was associated in a way with "some of the things that have made us feel that our age is touched in an unusual degree with a stain on the human record." He explained that the engineer understood perhaps above all men that if his work was touched with "graft" it will sooner or later vitiate what you do.

Governor Wilson drew a parallel between the work of the engineer and the literary man, pointing out that in both and in all affairs, "a great man must be master of men, of opportunity and of circumstances."

The Governor pronounced his creed for the man of affairs when he said: "In affairs, we must not be impatient of slow processes, and of tradition. The leader must look forward to things not yet done as things done, and carry the thought of his generation forward to them.

"The engineer of human affairs and fortunes is the sympathetic interpreter of evisting [existing] affairs and fortunes."

In conclusion he said that the success of the engineering profession[,] like that of the man of affairs, lay in the determination "not to think of money, but of service."

Richard H. Rice, '85, "Steam Turbine"[1] Rice to the alumni, presided.

Printed in the Trenton *True American*, Feb. 9, 1911; some editorial headings omitted.
[1] Richard Henry Rice, an engineer who was general manager of the turbine department of the General Electric Company's works at Lynn, Mass., and was principally engaged in perfecting General Electric's steam turbine.

To Robert Bridges

Personal.

My dear Bobbie: [Trenton, N. J.] February 8, 1911.

Friends with more political sense than I have, have looked over the correspondence you sent me[1] and see no harm in the movement which [Henry Skillman] Breckenridge has set on foot. Of course unwise things may be done in the course of it, but there is nothing in the movement itself that seems unwise and certainly it is from the young men of the country that the new parties are going to draw their vim and their success. I hate to see Cleve drawn into any expense on my account, but I must answer your questions as I have.

In haste,   Affectionately yours,   Woodrow Wilson

TLS (WC, NjP).
[1] It is missing. Wilson probably returned it to Bridges.

To Ray Stannard Baker[1]

My dear Mr. Baker: [Trenton, N. J.] February 8, 1911.

Your letter of the seventh is very gracious and I warmly appreciate the compliment paid me by the desire of the Insurgent's Club[2] to have me attend one of their meetings, but it is literally true that I have reached my limit. I cannot without endangering both my health and the performance of my public duties add to the already foolishly large speaking list that I have permitted myself to make.

I am in warm sympathy with the objects of the Club and wish very much that I could show my sympathy in some definite way.

        Cordially yours,   Woodrow Wilson

TCL (RSB Coll., DLC).
[1] Journalist and muckraker, at this time one of the editors of *American Magazine*; later friend and authorized biographer of Woodrow Wilson.
[2] This organization, while supposedly nonpartisan, consisted largely of insurgent Republicans. Among the leaders were Amos Richards Eno Pinchot and Gifford Pinchot, Francis J. Heney, Gilbert E. Roe, Lincoln Steffens, Baker, and Frederic C. Howe, who served as president of the club in 1912. Baker's letter of February 7 is missing, but he later recounted the details of the invitation. In January 1911, a committee of the Insurgent Club was planning a rally at which they hoped Wilson and Senator Robert M. La Follette would be the main speakers. Upon receipt of Wilson's letter of February 8, Baker telephoned the Governor, urging him to reconsider and stressing that the group was nonpartisan and focused on progressive issues. According to Baker, Wilson said, "I am heartily in sympathy with the movement, but I am convinced that I must make my fight within the Democratic party. It must be a party movement." By the time the rally was eventually held—on January 22, 1912, in Carnegie Hall in New York—the Insurgent Club had become primarily a vehicle for La Follette's presidential movement. At the meeting on January 22, 1912, the Wisconsin Senator was the featured speaker and stressed that the recall should be extended to judges. *New York Times*, Jan. 23, 1912; Ray Stannard Baker, *Woodrow Wilson: Life and Letters* (8 vols., Garden City, N. Y., 1927-39), III, 184-85; Belle Case La Follette and Fola La Follette, *Robert M. La Follette* (2 vols., New York, 1953), I, 362, 389.

From John Wesley Wescott

My dear Governor Wilson: Camden, N. J., Feb. 8th,1911.

You have made three appointments,[1] not only unexception-
able, but exceptionally strong. The comments on every hand
are gratifying.

In reference to the appointment of Mr. Nowrey,[2] I beg to say
that, while he may not be an ideal appointee in every respect,
I believe that he will size up to the responsibilities of the office.
Unless you secure a man conspicuous for his mechanical and
technical ability, further reflection convinces me that William A.
Logue, of Bridgeton, would be an ideal selection.[3] If he lacks at
all, in any respect, it would be a want of technical and mechanical training. He is a scholarly man with considerable mathe-
matical capability, and, in my judgment, would readily master
the office with respect to these matters; but, in all other regards,
I doubt very much whether you could find his equal throughout
the state.   Affectionately yours,   John W. Wescott.

TLS (Governors' Files, Nj).
    [1] Wilson had nominated Clarence Lee Cole of Atlantic City to be judge of the
Circuit Court for Atlantic, Burlington, Gloucester, Salem, Cumberland, and
Cape May counties, and Frank Smathers of Atlantic City to be judge of the
District Court of Atlantic City. He had also re-nominated Mark Anthony Sullivan
to the Court of Errors and Appeals. The Senate confirmed the three nominees on
February 7, 1911.
    [2] Joseph E. Nowrey, Mayor of Camden, 1902-1905, who had been defeated
for Congress in 1910. Wilson had considered naming him state Commissioner of
Roads.
    [3] William Augustin Logue, lawyer of Bridgeton, N. J., and member of the
New Jersey Board of Fish and Game Commissioners. Wilson appointed Logue
to another term as a fish and game commissioner in 1912.

Two Letters to Walter Hines Page

My dear Page: [Trenton, N. J.] February 10, 1911.

I have a very warm friend, Colonel James C. Sprigg, of Essex
Fells, New Jersey, (otherwise Caldwell), whom with Mr. Walter
McCorkle[1] and other Southern friends of mine in New York, is
bent upon getting up some kind of organized movement to advocate my claims for the nomination for the Presidency. Colonel Sprigg does not seem to me a very wise person and he
certainly is not considered in this State a practical man. His
schemes are generally good, but for some reason are generally
smiled at. I myself think that he is underrated and that it is
chiefly his manner that stands against him. At the same time I
am a little uneasy about any movement that he might start (but
any movement at all for that matter of this ambitious kind). I

have, therefore, taken the liberty of advising him to send Mr. McCorkle and others interested to you for hard headed advice. I hope that you will not mind my taking this liberty.

With warm regard,

Cordially yours,   Woodrow Wilson

¹ Walter Lee McCorkle, a Wall Street lawyer originally from Virginia.

My dear Page: [Trenton, N. J.] February 10, 1911.

It will be a novel experience to have a man like Mr. Hale¹ spend a week seeing how I go through the paces, but he is most welcome and I am most happy to have a plan set afoot which may serve to keep the witches off.² It is certainly generous of you to wish to have this done in the World's Work.³

Most faithfully yours,   Woodrow Wilson

TLS (W. H. Page Papers, MH).
  ¹ William Bayard Hale, former Episcopal priest who entered journalism in 1900 and demitted the ministry in 1909, at this time a member of the editorial staff of *World's Work*. He wrote a campaign biography, *Woodrow Wilson: The Story of His Life* (Garden City, N. Y., 1912) and edited a selection of Wilson's speeches during the preconvention and presidential campaigns of 1911-1912, *The New Freedom* . . . (Garden City, N. Y., 1913).
  ² For the meaning of this phrase, see WW to Mary A. H. Peck, Feb. 19, 1911.
  ³ The article was W. B. Hale, "Woodrow Wilson: Possible President," *World's Work*, XXII (May 1911), 14, 339-53.

To William Bayard Hale

My dear Mr. Hale: [Trenton, N. J.] February 10, 1911.

I am afraid that you would find a week with me very dull indeed, but if you are willing to undertake it, you will certainly be most welcome to be here with me.

I shuttle between Princeton and Trenton, spending my nights in Princeton and my work day in Trenton from one-half past ten in the morning until about five in the afternoon, generally. I do not know whether you would care to go back and forth also, but in any case you will be welcome and next week is as clear from engagements away from work as any that I can forsee.

Sincerely yours,   Woodrow Wilson

TLS (received from W. H. Hale).

To John Wesley Wescott

My dear Judge Westcott: [Trenton, N. J.] February 10, 1911.

I am sincerely glad that my appointments so far have had your approval[.] There is no one whose approval I more desire.

I hope that you will think my appointment of the Road Commissioner[1] also was the right thing. I am delighted to hear of Mr. Logue of Bridgeton. He is the kind of man it is worth while keeping in mind for other things. I wonder if you could some time have somebody send me details about him; his profession, etc.   Cordially and faithfully yours,   Woodrow Wilson

TLS (J. W. Wescott Coll., NjP).
[1] Wilson had just appointed Edwin Augustus Stevens as Commissioner of Roads for a term of three years.

To Joseph Stanislaus Hoff[1]

Ny [My] dear Mr. Hoff: [Trenton, N. J.] February 10, 1911.

I meant to make a point of seeing you before announcing the nomination I would make for the Commissionership of Roads, but I was so rushed it turned out to be impossible for me to do so.

I hope I need not assure you that my failure to appoint you was not due in the slightest degree to any doubt as to your character or ability. The post is of such capital importance that I thought it right, if possible, to find an engineer of State wide reputation to fill it, and I am happy to feel confident that your own judgment will sustain me in this instance.[2]

With cordial regard and sincere respect,
Very truly yours,   Woodrow Wilson

TLS (received from Mrs. John Woodruff).
[1] Meat and vegetable dealer of Princeton, chairman of the Mercer County Democratic Committee.
[2] While Wilson's selection of Stevens certainly fulfilled his requirement of "an engineer of State wide reputation," personal and political considerations may also have entered into the appointment. Stevens was not only Wilson's classmate at Princeton but also a close personal friend. As for political considerations, Hoff, along with the other members of the Mercer County Democratic Committee, had supported Frank S. Katzenbach, Jr., for the gubernatorial nomination in 1910. Moreover, according to an article in the Hoboken, N. J., *Hudson Observer*, Feb. 1, 1911, Hoff's appointment was strongly opposed by a rival Democratic faction within Mercer County. George Opdyke Vanderbilt of Princeton, former state senator and former Speaker of the House of Assembly, sought the Democratic congressional nomination in 1910 and was angered by Hoff's support of the Princeton professor, William Libbey, who received the nomination but was defeated in the November election. When Hoff appeared as the leading contender for the commissionership of roads, Vanderbilt opposed him and enlisted the aid of Garret Dorset Wall Vroom, judge on the Court of Errors and Appeals and a long-time power in Mercer County Democratic politics. Hoff had supported Katzenbach against Vroom for the Democratic gubernatorial nomination in 1907. While there is no evidence that Wilson took this internecine party warfare into consideration, he did decide to appoint Stevens instead of Hoff, wrote this letter of explanation to the Mercer County chairman, and consoled him with an appointment to the state Civil Service Commission on May 8, 1911.

To John Fairfield Dryden

[My dear Senator Dryden: Trenton, N. J., c. Feb. 10, 1911]

I am sure that the project to erect a noble monument to Mr. Cleveland at Princeton must appeal to men of all classes and of all political affiliations throughout the country.[1] Mr. Cleveland had the happiness before he died of knowing that the whole country recognized his sterling worth and his great and conscientious services to the country. Partisan feeling died entirely away, and men everywhere saw in him a great character which had given him eminence and commanding influence in our politics and in our national policy. A monument to such a man, erected in a university town, where young men from all parts of the country may see it and reflect upon the lessons of conduct it represents, would surely be one of the most fitting inspirations of patriotism and public duty that could be conceived.

[Sincerely yours,   Woodrow Wilson]

Printed in the *Trenton Evening Times*, Feb. 10, 1911.
[1] About this matter, see WW to J. F. Dryden, June 16, 1910, n. 2, Vol. 20.

An Appeal for Manchurian Relief

[Feb. 10, 1911]

The tragical famine now prevailing in Manchuria, China, calls for special effort on the part of humane and Christian people everywhere to contribute to the relief of the suffering. The Commercial Club, of Seattle, Wash., has undertaken, under the auspices of the American Red Cross Society to ship food and clothing. Flour, rice, dried fish and coarse cotton cloth and cotton wadding for clothing will all be most gratefully received and will be promptly forwarded by the club in an army transport granted by Congress for the purpose.

Such gifts should be directed to the "Commercial Club, Seattle, Washington. In the care of the Red Cross Agency." Money will also be very much needed and immediately sent to the American Red Cross Society at Washington, D. C.

I would most earnestly commend this call for aid to the attention of all citizens of the State who can contribute supplies or money and would respectfully urge them to lend their assistance as freely and as promptly as possible.

America has always been among the first in the great family of nations to give generous aid in such works of humanity, and I am sure that the people of New Jersey will be as quick to act and as generous in an action as the people of any of her sister States.

Printed in the *Newark Evening News*, Feb. 10, 1911.

An Address on Behalf of Berea College[1]

[[Feb. 10, 1911]]

President Frost, Mr. Low, Ladies and Gentlemen:

I always wonder why it is necessary to make speeches for Berea. The case is so obvious, the object to be sought so admirable, the things at stake so momentous, why should we need to be persuaded to support an enterprise like this? All that I have come here for is to add my little part in pointing out to you what it means. I wonder if any of you have ever been in the mountains of Kentucky and North Carolina. I wonder if you realize the life, the simple life, that is set amidst those magnificent and beautiful surroundings, and I wonder if you realize how that life waits for the touch of help to spring into an energy which it is impossible it should know otherwise.

I used to know the mountains when I was a boy, and did not think seriously about these things, but in all the years that have followed the picture of those simple people, the image of the beautiful surroundings in which they live, has seemed to grow upon the sensitive surface of my memory, until it means more and more with regard to the interpretation of life and the development of it. When you are asked to subscribe for Berea you are asked to subscribe for a renewal of the life of the country at its sources. Do you never reflect where the sources of the nation's life lie? Do you suppose that the life of a tree is derived from its fruit? Do you not know that the life of a tree is derived from these unseen origins which lie beneath the soil, where everything is dark and hidden and silent, and if you choose to regard it so, unbeautiful? But here all the sources of vitality lie, and are sent forth into the roots, into the trunk, into the vibrant branches, and finally into the flower and fruit. So it is with the nation. Our sources do not lie where distinction is revealed in this, that and the other man. They lie in the places whence he, it may be, came, or whence his forbears came, and whence the people whose stock he represents came and all the sources of strength and renewal come from the bottom up, not from the top down. (Applause.)

[1] Delivered in Carnegie Hall, New York. William Goodell Frost and Seth Low also spoke, and Josiah Cleveland Cady, New York architect and trustee of Berea College, presided.

That man is no friend of the country who works with regard to the things that have been accomplished. He is a friend of the country who works with regard to making sure that other like things will be accomplished in the future, and that can be done only by educating the silent undeveloped masses in whom the strength of the nation resides (Applause), in which all these sources lie hidden, from which will come the streams of influence and of energy and of initiative which will make us go upward from generation to generation.

These men and women are quiet peoples of the inland empire of the mountains.

Now, in those little pockets of those splendid mountains lie some of the future sources of our strength, there in a sort of sequestered store, an unspoiled stock, stock of the original stuff of which America was made, for the most part. And you have only to touch this source with the magic of a little subscription of money to see the strength leap forth. Why should a man come and argue to a body of intelligent people that this is desirable?

There is another thing which I wonder if you have thought of. There are forces lying there which cannot in any other way be released. This is a sharp, competitive age. A man without some degree or [of] training cannot enter the lists of modern competition and succeed unless he be gifted with a singular and unusual genius. And what you are seeking to do in helping Berea is to release forces which lie there imaginative, and yet sober, locked up in the hearts of an old stock which has been set apart in places where the mind broods. You know that many of these people come of Scotch-Irish stock, a stock which I like to praise because in praising them—since I come from that stock, I am praising myself by proxy (laughter). This stock, a portion of it long ago wandered into the hills, and made its ways up those quiet and sequestered valleys, and has remained there ever since, unspoiled, untouched, unchanged. They are a very imaginative people; how could it be otherwise? How could the imagination, how could the soul of man fail to be touched by those elevating surroundings where the air itself seems suffused with imaginative color, where it seems impossible that a man should be there and not think in images, in images of the majesty of nature, of the might and majesty of God himself, where all nature is arrayed to quiet the thought and yet to stimulate it. But while the thought is stimulated, it is Scotch-Irish thought, and therefore it is sober, stubborn thought. It is not thought that leaps easily into new channels. On the contrary, it is thought that comes conservatively in the old roads, in the old ways of thought, touched, no doubt, I think, with color, but touched with a very sober Quaker color. Now, you are asked to release this, to release the mind that broods there, upon the modern field of endeavor, of sharp, hot, competitive endeavor.

If I were to choose again a man to inject into modern American life, I would take some man who in his youth had had time to think. (Applause.) A man who had spent his boyhood in some quiet covert, where it is possible for the mind to indulge in what most Americans never indulge in—that is to say, reverie, contemplation, those silent processes of the mind by which the impressions of life penetrate and saturate, so that never afterwards he can stand in a position where life is a retrogression, but always a movement forward; where he can always look back and see the image of the quiet home, and the plodding of the day's work, of the simple and humble folk from whom he sprang. No matter how much brilliant movement there may be in the foreground, it never overshadows the background upon which the brilliancy shines forth. These men, like Lincoln, to whom Dr. Frost so suitably refers, these men like Lincoln, will never forget the feeling or shake off the prepossessions of the common folk.

Now a man who has not these prepossessions is not fit to lead or serve a free people (Applause), and I should expect the noble processes that are going on at Berea to produce for us in some day of critical exigency another man like Lincoln of that unconquerable stuff of the old stock of the continent and yet touched with the energy of a new age and with the vision of a new age and able to lead out of old things into new.

Moreover, this is a Southern enterprise and because I am a Southerner perhaps I have a strong prepossession in its favor, because by enriching the life in the South, what are you doing? You are strengthening the life of the country in that portion of it where there is pretty sure to be a reversion to type. The South is the least changed part of this country, so far as the make-up of its population is concerned and that population is the portion of our population by which we have our oldest unaltered connection with our institutional development. Here is the straightest strain of American political tradition. Do you want to enrich that strain or do you not?

You have had your quarrels with the South, but you at least own that the South knows how to quarrel, that the South knows how to argue its case and that the South stubbornly based its cause upon what it believed to be political traditions and with that stubborn political conservatism there nevertheless goes the most radical sympathy with the common ordinary people of this country, with what I believe is, using a small "d" and not a big one, the real democratic foundation of our life. (Applause.)

You speak of the South as if its traditions were aristocratic, and yet you know that more stubbornly than any other part of the country it has been persistently democratic. No[w] I do not know whether you want to subscribe to increase the strength of democracy or not (Laughter and applause) but I would commend it to you as a hopeful enterprise. (Laughter and applause.) And I can guarantee it to you, I think, that if you will strengthen the democracy that will come out of the mountains you will be again renewing the sources of our political life, because I do not know where else you will find a straighter tradition, leading you back to the origin of our liberty.

There is one singular feature about the remote Southern mountains, from which Berea draws her students. It has all the characteristics of the frontier and yet it is an interior. It is as if the life of the country had surrounded its frontier and left an unaltered strip of it running along the coast. What is the characteristic of the frontier? Until 1890 the census makers were always able, in drawing their maps, to draw a frontier between us and the Pacific. After gold had been discovered in California great populations hurried to the Pacific Coast, but there was still, until 1890, an unchartered strip between us and the Rockies, which constituted our Western frontier.

Until twenty years ago therefore the most characteristic part of the life of this country was that its energies always had an outlet on a frontier, and that the frontier was the place where its energies re-appeared and tested themselves, because on a frontier there is nothing to rely on except your own wits. There are no finished institutions for you, there are no facilities of life —you have got to make everything you use, and raise everything you eat and organize everything you undertake; and the rank and file have to be drawn into vital processes of political renewal. That is the character of a frontier and it was that character that kept us vital, and left the West till this day the most characteristic and American part of America (Applause), the part of America which constantly has to remind us that there are a lot of things to be done yet. (Applause.) Very well, here is, so to say, an unused cistern out of which we can draw in our own immediate neighborhood the enegery [energy], the initiative, the versatile adaptability that can be made upon a frontier. Here is our interior preserved frontier, and here are these immediate contacts, just next our doors, with the necessities and pressure of nature. Do you wonder then that a great spirit enters into men like Dr. Frost, that obliges them to spend themselves until there is hardly anything left in them except the will that originated the whole thing to serve this consummate purpose? Do you need to be detained to be told that this is an interesting thing to do? Can you think of anything more interesting or promising upon which to spend your resources, and can you think of any resources that will exceed the interest and the necessity? I am sorry that I have only my tongue to lend to this enterprise. I wish that I had the privilege, which, I dare say, a great many men in this audience might exercise, of lending the sinews of war, of contributing money, and so joining the patriciate, the only patriciate of America, of those men who serve their country. (Great applause.)[2]

Printed in the *Berea Quarterly*, xv (April 1911), 23-28; with corrections and one addition from the partial texts in the New York *World*, Feb. 11, 1912, and the New York *Evening Post*, Feb. 11, 1912.
[2] There is a brief WWhw outline of this address, dated Feb. 10, 1911, in WP, DLC.

A News Report of an Address
to the Kentuckians of New York

[Feb. 11, 1911]

300 KENTUCKIANS DINE

Pay Tribute to Lincoln and Hear State's Spirit Lauded.

Three hundred Kentuckians dined at the Hotel Plaza last night to celebrate the birthday of Abraham Lincoln, whom, in the words of one of the speakers, "Kentucky gave to Illinois, Illinois gave to the Republic, and the Republic gave to the ages." Gov. Dix welcomed the "Kentuckians who are New Yorkers" to this State, and Gov. Woodrow Wilson hailed them in behalf of New Jersey, and pointed out the country's great need of men of the strenuous yet sporting spirit that characterized the early pioneer Kentuckians. . . .

Gov. Wilson, who followed Gov. Dix, said he always thought of Kentuckians as embodying, even as did their thoroughbreds, "mettle and spirit, a combination of free, beautiful movement and willingness to labor—the spirit of the sportsman and of the man of enterprise and ambition."

"Nothing is more needed in our country to-day," he said, ["]than that spirit of the frontiersman which Kentucky produced. We need audacity in public life—not mere destructive audacity and willingness to work that vanquished the Indians, but a constructive gift as well, a spirit of wisdom and high ideals. There are frontiers of politics, too, which we must push beyond.

"The men who have dreamed have built up our industries, our knowledge, our politics. In every generation we have seen the forces of greed and ignorance combine themselves against the forces of the ideal.

"In her early days Kentucky touched the feudal forces of France, the arbitrary and feudal power that had taken a hold on part of our country. To-day, as then, it is her duty and the duty of all Americans to drive out these arbitrary and feudal powers. They are many and infinitely varied, but we thank God for that. To-day, as in the frontier days of Kentucky[,] you want to sink your teeth in flesh, not in pemmican; you want to hit something that is tangible and will resist; you want to cut something in a way that will draw blood.

"Are you proud of being American—intensified Americans, Kentuckians—simply because America has been great and Kentucky has been famous? Do you want to be a hiatus, a parenthesis, a pause in the history of mankind? Don't you want to invest all those splendid traditions? Do you want to be in the old, played-out game of looking backward on the ever-young game of lifting men to higher levels and cheering them on to ever higher achievement? Kentucky has rich blood and splendid power. On what are you going to spend it? Is not all life the spending of such power, not on ourselves but on others?"[1]

Printed in the *New York Times*, Feb. 11, 1911.
　[1] There is a brief WWhw outline of these remarks, dated Feb. 10, 1911, in WP, DLC.

From Lindley Miller Keasbey[1]

My dear Dr. Wilson:　　　　　[Austin, Tex.] Feb. 11th. 1911

Hon. Thos. B. Love, whose letter to me I enclose, is now Vice President and Counsel of the Southwestern Life Insurance Company. Mr. Love was for two sessions of our Legislature Speaker of the House and under the last Campbell administration,[2] our Commissioner of Banking and Insurance. In these political capacities, Mr. Love was the author of and responsible for the passage of our insurance and bank guaranty laws. For some years I have been in close personal and professional contact with Mr. Love and know him to be a remarkably efficient constructive statesman and withal, an astute politician. But, what is much more important, Mr. Love is genuin[e]ly and honestly interested in sure-enough democracy; that is: he has the cause of the common people,—the consumers and among the producers the workers, farmers and laborers,—at heart. During the last few years,—especially during the last gubernatorial campaign,— I have seen him sorely tested and found him firm.

I enclose his letter and write you this to bring you two in touch. From my long acquaintance with you and your work, I am sure of the "tendency of your views,"—the evidences of your being on the people's side are open and before us all. I have written Mr. Love my conclusions on these points. Perhaps you will find it in your way to endorse these conclusions. I should like a letter I can enclose to Mr. Love.

You should know I am not in active politics out here. But from my academic position I have been called upon a lot for advice and for political copy. In Texas I have advocated and stood for the so-called radical legislation of the last administration, especially that concerning insurance and bank guaranty. The prohibition question at present before us seems to me, immediately at least, neither economic nor political, so I have taken no part in it one way or the other. This winter I have been devoting my entire attention to Arizona and her constitution. Under separate cover I am sending you a series of stories I have written on the subject for the press. The issue in this country, or so it seems to me, between oligarchy and democracy is narrowing itself to the pros and cons of the initiative, referendum and recall. In Arizona now this issue is drawn.[3] It soon will be in Texas, judging from the Governor's[4] assurance of vetoeing these features in the Texarkana charter now before the House. It is too early, perhaps, to say whether these issues will be up in national politics in 1912. I do believe, however, that the progressive Democrats and Republicans at Washington will support the Arizona constitution. If you find it in your way and can conscienciously do so, I wish you would say a good word for this democratic document.

With appreciation of your splendid political conduct in my native State and best wishes for your continued success, I am,

Very sincerely,   Lindley M. Keasbey

TCL (T. B. Love Papers, Dallas Hist. Soc.).

[1] Professor of Political Science at the University of Texas since 1905.

[2] That is, the administration of Thomas Mitchell Campbell, Governor of Texas, 1907-11.

[3] See G. W. P. Hunt to WW, Jan. 2, 1911, n. 2.

[4] Oscar Branch Colquitt, elected in 1910 to his first of two two-year terms.

From Josiah Cleveland Cady

My dear Gov. Wilson: New York, February 11, 1911.

Dr. Frost can more suitably thank you for your address at Carnegie Hall last night, but as one of the audience,—one having no personal ends to seek,—you may be interested to know my impressions.

I should mention clarity as a striking feature of your talk;—clarity of voice, of thought, and impression.

Both Seth Low and Dr. Frost are experienced public speakers, and Dr. Frost one that especially carries his audience,—but neither was heard as clearly or distinctly as you—the difference was marked. My family tell me that not only no word of yours was lost, but there was great ease and comfort in listening to you.

In regard to the second item,—the way the audience closely followed you, although you spoke seriously, without attempt to amuse them, showed how they grasped and were held by your thought.

As to the expression of it,—Dr. Frost who is an unusually scholarly man, often nudged me, saying "that's a classic" or "admirably put."

Those of us who rejoice that a man of high principal is at the head of the government of an important state, are greatly heartened that he is so unusually equipped for impressing his ideas and policies upon the people.

Very sincerely yours, J. Cleveland Cady

TLS (WP, DLC).

To Mary Allen Hulbert Peck

Dearest Friend, Princeton, N. J. 12 February, 1911.

I do not feel that my letters pay you back in anything like equal coin for the letters I enjoy so much, and look forward to so eagerly, as the steamers come. I have to write so hurriedly and when I am so tired that there is no ginger in me, no vivacity, no invention,—nothing but dullness and more than a touch of weariness of the things that are, after all, all there is to tell you of, —for they fill my days. I am not really as dull as I seem! And when I am at them the things I deal with day by day do not pall upon me at all. I take them, on the contrary, with zest and unflagging interest. But somehow they do not seem to lend themselves to an interesting narrative, in a letter intended to please and entertain a dear friend to whom I owe every pleasure I can give in return for the pleasure she has given me. One always likes to talk his best to one whose gift for delightful talk is one of the things that qualify her for being the best companion in the world. By the way, the other evening after a banquet with The Kentuckians in New York at which ladies were present a very charming young person whose name I did not catch spoke of you in glowing terms. "I think I met a dear friend of yours in Bermuda a couple of years ago," she said. "Mrs. Peck?" I asked. And then we both went into rhapsodies about you; and I liked her all the better for it. She at once seemed to me both interesting and charming. But it was a handshaking "reception" and she drifted out of range in a moment. I did stunts that night! I had absent-mindedly (to put it kindly) made two promises to speak for the same evening. I had promised to speak at a meeting in behalf of Berea College at Carnegie Hall (Berea College is in Kentucky and is for the poor whites of the Southern mountains, —an enterprise that has my deep sympathy and whose chief man, Dr. Frost, the president, is of the salt of the earth, a man who thinks always of his duty and never of himself) and I had also promised to attend the banquet of the Kentuckians; so I had to do both. It was like campaigning again, hurrying from audience to audience in an automobile, in charge of anxious committees. But it lacked the excitement of campaigning and rather took it out of me. Mrs. Wilson and Margaret went with me to the dinner, and Margaret had a bully time dancing into the small hours of the morning with the sporting Kentuckians after the dinner *and* reception were over, while we sedate elders went discreetly to bed. We were lodging for the occasion in the Plaza Hotel, where the dinner and dance were held. I hurried home the next day (yesterday) to attend the presentation, in Old North,[1] in the Faculty Room, of a portrait of Dr. Shields,[2] a former teacher and colleague of mine whose daughter[3] is a friend of ours. I wish I could describe the scene to you! I rushed up from the train to find a most interesting audience made up almost entirely of the people who fought me while I was President here and who were rejoiced to get rid of me, and all banked on one side of the room, the side opposite the portrait. There was no place for me to sit but upon the empty seats opposite, where I faced the crowd in dignified isolation, sitting almost under my own portrait. To complete the picture, to complete the situation, Dr. Patton, the other

[1] That is, Nassau Hall.
[2] The Rev. Dr. Charles Woodruff Shields, Princeton 1844, Professor of the Harmony of Science and Revealed Religion, 1866-1903, who had died in 1904.
[3] Helen Hamilton Shields (Mrs. Bayard) Stockton.

rejected president, presently came and sat near me. No one joined us but old Chancellor Magie[4] and lovely Mrs. Marquand,[5] both of whom came in even later than I did. There I sat and heard discourses from men whom for one reason or another I despise. The portrait was accapted [accepted], for the University (why, in Heaven's name, I cannot guess, except that his faction is now in the saddle) by Hibben. He played the part *I* would have played, had I not been,—Governor of New Jersey! Why will that wound not heal over in my stubborn heart? Why is it that I was blind and stupid enough to love the people who proved false to me, and cannot *love*, can only gratefully admire and cleave to, those who are my real friends by the final, only conclusive proof of conduct and actual loyalty, when loyalty cost and meant something? Such scenes as that of the other day affect me very deeply. My best course, the course I instinctively follow most of the time, is to think always of my new job, never of my old, and to relieve my heart by devoting all its energies to the duties which do not concern friends but that great mass of men to whose service one can devote himself without thought of the rewards of personal affection or friendship. Perhaps it is better to love men in the mass than to love them individually! We are in the midst of the serious work of the legislative session now, and my whole thought is of "bills," and the means of getting them through without mishap or mutilation. It is an absorbing, and on the whole fascinating, occupation.

It makes me sad when your letters reveal you tired and discouraged and a bit weary of the empty round of this that and the other that makes no real difference and sets forward nothing in particular; but, on the whole, I think that your letters show your *tone* all the while improving,—show you more soothed, more secure and happy in your sense of freedom, more conscious of your own real soul and taste and alliance with what you find in the wind and the sea, in books and in old, true friends, in your own heart, in the nature that suffering for a little while crusted over; and that makes me very happy. As the days go on I know that you will more and more *find* yourself. Your mind and heart will more and more demand sat[is]faction of you in the things that are permanent. And then you will do something like what I once made you promise to do: you will give yourself some definite object and occupation,—will probably write a sort of autobiography in which you will release your heart; and then more and more enrich the subject matter of what you write

[4] William Jay Magie.
[5] Eleanor Cross (Mrs. Allan) Marquand.

by doing things for the people who need you and who are to be found everywhere. See if my prediction does not come true. I know the friend I have found, perhaps better than she knows herself.

Good night. I wish my letters to you were like my thoughts of you! All unite in affectionate messages.

Your devoted friend,   Woodrow Wilson

WWTLS (WP, DLC).

A Statement on a Proposed Increase in Postal Rates

[[Feb. 12, 1911]]

It must be that those who are proposing this change of rate do not comprehend the effect it would have. A tax upon the business of the more widely circulated magazines would be a tax upon their means of living and performing their functions.[1]

They obtain their circulation by their direct appeal to the popular thought. Their circulation attracts advertisers. Their advertisements enable them to pay their writers and enlarge their enterprise and influence.

This proposed new postal rate would be a direct tax and a very serious one, upon the formation and expression of popular opinion—its more deliberate formation and expression, just at a time when opinion is concerning itself actively and effectively with the deepest problems of our politics and our social life.

To make such a change now, whatever its intentions in the minds of those who proposed it, would be to attack and embarrass the processes of opinion. Surely sober second thought will prevent any such mischievous blunder.

Printed in the Trenton *True American*, Feb. 13, 1911.

[1] Wilson's statement was evoked by a controversy over President Taft's proposal to increase the postal rates on magazines. As early as 1901, President Roosevelt had pointed out to Congress that newspapers and magazines constituted three fifths of the weight of the mail but paid only a fraction of the cost of the postal service. As the Post Office Department continued to run deficits, Congress appointed a series of commissions after 1905 to study the problem; the most significant report was completed in 1909. Taft inherited a postal deficit of $17,500,000 in 1909, as well as an imminent deficit in the national budget. In his Annual Message of 1909, the President attributed the postal deficit to the cost of carrying second class mail but called for an increase in rates only on magazines.

Taft's proposal was cumbersome, for it stipulated a rate of one cent a pound for that portion of a magazine devoted to educational materials and four cents a pound on advertising materials. In addition, the need for higher rates was considerably dampened by a lower postal deficit in 1910—only $6,000,000 —and a surplus of $219,000 in 1911. Taft's position was also weakened by his singling out magazines as objects of the rate increase. Magazine publishers, along with his political opponents, accused the President of a political vendetta in response to hostile muckraking articles, especially the series in *Col-*

lier's in 1909 on the Ballinger-Pinchot controversy (about which see n. 3 to the address printed at Nov. 4, 1910, Vol. 21). Taft privately admitted that he was angry with some of the muckraking magazines operating with public subsidy at his political expense.

The President's rate legislation languished in the Sixty-first Congress, and intensive lobbying by publishers defeated its passage in the closing days of the session during late February and early March 1911. However, Taft managed to secure the appointment of another postal commission. Its final report in 1912 recommended a rate increase on both newspapers and magazines, but by this time the President was chastened by his conflict with the publishers and took no action. He later realized that he had made a serious political blunder by indirectly attacking the periodical press; by 1912 the issue had combined with many others to undermine his relations with insurgents in his own party and other progressives. See Donald F. Anderson, *William Howard Taft: A Conservative's Conception of the Presidency* (Ithaca, N. Y., and London, 1973), pp. 146-47, 209-11, and Wayne E. Fuller, *The American Mail: Enlarger of the Common Life* (Chicago and London, 1972), pp. 141-47.

From Sherman Montrose Craiger[1]

My dear Governor Wilson: Albany, N. Y., Feb. 14, 1911.

Your letter of the 8th instant was duly received and is highly appreciated. Among other things I note that you say:

"You are quite right in assuming that the purposes of the proposed National Independent Democratic League have my heartiest sympathy and I should like [it] very much if I were free to lend my active aid to the Association, but the fact of the matter is that I have all my life long refrained from connecting myself with anything to which I could not lend myself with energy and to which I could not give the attention which its importance required. I am in conscience bound to decline, therefore, the very high compliment you have suggested of making me the honorary president of the League."

You add:

"I cannot help hoping and believing that the Democratic party itself is becoming a very effectual independent league to which men of progressive opinions will more and more attach themselves, and the work of your League will I think be sure to assist in its progress."

While it is a great disappointment, of course, that such a movement could not enjoy the benefit of your leadership,[2] everyone seems to feel pleased that in the larger sense the people regardless of party are to profit by your inspiring example as leader of your party in your locality. "Governor Wilson," a distinguished lawyer said to me recently, is "the best exponent of true Democracy and the most effective flagellator of false Democracy that these later years have developed." There is a growing number of New Yorkers who are delighted to be known as the "Wilson-brand" of Democrats.

Among them there is an intense desire to help rid politics of the so-called "machine" or "corporate" control. The sentiment of prominent men here is well summed up in the following expression of opinion by a leader of the New York bar. He said:

"I should be glad to do what I can to aid in putting the Democratic party in a position to retain the support of that great body of independent voters who have heretofore supported it when its principles and methods have been such as to commend it to their intellect and conscience."

The problem to be wrestled with is to bring about a condition so that the policies of the party and its leading candidates for public office shall be heartily in accord with true Democratic principles, and will successfully fight for their success. The party organization must be held entirely independent of the so-called "bosses." If this savors of that "audacity in politics" to which you so admirably have referred, it is certain to become fashionable in New York!

An evening paper points out that Democrats are becoming restive. This does not mean a split but that the fight will be waged until the "special interests" are driven out of the party. They have no logical standing in our ranks, and should feel more at home in our opponent's fold, especially when Lincoln Day dinners brings men like Theodore Roosevelt, William Barnes and Timothy Woodruff into sweet concord! Is there any contradiction in a man like William F. Sheehan enrolling himself with the party whose senators and assemblymen carry out the orders of the Republican "bosses" by voting solidly for Chauncey M. Depew?

I believe the day will come when the Democratic party will hold out no hope of reward to men of Mr. Sheehan's type and their friends. No doubt he and Mr. [Thomas Fortune] Ryan both have a right to participate in the political affairs of the country. But I submit that there is nothing democratic in the latter suggesting that Mr. Sheehan would make a good governor, and then acquiescing in his stand for the senatorship. Nor do I think that Mr. Sheehan's services in collecting six hundred thousand dollars, as reported, for the expenses of political organization work, constitute him as the ideal candidate of a party whose past greatness has nothing in common with such activities. The place of the commercial politician is among the Republicans, not in the Democratic organization.

Believe me, with the greatest respect,

Very cordially and sincerely yours,

Sherman Montrose Craiger

TLS (WP, DLC).

¹ Colonel in the United States Army Reserve and an investment counselor in New York, at this time involved in the fight against the election of William F. Sheehan to the United States Senate.

² Insofar as the Editors know, the National Independent Democratic League never materialized.

From Maitland Dwight

Dear Dr. Wilson: Princeton, N. J., Feb. 14th. 1911.

At a meeting of the class of 1911 held a short while ago it was unanimously decided that you should be asked to take some part in the Commencement Exercises this year. I believe that Dean Fine has already spoken to you of this desire, and it is only my purpose to let you know that every one in the class hopes very much that you will be able to do this.

It seems to me that some time on Class Day, probably in the morning, would be the best time, if that were convenient for you, but of course that can be decided later.

Hoping very much that you will be able to do this,¹

Very sincerely   Maitland Dwight

TLS (WP, DLC).

¹ Wilson did not participate in the commencement exercises in 1911. However, Dwight, president of the Class of 1911, took the diplomas to Trenton, where Wilson signed them. *Princeton Alumni Weekly*, XI (June 14, 1911), 580.

A Statement on the Geran Election Reform Bill

[Feb. 15, 1911]

As legislation begins to take shape I recall two of the most important promises I made to the people of the State during the recent campaign. I promised in the first place that during the legislative session I would speak to them very freely and frankly about the more important bills pending in the Legislature, and I promised that I would do everything in my power to promote such legislation as was likely to put the government of the State into their hands.

In speaking of the bill which has been introduced into the House by Mr. Geran, of Monmouth, I can fulfil both promises at once. That bill embodies an attempt to redeem, with the utmost frankness, the most important pledge of the campaign.

The main issue of that campaign, if I understand it, was whether the business of the people should be privately managed by groups of politicians, or publicly managed entirely in the open and in a way to give the people themselves the freest possible access to everything that was done or proposed.

The evils of our politics have existed largely because public affairs could be controlled by private understandings arrived at in ways which the people could not comprehend; and the basis of all this private management has been the choice of candidates for office and of those who were to conduct the affairs of the parties in such a way that the people felt themselves unable to take part with effectiveness and intelligence.

The Geran bill is intended to clear all obstacles away and to put the whole management, alike of parties and of elections, in the hands of the voters themselves. Every part is essential to the frank and candid carrying out of the most sacred promises of the campaign. Its purpose is to make the government in every part the people's government.

It is not an experimental bill; it is based upon abundant experience elsewhere by our fellow-countrymen and cannot fail when adopted in its integrity to accomplish the purpose it seeks.

What it does is: First, to purify the processes of election and of the choice of candidates by vastly improving the method of selecting election officers; and, second, to put all selections, whether of those who are to serve the State, or of those who are to serve the parties as managers and directors, immediately into the hands of the people themselves, without the intervention of unnecessary machinery.

It extends the primaries, not only to the selection of Congressmen and Governor, but also to the choice of the men who are to direct the committees of the parties, and to the selection of the delegates who are to represent New Jersey in the conventions which make choice of Presidential candidates.

It goes beyond that and affords the people the right to express their preference with regard to candidates who shall be considered for the Presidential nominations. Some of the provisions of the bill have already passed the Senate upon the initiative of Senator Nichols.[1]

The present Legislature is one of the freest legislatures the State has ever seen. Its members are actuated by a sincere desire to serve the best interests of the State and of its politics, and to carry out in the fullest and frankest manner the expectations of the people. I think that the whole Legislature rejoices in its consciousness that it is free to do these things.

Opposition to this bill, which puts the government in the hands of the people, will not come from the Legislature. It will come from outside the Legislature, and will admirably serve to distinguish the friends of the people from the friends of private management.

It will be thoroughly worth while to observe the persons who interest themselves to oppose it. Their names will make an excellent list, easily accessible, of those who either fear to establish the direct rule of the people or who have some private and selfish purpose to serve in seeing that the more concealed and secret methods of politics are not taken away from them and made impossible.

It is, in one sense, the main bill of the session. It will afford an excellent test as to whether the recent campaign meant what it seemed to mean or not.

Public opinion has now an opportunity to assert itself in triumphant fashion against those who would seek to deter the Legislature from this wholesome and admirable legislation upon which the future of free administration in the State will directly depend. Its passage will mean that we shall regularly and always have free legislatures, and not depend upon exceptional circumstances to give them to us.

The bill is now in the hands of the Judiciary Committee of the House. There is every reason to believe that it will be perfected in its details by that committee, and that it will be promptly reported out to the House itself.

No doubt there are details of the bill which need reconsideration, but all its essential features are sound, and it is to be hoped and expected that it will come from the committee without any alteration, except changes of detail.

If I may speak for myself, I would say that I am deeply and earnestly interested in the measure; that I regard it as essential to the political purification and advancement of the State, and that I shall be very glad, from time to time, to discuss this and other legislation in public as time and opportunity may allow.

I shall take the liberty from time to time to speak of other bills hardly less essential to the reasonable programme of reform to which the present Legislature is pledged than this bill concerning the primaries and elections.[2]

Printed in the *Newark Evening News*, Feb. 15, 1911, with an addition (the final paragraph) from the text in the New York *Evening Post*, Feb. 15, 1911.
[1] Isaac T. Nichols, Republican of Bridgeton, Cumberland County, author and journalist.
[2] The progress and final provisions of the Geran bill, as well as of all other important legislation of the session of 1911, will be recounted in subsequent documents and notes.

To Lindley Miller Keasbey

My dear Professor Keasbey: [Trenton, N. J.] February 15, 1911.

I am sincerely gratified to know that Mr. Love should be interested in my political fortunes, because I know independently of your letter what and how much Mr. Love stands for and he is just the kind of man I should wish to have believe in me.

You may be sure that I am heart and soul for all the measures which will put the people again in control of their government and enable us to conduct politics in the open instead of by private and secret management. I believe that the crisis in our affairs is a very serious one, not that I think there is any element of hopelessness in it. On the contrary, I believe that by a combination of patriotic men our affairs can be brought to a very sound and entirely democratic footing again. But this must be done by taking the situation seriously and by standing together for everything that will advance the cause of democracy, that is to say, everything that will square the government with the common interest.

Undoubtedly, though I was somewhat slow to be convinced of it, the Oregon plan of direct legislation is a necessary and efficient plan for accomplishing what we are after. I believe that it will be best used and worked out in our State governments, and there is every evidence that the attention of the country is very much concentrated upon it. It is interesting that more state platforms refer to the initiative and referendum and recall than to primary laws even.

The Arizona situation I have not yet been able to study.

With warm appreciation of your kindness,

Cordially and sincerely yours,   Woodrow Wilson.

TCL (T. B. Love Papers, Dallas Hist. Soc.).

From Walter Hines Page

My dear Wilson: Garden City, N. Y. February 15, 1911.

By all means send Colonel Sprigg or anybody else who will come on this errand to see me, but suggest to them that they make an engagement out here by telephone. I think I can promise them a pleasant hour or two in our new establishment,[1] which seems to interest everybody who comes to see it.

I have some very definite notions about such work as McCorkle and Colonel Sprigg seem to have in mind. They are very simple and very old-fashioned notions, but they are based upon a life-long study of the fickle thing that we call public opinion. I have followed and brooded and toiled over its ebbs and flows so long that I do sometimes believe I have some notions about it.

If you will permit me to say so, I think I know you well enough to have some ideas on the subject from that side also.

It would delight me more than anything else to have a chance to talk with you, and almost any time that you have an hour or two to spare, preferably towards the end of a week, I should be glad to run down to Trenton.

You may trust Hale entirely. Among his other virtues he has a good degree of prudence.

Very heartily yours,   Walter H. Page

TLS (WP, DLC).
    ¹ The offices and physical plant of Doubleday Page & Co.

To Thomas Bell Love

My dear Mr. Love: [Trenton, N. J.] February 16, 1911.

Your letter of February seventh has given me the deepest pleasure and gratification. It encourages me greatly to know that I have your approval in the things I have been trying to do.

I am taking the liberty of sending you a copy of our legislative manual which happens to be the only form in which I have at hand our campaign platform. I shall take pleasure in having sent you, under another cover also, a copy of my inaugural address. I have as yet sent no messages to the Legislature.

I am heartily in favor of the adoption by the Legislature of New Jersey of the income tax amenement [amendment] to the Constitution. I have sent no message to the Legislature on the subject, but I am planning to hold a conference with my colleagues in the Legislature at an early date and hope that I shall be able to pursuade them to vote for the amendment. I find that there is a good deal of honest difference of judgment among them about it. Many of them fearing to practically deprive the State of this source of income by opening it to the Federal government.

You judge me very generously with regard to my political capacity. I feel a genuine modesty about the whole thing but cannot refrain from expressing my gratitude to you that you should feel inclined to commend me to the consideration of the party. I wish very much that business or other opportunity would bring you in this direction so that I might have the advantage of a personal conversation with you.

Cordially and sincerely yours,   Woodrow Wilson

TLS (photostat in the T. B. Love Papers, Dallas Hist. Soc.).

From Francis Fisher Kane

Dear Doctor Wilson: Philadelphia. Feb. 16, 1911.

Thank you for yours of the 13th. I understand your position perfectly with regard to Mr. Bryan's being invited.[1] I thought the matter safe in [Roland S.] Morris's hands. There are times when it is best not to stir things up, and I was content to leave the matter in his hands, he being on the sub-committee on Speakers and Invitations and he being also a true friend of yours and of Mr. Bryan.

Just at present I do not want to see you more drawn to that end of the party. There has been too much talk along that line.

Have you any desire as to the toast to which you will respond? Preachers on such occasions may stray far from their texts. This is generally the practice, but you may have some wish in the matter. If you have, please let me know.

I am sorry to hear that you will probably have to remain in Trenton until late in the afternoon. You will of course in due time let me know your train so that I can meet you at the station, and if you can get away earlier and so give me the chance to gather two or three of your friends together at my house in the afternoon, you will let me know.

Yours faithfully,   Francis Fisher Kane.

ALS (WP, DLC).
[1] To speak to the Democratic Club of Philadelphia on February 21, 1911.

To George Brinton McClellan Harvey

My dear Colonel Harvey: [Trenton, N. J.] February 17, 1911.

Thank you sincerely for your little note enclosing Marse Henry's note[1] and the editorial from the Raleigh News and Observer.[2] It was kind of you to think of me. I am heartily sorry that your ashma is so stubborn and hope sincerely that you get the best of it.   Cordially yours,   Woodrow Wilson

TLS (WP, DLC).
[1] H. Watterson to G. B. M. Harvey, Jan. 29, 1911, ALS (WP, DLC), the main part of which read as follows: "First blood for Wilson! How could it have been otherwise? If he goes on successfully 'cleaning house,' what can you do but hold to your bargain and not repent it? The Martine incident may after all serve a purpose with certain elements needful at the critical moment. Smith is a fool—an old fool—and deserves what he has got. The case was as clear as a chunk of sunshine and he should have seen it. I shall be in London from the 1st to the 12th of May, and shall live in the hope of finding you there."
[2] It is missing.

From Cleveland Hoadley Dodge

Dear Woodrow,   New York Feb'y 17th 1911

I would give all my old books to see you & have a good talk with you before I leave for Arizona next Wednesday but I fear it is not possible as we are both so busy.

I must however drop you a line to cheer you up about Princeton (you don't need any cheer about politics—you have laid the enemy out so bravely—poor Nugent[1]) in view of what [Edwin Grant] Conklin has just told me of his talk with you & your general blueness regarding the situation. I wish I could tell you *all* that has transpired in our "Committee on the Presidency" but I cannot do that. I can say however that we have ransacked the country with a fine comb & have examined with great thoroughness the merits of about fifteen men of great distinction, but all agree that no one of them will do.

The conviction is steadily growing on Momo[2] that any man of strong convictions from the outside who should accept the Presidency, would doubtless be more of a stumbling block in the way of West's plans than a man like Fine, about whom the worst is known and it only needs a slight degree of rapprochement between Fine & West to bring about what we most desire. Cadwalader is solid for Fine, so is Jacobus & Cyrus & myself— not to speak of Mr Stuart.[3] Momo made the awful mistake, as early as last November, of asking Fine to apologize to West. The other day Cadwalader sat all over him for his stupid blunder & I hope made some impression.

In my opinion it only needs a little more time before the inevitable takes place & West & Momo yield. This thing is *sure* however that if we wait two years or longer there will be no other President elected if Fine is not & I trust that our friends the enemy will tire out long before then

What I tell you is of course in *strictest confidence*, but I want you to know how really hopeful the situation is. If I was a betting man, I would give odds that Fine would be chosen within another twelvemonth. Meanwhile he is in the saddle & winning golden opinions, and slowly but surely breaking down & wearing out or winning over those opposed to him.

In a nutshell, it is Fine or nobody, and Mr Stuart is so anxious to have the matter settled that I do not think Momo can hold out much longer. [Luther P.] Eisenhart, Fine tells me, is persona grata to West & I hope he can reconcile them.

So don't despair, old man, but help us all you can

God bless you in your glorious fight & keep you & yours well & happy is the earnest prayer

of your's aff'ly   C. H. Dodge

ALS (WP, DLC).
[1] Nugent had been much in evidence in the State House and about Trenton since the legislature convened. Anti-machine legislators were so irritated by his presence that Wilson called him into his office on February 17 and advised him to return to Newark. See Link, *Wilson: The Road to the White House*, p. 251.
[2] Moses Taylor Pyne.
[3] John Aikman Stewart.

From Clarence Hamilton Poe[1]

My Dear Sir: Off Port Said, Feby. 17, 1911.

I am just on my way home, having been in the Orient since last September; and it may interest you to know that among the Americans I have met abroad—tourists and temporary residents in foreign lands—there is no such enthusiasm for any other possible candidate for the next Democratic Presidential nomination as there is for Governor Woodrow Wilson of New Jersey.

Moreover, some of your staunchest advocates are from Ohio—men who admire the Ohio candidate[2] but yet think you the safer leader.

My letters from North Carolina also indicate a rapid crystallization of sentiment in your favor in the South—as was to have been expected. Your fight to put a clean, able man in the New Jersey Senatorship has helped you everywhere.

I am not a politician—at least not in the office-seeking sense, for I have done more dodging than seeking, no seeking in fact—but I have a paper of 100,000 circulation among the foremost planters and farmers in the South, and I think I shall be able to help along the Wilson boom when I get home next month—partly for your sake but more for the sake of the party and the Nation.   Sincerely yours,   Clarence Poe.

(Editor "The Progressive Farmer." Raleigh, N. C.)
Home by March 10th.

ALS (WP, DLC).
[1] Chief owner and editor of the Raleigh, N. C., *Progressive Farmer*.
[2] Governor Judson Harmon.

To Cleveland Hoadley Dodge

Dear Cleve.,   Princeton, N. J. 18 February, 1911.

Thank you with all my heart for your letter. It was not the specific question of the presidency that was weighing on me like lead, but the perception that, with the ascendency of West and his counsels, a veritable blight has descended on the dear place. I never saw so depressed a set of scholars as now inhabit it.

But I know that you are true to the core and that anything that you can do will be done. I would trust any ideal or any institution in your hands. Do not go out to Arizona with me on your mind. I am a firm believer in the triumph of the right in the long run. God send it may not be too long a run! Bless you! May you have a refreshing trip in the midst of business.

With deep gratitude and affection,

Faithfully Yours,   Woodrow Wilson

WWTLS (WC, NjP).

To Mary Allen Hulbert Peck

Dearest Friend,   Princeton, 19 February, 1911.

The days go quietly by, all sorts of interesting things happening, but only of the sort that do not lend themselves to the genius of a dull letter writer, like your humble servant. They are things of counsel and of incident: things discussed by delegations that come to my office almost every day; amusing vagaries of character and behaviour on the part of those who come seeking office for themselves or for their friends; long conferences on pending bills (on Friday, for instance, when I wanted to be writing a letter to get off on the Saturday steamer, I was in conference on a bill from three in the afternoon till half after ten at night, dinner hardly excepted, since the conferees dined together); interviews with newspaper men; talks with legislators, to keep them in line for necessary legislation; etc., etc. I would bore you to death if I went into details,—if I told you, for example, what the real merits of the question of regulating cold storage seem to be, or explained to you what the clauses are that are most in debate in the elections and primaries bill. And yet, if you were here and could look on and listen, you would find it as absorbing as I do, and as amusing; and, if I had the gift I could put much of it into my letters in the colour it has in life. Speaking of sitting by and looking on, that is just what a very interesting chap has been doing whom the editor of the World's Work sent down to study me. He sat about the office, heard interviews and delegations, saw me sit with commissions of one sort or another, and listened quietly throughout long conferences on bills; went to lunch with me day after day for a half week; talked his fill with my Secretary at such in-between-times as there were; and then went off,—with what impressions I do not know. I only know that he seemed a singularly fine and intelligent fact of a *man*, undoubtedly cultured and able to distinguish this from that, and that he saw me as I really am from day to day, with absolutely no stage setting or variation of the day's work arranged for his benefit. I think you will be amused to hear the terms in which Walter Page, the editor of the World's Work proposed that Mr. Hale (William Bayard Hale was the name of the patient watcher and listener) should come down and observe me. He said that so long as the Evening Post and Harper's Weekly continued to praise me I must remain under a certain cloud, unless others came to the rescue, and that he was sending Hale down because he hoped that something printed in the World's Work would serve to "keep the witches off." All these men are strangely interested in the enterprise of making me President of the United States. I cannot help them in the least. There is something in me that makes it inevitable that I should go on as I have begun, doing things as it seems to me they ought to be down [done], square with my own individual sense and conviction of right, whet[h]er it is expedient or not; and I may, by that token, at any moment spoil all they are generously trying to do! I think every man instinctively likes to play the role of king-maker. I am at present, apparently, suitable material for their favourite sport, and so the game is put on the boards. I do not mean that they are not generously interested in me, personally; but I must, for the working of my own mind, have something in addition to that to explain their enthusiasm. Two newspapers that have been sent me say a rather amusing thing. They say that it is necessary to praise me so often that they mean, for fear of making the thing trite and tiring their readers, to bunch it all in one article a week! It is amazing that so little performance of one's mere duty should raise such a smoke! I do not see what else I could have down [done] than what I have done.

Full as my weeks are, the most interesting event in them is the arrival of your letters. They have first of all the wonderful charm of your own person, your own mind and fancy and sweet friendship, and, besides that, the charm of seeming to come out of a past life of my own,—the life in which vacations in Bermuda and the leisurely pursuit of dear friendships were possible,—the life in which my character seems to have been formed, amidst the influences that were of my own choice and deliberate preferring, and in which I had the sort of freedom now denied me, the freedom to stop and reflect and to choose and enjoy,—with a *conscious* enjoyment. Such reminders are like thrills from the *sources* of one's life. *Now* there is time to think deliberately of nothing. I do not see how a young man, thrown into such a steaming caldron, can get or keep his bearings at all. What established judgments, what fixed points of experience, what tested tastes and instincts has he to steer by? Where are the old lessons of friendship, and the old lessons of reasonable distrust and caution, and the firmly rooted confidence in cert[a]in principles of choice and action that serve to guide and steady a man of fifty, who is seasoned to life and to dealing with men? The older man has done his thinking and established his landmarks and ascertained his ground, and need not be confused by the whirl of the day's breathless business. He goes to bed at night tired out, and without having had so much as a sweet quarter of an hour to think deliberately or consciously of his friends and of all the things that tie him to his faith and his happiness; but is he conscious of them as of course: they are part of his fibre—they are with him all the time: he does not *have* to recall them or to summon them. What a thrill, then, is there in the letter that comes as if it were a dear, authentic voice out of these central, permanent influences of his heart and mind! How it heartens him and clears away his slight confusions and chases away his fatigues and renews him at the very core of all that makes a man of him, and worth the trust and confidence of his fellow men!

I am perfectly well, and get all too few letters,—from you! All join me in affectionate messages, and I am, as I think you will see,   Your devoted friend,   Woodrow Wilson

WWTLS (WP, DLC).

To William Goodell Frost

My dear Professor Frost: [Trenton, N. J.] February 20, 1911.

I am deeply grateful to you for your letter.[1] It affords me the greatest pleasure to know that I was of some sergice [service] and certainly am gratified for the cordial terms in which you speak of it.

Do take care of yourself. It will not do for you to risk anything and I hope sincerely that the grippe will release its hold
upon you quickly in the South.

With warmest regard,

Cordially and faithfully yours, Woodrow Wilson

TLS (W. G. Frost Papers, KyBB).
[1] It is missing.

An Address to the Democratic Club of Philadelphia[1]

[[Feb. 21, 1911]]

MR. TOASTMASTER[2] AND FELLOW DEMOCRATS: I was interested
to see in looking at the list of speakers[3] that my subject was to
be announced. The Toastmaster has not announced it, for he
has spoken of nothing but myself, and certainly that is not my
theme. There is one thing that I am not, I am not a Wilson man.
I was interested in the latent contrast drawn by Mr. Norris between Senator Gore and myself. He said that you were to hear
the scholarly oratory of the Governor of New Jersey, and the,
perhaps, radical doctrine of the Senator from Oklahoma, thereby proclaiming himself of the number of those whom I regard
as doubly heretical in believing that scholarship is of necessity
retrogressive, and the scholar cannot be a radical. The one
thing that scholarship cannot do, if it be true scholarship, is to
stand still. The one thing that scholarship reveals to men is the
inevitable progression of affairs. No man can see, in the least,
beneath the surface, who does not see that men must press forward from stage to stage in an unending struggle for things
which they have not yet obtained; that in the intellectual sphere,
as in the social sphere, there is a constant, hopeful pursuit of
the ideals that lie just beyond the touch. I do not see myself how
a scholar can be a conservative.

Moreover, I have been a scholar (if I be a scholar—we could
put that to the jury), if I be a scholar, I have been a scholar constantly enjoying the advantage of being associated with very
young men. I am sorry to see how many men present share with
me the disadvantage of being no longer young; so let me tell
you that the immediate future is to be made by the young men

[1] Delivered in the Bellevue-Stratford Hotel.
[2] Francis Fisher Kane, president of the Democratic Club of Philadelphia.
[3] George Wilkins Guthrie, former Mayor of Pittsburgh, a leader of progressive
Pennsylvania Democrats at this time seeking to revitalize and reorganize their
party; Senator Thomas Pryor Gore of Oklahoma; Representative Alexander
Mitchell Palmer of Pennsylvania; George Washington Norris, a Philadelphia
banker active in Democratic politics; and, of course, Wilson.

of this country and not by ourselves, for we have, most of us, inveterate prepossessions which are a clog on progress. There was something said recently by a very witty Englishman, which seemed very cynical, but which, I am afraid, is painfully true. He said: "It is not true to say of a man who has attained a distinguished position in his profession or undertaking, that you cannot bribe a man like that, because the truth is, he has been bribed. The existing order of things has made him, and he dare not touch the existing order of things for fear it should wreck him; the existing order has put him under bonds not to change it. He has been bribed."[4]

Now it is time that notice should be served upon all these gentlemen that the existing order of things is going to be changed. The warning is only fair because it is only equitable that they should have time to make their preparations. I have known for a long time that it had to change because I have, of necessity, been associated with generation after generation of the young men who are going to change it, and who were, year by year, serving notice on me that they were changing it.

I do not suppose that you realize how college life has changed within a generation. College boys used to be taken care of, and college faculties used to be in the position which the Republican Party constantly desires to occupy. They used to be *in loco parentis*. The rule is discontinued both for college faculties and for the Republican Party. It is no longer possible for them to act *in loco parentis*, for the family has grown up and has taken charge of its own affairs.

What is radicalism? I very much suspect that if the Senator from Oklahoma and I were to hold a private conference we should not have very much difficulty in coming together on the same platform. An interesting circumstance about the radicalism of our time is that it purposes a restoration. Do not deceive yourselves, gentlemen, by the literary theory of American institutions. If you contrast what is called the radical programme, let us say the programme which has been so successfully and admirably carried out in the State of Oregon with the literary theory of our institutions, you see a very radical contrast. The literary theory of our Constitution is that we are living under a representative government. The fact of our institutions is that we are not living under a representative government, and those who seek to bring the people—the will, the opinion, the purpose

<hr>

4 Wilson was paraphrasing a passage in Gilbert K. Chesterton, *Orthodoxy* (New York and London, 1908), p. 219.

of the people, directly to bear upon affairs, are trying not to destroy, but to restore representative government.

It is very interesting to see how an audience like this responds and thrills at those old words, consecrated throughout many generations, whose music we have heard repeated by Mr. Guthrie, those old formulas of liberty that have rung in this country from generation to generation on the lips of public orators. I believe, and hope, that my own pulse leaps to respond to them as yours does, but what I am interested in is the translation of liberty into experience, and my blood would leap much more quickly to the details by which we were to get it, than to the general statement of what it is we want to get. For our task at present is not to bring about, or, rather, I would say, it is not to determine what specific readjustment and reforms we want, but it is to determine how we are going to get them. We know what we want and both parties promise what we want, but we have not yet got it. I am practical enough to be interested in the *modus vivendi*. It is all very well to say what we want. We want liberty. Of course, we want liberty, but what is liberty?

I see gentlemen sitting here who have been obliged, at certain specified hours of the day, to come and hear me speak, and they will recognize the illustration that I am about to use. Liberty consists, if I understand it, in the best adjustment possible in society. Liberty does not consist of having your way. It does not consist in any class having its way. It does not consist in serving any particular interest, though it be the greatest interest in the country. It consists in the reasonable and most equitable adjustment of all the interests of the country with each other. When you say of a piece of splendid, powerful machinery, that it runs free, do you mean that one part is prevailing over the other parts? On the contrary, you mean that there is such a perfect adjustment between the parts that friction is reduced to a minimum, and that it is the exquisite accommodation of the parts to each other that constitutes the freedom. If you say that a boat sails free, what do you mean? Do you mean that she is resisting the forces of nature and beating about to have her own way? No, you mean that she has yielded to the movement of the wind, is obedient to nature, has adjusted herself to the great force which is abroad in the heavens, and that her adjustment is her freedom, for she is harnessing the free forces of nature that she may have her pleasure in the run. Your best skipper is the man who knows the best adjustment. The best sport in modern yachting consists in races between boats of identical models and identical rigging, to see which skipper can get the most out of the wind. It means which skipper can make the most perfect adjustment to the force which he is using. That is liberty, the perfect adjustment of the parts to each other. That is what we are seeking.

There are different ways of getting it. I have a certain respect for the Republican Party. A party which has, through a long series of years, accomplished an extraordinary sequence of successes, is deserving of respect; and a party which, through a portion of that long period, has kept up a successful bluff is worthy of some respect. To maintain the appearance of service after you have given up the reality, at any rate shows some histrionic gift. But the theory of the Republican Party, as the Republican Party has been guided in recent years, at any rate, is an impossible theory by which to obtain the right adjustment of society. The theory of the Democratic Party is that you are to serve the general interest by bringing the will and purpose of the whole people to bear upon affairs. In other words, you are to bring the whole free force of Democracy to bear in order to gauge your force and to adjust your institutions to that force; whereas, the theory of the Republican Party has been that you must put the power of the people into commission, that you must entrust it to those persons in the community who have the largest stake in the community, and who, because they have the largest stake in the community, may be supposed to understand the interests of the community best. In other words, it is the intervention of a steering committee between the power that is to be used and the instrumentality through which the power it is to be used.

The Republican Party ought not to be too severely blamed. The Republican Party started out upon a very handsome mission; namely, to substitute free for unfree labor. It started out to serve one of the fundamental principles of liberty; but, in order to do so, it had to fight and carry to an end a very expensive war. In order to pay for the war it had to enter into certain partnerships with capital. Do not let us put the terms of our history wholly in parlor language. Let us face the facts as they are. One of the greatest statesmen that this country has ever had, though a statesman with whose fundamental tenets of government we must most of us dissent, namely, Alexander Hamilton, started out with the idea that if this government was to be stable it had best have a public debt which might be held by the most substantial men in the country, so that the most substantial men in the country would have a stake in the stability of the government. A very respectable theory as a working basis for starting a new experiment. He said: "Do not depend on the volatile material which makes changes, because you are starting a new government, but depend upon the conservative citizens whose fortunes are staked upon stability and then the government will be an investment." The Republican Party, having to pay for a very expensive war, had to see to it that the government and the success of the Republican Party became an investment for somebody, and in order to make it a permanent investment for somebody, they had to make it worth the while of large bodies of moneyed men to stand by the Republican Party. I do not need to tell you by what means they did so. It was a very expensive partnership for the Republican Party, because they had to keep raising the ante. They had to keep increasing the productivity of the investment in order to keep the investors satisfied; and therefore the amazing progression of the use we have made of the doctrine of protection has been an absolute necessity on the part of the Republican Party if they were going to keep up the partnership.

I remember hearing a very ingenious speaker from Kentucky use a very interesting illustration. He was talking about a famous four hundred thousand dollar campaign fund that was once raised. In those days four hundred thousand dollars seemed an enormous campaign fund, but the partnership has had bigger operations since. This speaker was insisting that of course the men who subscribed the four hundred thousand dollars expected to get something for their money. He said: "I do not mean to suggest direct and gross forms of corruption, or any corruption at all, necessarily, in the ordinary sense of that term. I can illustrate what I mean by this. Down where I live in Kentucky a prudent housewife, before she goes to bed, for fear the pump should not suck in the morning, pumps a bucket of water and leaves it to stand there, so that if the plunger is dry in the morning she may pour in some of that water to expand it and make it suck again. Now of course, when she has to do that, and pumps, the first water that comes out is that same water that she poured in. All I mean to suggest, therefore, is that the four hundred thousand dollars was water poured in to make the pump suck." It has been a very dry pump. A great deal of water has had to be used to keep it going; and that has been the process of government in recent years, a process, I have no doubt, maintained in many instances with perfectly pure motives. I am not impugning the honesty or the integrity or the patriotism of many of the distinguished men who have been connected with the Republican Party. Still less am I questioning for a single moment the great body of my fellow citizens who have voted the Republican Ticket. That is not the point. The point is that we are now beginning to perceive that the whole partnership was based upon a vicious principle, a very dangerous principle, and that in order to get a new adjustment we must bring all the parts of the social machine into the rearrangement, and must see to it that henceforth there is no particular partnership between government and selected interests of any kind.

How are we going to do it? You know that in order to maintain this partnership a very interesting body of machinery has grown up, machinery which had a most plausible appearance of being necessary, and which grew from stage to stage almost unobserved until we found that instead of using it, it was using us; the machinery by which we thought we were holding opinion together, and then found that we were only holding offices together—the machinery of nomination, the machinery of arrangement. It is an unpleasant matter to talk about, but it is an open secret. You know that the members of state legislatures have again and again found themselves obliged, with regard to all the important measures of the session, to take their orders from persons who were never elected to anything, but who constituted the nominating machinery by which the representatives obtained their positions, and hoped to retain them. The men who constituted this nominating machinery received their orders, in turn, from the interests which were involved, because the organization which had selected them had received the money for its operations from the interests whose orders were carried out in the legislature, either by stopping this bill or by promoting that. It has been suggested in certain quarters that gentlemen who live secluded in universities never heard of these things. It has been supposed that the men whose business it was to understand them did not understand them. I remember traveling in a train once with a young gentleman who was a member of the legislature of a neighboring state, which was then contemplating doing what it took it a long time to do, namely, setting up a railway commission which was expected to have powers of regulation, and I said: "How do you mean to constitute the commission?" He said, "Oh, we expect to leave that to the people." I said: "Do you mean have them elected?" He said: "Yes." I said: "Is that leaving it to the people?" "Why, yes," he said. I said: "Now let us get down to business. Were you selected by the people? I know who is the boss in your county. Stripped of all verbiage, is it not true that he picked you out to go to the legislature?" He said: "Yes, if you put it that way, that is so." I said: "Then is not your choice between having these commissioners chosen by certain bosses privately or chosen by the governor publicly?" He said: "Well, Professor, I see you understand politics." I said: "I would be ashamed of myself if I did not, because I try to teach it." We all know, without the least degree of discouragement, for I am not discouraged even if you are, and without the least touch of cynicism, that this has been the fact, and that in order to have the people brought into the game again, we have got to sweep something away and sweep it clean. Not organization, for organization is necessary, but that organization which does not derive its authority and inspiration from the people.

We have a primaries and election bill pending in New Jersey. It will not, I hope, pend long. It is no cheese-paring measure. It is no timid measure. It is no measure which says: "We will try a little of it." It is a measure which says: "We will try all of it. We will put this whole thing in the hands of the people, including the selection of their party committeemen and their party machinery at the primaries," and the proof that the thing will do it, is the persons who are opposing it.[5] There were certain persons in recent weeks in New Jersey who opposed the will of the people with regard to the choice of a Senator. These same people are now lining up to oppose this bill, and they have certain confederates and assistants who were not at their side in the recent controversy, certain other persons who did not care to defeat the will of the people in respect of the senatorship, largely because they did not care for that particular senator, but who do know that anything that they wish to do without the consent of the people will be made impossible if this measure should pass. It is going to be perfectly possible to make a list of those persons. It is going to be very pleasurably possible to publish a list of those persons if they wish to have their names published. I hope it will not come to that, not for my sake, but for theirs. I hope it, because I believe that their opposition is largely based upon what most opposition to measures of this kind is based upon, namely, plain ignorance.

There is another bill pending in New Jersey which illustrates the same thing, if I may put it in parenthetically. There is what we call a public utilities bill pending, in which New Jersey, very much belated, is trying to do what so many other states have

---

[5] About the opposition to the Geran bill, led by James R. Nugent and the Essex County Democratic organization, see Link, *Wilson: The Road to the White House*, pp. 250-256.

been very successful in, viz., set up a commission which will have a rate-regulating power and a power which goes beyond the regulation of rates to the regulation, to a certain extent, of the business, of public service corporations. The opposition to that bill on the part of representatives of public service corporations is largely based upon ignorance of what the effect of similar legislation has been in other states; and yet there are some clear-sighted men who see the point. They see that if the state can regulate and therefore vouch for their business, their securities will have a preference in the market which they could not have in any other way, for if by public scrutiny there is no secrecy and no possibility of manipulation, then the value of their securities is known and not speculative. A man who does not see the point of that does not know business, and a man who does not want his business put upon an unimpeachable footing ought to oppose such measures of legislation. A boss who wants to do legitimate things ought to be keen enough to see that he gets added power by being authorized by the people to do the legitimate things which he pretends he wants to do— not by choosing himself, but by going to the people and getting chosen. If he cannot stand that scrutiny he is not in a position to claim any public authority whatever.

What we are doing, therefore, in such bills, is to break down these barriers, or rather, to use a better figure, is to cut down the jungle in which all sorts of secret forces are lurking, to cut down the jungle in which there is covert secrecy and concealment, for every process which should be open and is, as a matter of fact, private. It is to break down all the private understandings of government and oblige them to be public understandings. There is nothing that illegitimate things wince at like the certainty that they will be known. There is nothing that will so test the integrity and validity of a man's purposes as his willingness or unwillingness to let it be known what he is doing. Therefore, everything that puts the axe to the root of the forest in which secret things lurk, and wait for us, is done in the interest of liberty, done in the interest of that necessary adjustment between the people and their instruments, which is what we seek.

See what a commonplace thing we are doing, therefore. We are simply trying to square the facts of our government with the theory with which we have been deceiving ourselves. We do not mean to live any longer in a fool's paradise. We mean to have the kind of government we supposed we did have. If we cannot get the kind of legislation we want, we will have the initiative and referendum, and where they have been tried, it is found that the people have just as discriminating a knowledge of what is necessary as any recent legislature, at any rate, has exhibited. My conviction is that when once this direct access of the people to the execution of their own purposes is accomplished, the initiative and referendum will not be the ordinary means of legislation. They will be the very salutary gun kept in the closet. The knowledge that if they do not represent, representatives will be dispensed with, will make representatives represent.

In these measures, therefore, we are not dispensing with representative government, but making sure that we are going to have it. What are we fighting for, then, in this so-called radicalism? Radicalism? Yes, because it goes to the root of the matter, but not radicalism in the sense that it is an insensate love of change, not radicalism in the sense that it is love of uprooting things. On the contrary, it is love of solidifying things and making them real instead of a sham. Do you suppose that we want to build stone superstructures upon card-board imitations of stone for foundations? We want to get the root of this whole thing, the radices, the roots, the radicals of it all, where we may hold fast. I like the image of the root rather than the image of the foundation, for the foundation takes nothing from the soil, whereas the root draws its whole sustenance from it, and I know the history of government too well not to know that all its vital forces come from the hidden earth, from the hidden origins, the hidden fountains that lie in the great body of the people. I have not seen in reading history the sources of strength coming from the top and flowing into the root. I have always seen them rising from the root into the branches. I have never read of any man who was really distinguished in the service of his kind, who could not either by direct origin or by the straight derivations of his sympathy, be traced back to the great heart and purpose of the people themselves. The great men of the world have always been the men who spoke for the rest of their fellow-men; have always been the men who gave voice to what otherwise might have been without articulation or utterance; the men who summed up in themselves, in their own energies, in their own hopes, in their own visions, what slumbered in the minds and hearts and aspirations of countless multitudes of men, who, if they had not found the outlet of such representation would have been dumb and powerless.

I tell you, gentlemen, that the so-called radicalism of our time is nothing else than an effort to release the energies of our time. This great people is not bent upon any form of destruction. This great people is not in love with any kind of injustice. This great people is in love with the realization of what is equitable, pure, just, and of good repute, and it is bound by the clogs and impediments of our political machinery. What we are trying to do is to release all its generous forces. They are not forces of envy. They are not forces which would seek to imperil the prosperity of a great country, even though it be merely the material prosperity of that country, but there resides in them what is the heart of all hopeful enterprises. Our forefathers were not uttering mere words when they spoke of the realization of happiness. Many men pile up great fortunes and fail to find happiness at the heart of them. Happiness comes with a pure heart. Happiness comes with unselfish motives. Happiness comes with the consciousness that you have served and sacrificed and done for men what you would have them do for you. It does not come, it never has come, it never can come, from the knowledge that you have trampled men under foot and spoiled human lives in order to attain it. Release the generous energies of our people and you will come upon a time of prosperity when the hearts of men will flower, when men will see that the true happiness of life is not in devising schemes of power, but in realizing in themselves the common aspirations of the race. Just as in great literature there come to expression the great emotions of mankind, so in politics there come to realization the great actions of mankind, so that men are partners with each other in the hopeful enterprises of human perfection and the hopeful enterprises of justice to which all government is consecrated. Let us not be jealous of the radicalism which seeks to derive all our forces from this single root of perfection.[6]

Address by Governor Woodrow Wilson of New Jersey, Delivered at the Dinner of the Democratic Club in Philadelphia, on Tuesday Night, February 21, 1911 (n.p., n.d.).

[6] There is a WWT outline of this address, with the composition date of Feb. 19, 1911, in WP, DLC.

From Louis Irving Reichner

Dear Governor Wilson   [Philadelphia] Feby 22nd 1911

I attended the dinner last night, as a guest of Roland S. Morris, and have already thanked him for the opportunity it gave me of hearing one of the ablest and most satisfying speeches I have ever enjoyed. Naturally I am always glad that I am a Princetonian but somehow you heightened the feeling of exultation in that Princeton claims you too as one of her family. I can't help but feel that you do not belong any more to any strictly party organization but represent the broader view of the whole people. Such a speech as you gave last night had running thro' it such truths and sentiments as appeal to and must be endorsed by all Americans no matter what their party affiliations.

I am only a small unit but I do want to express to you my gratification and pride in hearing such words and hearing them too from a Princeton man.

Yours very truly   L. Irving Reichner

ALS (WP, DLC).

John Wesley Wescott to Joseph Patrick Tumulty

My dear Tumulty: Camden, N. J. February 22, 1911.

I promised to write you about the dinner.[1] It is difficult to use moderation. The truth is that the only thing I stand in awe of in this world is intellectual power directed by great moral purpose. The further truth is that these qualities inspire me with a sense of fear as well as of awe. The result is that I am actually getting afraid of Governor Wilson.

The occasion was great, but the Governor's speech was greater. The audience, an unusually brainy one, rose in mass when he arose; it arose in mass when he sat down. If the highest eloquence is ability to convince permanently, then Governor Wilson has that marvelous gift. The speech will work endlessly in the minds of those who heard it. Perfect in logical method, transcendent in classic finish, omnipotent in simplicity, resistless in practical substance, I pronounce it greater than the immortal efforts of Demosthenes. While Governor Wilson is conscious of his power, he is not conscious of the wide reaching effect of his words. He was the Alps; the rest the vales beneath. The phenomenon is moral energy supplementing the clearest mental insight.

I know that the above is strong eulogy, but it does not, by any means, compass the situation. More than ever am I persuaded that this personalized force has a great destiny. The point is for smaller men to aid it. It is very clear to me that Governor Wilson should not allow to escape any opportunity to appear before an American audience at any place. The country is so vast, its energies so intense and practical, its brains so eager and absorbed that a great mind cannot, as in the small states of Europe, become generally known by a single effort. The country must know this man, not by distant comparison, but by actual presence. I make this suggestion as emphatically as possible.   Sincerely yours,   John W. Wescott.

TCL (WP, DLC).
¹ That is, the dinner of the Democratic Club of Philadelphia.

A News Report of Remarks in Trenton
to the New Jersey Consumers' League¹

[Feb. 25, 1911]

Governor Wilson Pledges Aid To the Consumers' League

The annual meeting of the Consumers' League of New Jersey was held in First Presbyterian Church yesterday afternoon, with an attendance of more than 200, comprising principally women interested in social work. The speakers were Governor Woodrow Wilson, John Spargo, a Socialist, known in America and Europe,² and Mrs. Florence Kell[e]y, of New York,³ a woman who has accomplished much for the cause of the oppressed. . . .

Governor Wilson was given a most enthusiastic greeting when he walked upon the platform, the people rising to greet him. After thanking the organization for the honor of addressing the members, he said he had taken a deep interest in the league and, though he had never taken an active part in the work, he nevertheless looked on with admiration at the work of the members.

Governor Wilson said he was in favor of the adoption of the messenger boy bill,⁴ as it has been termed. He said the bill had his sympathy and support. Continuing, he said: "There are many ways in which we can show real citizenship. Many people imagine that the ballot is the expression of citizenship. Citizenship is not merely an exercise of power. It is taking part in a vital process—that is the true meaning of patriotism. Sentimentality sometimes passes for patriotism. Your members are interested in seeing that your fellow beings are treated properly, that is patriotism and citizenship of the highest type. In helping shop girls and working women, you are seeing to it that principles of mercy and justice are carried out. The reflex upon yourself is the most handsome usury you can get out of it. Character arises out of self."

The Consumers' League may be said to be a society for self improvement. A society like this illustrates the real energy of a nation like ours. It is wholly voluntary. Our country is governed by organized opinion. The only object of going around making political speeches is to find out opinion. You are in a sense a pre-eminent legislature. You do not depend upon theory but get the facts and present them to the lawmaking powers. I sympathize with you, and in some degree understand and am ready to aid you in any way.

Printed in the Trenton *True American*, Feb. 25, 1911; some editorial headings omitted.

[1] Affiliated with the National Consumers' League, about which see Juliet C. Cushing to WW, Dec. 8, 1910, n. 1.

[2] He was at this time perhaps the leading theoretician and strategist of the right wing of the Socialist Party of America. Born in England in 1876, he emigrated to the United States in 1901 and made his home in Bennington, Vt. Child labor was one of his many concerns, expressed in such publications as *The Bitter Cry of the Children* (New York and London, 1906) and *Socialism and the Child Labor Problem* (Girard, Kan., 1906).

[3] Social worker, settlement house worker, and crusader for social welfare legislation. At this time she was a resident of Henry Street Settlement in New York and general secretary of the National Consumers' League. She was also a leading advocate of the amelioration of women's working conditions and the establishment of a federal children's bureau, about which see A. J. McKelway to WW, Dec. 16, 1910, n. 4.

[4] A bill prohibiting the employment between 10 P.M. and 5 A.M. of messenger boys under eighteen and twenty-one, depending upon the size of the city, was pending in the Senate at this time. Wilson signed the measure on May 2, 1911. *Acts of the One Hundred and Thirty-Fifth Legislature of the State of New Jersey . . .* (Paterson, N. J., 1911), Chap. 363, pp. 752-54.

To Mary Allen Hulbert Peck

Dearest Friend,   The Waldorf-Astoria New York. 26 Feb'y, 1911.

How often I am in New York on Sundays! It is just beginning to strike me,—because Sundays are the only days, in this time of extraordinary absorption in my new duties, when I have the blessed opportunity to write to you—and it begins to strike me how seldom I use my own stationery. It is a *blessed* opportunity,—for I do deeply enjoy thinking about you and talking to you. I think about you at all times, but writing intensifies the thinking and puts it into definite words—and it is very delightful to have you to think of,—a true, splendid, generous, loyal, charming friend—whom to think about is to gain every sort of reassurance and refreshment. It reëstablishes the heart.

I came to town yesterday to attend the dinner of a very jolly organization known as The Amen Corner. Four governors—Dix of N. Y., Baldwin of Conn., Foss of Mass., and myself—were present, chiefly to be tested, to see if they could stand being made fun of like Christians and gentlemen. I got off very easily (I will send you what was said if they put it in print),[1] but Dix was *terribly* roasted. It was all the more audacious and trying because what was said was all *true*! He stood it like an angel, I must say. He is a strangely *quiet* man—perhaps lacking in sensibility and therefore in the power to suffer. But nobody, I suspect, really lacks that.

To-day (after breakfasting at 10.30 after a *fine* night's sleep) I went up-town to see Margaret in her cosey little rooms, and took mid-day dinner with her at the odd little Bohemian club at wh. she takes her meals. She is enjoying her life here *immensely*, her music, new friends and old, and operas galore. How I wished there were some one worth seeing at 39 East 27th St.[2] Please take care of the dear lady who used to live there, as you would of a very precious thing. It distresses me deeply and makes me very, very nervous to have it even suggested that she has nervous prostration. Alas! alas! you *must* take care of her. Her letters do not read as if she were anything but her own delightful self.

Everything goes well with me. I am perfectly well, physically, apparently thriving on the work that has fallen to me, and my spirits are good because there is a good chance of all the bills I am most interested in passing—though the Republican Senate may block me yet. Monday nights I sit up with the legislature to all hours—for they sit in the evening,—but most other days I get home to dinner.

This is the season when I have generally gone to Bermuda—and how I long for it now—in spite of the genuine jest I have in the work I am doing! Somehow I have constantly in my mind an image of Salt Kettle ferry and its neighbourhood—and it seems to me a very delectable and romantic place! All cordial messages to Mrs. Allen and your son from

Your devoted friend   Woodrow Wilson

ALS (WP, DLC).

[1] Leading politicians, civic leaders, publishers, financiers, etc. of New York crowded the grand ballroom of the Waldorf-Astoria on this occasion. Wilson did indeed get off easily, as the only mention of his name came when one member rose to place him in nomination for the presidency. Wilson, he said, would get everyone's vote "except Jim Smith's." *New York World,* Feb. 26, 1911; *New York Times,* Feb. 26, 1911; *New York Daily Tribune,* Feb. 26, 1911. Wilson went prepared to speak with a handwritten outline entitled *"The Being and Powers of a Gov'r.,"* with the composition date of Feb. 25, 1911 (WP, DLC); however, none of the governors present spoke.

[2] The address of Mrs. Peck's apartment in New York.

To Oswald Garrison Villard

Personal.

My dear Mr. Villard: [Trenton, N. J.] February 27, 1911.

It is always a pleasure to hear from you[1] and it will give me genuine pleasure to look you up the earliest possible time and have a talk about the important matters you spoke of. They are of course giving my own thought a great deal of concern.

I wish sincerely that I could meet the invitation of the Insurgent's Club, but I really have put as many engagements on my calendar as I dare put upon it and I have no choice but to decline. I should consider it an honor if I could accept.

With warmest regard,

Cordially yours,   Woodrow Wilson

TLS (O. G. Villard Papers, MH).
1 Villard's letter is missing.

A News Report of Remarks to the New Jersey Editorial Association

[Feb. 28, 1911]

GOVERNOR TELLS PLANS TO EDITORS

Public Utilities, Corrupt Practices, Election Reform and Employers' Liabilities His Legislative Measures

The New Jersey Editorial Association had among its guests at its annual dinner yesterday afternoon Governor Wilson, Frederick W. Donnelly[1] and Don C[arlos]. Seitz, manager of the New York World, each of whom made addresses.

Governor Wilson emphasized his position in regard to bills pending in the Legislature and declared himself as non-partisan respecting legislation.

He explained that there are four measures in the Legislature which he is advocating. These embody platform pledges favoring the enactment of public utilities, corrupt practice and employers' liability laws, as well as an election law, such as provided for in the Geran bill.

"Any other measures," said the Governor, "I am not saying whether they have my support or opposition until they reach my hands."

The bills advocated by him, he said, take in not only pledges of the Democratic platform, but also of the Republican party, and he could not see how they could be called partisan measures. This the Governor took particular care to emphasize.

Printed in the *Trenton Evening Times*, Feb. 28, 1911.
1 Frederick William Donnelly, merchant and civic leader of Trenton, elected mayor of that city in 1911.

To Charles Andrew Talcott

My dear Charlie: [Trenton, N. J.] February 28, 1911.

It is mighty hard to decline anything that you want me to do,[1] but I really have made as many engagements as I dare make in view of my public duties. Do stop and see me on your way to Washington, or on your way anywhere else. It would be such a delight to see you for a talk with you.

Always affectionately yours,   Woodrow Wilson

TLS (WC, NjP).
[1] Talcott's letter is missing.

An Address to the West Hudson Board of Trade in Harrison, New Jersey

[[Feb. 28, 1911]]

I no longer come to plead a personal preference on your part; I come to do something which it is an honor to do, to speak to you about the things that we ought, as fellow citizens, to discuss between elections. Discussions at election time, gentlemen, too often mean very little; they too often mean that you are commending a party and a set of candidates by promises which you have no sort of confidence will be afterward redeemed. And so it seems to me that the business part of every political career is the part that follows the election. During that election I made a number of promises to my fellow-citizens for myself, as well as promises which I felt authorized to make for our party. I promised that if elected I would seek every proper opportunity to tell them what was going on in the business of the State, how their affairs prospered, just what questions were pending and just what part public opinion may be expected to play in the settling of those questions.

At Trenton, as in every other State capital, gentlemen, we are not conducting our own business, we are conducting your business, and only so far as we can have your support and approval can we make that government. Just so far as we can arouse your interest in public affairs, just so far is that the very essence of democratic government.

Now you know that discussion is centering at Trenton and in other quarters just now generally upon a particular bill, the bill introduced by Mr. Geran, of Monmouth County, called for short the primaries and election bill. The object of that measure is to do what? It is to fulfill the principal promise of the campaign, namely, to purify the machinery of election and to put the choice of representatives of every grade absolutely in the hands of the people themselves. We have been doing a great deal of investigating recently, gentlemen, of the processes of election, of those processes which would not satisfy you, and we know by abundant evidence scattered through all times, that [through] investigating committees this year and in previous years, that in order to get satisfactory elections you must have trustworthy election officers. If you cannot get men of a high grade and of trustworthy character, the whole process is vitiated at the root.

What does this bill propose to do? It proposes, in the first place—though the first draft of the bill as published does not show this—very greatly to increase the remuneration of election officers, so that it will be possible to have men who can leave their business temporarily for this duty. And then it proposes to see to it that we get a different grade of election officers in some places by requiring them to be submitted to a very simple examination by the Civil Service Commission.

You know without being told that many of our election officers cannot even read with ease and that they figure very slowly and with difficulty; they cannot tell at a glance whether a ballot is properly marked or not, or which names are marked on the ballot, and they cannot follow with rapid eye the making columns of figures or the adding up of columns of figures; they cannot check the absolutely fundamental processes of recording the vote.

What do we require that they shall be certified as being able to do—pass an examination to enter college? Certainly not. There is nothing literary about the examination proposed; the very simple requirement is that they should be able to read readily, that they should be able to write readily, that they should be able to figure readily, and that they should know colors from one another. Is there anything very academic or difficult about that examination? Would it take a man more than two or three minutes to pass that examination? Aren't those examinations held by any intelligent men who might be deputed to hold them? Couldn't a man who knew anything go and take an examination of that sort and qualify? It requires neither learning nor time, and therefore it is a perfectly reasonable fundamental minimum requirement.

Now, how are those officers going to be appointed, for here is where the crux of the whole thing comes in? Don't let us, even in words, gentlemen, deceive ourselves. The great majority of election officers in this State are honest men and return the vote by honest processes, but there are some who are not, and when they are not honest, what is the thing that happens? The thing that happens is that there is collusion among the election officers; that there is an arrangement—with sorrow be it said—between election officers representing the contesting parties; that they do not watch and check each other, but co-operate with each other in doing the things that ought not to be done. The difficulty with politics is not the partisanship of it, but the bi-partisanship of it.

Now, if we are going to be true to the people of this State we must give them impartial election officers. How are you going to do it? Well, there are various ways in which it can be done. I am not going to stop to debate those ways, but I can suggest several of them. You can do as they do in Oregon, for example— ask the courts, some one of the minor courts, to appoint those men from a qualified list; and if you have reason to believe that the court is partisan and that it will not give you impartial officers, establish a representative means of appeal, as for instance, the Circuit or the Supreme Court, which can review your complaint and tell you whether it has been proper or not.

Election officers do not belong to the parties; they belong to the people of the State, and the people of the State have a right to have absolutely impartial election officers. We have appointed two Republican election officers and two Democratic election officers because that seems the simplest and fairest way, but those men do not belong to the Democratic and Republican parties; they belong to the people. The election officers ought to be absolutely non-partisan, and I do not care to what length a bill goes to establish non-partisan methods of getting the votes out at the polls, I am for it, and the people of New Jersey are for it, and if they don't get it soon they will get it late, and the men who stand in their way of trying to get it soon will be put in such shameful oblivion that they will wish they had never entered on the stage of politics. The people of New Jersey are just as wide awake as any people in the United States.

Now, I am not going to debate with you the processes. There are legitimate differences of opinion as to the process of getting impartial election officers. All that I am going to say is that when we have got together, gentlemen, in Trenton upon a reasonably good way, then we are going to stand together and are not going to debate the matter any longer. You can object to any process established, and let me tell you that the favorite process of designing men to defeat a measure is to talk it to death by reasonable objections; they are not foolish enough to offer bootless objections, because they would not be talked about, but their object is to talk and talk and talk until the session is over and the thing is dead. Very well, then, let us insist, after one reasonably good method is suggested, that the talking shall stop and go to work and try that method and see whether it will work out or not.

But there are other things that this bill does. It puts everything into the primaries; it makes it the right of the people of this State to get directly at the choice of the persons who are going to represent them in every public function; and I want to say to you that I am for that with every ounce of force there is in me; and the challenge that I issue is this: Let no man oppose this thing unless he is willing to oppose it in public and for reasons.

I am not standing here to ask that I may have my way, but I am challenging every man who wants another way to convince the people of New Jersey that that is the right way; and I am perfectly willing to take the hazards of the battle. But we are done in this day, gentlemen, with private arrangements, and every man who wants to make out his case has got to make it out in public. If you want a particular kind of process, come out and say why you want it and let us see if your reason holds water; let us see if it is a reason that you can give in public without embarrassment; and if you blush or hesitate or involve your phraseology so as to conceal something, then you may make perfectly certain that the people won't swallow it.

The primaries and elections bill is a complicated measure; it has got to be studied as a whole and not in its parts; and as a whole it is a measure so sound that it is based in every portion upon abundant experience in other parts of the United States. Every part of that bill not only will work, but has worked; it is not new stuff, brought out by theorists; it is tested stuff, lived under by intelligent people all over the United States. So that no man can stand up and say, 'this is a measure that is conceived in a closet.' It is a measure that has been enacted in State after State and lived up to by populations which are now free of the process under which they used to groan and be ashamed.

There are other bills pending at Trenton which I deem it my duty to speak of, and to speak of very frankly.

I want you to understand, gentlemen, that, as your representative, as the only representative of the whole State—for such is the Governor—I am not trying to run the Legislature at Trenton. It might be an amusing thing to try to run it, but I couldn't if I tried. I know a majority of the members of that Legislature pretty well, and I respect them thoroughly; and let me tell you that those men are going to act upon their consciences and cannot be run by anybody. If I tried to run the Legislature I would have a great deal of fun, because I would have to come in contact and contest with a great many able men, and it would stir every wit there is in me. But that is not what I am trying to do. I am not backing up by my public utterances any bill in Trenton except the four bills which are the explicit redemption of our promises made in the platform of the Democratic party, and, for that matter, in the platform of the Republican party, too. There is not a measure of the four which any Republican in that Legislature has the slightest excuse for not voting for.

Now, what are the four measures? The measure that I have just mentioned; then a very thorough and efficient corrupt practices act, which limits the amount of money that candidates may expend in their campaign, which states the objects for which they shall expend the money, which makes it necessary that they should publish their campaign expenses in items whenever the items exceed a few dollars, and the sources from which they got the money.

If the sources from which they got the money are proper sources, it will be very difficult to convict them under that act; but if the sources from which they got the money are improper, it will be perfectly possible to find them guilty under that act. We want to make it just as uncomfortable as possible for the men who get their money from improper sources. The object of the bill is to make everybody uncomfortable who has anything to be ashamed of. Isn't that a fair proposition to the people? And to make nobody uncomfortable who has nothing to be ashamed of. That is another campaign promise, and the items of that bill correspond, item by item, with the special statement of that promise in the platform of the Democratic party.

Then there is a public utilities bill. How long and how patiently the people of New Jersey have fought for a real public utilities bill. They got a public utilities bill, but it was born without teeth. I do not know by what peculiar process the thing was managed, but it was conceived without teeth and was meant to be born without teeth.[1] I am talking about what I know, and I can prove to you that it was made to be born without teeth, that it was not intended to have any, for I can tell you where the bill was drawn.

Now we have got to get rid of that; we have got to have a new deal on the public utilities measure. Why? Because we are

---

[1] Again, see n. 2 to the address printed at Sept. 30, 1910, Vol. 21.

trying to do nobody, trying to get even with nobody, trying to put nobody at a disadvantage who is serving the public in a useful way. Nothing else. If I did not believe, gentlemen, that an effective public utilities bill was the best thing for the public serving corporations of this State I would not support it. I am not a friend of any part of the population of this State as against any other part of the population of this State. I am for the things which we can get together and do common justice all around.

Now, what has been the history of public utilities measures elsewhere? I don't like to say such things, gentlemen, but practically all opposition to the public utilities measure is absolute ignorance on the part of those who oppose it; they would suppose that New Jersey was a news tight and air tight compartment, and that they had never heard of what has happened in other parts of the United States.

Where did the first of your public utilities measures come from? From Wisconsin, introduced by that very able and very energetic man, Mr. La Follette; and the public service corporations of Wisconsin fight for Mr. La Follette as they would fight for life. What is the result? The men at the head of those corporations—I have it from their own lips—are absolutely converted to the belief that one of the best things that ever happened was the success of Mr. La Follette.

Why, don't you see the reason? Look at the present condition of the public serving corporations of this State; they are universally suspected that so much of their stock is watered stock that it is not worth what it is selling at. You know I am telling the mere fact. Now I believe that it possibly is worth what it is selling at, but everybody in the State outside of the directors of those corporations wants a public utilities measure that has powers. They can, by inquiry, show the people of the State just what their rates are based on, and by that means guarantee the business to investors. Don't you see that they can? What makes anything safe in the security markets is the confidence of the people who buy the securities, isn't it?

What has happened since the United States Steel Corporation has been making absolutely frank public statements of its affairs. Hasn't criticism of that corporation decreased and decreased? Now suppose public statements were vouched for, not only by the officers of that corporation, but by public examiners who had no interest whatever in the matter, don't you know that you would be perfectly sure what you were buying when you bought the stocks or bonds of that corporation? Why do the public service corporations of this State not wish their securities to be publicly guaranteed? Why do they not wish the suspicions of all kinds that exist to be removed by the only thing that can remove suspicion from anything, namely, absolutely frank publicity? If I am ashamed, and want you to stop suspecting me, the only way I can manage it is by giving you something by which you can make yourself conversant with the facts, so that you can judge for yourself. Denials won't do it. Assertions to you that I am honest won't do it. You have got to have the record of my life and judge for yourself whether I am honest or not.

These gentlemen don't understand what they are fighting. They are fighting the security of their own future. If I didn't believe every word of this, gentlemen, I would not support those measures, for I am not trying in the things I am advocating to damage two great bodies of business[2] in which the money of so many thousands of the people of this State is invested. That is not what we are trying to do.

Now take the other matter—the fourth measure—which you can call either the employers' liability or the workingmen's compensation act, for it is both. New Jersey is belated beyond most all of the States in establishing a just relationship of liability between the employer and the employe.[3] We have permitted to exist in this State until the present day common law defenses against liability which belong to an absolutely different state of society, which are just about as belated as chain armor. Chain armor has long ceased to be a fashionable dress. These common law defenses against liability ought to have gone out with chain armor. Not in order to leave the employer defenseless, but in order to bring about an equitable arrangement, by which there should be sort of an automatic insurance of workingmen against risk, an insurance which must be borne by the employer.

What insurance company will now, for reasonable rates, insure an employe against the absolutely incalculable risks of a suit at law? You have to go before a jury. The sympathy of the jury may give excessive damages if the case is pitiable. No one can calculate the result of a suit. You cannot establish a rate against which there is no basis of calculation, but if you will establish a definite schedule of liabilities and have that schedule extend to the insurance companies, then you can reinsure yourself in the insurance companies at a definite, fixed calculable rate, and you are not going to pay, for the whole community is

[2] That is, the Public Service Corporation of New Jersey and various railroad and traction companies.

[3] Again, see n. 9 to the speech printed at Oct. 5, 1910, Vol. 21.

going to pay it, and the whole community is willing to pay it, in order that there may be prompt, simple justice.

In the extraordinarily dangerous civilization which we have set up there is danger upon every side because of the use of terribly powerful machinery, the safety of which cannot, even by careful inspection, be always guaranteed. There are many defects that are latent, not discoverable by inspection, in great fly-wheels, in great bodies of moving machinery that no sort of careful inspection will always disclose, and we draw the bodies of our working men into factories and occupations which involve daily and constant risks. Society is perfectly ready, ought to be very glad, to insure great bodies, mounting up into the hundreds of thousands, of our fellow-citizens, for the risks that they take in sustaining modern life and modern civilization. That is the significance of the employer's liability and working men's compensation act, and there is an explicit pledge in the platform of the Democratic party that that legislation shall be enacted, too. Very well, then my program is to go out before my fellow citizens whenever I enjoy a privilege such as I enjoy this evening and talk over pieces of that sort of legislation to the fullest extent of the powers I command, because they are promises to the people not only, but because they cover things that ought to be done for the people whether they were promised or not.

We went through a campaign last autumn, gentlemen, when we had amusement and entertainment listening to all sorts of speakers, but that was not business; that was merely preliminary; that was setting up the machinery of government. But now we have got down to the business of government; we are conducting the government now, and what is going to be your attitude, to conduct business honestly and in the interest of everybody? Aren't you going to sustain us, aren't you going to stand back of us? Are you going to lag behind, or are you going to assist us in doing these fundamental things. And don't you realize that every one of these things is the right thing? These are not political policies, gentlemen; these are things which are fundamental to the whole structural [structure of] government and to the whole operation of human society as at present constituted.

I cannot imagine just men forming into parties and opposing each other upon these measures. They are in the common interest; they are in the interest of one party no more than they are in the interest of the other party, and therefore we can debate them as men debate those things which are intended, not for the revolution of society, but for its restoration. What we are doing now, gentlemen, is a very interesting thing in the United States. We have so complicated our machinery of government, we have made it so difficult, so full of ambushes and hiding places, so indirect, that instead of having true representative government we have a great mass of unintelligible organizations intervening between the people and the processes of government, so that by stages, without intending to, without being aware of doing it, we have lost the purity and directness of representative government, and what we are engaged in doing now is not upsetting our institutions, but restoring them. The processes we are engaged in are the most fundamentally conservative processes that were ever undertaken. If your tree is dying is it revolution to restore the purity of its sap and to purify the soil that will sustain it? Is this process of restoration a process of disturbance? No! It is a process of life; it is a process of renewal; it is a process of redemption.

These are the things that we are standing for, and is it not invigorating, gentlemen? Is it not worth living in an age when we are privileged, we who, knowing the glories of the great history of this country and the great physical achievements of the men who stood by this government, when we are privileged to play a part of that play, a constructive, renewing part in serving under the great banner of human liberty?

This is just as much a constructive age in politics as was the great age in which our federal government was set up, and the man who does not awake to the opportunity, the man who does not sacrifice private and exceptional interests in order to serve the common and public interests is declining to take part in the business of that heroic age. I am sorry for the man that declines, very sorry for the man who is so blind that he does not see the opportunity, and I am happy in the confidence that in this era, whether they miss it or not, the American people will not miss it.

There are places in this country where men slumber and are negligent, where men forget and do not see; but there are men the country over, and you will see the kindling eyes of millions of men who understand that liberty and mean at all costs to possess it. They will not be disappointed; they will not be defeated. You may be their salvation or their undoing, and then, when the records come to be written, how will the names be inscribed and upon what lists? Which side do you choose, the side of those who opposed and were defeated because they would not see the truth, or on the side of those who saw the truth and gloried in it and made themselves free by serving it? That is the choice which is being made in the United States. Do you not see the signs?

Can any man distinctly draw the lines of party separation in this country now? What is happening, gentlemen? Men by the millions, from ocean to ocean in this country, are saying: "We will not stop to examine the labels which we once wore; we will look for the truth and look for the leadership of men who will see the truth and who shall lead us into freedom." I entertain the ambition, the very reasonable ambition, that this commonwealth that we live in and which we love will be among those which will lead the commonwealths of the country in the discovery of those regions of achievement which are the regions of the redemption of the human spirit.

Printed in the Jersey City *Jersey Journal*, March 1, 1911, with additions and corrections from the text in the *Newark Evening News*, Mar. 1, 1911.

From William Jennings Bryan

My dear Sir: Lincoln, Neb., March 1, 1911.

I find your letter upon my return to the city, and am greatly gratified at your endorsement of the platform of 1908. It represents, in my judgment, the Democratic principles applied to present conditions. A number of the policies endorsed in that platform (and opposed by the Republicans during the campaign) have already been taken up by a Republican congress, and even by a Republican president. The bank guarantee is a more recent development of the Democratic idea, which is, I think, entirely in harmony with the party position on other questions. In providing for a guarantee fund we are simply looking at the banking question from the standpoint of the depositor, and compelling the banks to make good the promise of security by which they draw deposits to the banks.

I notice that you do not recommend the income tax, although I have heard it stated that you endorsed an income tax amendment, as you must do in endorsing the Denver platform. I hope that you will see your way clear to send a message to the legislature on that subject, for one state may be important. I think we are going to have enough states to ratify it, but it may be so close that one state will determine the result. I know that there is opposition to it among the financiers, but the fact that the President presented it to congress, the senate passed it unanimously, and the house with only fourteen votes in the negative, ought to be a sufficient answer to the criticism of the east.

I shall be in the neighborhood of New York early in March, and have promised Prof. Erdman[1] to come to Princeton. Shall arrange to see you while in the east if possible,[2] but if I do not see you there I shall meet you at Indianapolis on the 13th of April.[3]   Very truly yours,   W. J. Bryan

TLS (WP, DLC).

[1] The Rev. Charles Rosenbury Erdman, Princeton 1886, Professor of Practical Theology at Princeton Theological Seminary since 1906.

[2] As has been noted earlier, they met in Princeton on March 12, 1911.

[3] When they were scheduled to speak together at the Jefferson Day banquet of the National Democratic League of Clubs. Wilson's address is printed at April 13, 1911. As it turned out, Bryan was unable to be in Indianapolis because he was attending the funeral of Tom Loftin Johnson, Mayor of Cleveland, 1902-10, who died on April 10, 1911. Bryan's speech, "The Passing of the Plutocracy," was printed in the *Indianapolis News*, April 14, 1910.

From George Brinton McClellan Harvey

Dear Mr. Wilson   New York March 1 [1911].

The inclosed letter from Mr. House[1] has some significance. The writer is an exceptionally able man, well-to-do financially and, I think sound politically.

His reference to Bailey[2] recalls to my mind that I had a talk with Bailey when coming through Washington. He said that Texas would *naturally* be for you and that his own disposition lay that way. But "too much Oregon" seemed to be in his crop. I urged him to make no commitment and he said he wouldn't without letting me know.[3] I rather expect to find him in the Harmon camp eventually by advice of his friends here who lean that way. But he wouldn't enjoy going up against men like House the least little bit and he may not.

House, of course, misapprehends my diagnosis of the situation. I fully appreciate the importance of Bryan and in a speech at Savannah on the 17th[4] shall recognize him as the party leader until another Presidential candidate shall be named. But I also appreciate the danger of being regarded as exclusively or too distinctively "the Bryan candidate." Such an one would surely be beaten in the convention.

As ever   Faithfully Yours   G H

Yoakum,[5] one of your admirers and a broad man, asked me to send you the pamphlet.[6]

ALS (WP, DLC).

[1] Edward Mandell House of Austin, Tex., identified in E. M. House to WW,

Oct. 16, 1911, n. 1, Vol. 23. The enclosure is missing, and there is no copy in the House Papers, CtY.

2 Joseph Weldon Bailey, state-rights, conservative Democratic senator from Texas since 1901.

3 House and Harvey do not seem to have been au courant with the political situation in Texas. In fact, on January 17, 1911, Bailey had said that he thought that Harmon was the leader in the Democratic presidential race and the best man that the party could name in 1912, as the situation then stood. He went on to rule out a possible Wilson candidacy, saying: "I don't think he would do at all. His revolutionary policy would make a Greek democracy of the country." *Dallas Morning News*, Jan. 18, 1911. Bailey would soon become the chief spokesman of the anti-Wilson, pro-Harmon forces in Texas during the preconvention campaign.

4 Harvey addressed the Hibernian Society of Savannah at 2 A.M. on March 18, 1911. As the report in the *Savannah Press*, March 18, 1911, put it, he did not hesitate to analyze Bryanism and to state why he believed that Bryan's influence should not be exerted against the kind of Democratic presidential candidate for 1912 that he, Harvey, had in mind. Continuing, Harvey appealed to the South to resume its place in party councils and dictate the selection of a candidate. "The South," he said, "through your statesmen and your journalists, is to harmonize and amalgamate the party. What less in common fairness can the East do than produce the man? Gentlemen, we have him and he is yours. If there is a highly-Americanized Scotch-Irishman, descended from Ohio, born in Virginia, developed in Maryland, married in Georgia and now delivering from bondage a faithful old Democratic commonwealth, he is the man who ought to be selected."

5 That is, Benjamin Franklin Yoakum.

6 This pamphlet is missing.

To George Brinton McClellan Harvey

My dear Colonel Harvey: [Trenton, N. J.] March 2, 1911.

Thank you sincerely for your kind letter with its enclosures. I find it hard myself to get thoroughly interested in the Presidential matter, I am so genuinely absorbed and interested here. I have not had a chance yet to read the full text of your article in the North American,[1] but I have seen enough of it to know that you have been as usual, exceedingly generous in your judgment of me and I thank you most warmly.

What you tell me of Senator Bailey and of Mr. House is certainly most interesting. I have no doubt that your diagnosis of Senator Bailey's eventual position will be carried out by the facts.

In haste, with warm regard,
                    Cordially yours,   Woodrow Wilson

TLS (WP, DLC).
1 George Brinton McClellan Harvey, "The Political Predestination of Woodrow Wilson," *North American Review*, CXCIII (March 1911), 321-30.

An After-Dinner Address to the Hoboken Board of Trade[1]

[[March 2, 1911]]

Mr. President,[2] Ladies and Gentlemen—Your greeting is, indeed, most gracious and I appreciate the welcome that you accord me. I was very much touched by the last words of your president in introducing me. I have a very profound belief in the common people of this State and of this great country, and I always feel, in addressing an audience like this, that it is not in them, but through them, that I read the common people. For you gentlemen are not the common people; you are removed in circumstances, and sometimes in sympathy, from the great mass of the citizenship of this country; you are not among those that daily feel the absolute pinch of the necessity to work; you are, most of you, men who have between you and that necessity a certain margin of resources upon which you can depend—a certain leeway of leisure, a certain opportunity to do the things that you please rather than always the thing that you must; and it is absolutely necessary that you should regard the problems of government in their true light—that you should constantly recall for yourselves the circumstances of the great mass of your fellow citizens.

I was just now agreeing with one of the gentlemen at this table that probably the judgment—the independent judgment of a country like ours—is not much in the men who have thrust forward and risen to the top in business. A certain gentleman said, the other day, that he had hoped that he might have in one of the houses of Congress one more term in which he could end his life as a free man, "for," he said, "I have spent my life serving the rich." Now how true it is of many of us, gentlemen, that we are spending our lives serving certain interests to which our personal advancement is as what a slave is at the tail of a cart? And how many men can release their judgment upon a free field and look at the progress of the country as if their personal fortunes were not involved? How many men can be, through one hour of discussion, indifferent to the considerations which touch their personal fortunes? How, then, are you going to root your politics in the soil which is the real source of its purity and of its strength?

There is a great deal of prejudiced nonsence talked about the interests with a capital I. Nobody can be blind to the fact

[1] Delivered at the German Club.
[2] Claus Henry Carl Jagels, president of the Hoboken Board of Trade.

that there is a great deal to be said about men entering in a large way in business and manufacturing that is merely slanderous in character, as Judge Speer[3] so truly intimated, and yet there is a contrast in our lives obscure to explain to us, either between what we call the interests and the general welfare of the community, men who concentrate their attention too much and too long upon particular interests, that the great businesses they are engaged in do lose touch with the common people and do obscure their judgment with regard to the fortunes of the common people; and a very interesting thing has happened in our politics in recent years.[4]

Why is it that party lines in recent months have become so obscure and parties seem to have been dissolved? Why is it that there is talk of a reformation of parties? Why is it that there is a very slight difference between one party platform and another party platform, all sorts of men claiming to be for the same thing? Is it not because we are not now really debating political policies? We are debating nothing else than the fundamentals of government; we are debating nothing else than the question, Have we a democratic government; have we a representative government; have we a government whose connections are with the general body of the people and which respond to the impulses of the people and to the judgments that lie in their hearts?

What is the main question now pending at Trenton? There is not a party question now being discussed there that I know of. Is it a party question whether workingmen shall be properly protected, or, rather, compensated for the injuries necessarily incidental to our very dangerous modern processes of industry? That is a question of equity, of justice, of humanity; it is not a question of politics or of parties.

Is it a party question whether we shall control, in some fair and adequate fashion, those great corporations which serve the daily and hourly necessities of our life, the corporations that we call the public service corporations? There is no politics in that; there is merely the question of whether the communities shall have command of their own lives or not, or shall have those lives dominated by men who dominate them for private profit.

Is there any politics, any party politics, in the question whether

---

3 William Henry Speer of Jersey City, Circuit Court judge for Hudson County, who, along with William Robert Shepherd, Professor of History at Columbia University, also spoke.

4 There seems to be no way to correct the garbled phrases in this paragraph.

men shall spend the money for illegitimate purposes at election, whether elections shall be put upon a basis of purity and economy or not? There is no politics in that; there is merely the question of the purity of the function of government, of whether the men who are put into authority shall get there by fair means or foul; it is a question of the integrity of government. But that is not a political question at all, and that is not the main question which is being debated at Trenton. The main question is, Shall the people have access to their government?

The fundamental bill of this session is the bill that is called the primaries and elections bill, the bill which, for the present at any rate, bears the name of a very excellent member of the Assembly, Mr. Geran, of Monmouth County. What does the bill try to do? What is the difficulty, gentlemen, and the discouragement that we suffer under as a board of trade whenever you try to better political processes and municipal conditions? I have not asked you in fact this question, but I have heard this question answered all over the United States, as I have gone over it from one part to another. The attitude of the most busy and thoughtful men toward their government is an attitude of indifference because it is an attitude of despair, that we think, when we go to the primaries, how do we know our votes are going to be counted. If we take part in the elections what choice do we make except the choice between the nominees of one political machine and the nominees of another political machine, and so far as that is concerned we would as leave settle it by the toss of a coin, because then, if one set of men is elected to office they take their orders from the machine and we don't like the machine and can't put it out of business and therefore we cannot get access to our own government.

And why does the machine try to conduct its affairs through what would seem to be the very sources of its power? Because it has come about that the people are not the source of their power; the source of their power is in the main derived from the men who are conducting great enterprises of business. There are men in every board of trade who are partners—intimate and constant partners, with political machines, which the parties they are connected with are pretending to fight. I am not stating anything that you don't know; I am simply one of those rash persons who say out loud what everybody thinks.

Now the business of politics at this moment is to reconstitute our government by putting it upon its right basis again, which is the basis of the popular will and not the basis of private arrangement. The partnership is about to be dissolved by public process; the partnership is about to be made impossible by pitiless publicity; pitiless not toward those who are honest; pitiless not toward those who are seeking, even in some partial and blind and groping way, to serve the general interests, but pitiless toward those who are trying to follow the lines which serve only themselves[,] who are afraid that changes will be made because of the effect the changes may have upon their bank account.

Now the object of the Geran bill is to restore the government to the people; and the Geran bill is going to be adopted. I know that it is going to be adopted because I know that the people of New Jersey want it. I do not want it except as one of the people of New Jersey. It is not my bill; it is not any man's bill. The beautiful thing about it is that it is no man's bill. It is a bill that comes from that irrepressible demand of a people that has discovered that throughout decade after decade it has been duped and deceived.

There are going to be open primaries for every kind of office, and there are going to be men set to count the votes who will count them as they are cast, or we will know the reason why. And I want you to observe, and observe very critically, who are opposing this bill. They are not opposing it in public; they are opposing it chiefly in private. Most of them won't even venture to come to Trenton because there are wide open eyes in the Governor's office. They work with the Assemblymen and Senators at home. Now the beauty of the present Legislature is that it cannot be "worked." I have associated with these gentlemen long enough to have a perfect confidence that they are not going to be imposed on any longer and made the dupes of designing persons in order to disgrace themselves and disappoint their constituents. Every newspaper in this State that has habitually supported the wrong enterprises is opposed to the Geran bill, and every man who wants to preserve the private power of the machine is against the Geran bill.

Now, I dare say there are defects in the Geran bill; there are many parts of it open to the judgment of honest and practical men, who are agreed generally, but what we are going to do is to get it in such a shape that it is as good a bill as can be got, and then we are going to stand for it in its every section; and then, if experience proves that it needs amendment, it can be amended after. The present plan is to pick flaws in it, to get time to talk it to death, and nobody can talk more plausibly with regard to the practical parts of the bill than those who want to kill it. Some of them have been adepts in this kind of talking throughout their career. They are innocent persons, for the most part. They think they are imposing upon us; they think we don't know what they are after; they think that the cloven hoof is neatly hidden under the skirt of the garment; but there is every sign of peace in the argument, and they are deceiving no-body—not even themselves.

It is absolutely necessary, gentlemen, that in matters of this kind you should not resolve yourselves into a debating society, but should make up your minds whether the object of a bill like this is to serve the people, and when you have found out that it is to serve the people, to get back of it and sustain the men who are trying to put it through.

Any smart man can start objections, but only a great man can waive objections, and so I am not going to put my judgment against the common good; I am going to stand for this thing through thick and thin.

Now I am not saying these things because I have the least nervousness as to what is going to happen to the Geran bill; I have not. We have discovered some very interesting things in recent months in New Jersey. I believe a few months ago very few people believed that a serious discussion of public questions on a public platform would result in uniting the people on intelligent action, but anybody that wanted to believe that has been undeceived. If I may speak of my own experience I have found audiences made up of the common people of this State quicker to take a point, quicker to understand an argument, quicker to comprehend a tendency and to comprehend a principle than many a college class that I have led; not because the college class lacked intelligence, but because a class of college boys is not in contact with the realities of life, and a body of the common citizenship of New Jersey is in contact with actual life day by day, and you don't have to explain to them what touches them to the quick.

If you will go out and explain to these people what it is you are trying to do, they will waive all minor objections, and they will see to it that you are sustained in doing it. The only thing you have to prove to them is that you really mean to serve them, that you mean what you say and that you are not in the least afraid of the man that is crooked; that the only thing you have to do with the man who is trying to do the wrong thing is to make him stand up in public and explain it. If you find men buttonholing you and buttonholing representatives and criticizing the primaries and elections bill, hire a hall for them and get them to get up on the stage and tell you why they are ob-

jecting. They will decline the challenge. There is nothing that
so chills ardor for wrong as exposure to the open air. I have
been told that it requires courage to advocate a popular cause.
Unless I have misread history, the only thing that requires
courage is to oppose it, because the thing that a man ought to
fear is not the interruption of his personal prosperity, but the
prominent disrepute of his name.

In the years gone by, when I was a very literary fellow, I
used to enjoy a certain grim satisfaction in hearing certain public men make public excuses for their careers, for I used to
know that it was quiet men, like myself, sitting at study tables,
reading the records in which we are told how posterity ought
to think of those men; that their voices would die with the hour,
and that the record of history would rise up against them generation after generation and those who were descendant from
them would wish that they had never been born.

What are we trying for, gentlemen—the satisfaction of the little
span of time that we spend in this world? What are we trying
for—the comforts of our bodies, the things what we put in our
stomachs, the mere pleasures with which we try to kill time and
spend it? Or are we trying for the permanent satisfaction of
our spirits; are we trying for that peace that comes with the attempt, at any rate, the honest attempt to perform our duty; are
we trying to enjoy the things that money affords us while they
disappoint us, or are we trying for those things only which will
bring us only the honor and the love and the respect of our
fellow men? Do we wish to make government for private business for our own behoof, or do we wish to advance the interests
of the community? Do we wish for private satisfaction, for selfishness triumphant, or do we wish for that nobler thing which
seems to connect us with the whole spirit of humanity, which
seems to fill our lungs with a breath which blows through the
ages, the breath which is the breath of immortal principle?
Are we trying to live for a little time, or are we trying to beckon
to other men like ourselves up the long road that leads to final
achievement?

I am not leading those things that seem temporal in themselves to too high a level in this question; I am trying to tell you
what I believe with all my heart you are content [with] by way
of essential principle. Let no man mislead you or deceive you. In
this day by day struggle for the interests of the people we are
connecting ourselves with the long processes of history, with the
eternal purposes of Providence, proving ourselves akin to the
great spirits which stand for every country as the stars which

they follow through the dark night and blaze when the morning comes.

Printed in the Jersey City *Jersey Journal*, March 3, 1911, with additions and corrections from the partial texts in the Trenton *True American*, March 4, 1911, and the *Newark Evening News*, March 3, 1911.

A News Report of Remarks to the Annual Dinner of the New Jersey Senate

[March 4, 1911]

WILSON ANALYZES SPIRIT OF TIMES

Governor in Address to Senators Says This is Another Period of Reconstruction

NEW YORK, March 4.—Governor Woodrow Wilson of New Jersey, who was the guest of the State Senators of his commonwealth at a dinner in the Ritz-Carlton last evening, compared the present era in politics to the American Revolution. He called both reconstructive periods and insisted the people of the country, as shown by the recent election, are demanding progress rather than conservatism. He said the people are disregarding political parties in their demand for progressive legislation and that the period of reconstruction by which the people would reconstitute the connection between the Government and themselves was begun. In that respect he spoke of the American Revolution as a great constructive epoch.

Governor Wilson laid great stress on the way in which he analyzed the fall election, saying the voters were looking for progressives and where they found such Republicans they elected them to office and where they could not they fell back on progressive Democrats. The speech was made to eighteen of the twenty-one New Jersey State Senators, the only absentees being George W. F. Gaunt, Griffith W. Lewis and Joseph S. Frelinghuysen,[1] who were unable to attend. There were nine Republican and nine Democratic State Senators present.

The dinner of the Senators to the Governor is an annual affair. They are accustomed to meet the Governor in a social way and at the same time discuss such phases of politics and statesmanship as are uppermost in their minds, but in a purely friendly way. Ernest R[obinson]. Ackerman of Union, president of the Senate, presided at the dinner. He made a brief speech introducing the Governor and praising him. Governor Wilson said he had met the various Senators individually, but it was unusually pleasant to meet them together in such a friendly way.

He said he was not a cynic as to the tendencies of the times, and he considered himself specially fortunate that he was Governor of New Jersey at a time when party lines are not drawn severely. He said he was glad the measures in which he is interested greatly are those in which men of all parties in the country are interested. Although he admitted he was a Democrat both by birth and conviction, yet in state affairs party lines are not strictly felt.

"I am inclined to think," he said, "the only motive of state politics is to see who gets the offices, and that having been settled, we ought to go along peacefully until the next election."

He said he was not a good party man, because he was not a good hater of a man who believed opposite from what he did.

Wilson said the legislation he wanted to see enacted in Jersey was not party legislation, because it was favored by other parties in other states. From that point he went into an analysis of the recent election. He said:

"A rough characterization of the recent campaign is that the people have tried to prefer the progressives to the reactionaries. The voters took progressive Republicans where they could find them, and in other places they fell back on the progressive Democrats. The question which it seems to me is asked by the people, is, 'Do you mean to move forward, or do you stand pat?' In other words, 'Do you stand with the connections the government has with the people, or do you believe in changing them for the benefit of the people.'

"Many people stand with the conservatives. While I respect them, I cannot agree with them. The country does not agree with them. The people are not satisfied with the measures that have been enacted for them. Although they are demanding new legislation and more things for their interest, it is true they do not like wild talk or unmeasured charges. Neither does the country like to see men called rascals and to have abusive terms used.

"What the country does want," Wilson continued, "are concrete proposals in regard to the relation of the government with the people. What interests me, and what should quicken the pulse of every man, is the fact we have entered on a new constructive era. We must go ahead."

The Governor pointed out the tendencies of the time must be controlled and used for the best interests of the people, or those tendencies would prove harmful.

"The great age of American politics," he said, "has dawned because men are coming forward to reconstruct the Government.

The American Revolution was not a revolution, but a period of reconstruction, and so today we have another era of reconstruction. By this means, as it were, the blood of the people again will flow into the veins of the Government."

Here the Governor launched out in support of the primary measure he is eager to have the Jersey Leagislature enact. He pointed out he was interested in getting certain measures turned into law. He emphasized the fact he was not a party man; that part of the legislation he wanted was originated by Republicans, and he meant to fight for it.

"I don't care who gets the credit," he said, "I am not jealous. All I want is the goods. What will be for the benefit of the people of New Jersey is what I favor."

Governor Wilson was in a happy mood, and in telling the Senators how glad he was to meet them together, said that if he was called by his first name, he would feel more at home. "If some one across the table called me Woodrow," he said, "I would feel that I had become one of the family."

After Wilson finished speaking, Senator Robert Hand of Cape May wanted the Governor to explain the difference between a Democrat and a Republican.

"I can't answer that question for anybody but myself," the Governor replied. "I am a Democrat because I understand by history the Republican party takes the attitude the Government is a trusteeship that should be administered for the benefit of those who have the greatest amount at stake." He said the stewardship of any class is not broad enough for the people and insisted the Republicans are trying to stand a pyramid on its apex. He admitted the platforms of both parties are almost alike, and said they were framed chiefly to appeal to the people and get votes.

Senator John D. Prince,[2] the Republican leader, also spoke, and he said that that [he] agreed with what the Governor had said. The difference, he said, was one of method, rather than of principle.

Printed in the *Trenton Evening Times*, March 4, 1911; one editorial heading omitted.

[1] George Washington French Gaunt, farmer of Mullica Hill and Republican state senator from Gloucester County; Griffith Walker Lewis, president of G. W. Lewis & Son, shoe manufacturers of Burlington, and Republican state senator from Burlington County; and Joseph Sherman Frelinghuysen, insurance broker in New York, resident of Raritan, and Republican state senator from Somerset County.

[2] John Dyneley Prince, Professor of Semitic Languages at Columbia University, resident of Ringwood, and Republican state senator from Passaic County.

To Mary Allen Hulbert Peck

Dearest Friend, Princeton, 5 March, 1911.

Things are getting intense and interesting again. The bills for which we are pledged and on whose passage the success and prestige of my administration as governor largely depend are ready for report to the legislature, and the question is, Can we pass them? I think we can, and my spirits rise as the crisis approaches: it is like the senatorial contest all over again,—the same forces arrayed against me; and no doubt the same sort of fight will enable me to win. I have begun my speech-making (this time at various dinners of boards of trade, which afford me a convenient platform) and am pouring shot into the enemy in a way which I hope reaches the heart of his defences. To-morrow I meet all the Democratic members of the Assembly in conference and shall have my first shot at them direct. Besides that, I shall draw various individuals into my office and have talks with them. After the difficulties of the House are overcome, there is the Senate to deal with, which is Republican, by a majority of three. I do not know just how they will act. The senators gave me a dinner on Friday night (the customary thing, it seems) at the new Ritz-Carlton hotel, 46th. St. and Madison Avenue, and in the little speech I made them I established as natural and cordial relations as I knew how to suggest. They are good and honest men, for the most part, and I could warmly feel all the things I said. I am hoping for the best even with them,—though from just which of them I am to get the necessary votes I do not yet know. There are so many "personal equations" to bring into these puzzling calculations that I do not know till the last moment how the "sum" is going to work out. It's a fascinating, as well as nerve-wracking, business. And yet through it all I keep perfectly well and seem to thrive. It is deeply interesting: no one would wish to fall inattentive or to fall asleep over such business. I can realize at every stage and turn of it how you would dote on it, and how keenly you would follow and comprehend it all, with your singular intuitive knowledge of people. And somehow, through all of it, I keep my stubborn optimism. I cannot manage to think ill of my fellow men as a whole, though some of them are extraordinary scoundrels. Fortunately in this strange game most of the scoundrels are cowards also. The right, boldly done, intimidates them. Above all, they shrink away from the light. I spoke at three dinners last week: on Tuesday night before the West Hudson Board of Trade; on Thursday night before the Hoboken Board of Trade; on Friday night to the senators. Before I write again I shall have vis[i]ted Atlanta. On the tenth I am to speak before the Southern Commercial Congress, which the President is to attend, and where all the interests of the South and of the country are to be discussed. I am to speak at the closing evening session on "The Citizen and the State," speaking, I believe, just before the President,—not a very eligible position on the programme.[1] I am not going because I want to go, or because I have something in particular that I want to say, but, I am half ashamed to say, because I thought it wise (which, being translated, means politic) to go. I hate the things done for policy's sake! I do not do them with any zest; and I fear the address will lack distinction and fire on that account. But I shall do the best I can in the circumstances; and I am fortunate in the fact that none of the other men who are to speak that evening is an orator or within hailing distance of becoming one.[2] How satisfactory one's fellows limitations are to one once in a while! The President is popular in the South, and will, no doubt, have a very hearty welcome. Just now the whole country regards him with increased respect, because of his unexpected energy in forcing through the reciprocity treaty with Canada. You will by this time have heard that he is actually going to call the extra session.[3] And then

[1] Wilson's address is printed at March 10, 1911.

[2] The four other speakers were Secretary of War Jacob McGavock Dickinson; George Westinghouse, inventor and industrialist; John Hays Hammond, mining engineer; and Henry Simms Hartzog, southern educator who at this time was President of Ouachita Baptist College in Arkadelphia, Ark.

[3] The Sixty-first Congress had adjourned on March 4, and Taft immediately called the Sixty-second Congress, with the House of Representatives controlled by the Democrats, into special session for April 4 to reconsider a bill for trade reciprocity with Canada. Canadian-American trade relations had languished since 1866, when the United States abrogated the Elgin-Marcy Reciprocity Treaty of 1854. During the late nineteenth century, Canada made several attempts to obtain lower tariff rates between the two countries but was met by consistent rebuffs.

In his Annual Message of December 5, 1910, Taft announced his intention to obtain trade reciprocity with Canada, and a "legislative agreement" was negotiated by Secretary of State Philander Chase Knox and Canadian emissaries in Washington from January 7 to January 21, 1911. On January 26, Taft sent the agreement to the Senate, asking for its approval, and the Senate sent it to the House, requesting passage without amendment. The reciprocity bill permitted a lowering of the Payne-Aldrich rates on manufactured goods and placed on the free list most agricultural goods as well as some raw materials. Western Republicans immediately opposed the measure as an attempt to gain advantages for eastern manufacturers at the expense of farmers, and eastern Republicans eventually rebelled against the bill because it undermined the principle of protection. Through intense lobbying, Taft won House approval on February 14 by a vote of 221 to 92, but a majority of Republican congressmen voted against the measure. When it went to the Senate, a coalition of midwestern Republican insurgents, representing large agricultural constituencies, and eastern Republican protectionists resisted Taft's pressure and prevented a vote before the end of the session. The bill had fairly easy sailing in the Sixty-second Congress. The House approved it on April 21, 1911, the Senate on July 22.

During the debates over reciprocity, various proponents described the mea-

there will be some fun: for it will be the new, not the present, Congress. I shall hold my breath till I see just how the Democrats are going to use their majority in the new House. Champ Clark, their leader in the chair, is far from being a wise person. He is, on the contrary, a sort of elaphantine "smart Aleck." What A comfort to be able to say these things *entre nous* and without a sense of being, as usual, indiscreet! Colonel Harvey has again become eloquent, and ingenious, on the subject of my being the Democratic nominee for the presidency. I shall try to send you by the post that carries this a copy of the March number of the North American Review, in which he has an article entitled "The political predestination of Woodrow Wilson." The New York Times remarked upon it that it might very well turn out to be true that I would be chosen by the party as its presidential candidate, but that it was not necessary to prove it in so nonsensical a a [*sic*] way: that the probab[i]lity could not be increased by ingenious folderol. The whole thing is very amusing, and I, as usual, look on as if at what was taking place with regard to some one else. If the presidency is a governorship greatly increased in difficulty, I do not think that I want it! Enough, at any rate for the present!

And now I have talked enough about myself to tire even your sweet interest and generosity! What I am really thinking about is you. I am merely trying to entertain you, with the best and only things I have to give: the things that I see and experience from day to day. What makes it tolerable for *me* in spinning out these yarns is that I can imagine your comments and all the whimsical and delightful diversions you would make from the ordered course of them if I were telling them to you by word of mouth,—as well as the real light you would shed on them and the real, generous pleasure that would shine in your eyes. These

---

sure as a means of extending American economic influence in Canada. For example, Taft described Canada as "coming to the parting of the ways," having to decide whether to pursue closer ties with the British Empire or the United States. Champ Clark said that he hoped to see the day when the American flag would float "over every square foot of the British North American possessions clear to the North Pole." Such statements so alienated Canadian public opinion that the reigning Liberal government of Sir Wilfrid Laurier was forced to dissolve Parliament over the issue of reciprocity. In the ensuing election, on September 21, the Conservative party, pledged to oppose reciprocity, came to power.

Taft's espousal of reciprocity and his reliance upon Democratic support for passage of the reciprocity bill widened the split in the G.O.P., while his heavy-handed tactics embittered representatives and senators in both parties. What the President had described as one of the most important measures of his administration proved to be a political disaster for himself and the Republican party and a boon for the Democrats. The authoritative monograph on this subject is L. Ethan Ellis, *Reciprocity, 1911: A Study in Canadian-American Relations* (New Haven, Conn., and Toronto, 1939).

are the real pleasures of correspondence: what the letters you write bring back to you of the personality and abiding charm of the dear friend to whom you are writing. May God bless you!

> Your devoted friend,   Woodrow Wilson

WWTLS (WP, DLC).

To Reginald Rowland[1]

My dear Master Reginald: [Trenton, N. J.] March 6, 1911.

You set me really an impossible task. I have never known how to assist anybody in forming a jusgment [judgment] about myself and I should be at a loss to point out to you the proper magazine articles. If the Library at Clinton has a copy of Poole's Index of Periodical Literature, you can easily find by its means practically every article that has appeared in the magazines about me. Supplements to the index are published every month.

I am very much complimented that you should make me the subject of your oration.

> Sincerely yours,   Woodrow Wilson

TLS (de Coppet Coll., NjP).
  [1] A schoolboy of Clinton, N. J., whose letter to Wilson is missing.

From Hoke Smith[1]

Atlanta Ga, Mch 6, '11

Please wire me when you will reach Atlanta and how long you will stay   without interfering in any way with plans of Commercial Congress a number of Democrats here desire the privilege of meeting you and expressing their appreciation of your distinguished services.   Hoke Smith

T telegram (Governors' Files, Nj).
  [1] Secretary of the Interior, 1893-96; president of the Atlanta Board of Education, 1896-1907; Governor of Georgia, 1907-1909; at this time Governor-elect of Georgia for the term 1911-13. He was one of the leaders of the Wilson movement in Georgia during the preconvention campaign.

A News Report of a Conference with the Democratic Assemblymen of New Jersey

[March 7, 1911]

WILSON CONFIDENT HE'LL GET REFORM

Has Four Hours' Conference With Assemblymen—
Will Meet Committee Tomorrow

After spending four hours in conference with the Democratic members of the House of Assembly yesterday afternoon Governor Wilson declared that he was confident in the belief that the Geran bill would be passed by the Legislature substantially as it has been agreed upon in the meeting between himself and the Democratic legislative leaders.

The meeting of the Governor with the Democratic Assemblymen, which was the first conference of its character ever held in the State House, was behind closed doors. According to Speaker [Edward] Kenny,[1] the Governor was on his feet continuously for two hours and ten minutes explaining the four "administration" measures. These, besides the Gearn [Geran] bill, are the Egan Public Utility Rate Making bill, the Simpson Corrupt Practices bill and the Edge Employers' Liability bill. The latter measure represents the conclusions arrived at by the commission investigating the subject last year.[2] For nearly an hour and a half of the time that the Governor occupied the floor he was engaged in answering questions asked of him by the various Democratic Assemblymen. The Governor referred to the affair as a "conversational conference."

There was little difficulty in the conference coming to an agreement to support the Egan, Simpson and Edge bills. These three measures, as a result of this agreement will be put through the House at the earliest possible moment.

After the Geran bill had been under discussion for a long time, it was decided to delegate the Democratic Assembly "Steering" committee to continue the consideration of it with the Governor. The "steering" committee, composed of Messrs. Matthews, La Monte, Backus, James, Meyer and Ramsay,[3] will meet the Governor in the latter's office tomorrow morning at 9 o'clock.

"These gentlemen and myself will try to get the Geran bill in such form as will be satisfactory to the Democratic majority, and the committee will then report back to another full conference of the Assemblymen," said the Governor to this arrangement.

After the conference concluded at 7 o'clock last night, many contradictory rumors concerning what had happened between the Governor and the Democratic Assemblymen were circulated through the State House corridors. One story had it that a number of Assemblymen had made some caustic remarks concerning the Governor's policies. The Governor said there was not a word of truth in such a report. While he was talking with the newspaper men concerning the conference Assemblyman Egan[4] rushed into the executive chamber to deny a rumor that quoted him as saying that some of the Assemblymen in the conference had "put it all over the Governor."

"I want you to understand that I never said anything of the sort," excitedly declared Mr. Egan to the Governor. "I am with you heart and soul for these measures," added Mr. Egan.

"While there were more or less suggestions for changes in various features of the bill to meet individual ideas," explained the Governor, "I took it that all of those who advanced such suggestion would vote for the bill whether or not their ideas were accepted."

Speaker Kenny wanted the Geran bill referred for further consideration to a committee composed of the Speaker of the House, the Democratic Assembly and Senate leaders, the Governor and the introducer, Mr. Geran. He put his proposition in the form of a motion and it was lost by a vote of 13 to 17.

Printed in the *Trenton Evening Times*, March 7, 1911.
1 Lawyer of East Newark, Hudson County.
2 See WW to Mary A. H. Peck, April 9, 1911, n. 5.
3 John Joseph Matthews, farmer of High Bridge, Hunterdon County; George Mason La Monte, civil engineer and farmer of Bound Brook, Somerset County; Harry F. Backus, wholesale milk and cream dealer of Caldwell, Essex County; Peter H. James, lawyer of Jersey City, Hudson County; Charles Anthony Meyer, civil engineer of Andover, Sussex County; and William Ernest Ramsay, physician of Perth Amboy, Middlesex County.
4 Charles M. Egan, lawyer of Jersey City, Hudson County.

A News Report of an Address to the Trenton Chamber of Commerce

[March 8, 1911]

Chamber of Commerce Dinner The Occasion of Significant Discussion of Public Affairs

... The applause which greeted the other speakers of the evening was as nothing compared with the ovation which greeted Governor Wilson when he was introduced by Toastmaster General Wilbur F. Sadler,[1] demonstrating most conclusively the hold the State's Executive has on the people of this great little State.

1 Wilbur Fisk Sadler, Jr., Adjutant-General of New Jersey.

In introducing Governor Wilson the toastmaster made casual mention of the fact that Governor Wilson was being talked of for President—a statement which was rec[e]ived with great applause.

"It is a great pleasure," said Governor Wilson, "to talk to you after being talked to all day. I am talked to on more subjects every day than I can comprehend. I get so much free advice that it neutralizes itself and leaves me just where I started."

Referring to the old Trenton Board of Trade, Governor Wilson said that it probably allowed its interest in public affairs to decay. It had to be revived. It is now reorganized to do just what the politicians dread to see done. They dread to see a community take charge of its own affairs. The awakening of public opinion is to them something to cause concern. And the particular thing which these gentlemen dread is that the public shall have access to their business.

Governor Wilson declared that it is true, as Ambassador Bryce had said,[2] that there is no country in which public opinion is so powerful as in the United States.

And, the Governor added, there is nowhere that the political jungle is denser than it is in America. It has to be cut through. Public opinion has to wade in boots in the small stream and open up and make way for the navigation of the ship of State.

The Governor referred to the rec[e]nt campaign, and said that it was an easy thing to go about asking for votes, telling what ought to be done and making promises. But now comes the sober task of fulfilling those promises.

"And one of the promises," said he he [sic], "which most binds my conscience, is that I would tell you all I know about what is going on in public affairs."

The Governor then referred to the conference of a few days ago with the Democratic Assemblymen. He said that the newspaper men were not admitted to that conference, and, as a result, they got a distorted view of what took place. Nothing happened in that conference that ought not to have happened. No difference of opinion was expressed about what ought to be done, and about the neces[s]ity of fulfilling the party's promises. But the newspaper men got the idea that the politicians desired to be believed, that there was serious opposition to reform legislation and that the Democratic members of the Legislature were disposed to balk at doing their duty.

The politicians are opposing the Geran bill, the Governor said, on the ground that it will break up parties. It will do nothing

2 Who also spoke.

of the kind. It will break up some things. It will break up unworthy party machines. And it will give the people direct access to their government and the machinery of government.

The trouble with the politician[s], declared the Governor, is profound and impenetrable ignorance. They fancy that certain consequences will result from a given thing, but they don't know. They have no knowledge by which to be guided. For example, said the Governor, we are debating things here that have ceased to be debated in all but two or three States. There is not a thing contemplated in the chief measures now before the Legislature that has not been tested elsewhere and found to work well for the common good.

Turning to Mr. Post[3] Governor Wilson declared that he had not found the highest knowledge of public affairs coming from men of business. "Their noses are so close to their ledgers that they can't see anything but the figures. They are so enmeshed in their own affairs that they don't know their country. They have ideas about politics and propositions of government that experience elsewhere has taught will not happen.

"There is no disposition on the part of the legislature or of the people to wrong anybody. No more just or generous sentiments are to be found anywhere than among the common people."

The Governor rather startled his audience of business men when he told them that his experience had shown that the very best and wisest judgment on matters of public policy was to be found among those men that earn about $2,500 a year.

Further on, speaking along the same line, the Governor again addressed Mr. Post with the declaration that everything he had learned from experience had taught him that "the real wisdom of human life is compounded out of the experiences of ordinary men."

Further discussing the Geran bill, Governor Wilson declared that there is not a provision in it that has not been tested in other States and found good.

[3] George Adams Post, president of the Standard Coupler Co., one of the founders and president of the Railway Business Association, who, according to the report in the Trenton *True American*, March 8, 1911, in his speech had "protested vehemently, eloquently, almost savagely, against a system of government that gives into the hands of the average man the legislative supervision of the affairs of the empire of capital and industry"; "protested that only men of great minds and ideas are fit to manage the mammoth, intricate, Nation-wide affairs of the modern business enterprise"; and "protested against permitting men whose spheres in life are limited, who are inexperienced, and provincial, to deal with those propositions in public life which bear upon the mighty problems of commerce and capital and finance, and which affect the welfare of the millions."

"You don't want to put the politicians out of business," said the speaker, "because they are very useful sometimes when they are disposed to serve you faithfully. But you want to give them the right sort instead of the wrong sort of power. And they must be taught that all must derive their authority in government and poditics [politics] from the people speaking through the primaries and elections."

Speaking of the opponents of the Geran bill, the Governor said that all he wanted was for its opponents to stand up and give their reasons for their opposition. He admitted, as Mr. Post had said, that the politicians, some of them, do a lot of irresponsible talking. But let the men [man] who has objections hire a hall and give his views to his fellow men, and he'll know himself in five minutes whether he is talking sense or nonsense.

Governor Wilson, in further defense of the Geran election bill, said that one of the great aroubles [troubles] with American politics is that men say, "What's the use of voting when we don't accomplish anything." And these men don't go to the polls. He said that he was not going to criticise men for not going to the polls when they vote and vote and vote and the things that they are voting for don't happen.

He sounded a gra[v]e warning against the practice of fooling and tricking the voters. "You fool them and intrigue against them and defeat them too long," said he, "and they will turn and rend you and in rending you may rend government itself."

"Let any man," exclaimed Governor Wilson, "who now stands in the way of popular government look to it, for a day of reckoning is coming if he refuses to stand aside."

The Governor expressed the greatest confidence in this legislature. He declared that it was made up of honorable, capable men, who knew their duty and will do it fearlessly.

The Governor also referred to the public utilities bill, declaring that it had been long in operation in the State of Wisconsin, where it was originated by Senator La Follette, and he said that recently a business man from that State had told him that while he fought the measure at first from an honest fear that it would damage industries, he was willing to admit now that nothing better had ever happened to business in Wisconsin.

The Governor argued that the public utilities bill will benefit business because it will give the people an insight into the affairs of those great public corporations which they now distrust and dislike. We are jealous of the great public service corporations now because we don't know whether their charges are legal or illegal. But when they are required to open their business to the inspection of the people's representatives and show the basis of their charges instead of suspecting we will know. Instead of fearing we will have confiddence and be satisfied. And as for the corporations themselves, their securities instead of having a speculative value, will have a certain value, and their stocks will become marketable because the value of their stocks will become known.

Governor Wilson's closing remarks were devoted to an eloquent representation of how much more desirable it is to live a life of honesty and truth than it is to live the life of the politician who cheats the people, of the business man who uses short weights and measures, of the judge who is unfaithful, of the public prosecutor who shirks his task, of the sheriff who pads the jury list, of the manufacturer who misuses his power to wring wealth from the weak, of the man whose conscience is not at ease. It was a mighty appeal for honesty and integrity in public and private life, and his audience, although it had applauded time and time again, burst forth into applause that shook the big hall.

Governor Wilson declared that he had never sought nor desired public office, but he was glad to devote a brief term to the public service of his fellow citizens, and declared that if in that service he would be able to satisfy his own heart he could afford to be indifferent to the world's judgment.

Printed in the Trenton *True American*, March 8, 1911; many editorial headings omitted.

From Francis Fisher Kane

Dear Governor Wilson: Philadelphia March 8, 1911.

Thank you for your note of yesterday. The printing of your address goes ahead, but not as rapidly as I could wish. The number of copies you ask for will be sent you. We are planning to print 2,000 in all.

Champ Clark lectured at the Baptish [Baptist] Temple here on Monday and we gave him a little dinner before his talk. He told me that, as he saw it, Taft had by his Reciprocity Message broken his party in half, and that there was little prospect of the halves coming together. Champ is not a radical and his references to your speech were not sympathetic. He had read the newspaper accounts, and "he understood you had gone the whole hog"—meaning that you had endorsed the entire radical programne. This was said across me at dinner to Harrity,[1] who sat on my other side, and I did not like it. It wasn't good taste on Mr. Clark's part to say the least, and I dare say the others argued, as I did, that he was just a little jealous of the New Jersey Governor.

I was at the Princeton Dinner last Friday and heard West's speech.[2] I felt untrue to you when I spoke to him cordially, and yet good manners seemed to require it. When I see you I'll tell you exactly what he said about the Graduate College. He has the lists to himself, and he brandished his spear right valiantly. Where was the Knight-errant of Democracy? Some of us missed him sadly.   Yours sincerely,   Francis Fisher Kane.

I did not like one thing particularly in West's speech.[3] More of this later.

TLS (WP, DLC).
  [1] William Francis Harrity, a lawyer of Philadelphia, who had been a powerful figure in the Pennsylvania Democratic party in the 1880's and 1890's.
  [2] Dean West was the principal speaker at the forty-third annual dinner of the Princeton Club of Philadelphia held at the Bellevue-Stratford Hotel on March 3.
  [3] It is difficult to know exactly what Kane found objectionable. West began by praising two of Wilson's major achievements at Princeton—the reform of the curriculum and the preceptorial system. He added, however, that Princeton was perhaps being too demanding in its entrance requirements by requiring preparation in too many fields. West predicted that the controversy over the graduate college would subside once it was built and said that the purpose of the Graduate School was to provide studies for the sake of knowledge, not "bread and butter studies." "By means of the Graduate College," he went on, "the Princeton spirit in the best sense will be perpetuated in the Princeton faculty. Here we will develop also the high-class teachers for the best colleges and schools." Warning that the danger of graduate education was concentration on "a too formal type of scholarship," he urged the training of personality as well as of mind. *Princeton Alumni Weekly*, XI (March 8, 1911), 345-47.

A News Report of Two Speeches in Atlanta

[March 10, 1911]

WOODROW WILSON FINDS OPEN ARMS OF WELCOME HERE

Atlanta Showers Distinguished Democrat from New Jersey With Attention—Hails Him as Party's Leader

Excepting presidents and ex-presidents, there has never been a visitor to Atlanta who has received more marked attention and been more warmly greeted than Gov. Woodrow Wilson, of New Jersey. Everywhere he is being hailed as one of the foremost members of his party. But his unusually hearty greeting in Atlanta is due to the fact that he is a southern man, and a former resident of Atlanta, where he began the practice of law.

Governor Wilson was tendered a luncheon Thursday evening [March 9] by Gov.-elect Hoke Smith, on which occasion he was hailed as one of the greatest men in the Democratic party and the most likely man for the presidential candidacy.

At a breakfast tendered him by the Young Men's Democratic League Friday morning Governor Wilson was again eulogized as the next president. Everywhere tribute is being paid to him as the leader of the party.

Following the breakfast of the Democratic league, Governor Wilson attended a reception at the home of Hugh Richardson[1] Friday morning, and later attended the Taft luncheon at the Capital City club. . . .

That Woodrow Wilson is one of the strongest and most significant figures in the Democratic party is evidenced by his cordial reception in Atlanta. At the breakfast Friday morning the speakers,[2] without exception, paid tribute to him as one of the most likely candidates for the presidential chair. . . .

Governor Wilson skillfully outlined the ideals of the Democratic party. He said that he believes that there are only two sets of men who can lead in politics—young men and men who never grow old. "The country," said he "is not measured by what it has been, but what it is, and what it hopes to be, and only in a determined, definite looking-forward is there hope."

He said that it has been significant of the south that it has had a tendency to shut itself in with the glories of the past, which are the finest in history. He said that there had been in the past an imagined hostility between the north and the south, but that he could now see no traces of this imagined attitude of the north toward the south, and that there seemed to be a universal desire that the south should come into her own again.

He said that the future of the party depends upon the young men and that the party should endeavor to attract them. In speaking of the two leading parties he said that their theories are directly opposed to each other; that the Republican party wishes to govern by trusteeship, putting affairs in the hands of those who are wealthiest, but that the only safe government is one in which all the people participate.

"Every time I deal with the present trustees of the United

[1] In real estate and investments in Atlanta. He had attended Princeton as a special student in 1891-92.

[2] Among them was Judge George Hillyer of Atlanta, retired, who had presided at Wilson's examination for admission to the bar in 1882 and signed his license to practice law. Hillyer said: "Last evening we listened to a man who has been president; this evening we shall hear a man who is president; but we have with us this morning a man who is going to be president."

States I see that they lack a vision of the people as a whole. The most serious thing facing us today is the concentration of money power in the hands of a few."[3]

He spoke of New York city as one of the most provincial places in the world, always looking out for New York, and, in contrast with this declared: "Our whole problem is to bring the people of the United States into the game."

He spoke of government as fundamentally a matter of "whom do you want to serve?" He said that business interests should be subservient to public interests, and that all should have intentions of public service. He said that the chief asset is confidence.

His closing remarks were a tribute to the Democratic party as standing for honest, wholesome, compact progress. . . .

Governor Woodrow Wilson, of New Jersey, was extended a most cordial and enthusiastic welcome to Atlanta and the south at an elaborate dinner given in his honor by Gov.-elect Hoke Smith in the banquet hall of the Piedmont hotel Thursday evening. Gathered around the festive board was a most representative assemblage and in short addresses of welcome Governor Wilson was repeatedly referred to as the next Democratic nominee and president of the United States, and his host, Gov.-elect Hoke Smith, as the most suitable man for vice president of the United States.

In response to the warm welcome extended to him Governor Wilson delivered an eloquent address, in which he spoke of the bright prospect of true Democracy in the immediate future and in which he defined true Democracy. . . .

Governor Wilson first stated that he was not a Wilson man. Continuing, he said: "There is a great difference between the south and the region in which I now live. This fact was brought more clearly to my notice on a recent visit to Trinity college, Durham, N. C.[4] No man can live long enough to solve all the mysterious parts of life which he does not understand.

"In riding on the train I entered into conversation with a North Carolinian, who upon learning that I was from New Jersey asked what the people of that state thought of Grover Cleveland, who was at that time president of the United States.

"I was forced to reply that I did not know. He immediately set me down as an ignoramus, but as a matter of fact fact [sic],

3 The first time, insofar as the Editors know, that Wilson mentioned this then highly controversial subject.
4 Wilson's only visit to Trinity College (now Duke University) had not been exactly recent. He spoke there on March 22, 1894. A news report of his address is printed at March 23, 1894, Vol. 8.

it is impossible to ascertain political feelings in some sections of the north as easily as they may be learned in the south.

"The south is noted for homogeneity and talkativeness. There is more politics talked to the square mile in the south than in the entire nation. The south can be sampled very much like a bale of cotton. You can pluck a piece here and find the value of the entire bale.

"In the south and in New England, the old country life of the mother country has been brought over. They are substantially English. In the states of New York, New Jersey and the middle north this is not true. The population is mixed to that degree commonly termed the American mixture.

"The present is a time of rejoicing for the coming back of the south into national politics. The south is certainly coming back to its former position as may be seen from glancing at the house of representatives and beholding the power of the southern party in that body.

"The return to power of the south is looked upon by some in the north with a peculiar feeling. To a certain extent the south is misunderstood. Many think that the south is conservative to the point of being reactionary. But how can a region be conservative which has such a community?

"The older I get the more radical I get along certain lines. Radical in the literal sense of the word, and I long more and more to get at the root of the whole matter.

"A short while ago I was a guest at dinner with a company of comfortable looking New York successful business men.[5] They wore that air of comfort which is not seen outside of New York.

"They seemed to be of the opinion that in my educational work I was trying to make their sons just as different from their fathers as possible. Now success in particular lines had narrowed their scope from habitual concentration. Absorbed in particular lines of business they had lost touch with the country and the world at large. My idea was to have their sons make a new start, not to take up life where their fathers had left off, but to enter it with a new and broader vision.

"I have studied politics all my life, and have found that the successful men are not the ones from whom best advice and information is to be learned. The man who is making $1,500 or $2,000 a year in most cases is better prepared to give information in regard to a business than the successful owner.

"Everything must be carried back to the people themselves.

[5] A meeting of the Williams College alumni in New York on February 5, 1909. A news report of this affair is printed at Feb. 6, 1909, Vol. 19.

This is true of business and politics and is the only basis which acts as a safeguard to human intere[s]ts.

"Have you ever noticed that society is never renewed from the top. It is from the bottom that the rise is made. The old families burn out and their places are filled by men from the unrisen sources.

"Did you ever stop to consider that the Roman Catholic church in the middle ages was an example of pure Democracy? There was no peasant who was too humble to become a priest and this democratic condition kept the government from going to dry rot during the period of the world's greatest addiction to aristocracy.

"The machine refer[r]ed to by Mr. Stovall,[6] in New Jersey, was not a powerful organization supported by the people. It was merely a selfish private close corporation and the only power it had was compelled by fear.

"Party organization is necessary. It is only when the organization becomes implicated with business to such an extent that the people and their interests are overlooked that part[y] organization becomes an evil.

"It will be dead easy for the Democratic party to win victory if they convince the people that they are working for them. There has been a great deal of talk among dissatisfied Republicans of the organization of a third party. These men cannot quite take to the name 'Democratic,' but if men are put up in the next election in whom the people believe, the Republicans themselves will form an integral part in casting votes for their election.

"It is only necessary for the Democrats to show that they are playing a square game and are consistent in saying that their purpose is to serve the people of the United States."

Printed in the *Atlanta Journal*, March 10, 1911; some editorial headings omitted.
6 Pleasant Alexander Stovall, editor of the *Savannah Press* and boyhood friend of Wilson's in Augusta, Ga.

An Address to the Southern Commercial Congress[1]

[[March 10, 1911]]

You are waiting to hear the President of the United States. I would consider it an act of presumption on my part if I were to detain you from that pleasure. I cannot refrain, however, from expressing the very great pleasure with which I face this

1 Delivered in the Atlanta Auditorium. Wilson was introduced by Governor-elect Hoke Smith.

magnificent audience, an audience gathered here where I like to remember that some of the most inspiring years of my life were spent.

It is a very stirring thing that a great body of people like this should be gathered together to deliberate upon the more serious purposes of their life as a section and as a Nation. I have listened, during the thirty-six hours that I have been here, to many comments upon this great gathering; and I have heard it spoken of as a symptom of the "awakening of the South"; but I don't think that the South has been asleep. It was not necessary to cry to the South "Awake"; for she was already tense with the consciousness of her own life. This is merely a beginning of the release of her power. She has known that she possessed it. She has known what her place was in the national situation. She has bided her time; and now, in the fullness of that time, she expects to take her place in the councils and in the exercise of the power of a great country.

When my subject "The Citizen and the State" was assigned me, it seemed to me that those who had framed it conceived that there was some contrast, some antithesis between the citizen and the State. The citizen is the State. The State is merely his instrument for expressing that part of his life which he shares with his fellowmen. As the citizen is, so will the State be. As the people of the South are, so will the life of the South, and the politics of the South, and the development of the South be.

It is true that these people have seemed to those who did not know, to be asleep during some of the decades that lie immediately behind us. It is true that the South has seemed lethargic and indifferent. There are some things which disturb us in thinking of the political history of the South, in recent years particularly. Her total vote has fallen tremendously below the number of her qualified voters; as if her voters were not eager to take a part in her affairs. And those who have known the explanation have seen that it was because the voters of the South supposed that the rest of the Nation was unwilling that she should enter the political arena and take the part that belonged to her. It has been thought that the Nation did not expect self-assertion of her; and therefore, with a sort of sensitive pride, she has refrained from playing her full part in public affairs. And she has required of her leaders, not that they take an aggressive part, but that they express merely her character, her pride, her reminiscence of the great past which has made illustrious so much of the record of this country.

It is as if the South had asked her leaders to represent what she has been, and what she is, rather than what she hopes and expects to be.

The South has not consciously connected its material growth with the general development of the United States, and has not asked her statesmen to plan that she should have a formative part in the conduct of affairs. That is due to something in the Southern character which we love, and those of us who understand it cannot for a moment criticise it. It is due to an exquisite sensitiveness of pride. You have thought that you were not welcome in the life of the Nation.

Now there has in recent years been a hopeful change. It is that change which blows like a fresh current of air through an assembly like this. If I read the opinion of other parts of the country correctly, you have long been mistaken. There is nowhere that I go any jealousy of the South asserting her old birthright in the affairs of the country. There is nothing but the most cordial feeling of brotherhood displaying itself throughout this country toward the waiting, the patient, the as yet unrealized energy of the South. There is no part of the country that I have been to where you are not regarded as warp and woof of the national life; and I have heard men say that there was spread upon the South as a sort of precious asset, some of the noblest, choicest and most honorable traditions of our national life. Nowhere else in the country has there been a more unbroken and continuous tradition, reaching back to the great formative period of our Republic.

There is a homogeneity in the South; there is a sense of community in the South; there is a consciousness of sympathy and neighborliness and common understanding, which makes this the very reservoir of that old emotion which lies at the head, at the source, of all true patriotism. I do not believe that patriotism is a mere sentiment. Patriotism sometimes seems to me anything but a sentiment. It expresses itself, it has its emotional outline in service. But patriotism rightly conceived is a certain surplus of character over and above what you spend on yourself. You know that we are very free in our use of the a[d]jective "great." We say of any man who has succeeded on a large scale that he is "great," no matter how selfish he has been. We may recognize his power by the adjective "great"; but there is one adjective which we reserve for a particular sort of man, and that is the adjective "noble." No man has ever won that beautiful encomium who has spent all his powers within the narrow circle of his own self-interest. No man is of the patriciate of this Nation who has not spent his powers upon the community, upon the State, upon the country; and it is this expenditure of force for the things that are not selfish that makes the patriotism of every race. The large-souled, noble men that we want in our land are the men of altruistic impulses, refraining from seeking their own individual interests because of their unconscious realization of, and regard for, the neighborhood and community of interest and the things which their neighbors expect and experience and need.

There is a very disturbing circumstance about separation from the people you know. If you have ever been in a distant foreign city, under circumstances which made you believe that nobody from anywhere near where you lived was anywhere within reach, you know how your character begins to break down. You begin to realize the awful fact that your character is really sustained by the opinion of the people you know. Now the peculiarity about a Southerner is that he knows the standards which every other Southerner will exact of him; and there is a very noble power to sustain you in this consciousness of your community standards. You can not fall below them without losing caste. And what is expected of a Southern man is one of the compulsions of your career. There are very few parts of the country where there are so many persons to buttress up your character as there are in the South. In most of the Northern communities the competition and the selfish rush for gold in the many large cities is so strenuous and so fierce that the number of people who know you, and watch you, and upon whose good opinion you must depend, is very much smaller than it is in the South. You must be able, when you come back to the South from Paris, to face the whole village or the whole town. And you don't want any questions asked about it.

That, it seems to me, is now the course that is about to go back into the great stream of national life. This tradition that runs back to the great days of the Republic and has continued until now unbroken, is going to be turned into the channels that make for the purification and energizing and advancement of the whole of a great country.

Did you never reflect upon the changed condition of the South now, as compared with the old days? There was a time when the South was dominated by a single interest. I am not now speaking of slavery, but something that slavery was incidental to. There was in the old South a fixed social order, from which a great many of these standards (which I have just been speak-

ing of) sprang, and the whole interest of the South was to preserve intact, first, that structure itself, and then, after that
structure was destroyed, the social standards which had been
produced by that structure. And the South may be said to have
been the place of a single interest. And now the South, having
seen almost two generations go by since that order was destroyed,
is face to face with many other interests. When we make campaign speeches, we spell those interests with a capital "I"; we
abuse them as "Big Business," as "The Interests," or, to sum
the whole thing up in one sinister suggestion, we speak of them
as "Wall Street."

The South is now face to face with "the interests." What, so
far as the South is concerned, are "the interests"? They are
those great bodies of capital, impersonated in individuals that
control them, that are coming down into the South to exploit
her resources. And how magnificent the resources of the South
are! When you reflect upon the mere physical conformation of
the South, her various coast lines, her inviting harbors, the great
navigable streams that thread her territory, the broad acres that
are only just now beginning to be made to yield their rich har-
vests of food for the human race, her gracious rainfall, her long
grazing season, the unexhausted and perhaps inexhaustible
stores of her mineral wealth, her great forests—all those things
which men covet to change into wealth and into power—such
are the resources of the South, at which the imagination kindles.
And great bodies of capital, impersonated by the men who can
control it, are coming down to exploit the resources of the South.

What are you going to do with these "interests"? You enjoy
a singular advantage, gentlemen of the South. You have before
you the record of experiments and of mistakes made in the rest
of the country, and you have something which the rest of the
country does not possess in equal degree. What you possess I
have just now been trying to point out to you. You possess a
common consciousness of your interests as communities, of your
solidarity as communities, of the obligations of honor and of
necessity placed upon you by neighborhood and State and re-
gional opinion. Very well, then; put these things into operation,
and bid your public men do a unique thing.

What are we seeking in our national life now? Are we seeking to defeat the profitable use of capital? Not at all. Are we
seeking to stop and embarrass and turn aside the great streams
of power, both personal and material which have been making
this country one of the greatest countries in the world? Are
we seeking to offset antipodal things against each other? Are

we seeking to offset popular passion against private property and individual interest? God forbid.

I am the friend, if I know my own heart, of the humblest people living, but I am not their friend in the sense that I am anybody else's enemy. I am the friend of honest capital, but that doesn't mean that I will league myself with any sort of capital to do harm, or to disparage the prospects of anybody else.

Do you know that we are seeking, in our politics, a missing term that we have not yet discovered? That term is "the common interest"—the interest which is just as much the interest of capital as the interest of labor, just as much the interest of the poor as the interest of the rich. And there is only one way to find it—we shall not find it until everybody wants to find it.

I do not object to those men who are pushing their interests as investors and capitalists, *because* they are pushing their interests. I object to them because when I talk to them I find that they do not understand anybody else's interests. And the trouble with them is not their greed, not their covetousness, but their extraordinary and impenetrable ignorance. They do not know that the stuff they work in is human life, and that unless human life be pure and prosperous they themselves cannot have what they covetously desire.

Every kind of business seems to be a sort of service when it is properly conceived. Conceive it correctly, and every great business is the service of the public for private profit, and the profit is illegitimate unless the public is served. What our men of means, therefore, have now to study, if their prosperity is to continue and to be sound, is the interests of the communities which they are serving. We will not grudge them one cent of their profit—though they pile it to high heaven—if they have got all of it by the honorable means of serving their fellowmen. But we will grudge them every cent of it which they get thinking only of themselves.

There are two theories of government. There is the theory of government which we call the aristocratic theory of government. It doesn't make any difference how you organize your aristocracy, the point is just the same. It is this: That you think there is a certain class of persons who have more money, or more intelligence, or more education than the rest, who are fit to be trustees for all the remainder. I want to ask you if we have not been in danger in this country of acting upon that idea? We have thought that the men whom we were sustaining by our national policies of taxation, in their efforts to build up great industries, were the men to whom we should look as the trustees of the national welfare.

I dissent absolutely from the theory. And I not only dissent, but if I had time and you had the patience, I could prove its absurdity. What do you do when you enable a man to build up a gigantic business and to make himself very rich thereby? You give him something so difficult to do that he becomes wholly absorbed in it, and does not think anything about the rest of the human race. He is the worst trustee of the public interest that I can imagine. His imagination has gone to wreck, his feeling of sympathy has been circumscribed, his vision has been bounded by the narrow limits of commercialism and the confining walls of his single undertaking; and because he is a great "captain of industry" he does not understand anything about the business of his captaincy.

A very witty Englishman once said that it was absurd to try to turn a man who had won eminent success and great wealth; you could not bribe that man, because, he said, the point about him is that he *has* been bribed. He has built up his success on the existing order of the national life, and he is under the biggest bonds that a man ever was put under to see that that order of life is not changed. He is under the biggest kind of a selfish obligation to see that nothing is altered, for fear his success might be interfered with.[2]

Now your rankest "standpatter" is your man who has the biggest permanent stake in standing pat. I do not expect to see those gentlemen moved with a derrick. I would be unreasonable and show ignorance of human nature to hope for it. When you want movement, you've got to take the movable part of mankind. And the movable part are not the men who are made, but the men who are "on the make." And inasmuch as they are in the majority, they can generally get the movement when they want it.

Let us have the movement; and let this great body of men representative of the South remember what it is that they have to work with. A great social tradition of honor, where only those are distinguished who embody in their own persons and in their own principles the judgments and conceptions of their neighbor! Where else in the country could there be better material for the sort of progress which will be not only movement, but fair movement, honorable movement—just to everybody concerned? Let no man deceive himself about the character of the affairs of this

[2] See n. 4 to the address printed at Feb. 21, 1911.

country and our day, ladies and gentlemen. We have come to a time when we are considering our life from top to bottom. And therefore we have come to a time which should quicken the pulse of every man who has the least imagination in him—for we have come upon a new constructive age, not an age when things are going to be pooled, but an age when things are going to be readjusted.

Did you ever think what liberty is? Liberty does not consist in every man's having his way—as I need not insist. I picture liberty to myself when I see a great and perfect piece of machinery, like a great railway locomotive. The freest locomotive is the locomotive whose parts are best assembled and adjusted and that runs with least friction. Many of you have sailed a boat. What do you do with her? Do you throw her head up into the wind? If you do, she will be caught and every stitch of canvas and every stick in her will quiver as if she were coming to pieces, and the sailor says she is in "the teeth of the wind." But let her veer off, let her yield to this great force that is blowing in her face, and what do you say of her? You say she goes very well, she sails free, she is adjusted to the great force that is blowing across the water.

And so with all government. It is adjustment; taking away the strains; assembling and unifying the parts. Now that is the kind of liberty we are seeking in our day. It is a more complicated task of construction than faced the great men who built our Republic. A time is now at hand when there is more room for statesmanship than there was in 1776—than there was in 1789. We shall adjust our minds and our lives to a great age, to which our children shall look back and say: "Then was a time when men thought upon public affairs, when they turned their eyes aside from selfish introspection, when they looked at the long, uphill road that lay before the toilsome advance of mankind, and sought with self-sacrificing philanthropy, with noble self-forgetfulness, with high consciousness of honor, with confident hope, to lead their fellowmen to new attainments and to the glorious radiance of a new day.[3]

Printed in LeRoy Hodges (ed.), *Proceedings Third Annual Convention Southern Commercial Congress Atlanta, Ga. March, 1911* (n.p., n.d.).
[3] There is a WWT outline of this address, with the composition date of March 5, 1911, in WP, DLC.

From Charles Henry Ingersoll[1]

My dear Governor: New York City. March 10, 1911.

I am writing you regarding your Trenton Chamber of Commerce speech, on the theory that sometimes a public speaker does not himself, appreciate clearly all that has happened. I regard your address as one of the most clear-cut presentations of democracy from fundamental standpoints, that I have ever heard; that it has applied to a complex phase of the subject under somewhat embarrassing circumstances, made it the more important and inspiring.

Your adroit and at the same time scathing answer to Post's various propositions, was very effective, and would have converted any but a well seasoned corporation agent.

But the most unique and perhaps the bravest thing you said, was regarding the business man, and as one in a position to know, I would say that you spoke with truth and accuracy.

With regards, I am,

Yours very truly,   C H Ingersoll

TLS (WP, DLC).
    [1] Secretary and treasurer of Robt. H. Ingersoll & Bro. of New York, watch manufacturers, single taxer and member of many reform organizations, who lived in South Orange, N. J.

From Clarence Hamilton Poe

My dear Governor: Raleigh, N. C., March 11, 1911

The enclosed interview in last Friday's News and Observer explains itself.[1] I am very much gratified to find the strong hold you have in North Carolina, and I am planning to hear your address before the South Carolina Press Association:[2] I had the pleasure of being the "outsider" to make their annual address last year. I also hope to hear you at Chapel Hill.

I shall be glad to do anything I can toward getting you the North Carolina delegation next year.

With best wishes, I am,

Sincerely yours,   Clarence Poe

TLS (WP, DLC).
    [1] The interview was about Poe's recent trip around the world and his assessment of the meaning of the elections of 1910. "The Democratic victory," he said, "was a source of great gratification to me, and there is much interest in Democratic policy all over the world. As the next Democratic Presidential candidate I have been surprised at the immense lead Woodrow Wilson has among people I have me[t]—not excepting men from Ohio. [']I should be all the gladder to see Wilson chosen,' a Northern ex-United States Senator said to me, 'because it would be a sort of recognition of the South; and I think the time has come for it.'" Raleigh, N. C., News and Observer, March 10, 1911.
    [2] This address is printed at June 2, 1911, Vol. 23.

To Mary Allen Hulbert Peck

Dearest Friend,   Princeton, 13[12] Mar., 1911

This time I am not in New York, but am just back from Atlanta, Georgia. I am *so* much distressed about the attack of bronchitis. What business have you to have bronchitis in Bermuda! You have simply been using yourself up,—forgetting that you went back to your paradise this time with no strength to spend, under the full reaction of the terrible strain of the past twenty years! You must *acquire*, not spend,—build up a new strength for new uses and a new world. *Please* remember! Please take the time to make yourself over, physically, for the sake of the new things, to which you are at last emancipated.[1] And, meanwhile, be just to yourself. Do not say, or *think*, what you have more than once said when speaking of the sad Colonel's wife[2] and of Mrs. Chief Justice.[3] You are *not* counselling them to do what you yourself did not do. On the contrary, you are urging them to do what you steadfastly attempted for twenty heartbreaking years,[4]—what you spent your youth and strength and all but your life itself in trying to do—to try, as you did, the heroic things for which you are now paying so heavy a penalty. You did nothing less than exhaust your splendid vitality in trying to keep faith, as you wish them to do. You have a better right than any one I know to give the advice you are giving them. *Do* not be so unjust with yourself! It only distresses me. Above all, rest, be careful, eat the good things the dear "Christians down stairs" so lovingly urge upon you, and live for the new duties, wh. are so much happier than the old.

I went down to Atlanta to attend the Southern Commercial Congress. I spoke on the last evening of the Congress, Friday, the tenth. The Secretary of War, President Taft, and I were all on the programme for the same evening, besides three other gentlemen who contributed their part also to overloading the programme. The poor President, who was last on the list, did not get a chance at the audience until nearly midnight. Mr. Roosevelt had spoken the evening before, in the same place, an enormous auditorium in which, both evenings, was collected an audience of not less than eight thousand people! It was a great sight and a great inspiration. On the whole the reception accorded me was finer than that accorded either Mr. Roosevelt or Mr. Taft. I spoke only half an hour but seemed to make a deep inpression [impression]. I was given a dinner, a breakfast, and a reception, and on every possible occasion was nominated for the presidency! It is all very gratifying, but a little disturbing to a gentleman who is trying to do his duty without fuss or display! I hurried back to greet Mr. Bryan! He was in Princeton to-day, to address the Theological Seminary, at their Sunday afternoon conference. They held it in Alexander Hall, which was packed; and the address, which was on Faith, was most impressive. He held the audience easily for an hour and a half. It was the first time I had ever heard him speak, and I was exceedingly pleased. After the meeting he came over to the Inn and dined with Ellen, Jessie, Nellie, a Mr. Birch[5] (in whose car he had come up from Burlington), and me, and I feel that I can now say that I know him, and have a very different impression of him from that I had before seeing him thus close at hand. He has extraordinary force of personality, and it seems the force of sincerity and conviction. He has himself well in hand at every turn of the thought and talk, too; and his voice is wholly delightful. A truly captivating man, I must admit. He had to be off by half past seven, so I had only a little while with him,—only through the short dinner.

To-morrow I return to the struggle at Trenton: and a struggle it is. There is much balking at the adoption of one of the chief bills pending, because it takes the control of things out of the hands of the politicians. I shall, apparently, have to use "the big stick." If necessary, very well! That is not my nature, as you know; but when the opposition is dishonest, not such as those who show it would dare ventilate in public, someone must champion the cause of the voiceless people, no matter what the consequences. I keep astonishingly well, considering the constant strain I am under. There must be some wholesome stimulation in it, as I think have sagely remarked before. Obvious remarks are so much the easiest to repeat!

I am very tired to-night. I just came off my long journey from the South at noon, leaving my train at Trenton and coming over in a motor car, and am so sleepy now that I can scarcely see the type I am hammering. All join me in affectionate messages, and I am (with warmest regards to your mother and your son) always   Your devoted Friend   Woodrow Wilson

WWhw and WWTLS (WP, DLC).
1 By her separation from her husband, Thomas Dowse Peck.
2 Wilson referred to the wife of Colonel Wright, whose brutish ways are discussed in WW to EAW, Feb. 25, 1910; WW to Mary A. H. Peck, Feb. 25, 1910; and Mary A. H. Peck to WW, Feb. 25, 1910, all in Vol. 20.
3 Marie Louise Norris Gollan.
4 That is, to make a success of her marriage to Peck.
5 Thomas Howard Birch, identified in H. E. Alexander to WW, Dec. 20, 1910, n. 1.

A News Report

[March 13, 1911]

Bryan Meets Wilson at Latter's Home in Princeton

William J. Bryan and Governor Woodrow Wilson met for the first time in their lives yesterday. It is the simple truth to say that each of these two greatest of Democrats was impressed with the other's splendid personality.

They will meet again soon, for it was arranged yesterday that they should both speak at the Jefferson dinner which is to be given in the big auditorium in Burlington, on April 5.[1]

Thomas H. Birch, of Burlington, is the inspiring genius of this April celebration. He suggested both to Mr. Bryan and to Governor Wilson that they pay his city a visit on that occasion, and both agreed to the proposition with evident pleasure.

This will be a great Democratic meeting, for it is proposed to have present not only these two champions of Democracy, but other prominent Democrats from various sections of the country, and the celebration promises to be one of the most significant of the many great celebrations with which the Democrats of the nation will this year honor the memory of Jefferson.

Governor Wilson hastened home from Atlanta, Georgia, in order to extend a fitting courtesy to Mr. Bryan.[2] The Governor was present at the meeting which Mr. Bryan addressed in Alexander Hall yesterday, and at its close warmly congratulated the distinguished speaker. Mr. Bryan was entertained at a family dinner by Governor and Mrs. Wilson.

Mr. Bryan Meets Governor Wilson

Although Mr. Bryan did not care to say much about the meeting, it is understood that he expressed himself privately as being very favorably impressed by Governor Wilson, and was glad to [have] had the opportunity of dining with him.

Asked by a True American correspondent to give his impression of the Governor, Mr. Bryan replied:

"I do not like to discuss men under these conditions. Whatever I should say in a personal sense would be construed in a political sense as having to do with the national situation. I am indeed very glad to meet Governor Wilson and his family at their home in Princeton."

The pos[s]ibility of Governor Wilson being the Democratic candidate for the Presidency was suggested to Mr. Bryan. This he refused to discuss but he did lay stress upon the fact that he himself would not be a candidate. When asked about his own candidacy and if it were true that he has declared himself out of the race, Mr. Bryan shook his head affirmatively and slowly replied with emphasis: "I have said several times that I am not a candidate, but I am still in politics."

"You have been quoted as not approving of the candidacy of Governor Harmon, of Ohio. Is that true?" Mr. Bryan was asked.

"I have made no statements relative to Governor Harmon," was the answer.

"The Commoner has discussed the matter, but I have not in a personal way."

Mr. Bryan declined to quote the article in The Commoner which had reference to Governor Harmon's candidacy.[3]

To reporters who inquired about it, Governor Wilson was as reticent as Mr. Bryan about the brief conference at Princeton Inn, and gave his personal assurance that as far as he was concerned the meeting had no political significance. "It was merely an opportunity to meet Mr. Bryan in a social way," said the Governor, "and I welcome it. Strange to say that in all these years Mr. Bryan and I never met."

Printed in the Trenton *True American*, March 13, 1911; some editorial headings omitted.

[1] Wilson's speech is printed at April 5, 1911; for a description of the affair, see WW to Mary A. H. Peck, April 9, 1911.

[2] According to Kerney, Wilson hurried home in response to a telegram from his wife. " 'It was surely the first time that these two men met, and the meeting was due entirely to the desire and planning of Mrs. Woodrow Wilson,' Dr. Erdman recently wrote me. And he added, 'Mrs. Wilson in later years said to Mrs. Erdman, "that dinner put Mr. Wilson in the White House." ' " Kerney, *The Political Education of Woodrow Wilson*, p. 163.

[3] *The Commoner*, II (March 3, 1911), 2, had said in an editorial that, although it would feel free to commend such actions of Governor Harmon as seemed worthy of approval, it did not consider the Ohio Governor "as an available man for the democratic nomination for reasons that will be given when the discussion of the subject seems proper."

To Clarence Hamilton Poe

My dear Mr. Poe: [Trenton, N. J.] March 13, 1911.

Your letter from "Off Port Said" has I need hardly tell you given me the deepest gratification; it was very delightful that you should think of me. I am both surprised and gratified at what you tell me of the wide spread attention attracted outside the country as well as in it by my campaign. I am a bit daunted to have been brought so much into the public eye but am trying to saw wood with diligence and close attention to the matters immediately at hand.

With warmest appreciation of your generous kindness,
        Cordially and faithfully yours,   Woodrow Wilson

TLS (received from Clarence Poe).

A News Report of a Conference with the Democratic Assemblymen of New Jersey

[March 14, 1911]

GOVERNOR WINS CONFERENCE AGAIN

Strongly Advocates Geran Bill and Democratic Assemblymen Promise Support

Following a three-hour conference yesterday afternoon with the Democratic members of the House of Assembly—the second of its character within a week—Governor Wilson's advocacy of the Geran election and primary bill was vindicated by the majority members of the Legislature deciding by a vote of 27 to 11 to support the bill in the revised form.

In the conference Governor Wilson made a long talk expla[i]ning his attitude on the Geran bill. At the conclusion of his talk, the Governor said:

"You can turn aside from the measure, if you choose; you can decline to follow me; you can deprive me of office and turn away from me, but you cannot deprive me of power so long as I steadfastly stand for what I believe to be the interests and legitimate demands of the people themselves. I beg you to remember, in this which promises to be an historic conference in the annals of the party of the state, you are settling the question of the power or impotence, the distinction or the ignominy of the party to which the people with a singular generosity have offered the control of their affairs."

The Governor expressed himself as particularly happy that the conference had voted as it did, and that he was not obliged even to seem to bring himself into contest upon the public platform with the representatives of his own party. . . .

It is understood that in his speech the Governor first called attention to the fact that there seemed to be serious objection in the minds of some of the members because of the way in which this bill had been prepared and suggested to the Legislature. He called the attention of the members to the fact that it was his clear prerogative, under the Constitution of the state, to suggest at any time measures for their consideration, and that it was clearly within the meaning of the Constitution that his suggestions might be in the form of regularly formulated bills. He said that it would have been within his choice, therefore, to send to them the pending primary and election bill in a special message and to ask them to vote upon it directly, as his suggestion, and so go on record whether they were willing or unwilling, as the case might be, to adopt it.

He said that rather than exercise this prerogative, he had preferred to co-operate with his colleagues in the Legislature and in conference after conference he had invited in those members of the Assembly who were officially or otherwise interested and taken advantage of the kindness of individual members to introduce this and other bills which he felt it his duty to urge, so that they might go out in the regular order of legislative procedure. He had done this so that he might not even seem to force the Legislature the choice, whether they would follow his lead or not.

The Governor pointed out to them that the bill which Mr. Geran had introduced had been objected to by those who opposed it only upon the grounds which went to the validity and efficacy of the whole matter. He maintained that it was absolutely necessary, in order to keep faith with the voters of the state and with public opinion, that the bill should substitute for the existing method of selection [selecting] election officers a method which would be a very much nearer approach to what was impartial and open and without taint of machine management, and that the other essential feature was that ballots should be of such form that the voters would have an opportunity to select individuals rather than tickets, and so be in a position to demand and expect of every political organization that they should put up candidates whose names would bear individual scrutiny. He urged that the Democratic party had for sixteen years been a minority which was assured to it because it would not open its processes to popular choice and to the free control of public opinion. Because, in short, the people had not believed that the Democracy was their servant but had feared that it was the servant of selfish political interests. The recent election, he pointed out, had been won because Democracy had challenged and obtained the support of independent voters.[1]

Printed in the *Trenton Evening Times*, March 14, 1911.

[1] Burton J. Hendrick, "Woodrow Wilson: Political Leader," *McClure's Magazine*, XXXVIII (Dec. 1911), 229-30, gives a more detailed account of the Democratic Assembly caucus on the Geran bill. "Why not invite me to the caucus?" Wilson asked when he heard that it was to meet. "It's unprecedented, I know. Perhaps it's even unconstitutional; but then, I'm an unconstitutional governor." Hendrick's account continues:

"Somewhat dazed by the proposition, the Democratic members agreed, and the Governor promptly appeared. There was a minority that sullenly rebelled against his presence. Hardly had the Governor begun to talk, when some one [probably Thomas Francis Martin of Hudson County] interrupted. He bluntly told Mr. Wilson that he had no business in the caucus. What 'constitutional' right had the Governor to interfere in legislation, anyway? His duties were of an entirely different 'constitutional' kind.

" 'Since you appeal to the constitution,' replied Mr. Wilson, 'I think I can satisfy you.' And he drew from his pocket a copy of the New Jersey Constitution and read the following clause:

" 'The Governor shall communicate by message to the legislature at the opening of each session, and at such other times as he may deem necessary, the condition of the State, and *recommend such measures as he may deem expedient.*'

"Naturally, that silenced all protests of this kind. The submerged reactionaries, however, were far from cordial in the early stage of the discussion. They accused the Governor to his face of 'playing' for the Presidency—a charge, however, that did not greatly disturb him. He wished rather to limit his attention to the merits of the particular bill under consideration. For three hours the Governor stood there, explaining the bill in detail to his party associates. He took it up clause by clause, rehearsed the experience of other States along similar lines, seemed, indeed, to have the political history of every cranny of the United States at his finger-tips. 'Where did this schoolmaster learn so much about politics?' the legislators asked themselves—'not only legislation, but practical politics?' After his explanation Mr. Wilson was submitted to a steady fire of questions. In answering these, he acted like a small boy playing his favorite game; he certainly enjoyed the proceeding to the full.

"At the conclusion the Governor launched into an impromptu appeal for support. The eloquence of which he is so great a master now shone at its best. Several of the legislators present have described this experience to the writer. 'I have never known anything like that speech,' said one. 'Such beautiful Saxon English, such suppressed emotion, such direct personal appeal—it was all wonderful, simply wonderful. The Governor talked for at least an hour, his speech flowing smoothly, readily, never pausing for a word or an idea. It was like listening to music. And the whole thing was merely an appeal to our better unselfish natures. The State had trusted us, as Democrats, with great duties and responsibilities. Would we betray the people or would we seize this splendid opportunity? But it is useless to attempt to describe the speech or the effect that it produced. We all came out of that room with one conviction; that we had heard the most wonderful speech of our lives, and that Governor Wilson was a great man. Even the most hardened of the old-time legislative hacks said that. It has been said that debate no longer accomplishes anything in American legislation, that nobody is now persuaded by talk. Here was a case, however, which refutes this idea. When we went into that caucus we had no assurance as to what the result would be. But opposition melted away under the Governor's influence. That caucus settled the fate of the Geran bill, as well as the whole Democratic program.' "

According to the Trenton *True American*, March 14, 1911, Allan Bartholomew Walsh of Mercer County also spoke strongly in favor of the Geran bill. "Mr. Walsh, in his address," this report continued, "said something about the necessity of preventing the domination of politics by organizations. Assemblyman Martin, of Hudson, jumped to his feet at the close of Mr. Walsh's address, and said something about Democrats forgetting the lesson of the [Democratic state] convention in Taylor Opera House [in Trenton on September 15, 1910]. He declared that every man present owed his nomination and election to a political organization.

"Mr. Walsh arose to reply, but he was interrupted by Governor Wilson, who declared that he understood Mr. Martin's reference to refer not to Mr. Walsh but to himself. He declared that he believed in organization, and he believed in parties. But he took issue with Mr. Martin's statement that every man present owed his position to an organization. The Governor said that while organizations may have been instrumental in bringing about his nomination, he owed his election to the people and to the people only, and he would refuse to acknowledge any obligation that transcends his obligation to the people who elected him."

From James Richard Gray[1]

PERSONAL.

My dear Governor: Atlanta, Ga., March 15th, 1911.

I am enclosing herewith the editorial page of the Sunday Journal, of March 12th.

This may possibly interest you, particularly the marked editorial.[2]

I need hardly state that the editorial was written in the utmost sincerity and it is a fair expression of the appreciation aroused by your visit to Atlanta.

I trust you suffered no illness or inconvenience from your visit and that upon your return you found your family and friends enjoying the best of health.

With cordial regards, I am,

Very truly yours, J R Gray

TLS (WP, DLC).

[1] Editor and general manager of the *Atlanta Journal*, Wilson's leading editorial champion in Georgia during the preconvention campaign.

[2] The editorial "Woodrow Wilson, Southerner, American," traced Wilson's roots in the South and the development of his career, and hailed his speech before the Southern Commercial Congress. "Few men, if any of the present day," the editorial said, "are so truly fitted to interpret the south in terms of the broadest Americanism. Indeed, there are impersonated in his thought and speech the most admirable and wholesome elements of the south and the nation." Continuing, the editorial asserted that Wilson was doing for politics what he had done for education: "He is interpreting to the people the best there is in them and is stimulating them to achieve this best in their government. He embodies the breadth and vigor of those forces that are bringing this nation into a new era of constructive progress, and his leadership may well be trusted." *Atlanta Journal*, March 12, 1911.

From William Elliott Gonzales[1]

Dear Governor Wilson: Columbia, S. C. March 16. 1911

The Executive Committee of the South Carolina Press Association met today and fixed the time for the Press Association meeting to fit with your engagement at Chapel Hill—our meeting being on May 31, June 1 and 2. You will speak in Chapel Hill at noon, May 31, and can leave there that evening, reaching Columbia the following morning, June 1.

With the consent of President [August] Kohn of the State Press Association I ask that you do me the honor and give me the pleasure of being my home guest while here. We would like more than a "flying visit." Numbers of Columbians knew you as a boy, and all of us knew and loved Dr. [James] Woodrow. I met you in his office in the Central National Bank many years ago.

Columbians and other South Carolinians wish to know you, and I am coming to think it the duty of everyone having a message for the good of humanity to establish a "personal" connection in as many places as possible.

I hope, Governor, you will bring Mrs Wilson with you.

Very sincerely yours, William E. Gonzales.

ALS (Governors' Files, Nj).
  1 Editor of the Columbia, S. C., *State*, Wilson's most vigorous editorial exponent in South Carolina during the preconvention campaign.

A Veto Message

To the House of Assembly: [Trenton, N. J.] March 17th, 1911.

I herewith return to the House of Assembly, in which it originated, Assembly Bill No. 163, entitled "An act concerning the pay or salary of officials, firemen and other employes of paid fire departments in cities of the first class of this State,"¹ without my approval.

This bill applies to cities of the first class in the State, and provides for a large increase in the compensation of all officers and employes of the fire department in such cities. I am informed that it would entail an additional expense of at least $65,000 a year in Jersey City, for which municipality it was especially designed. A careful examination of the bill discloses the fact that there is no provision for affirmative action on the part of the mayor and board of finance, who are the responsible financial authorities of the city; and submission to a popular vote is ordered without their concurrence or advice.

The bill deprives the proper responsible officers of the city of the power to determine whether or not the expenditure provided for is within the resources of the taxpayers or is a proper measure of local administration.

In view of the increasing burdens of taxation, under which the citizens of our municipalities are laboring, it seems to me a particularly questionable use of legislative power to intervene without their solicitation to increase these burdens. Every endeavor should be made to assist the cities in carrying out a systematic policy of retrenchment and economy. Anything which overrides their constituted authorities is inconsistent with the principle of home rule and with the just encouragement of efforts to effect reasonable reform.

Respectfully,   Woodrow Wilson,   *Governor*.²

Printed in *Minutes of the N. J. House of Assembly, 1911*, pp. 602-603.
  1 That is, cities of over 150,000.
  2 The New Jersey legislature could override a veto by simple majority vote. This veto was sustained.

To Clarence Hamilton Poe

My dear Mr. Poe: [Trenton, N. J.] March 17, 1911.

Again I have to thank you for your thoughtful kindness. The clipping from last Friday's News and Observer is certainly most gratifying. It is delightful to know that I am to have a chance of seeing you at Chapel Hill and at the meeting in South Carolina.

In haste,   Cordially yours,   Woodrow Wilson

TLS (received from Clarence Poe).

To Mary Allen Hulbert Peck

Dearest Friend,   Princeton, 19 March, 1911.

Please pardon me! It has been my fault that the North American Review did not go to you. When I spoke of it in my letter it had not been published: only advance sheets of it had gone to the newspapers and been extensively copied by them. By the time it came out I had been swept along in this overwhelming tide of work that hurries me from one week's end to another, and the thing went out of my head! It is the old story, that I have repeated so often to you: all this fuss about the presidency seems to make no real impression on my consciousness; seems to concern some third person! If the article had been about *you* or about anything else real and absorbing, I would have continued alive to it, and it would have reached you as soon as the post could carry it. Yesterday I had to go into New York for an hour or so. I bought the magazine and to-day have done it up with my own hands and shall send it by the same post that is to carry this letter. Again I beg that you will forgive me. I was very stupid, and very negligent of your pleasure, to forget and neglect. The World's Work article has not yet been published.

The work goes more strenuously with every week, as the session approaches nearer and nearer to the point where it is to be decided whether the main bills (the administration bills) are to pass or not. I am confident that they will pass, but the machine is dying exceeding hard, and nothing will be absolutely certain until it is done and my signature on the bills. Some time I shall have a chance to describe to you a session day: it is too complicated a narrative for a letter. But I can give you an idea of what *some* of my days are like by describing last Friday. Until noon I worked at my correspondence, dictating something over an hundred letters,—for the legislature sits in the early part of the week and while it sits my letters pile up, unanswered. At noon

I began to see the people with whom my Secretary had made stated engagements for interviews,—most of them with some axe to grind, and with no gift for stating their errands promptly, clearly, or frankly. At half past twelve that routine was interrupted by the sitting of the State House Commission, of which I am ex officio chairman, which passes on all sorts of business matters, as a sort of clearing house for everything that does not fall within the statutory duties of some one of the regular Departments. A little after one I hurried out with Tumulty (my delightful young Secretary and political mentor) to lunch. At two I went to one of the larger court rooms in the capitol and held a hearing on a certain milk bill which has passed the houses but which certain persons, chiefly members of Boards of Health, are very anxious I should not sign. The farmers are unanimous in wishing me to sign it. It lowers the total amount of solids milk is required to show under test from twelve per cent to eleven and a half, the farmers maintaining that the latter is the natural limit of the variation in perfectly pure milk coming from ordinary normal cows. There must have been an hundred persons at the hearing. Almost everybody present had something to say, and I did not get away from them until a few minutes after five. After that I had a long interview with a very serious young writer on the tendencies of State governments; and then a long conference with some important men from South Jersey on judicial appointments. They did not release me (though I was nearly blind and crazy with fatigue) until after seven. I crawled out to dinner; and then came back to shut the doors of my office and address myself to the real business of the day: the study of the bills that had been sent me and the signing of a great number of important orders! The bills had to be carefully scrutinized and considered; three of them I vetoed (though the milk bill I signed); and in connection with one or two of them past legislation had to be looked up. On top of all, there was the correspondence to finish. I crept home on almost the last trolley before midnight, worn out and utterly indifferent to the public welfare!

Ouija was quite right about James W. Alexander. He is one of "the other side" in our university affairs whom I most despise, —a man at once plausible, stupid, and weak. I am sorry that you should be burdened with him, and that he should be privileged to enjoy you. He deserves nothing. I hope that he is not to stay much longer. I rejoice in your resolution to take a rest, and deny yourself to those who daily use and exhaust you for their own pleasure. You are the best company in the world, and you give all that is delightful in you to any one who requires it, and give with utter lavishness. You can never grow strong if you do not spare yourself, and spare yourself systematically. It fills me with dread and foreboding to see how little you have gained in all these weeks at Bermuda, where you should thrive and regain your strength as nowhere else. No doubt the mean chilliness has had a great deal to do with it. As the Spring comes on you will thrive better. When I was in the South the blossoms were show-ing in fine glory on the peach trees, and I thought of what must surely be happening in Bermuda, for your delight and re-freshment. It made me very happy. For you need more than you have had. I have seen from your letters that your remaining friends there did not satisfy you as they used to. It is particularly sad that trouble should have crept into the Gollan household, which seemed so full of all that ought to make people content and happy. Is She not going to follow him?[1] I always thought her very proud of him, and have found her eager to talk about him and quote him. Let us hope that it is all just a process of settling down to what was begun at little too late in life.[2]

We are all perfectly well. Give my love to Mrs. Allen and your son; and think of me always as, with all my heart,

Your devoted friend,   Woodrow Wilson

WWTLS (WP, DLC).
[1] Judge Gollan had been transferred to Trinidad, where he served as Attorney General from 1911 to 1918.
[2] The Gollans had been married in 1908, at which time he was forty.

To the Legislature of New Jersey

To the Legislature: [Trenton, N. J.] March 20th, 1911.

I take the liberty of calling your attention to a very important matter awaiting your decision—the question of the ratification of the proposed amendment to the Constitution of the United States which gives to the Federal Congress the right to impose an income tax.[1] Liberal opinion throughout the country clearly expects and demands the ratification of this amendment.

It will undoubtedly be an act of great liberality on the part of the States to concede it. They will thereby be sharing with the federal government one of the few powers of taxation which, under the latest decision of the Supreme Court of the United States in that matter,[2] they may now regard themselves as en-titled to exercise, to a certain extent, exclusively,[3] but it is clearly in the interest of the national life that the power should be con-ceded. It will free the government of the United States to put its fiscal policy upon a much more enlightened, a much more modern, a much more elastic basis than it now rests upon, or apparently can rest upon so long as this power is withheld. If this power be granted, the general government may adapt its whole system of taxation to the actual economic life of the country much more favorably than it is now adapted. It may make it more just and may adjust it more nicely to the interests of the people at large.

May I not urge upon you as earnestly as respectful the prompt adoption of this exceedingly important amendment, that New Jersey may be put among the number of those States which do not prefer their own interests to those of the nation as a whole?[4]

Respectfully,   Woodrow Wilson,   *Governor.*

Printed in *Minutes of the N. J. House of Assembly, 1911,* pp. 601-602.

[1] A bill to ratify what became the Sixteenth Amendment permitting the federal government to tax incomes without the limitations imposed by the direct-tax provision of Article I, Section 2 of the Constitution (about which, see WW to the New Jersey Senate, April 4, 1911, n. 2) had been introduced in the New Jersey Senate on January 10, 1911, by Isaac T. Nichols, chairman of the Finance Committee, who had reported the bill favorably on January 30, 1911.

[2] Flint v. Stone Tracy Co., in which the court ruled on March 13, 1911, that the corporation tax of the Payne-Aldrich Tariff Act of 1909 was constitutional. The Supreme Court ruled that the tax was an excise, rather than a direct, tax, and that it neither violated the direct-tax provision of the Constitution nor was an unconstitutional invasion of state sovereignty over corporations, since they were involved in national rather than state economic activities and were therefore subject to the federal government's taxing power.

[3] That is, the taxation of personal incomes.

[4] The Senate voted, eight to twelve, to reject the income-tax amendment on the same day that it received Wilson's message. The New Jersey legislature did not approve the Sixteenth Amendment until February 4, 1913.

A Statement About an Altercation
with James Richard Nugent

[[March 20, 1911]]

I sent for Mr. Nugent, and when he came to my office I told him I had sent for him as chairman of the State committee to learn his attitude on the Geran bill. He said he would line up a majority against the Geran bill, if possible.

I told him he was following a suicidal course.

He replied that the whole of the "regular" Democratic organization in the State was opposed to the bill.

I told him he was mistaken about it, but he pooh-poohed the idea, and reiterated his statement, and said I would see all right. Then I said to him:

"You understand, of course, that the bill will pass?" He replied: "I understand that you have certain votes pledged to the bill. I do not know by what means you got them."

"What do you mean?" I asked him.

He replied: "The talk is that you got them by patronage."

I got to my feet at once, and said to him, "Good afternoon, Mr. Nugent," waving him to the door of the office.

As he walked out he continued to talk, and to everything he said I responded, "Good afternoon, Mr. Nugent."

He did manage to say that he knew I was no gentleman, to which I calmly replied, "Good afternoon, Mr. Nugent."

I invited him here and he insulted me.[1]

Printed in the *Newark Evening News*, March 21, 1911.
[1] For the background and an account of this affair, see Link, *Wilson: The Road to the White House*, pp. 251-53. For Wilson's own extended account, see WW to Mary A. H. Peck, March 26, 1911.

From Thomas Littlehales[1]

My dear Governor: Camden, N. J. March 21, 1911.

In the daily papers Mr. Nugent is credited with having said that the only people who are "with you" are those affiliated with the independent Republican movement, who drift from one party to another.[2] I am sure that were it possible at this time to put the question to a popular vote, Mr. Nugent would be a very much surprised man. The "line-up" would be overwhelmingly in favor of your efforts for the general uplift of New Jersey politics and the measures you are trying to have enacted into laws; it would show on your side not only the independent Republicans, but the right thinking people of all parties; and arrayed against you,—but very much in the minority,—the "organization" forces, largely controlled by the "Interests" they represent, and who see in the consummation of your plans the waning—let us hope the end—of their power.

It is fortunate indeed for the people of New Jersey that we elected a *real man* for Governor, one with convictions of the right and the courage to carry them out. No person with a grain of common sense could misunderstand your campaign utterances. The Nugents, the Smiths, and those of their ilk were given due notice that you were after a new order of things. They are just discovering that we elected a man with a good stiff back-bone, and not a common piece of clay which they could mould at will.

More power to you Governor, and may your shadow never grow less until you have all your enemies and detractors confounded, and such laws on the Statute books of the State as shall place its government where it belongs, i.e., in the hands of the governed; and its burdens *fairly* distributed among those reaping its benefits.

The writer has been a consistent Democrat since casting his first vote for Grover Cleveland in 1884, and is proud to feel that under your banner equity and right must and will prevail.

Hoping to have the pleasure of seeing you at the Americus Club[3] banquet on the 27th instant,[4] I beg to remain,

Very respectfully yours,   Thomas Littlehales

TLS (WP, DLC).

[1] Engineer and manager of the American Coke and Gas Construction Co. of Camden, N. J.

[2] Nugent's statement on the altercation is printed in the *Newark Evening News*, March 21, 1911. In it, Nugent said that Wilson had sent for him and asked whether he, as Democratic state chairman, was opposing the Geran bill. Nugent replied that he was not opposing it in his capacity as state chairman but as a member of the Democratic State Committee and of the Democratic Committee of Essex County, the members of both of which were overwhelmingly opposed to the Geran bill. Nugent said that Wilson "very dramatically" declared that the people were with him and against Nugent, as they had been during the senatorial fight. The balance of Nugent's statement follows:

"I said to him: 'Governor, the only people who are with you, are the people who are generally affiliated with the independent Republican movement, and who drift from one party to the other.[']

"He seemed to get very warm at this statement, and reiterated his assertion that my information was not correct.

"I said: 'Governor, there is a great deal of talk about this bill and the means that are being used to pass it. You have not heard the talk, but I have.'

" 'What do you mean,' he asked.

" 'There is talk,' I said, 'that you are using your patronage to obtain votes for this bill.'

"He said: 'Did you mean to come in here to insult me?'

" 'No,' I replied, 'but I think you brought me in here to insult me—at least, your actions show it, and I consider it very characteristic of you, and indicative of your qualities as a gentleman.' Then he said, 'Good day, sir,' and I said, 'Good day.' "

[3] The Editors have been unable to discover anything about the Americus Club other than that it was located at 540 Mt. Vernon Street in Camden.

[4] If invited, Wilson did not attend.

From Andrew Carnegie

My dear Governor,   New York March 21, 1911

You stand for the highest in political life and hav no dout notist how the proposed treaty for arbitration of all disputes has been receivd in Britain,[1] where the leaders of both parties welcome it with outstrecht hands as a step to higher things. Is it not possible for us to imitate that in our country. I think we should be able to do so.

The Archbishop of Canterbury[2] announces a great meeting in Albert Hall, where the leaders of all sects are to join in support of the treaty. We are about to arrange a similar meeting here in Carnegie Hall, over which we hope Bishop Greer[3] will preside, with all sects invited.

Now for the point! Are you prepared to welcome the proposed treaty as something above party? I hope so.

You know that a two-thirds majority is needed in the Senate, which is difficult to obtain. The President has exprest his belief publicly that the Senate will welcome the treaty, but we are all somewhat apprehensiv. Here is an occasion for you to show that you are in great issues above party. Surely an agreement to settlement all disputes that may arize within the boundaries of the English-speaking race is a subject worthy of your support, not only as a party man but as a leader of mankind.[4]

Very truly yours, [Andrew Carnegie]

CCL (A. Carnegie Papers, DLC).

[1] President Taft had announced his intention to broaden the basis of the Root arbitration treaties of 1908-1909 (about which see Richard W. Leopold, *The Growth of American Foreign Policy: A History* [New York, 1962], pp. 286-87) by making them cover questions of national honor. Carnegie in late 1910 had established the Carnegie Endowment for International Peace, in part to promote Taft's plan.

[2] The Most Rev. Randall Thomas Davidson, Archbishop of Canterbury, 1903-28.

[3] The Rt. Rev. David Hummell Greer, Bishop of New York.

[4] As it turned out, Carnegie was unable to hold his meeting in Carnegie Hall until December 12, 1911. German sympathizers, led by Alphonse G. Koelble, New York lawyer, and head of the German-American Citizens' League of New York, disrupted the meeting, charging that arbitration treaties, which had been negotiated with Britain and France and were then before the Senate, were in fact instruments of an alliance against Germany. The meeting was adjourned in an uproar before Carnegie had an opportunity to speak. *New York Times*, Dec. 13, 1911.

To Andrew Carnegie

My dear Mr. Carnegie: [Trenton, N. J.] March 23, 1911.

Of course I am in favor of the arbitration treaty. I am in favor of every treaty which puts international affairs upon the basis of reason and accommodation. I wish I were free to attend the meeting in Carnegie Hall, but I am bound here hand and foot.

Cordially and sincerely yours, Woodrow Wilson

TLS (A. Carnegie Papers, DLC).

To Walter Hines Page

My dear Mr. Page: [Trenton, N. J.] March 23, 1911.

I drop you just a line to say that I shall be at your house by ten o'clock on Saturday morning.[1]

Cordially and faithfully yours, Woodrow Wilson

TLS (W. H. Page Papers, MH).

[1] See WW to Mary A. H. Peck, March 26, 1911.

To John Wesley Wescott

My dear Judge Westcott: [Trenton, N. J.] March 24, 1911.

I feel that I ought to write you at once about my change of mind with regard to Cape May County. When you were with me you must have seen that you practically convinced me that it would be best to appoint Mr. Matthew Jefferson[1] to the Court of Common Pleas. Since I saw you it happens that I have been able to get very vivid impressions of the state of opinion in Cape May County from a number of new sources from which I had not drawn impressions before. I an [am] now convinced, my dear Judge, that in spite of my inclination to the contrary, it is my wise and proper course to appoint Mr. Curtis Baker.[2] I believe that the appointment of Mr. Jefferson would be regarded as a whimsical and an aebitrary [arbitrary] act on my part and would create a greater antagonism than it is at all reasonable to create, in view of Mr. Jefferson's only moderate legal attainments and ability. He has no marked superiority of gifts over the other candidate and there is evidently a distinct feeling in the County that to appoint him would be to deliberately go contrary to the whole feeling of the County without strong convincing grounds.

It was my strong desire to act upon your judgment in this matter, but I have been thoroughly convinced that the wise thing to do is to appoint Mr. Baker.

With warmest regard,

Faithfully yours,   Woodrow Wilson

TLS (J. W. Wescott Coll., NjP).
  [1] Lawyer of Camden, N. J.
  [2] Curtis T. Baker, lawyer of Wildwood, N. J. Wilson appointed him on April 5, 1911.

From Pleasant Alexander Stovall

Dear Governor: Savannah, Ga. March 25th, 1911.

I enclose you the report in full of Col. George Harvey's speech in Savannah on the night of Friday, March 17th.[1]

With best wishes, I remain,

Yours very truly,   Pleasant A Stovall

TLS (WP, DLC).
  [1] A clipping from the Savannah Press, March 18, 1911. See G. B. M. Harvey to WW, March 1, 1911, n. 4.

From George Howe III

Dear Uncle Woodrow: Chapel Hill, N. C. Mar. 25, 1911.

I have persuaded the President[1] to let your family have you for one meal while you are here at Commencement, and I write long in advance so that you will not give to somebody else the little time we are to be allowed to have. Of course I am not keeping house,[2] but my second home is with my intimate friends, the Pratts,[3] whom I am eager to have you know. They are no less eager to know you, and are going to entertain you for our one permitted meal. Mother and Annie[4] will also be here: do not fail this family party. Save for us supper time on the Monday evening before your speech. You will have nothing else to do at that time, but a reception follows at about ten o'clock. Pratt will write to you himself as soon as he knows that I have written.

I am looking forward to your coming with more feeling than I dare express—peculiarly deep feeling at this time. And a tremendous Commencement is prepared for your coming. I wish you could bring Aunt Ellie with you. Is there any possibility of it? All invitations apply equally to her of course.

With a great deal of love to all,   George Howe

TLS (WP, DLC).
[1] Francis Preston Venable, President of the University of North Carolina.
[2] He was now separated from his wife, Margaret Smyth Flinn Howe.
[3] Joseph Hyde Pratt, Professor of Economic Geology at the University of North Carolina since 1904, and his wife, Mary Dicus Bayley Pratt.
[4] Annie Wilson (Mrs. George, Jr.) Howe and Annie Wilson Howe (Mrs. Perrin Chiles) Cothran.

To Mary Allen Hulbert Peck

Dearest Friend,   Princeton, 26 March, 1911.

It is delightful to feel the Spring coming on,—for it will bring relief to you and a chance to rest. The crowding Americans will begin to thin out in Bermuda and you will have a respite. The drain upon your strength makes me most uneasy. I suppose it never occurs to you to excuse and spare yourself! You must not distress your friends by utterly wearing yourself out on your acquaintances. I do not wonder that you go on as you do: it must be a constant delight to please people as you do, and deserve their affectionate admiration; but there is such a thing as prudence, though you may not know it!

Another week has brought me another success. After a very hard struggle, again against both the Democratic and the Republican state machines, I got the chief reform bill of the ses-

sion through the Assembly, by a vote of 34 to 25.[1] It has still to
run the gauntlet of the Republican Senate, but I have reason
to think that it will pass even there. It has been almost as bitter
and interesting a business as the fight for the Senator, and the
victory, everybody seems to think, was quite as marked and
significant. Just before the vote I sent once more for James
Nugent, the chairman of the Democratic State Committee, to
make a last effort to bring him to his senses, and turn the fight
into something like a genuine party action, in which the party
minority should yield to the party majority; but it was no use.
He was beligerant and offensive, and pretended to think that
he had the votes to defeat me. When he spoke of "the organization's" opposition to the bill (which affects primaries and elections), I said "surely you know that you will be beaten in this,
as you were in the senatorial fight." He said that he did not know
anything of the kind. "I know," he said, "that you have a certain
number of votes,—or think you have: I don't know how you got
them." "What do you mean," I exclaimed. "Why, it's the talk that
you got them by patronage," he said. I fairly sprang to my feet,
and, bowing and gesturing most emphatically towards the door,
said, I have no doubt with blazing eyes, "Good afternoon, Mr.
Nugent." Upon every effort that he made to say something more
I repeated, with increased emphasis, "Good afternoon, Mr.
Nugent." He lingered long enough to tell me that I was no gentleman, and that he had expected nothing else from "the like of
me." It was a most unpleasant incident, which I did not at all
enjoy; but apparently it did a lot of good. It has been spoken of
with glee all over the country, and editorials written about it,
of which the enclosed[2] is a specimen. One paper had a cartoon
entitled "Good afternoon," in wh. Nugent was to be seen flying
head foremost from a door out of which protruded a foot marked
"Wilson." In the distance, nursing his bruises, sat Smith. It is all
very well to get applause and cre[d]it for such things, but I need
not tell you that they are not at all to my taste. I cannot help
feeling a bit vulgar after them. They commend me to the rank
and file, and particularly to the politicians themselves, I believe,
but they do not leave me pleased with myself. I feel debased to
the level of the men whom I feel obliged to snub. But it all
comes in the day's work.

I had a strange conference yesterday in New York.[3] There is
a group of generous men there who are going to collect a fund

---

[1] The Geran bill, which the Assembly had adopted on March 21.

[2] It is missing.

[3] The conferees were Wilson, Walter Hines Page, Walter Lee McCorkle,
and William Frank McCombs.

and effect an organization to promote my chances for nomination for the presidency.* They wanted to see me to arrange for a western trip in May, when they want me to go all the way to the Pacific coast and make a series of addresses, in Missouri, in Iowa, in Colorado, in California, and in (the State of) Washington. They are going to hire a man who is to devote himself to the business, with an office in New York (though, of course, there is to be nothing about it to attract attention to it or make it appear deliberate and systematic; it is to be quiet and unadvertised) and who is probably to go West with me, as anything I choose to call him. The addresses are to be arranged for chiefly through Princeton men, and the trip is not to wear the look of being anything political. It is all a very strange business for me, and not very palateable. I feel an almost unconquerable shyness about it. I dare say I shall grow brazen enough, however, before it is all over. Whether I am nominated or not, my maiden coyness will, all too probably, have worn off! Does it seem to you ridiculous?[4]

Friday night I dined in New York, at Billy Isham's house, with forty-one of my classmates. Isham has given class dinners for the last thirty years, and has kept us together, like a family. This dinner was, in a way, to me. They drank my health and I made a little speech. When I am with those fellows, the thirty years since our graduation seem to fall away, and I *cannot* make such a speech as I would make in any other company. I feel like a boy again, and, I dare say, speak like a boy. But it was very delightful to be with them again. It was a refreshing interlude in the work at Trenton.

And so I have written another letter about myself, while think-

---

[4] According to a later account by Frank Parker Stockbridge ("How Woodrow Wilson Won His Nomination," *Current History*, xx [July 1924], 561-64), who was hired to make arrangements for the western tour and serve as Wilson's general publicity agent, Page, McCorkle, and McCombs raised an initial fund of $3,000 to finance the trip and to pay Stockbridge's salary for a time. Stockbridge soon made arrangements for Wilson to speak in Kansas City, Denver, Los Angeles, San Francisco, Portland, Seattle, St. Paul, and Minneapolis. Lincoln, Nebraska, was later added at the request of Charles Wayland Bryan, brother of William Jennings Bryan.

While Stockbridge was making preparations for the tour and a nation-wide publicity campaign, Wilson allegedly told him: "I am not to be put forward as a candidate for the Presidency. No man is big enough to seek that high office. I should not refuse it if it were offered to me, but only if the offer came from the people themselves; no man is big enough to refuse that. You must not ask any one to say a word or print a line in my behalf. Confine your activities to answering requests for information. When such inquiries come, tell them the whole truth; there is nothing to be concealed or glossed over. If you are in doubt as to where I stand on any question of public policy concerning which you are asked, come and see me or telephone. I shall refer all inquirers to you."

Wilson's western tour and the beginnings of the organized movement to make him the Democratic nominee in 1912 will be chronicled in some detail in Vol. 23.

ing of you. I am so sorry that you should feel that there is any cause for anxiety about Allen. I am sure that you will find that it is only catarrh that is troubling him. I cannot imagine his developing anything worse in Bermuda, with you and Mrsa [Mrs.] Allen to care for him as you both do. But if you want to take care of him, you must first be sure to take care of yourself. Do write and say that the weather is again sweet and invigo-rating and that you are constantly out of doors and entirely well! All unite with me in affectionate messages. Remember me to both your dears [dear] ones; and think of me always as

Your devoted friend,   Woodrow Wilson

* The leading spirit is Walter Page of *The World's Work*

WWTLS (WP, DLC).

From Joseph Hyde Pratt

My dear Dr. Wilson,   Chapel Hill, N. C. March 26, 1911.

I am delighted that you are to visit Chapel Hill at our Univer-sity Commencement and I am looking forward with a great deal of pleasure to meeting you again. I know your time will be very thoroughly occupied while you are here, but I hope you will be able to give us a little time.

Mrs. Pratt joins with me in a most cordial invitation to you to take supper with us on the Monday night you are in Chapel Hill.

George has seen Dr. Venable and it will not interfere with any of his arrangements.

Trusting that we will have the pleasure of having you with us, I am,   Yours sincerely   Joseph Hyde Pratt.

ALS (WP, DLC).

To John Wesley Wescott

My dear Judge Wescott: [Trenton, N. J.] March 27, 1911.

I am truly distressed by the situation. I have come to enter-tain the warmest affection for you and the highest opinion of your judgment, and yet the analysis made of the situation in your letter[1] is not complete. The Camden lawyer to whom you refer is of course Mr. Nixon.[2] If it had been Mr. Nixon alone who came to me about the matter, I should have seen the thing as you do, but I think you would be very much surprised to know the variety of sources from which the impression has come to me that the whole county would regard the appointment of Mr. Jefferson as a willful disregard on my part of the choice which opinion has made in that county.

I feel only too keenly, as you do, my liability to be misled and deceived and it really distresses me to differ from you in judgment. I wish I could quote to you the representations that have been made to me, but they have come from so many sources and from so many different kinds of individuals, whose names I even did not know, that it looks to me like nothing less than a spontaneous exhibition of feeling on the part of a great variety of elements in Cape May.

I hope that the event will show that I have not been mistaken in these impressions, and yet I do not feel the least confidence in my own judgment.

Cordially and faithfully yours,   Woodrow Wilson

TLS (J. W. Wescott Coll., NjP).
    1 It is missing.
    2 Horace Franklin Nixon, Princeton 1894, lawyer of Camden, N. J.

To Samuel Huston Thompson, Jr.

My dear Mr. Thompson: [Trenton, N. J.] March 27, 1911.

I sincerely appreciate your kind letter of March twenty-first.[1] My attitude towards the initiative, referendum and recall is this. My judgment was at first very much against them, but I have been very much impressed by the success with which they have been used in Oregon and in my Inaugural address to the Legislature I commended the Oregon system very warmly to their study and consideration. The adoption of these measures in any particular State is of course a matter to be based upon the conditions obtaining in that State. The people are certainly here justly tired of their inability to secure the fulfillment of campaign pledges, because of the intervention of machine management and control and I think the universal feeling is that it may be necessary for them to assume upon occasion, at any rate, direct control of legislation themselves.

I am hoping that it may be possible for me to come out to Denver in May, and if it is, I shall look forward to the greatest pleasure to seeing you again.

Always cordially and faithfully yours,

Woodrow Wilson

TLS (photostat in RSB Coll., DLC).
    1 It is missing.

From Warren Worth Bailey[1]

Dear Sir: [Johnstown, Pa.] March 28 [1911].

Permit one who has watched your course ever since your nomination with profound interest to congratulate you most cordially on the record you are making. I am free to say that when you were nominated I had an impression of you that your course since then has quite discredited. In common with many others I had associated you with the reactionary element of the party and possibly we who held this notion were indebted for it more to some of the newspapers and periodicals which were your especial champions than to any word or act of your own. Some of us have grown chronically suspicious of any man who finds favor in the eyes of certain publications known to be affili-[a]ted in sympathy or in fact with the "interests."

It may interest you to know that there is a strong and growing sentiment in Pennsylvania in your behalf with reference to 1912. I was the secretary of the Bryan Democratic league in 1908 and in this way I was brought in pretty close touch with the progressive element of the party. I am still in fairly close touch with that element and I think it is within the mark to say that the Wilson sentiment to-day is about equal to the Bryan strength three years ago. You may recall that in the contest at the primaries we elected 52 of the 64 delegates to the national convention under Bryan instructions. This was in face of the open and violent opposition of the party organization led by Mr. Guffey.

I should be glad of a chance to discuss the situation with you and it has occurred to me that the opportunity may arise on the 13th prox. at Indianapolis, where I understand you are to speak. It is my purpose at present to attend that celebration, traveling from here with Mr. Bryan, who is to speak in Johnstown the evening of the 12th. We shall go by the Chicago and St. Louis express (No. 21) on the Pennsylvania and I have thought it possible you might travel by the same train, in which case a chance to pay my personal respects to you might present itself.

Believing that you are most happily disappointing others as you have disappointed me and feeling that the work you are doing is precisely the sort of work which needs to be done in bringing the government back under the control of the governed, I have the honor to remain

                    Sincerely yours,   Warren Worth Bailey

TLS (WP, DLC).

1 Proprietor and editor of the *Johnstown*, Pa., *Democrat* and, as has been noted earlier, a leader of the progressive, anti-Guffey wing of the Pennsylvania Democracy.

To Warren Worth Bailey

My dear Mr. Bailey: [Trenton, N. J.] March 29, 1911.

Your letter of March twenty-eighth is very generous and has given me a great deal of pleasure. I hope sincerely that it will be possible for us to have a talk at Indianapolis; if not, perhaps we can seek some other occasion. I cannot tell just now by what train I shall be able to get away, but I shall keep the memorandum in mind that you are going by the Chicago and St. Louis express No. 21, and I shall try to take that train.

What you tell me about the sentiment in Pennsylvania is certainly as gratifying as it is surprising to me.

Cordially and faithfully yours, Woodrow Wilson

TLS (W. W. Bailey Papers, NjP).

To Samuel Huston Thompson, Jr.

My dear Mr. Thompson: [Trenton, N. J.] March 29, 1911.

Your telegram on behalf of the Mile-High Club[1] has given me a great deal of pleasure. I am sorry to say I cannot give an absolute definite answer, because I am referring the arrangements of my schedule while in the West to some friends in New York who have kindly undertaken to superintend the matter for me, but I shall let you know later.[2]

Cordially and faithfully yours, Woodrow Wilson

TLS (S. H. Thompson, Jr., Papers, DLC).
 1 It is missing.
 2 See WW to S. H. Thompson, Jr., March 31, 1911, n. 2.

From Henry Skillman Breckinridge

My dear Gov. Wilson: Baltimore, Md. March 29. 1911.

The initial stages of the local "Woodrow Wilson Democratic Association["] have passed. First we organized with about 100 young professional men and graduate students of Johns Hopkins University. Within the next few days we are sending out a thousand circulars inviting men to become members. I am inclosing a copy of the circular and articles of association as they will be issued.[1]

The most important problem facing us at this time is the obtaining [of] good speakers for our first public meeting. It is essential to get a man whose words will carry weight, who can arouse enthusiasm, and at the same time enunciate principles acceptable to yourself. My mind turned first to Senator Martine as being the man most under obligation to you, but I know nothing of his abilities as a speaker. I have written Mr. John E. Lathrop for suggestions along this line and hope that you may be able to suggest some one. Of course I should not divulge the source of the suggestion.

It is most important, in my opinion, that this Baltimore Association be a marked success, for the reason that if successful, it will stir other communities to follow suit. I have received most encouraging reports from Ohio, Kentucky and California. I am convinced that all that is needed is a match to set the fire going in many places.

Please tell me the name of the Princeton editor in the South who desired to start a "Wilson Boom" two or three years ago.

Mr. Lathrop, of Washington, was very cordial in his reception of this plan of associations, and I hope to get valuable assistance from him.

This morning's N. Y. Times reported a visit to you by Senator Owen and said he favored you as a candidate for the nomination.[2] I sincerely hope that this report may be true.

With great respect,
Very sincerely yours,   Henry S. Breckinridge

ALS (Governors' Files, Nj).
  [1] They are missing.
  [2] After the visit, Owen declared that Wilson was the presidential choice of Oklahoma. *New York Times*, March 29, 1911.

A Veto Message

To the House of Assembly: Trenton, March 30th, 1911.

I herewith return, without my approval, Assembly Bill No. 245, entitled "An act authorizing any borough of this State to appropriate moneys for the celebration of the fiftieth anniversary of the founding or settlement of the place where said borough is located."

It seems to me very unwise to authorize any community to saddle itself with debt in order to enjoy the pleasure of a celebration. The very spirit of a celebration is spontaneity, and when a celebration is genuinely desired by the citizens of a locality, it can easily be paid for by private subscription. Private subscription, moreover, will probably be limited to the sums actually needed, whereas appropriations out of the public treasury, or moneys borrowed, seem so easily obtained that the same care is not likely to be used in regard to expenditure.

Respectfully,   Woodrow Wilson,   *Governor*.[1]

Printed in the *Minutes of the N. J. House of Assembly, 1911*, pp. 877-78.
[1] This veto was sustained.

To Benjamin Barr Lindsey

My dear Judge Lindsey: [Trenton, N. J.] March 30, 1911.

Your letter of March twenty-second[1] is more than generous and I thank you for it very heartily.

I am now planning to come out to Denver some time in May and shall look forward with the greatest pleasure and gratification to the possibility of seeing you when I come. A talk is worth all the letters in the world.

Your friendship gratifies me and supports me.

Cordially and faithfully yours,   Woodrow Wilson

TLS (B. B. Lindsey Papers, DLC).
[1] It is missing.

To Henry Skillman Breckinridge

My dear Mr. Breckinridge: [Trenton, N. J.] March 30, 1911.

You are certainly doing most admirably and unselfish work and you know I need not tell you how deeply I appreciate it. The circular makes me blush, but the one essential part is that you really believe it yourself. This makes me very deeply glad.

I do not believe that Senator Martine would be the man you are looking for. He is an admirable fellow but he is somewhat flambouyant in style and has to be heard more than once to be appreciated for what he is.

I am ashamed to say the name of the Princeton editor in the South who desired to start a Wilson boom two or three years ago has utterly gone out of my head. The best I can suggest is this: That you write to Mr. Williams of '74, the editor of the Indianapolis News (I think his full name is Charles L. Williams),[1] who probably knows Princeton material in editorial offices in the South. Possibly if you send your circular to him you could get a response that would answer your question. It is very stupid of me to have forgotten.

When it comes to suggesting a man to speak at your meeting, the embarrassment is that it would be practically asking the person invited to identify himself with the movement, and most public men might feel a good deal embarrassed. Perhaps you could inquire and find out whether it is true that Senator Owen expressed himself as in favor of my nomination. If he did, then you could find no better man, I should think, than he.

I am ashamed to be so sterile of ideas on the subject that so nearly concerns myself, but it is at least proof of my good faith when I say that I do not know how to promote any movement of this kind.

With affectionate regard,

Sincerely yours,   Woodrow Wilson

TLS (H. S. Breckinridge Papers, DLC).
¹ Charles Richard Williams, Princeton 1875.

To William Bayard Hale

My dear Mr. Hale: [Trenton, N. J.] March 30, 1911.

I have taken the liberty of making one or two excisions in the article, and yet it is so generous an estimate of me and is so admirably done, that I do not like to touch it. I can only thank you with all my heart for your partial and generous judgments.

The article was returned by special delivery post this morning to "The World's Work, Garden City, Long Island."

Cordially yours,   Woodrow Wilson

TLS (received from W. H. Hale).

A Veto Message

To the Senate: [Trenton, N. J.] March 31st, 1911.

I herewith return, without my approval, Senate Bill No. 148, entitled "A further supplement to the act entitled 'An act to establish public parks in certain counties in this State, and to regulate the same,' approved March fifth, one thousand eight hundred and ninety-five."

Undoubtedly the expenditure sought to be authorized by this bill is a very proper one. I return the bill without my approval because of its mandatory form. It leaves the financial authorities of the counties concerned without any choice in regard to the appropriation of moneys called for. They are obliged to appropriate them and to borrow money to meet the appropriation, upon the mere request of the Board of Park Commissioners. If this bill were permissory in character, I should not hesitate to sign it.

I return it without my signature because of my very clear conviction that it is a serious interference with the self government of communities that mandatory action of this sort should proceed from the Legislature of the State. I feel that we are in danger of drifting away from some of the essential practices of local self government and that the tendency is to have all initiative in matters of expenditure and of the exercise of authority proceed from Trenton.

Respectfully,   Woodrow Wilson,   *Governor.*[1]

Printed in the *Journal of the Sixty-Seventh Senate of the State of New Jersey* . . . (Trenton, N. J., 1911), pp. 602-603.
[1] This veto was sustained.

To Samuel Huston Thompson, Jr.

My dear Mr. Thompson: [Trenton, N. J.] March 31, 1911.

Your letter of March twenty-seventh[1] comes to me to-day. It is very generous of you to offer me the hospitality of your home, but I feel that I ought not to accept it but ought to go to a hotel, because, as you say, it is only too certain that I shall be besieged the moment I get there, and I should feel very much embarrassed to feel that I was merely making a convenience of your home. Moreover, I think it would make those who wanted to see me feel a little hesitancy also. It would be very delightful to be your guest, if only I could feel I was doing so with perfect propriety.

I dare say, from present appearances, that it will be quite possible for me to be the guest of the Mile High Club. The tentative schedule we have made out would bring me to Denver early on the morning of May eighth, and would give me the evening of the eighth to dine with the Mile High Club and the evening of the ninth to dine with the Chamber of Commerce.[2] It may be necessary to make a slight alteration in these dates later, but at present I suggest them to your consideration.

Cordially and sincerely yours,   Woodrow Wilson

TLS (S. H. Thompson, Jr., Papers, DLC).
[1] It is missing.
[2] News reports of these affairs are printed at May 9 and 10, 1911, Vol. 23.

Remarks to the New Jersey Conference of Charities and Correction[1]

[[April 2, 1911]]

Mr Chairman,[2] Ladies and Gentlemen:

The most obvious dictates of discretion would have bidden me not come to this meeting, because I cannot pretend to any intimate knowledge of the subjects discussed in a conference of this sort. I stand defenceless in my ignorance. And yet it would have been to display an indifference which I do not feel if I had declined to be present in this, my own home, to take some part, though a very slight part indeed, in the deliberations of this Conference. For the matters with which it concerns itself are of the greatest moment, and no student of the forces of society can fail to realize the extraordinary significance of forces that display themselves in a gathering like this.

The only real forces of society, it seems to me, are the voluntary forces—the forces that display themselves unbidden, that come out of a real genuine appreciation of the needs of men, and a genuine impulse to meet those needs without the whip of law, or without the compulsion of any system of government. A conference like this is a voluntary effort on the part of those who are not obliged to interest themselves in this sort of thing, to assist their fellow men where they most sadly stand in need of assistance.

I have sometimes thought that the real difficulty of movements represented by such a conference is that they are apt to be touched with too much sentiment. You can show sentiment with regard to individuals you know; but, unfortunately, if my experience is any guide in the matter, you cannot show too much sentiment towards persons you don't know, because sometimes the superficial manifestations of life are not the manifestations of the reality. And when, in addition to that, you have to deal with masses of men, with tendencies, with those human forces which display themselves in statistics, in the mere number of persons, for example, who commit suicide within the year, and the seasons of the year in which most suicides occur, and you stand in the presence of that vague, intangible thing that you call a tendency, then you must do some very stern thinking. You must not allow yourselves to forget the original and fundamental meaning of the word charity, which, if I am not misinformed, comes from the word which means love; and love is not based

[1] The opening session of the tenth annual meeting, held in Alexander Hall on the Princeton campus, April 2, 1911.
[2] Dean Henry B. Fine, who was presiding at this session.

upon an unintelligent sympathy. Love is based—untimately [ulti-
mately], at any rate—upon nothing less solid and enduring than
justice. The only way to be a true friend, I suppose, is to comprehend your friend and to do him justice, whether it hurts him
or not, whether it pleases him or not.

And so with the judgments with regard to society; we must not
allow ourselves to be misled by mere sympathy. We must not
allow ourselves to be led into following those impulses of pity
which may not be impulses of help. Because, to pity a weak man
is not to help him, is not to stimulate him. If you say to a
man who is sorry for himself that you are sorry for him, you
decrease his strength in just that proportion; you make him just
that much more pulpy than he is when he begins to exhibit the
ultimate weakness of being sorry for himself. So that what we
have to study in our processes of charity are processes of stimulation and processes of correction; and it is just as charitable,
just as valid evidence of love, to correct as it is to sympathize.
So that there is not a mere chance in the connection of the two
words which constitute the title of this Association: charity and
correction go hand in hand; and what we are trying to correct
is not so much the individual as the forces—chiefly social forces—
which are producing the mischief.

One of the most extraordinary features of our time, as it
seems to me, is that society seems, with respect to every portion
of its life, to be looking itself over—to be holding itself off at
arm's length and examining what characterizes its life, what
the tendencies are that should be encouraged and what the tendencies that should be corrected; what the forces are that are
making for good and what the forces that are making for evil.
And the forces of society are better corrected by this self-comprehension than by any amount of sympathy, by any amount of the
old-fashioned charity, which is the mere pouring out of money
to those who happen to stand in need of money, whether they
ought to be in need of it or not.

It is this self-comprehension which is not weakened by too
much sentiment which is the hope of society; for ladies and
gentlemen, we must not think of the present generation only. We
are in this world for only a little time, and it is a matter of com-
parative indifference how soon we go out of it, or how we get out
of it. Each generation is a mere transient item in the great process
of the development of humanity. We cannot afford to waste
sympathy on ourselves or on our contemporaries. The thing we
must do, whether it kills us or cures us, is to study the remedies;
to apply the disciplines as well as the ameliorations; because

there is only one thing that is ever going to elevate society, and that is the human will. Society must always be governed by law; and the major premise of law is moral responsibility—the moral responsibility of the individual. If there is no choice, then there should be no punishment. If there is no freedom of the will, then the penalties of the law are intolerable, for they are unjust. Except as you can produce independence and freedom of the will, you cannot justify a system of law. For every punishment is based upon the hypothesis that the will of the individual punished could have chosen the other course. If it could not, if social conditions are such that it was out of the question for it to choose it, then the punishment is unjust; and inasmuch as society cannot conceivably live except by a system of law, society can live only by the stimulation and freedom of the human will. You must liberate the individual, you must put him upon his mettle, you must put him in such shape that he can discriminate between right and wrong, and make him physically and mentally and morally strong enough to choose the right in preference to the wrong; or else you have not accomplished the fundamental work of society.

Now, all of these things are easy enough to say. These are the kind of generalizations upon which anybody falls back who does not know anything in particular about the subject that he is discussing. But, nevertheless, though they may be a refuge in my case, they are, nevertheless, valid propositions; and it seems to me they are propositions which should lie back of all the endeavors which we are blindly undertaking.

Now, the last thing that I have to say is that nothing of this sort can be isolated. No studies of this sort can stand apart, and by themselves. Mrs. Alexander[3] was speaking of the increasing burden of taxation; and it is a very grievous thing, indeed. Apparently there is nothing that can be done to ameliorate existing conditions that does not increase the public expenditure; and the increase of the public expenditure involves, of course, the increase of taxation. Very well, then; if you are going to push this thing home, you must be fair in your system of taxation; and the trouble now is, not the amount of money raised by taxation, but the people from whom we get it. There is not an equitable system of taxation; and therefore if you wish to push philanthropy through, you must become reformers of taxation. We must get more money; but we must get it from different people than

---

[3] Caroline Bayard Stevens Alexander, president of the New Jersey Conference of Charities and Correction in 1911. She is identified in Caroline B. S. Alexander to WW, Sept. 21, 1910, ns. 1 and 2, Vol. 21.

those from whom we are getting it. We are squeezing and squeezing and squeezing the poor; and we are not, in anything like the same proportion, laying our excises upon the rich.

Now, then, there are those who are noble among the rich. For they are very fond of revenge upon us by giving us the money. But that very impulse—that very impulse of generosity is, I venture to think, at the bottom an impulse of redress. "You won't exact it of us; therefore, we will show you where you ought to get it, and give it to you"; and I must say that those persons seem to me to elect themselves into our nobility—our natural nobility; for only that is the noble class in any community that recognizes and carries and rejoices in its public responsibilities.

We are cheating the rich people of their just share in the great things that we are trying to undertake. You cannot touch any part of the body politic, therefore, or of its processes of reformation, without touching all the rest; and your quest of justice will lead you to the confines of politics.

Printed in *Proceedings of the New Jersey Conference of Charities and Correction . . . 1911* (Trenton, N. J., 1911), pp. 22-25.

To Mary Allen Hulbert Peck

Dearest Friend,   Princeton, 2 April, 1911.

The days go as usual: I have got used to a confusing variety, though my nerves sometimes feel the incessant strain. The legislature still sits (and is likely to sit, alas! for three or four weeks longer), and the interminable fight still goes on for the bills that must be passed if we are to keep faith with the people. There is nothing to relate, except incidents; and there was one very amusing incident last week.

The Senate of the State has, you must know, a Republican majority of two:[1] I must obtain at least two votes to get my bills through. The senator from Cumberland County is one Nicholls,[2] a sly old fraud who likes to increase his consequence by posing as something of an independent. At an early stage of the game he came to me and intimated that he was going to stand by me and vote for the administration measures. He dropped into my office frequently, and I began to realize that something was in the wind. As if to assist my diagnosis, the sheriff of Cumberland[3] up and died. The senator promptly showed his hand. He came to me

[1] The Republican majority in the Senate was, actually, three.
[2] Isaac T. Nichols.
[3] George W. Payne.

and said very plainly that, since he was going to vote for my bills, he expected to be allowed to say what the appointments in his county should be. Needless to say, I did not indulge him. I appointed the man who seemed to be most acceptable to the Democrats of good standing in the county.[4] He thereupon renounced me. I was not the broad man he had taken me to be, he said. He was loud and not at all parliamentary in speaking of the breach. He certainly would not vote for the bills. A day or two after his dissapointment, I was invited, by the Adjutant General, Sadler, to go out with the senators to the [Trenton] country club and eat a fried chicken and waffle supper (which was delicious, by the way), and at the supper things happened! The senators are as jolly as boys when they let themselves "go" on such an occasion, and that night they were in fine fettle. In the middle of the meal Frelinghuysen, of Somerset, got up and said, "By special request, Senator Nicholls has consented to sing 'I Love Him No More.' " Then the fun began! Nicholls got up to speak, but for almost five minutes they would not let him, throwing all sorts of jibes at him, very good natured and very witty, but very teasing. When they let him, he said that the trouble was, not that he did not love me more, but that I loved him less. I reminded him that I had high example, for "Whom the Lord loveth he chasteneth,"—and then we were off! The rest of the evening was one unbroken romp. After we got up from the table we danced in every comical combination any one could think of, and I led Senator Nicholls several times around the big dining room in a cake walk, in which we pranced together to the perfect content of the whole company. He seemed quite mollified before we got through with him. Such are the processes of high politics! This is what it costs to be a leader! But it remains to be seen whether the sly old fox votes for the bills or not. I would not trust him out of my sight.[5] But this at least seems gained: I am on easy and delightful terms with all the senators. They know me for something else than "an ambitious dictator."

Colonel Harvey has broken loose again. This time I actually *do* send you a copy of the April number of the North American Review, in which he pays me a really beautiful tribute. I wish that it were deserved. I should like to be the true original of such a portrait![6]

[4] Harry J. Garrison.

[5] For the political results of this *pas de deux*, see WW to Mary A. H. Peck, April 16, 1911.

[6] "The Problem, the Solution and the Man," *North American Review*, CXCIII (April 1911), 481-93. This editorial in part came from the advance text of

The presidency business seems to be ripening into a veritable movement. A small group of indulgent friends in New York have actually employed (in a way to attract no attention) a man named Stockbridge, who is to be my publicity agent. Already he is giving me no end of trouble to supply him with "copy." I do not know how to play my part of the unpalateable game. The trip through the West is planned. I leave on the third of May and get back (what may be left of me) on the 28th. My itinerary includes Kansas City, Des Moines, Denver, Los Angeles, San Francisco, Portland, Seattle, Indianapolis, and Chicago. It will be quite like a campaign speaking tour. It will at least serve to test my power of enduring such things. The chief antidote, no doubt, will be to get as much fun out of it as possible. I shall try to get off frequent little notes to you, if no more.

I suppose you will still be in Bermuda, even then. I hope so.

Harvey's speech to the Hibernian Society of Savannah cited in P. A. Stovall to WW, April 5, 1911, n. 3.

In "The Problem, the Solution and the Man," Harvey wrote, "The vital problem now confronting the people of the United States, the problem involving the perpetuity of free institutions, the problem which transcends all economic, political and moral issues, is how to make equitable distribution of the combined earnings of labor and capital without rending the fabric of popular government." The solution, Harvey argued, lay in "co-operation, a drawing together in frank and unselfish tolerance of one another's opinions," and he looked specifically to the South as the "teacher" of the nation. Harvey's unsurprising conclusion was that Wilson was the man, who, through the support of the South, could bring unifying leadership to the country, and he concluded with the following tribute:

"Great occasions find great men. Here is one who, if he had lived in the days of Jefferson and Madison, would have rivalled the one as a champion of the people and would have equalled the other in comprehension and lucid expression of fundamental law. No other living personality so happily combines the dominant traits of those two great statesmen; no other has evidenced so perfect a blending of profound knowledge and simple devotion to humanity; no other has shown so clearly how quickly the old truths will spring into new light and power when touched by the magic wand of full sincerity; no other more surely embodies the authority of sustained thought, of unremitting labor for unselfish ends, the spirit of sacrifice and devotion, the instinct of independence, the love of perfect freedom. Born a polemic and controversialist, intellectually combative and self-reliant; fearless to the verge of temerity; indifferent to applause or censure for its own sake; incapable of intrigue; prompt to accept conclusions based upon right *versus* wrong without inquiring or caring whether they be politic or even expedient; persuasive in oratory, but devoid of artifice; too intent, too earnest to employ cheap and paltry devices; his pockets filled with moral dynamite; his every thought springing from knowledge that all of the basic principles in our political order, including conservatism, emerged from the well of the most radical democracy, and that democracy itself is only letting in light and air; at the height of his powers of intellect and judgment; upon the high plateau of middle life, best adapted to noble and enduring achievement, stands the man, the liberal, the progressive, the radical, if you will, wide-eyed, open-minded, calm, resolute, exact in thought, effective in action, the most vivid and virile personality, save one, developed on American soil in half a century. Such, without exaggeration or undue emphasis, is Woodrow Wilson."

Crazy as I am to see you again, I am still more anxious to have you get rested and restorad [restored] to your old tone. I hope with all my heart, therefore, that you will stay after the place empties, and get its sweet calm into your system, so that whan I see you again I shall have the happiness of seeing some of the colour of dear Bermuda in your cheeks, and see you full of your old vigour and contagious high spirits. Come back ready to bid defiance to any fatigues that America in its bigness and its restlessness may have in store for you. That is at present my dearest wish. I want you to have the best there is to get in the world, and the prime good of all is the health that makes enjoyment possible, and straightens out all perplexed thinking. Possibly we shall break up here when I start West. Ellen and the girls may go at once to Lyme. After I return I am booked for two addresses in the South, and then, I hope, I can join them, and feel free to do a little heavy resting! Faith, I shall need it! And yet I stand the pace wonderfully well. I keep well and each morning sees me fresh and vigourous again. If the pesky legislature would only do its work and be gone, I could be happy.

All join me in affectionate messages. Give my love to Mrs. Allen and your son.

						Your devoted friend,	Woodrow Wilson

WWTLS (WP, DLC).

To the Senate of New Jersey

To the Senate:					[Trenton, N. J.] April 4th, 1911.

I trust that I may with perfect respect call the attention of the Senate to the resolution passed unanimously by the House of Assembly ratifying the proposed amendment to the Constitution of the United States, which confers upon Congress the right to lay taxes upon incomes.

This amendment has no partisan color whatever. It was suggested by a Republican President and passed by a Congress of which both houses were Republican, but it received the cordial support of Democrats in both chambers of the Federal Congress and has been endorsed by the National platforms of both of the great political parties of the country. It seems clearly sustained by the public opinion of the Nation.

Our own House of Assembly has agreed to it without a single dissenting voice.[1]

It is a matter of great consequence to the whole future policy of the government of the United States that this amendment should have the sanction of the States. A large majority of them have already ratified it. The State of Maine has just reversed her former action and accepted it. New Jersey should forego all considerations of self-interest and confirm it, to enhance her credit as a progressive and patriotic commonwealth, to further the right adjustment of the burdens of National taxation, to enable the Federal government to liberalize its financial policy without loss or embarrassment and to consolidate the interests of State and Nation upon a real reciprocal footing. One decision of the Supreme Court of the United States, based upon erroneous economic reasoning,[2] has made this amendment necessary. The powers of the Federal government in this important matter should be restored to their first integrity.

I take the liberty, therefore, with all respect and with the deepest earnestness, to urge upon the Senate concurrence in the resolution now sent up to it from the House. I am convinced that the honor of the State would be greatly enhanced thereby.
Respectfully,   Woodrow Wilson,   *Governor.*[3]

Printed in the *Journal of the Senate of N. J.,* *1911,* pp. 639-40.
[1] On March 29, 1911.
[2] Pollock *v.* Farmers' Loan & Trust Co., 1895, in which the Supreme Court had ruled the income tax provision of the Wilson-Gorman Tariff Act of 1894 unconstitutional on the ground that an income tax was a direct tax on real and personal property and therefore violated Article I, Section 2 of the Constitution requiring that direct taxes be apportioned according to population.
[3] Wilson's appeal was, once again, in vain.

An After-Dinner Political Address[1]

[[April 5, 1911]]

Mr. Chairman, ladies and gentlemen: I must admit that I feel very much more comfortable to-night than I did the last time that I appeared in this room.[2] I was then, as I supposed, invading the enemy's stronghold. I knew how ill Democratic doctrine would sit upon some Republican stomachs. I saw the look of apprehension in the faces of the men gathered; moreover, I was asking them for their suffrages, and since that time they have been generous enough to accord them to me. Burlington County broke its record, repented of some of its errors and mistakes, and showed that it had its face toward that glorious future that Mr. Bryan has so eloquently painted for us.

[1] Delivered at the Jefferson Day dinner of the Burlington County Democratic Club in the Auditorium, Burlington, N. J. Thomas H. Birch presided; William Jennings Bryan, Senator James E. Martine, and Frank S. Katzenbach, Jr., also spoke.
[2] About Wilson's earlier speech in Burlington, on October 6, 1910, see the news report printed at Oct. 7, 1910, Vol. 21.

I share the feeling of pleasure, ladies and gentlemen, that Mr. Birch and Mr. Bryan have expressed in facing this audience upon this occasion, and yet I feel that my pleasure, as compared with Mr. Bryan's, has a touch of selfishness in it. Mr. Bryan has borne the heat and burden of a long day; we have come in at a very much later time to reap the reward of the things that he has done. Mr. Bryan has shown that stout heart which in spite of the long years of repeated disappointments has always followed the star of hope, and it is because he has cried America awake that some other men have been able to translate into action the doctrines that he has so diligently preached. It is just that he should feel glad upon such an occasion when we celebrate the triumph of democracy in New Jersey, and yet I have always felt a certain embarrassment in speaking in party terms with regard to the things that have happened in New Jersey. For you know, ladies and gentlemen, that last November there were thousands upon thousands of men who up to that time had voted the Republican ticket who then voted for the Democratic candidate. I do not feel as if it were exactly a Democratic party victory which was then achieved. Mr. Bryan has given you the key to the matter.

What happened? The doctrine of the people had been preached in season and out of season by men who comprehended the needs of the people, and then, presently, a Republican President[3] and other men associated with him began to see the moral of the lesson, began to see the great things that waited to be done, and swung into the great line of men who were turning their faces toward the light, and so built up, year by year, that great triumph of the people which has now expressed itself in their confidence in the particular party which without division has devoted itself to that great cause. For the trouble with the Republican party at the present moment is that it is divided, and the strength of the Democratic is that it is united, and it is united in the pursuit of the purposes which the more enlightened and progressive ranks in the Republican party are seeking themselves to promote.

There had been a union of parties in the pursuit of a purpose, and it is the triumph of the purpose which we celebrate in this gathering to-night. And I tell you, gentlemen, the purpose has triumphed, is triumphing and shall go on from achievement to achievement.

I was not myself permitted to attend the hearing before a committee of our Senate yesterday afternoon upon the Geran

[3] Theodore Roosevelt.

bill—the primaries and election bill—but I want to tell you that
that hearing marked an epoch in the political history of New
Jersey. What happened at that hearing and what was the scene?
The hearing was held upon a bill which proposed to give the
people of this State access to their own government at every
point. A few gentlemen came into that presence, sullen, embarrassed, knowing not how to speak with any degree of force
to oppose the bill, and before the hearing was one-third pro-
gressed they left the room,[4] for, from every quarter of New
Jersey, men of the first talent and character had rallied to the
defense of the people in that room. They did not come there to
utter sentiments; they did not come there to promote mere
party program. They came there with briefs for the people of
New Jersey and they showed that the only way in which the
people of New Jersey could be let into their government was
by the wide open doors of this particular measure.

I had a gentleman tax me the other day with the accusation
that this measure went very much beyond the promises of the
Democratic platform and of the Republican platform. I know
the promises of the Democratic platform more familiarly than
I do the promises of the Republican platform, because I knew
that I had to stand with both feet on all of them and I wanted
to see if they would bear my weight. Now, the promises of electoral reform was that the processes of election should be simpli-
fied, and this gentleman said that in fulfilment of that you gave
us a bill forty-two pages long, so complicated that it has to be
read again and again for the ordinary mind to comprehend it.

That was a simplification of the electoral processes of this
State. How do you simplify a jungle? You simplify it by putting
the ax to the root of everything that grows in it, and if you have
got a jungle so thick that the liberties of mankind can never
find a pathway through it, you have got to have axes enough
to lay to those roots. And every page of that bill contains an
ax, and every ax will be laid to the root of some rank growth
in that abominable jungle.

I wonder if you ever saw the book written by Judge Ben Lindsey, that lover of mankind and of children, who presides over the
juvenile court in Denver, Col.? That book is a narrative of his
contest with the political machine that was crushing out the life
of men and the life of the children in that great city and in that
great State, and the significant title that he gives the bo[o]k is

[4] The only opposition to the Geran bill on this occasion came from an Essex
County delegation composed of representatives of both the Republican and
Democratic county committees. Trenton *True American*, April 5, 1911; *Newark
Evening News*, April 5, 1911.

"The Beast." This is "The Beast" of the jungle, this secret covert control of the processes of the politics and of the fortunes of mankind, and the removal of the jungle is an infinitely sweet and wholesome process of the simplification. We shall now know the paths that we walk; we shall know the men that we are dealing with, and God's sun shall shine upon every footfall that He gives.

It is delightful to be accorded an occasion upon which I can speak of these things and report to you the progress we are making at Trenton. There are gentlemen in front of me and gentlemen behind me who have done all the talking in recent weeks down in Trenton, and it is a luxury to be let loose myself. I have become the best listener in the State of New Jersey. I have listened to the applications for more offices than I knew existed, and I have listened all day long and I have listened with intense interest and deep pleasure to the echoes that I could catch occasionally of the transactions in the committee rooms and the debates on the floor of the two houses. For I want to bear my testimony that the gentlemen in the Senate and House at Trenton are trying to serve their constituents, and that it is a pleasure and a profit to me daily to learn in their company what the interests of the State of New Jersey are. One of the hearings in Trenton I was privileged to hear. There had gathered a great company of men in the Senate chamber—not to discuss any political matter, not to discuss any matter of controversy, but to discuss one of the fundamental interests of the people of New Jersey, namely, their processes of transportation.

It was the hearing on the project for a great inland waterway, paralleling the ocean and opening, as it were, all the arteries of New Jersey to the free flow of her vigorous material blood. That was the sort of hearing that collected the audience; that was the sort of hearing to which men were bidden to come as if they would hear something interesting and profitable and lying at the real heart of the business of public affairs. And men gathered there from different parts of the country to tell New Jersey what her chance was to take part in these great enterprises. And you know what that means, gentlemen.

I am not going to indict the persons who have hitherto controlled the processes of transportation in New Jersey. I know so many of those men, and I know so well that they are just as honest as I am, that I am not going to impeach their character in any respect. But I do want to point out to you that the railways of New Jersey have so monopolized the traffic of New Jersey that many of her best energies have been cabined and confined until she has had an artificial growth in some parts and a natural growth in very few parts. And these men had gathered together to show her how she had to but open her arteries and let her blood flow, how she had to but make a little link here and a little link there, and nature's great fluid highways would carry her boats and her cargoes, link her processes of trade with every part of the country, North and South, keep away from the winds and the dangers of the outer coast, and see her factories grow thick along the lines of a great highway where no man could establish a monopoly and where the people would have their rule and their opportunity. That was what interested this great company; those are the things that are gathering audiences in the capital of Trenton.

Now I know that a great many people say that New Jersey has awakened in these recent weeks to her opportunities and to the occasions that she has to show her strength. I do not think that such language describes what has happened. New Jersey was not asleep. This is not a stolid and indifferent people. New Jersey has been just as wideawake as any other State in the Union; but New Jersey was sick at heart with discouragement; she knew what she wanted to do, but no man would lead her and show her the way. Those who promised to show her the way broke their promises and themselves lost their way. Go back and look at the history of legislation in recent years at Trenton and see what has happened there again and again. We have a little band of men in the House of Assembly at Trenton who undertook to fight for the rights of the people. Their opponents were abashed and silenced, and men who had promised and were bound by every interest except the public interest to vote against them found it impossible when the light of day shone upon the process to refrain from redeeming their pledges to the people. Whenever anybody has spoken for the people at Trenton, the great forces of opinion in New Jersey have sustained them and no man has dared to stand in the way. Search the legislative records of New Jersey, gentlemen, and make up your roll of honor. It is a long roll of honor. You know the men. You will steadily, as you know them better, advance them from stage to stage in their career until they shall find that the old saying that a democracy is ungrateful is deeply false.

Let but a great people know who their real servants are and they are lavish in their gift of power, they are lavish in their praise, they make heroes of little men if those little men but do them honorable service. And so I say that the happy day has come in New Jersey, not when she has awakened, but when she has realized her power. And in such hearings as took place in Trenton yesterday she is showing that she has now found how easy it is to force her way along the track of progress. I think it very important, ladies and gentlemen, that we should know very distinctly what it is that we are about. Mr. Bryan has stated in language more eloquent than I could frame what the time-old struggle has been of men against those privileged forces that were crushing the life out of them and dimming their lamps of hope so that they could hardly grope their way along the dark highway upon which they struggled.

Mr. Katzenbach has spoken to you of the immortal author of the Declaration of Independence but the Declaration of Independence does not mention the issues of the year 1911, and the men who are the real children of the Declaration of Independence are the men who are translating its terms into the language of our own day and its problems. What is there that we fight in our day? We fight the Interests, we say, and there is a sinister capital at the front of the word; we fight Big Business, we say, and there again the capital affords the emphasis, and we say we are going to master the Interests. I entirely subscribe to the program, but I first want to know what it is I am going to tackle, and then I want to know how it is I am going to tackle it. And when I ask myself am I going to tackle men or am I going to tackle conception, I know that the wrestling is to be with invisible powers. It is not to be with persons; it is to be with ideas.

I know that when I grapple, in the small part that I play, with the great interests which have permitted themselves to become sinister in the affairs of our country, I am not dealing with in-[d]ividuals. There are individuals who represent the interests in our day who are men of noble mold; who are men of statesmanlike scope of conception. There are men among them who mean to do a service to you and to me, but they are not in the majority; they lurk in any company. There are men of that kind in the hosts that are now marching to achieve the victories of the people also.

I have a great many more friends now than I had before some of them were beaten, and I want to serve notice on them here and now that I know them at heart; I have got them labeled. I know the original from the spurious imitation. And I think I know the original from the spurious imitation of the real captains of industry. The captains of industry are very easily distinguishable from the captains of graft, but even the captains of industry have done this country a service which they are now only beginning to realize. What I am afraid of is not the men, but the point of view at which they stand. What we have got to grapple with is not a body of persons, but a very formidable array of ideas.

How true what Mr. Bryan and Senator Martine said when they spoke of the sovereignty and majesty of the idea and of the truth and its magnitude, as compared with the individual. The power of any man who exercises power in the world of thought and activity is only the power that he gets by embodying some truth or some idea, and these men of the interests are formidable only because they embody an idea, and it is the idea that I hate, it isn't the men.

What is this idea? The idea that is fundamental to all of it is that the people cannot take care of themselves and that the people who have the most money are intended by God to take care of them. That is the fundamental idea. These gentlemen do not believe in democracy, they distrust it fundamentally. You have sat at dinner tables, as I have sat, and heard the unguarded conversation of the last two or three years. You know that it was said in connection with a great statesman in this country, that it was possible that a monarchy might be set up in America. And what was their talk, the unguarded talk at dinner tables? It was that it might be a very good thing to set up a monarchy in America because, they said, in order to govern this great country with its accumulations of wealth and power the votes of masses of men are too difficult to manage and direct and control; it is necessary to have concentration of political power where there is concentration of material power.

I heard that doctrine again and again by men who ought to have known better, and I learned by listening to such talk that these men fundamentally distrusted the principles of democracy, that, therefore, they were ready to make secret alliances with political machines to see that legislation that they did not want was prevented and legislation that they did want was promoted. It was for that reason that they were afraid of primary laws and free access of the people to their own government. They want them shut out, because they fear what they would regard as the horde of common men. And corrupt political machines have been the instruments of that kind of covert oligarchy.

We believe in political organization; we believe in political leadership, but we do not believe in those political machines whose power comes from money intended to be used for special interests and not in the common cause. Nobody can watch the lobby in any Legislature without seeing who are behind the lobbyists. These gentlemen sometimes think they conceal themselves. They are as silly as the ostrich, with its head in the sand, for there bulks the ugly, awkward body. I say we are opposed to this very conception; we take exception to their alteration, their fundamental alteration, of the immortal utterance of Lincoln. They believe in government for the people, but they do not believe in government by the people. They say we will be the trustees in this important business and we will let you share in the droppings from the table.

Now, I want to utter this doctrine as an interpretation of your thought. I want to say that industry is not for the communities in which it is set up. Industry, if it be wholesome and genuine, is of the communities in which it is set up. Do you mean to tell me that the factories at Trenton are established for the workmen in those factories and for the people in Trenton? They are established and maintained and given their energy by the workmen who are in them and by the people in Trenton. The only vitality of any kind of industry, ladies and gentlemen, springs out of this common soil of the brain and sinews and intelligence and instincts of common men.

This country is as great as her rank and file. The flower that blooms on the stem is merely the evidence of the vitality of the stem, and the real source of its beauty, the very blush that it wears upon its tender cheek, comes from those silent sources of eternal life that lie hidden in the chemistry of the soil. And so the flower of every civilization derives its beauty, its significance, its mortality from the people from which it springs. No man in his senses would seek to represent a people in order to mislead them. As easily, as readily think of sapping the blood of a generation as mislead their thoughts. As quickly think of betraying every secret application of human relation as deceive a great people. For what do you do? What was upon the verge of happening in recent years in this country? You make deep cynics of them. You sow those fearful seeds of despair, which will spring up like dragons' teeth and destroy any civilization. And so the thing that we have come to celebrate to-night—the flower we have come to pluck to-night—is not the flower of party triumph, but that flower we would always wear at our heart, the flower that springs out of and is made fertile by the blood of humanity.[5]

Printed in the *Newark Evening News*, April 6, 1911.

[5] There is a WWT outline of this address, with the composition date of April 1, 1911, in WP, DLC.

From Pleasant Alexander Stovall

My dear Governor: Savannah, Ga. April 5th, 1911.

I have received your letter of March 27th asking me how the speech of Col. George Harvey "impressed the men who actually heard it."

Now this brings out the whole story and it is sufficiently dramatic and interesting to be told right here.

I enclosed you the article which I wrote just after the dinner,[1] when Col. Harvey was prevented by the rules of the Hibernian Society from making a political nomination.[2] However he delivered his corrected speech[3] with splendid effect. He was the last man on the list and it was 2 o'clock a.m. before he began. When he got to the personal part he described you and the men called out "the name, the name, give us the name!" Finally one fellow shrieked "Woodrow Wilson" and there were cheers, except from the throats of two republicans. One is collector of ports and the other is post-master (of course).

The crowd was for you; Savannah is for you, and I believe the whole state of Georgia and the South. Incidentally I may add the Nation is with you. That follows as a matter of course.

    With best wishes, I remain,
                    Yours very truly,   Pleasant A. Stovall

TLS, (WP, DLC).
  [1] A clipping of the news report in the *Savannah Press*, March 18, 1911, which Stovall had in fact already sent to Wilson.
  [2] Stovall's report described the reasons why Harvey had to omit explicit reference to Wilson in his speech to the Hibernian Society. Peter W. Meldrim, president of the organization, greeted the dinner guests and warned that the society did not tolerate any references to political or religious issues. "Any reference," he said, "to living public men, whether in praise or dispraise, would be manifestly out of place." As the account of Harvey's speech given in G. B. M. Harvey to WW, March 1, 1911, n. 4, reveals, Harvey certainly did not refrain from discussing political issues, and only an ignoramus could have failed to perceive that he was talking about Wilson when describing the ideal Democratic candidate for 1912.
  [3] The advance text of Harvey's speech, which ended with a glowing tribute to Wilson, was printed in the *Newark Evening News*, March 18, 1911.

To Mary Allen Hulbert Peck

Dearest Friend,   Princeton, 9 April, 1911.

The incident this week (besides the receipt of your letter) was a big political meeting at Burlington. It was got up, really, in order to bring Mr. Bryan and me together on the same stage. I told you, did I not? of my first meeting with Mr. Bryan two or three Sundays ago, when he came here to make a religious address, at the invitation of the Theological Seminary, and dined with us here at the Inn afterwards, before rushing off to Trenton, to speak in the evening. I must admit that he impressed me as a man of real power, an extraordinary person. It was at that time that Mr. Birch of Burlington, his host, who had brought him up in his car for the meeting, proposed a grand Democratic rally for the fifth, and on the fifth we had it. Ellen, Jessie, Nellie, and I all went down and stayed with the Birches over night, and all had a very good time. I had been really ill for about twenty-four hours with a wretched upset in my bowels (the result, no doubt, of too long continued strain and fatigue) and was very nervous indeed about the speaking. I had never been matched with Mr. Bryan, or any other speaker his equal before, and had my deep misgivings as to how I should stand the comparison. I felt dreadfully weak, because of my physical condition, but put on a forced draught and came off, I am happy to report, without discredit. Unless there was a general conspiracy to lie to me, I spoke as well as Mr. Bryan did, and moved my audience more. Ellen said I was "more of the orator" than she had ever seen me before: that is, that I put more colour and emotion into what I said than usual. I know that I was much more excited than usual, and so the result remarked by her was natural enough. First of all we men (while the ladies dined with Mrs. Birch[1]) went to a dinner at the hotel; but we sat down early and rose from the table in time to be at the opera house by eight o'clock, where we found the ladies already in their boxes. The audience numbered about twenty-five hundred. It was the same place I had spoken in when I visited Burlington on my campaign. Mr. Bryan spoke first, and spoke for an hour and a half! It is wonderful how he can hold an audience as long as he wishes to. He has extraordinary force and magnetism. For one thing, he has perfect command of himself, and perfect familiarity with his subject, and an admirable command of language. The whole thing comes from him freely and perfectly coined. After him our (my) new Senator, Martine, spoke for about fifteen minutes. He had been hurried up from Washington, where the special session of Congress had but just organized the day before, for the purpose. Champ Clark, too, had hoped to come, the new Speaker, but could not get away. By the way, did you know that "Champ" is an abrieviation of Beauchamp? He found his christening burdensome out in Missouri,— at any rate in politics. Martine did very well. Everybody was pleased with him. In the course of his little speech he did what seems to have become a favourite amusement with speakers, at

[1] Helen Barr Birch.

any rate when I am present: he spoke of me as the next President of the United States,—at which the audience went wild, and Mr. Bryan seemed not a little impressed. By the way, I forgot to say that in his own speech Mr. Bryan paid me a very handsome tribute of generous praise,[2] which my sanguine friends thought quite significant and were immensely pleased at; for of course no Democrat can win whom Mr. Bryan does *not* approve. After Martine Frank Katzenbach spoke, the very weak brother who ran on the Democratic ticket for the governorship three years ago. He gave us a dull biography of Jefferson. This is the month of Jefferson's birth, and all Democratic gatherings in April are supposed to be in commemoration of him. Then spoke your humble servant, very much excited, but on his mettle. I spoke for about half an hour, and sat down relieved but almost exhausted, and not a bit fit for the inevitable reception which followed at the Birch's. The only thing that made it bearable was a very beautiful and delightful woman, who almost made it enjoyable. Did you ever hear of Mrs. E. Burd Grubb[3] (terrible name), and did you ever see her? She is an English woman, one of a family of seven famous beauties, it seems. She seems a true, noble sort of creature. I had met her before, but had never had a chance to have a real talk with her. She is General Grubb's second wife.[4] He pointed out to us at Burlington a house just next the Birch's (both houses stand, delightfully placed, just on the bank of the great spread[ing] Delaware) from whose river piazza he was married, but "not to this dear young thing," he said, turning to the beauty, "she was flying about in Heaven then." He seems very deeply devoted to her. As he approached us, once, during

2 Speaking on the subject, "Watchman, What of the Night?", Bryan spoke about Wilson as follows: "I think no one in New Jersey rejoiced more than I did when the returns came in and we learned that Governor Wilson was elected Governor of New Jersey. His campaign raised expectations and his administration has satisfied expectations. The speeches in his campaign were pledges and he has fulfilled them as an Executive. It is necessary to promise great things in order to attach the people to you on election day, and it is necessary to keep the promises in order to keep the people with you after election. . . .

"Our hopes in the West were raised when we found that Dr. Wilson was making his campaign in the good, old-fashioned democratic way, and we have rejoiced day by day to find that he recognized the responsibility of leadership, and was not afraid to risk his future doing right. I am glad, therefore, to be at this meeting, and to be upon the program with him, and to assure him that none of these constituents who regard him with pride and watch him with interest are more interested in his doing well, and in his serving well of his people, than I.

"I think one of the best things that he has done was to send Martine to Washington, and when I give him credit for doing it I think that I am not overstating the case, for, if I understand the situation, we would hardly have had Martine if we had not had Wilson."

3 Violet Sopwith (Mrs. Edward Burd) Grubb.

4 General Grubb's first wife was Elizabeth Wadsworth Van Rensselaer Grubb, whom he married in 1863 and who died in 1886.

the evening, she extended her hand to him, and he kissed it like a knight.

We are all well. I have not entirely recovered tone from that little attack, but I am taking good care of myself and am getting further and further away from it every day. As usual, I slept until midday to-day, and feel very fresh, in consequence. One of the bills (the one providing for compensation of workingmen for accidents)[5] has passed and become law. The most important

[5] Both parties had pledged support for workmen's compensation during the campaign of 1910, and the controversy over the legislation of 1911 basically revolved around the nature and extent of employer liability and employee protection. The measure adopted (*Laws of New Jersey, 1911*, Chap. 95, pp. 134-45) grew out of the work of a commission appointed by Governor John Franklin Fort in 1910. The commission, composed of representatives of business, labor, and the legislature, was headed by William Dickson of Montclair. Other members included Walter Evans Edge, Atlantic City; J. William Clark, Newark; Samuel Bolterill, East Orange; John T. Cosgrove, Elizabeth; and Edward Kirkpatrick Mills, Morristown. For additional background on the appointment of this commission and previous workmen's compensation legislation in New Jersey, see n. 9 to the speech printed at Oct. 5, 1910, Vol. 21.

After the election of 1910, George L. Record submitted a workmen's compensation bill to Wilson, but it was never introduced in the legislature. Kerney, *Political Education of Woodrow Wilson*, p. 105. Instead, Republican State Senator Edge, on January 16, 1911, introduced a bill which the commission had prepared and Assistant Attorney Nelson Burr Gaskill had put into final form. Shortly afterward, Edge and Gaskill conferred with Wilson about the measure. Edge explained that its provisions were made elective to prevent the possibility of its being declared unconstitutional. According to Edge, Wilson replied, "I have no patience with either the Constitution or the Supreme Court," adding that he wanted the provisions made compulsory and was willing to risk a court test. Gaskill then informed Wilson that the bill contained a provision stipulating that, if the parties involved did not say within a stipulated period that they would not be bound by the act, its provisions would go into effect automatically. This conversation led Edge to believe that Wilson would not support his bill. Walter E. Edge, *A Jerseyman's Journal: Fifty Years of American Business and Politics* (Princeton, N. J., 1948), pp. 73-75.

Edge's bill, referred to the Committee on Corporations, of which he was the chairman, was reported out of committee on February 28 with some amendments, including several that specified precisely the amounts of compensation for various injuries. The bill came up for a vote on March 14, and during five hours of sharp debate several amendments were proposed by Senator William C. Gebhardt, who frequently spoke for Wilson on the floor of the Senate. Gebhardt's chief complaint was that the specification of compensation for various injuries prevented a worker from winning a more generous award from a jury. Edge countered that the bill specified compensation in order to relieve workers of the cost of litigation. The Senate adopted the Edge bill on March 15 with only minor changes. Trenton *True American*, March 15, 1911; *Newark Evening News*, March 15, 1911; *Journal of the Senate of N. J., 1911*, pp. 45, 219-21, 341-44, 374-75.

Meanwhile, Cornelius Ford of Hudson County had introduced two bills in the Assembly on January 16, 1911, one concerning workmen's compensation, the other defining employers' liability. Ford, who was president of the New Jersey Federation of Labor and chairman of the House Committee on Labor and Industries, reported his employers' liability bill on February 6. Then Allan B. Walsh of Mercer County proposed his own measure providing for an elective schedule of compensation. It was buried in Ford's committee. Ford's two bills eventually came to the floor, but a vote upon them was never taken. *Minutes of the N. J. House of Assembly, 1911*, pp. 52, 122, 133, 152, 210, 284, 310, 314, 399, 405, 511, 1487, 1493, 1725.

Ford now became preoccupied with the Edge bill, which was introduced in the House on March 21. Ford kept it bottled up in his committee in the

of all, the primaries and elections bill, will, I now feel confident, pass this week. The other two[6] are in more or less of a legislative tangle, but I hope will come out in more or less ship shape this week or next for final passage. If they all go through, I shall feel that the struggle has been worth all it cost of fatigue and anxiety. There is a grim satisfaction in the whole thing: for now no one expects me to pull up, falter, or alter my purpose in the least, and there is a tonic air in the whole process. God bless you. All join me in affectionate messages. Write me as full letters as you can, *all* about *yourself*. Give my love to Mrs. A. and Allen.

Your devoted frieod [friend],   Woodrow Wilson

WWTLS (WP, DLC).

---

hope that his own legislation, which provided more generous compensation than the Edge bill, would be enacted. At some time during late March, Wilson decided to support the Edge bill. As Ford later recalled, the Governor called him into conference and asked him to support the Edge bill. Wilson indicated that he feared that Ford's measures would not pass the Senate. "Don't you think it would be the part of wisdom to accept the Edge bill and make sure of getting something?" Wilson asked. After consulting with labor leaders in the state, Ford brought the Edge bill to the floor of the Assembly on April 3. The Assembly approved it unanimously, and Wilson signed it on the following day. New York *World*, June 5, 1912; *Newark Evening News*, April 4, 1911; *Minutes of the N. J. House of Assembly, 1911*, pp. 619, 621, 902-903.

The workmen's compensation act of 1911, like the act of 1909, specifically abolished two grounds which had exempted employers from liability—negligence by a fellow employee and the assumption of risk by the employee. The law covered workers under sub-contract and stipulated that employers had to prove willful negligence by an employee in order to avoid paying damages. Section II, which caused the most legislative controversy, provided an elective system of compensation. Once an employer and his employee had agreed to the provisions of this section, the employer was compelled to pay compensation for injuries, whether or not the employee had been negligent. Employers and employees were assumed to have made such an agreement unless they specifically stipulated to the contrary. The only exception to the liability of the employer was when death or injury were self-inflicted or due to intoxication. Workers surrendered the right of obtaining additional compensation by other recourse, for example, trial by jury. However, if the amount specified in the law was disputed by the employer or the employee, either or both parties could take the case to court. The act spelled out in detail the compensation for various injuries—loss of a thumb, 50 per cent of daily wages for sixty weeks; loss of an index finger, 50 per cent of daily wages for thirty-five weeks, etc. In cases of death, the law provided a sliding scale of benefits based upon the number of dependents, and, if there were no dependents, the employer paid for the cost of the last illness and the worker's burial.

The legislature also approved two more Edge-sponsored bills expanding the coverage of the law to employees hired before the act was passed and establishing an employers' liability commission to investigate and report on workmen's injuries and the implementation of the law. *Laws of New Jersey, 1911*, Chaps. 241 and 368, pp. 520-522, 763. Shortly before adjournment, the legislature adopted a bill permitting employers to form their own insurance companies to cover the costs of liability. *Journal of the Senate of N. J., 1911*, pp. 914, 1024, 1053, 1131; *Minutes of the N. J. House of Assembly, 1911*, pp. 1384, 1387, 1446, 1447, 1451-52, 1660, 1725. Wilson gave this measure a pocket veto.

6 The corrupt practices and public service commission bills, about which see ns. 3 and 4 to the statement printed at April 21, 1911.

From Henry Smith Pritchett

Personal

My dear Governor,   Bermuda April 9, 1911.

Having come down here to recover from a somewhat painful illness I ran across today a N. Y. paper containing a statement of the admirable way in which you dealt with the man[1] who charged you with using patronage to make votes. I cannot refrain from telling you my pleasure in this incident. For too long has it been tacitly assumed that offices could be used to trade with in this way that good men had forgot the shame of it—presidents, senators and governors have simply fallen in with the custom exactly as good men in England 100 or 150 years ago dealt openly in the sale of office and of title. I am glad to see you hit this thing. Good fortune to you in your fight for clean government.

I hope to return to N. Y. in ten days in good health. I have met here some very good friends of yours who speak in warm terms of your visits here and among others Mrs. Peck.

                    Yours faithfully   Henry S. Pritchett

ALS (WP, DLC).
[1] That is, James R. Nugent.

A Veto Message

To the House of Assembly: [Trenton, N. J.] April 10th, 1911.

I return, without my approval, Assembly Bill No. 197, entitled "An act to provide for the legal commitment and reformation of wayward females."

I return this bill because I am informed by the Attorney-General that its title is, under the terms of the Constitution of the State, seriously defective, and also because the processes of commitment provided for in the bill seem to be inconsistent with constitutional guarantees as to methods of trial when individuals are deprived of their liberty.

                    Respectfully,   Woodrow Wilson, *Governor*.[1]

Printed in the *Minutes of the N. J. House of Assembly*, *1911*, p. 1035.
[1] This veto was sustained.

To John Wesley Wescott

My dear Judge Wescott: [Trenton, N. J.] April 10, 1911.

Thank you sincerely for your letter of April eighth.[1] I am always grateful to you for your generous assistance and I need not tell you how I appreciate your attitude towards me personally. It has given me pleasure not only, but strength.

Cordially and faithfully yours,   Woodrow Wilson

TLS (J. W. Wescott Coll., NjP).
    1 It is missing.

To the House of Assembly of New Jersey

To the House of Assembly: [Trenton, N. J.] April 11, 1911.

There are two subjects which have taken shape for consideration since the opening of this legislative session which are of such far-reaching importance that I take the liberty of calling your attention to them and of earnestly commending them to your very careful consideration.

One of these subjects is the form of our system of public school administration. The other is the reform of our city government.

Since the opening of the present session the Senate committee, appointed two years ago to investigate the whole matter of the methods of our public school teaching and administration and the expenditure of money both by the State and the several localities of the State in connection with education, in the erection of buildings for educational purposes and in the supplying of the various physical means of conducting our public instruction, has completed its work and submitted to the Senate a very notable report.[1]

The report is singularly complete. It is the result of an investigation which has attracted the attention of the whole State. The method of the investigation, its thoroughness and its result have won applause on all hands. No one can read the report now submitted without admiring the work which has produced it or without feeling that every recommendation it contains is sustained by reasons which are quite unanswerable.

The Committee has introduced into the Legislature bills intending to give these recommendations effect in law, and I must say that it is my clear conviction that the measures represent reforms which are not only necessary, but exceedingly advantageous. If carried into effect, they would put the educational system of the State upon a footing of economy and efficiency such as it has never known before.

The State annually spends vast sums of money upon the schools, and yet has never had any means of making sure of how

---

1 *Report of Senate Committee to Investigate the Methods and Practices, Expenses and Disbursements of the Public Schools* (Trenton, N. J., 1911).

it was spent, with what wisdom, with what economy, with what careful attention to the objects for which it was intended to be used. The State cannot be said to have had any legal arrangement in this matter which deserved the name of system. The measures now pending before you will not deprive localities of their much prized autonomy and should not do so, but they will give the State opportunities to exercise a systematic supervision, and will afford means by which the public instruction of the State may be intelligently co-ordinated and directed. It has seldom happened that reforms of this sort could be put upon a more solid basis than these changes will have, as sustained by the admirable report of the Senate committee. I cannot too urgently commend them to your favorable attention. I think the judgment of every person familiar with matters of this kind, if addressed to this matter without bias, must recognize both the necessity and the desirability of effecting the reforms suggested. They are, without exception, admirable.[2]

[2] This comprehensive report, which was submitted to the Senate on March 28, 1911, was the product of a two-year study by a committee appointed in 1909 to examine the public school system in New Jersey and recommend reforms. The committee consisted of state senators Joseph Sherman Frelinghuysen of Somerset County, William James Lee Bradley of Camden County, and George Sebastian Silzer of Middlesex County, as well as Samuel St. John McCutcheon, a lawyer of Plainfield; William H. Morrow, a lawyer of Belvidere; and William Gray Schauffler, a physician of Lakewood. The last three men were appointed to the committee by the state Board of Education in 1909 and 1910, but they served at the behest of the committee itself in 1911.

The report's twenty-nine recommendations represented an attempt at a thorough reform of the New Jersey public school system by extending state control over many aspects of public education. The report focused primarily on four major areas—the financing of public education, administration of the state school system, improvement of educational standards, and correction of political abuses. The committee was especially critical of the trustees of the state school fund, about which see n. 1 to Wilson's draft of a proposed state Democratic platform, printed at Aug. 9, 1910, Vol. 21. The report stated (p. 23), "There has been carelessness, we might even say gross negligence, if not actual dishonesty, connected with some issues of bonds." For example, it cited cases of local school boards selling bonds to public dealers instead of the trustees of the school fund. These dealers in turn sold the bonds to the school fund at a nice profit. The committee also revealed that the trustees of the school fund deposited money collected for educational purposes in banks of which they were officers, directors, or stockholders. This money was usually placed in accounts that bore only 2 per cent interest. The trustees were slow in releasing such money; as a result, local school boards were frequently forced to borrow money at 6 per cent in order to cover expenses until they received their allotment of state funds.

Most of the committee's recommendations were embodied in a group of laws passed by the legislature in April 1911. The existing state Board of Education and the office of state superintendent of public instruction were abolished, and a new board with vastly extended powers, and a commissionership of education, were created. The new board was authorized to appoint a state inspector of school buildings, an inspector of school accounts, and supervising principals; establish a uniform system of bookkeeping for all public schools; grant accreditation to secondary schools; fix tuition rates for students who attended schools outside their districts; and compel, by subpoena if necessary, the production of any materials related to the administration of local schools. The new commissioner of education, who could be recruited from outside New

There is also pending before you a bill permitting the cities of this State, great and small, to adopt such changes in their organization of government as will enable them to simplify the processes by which they choose their officers, and thus concentrate responsibility in the interests both of purity of administration and of efficiency. The bill is not mandatory; it is meant merely to afford the cities the right to determine whether they shall adopt the so-called commission system of government or not.[3]

Upwards of one hundred cities of the United States have already made this change in their organization. I have yet to hear of any instance in which those who advocated the change have been seriously disappointed in its results. It has resulted in purifying and clarifying and perfecting every process of local government. It has concentrated responsibility, has enabled the voters to exercise a real control and has stimulated efforts at economy and business-like reorganization.

Jersey, was empowered to appoint four assistant commissioners, three of whom would supervise elementary, secondary, and industrial education, and one of whom would arbitrate disputes arising out of the school laws or rulings by the commissioner or the state board of education. The commissioner could also prescribe minimum examinations for graduation from grammar schools and admission to high schools; require a minimum course of study for elementary and high schools; and direct a county collector to withhold funds from any school which did not comply with the law or the rulings of the state Board of Education (*Laws of New Jersey, 1911*, Chap. 231, pp. 506-510).

Other laws regulated the sale of school bonds, about which the committee had expressed great concern. Private sales of such securities were prohibited, unless the trustees of the school fund refused to purchase them, and all bonds had to be signed, sealed, and delivered within the state. All private sales were required to be made in cash or by certified check (*ibid.*, Chaps. 235 and 236, pp. 514-15). In addition, the legislature directed counties to provide county superintendents of schools with offices and clerical assistants to assure adequate record-keeping (*ibid.*, Chap. 232, p. 511); regulated the appointment of members to local school boards (*ibid.*, Chap. 233, pp. 512-13); directed local boards to establish special classes for subnormal, blind, and deaf children (*ibid.*, Chap. 234, pp. 513-14); required the state comptroller to distribute state funds to local districts on a regular and prompt basis (*ibid.*, Chap. 237, pp. 516-17); and provided for standardized plans and specifications for school buildings of various sizes and mandated approval of building plans by the state Board of Education prior to construction (*ibid.*, Chap. 369, pp. 764-65). Although not explicitly recommended by the committee, the legislature also placed the employees of school districts under the civil service, provided such coverage was approved by the voters of the district (*ibid.*, Chap. 346, p. 727).

The legislature of 1911 failed to take action on several key recommendations of the committee, including preventing trustees of the school fund or local school districts from concentrating all the money at their disposal in one bank or in any bank in which a trustee or school board member had a financial interest; limiting the size of classes to forty-five students; prohibiting political contributions by school employees; building more facilities for retarded children; and supporting a state constitutional amendment to allow women to vote in school board elections.

[3] Wilson referred to Assembly bill No. 321, "An act relating to, regulating and providing for the government of cities, towns, boroughs and other municipalities within this State." For a description of the measure as adopted by the legislature, see n. 5 to the news report printed at April 18, 1911.

The reforms suggested for the adoption of the cities do not consist merely in putting their government into the hands of a small commission. Back of this change and in addition to it are the initiative, referendum and the recall, measures which enable the people to correct the mistakes of their governors, to adopt measures upon their own initiative, when necessary, and to recall from office unsatisfactory officials. These have proved not only efficient, but absolutely necessary parts of what is now known as the commission form of government in the various cities of the country.

There can be no doubt that these reforms are desired and even demanded by intelligent opinion in the cities of our State. We have abundant evidence that there is an extraordinary body of opinion behind them. The demand for them grows from day to day with extraordinary volume. It does not proceed from unthinking agitation. It proceeds from a very careful and thoughtful consideration of the problems involved and of the reforms which are necessary to meet and settle these problems. The changes proposed are not experimental; they have been tested by abundant experience elsewhere, and I am sure that it would afford all thoughtful persons cause for serious disappointment if the Legislature should not avail itself of this opportunity to show itself allied in this matter, as in all matters, with the impulses of progress now so handsomely manifest in our bodies politic.

Respectfully,   Woodrow Wilson,   *Governor*.[4]

Printed in the *Journal of the N. J. House of Assembly, 1911*, pp. 1060-1062.

[4] He sent an identical message to the Senate on April 11, 1911. It is printed in the *Journal of the Senate of N. J., 1911*, pp. 768-70.

From Marion Jackson Verdery

My dear Governor Wilson: New York, April 11th, 1911.

In so far as newspaper reports have enabled me to do so, I think I have read every speech you have made since your inauguration. I also followed closely the brave fight you made for Senator Martine's election. I congratulate you heartily upon all you have said and done.

You are measuring fully up to the high standard of courage, wisdom and patriotism which my enthusiastic admiration and jealous affection have set for you. Your future public usefulness, in my opinion, will be limited only by your power of physical endurance and your continuance in the public service.

I honestly believe you have the most intelligent grasp on the fundamental principles of our form of government, and the most comprehensive understanding of true republican democracy of any living American citizen. This is superlative language, but it only fairly expresses my unbounded confidence in you, and I have no misgiving but that your future course and conduct will fully justify my abiding faith.

I verily believe that before the National Democratic Convention of 1912 assembles you will have so conspicuously demonstrated to the whole American people your consummate ability, your dependable conservatism, your political wisdom, and your exhalted patriotism that your nomination for the Presidency by that Convention will be assured.

There is but one thing, in my judgment, which may hinder that consummation of your brilliant prospects, viz: the finger of the "Peerless One"[1] being put in the pie.

I pray God he may let you alone and that you may not by any combination of circumstances be forced or drawn into any entangling alliance with him.

He never preached a sound doctrine in his life. His greatest power has been through a God-given personal magnetism, which he has used to afflict the mind of the people with inflammatory sensations and then to draw them after him into the lamentable consequences of misplaced confidence in false leadership.

If I have written with too great familiarity and freedom, forgive it on the score of my whole-hearted loyalty to you.

With best wishes and highest hopes for you, I beg to sign myself,   Sincerely your friend,   Marion J. Verdery

TLS (WP, DLC).
[1] William Jennings Bryan.

To Marion Jackson Verdery

My dear Verdery: [Trenton, N.J.] April 12, 1911.

Thank you for your letter of the eleventh. You are perfectly right. The hazard in the whole case is what Mr. Bryan may do and say, but I do not see how I can control that at any degree. I can only go my own way and speak my own thoughts, and let the rest be taken care of by the powers which really preside.

Your letter is very generous as usual, and I thank you for it with all my heart.

Cordially and sincerely yours,   Woodrow Wilson

TLS (de Coppet Coll., NjP).

A News Report About Wilson's Arrival in Indianapolis

[April 13, 1911]

WILSON ARRIVES FOR DEMOCRATIC FEAST

New Jersey Governor Is Greeted by Governor Marshall
and Other Party Men.

Woodrow Wilson, Governor of New Jersey, arrived in Indianapolis shortly before noon today. He is to be the "headliner" at the "national Democratic achievement" banquet at the Murat temple tonight, under the auspices of the Democratic League of Clubs. Governor Wilson was met at the station by Governor [Thomas Riley] Marshall, Hugh Dougherty, chairman of the general executive committee of the banquet,[1] and William C. Liller, president of the league.

As definite word has been received that William Jennings Bryan will not be here, and several other prominent Democrats who had been invited to speak have sent their "regrets," Governor Wilson will have to stand the brunt of attention as the most distinguished guest present. He will be entertained while here by Governor Marshall, who gave a luncheon this afternoon at the University Club in honor of Governor Wilson and other guests.

Printed in the *Indianapolis News*, April 13, 1911; some editorial headings omitted.

[1] President of the Marion Trust Co. of Indianapolis, who was much involved in construction of the Fort Wayne, Cincinnati, and Louisville Railroad and the Toledo, St. Louis and Kansas City Railroad.

An Interview in Indianapolis

[April 13, 1911]

PEOPLE LOOK TO MAN, NOT TO PARTY—WILSON

Governor Woodrow Wilson, of New Jersey, who came to attend the Democratic banquet, tonight, is not saying a word about himself as a presidential possibility. He was asked whether his name would go before the Democratic national convention next year for that nomination and he answered:

"I am engaged in the interesting occupation of sawing wood. I do not know anything about that, and I am not worrying about it."

And that was all he would say on the subject. But he talked in an interesting manner about other things, especially political conditions. On his arrival in the city at noon he was met by Governor Marshall and taken to the latter's home in North Pennsylvania street.

Three leading points were set out in his talk. First, that party lines rest lightly on the people in these days; second, that the spirit of progressiveness is not confined to any one section of the country, but that it is as strong in the east as in the west; third, that he believes the man of the so-called middle class is better able to meet conditions and to advise in regard to proper legislation than the man of leisure and culture.

"I believe that the man who is on the make recognizes a condition more quickly than the man who has reached the point where he does not need to progress," he said. "For that reason I should say that it is safer to take the advice and counsel of the common man. He understands life. He knows what it means to be close to the people. He understands what the people need, because he is one of them himself and feels what they feel. He is in the current, and he knows the current and feels it and understands it better than the man who stands on the bank. That is the way I might illustrate what I mean. I have noticed since I was inaugurated Governor of New Jersey that when men come before me on hearings on matters of legislation most of them know the legislation only as it affects them or their business. They do not know anything about the legislation as it affects the entire community. Now, these are not the men to depend on for advice in framing legislation. What we need is men who are interested in legislation for the general people.

"I noticed in my campaign in New Jersey that when I spoke to a crowd of workingmen—the men who are on the make—I could get along faster with my speech than when I addressed men of leisure. The former understood at once what I was telling them, while I felt when addressing the latter that I had to explain to them the rudiments of what I was telling them. There you have the difference.

"It is true that party lines are resting lightly on the people in these days. I do not mean by this that there will be new parties. I do not believe there will be any new parties, but I believe there will be a redistribution of the voters between the parties. The people now look more at the man and what he represents than at the party label on his ticket. This has been more apparent in the west than in the east, but this is because there has been better opportunity for it to come to the surface in the west. But I am sure that it is just under the surface in the eastern states, and that it will come out when given the slightest opportunity.

"The reason why this spirit of independence has not been more pronounced up to this time is that generally there has been so little difference in men and what they represented that it made little difference which way the people voted. The two parties have been nearly alike. The last national platforms of the two parties were so nearly alike that it was difficult to tell them apart. Therefore, it has reached the point where the people look more to the man and what he personally represents than to anything else, when they get ready to vote. This was demonstrated in Massachusetts, and to a certain degree in Maine. It was shown plainly in New Jersey, where a hundred thousand independent voters asserted their independence on election day.

"Progressiveness is not confined to one party, but the distinction between progressiveness and standstillism is more marked in the Republican party than in the Democratic party. This is due to the fact that the Republican party has always been more closely allied with the special interests, so that when the progressive spirit developed there it was more noticeable. The cleavage between the two factions in the Republican party, therefore, is very marked. The cleavage between the two elements in the Democratic party is not so clearly marked, because the Democratic party has always been the more progressive party of the two.

"This country can not stand still. The policy of standstillism should not prevail. I remember that when I was president of Princeton university some members of the board thought I was going too far and too fast with the institution. They said we ought to stand still a while—that everything was going all right and that we ought to let well enough alone.

"I told them that if they would guarantee me that we would stand still I would be satisfied and would agree to that policy. But I said they could not stand still. When you think you are standing still you are going backward. It would be all right if you could stand still in your business and walk around with your hands in your pockets and whistle, knowing that you were safely standing still. But you can't do this. You must make progress. You must go ahead. You must do things.

"What will be the leading issue in the next national campaign? It is difficult and dangerous to make a prediction at this time. It is too far ahead. Of course the tariff will be one of the great issues, but just how much of a figure it will cut is a question. Further than that I should not care to go."

Printed in the *Indianapolis News*, April 13, 1911.

A Political Address in Indianapolis[1]

[[April 13, 1911]]

Mr. Toastmaster,[2] Governor Marshall, Ladies and Fellow-Citizens—I hardly recognize myself in the description I have just heard. I am very grateful indeed that there are very few Princeton men present, for in their presence it would be hard for me, knowing what they do of me, to live up to the role that has been created for me. I feel very much like the old woman who was in a side show of a circus, and saw, or thought she saw, a man read a newspaper through a board, and she said: "Here, let me out of this place; this is no place for me to be with these thin things on."

In the presence of a Princeton man[3] this disguise of greatness must be very transparent. But any man who enters public life must try to live up to anything that he is called upon to do, and I am not in the condition of the old colored man I heard about the other day, who fell asleep in a railway car and sat with his head lolling back and his mouth wide open. A fellow-passenger, who had a vial of quinine in his pocket, went over and quietly dusted a lot of it over the darky's tongue. The old man slept on for a time, none the wiser, but presently he closed his mouth and sat up quickly, and as the conductor passed along he stopped him and said. "Boss, is there a doctor on this train?" "I don't know. What do you want a doctor for?" "Well, boss, I done busted my gall." Well, I haven't quite busted mine yet!

Seriously, gentlemen, it is with peculiar pleasure that I face this company to-night. And yet the pleasure is in very great part marred by the absence of Mr. Bryan[4] because the spirit of this meeting is the spirit of rejoicing; the consciousness of the men present is that after a long series of defeats, Democracy is about to realize its strength and to come into its own; and it is a pity, when there is such rejoicing afoot, that the gallant man who has borne the heat and burden of the day should not be present to contribute his wit and cheer in the time of triumph. It is a pity that only those of us should be present who have taken up the labor in the later and easier days.

[1] Wilson was addressing a Democratic achievement banquet given under the auspices of the National Democratic League of Clubs at the Murat Temple in Indianapolis.

[2] James Hamilton Lewis, a prominent lawyer and Democrat of Chicago, who had just introduced him. Lewis, congressman from the State of Washington, 1897-99, served as senator from Illinois, 1913-19, and again from 1931 until his death in 1939.

[3] Probably Charles Richard Williams, Princeton 1875, editor of the *Indianapolis News*.

[4] Who, as has been noted earlier, had been scheduled to speak and had gone to Cleveland to attend the funeral of Tom Loftin Johnson.

I feel, in the field of practical politics, like a new recruit. I suppose that you gentlemen do not realize what is going on in the universities of our day. I suppose that there are still men who think of universities as remote and cloistered places, where men think of that imperfect account of life which is contained in books and do not look directly upon the actual facts. But that is not the kind of university that I have known. I remember of telling a body of gentlemen who looked particularly well dressed and comfortable, in New York, not many months ago, that I understood the business of a university to be to make young gentlemen just as unlike their fathers as possible. Of course I hastened to explain that I did not mean any disrespect to the fathers; but that by the time a man had got old enough to send his son to college, he had established himself in some kind of success and had got the point of view and separation of some particular occupation, and in that degree he had rendered himself unable to see the general conditions of the country, and that I understood the business of the university to be to regeneralize the generation; to take them away from the prejudices of their fathers and lay before them afresh the map of life which men had traveled generation through generation, making their own fortunes, unassisted by previous generations, except in so far as the experience of previous generations had afforded them a standard of conduct; so that each generation might look afresh upon the fortunes of mankind and know that the work was an unending work of lifting men from level to level of new achievement and of fresh discovery.

That is the spirit of the modern university—not to keep men anchored in the prepossessions of the past, but to take them to some quiet upland where they may see the visions of the future.

I would not have you forget that the patron saint of Democracy conceived it as one of his greatest achievements, that he had founded the University of Virginia; that he had searched the world for learned men, in order to bring to that ancient commonwealth competent teachers of youth, and that as he sat upon the hill of Monticello and day after day, through his powerful field glass, watched brick put upon brick in the construction of the buildings of the university, he saw that he was piling there that house of vision in which the young men of Virginia should subsequently see the things which had been taught in his philosophy of government, and things which he had learned in his converse with the men who were putting the blood of revolt and of fresh achievement in the veins of the people of France, when he visited the French republic, and that he felt secure that learning should sustain patriotism, and that the great university which had risen at his touch should be the school of free men. It is an interesting circumstance to me that on these occasions we recall more than the names of any others the names of Jefferson, the philosopher, the student, the profound man of thought, and that other son of the people, Andrew Jackson. These are the two types of Democracy. Democracy is based upon deep insight into human nature on the one hand, and those unconquerable impulses of manhood which exemplify themselves upon fields of battle, in sons of the soil like Andrew Jackson.

The other day I was dining with some of my colleagues in the senate of New Jersey, and I had said in a little speech I made to them, that I was two kinds of a Democrat—I was born a Democrat, and then when I got old enough to think about things, I became a convinced and converted Democrat. One of the most plain spoken of my colleagues—a Republican—got up and said: "I wish the Governor would tell me what he understands a Democrat to be." I said:

"I am perfectly ready to tell you what I understand a Democrat to be, and how I understand him to be distinguished from a Republican. A Republican believes, I will concede, in government for the people, but he does not believe in government by the people. He believes in establishing a body of trustees, who shall administer the affairs of the nation for the benefit of those who haven't sense enough to conduct it themselves. He believes that the vested interests of the country, if they prosper, will transmit their prosperity to the rest, and that they, better than the rest, understand what the true foundations of prosperity are. Now, I absolutely dissent from that theory. I am not willing to put myself in the hands of any body of trustees for the benefit of the people. I believe that the only persons who understand the nation, as a whole, are the people of the nation as a whole. Moreover, the very men who do not understand the conditions of the nation as a whole are the men who have immersed their thought in the great transactions of modern corporations. The men who understand the life of the country are the men who are on the make, and not the men who are made; because the men who are on the make are in contact with the actual conditions of struggle, and those are the conditions of life for the nation; whereas, the man who has achieved, who is at the head of a great body of capital, has passed the period of struggle. He may sympathize with the struggling men, but he is not one of them, and only those who struggle can comprehend what the struggle is. I would rather take the interpretation of our national life from the general body of the people than from those who have made conspicuous successes of their lives.

The man who is in the water knows the strength of the current; not the man who has won his way to the bank. The man who knows that he must use his utmost wit from morning till night to support and feed those whom he loves, knows how hard it is to live; he knows what it is that cheats him; he knows what it is that harasses him and balks him; the other men do not know. Therefore, I will seek counsel of those who are in the struggle, and not of those who have won their way out of it. (Applause.)

This is the night, gentlemen, upon which we assemble to renew our vows and to utter our creed, and I want to ask you what your creed is, as Democrats? I am not interested in abstract phrases; I am not interested in a creed which can not be put in the language of the man of the street; I am not interested in principles which can not be translated into a program. Nobody is debating, any longer, the general ideas of freedom. We think we know what they are. But it is a very different and a very much more difficult matter when you debate the methods of freedom. I subscribe, and every other American I ever met, subscribes to the Declaration of Independence; but the Declaration of Independence did not mention the problems of the year 1911, and I do not find the problems of the year 1911 solved in the Declaration of Independence. (Applause.) There is only one way in which we can be of the stature of the men who uttered that great declaration. Did you never notice that we only quote the introductory portions of that great document? The rest of it is a recital of actual facts, of grievances, of things that constitute an intolerable condition of affairs, and is a challenge to the civilized world to bear witness that we do not mean to endure those things any longer. It is a bill of specifications. Very well, then. If we are to be of the stature of the men of that generation, we must not stop with the preamble; we must draw up our bill of specifications, and in proportion as we show that we know what is the matter and know how to cure the ills of our day, so shall we be true sons of those great sires.

We say that we are Jeffersonians and Jacksonians, and we say that Jefferson and Jackson were the enemies of privilege and the friends of the common people. Well, what is the guise of privilege in our day? It doesn't wear any of the guises that were worn in the days of the Declaration of Independence. This is a day utterly unlike that; this is a day when we must put in plainest speech what it is that we fight, and when we come down to the statement of what it is that we fight, it is very difficult, indeed, to discriminate between some of the things that have been done by Democrats and some of the things that have been done by Republicans.

What I am particularly interested in fighting, where my fight is, is the machinery that is nonpartisan; the machinery that is bipartisan. The men I have been fighting in New Jersey are no more Democrats than the men who fight shoulder to shoulder with them, against me, are Republicans. They are nothing except men banded together to have their own selfish purposes prevail, regardless of the public interests.

You remember what a certain politician in New York once said—"There aint no politics in politics"—by which he meant "There aint no practical distinction as between the men who are seeking the offices for the sake of the offices." The most sinister thing that we have had to fight is the agreements between the machines of the two parties, to divide the offices, and to see to it that the men who are banded together for a common purpose are not discriminated by party labels. Now, how has it proved possible for these men to make these combinations against the public interests? Our thought does not travel as fast as the facts. Some of us talk about the political machine as if it were the machine of twenty years ago. It is not the machine of twenty years ago. The machine of that day was merely a combination of persons who did the nominating and controlled the tickets. That is not the machine of today. The machine of today is a body of men of both parties, subsidized by certain great interests, to see to it that nothing is done in the legislatures, or adjudicated in the courts, that is contrary to their interests.

Why do we want the direct primary? Why are we so keen to open this whole process of nominations so that the people can get at it? Because the old style of nomination and election was an impenetrable jungle, in which this particular beast roamed, for which we have got out our gun.

Every measure that we are seeking to put in force in New Jersey and everywhere else is an ax to be laid to the root of every pestiferous thing that clogs that jungle. (Applause.) Here is a marvel that was referred to by our distinguished toastmaster—a primary elections bill that goes the whole hog, that is as advanced, as a body of law, as any legislation that has been attempted anywhere in America adopted by the unanimous vote of a Republican senate, under the impulse of a Democratic victory.[5] (Applause.) Not because I was making life miserable for

---

[5] News had just been received that the New Jersey Senate had unanimously approved the Geran bill. See the news report printed at April 14, 1911.

those gentlemen—I was trying to, but that was not the reason. The reason was that the voice of the people of New Jersey was absolutely clear, dominating the whole life of the state, like a ringing note, that no man could fail to heed or could dream for a moment of resisting.

I presume you have thought of New Jersey as the home of trusts, because the people of New Jersey were in love with trusts. The people of New Jersey hate their own kind of trusts just as much as you do, and the people of New Jersey have never been asleep; they have merely been discouraged. They have simply waited to have a chance, and the minute they got a chance they got up on their hind legs and were as active as anybody in the Union. These are the things that are happening to cheer us; these are the breaths of hope which blow through the country like a great trade wind, and every man is obliged to trim his sails to it.

When we think of privilege we must realize that we must translate it into terms of fact. Now, the terms of fact are these: That the machine is the instrumentality of privilege, not the organization. There is a distinction between the organization of a party and the machine that runs the organization of the party. But the machine is their instrument and they have got more hiding places than you can find out in a generation, and some of their principal hiding places are the committee rooms of our legislatures. Our legislative measures are not devised and are not debated upon the floor, for the most part—particularly those that the machine is interested in. They are debated behind closed doors, and where all the mischief is done is where nobody can listen and nobody can see.

Do you know that there has been a singular change in the attitude of the people, recently, toward their executives? It is not hard to find the explanation of that. I remember meeting a senator from New Jersey one day, a good while ago, while Mr. Roosevelt was President. We were in a railway car and the senator was evidently in a very bad humor. I said, "Senator, what is the matter?"

"Oh," he said, "I wish the Constitution had not given the President the right to send messages to congress."

"Why," I said, "senator, I think you are barking up the wrong tree. That is not what is the matter. The trouble is that he publishes his messages, and if the country happens to agree with him it doesn't stop to hear what you have to say. Now you can not imagine a Constitution which doesn't give the President the right to tell the people what he thinks, and if he ever once gets them to thinking the same way he does, the case is closed, and you are not afforded a hearing, and the reason the people are looking to the President of the United States is that he must do his debating in public, that he is the only national representative, that his is the only voice that has been bidden to give itself utterance by the whole body of free Americans, and, therefore, by the analogy of the President, the people are turning to their Governors and saying, 'We don't know what is going on in these committee rooms; we don't understand the things that are put upon us as laws, because they are not debating and we don't see anything in the newspapers that explains this; we want somebody to undertake to deal with this matter, who will speak to us, and for us, and bring these things out in the public forum.' "

The wonderful thing is that the minute you invite men who are intending to do things that are contrary to the public interest to come out and present them upon the public platform, they change their tune, they change their mind, they change their measures.

We are fighting privilege in another form also, gentlemen. The eloquent gentleman from New Mexico[6] said that we were not fighting property. We are not fighting property, but we are fighting wrong conceptions of property. There are some things that men pretend to own, which they can not, in any proper sense, be said to own. Did you never reflect upon the character of a modern joint stock company, such as our great corporations and trusts are? Who knows the partners in any one of these great corporations of capital? The partners, I suppose, are the stockholders; though you would not think it from some of the court decisions, and these stockholders are never any fixed body of men, because the stock is sold from day to day and the partners are changing and the investment in these stocks constitutes the means of livelihood of thousands of persons who never have any real voice in the votes of the boards of directors. It is as if the whole country said, "Here are our earnings, here a little pile, there a little pile, there a little pile. We will scrape them all together and we will make a great body of capital and we will let ten or a dozen gentlemen sit around a board and say what is going to be done with this capital." And these gentlemen, sitting around that little board, talk about the franchise and the capital of the corporation as if it were their private property. It is nothing of the kind. Those men are simply licensed and privileged by the community to act as trustees and representatives

[6] Harvey Butler Fergusson, lawyer of Albuquerque, who had spoken on "Militant Democracy." Fergusson had been a delegate to Congress from New Mexico Territory, 1897-99, and after statehood served as congressman from 1912 to 1915.

of the community in the combinations of the power of wealth. So far from being the owners of the property, they are trustees of other people's goods and they are responsible to those other people.

I wish you would reflect upon this definition of business in our day. It seems to me that business upon the great scale upon which it is now conducted is the service of the community and the representation of the community for private profit, and the profit is legitimate only in proportion as the service is genuine. I utterly deny the genuineness of any profit which is gathered together without regard to the serviceability of the thing done. These men are trustees of the wealth of thousands of persons, and only as trustees can they justify their private accumulations of wealth. Let them act in the spirit of trustees; let them render genuine service to the communities in which they live, and no man will begrudge them one penny of their wealth. (Applause.) We are ready to stand sponsors for every man who will serve the country in his business, and we are ready to fight any man who does not serve the country in his business. Men have got to learn that in a certain sense, when they manage great corporations, they have assumed public office and are responsible to the communities for the things they do. That is the form of privilege that we are fighting.

Now, there is another matter. You know that recently a workingman's compensation act has gone by the board in one of our great states because it seemed to the supreme court of that state to be compulsory in its operation.[7] Why, in their judgment, was it unconstitutional if it was compulsory? Because, being compulsory, it seemed to violate the principle of free contract. The principle of free contract being guaranteed by most of our state constitutions, it is held by most of our courts that the legislature can not impair it or take it away, and can not say to the employer and to the employe: "You must enter into a contract of employment under such and such conditions." Now, I want to suggest to the lawyers present that they ask themselves this question: Is this an interference with real freedom of contract? That goes back to the question: Has the workingman of this country real freedom in making his contract? Here is a great

[7] The New York legislature in 1910 had passed a workmen's compensation act compelling employers to compensate workmen injured in the course of employment in any of eight specified hazardous occupations. The employees concerned had the option of accepting the stipulated compensation or of suing for more. On March 24, 1911, the state Court of Appeals declared the measure unconstitutional on the ground that its compulsory feature violated both state and federal constitutional provisions against the taking of property without due process of law.

industrial community; here are half a dozen factories, or, rather, half a dozen combinations of factories in one community. These men must take the labor offered them by those factories or let it alone. They must work upon the terms offered them or starve. Is that freedom of contract? Do you mean to say that you believe, in the face of the existing conditions, that the workmen of the year 1911 are in the condition of the workmen of the year 1850, when the individual workman went about and dealt with individual employers, and there was really freedom and circulation of freedom of contract? Those conditions have gone by, and we must see to it that men working in masses, under conditions that are not really conditions of free contract, are safeguarded in their lives and rights by our legislatures. (Applause.)

That is the reason that the program of our party is so definite. I pause, because I think I was wrong in saying "the program of our party." Gentlemen, we must be broad in the politics of this year and of the years that are coming. Democrats are not peculiar in seeing this vision of existing affairs and of the reforms which must be set up. The real difference in this country is between the men who see and the men who do not see; the real difference is between the progressives and the men who want to stand still. There are standpatters among Democrats as well as among Republicans. There are more standpat Republicans than standpat Democrats, because more Republicans have gotten into the habit of standing pat, and it is largely a matter of personal disposition and of the ability to see existing conditions. We must see to it that there is no niggardliness in the way in which we speak of one another. We must see to it that there are no artificial distinctions. We must see to it that we welcome, and welcome with an open heart, all men of all kinds and all labels, who want to work for the progress of justice and the liberation of the people in this country. When I talk with progressive Republicans and have them lay down their creed for me, I can not see where their creed differs from mine. I can only say to them, "I wonder that you retain your label." (Laughter and applause.) I can only say to them: "We are allied together by spiritual connections which we ought not to be so stupid as to deny in the alliances which we form." Let us say, then, therefore, gentlemen, "that progressives in this country have a definite program," for the program is the same all along the line. The program consists in these items, if I am not mistaken:

First, to give the people free access to their political machinery; to give them the absolutely free selection of the persons who are to represent them, and free control of those persons, after they have been chosen to represent them. (Applause.)

Then, in the second place, we are going to do everything that is necessary to put society once more in control of its own economic life. We are going to see to it that the economic life of the country is not controlled by small bodies of men, who, however honest they may be, are, nevertheless, blind to the real interests of men and to the real movements and currents of human nature and of society. I know a great many men whose names stand as synonyms of the unjust power of wealth and of corporate privilege in this country, and I want to say to you that if I understand the character of these men, many of them —most of them—are just as honest and just as patriotic as I claim to be. But I do notice this difference between myself and them: I have not happened to be immersed in the kind of business in which they have been immersed; I have not been saturated by the prepossessions which come upon men situated as they are, and I claim to see some things that they do not yet see; that is the difference. It is not a difference of interest; it is not a difference of capacity; it is not a difference of patriotism. It is a difference of perception.

A witty Englishman said that if you tied a man's head to a ledger and take something off his wages every time he stops adding up the figures, you can not expect him to have an intelligent idea of the antipodes. Now, these men have so buried their minds in these great undertakings that you can not expect them to have reasonable and rational views about the antipodes. They are just as much chained to a task as if the task were little instead of big. Their view is just as much limited as if their business were small instead of colossal. But they are awakening. They are not all of them asleep, and when they do wake, they are going to lend us the assistance of truly statesmanlike minds. We must not be intolerant in this great country. We must see that we are dealing really with the hearts of men and with their intelligences, but we must say to those gentlemen and to ourselves, "Our program, from which we can not be turned aside, is that we are going to take possession of the control of our own economic life." (Applause.)

The third thing is that we are going to conserve, quicken and stimulate our national life, not merely by what we call conservation, which means the conservation of water and of growing trees, and the renewal of the natural resources of the country. That is not all. We have got to conserve the lives of the country. We have got to see that men's lives are safeguarded, that women are guarded against the work which kills and deteriorates, that the children are kept out of the factories at a tender age, when they can not bear the burdens, and that they are kept out of the saloons and out of the vicious shows that demoralize their minds. We have not [got] to see that the morals and the wholesome blood of the country are conserved and safeguarded. That is part of our program—that great physical and moral sanitation, which is the hope of the country.

And then we have got to see to it that we do not falter or hesitate in the great task of seeing to it that our fiscal policy is one of equality and justice, and not a policy of favoritism. That is the trouble with the tariff, gentlemen. The tariff is not marred by being protective; it is marred by being a perfect nest of patronage. There was not a member of either house of the national congress, outside of the ways and means committee of the house and the finance committee of the senate, who understood the Payne-Aldrich tariff bill. Ever since that bill was passed, magazine writers and editorial writers, members of congress themselves, have been finding the jokers that lurked in it. They have been finding the little changes of clauses, the little changes of phraseology, the little changes of figures that meant colossal fortunes for men who, under the ambush of the political machine, smuggled those things into the law of the land. You have got to see that whichever policy is pursued, it is pursued honestly, and in the interest of the whole country, and then you have got to see that the burdens of taxation are made more equal than they are. In short, gentlemen, the program of the Democratic party is a program of opportunity. We want to open the gates to mankind. They have been standing against closed doors looking with longing eyes through the little chinks that showed them the land of promise and justice and equality. Those doors have been barred against them; they should not pass through. I wish that every man in the country might realize that this program is his only conceivable program, because any other program ties us like slaves to the conditions of the past, whereas, this program of progress and of change is the program of opportunity, the program of adjustment, the program of progress.

Did you ever conceive what liberty means, gentlemen? Liberty is not an abstract thing. Liberty is not the absence of restraint. What do you mean when you say a great powerful engine, propelled by steam, runs free? What do you mean by the freedom of that machinery? You mean its perfect adjustment; the parts are so assembled and united that friction is reduced to a mimimum [minimum]. Let it serve as a picture of what you mean by political liberty. It means the interests and powers and passions of men are so adjusted to each other that the friction is minimized.

Now your whole process of reform, your whole process of legislation is a process of adjustment, a process of accommodation, a process of bringing things together in handsome co-operation, instead of in ugly antagonism. That is your vision of the thing that is to be done, not destroying any part of the great body politic, or the body social, but uniting those living and sensitive things into one organism, through which will flow unobstructed the life blood of a free people. That is the vision that we have to offer ourselves.

And so it seems to me that that is the hope we are offering the country. Why is the Democratic party the party of hope, rather than the Republican party, with its progressive elements? Because if [it] fortunately happens that during these years, when the great alliance between vested wealth and political power has been cemented, the Democrats have been out of power and the party in power has entered into the alliance. (Applause.) I won't venture to conjecture what the Democrats would have done. I will only say that they have not done it, and that the Democratic party is the party of hope because it is the free and disentangled party. (Applause.) We haven't made any embarrassing promises; we haven't made any entangling alliances; we are ready to go in any direction that we want to go, and we want to go in the direction of the light. We have seen the light and we have seen the growing dawn of a new day; our faces are alight with the reflection from that kindling sky. We know that there are steep and rugged paths ahead of us, but we have the blood, the full blood and the hope of youth in us, we have the confidence that the people believe in us and are going to support us, and we shall struggle up those h[e]ights to the levels and until tableland after tableland has lifted up [us] above the noisome plain, and we have carried man another stage forward in that great progress of humanity in whose cause America was set up.[8]

Printed in the *Indianapolis News*, April 14, 1911.

[8] There is a WWT outline of this address, with the composition date of April 1, 1911, in WP, DLC.

A News Report

[April 14, 1911]

GOVERNOR TALKS ON GERAN BILL'S PASSAGE

INDIANAPOLIS, Ind., April 14.—"The passage of the direct primary bill by the Republican Senate of the New Jersey Legislature is the result of a popular uprising, in which the voice of the people made their demands so clear that there was no escape," said Governor Woodrow Wilson, of New Jersey, here to-day. During the Democratic banquet in this city last night Mr. Wilson received a telegram advising him that the primary bill had been passed unanimously.

"The men who are fighting me in the Legislature are not Republicans or Democrats," said Mr. Wilson. "They are merely a body of men banded together for selfish interests. One of the hiding places of those seeking special privilege is in the old State convention.

"The primary bill passed by the Senate is as progressive a piece of legislation as has been enacted in any State in the Union."[1]

Printed in the *Newark Evening News*, April 14, 1911.
[1] The Senate had passed the Geran bill with a few clarifying amendments on April 13. This version the Assembly accepted on April 19. Geran took the measure to the governor's office on that day, and Wilson signed it at once, saying, "This is certainly a grand consummation." Jersey City *Jersey Journal*, April 20, 1911. The act had sixteen sections, the most important of which were as follows: candidates for positions as officers of district boards of registry and election had to be certified as qualified by the State Civil Service Commission on the basis of examination; delegates and alternates to national party conventions and candidates for governor and congressmen were to be nominated by direct party primaries (earlier legislation had provided for the direct nomination of candidates for the legislature and municipal offices); candidates for senator or assemblyman were required either to sign a pledge that they would support for United States senator the people's choice in the party preferential primary or issue a statement that they would consider the primary choice only as a recommendation which they would be at liberty to disregard if their judgments so dictated; personal registration by all voters was compulsory in all cities and towns of more than 5,000; an official uniform ballot was to be used in all general elections in place of the old party ballots, and samples of these official ballots were to be sent to registered voters a week before the election; the membership of the annual party conventions to be held in Trenton was to include only candidates for the Senate or Assembly, the governor in office or the candidate for governor, members of the Senate holding office, and members of the state party committees. Other provisions dealt with definition of election districts, procedures for primaries and other elections, eligibility of voters, registry lists, the method of voting, the make-up and protection of ballots, petitions of various kinds, and the election of county party committees. *Laws of New Jersey, 1911*, Chap. 183, pp. 276-325.

To Henry Smith Pritchett

My dear Pritchett: [Trenton, N. J.] April 14 [15], 1911.

Your letter of April ninth from Bermuda gratified me very deeply. I was sincerely sorry to hear of your illness. I am afraid you have not been taking very good care of yourself. I sincerely hope that this will find you well again when you come to your desk.   Cordially and sincerely yours,   Woodrow Wilson

TLS (H. S. Pritchett Papers, DLC).

From William Lustgarten[1]

My dear Governor: New York, April 15th, 1911.

I read with a great deal of pleasure and profit your address at the National League of Democratic Clubs at Indianapolis.

The Democratic victories of 1910 have been all but frittered away; yours has been the notable exception; your actions have squared your professions.

The more we Progressive Democrats of New York look about us, the more we realize that you are the only salvation for the Democratic Party for 1912. Democracy "with all its fears, and all the hopes of future years, is hanging breathless on thy fate."
        Very respectfully yours,   William Lustgarten

TLS (Governors' Files, Nj).
[1] Lawyer and chairman of the executive committee of the Progressive Democrats of New York, an ephemeral organization about which nothing can be found.

To Mary Allen Hulbert Peck

Dearest Friend,   Princeton, 16 April, 1911.

Your sweet letter of Sunday tells me only what I had already divined: that you have been "overdoing" all winter, considering the state of your health, and that you have been really very ill, even when you did not yield to it and admit that you had given out. I knew it from the little scraps of letters; I knew it from the constant fatigue they disclosed; I knew it by the ebb and flow of your spirits; I knew it, in short, by a thousand signs which a devoted friend will see, and have been oppressed all the while by an undercurrent of anxiety about you. How deeply delightful it is, therefore, to hear you say now that you feel that you are really out of it, and are coming to feel like your old vital self again! It lifts a burden from my heart, and makes my own tasks easier!

I did not see your letter till last night. I have just got back from Indiana. On the thirteenth (which was Jefferson's birthday) they had a big Democratic "Achievement Banquet" at Indianapolis. Mr. Bryan had been booked to be there, but was kept away, at the last moment, by the death of Tom. Johnson, the famous one-time mayor of Cleveland, who was a life-long friend of his, and whose funeral he felt it his pious duty to attend. And So I, as a new "national figure" (!), had the centre of the stage to myself. It was a big affair. Some twelve hundred Democrats of that region of the country (plus Colonel Harvey!) were there, and were in fine spirits for the celebration. I do not know how good a taste of my quality I gave them (I can seldom tell when I am at my best or even doing myself justice), but they listened as well as any speaker could have desired and seemed to feel genuine enthusiasm about what I had said and what I had shown myself to be. I was the only Easterner who spoke, but did not feel at all lonely. I have always felt thoroughly at home in the West, as you know. It seems to me the genuinely American part of America. And Indianapolis is a remarkable place. I do not know any American city of its size that is the home of so many interesting people, whom it is thoroughly worth while to know; and at a reception given me by Mrs. Kern,[1] the wife of the new Senator, apparently every notable of the town, as well as others, were on hand to be enjoyed. If it were only possible to enjoy people at an afternoon reception, when you are made to stand in "the line"! I stopped with the Governor, Thomas R. Marshall, himself "prominently mentioned" for the presidential nomination, and a capital and very able man. If the sphere of his thought and action had been a little bigger than Indiana, he would be a big man. He has the brains and the sagacity. Mrs. Marshall[2] is a dear, and uncommonly pretty. Her mouth is adorable,—singularly like yours! They have no children, and live, with delightful simplicity, in a little house which they hire for themselves, Indiana, like New Jersey, not supplying her governor with an "executive mansion." While I was gone our Republican Senate passed the chief administrative measure, the elaborate and radical primary and elections bill, which puts the "machines" out of business, without a single dissenting voice! That is regarded here as something little less than a miracle. I seem to have won the confidence of my Republican colleagues in the Senate in an unusual degree. I think that they realize that I have almost no partisan motives in what I do: that I am not trying to win advantages for my party, but only reforms for the people. It has been delightful to see them come around. But the old fox, Nicholls, was absent when the vote was taken. He "ducked," as the saying is in Trenton. It is hoped that the session may end this week. No one hopes it more fervently than I do, for I am very weary of the constant strain and vigil, to see that nothing goes wrong, and nothing that is improper slips by me. I reached Trenton just after breakfast yesterday morning, and put in some eight hours on bills

What pleases me most in my journies is that very plain men (like railway conductors and brakemen, for example) come up to me with cordial greetings, their eyes shining with a sort of enthusiasm, as if they were approaching a friend whom they knew and trusted, and express the deepest confidence in me, and in my future. And they say immensely interesting things, too, which show great thoughtfulness. A conductor, on this journey, expounded to me his theory of the relation of the States to the general government; and a most sound and intelligent theory it was, too. I would rather have the trust of such fellows than that of all the swells in the world. These men are "up against it" and know what life means. They know the men who comprehend and sympathize, and only such men can help them or the nation!

But how stupid it is to have to talk of myself (to let you keep up with me) when I might be talking of you! My friend Pritchett (whom you speak of as Prichard) wrote me a little note from Bermuda, of kind congratulations, which ended "I have met here some very good friends of yours who speak in warm terms of your visits here, and among others Mrs. Peck." "Among others"! I like that! For my own part, I cannot think of anyone else in Bermuda. Mrs. Peck *is* Bermuda, not only for me but for scores of others, to whom she seems a sort of presiding spirit, an ideal embodiment of the place, with its vital airs, its vivid beauty, its infinite variety, its spirit as of constant youth, its friendliness and intelligence! What his words meant was that "Mrs. Peck" was the only one that had made any real impression on him. Alas! if you are to be as far away as the Adirondacks, how is a fellow who must go part of each week to Trenton to see anything of you? Above all things else, take care of yourself. Write me that the conscious recovery goes on apace, and so contribute to the peace and strength of

Your devoted friend, Woodrow Wilson

Love to Mrs. A. and your son. Affectionate messages from us all.

WWTLS (WP, DLC).

[1] Araminta Cooper (Mrs. John Worth) Kern.
[2] Lois Kimsey (Mrs. Thomas Riley) Marshall.

To Jenny Davidson Hibben

My dear Mrs. Hibben,   Princeton, New Jersey 16 April, 1911.

I did not hear until yesterday, when I returned from a trip to the West, of the death of your father.[1] May I not express my warm sympathy? I know how much your father meant to you; I know what a remarkable man he was, for strength of character, vigour of mind, and depth of affection; and I know what such a separation must mean to you now and must continue to mean to you for the rest of your life. It grieves me to think of what it will cost you.   Sincerely Yours,   Woodrow Wilson

ALS (photostat in WC, NjP).
    [1] John Davidson, who died at his home in Elizabeth, N. J., on April 14, 1911.

From Bowdre Phinizy[1]

personal

Dear Governor: Augusta, Ga. April 17th/11

As you will see from the enclosed[2] we are very anxious down here in Georgia and particularly in Augusta to make you the next President of these United States. It has occurred to me that unless you can and do show very good and prompt cause why this should not be done, that the Herald and myself along with a great many others will interest ourselves in seeing that this is done.

I already have the promise of a very distinguished Republican of nation wide fame and acquaintance, one of the most brilliant men I know, to use his voice and pen and hand in your interest and against the present Taftian policies.

With sincere good wishes for Mrs Wilson and for yourself in all things and with the kindliest remembrances of the old days at Princeton,
                    Sincerely and cordially yours,   Bowdre Phinizy

TLS (WP, DLC).
    [1] Princeton 1892; publisher and editor of the *Augusta*, Ga., *Herald*.
    [2] A clipping of an editorial in the *Augusta Herald*, April 16, 1911. It said, among other things, that Wilson was easily the most commanding figure in the Democratic party, if not, indeed, in the United States. "As the democratic nominee for the presidency," the editorial continued, "there is but little doubt that he would be overwhelmingly elected, as the progressive, independent vote of the entire country would gladly rally to the support of such a man in the presidential election."

To Samuel Huston Thompson, Jr.

My dear Mr. Thompson: [Trenton, N. J.] April 18, 1911.

Thank you sincerely for your letter of April tenth.[1] I wish I could have answered it more promptly, but we are in the rush of the last days of our legislative session.

I warmly appreciate the suggestions your letters contains and am very much gratified at what you tell me about Governor Thomas' attitude in the things which were giving you some anxiety.

I am sorry to say that it seems impossible for me to state beforehand just what my topics will be. I wonder if the committees in charge would not be willing to simply announce addresses without subjects?

In haste,   Cordially yours,   Woodrow Wilson

TLS (S. H. Thompson, Jr., Papers, DLC).
[1] It is missing.

A News Report of Remarks About the Commission Government Bill

[April 18, 1911]

COMMISSION BILL NOW IN SENATE, FREED OF GRIFFIN'S AMENDMENT

Senator Leavitt, chairman of the Senate Committee on Municipal Corporations, this afternoon reported the Trenton bill for a commission form of government,[1] with the obnoxious Griffin "40-per cent. majority" amendment[2] stricken out.

In place of the Griffin provision that the bill must be adopted by a majority equal to 40 per cent. of the votes cast at the last general election, Senator Leavitt reported an amendment that a majority of the majority of the votes cast at the last election should be cast for the bill.[3]

In other words, the Leavitt proposition is that it will require only a few more than 25 per cent. of the total vote cast at the last general election to adopt the new law for this city.

It is believed that the bill will be passed by both houses in this form.

Assemblyman Walsh and H. G. Stoddard[4] called on Governor Wilson this afternoon in reference to the commission bill. In the conversation Governor Wilson expressed his approval of the majority of the majority plan. The Governor said that this was especially pleasing to him.

Governor Wilson is heartily in favor of the enactment of a real commission government law by the present Legislature. He is vigorously opposed to the "forty per cent. majority" amendment which the machine members of the Assembly tacked to the Trenton commission bill when it was passed in the House last week.

"Majority should rule," said the Governor last night, "and any majority should be sufficient for the adoption of a referendum question. If ten citizens vote on commission government and six of them favor the plan, commission government should prevail. If the people wil[l] not turn out to vote for such propositions it is their own lookout and their failure to act should not be allowed to result disadvantageously to those who do participate.["]

The Governor said that he was surprised upon his return from Indianapolis to learn that the bill had been amended by Assemblyman Griffin.

"I think it was a very grave mistake to amend the bill," he said, "and I fear there could have been no other purpose than to render it nugatory. There seems to be a difference of opinion just as to what the amendment does. The obvious intent would appear to be that forty per cent. of the vote cast at the last Assembly election is necessary in order to adopt the measure, but another interpretation is that it would require a majority of the forty per cent. of the voters. I sincerely trust that the mistake will be remedied, and that the Legislature, before adjournment, will pass a proper commission government bill."[5]

Printed in the *Trenton Evening Times*, April 18, 1911; some editorial headings omitted.

[1] A committee of the Trenton Chamber of Commerce had prepared a bill to permit cities and towns to adopt the commission form of government if a majority of the majority of the voters in the most recent general election approved. Senator Harry D. Leavitt and Representative Allan B. Walsh, both of Mercer County, introduced the measure on February 20, 1911.

[2] In an effort to render the bill not viable, Thomas F. A. Griffin, Democrat of Jersey City, had introduced an amendment on April 11 requiring approval by at least 40 per cent of the voters in the most recent general election before the commission form could go into effect. Griffin had acted at the behest of Thomas F. McCran of Paterson, minority leader in the Assembly, and of Nugent, who was still much in evidence about the State House. The Griffin amendment was so obscurely worded that most legislators did not understand its import, and the Assembly approved it on the same day that it was introduced by a large majority. *Minutes of the N. J. House of Assembly, 1911*, p. 1066; Link, *Wilson: The Road to the White House*, p. 265.

[3] The Senate struck out the Griffin amendment on April 19.

[4] Harry Galpin Stoddard, president of the Trenton Iron Co., chairman of the committee which had drafted the commission government bill.

[5] In the vote on the Leavitt-Walsh bill on the last day of the session, April 21, the Democratic majority leader in the Assembly, John Joseph Matthews of High Bridge, came out in support of the Griffin amendment. A conference committee of the two houses hastily convened and effected a settlement that yielded a substantial victory for the progressives. It required approval by 30 per cent of a municipality's voters in the most recent general election for adoption of

commission government. An integral part of the bill were provisions for the initiative, referendum, and recall. *Laws of New Jersey, 1911,* Chap. 221, pp. 462-83; Trenton *True American,* April 22, 1911.

From Thomas Bell Love

My dear Governor: [Dallas, Tex.] April 18, 1911.

I am writing to congratulate you on your excellent address at Indianapolis, as well as upon your downright course with the legislature of your State. I have made it a point for some months past to carefully test public opinion among Democrats as to the Democratic nomination for President in 1912, and I find the sentiment in favor of your nomination to be strong and steadily growing. I have not as yet begun to organize, for the reason that I have deemed it best to postpone organization until after the prohibition election which occurs in this State on July 22d. My present judgment is that it is best to let matters drift until about August, but it may be that circumstances hereafter arising will make it expedient to act before that.

I am very desirous of arranging for you to deliver an address in this city during the Texas State Fair in October of this year, and I will be glad to have you indicate your disposition and probable ability to meet such an engagement. If you can arrange to be in Dallas about that time, we can arrange to bring together to hear you a great throng of people from all portions of the State and make a great opportunity of the occasion.

I sincerely hope that you will succeed in procuring the enactment of a satisfactory direct primary law, and generally in carrying out your legislative program. I only see in our newspapers fragmentary accounts as to what is going on in New Jersey, and these do not keep me promptly and well advised, but they have impressed me, as I am sure they have the people of this State, most favorably with your patriotic determination to keep faith with the people.

With best wishes, I am

Yours very truly,   Thomas B. Love.

TCL (T. B. Love Papers, Dallas Hist. Soc.).

From Thomas Smith Bryan[1]

Dear Mr. Wilson: Columbia, S. C. April 18, 1911.

Some two years ago Mrs. Woodrow[2] gave the Y.M.C.A. of Columbia a beautiful lot adjoining her home for the purpose of putting up a Y.M.C.A. building. Some months ago we made a canvass of the city and raised the money for the purpose. We will in the course of the next few weeks be ready to lay the corner stone, and I am writing to ask if you will not be the speaker on that occasion. I notice with a great deal of pleasure your being in our city on the 1st of June and we will have the corner stone laid any time during that day that will be convenient for you. I trust, therefore, for the sake of Mrs. Woodrow as well as the Association that you will consent to deliver this address for us.[3]

I do not care to work a willing horse, but at the meeting of the Trustees of the College for Women[4] held last week resolution was passed to ask you to deliver an address before the graduating class on the night of June 1st, and I promised our very worthy President, Miss McClintock,[5] that I would write you and urge you to accept the invitation. I can assure you it will be a great treat to all of the people, especially to the girls of our College if you will make the address.[6]

With kind regards to you and yours, I am,

Yours very truly,   T. S. Bryan

TLS (Governors' Files, Nj).

[1] Owner of a book store and an affiliated printing establishment in Columbia, S. C.; banker; and general secretary of the Columbia Y.M.C.A.

[2] Felixiana Shepherd Baker (Mrs. James) Woodrow, Wilson's aunt.

[3] A news report of Wilson's address on this occasion is printed at June 2, 1911, Vol. 23.

[4] The College for Women in Columbia, chartered in 1887 as the South Carolina Presbyterian Institution, for Young Ladies; founded in 1890 as the Presbyterian College for Women; reorganized about 1910 as the College for Women. Actually, the institution had no formal connection with the Presbyterian Church until 1915, when it was absorbed by Chicora College, a Presbyterian institution that moved from Greenville, S. C., to Columbia in 1916. F. D. Jones and W. H. Mills (eds.), *History of The Presbyterian Church in South Carolina Since 1850* (Columbia, S. C., 1926), pp. 374-77; Daniel W. Hollis, *University of South Carolina* (2 vols., Columbia, S. C., 1951-56), II, 308.

[5] Euphemia McClintock, president of the College for Women since 1902.

[6] Wilson was unable to accept this invitation, but he was given a reception at the College for Women after his address to the Y.M.C.A.

To Samuel Huston Thompson, Jr.

My dear Mr. Thompson: [Trenton, N. J.] April 19, 1911.

Your letter of April thirteenth[1] is certainly very kind. I appreciate heartily the arrangements you are making and hope you will use your own discretion about arrangements consented to. I am sure that it is an excellent discretion.

I think I had better be as quiet on Sunday as possible, but I shall certainly hope to attend the principal Presbyterian Church of the City. I shall get you to coach me as to which one to go to when I come.

This is an additional memorandum to my letter written yesterday.

Cordially and faithfully yours,   Woodrow Wilson

TLS (S. H. Thompson, Jr., Papers, DLC).
¹ It is missing.

From Daniel Kiefer

My Dear Sir: Cincinnati, O. April 21 1911

The progressive citizen is neglecting his duty who fails to congratulate you on the magnificent democratic address you delivered in Indianapolis.

Since your election you have been furnishing each day new evidence of devotion to pure democracy, so that even those who, like yourself, once looked upon you as reactionary of the most pronounced type, have realized that there is not a better representative of true democracy in high official positions.

In the space of a few months, your efforts have resulted in advancing such democratic measures as direct election of United States senators, and the progressive legislation which has made Oregon famous, to a position that makes early adoption even in the states long considered hopelessly conservative, a strong probability.

Your recent endorsement of the Initiative & Referendum after having been a strong opponent, marks you as a kind of man in public life, that is much too rare, a man with the moral courage to openly admit that a position once assumed was a mistaken one.

The State of New Jersey is fortunate and should be proud of having such an official head. Democrats who would like to see the democratic party champion democratic principles in 1912 cannot help but wish that the party in the country may enjoy that same good fortune when the time for it arrives.

With assurances of my great respect, I am, with best wishes,
                              Yours very truly,   Daniel Kiefer
TLS (Governors' Files, Nj).

A Statement on the Work of the New Jersey Legislative Session of 1911

[[April 22, 1911]]

I think it will always be remembered as extraordinary in this, that it witnessed the fulfillment by the Legislature of every important campaign pledge.

Much remains to be done in the way of effecting such reorganization of the State government as may result in increasing economy and efficiency, and many reforms of consequence remain to be prosecuted and put upon the statute book, but no single Legislature could possibly be expected to accomplish more than this one has accomplished. It has acted not only with unusual diligence and sobriety, but with singular absence of party feeling and party contest. It has had about it the freedom which characterizes men who are acting in the public interest and without regard to private connections or personal interest. In no other way can I account for its extraordinary record.

The Employers' Liability and Workingmen's Compensation act has given the State a statute more serviceable and more consistent with justice in the field to which it applies than perhaps any other in the Union.[1]

The Primary and Election bill has worked a thorough going reform of the whole electoral process of the State, and has put every process of choice directly in the hands of the people.[2]

The Corrupt Practises act is singularly thorough going, and will undoubtedly prove most effective. It will do, perhaps, more than any other piece of legislation on this notable list, to purify elections and secure unbiased action of the people at the polls.[3]

The Public Utilities act goes the full length of reform in respect of the control of public service corporations. It is a thoroughly business-like act, well conceived and well constructed, and ought to afford a means of settling some of the most perplexing questions connected with the control of corporations.[4]

Add to this list the regulation of cold storage,[5] the substitution of indeterminate for determinate sentences for criminal offenses;[6] the rectification of the abuses in connection with false weights and measures;[7] the administration reform of the school system;[8] and it must be admitted these constitute one of the most remarkable records of legislation, I venture to think, that has ever distinguished a single legislative session in this country.

Printed in the *Newark Evening News*, April 22, 1911, with corrections from the texts in the Trenton *True American*, April 22, 1911, and the *Trenton Evening Times*, April 22, 1911.

[1] For a summary of the provisions of this act, see WW to Mary A. H. Peck, April 9, 1911, n. 5.

[2] The primary and election reform bill is summarized in n. 1 to the news report printed at April 14, 1911.

[3] The corrupt practices act, which passed both houses of the legislature on April 20, 1911, was comprehensive and stringent. It required each candidate for office to appoint a committee which would be exclusively responsible for collecting, auditing, and disbursing all funds donated on his behalf. Within a specified time after an election, the treasurers of such committees had to file itemized, sworn statements of all monies contributed, the names of all donors (including the candidates themselves), and how and to whom the funds had been disbursed. Limits were placed on the amounts each candidate could spend, and any candidate who refused or neglected to file the required statements

would suffer certain penalties and if elected forfeit his office. All campaign literature had to bear the name and address of the source. None of the money collected on behalf of a candidate could be spent to hire vehicles to transport voters to the polls or to hire poll watchers, and the colonizing of voters was specifically forbidden. The act prohibited candidates from making unusual contributions to any clubs or religious or charitable organizations, and forbade majority stockholders in corporations, and corporations and businesses themselves, to contribute to campaign funds. The act also outlawed a number of practices, such as buying votes or influencing votes with money or promises; false registration; fraudulent voting; stuffing ballot boxes; betting on the outcome of elections; and intimidation or threats by employers to influence employees. For the background and drafting of this bill, see Link, *Wilson: The Road to the White House*, pp. 259-61; for the act itself, see *Laws of New Jersey, 1911*, Chap. 188, pp. 329-49.

⁴ The act, one of the most thoroughgoing in the nation to this time, passed both houses of the legislature during the morning of April 21. It created a Board of Public Utility Commissioners of three members appointed by the governor with the consent of the Senate. The commissioners were required to publish periodic reports of their findings and decisions and to make annual reports with recommendations to the governor. The act forbade members and employees of the board to have any professional relationship with or to hold securities in any public utility in the state. It also defined utilities subject to the board's supervision as "every individual, co-partnership, association, corporation or joint stock company . . . that now or hereafter may own, operate, manage or control within the State of New Jersey any steam railroad, street railway, traction railway, canal, express, subway, pipe line, gas, electric light, heat, power, water, oil, sewer, telephone, telegraph system, plant or equipment for public use, under privileges granted or hereafter to be granted by the State of New Jersey or by any political subdivision thereof." Among the board's powers were the right to investigate either on its own initiative or upon written complaint any matter concerning any public utility; to appraise and evaluate the property of any utility and to fix just and reasonable rates based upon such evaluation; to require all public utilities to file complete schedules of their rates; to establish standards of service for electric companies; to compel any railroad or street railway to establish and maintain junction points and intersections with other lines and switch connections with private sidings; to suspend any rate increase pending investigation and approval by the board; and to require any public utility to comply with state and municipal laws and the provisions of its charter and to maintain its property and equipment in such condition as to enable it to provide safe and efficient service. The act also gave the board far-reaching supervision over the financial transactions of all companies under its jurisdiction by a series of prohibitions against various activities including the issuing of stocks and bonds without the board's prior approval. Procedures for hearings and investigations were outlined in detail and included the power to subpoena witnesses and compel the production of relevant documents. The orders of the board were subject to the review of the state supreme court, and that body was empowered to set aside orders when they were deemed to be unreasonable or outside the jurisdiction of the commission. For a discussion of the background of this legislation, see Link, *Wilson: The Road to the White House*, pp. 134-39, 261-63. The act is printed in *Laws of New Jersey, 1911*, Chap. 195, pp. 374-89.

⁵ This measure required all cold storage operators to brand and stamp the date of receipt of all solid foods; forbade operators to keep or sell any food in cold storage for longer than ten months without the permission of the State Board of Health or its agents; authorized that agency to inspect all cold storage plants, to maintain reasonable standards of sanitation, and to enforce the act; required cold storage operators to submit quarterly reports listing in itemized particulars the quantity of all food in storage to the Board of Health; forbade operators to transfer food from one plant to another for the purpose of evading the act or to put food in cold storage once it had been removed from it; provided for the sale by public auction of food kept longer than ten months; and provided penalties for violation of the law. *Laws of New Jersey, 1911*, Chap. 189, pp. 349-53.

⁶ *Ibid.*, Article 191, pp. 356-60.

⁷ *Ibid.*, Chap. 201, pp. 414-27.

⁸ See WW to the House of Assembly, April 11, 1911, n. 2.

From William Frank McCombs

My dear Governor: New York April 22, 1911.

I am very glad to know that you are pleased with Mr. Stockbridge and I hope that in addition to his other active duties he will be able to relieve you of much detail. I am going to have Mr. Brougham[1] in to see me on Monday. I have an idea that he may be of service. Last week I had a long talk with Daniel Altland, '98 of Detroit.[2] I think he can be of assistance in Michigan. He has promised to keep in touch with me.

You expressed in your letter a feeling that what I am undertaking in the matter of the western trip may become burdensome to me, and say that you have a conscience in the matter. I also have a conscience on the general question, which operates in this way: I should feel that I was not discharging the functions of a good citizen if I did not make every effort to assist in bringing about your nomination and election to the presidency, and it gives me great pleasure to devote myself to that proposition.

With warm regards, I am,
                    Yours sincerely,   Wm. F. McCombs

TLS (WP, DLC).
[1] Herbert Bruce Brougham, editorial writer for the *New York Times*.
[2] Daniel Fickes Altland, Princeton 1898, lawyer of Detroit.

To Mary Allen Hulbert Peck

Dearest Friend,   Princeton, 23 April, 1911.

The Legislature adjourned yesterday morning at three o'clock, with its work done. I got absolutely everything I strove for,—and more besides: all four of the great acts that I had set my heart on (the primaries and election law, the corrupt practices act, as stringent as the English, the workingmen's compensation act, and the act giving a public commission control over the railways, the trolley lines, the water companies, and the gas and electric light and power companies), and besides them I got certain fundamental school reforms and an act enabling any city in the State to adopt the commission form of government, which simplifies the electoral process and concentrates responsibility. Every one, the papers included, are saying that none of it could have been done, if it had not been for my influence and tact and hold upon the people. Be that as it may, the thing was done, and the result was as complete a victory as has ever been won, I venture to say, in the history of the country. I wrote the platform, I had the measures formulated to my mind, I kept the pressure of opinion constantly on the legislature, and the

programme was carried out to its last detail. This with the senatorial business seems, in the minds of the people looking on
little less than a miracle in the light of what has been the history
of reform hitherto in this State. As a matter of fact, it is just
a bit of natural history. I came to the office in the fulness of
time, when opinion was ripe on all these matters, when both
parties were committed to these reforms, and by merely standing fast, and by never losing sight of the business for an hour,
but keeping up all sorts of (legitimate) pressure *all the time*,
kept the mighty forces from being diverted or blocked at any
point. The strain has been immense, but the reward is great.
I feel a great reaction to-day, for I am, of course, exceedingly
tired, but I am quietly and deeply happy that I should have
been of just the kind of service I wished to be to those who
elected and trusted me. I can look them in the face, like a
servant who has kept faith and done all that was in him, given
every power he possessed, to them and their affairs. There could
be no deeper source of satisfaction and contentment! I have
no doubt that a good deal of the result was due to the personal
relations I established with the men in the Senate, the Republican Senate which, it was feared at the outset, might be the
stumbling block. You remember the dinner in New York and
the supper at the Trenton country club which I described to you.
Those evenings undoubtedly played their part in the outcome.
They brought us all close together on terms not unlike friendly
intimacy; made them realize just what sort of *person* I was.
Since then Republicans have resorted to my office for counsel
and advice almost as freely as Democrats (an almost unprec-
endented circumstance at Trenton) and with several of them
I have established relations almost of affection. Otherwise I do
not believe that the extraordinary thing that happened could
possibly have come about: for all four of the great "administration" measures passed the Senate *without a dissenting voice*!
The newspaper men seem dazed. They do not understand how
such things *could* happen. They were impressed, too, with the
orderly and dignified way in which the session ended, despite
the long strain of the closing night, when the houses sat from
eight until three. Generally there is wild horseplay, like that on
the stock exchange, but this time everything was done decently
and with an air of self-respect. I took several naps in my office
during the long hours of the session, coming out into the outer
office in the intervals to talk and swap stories with the men who
were sitting there, my secretary, the reporters who were coming
and going, and interested friends who had come down to see

how things ended. Then a committee from each House called
on me to ask if there was anything more I had to lay before
them before adjournment,—and the session was over. Most of
the members dropped in to say good by, and by four o'clock
your tired and happy friend was in bed in the noisy little Hotel
Sterling, with the strong odours of late suppers in his nostrils,
floating in at the open window. It's a great game, thoroughly
worth playing!

I literally have not had five minutes time to drop in and see
the Roeblings.[1] I have thought of them almost every day, and
have wanted to go very sincerely. I think Mrs. R. charming. But
I have not felt that I could relax my attention for a moment
while the session lasted,—and it had already begun when I was
inaugurated, you know, and plunged into the first fight, the fight
for the senatorship. Winning that, by the way, made all the rest
easier; but it also made the session some two weeks longer than
usual. What a vigil it has been! I am certainly in training for
almost anything that may come to me by way of public tasks.
There are serious times ahead. It daunts me to think of the
possibility of my playing an influential part in them. There is
no telling what deep waters may be ahead of me. The forces
of greed and the forces of justice and humanity are about to
grapple for a bout in which men will spend all the life that is
in them. God grant I may have strength enough to count, to
tip the balance in the unequal and tremendous struggle! This
week I turn to speechmaking again (much the easier task of
the two) and to preparation for my western trip. All through
everything, as the days come and go with their tale of tasks,
runs a constant thought of you, a constant solicitude for you,
and an abiding consciousness of being (and of being blessed by
being),   Your devoted friend,   Woodrow Wilson

Affectionate messages from all to all.

WWTLS (WP, DLC).
   [1] Washington Augustus Roebling and his wife, Cornelia Witsell Farrow
Roebling, a close friend of Mrs. Peck. The Roeblings lived at 191 West State
St. in Trenton.

To Thomas Bell Love

My dear Mr. Love: [Trenton, N. J.] April 24, 1911.

   Your letter of April eighteenth has lain unanswered because
of the rush of the last days of our legislative session.

   You will be interested to know that my entire programme of
legislation was carried through. It is thought here that this has

been the most extraordinary session of our Legislature within the recollection of those now living. It is a wonderful example of the effect of public sentiment.

You are very kind to be so thoughtful of me. I have received a number of letters about the State Fair in October and am keeping it in mind. I shall certainly try to keep myself free to go, and so far as I can now see, nothing is likely to arise which will prevent it.

I greatly appreciate your kindness and shall look forward with the greatest interest to seeing you when I do manage to get to Texas. I need not tell you how much it gratifies me that a sentiment should be growing as you find it. I do not feel that I deserve it but it gratifies me none the less on that account.

Cordially and sincerely yours,   Woodrow Wilson

TLS (photostat in the T. B. Love Papers, Dallas Hist. Soc.).

From Benjamin Barr Lindsey

My dear Governor: [Denver, Col.] April 24, 1911.

When you are in Denver I hope you can see some of the Progressive Democrats. Among the strongest of these is Ex-Governor Thomas. In my judgment he is the hope of progressive Democracy in this state. Others are former U.S. Senators [Thomas MacDonald] Patterson and and [sic] Frank J[enne]. Cannon, owner and managing editor respectively of The Rocky Mountain News and Mr. Boyd F. Gurley part owner and Manager of The Denver Express. These two papers will undoubtedly fight the "special interest" Democrats lead by Mayor Speer, Billy and Frank Adams[1] (brother[s] of Ex-Governor Adams)[2] and Gerald Hughes (son of former U. S. Senator Hughes)[3] in their present effort to send a delegation to the next Democratic convention pledged against candidates regarded as progressive. If they consider their plan hopeless they will no doubt pretend to support some progressive.

The corrupt special interests in the State have used the Democratic organization in Denver for all their big steals and legislative betrayals of the people. They have been forced to yield any election reform measures so far secured. Governor Shafroth is a good man but by no means militant, and so far any progressive measures have been obtained largely through the power of public sentiment in which the News and Express have done most without the same help from Governor Shafroth that you have so signally rendered in New Jersey.

I am very sorry that my lecture period this year brings me home just after your visit in Denver, and I shall not have the anticipated pleasure of seeing you.

A great reception awaits you in the West, and I am glad you are making the trip.   Sincerely,   [Ben B. Lindsey]

CCL (B. B. Lindsey Papers, DLC).
    [1] William H. Adams, cattleman of Alamosa, Col., and governor, 1927-33, and Frank Adams, businessman of Denver.
    [2] Alva Adams, the oldest of the three brothers, who had prospered as a merchant in Pueblo and served as Governor of Colorado, 1887-89 and 1897-99. He was elected a third time in 1904 but was unseated on March 20, 1905, by the Republican-controlled legislature on the ground of fraud in his election.
    [3] Charles James Hughes, Jr., Democratic senator from Colorado from 1909 until his death on January 11, 1911.

A News Report of Remarks at the Free Synagogue in New York

[April 25, 1911]

WILSON TALKS "SQUARE DEAL"

Refers to Evils of American Business in Address at Free Synagogue Banquet.

TRIBUTES FOR THE GOVERNOR

NEW YORK, April 25.—Governor Wilson, of New Jersey, was the principal speaker last night at the Hotel Astor, in honor of the fourth anniversary of the founding of the Free Snyagogue [Synagogue]. Rev. Stephen S[amuel]. Wise, the founder,[1] also was present.

Dr. Wilson listened attentively to all the praise poured upon him by the ten speakers who preceded him. When his turn came, about midnight, he was greeted with prolonged applause.

The Governor made clear to the audience his opinions about business and politics. He requested that if there was a business man in the audience who conducted his business unjustly he should leave the room. There was not even a stir among those present.

"My idea of right," he said, "is not an opportunity to be selfish, but a duty to be serviceable. If right implies selfishness, then I deny that my constituents possess any rights.

"I hate that old maxim, 'Business is business,' for I understand by it that business is not moral. The man who says 'I am not in business for my health' means that he is not in business for his moral health, and I am the enemy of every business of this kind. But if business is regarded as an object for serving and obtaining private profit by means of service, then I am with that business. America simply demands that wealth which is made shall be made by distinct business service, giving honest weight, honest measure and without deception. If your business is detrimental to the community it has stopped being serviceable, and then we must put you out of business.

"I don't care a peppercorn as to the difference between a nominal Democrat and any ordinary Democrat, but I do care a vast deal about the difference between a progressive and a reactionary. Bosses are of the latter rank. They are all in the same family and of the same gang. They belong neither to one party nor to another, and their strength lies in their secret meetings where they connive to selfishly advance their own interests. It is when they introduce our large business men into these private meetings that our trouble of regulation begins.

"The corporations must be regulated, and I have discovered that fines do not constitute a pressure but a relief from pressure. Therefore I am not in favor of fining the corporations, but I am very much in favor of jailing the gentlemen who misguide the corporations. The reflections of confinement are soul-inspiring.

"I come to you from an atmosphere of serenity where things are discussed as if nothing had to be done on the instant. For six months I have been in ceaseless vigilance for fear that something might be done which ought not to be done.

"We are in the presence of a great body of changing opinions, and with this will come a change of atmospheric conditions, a general readjustment of our economic and political relations with each other. There is no reason for being afraid of the prospect, however, for if there will be a revolution it will be a revolution carrying sympathy with it, and that which breeds sympathy makes for reform. Many men are truly great, but we call that man truly noble who works for the benefit of his fellow-men. By the same test we judge nations. A nation can gain distinction only by the use of its moral powers. That nation is not only great but is truly noble which uses its power in the direction of the right.

"Influences are at work to recreate out of the debris of debauchery and misuse a nation with a higher tone of individuality, with a greater moral certitude, and with greater emphasis on its unlifting [uplifting] supremacy. It will be a reconstructed age."[2]

Printed in the *Newark Evening News*, April 25, 1911.
[1] He was also active in numerous social reform organizations and a leading Zionist.
[2] There is a WWhw outline of this address, dated April 24, 1911, in WP, DLC.

From Benjamin L. Farinholt[1]

My dear Sir: West Point, Va. April, 26, 1911.

I notice from the press that you propose to make a visit to the South West and to Lincoln, Nebraska, and will there be entertained by Mr. W. J. Bryan. Mr. Bryan is the nemesis of the Democratic Party, and as a lifelong democrat and a Southerner, from cuticle to core, we beg you to keep away from Mr. Bryan. Any association with him, and the acceptance of his hospitality will cost you, in whom we had centered our hopes as leader of our banner for 1912, half million votes in the South, and more in the North.

For the good of our overburdened countrymen and the hope they place in you for relief do not make this mistake. The reasons are too obvious and too many for me to name to a man of your extraordinary discernment, and I voice the opinion and wishes of hundreds of true democrats around me who sincerely deplore that such an announcement has been made, and for the good of the party and our whole country trust you will recall any engagement.

Mr. Bryan is as dead with the great mass of the Democratic party as with the Republicans, and nothing would please the Republicans better or solidify and give them them [sic] greater cheer than to have you affiliate with Mr. Bryan, who will undoubtedly endeavor to make the impression that he favors and fosters your nomination, and although I and many friends have voted for him twice and three times, we know you can carry no heavier weight in the campaign should you be nominated, nor one which would so surely prevent your being the great instrument for good to the whole country as to be patronized by the three times repudiated Nebraskan.

I have the honor to be sincerely your political friend,

B. L. Farinholt.

TLS (Governors' Files, Nj).

[1] Born near Yorktown, Va., on May 26, 1839. A colonel in the Confederate Army, he moved to Baltimore in 1884 where he was in the mercantile business. At this time he was living in retirement in West Point, Va., and died on December 24, 1919. He was a close friend of Robert Hunter Fitzhugh, Wilson's long-time correspondent of Lexington, Ky.

A News Report of an Affair in New York

[April 27, 1911]

TOAST WILSON AS PRESIDENT

New Jersey Senate Indorses Executive at Dinner
Given in New York.

NEW YORK, April 27.—New Jersey's State Senators, Democrats
and Republicans alike, drank a health last night to Woodrow
Wilson, the next President of the United States, at a dinner
given at the Hotel Astor in his honor by Ernest R. Ackerman,
President of the Senate. Twenty of the twenty-one Senators
and the Governor, as well as his private secretary, Joseph P.
Tumulty, and others, were present.[1] The dinner was marked by
enthusiastic outbursts of good feeling. . . .

During the dinner the guests, including the Governor himself,
joined in robust chorus in all the selections furnished by the
orchestra, singing with equal fervor everything from "When good
fellows get together" to "Any little girl that's a nice little girl
is the right little girl for me." . . .

Governor Wilson, who had not intended to make a speech
at the dinner, rose amid hearty cheers from every diner at the
great round table.

"I cannot tell you how gratified I am to see the wish I hazarded
at our first dinner some time ago now fulfilled," he said. "At that
time, you may remember, I expressed the wish that I might grow
into intimate acquaintance and friendship with all of you, and
to-night I may proudly and contentedly say I am not only among
acquaintances, but among friends, and many intimate friends,
and for not a few I have formed a true and deep affection. It is
fortunate for New Jersey that her Senate is a small body, small
enough to come together just as we are together to-night—to
come together and understand each other, each other's character
and motives.

"It has grieved me much to find newspaper correspondents
in the last year reporting that the Senate had yielded to reform
measures under pressure of the Governor, as if I had exerted
pressure and found the Senate unwilling of its accord to espouse
the reform measures it finally passed. That has not been the
case. I am aware of no pressure exerted by me, and I know
only of the earnest and hearty co-operation I have ever met in
the Senate. Never have I found anything more than honest difference of opinion existing between some members of the Senate
and myself.

"Most men are beginning to realize that it is only an artificial process that divides Democrats from Republicans in the State Senate, or in State politics, as, in fact, in city and county politics and issues, which have little or no connection with the great party divisions in national politics. We have realized that in the present session of the Senate, and realized, too, that we are living in a day that differs from the days that have gone before and requires different political attitudes and measures.

"The only essential difference in American politics to-day is the difference between progressives and reactionaries. We have in the last ten years come out of the period of merely negative politics, politics which consist wholly of attacking abuses and heaping objurgation upon men and measures of other political faith.

"We have passed out of that earlier period into one of constructive legislation. Formerly we contented ourselves with pointing out what things were to be feared. To-day we no longer need merely to point out what is to be feared; we have learned how to escape and master our fears and build up positive measures of reform and solid achievement in politics.

"New Jersey is not backward in her thought—she may have paused longer than others, but it was only to consider her course better while she paused. We have not done everything in the way of reform, as Senator Johnson[2] seemed to think a few moments ago; we may still be able to find more things to do when the Legislature convenes again. But if we have not done everything, we have at least done everything in sight at the last session. We have done, and done thoroughly, all the main things that were waiting to be done—and we have accomplished them with a perfect unanimity of counsel.

"It pleases me especially, and beyond the power of words, that you have come to credit the professions made by me when I sought the office I now hold, that you feel that I seek and will support reforms irrespective of from what political house they come. Your confidence in me is my greatest happiness. It has been a real delight to me to see Republicans in the Legislature resort to my house as freely and often for conference as members of my own party.

"All these things weave us together as a common family, seeking to serve well, as we have served, our great commonwealth."

Printed in the *Newark Evening News*, April 27, 1911; some editorial headings omitted.

[1] Actually, only nineteen senators attended. Walter Evans Edge, Republican of Atlantic City, Atlantic County, and Johnston Cornish, Democrat of Washington, Warren County, were unavoidably absent.

[2] James A. C. Johnson, Democrat of Englewood, Bergen County.

A News Report of an After-Dinner Address
to the Phillipsburg, New Jersey, Board of Trade

[April 28, 1911]

GOVERNOR ILL OF INDIGESTION

Attacked at Phillipsburg Banquet,
but Was Able Later to Conclude Address.

PRAISES LEGISLATURE'S WORK

PHILLIPSBURG, April 28.–While delivering his address at the
Board of Trade banquet here last night, Governor Woodrow Wilson was taken ill from acute indigestion. He was compelled to
retire to a private room for half an hour before he was able to
resume speaking. Governor Wilson remained in Phillipsburg
over night as the guest of Dr. J. M. Reese.[1]

During the reception which preceded the banquet, at the
home of Dr. Reese, hundreds of citizens greeted the Governor.
The decorations in the banquet hall were the most elaborate
ever undertaken in this city. Several times during his address Governor Wilson was interrupted by applause.

He took occasion to state that this was his first opportunity
to report to his constituency since the adjournment of the Legislature, and that it afforded him great pleasure to give an account of his stewardship.

"In the first place, a measure to give full justice to the workingman in the matter of compensation for injuries.

"In the second place, such a reform of the election laws as
will open to the people in the freest possible manner the right to
nominate to office and to elect to office without the intervention
of political machines and private caucuses and such an improvement of the form and use of the ballot as will insure secrecy of
voting and, above all, freedom of choice to the voter.

"In the third place, an act to regulate expenses at elections,
to provide for a publication of the accounts of candidates and
campaign committees and to punish corruption in as thoroughgoing a way as possible.

"And in the fourth place, what the State had long waited and
striven for, a measure which will give to the Public Utilities
Commission genuine powers of regulation over public service
corporations, whether railway and trolley lines or gas companies
and electric light and power companies. The measures framed
and passed in the pursuance of this program are singularly
complete and thoroughgoing. No State in the Union has more
progressive laws now as respects these fundamental matters
upon its statute books than New Jersey has.

"In a single session these four great matters were thoroughly and, it is to be hoped, finally dealt with. But that was not all. Besides these great measures a very much needed act was passed regulating the cold storage of foods. The old-fashioned and discredited system of definite, inelastic sentences for criminals was done away with and indeterminate sentences substituted. The administration of the school system of the State was reformed by a series of measures which will certainly make for increased efficiency and for invariable honesty and responsibility in the administration of the school funds and of the methods of instruction. An act regulating weights and measures more thoroughly, providing for their inspection throughout the State and penalizing deception in their use, was passed. And the cities of the State were authorized at their pleasure to adopt the commission form of government, which concentrates responsibility, and which, whenever adopted, has had the effect of simplifying and purifying local administration. The purchase of the rights of way for the great intracoastal waterway was authorized.

"The only acts of importance missing from this list are an act to liberalize the laws regarding automobile licenses and a resolution fulfilling the pledge of both national parties to grant to the federal government the right to impose income taxes.

"I think this is a record of which to be proud and it is with the greatest pleasure that I record my impression that the Legislature felt a great zest and pleasure in carrying out this extraordinary program. The members of the House seemed to vie with one another in giving their constituents abundant evidence that they were free men devoted to the real interests of the State. New Jersey is happy in having turned her face to the light and set out upon the path of modern progress with a stride that will certainly carry her forward very rapidly to a place alongside the leading Progressive States of the Union."

Printed in the *Newark Evening News*, April 28, 1911.
[1] James Mitchell Reese, physician of Phillipsburg, N. J.

An Interview in Norfolk, Virginia[1]

[April 30, 1911]

GOV. WILSON COMMENTS ON DEMOCRACY'S CHANCES

Governor Wilson was disinclined to discuss national politics when he granted an interview to a Landmark reporter yesterday. He did not think, he said, that there was much danger of a split in the Democratic party, although some elements in the party might not care to follow past leadership as the people are demanding.

"The hour of opportunity for the Democratic party is now here," he said, "and I believe the party will take advantage of it; that it will furnish the means for fulfilling the country's needs along progressive lines." The Governor thought that while there might be some shifting both parties will remain intact, virtually, and that no new party will be formed. He was not willing to suggest the probable paramount issue in 1912, saying that the subject was too big and that things move rapidly.

"The Democrats," he said, "have adopted an excellent program and they are living up to the expectations of the people. I hope they will keep on honestly and sincerely striving for the welfare of the people instead of striving for party advantage. That policy will win because it is right."

The Governor thought the reciprocity bill and the farmers' free list bill[2] good political moves, because they are right. He thinks better results can be had by revising the tariff schedule by schedule rather than as a whole. There will be fewer opportunities for log rolling, combinations and deals, and when each schedule is taken up in a separate bill it is more likely to be considered solely on its merits.

"While I am a low tariff man, I believe that the tariff question ought to be handled carefully and with good judgment so as not to destroy any legitimate industry and not to unsettle business conditions any more than necessary."

The Governor said he favored the election of United States Senators by the people and the initiative, referendum and recall, authough [although] this ought not to apply to judges, as in the Arizona constitution.

Printed in the *Norfolk*, Va., *Landmark*, April 30, 1911.

[1] He had just arrived to address the Pewter Platter Club.

[2] A measure to put agricultural implements, cotton bagging, cotton ties, fence wire, and various other articles on the free list. Taft vetoed this bill on August 18, 1911.

Two News Reports of an Address in Norfolk, Virginia

[April 30, 1911]

ACCLAIMED DEMOCRACY'S GIANT OF THE HOUR AT
PEWTER PLATTER DINNER

Hailed as the most commanding figure on the American political horizon and wildly greeted as the giant apostle of modern and progressive Democracy upon whom the nation will call to again intrench in power at Washington the party of Jefferson,

Woodrow Wilson, the militant Governor of New Jersey, came back yesterday to Virginia, his native land and last night before the Pewter Platter Club and a distinguished gathering of railroad presidents, bankers, doctors, lawyers, business men and political leaders, he signalized his return with a terrific arraignment of "machine" politics and bosses, of secretive business methods of public corporations, of "standpatters" in the political and commercial world and then in another breath he upheld free and open criticism of public institutions and political conditions, and advocated publicity as a remedy of economic evils.

There were dramatic touches to the scene. Around Dr. Wilson were gathered an audience of men prominent in State and municipal affairs, men of prominence in the business world, men whose word is power in politics and men high in financial and corporate institutions. The boldness, the directness, the incisiveness, the fearlessness and the force of the "Virginian-Jerseyman's" words crashed at times through the throng like a series of thunderbolt jolts. At the same time his frankness and eloquence aroused the crowd into a storm of enthusiasm. . . .

Dr. Wilson, as he did once before when he spoke to a Norfolk audience at the Jamestown Exposition some years ago,[1] tossed aside his prepared address and in words eloquent and vivid he discussed business conditions of the nation, political affairs of the country and made several allusions to his work as New Jersey's chief executive. . . .

In the course of his remarks Dr. Wilson plainly told his hearers that the future of the nation did not lie so much in men composed of the company before him, but in the masses. He said the nation should conserve its moral integrity by seeing that its women are not overworked and its children are not crushed in the industrial world.

"We are now reconstructing our economic life," said Dr. Wilson at one point in his address. "This doesn't appeal to the banks, it doesn't appeal to the manufacturer; it disturbs trade, but it has got to be done. The time must return when there will again be a free use of individual effort and resources."

Touching upon wealth and capital, Dr. Wilson said a new system has arisen with the development of America. No longer does a man or company of men do business with their own money, but big corporations are organized, stock is sold and people's money brought under the control of a few men who sit around a table. He contended with some vigor that a corporation, doing business with people's money, should conduct its

affairs within the glare of publicity and keep nothing of its transactions hidden.

Dr. Wilson came out flatfootedly for the initiative, referendum
and recall, which he said were instruments that placed in the
hands of the people true representative government and took
government out of the hands of bosses and machines. He told
of how men of wealth control Legislatures and how the legislators are tied up with notes in banks and held in subjection.
Touching upon conditions in New Jersey, he said his part of the
reform work there had been magnified and he was only instrumental in breaking the stranglehold of the machine upon the
legislators. He declared at another point that he would esteem
himself a recreant and a coward if he did not stand ready to
criticize anything.[2]

Printed in the Norfolk *Virginian-Pilot*, April 30, 1911; several editorial headings
omitted.

[1] A news report of Wilson's address on that occasion and the address itself are
printed at July 4, 1907, Vol. 17.

[2] Here follows the text of the press release which Wilson had tossed aside.

✧

[April 30, 1911]

WILSON TELLS WHY PROGRESSIVE POLICIES WILL REDEEM GOVERNMENT FOR PEOPLE

WILSON EPIGRAMS.

Our attitude is one of hope instead of fear. This is an age
that proposes everything for itself.

We do not find any one kind of Democrats or any one
kind of Republicans—they are progressives or standpatters,
and there are standpatter Democrats as well as standpatter
Republicans.

There are the Liberals, who believe that because there is
to be a change things are not going to be torn down; and
there are Tories who are satisfied with the deterioration of
the past.

The preservation of the race as a whole is the policy of
conservation. See that women are not overworked and that
children are not crushed in their childhood and you will
develop leaders to preserve the forests and the mines.

The words safe and sane have been much abused. By safe
they believe in consulting their grandmother about everything, and by sane they mean to sit still and do nothing.

We are tired of talking in the formulas of the days that are gone, and gone never to return.

Books are not safe; they are not trustworthy. I never knew a man who knew enough to write more than one chapter and I never knew a book that was accepted as a whole.

This is a life of illogical connections.

I revere the spirit of the Constitution, but not the text. I would be willing for the framers to speak for themselves as to the way their work is construed.

The same organs that govern the body physical govern the body politic.

We are reconstructing our economic life. That does not encourage the banking business nor stimulate manufacturing. But it has got to be done and it is not finished until it is done right.

Do not deceive yourself that modern labor is seeking his own employer. He never sees him. Do you believe those are the terms of the free contract of the Constitution?

Are we afraid of the radicalism that goes to the root of these facts?

I challenge every manufacturer and business man to answer these questions by opening the books. And for those who refuse there is no cover he can seek.

The point is, have we representative government? Every radical I know is a radical because he wants to restore representative government.

Legislators are used as puppets. Many legislators cannot vote as they want to because their bosses control the banks that hold their notes.

After an introduction by President E. A. Alderman, of the University of Virginia, as the foremost man for the Presidency of the United States, as the greatest exponent of the age of the common rights of the people of this country, Governor Woodrow Wilson, of New Jersey, enunciated the doctrine of the progressives, whether Democrat or Republican, as the basis of the transformation of the economics of the nation.

Governor Wilson said his doctrine did not tend to encourage banking or stimulate manufacturing. Through the process of change, he said, the country must adjust itself to a new condition and the problem would not be settled until settled right. He adhered to the spirit of the constitution, but not to its text, and invoked the teachings and doctrines of the framers of the fundamental law in support of his statements.

The population was divided into Tories and Liberals. The Liberals do not think because there is to be a change things are to be destroyed. The Tories believe in the established order of things and are satisfied to do nothing.

"Let things alone and they deteriorate," he said.

"Are you a Liberal, allied with the future of the race, or are you a Tory, satisfied with the deterioration of the past?"

This was the proposition Governor Wilson put up to his audience.

"Did you ever hear of a tree that drew its substance from the flower instead of the root; did you ever hear of a plant that drew its strength from the top instead of the root? The foundation of this country does not lie in companies of men like this. It is in the masses you meet on the street whom you do not know.

"The preservation of the race as a whole is the real policy of conservatism—see that women are not overworked and that children are not crushed in their childhood. Then you will develop leaders to preserve the forests and the mines."

Both Governor Wilson and Dr. Alderman were liberally applauded. When the Governor had finished his speech the crowd arose, yelled and waved napkins and beer steins until the distinguished son of Virginia arose and bowed recognition to the ovation.

His speech was the most convincing argument that has probably been heard in Norfolk for the readjustment of the government to the needs of a new age—the establishment of capital upon a basis of a business of the people instead of private interests; a plane of common economy instead of private gain. He said the capital of the great corporations of this age is the capital of the people and no individual has the right to refer to the millions represented as private money or as the private business of the directors and officers. "It is public business and the directors are no more than trustees of the public funds they have solicited to carry on the enterprise for which stock subscriptions were solicited from whoever would buy the shares."

In the audience were the representatives of the great industries of Norfolk. The fact that they applauded the speaker's utterances may be taken as proof that they endorse the sentiments he expressed. The Pewter Platter Club is composed, as Judge Thomas H. Willcox, toastmaster, said, of the best interests of this city. The fact that they selected Governor Wilson as the principal speaker for the last function of the season has its own significance.

If the selection was made with the expectation that he would pander to the interests that were represented at the dinner, then they were mistaken. For in language as emphatic as the most accomplished linguist—which Governor Wilson is—could express he took his stand with the common people and against the powers that control the votes of legislators and make the rights inherent from the foundation of the government secondary to their pecuniary interests.

"Many legislators can not vote as they want to because their bosses control the banks that hold their notes," he said.

Governor Wilson took a bold stand for the initiative and referendum. He said for twenty years he lectured his classes against it and then he went to looking for the truth concerning it. Now he only regretted that he could not apologize to the classes for the lectures he had made before he looked into the facts.

"Believe in it? Of course, I do, because I believe we want to get control of our institutions again."

In conclusion Governor Wilson spoke of the symbolic colors of the American flag, growing eloquent as he described the white stripes as typical of the paper on which was written the fundamental rights of the people and alternating red as typical of the blood of the patriots in which those rights were concerned.

"America is great not because she is rich, but because of her mind and dreams of great realities."

He boasted that the reformation was to be made not by the people struggling blind through revolution, but without a single tear or the shedding of a drop of blood.

He said his ideas were adopted into law in the closing days of the New Jersey Legislature, not because he domineered over the legislators, but because they had awakened to the new form of the new age. . . .[1]

Printed in the *Norfolk*, Va., *Landmark*, April 30, 1911; several editorial headings omitted.
  [1] Here follow Alderman's introduction and Wilson's press release.

To Mary Allen Hulbert Peck

Dearest Friend,   On Board S. S. [*Virginia*] 30 April, 1911

I know that you will forgive pencil. This is the only chance I have to write—on Sunday, *en route*. I have just been down to Norfolk, Va., to dine with the Pewter Platter Club. I did not expect when I made the promise to go that the engagement would catch me at so desperately busy a moment. I then expected that the legislature would adjourn at least a week earlier than it did. It was jolly to get off, little as I could afford to give the time for the trip just at this juncture. I was glad to get away from Trenton and its pressure of work; and this particular engagement was very welcome to me because I wanted to say something at this particular time in the South. At this particular time because there seems to be gathering in the South a really big body of sentiment (*and* opinion) in favour of my nomination for the presidency. The South is a very conservative region—just now probably the most (possibly the only) conservative section of the country—and I am *not* conservative. I am a radical. I wanted a chance to tell my friends in the South just what I thought, just what my programme is, before they went further and committed themselves to me as a "favourite son." I do not want them to make a mistake and repent it too late. I hate false colours, false impressions. I made myself clear enough last night! The local paper said this morning that "the boldness, the directness, the incisiveness, the fearlessness and the force of the 'Virginian-Jerseyman's' words crashed at times through the throng like a series of thunderbolt jolts. At the same time his frankness and eloquence aroused the crowd into a storm of enthusiasm." How is that for newspaper writing? That, I should say, is "going it some"! The nearer I get to the possibility of a nomination the less I feel willing to *try* for it,—the more I see the necessity that I, being what I am, should *not* commend myself for the choice, but should go my own way of speech and effort and keep my thoughts free of entanglements. And how weary I get, how *very* weary of talk of myself and of the presidency. I am sick of such personal stuff. How delicious it would be get a letter full of *you*, —full of no flavour but your own! It would be like a tonic. I shall try to clear my thought of all else and hypnotise myself with images of my dear friend!

                    Your devoted friend   Woodrow Wilson
I am well & fit.

ALS (WP, DLC).

To Thomas Berry Shannon[1]

My dear Mr. Shannon: [Trenton, N. J.] May 1, 1911.

The question asked in your letter of April twenty-seventh[2] about mt [my] attitude toward the important question of local option is, of course, a perfectly legitimate one, and you are entitled to a very frank answer. I would have replied sooner had I not been prevented by imperative public engagements. I have explained my views to you in private but have, of course, no objection to your making them public.

I am in favor of local option. I am a thorough believer in local self-government and believe that every self-governing community which constitutes a social unit should have the right to control the matter of the regulation or of the withholding of licenses.

But the questions involved are social and moral and are not susceptible of being made parts of a party programme. Whenever they have been made the subject-matter of party contests, they have cut the lines of party organization and party action athwart to the utter confusion of political action in every other field. They have thrown every other question, however important, into the background and have made con[s]tructive party action impossible for long years together. So far as I am myself concerned, therefore, I can never consent to have the question of local option made an issue between political parties in this State. My judgment is very clear in this matter. I do not believe that party programmes of the highest consequence to the political life of the State and of the Nation ought to be thrust on one side and hopelessly embarrassed for long periods together by making a political issue of a great question which is essentially non-political, non-partisan, moral and social, in its nature.

Very sincerely yours,   [Woodrow Wilson]

CCL (Governors' Files, Nj).
1 Superintendent of the Anti-Saloon League of New Jersey and pastor of the Kilburn Memorial Presbyterian Church in Newark.
2 It is missing.

To Benjamin Barr Lindsey

My dear Judge Lindsey: [Trenton, N. J.] May 1, 1911.

I am deeply sorry that I am not to see you when I am in Denver. I thank you very warmly for your letter of April twenty-first giving me a clew to the various kinds of Democrats I shall find when I come to Denver. I am looking forward with confidence to seeing both Senator Patterson and ex-Governor Thomas and am heartily glad that they have your endorsement.

In haste, with warmest regards,

Sincerely yours,   Woodrow Wilson

TLS (B. B. Lindsey Papers, DLC).

A Response to a Toast, "Princeton Ideals"[1]

[[May 1, 1911]]

It is with a variety of feelings that I come here to-night. The last time I attended a PRINCETONIAN banquet,[2] I was connected with the University and therefore connected with you. Now, in accordance with what seemed to be an obvious duty, I have come to leave Princeton, but not in spirit and not in thought, and to separate myself from association with you.

The audience which I face here to-night is a very small, select number of persons who have special privileges and, therefore, special burdens and duties. If you do not acquit yourself as men when you go out into the world, you are of all men most blameworthy; and so when I was asked to speak of Princeton ideals the theme connected itself in my mind with the new things I have been doing lately rather than with the things I was doing some time ago.

I suppose that after having preached to you for twenty years, I could not have gone on with my doctrine of public duty unless I had attempted some of the practice. And the ideals of a university translated into the forces of public life are not easy to analyze. What I tried to do when I was lecturing to you men, was to speak of things as they are, not of things as they might be. For I believe if there is any one thing for which the mind as distinguished from the heart should have a passion, it is reality.

The real difficulty with public affairs now-a-days is that there are so few persons who have a stomach for facts. I have tried to tell many an audience the truth, and I have seen many an audience actually shiver, because it did not want to hear it. We have got to come down to realities. I agree with the Attorney-General[3] that the legislatures represent our population. They are a fair sample taken out of the bundle; and I agree that if they were free to represent the people in making our laws they would very fairly represent them indeed. The trouble is not with their character but with their circumstances.

Now I want you men to understand that college men are under a deeper obligation than anybody else to know what the realities are. A college man is a man who for a certain period of his life is set free from narrowing employment. He is at liberty to examine the facts. Moreover, he is in a situation where his faculties are trained to observe the relations of the facts; and therefore the particular thing that ought to be the college ideal is to make your minds so serviceable, so indispensable, so certainly of such temper as cannot be deceived, that a great torch will burn in every place of learning which will take the shadows out of every system, even the system of government; and make it plain where the scoundrels are lurking.

And so if there is one thought stronger than another in my mind, it is that it would be a very glorious thing if Princeton might measure her greatness by the number of thinking minds that she contributed to the life of the nation, not merely to public life, but to the great realm of discovery that we call scholarship, to the great body of helpful men that go out as engineers and fulfill the tasks of the mind in their concrete form; that it should contribute to every walk of life, the men who see more and can accomplish with more certainty and accuracy of touch than anybody else.

Printed in the *Daily Princetonian*, May 2, 1911.

[1] Given at the thirteenth annual banquet of the *Daily Princetonian* at the Princeton Inn.

[2] On April 29, 1910. See the news report printed at April 30, 1910, Vol. 20.

[3] George Woodward Wickersham, Attorney-General of the United States, who, responding to the toast, "The Future Citizen," had said, "We have a system of representative government. I have heard it said that it does not represent the people. I take issue with that statement. Our public officials are human agents and they have sometimes been untrue to their trust. Still, laws have to be administered by human agencies; no law will work automatically to work reform. The character of the men behind the law is after all what counts; and the character of the men who are going to make and enforce the laws is more important than forms or institutions of government."

A News Report of a Speech in New York to the National Democratic Club

[May 3, 1911]

CHEERS FOR WILSON AT O'GORMAN DINNER

Gov. Woodrow Wilson of New Jersey, introduced and cheered as "capable of filling any place in the gift of the Nation," was the dominant figure at the dinner of the National Democratic Club at the Hotel Astor last night in honor of United States Senator James A. O'Gorman, saving only Senator O'Gorman himself.

Both men were received with great cordiality by at least 600 of the leading Democrats of the city. Senator O'Gorman stirred his hosts and their friends to a high pitch of enthusiasm by declaring his profound faith in the wisdom of the party's stand for a revision downward of the tariff, the reciprocity treaty with Canada, and the election of United States Senators by direct vote. To all these policies he pledged his hearty support.

Gov. Wilson gave a graphic picture of how he had found the State of New Jersey gripped at the throat by both so-called Democratic and Republican machines, how he had sought to free the State and its Legislature of this hold, and how, when the smoke had cleared away, the Legislature found itself free at last to give the people the reforms they demanded.

Charles F[rancis]. Murphy, leader of Tammany Hall, with his chief political adviser, Daniel F[lorence]. Cohalan, was at the guest table only a few feet from Gov. Wilson, and his face was a study while Gov. Wilson was telling how he smashed machines which did not represent the people but the bosses. . . .

Toastmaster Farrelly[1] called Gov. Wilson a "scholar and statesman who had redeemed in a single year the pledges of his party which had been expected to be a three years' task." Before touching on his work in New Jersey, Gov. Wilson confided to his audience that he had picked O'Gorman for Senator three days before his selection was actually made. It was his only instance of prophetic vision, he said, and he was very proud of it.

"I was dining with some gentlemen in this city," he said, "and when the conversation turned on the difficulty the Legislature was having in making a choice, I said, 'I cannot see why they don't take Justice O'Gorman.' "

Gov. Wilson said that Senator O'Gorman was a "man of quality." Most men might be anybody, but Senator O'Gorman, for habits of thought and action, and for quality of mind and character, was somebody in particular. Turning later to a discussion of affairs nearer his own home, his conduct of which, in the evident opinion of many of those present, had made him a National character and something of a Democratic hope, Gov. Wilson said:

"It is sometimes said of me, by nature of compliment, apparently, that I 'forced' the Legislature of New Jersey to do acts of reform which otherwise it would not have done. I did no such thing. What I did, or tried to do, was to render the New Jersey Legislature free to pass the progressive measures which the people of the State of all parties demanded.

"When I entered the Governorship I found that two organizations had a strangle hold on the Legislature. One organization was the Democratic machine, the other the Republican machine, and the Republican machine was no more Republican than the Democratic machine was Democratic. Both were conducted for

[1] Stephen Farrelly, philanthropist and founder of the American News Co. of New York.

accomplishing the ambitious ends and carrying out the programmes of themselves and of certain men who were subsidiz-
ing them.

"We had a little skirmish over there," he went on, but was
halted by applause and laughter, for many remembered his
several heated tilts with State Chairman Nugent. "Then the
war was over," he said, when he could be heard, "and if I ever
saw a lot of self-respecting, patriotic legislators in all my life,
it was the Legislature of New Jersey. Some of the men came
to me, saying that if they did not do as the machine men wanted
them to do their business would be ruined, their notes in bank
would not be extended, and they were threatened on every side.

"I am not speaking in general terms, I am speaking of specific cases, and I can give names and figures if necessary, but
as I am out of my jurisdiction I won't do it. The thing to do was
to break the hold of these men on the members of the Legislature, and that done, the rest was easy. But the hold must be
broken if it has to be done with sticks of dynamite."

Gov. Wilson said that the grip of the machine on the Nation
must likewise be broken.

"Don't be squeamish," he shouted. "We are grown-up men."

"Right you are," came from several parts of the hall at once,
and Mr. Murphy, looking on, smiled faintly, as he had also
smiled when some one spoke of how wise the "Legislature" had
been in selecting O'Gorman for Senator.

Gov. Wilson poured oil on the wounds of the machine a moment later, however, by saying he was not indicting men for the
evil system which had sprung up, but the system itself. All the
people were more or less responsible, he said, and the thing
was to recognize that we were on the eve of departing from
one of the essentials of the Government.

The speaker declared himself enthusiastically for the popular
election of United States Senators, not because he believed that
any large number of Senators did not represent the States from
which they came but that a few did not, and this few indicated
a danger ahead for the Republic.

Gov. Wilson made a serious comment on what he declared to
be an evil growing out of the fact that this city dominated the
finances of the country. He said there was a side of humanity
in banking and currency, though many did not recognize it. He
was speaking of checks on opportunity.

"A real trouble in this country is the fact that the surplus of
our resources is in New York, and no one has access to that surplus who has not been accredited in New York," he said. "Such

is not the case in England or Germany. In those countries a villager may tap the resources of his country not in proportion to the extent he is known in London or Berlin but in proportion to his standing among his neighbors."

Such a condition of affairs, he said, had wrought injustice and limited opportunity in America.

Printed in the *New York Times*, May 3, 1911; some editorial headings omitted.

From Julius Daniel Dreher[1]

My dear Governor Wilson: Port Antonio, Jamaica. May 4, 1911.

Please let me take a few moments of your time to ask you to accept my warmest congratulations on the brilliant success of your administration. Apart from my profound interest in good government, I cannot help feeling a special interest in your success because you are a distinguished educator and I still belong, in attachment, to the college clan.

In The Springfield Weekly Republican, which is my main reliance for general news and information, I have read a part of your Indianapolis speech, which is by far the best thing of the kind I have read for years. Your democracy is a living thing, quite different from the traditional mummy so frequently exhibited by politicians who trim their sails to catch the favoring breeze.

It is refreshing to feel that we are in the dawn of a fairer and better day and that you are one of the prophets preparing the way of the people, which, I believe, is also the way of the Lord. May God spare you long in this high service!

Don't stop in the good work to answer this letter, but, always believe me,

With highest regards and all good wishes,

Faithfully yours,   Julius D. Dreher

I am very glad you sent a cheering word to the Roanoke faculty in the brave fight they are making.[2]

ALS (Governors' Files, Nj).

[1] President of Roanoke College, 1878-1903; American consul at Tahiti, 1906-10; at this time consul at Port Antonio, Jamaica.

[2] The "brave fight" being waged by the faculty of Roanoke College involved Herman Justus Thorstenberg, Professor of History and Social Science, and his use of Henry William Elson, *History of the United States of America* (New York and London, 1904), as the textbook for a freshman history course. The controversy began in the autumn of 1910 when Judge William Walter Moffett, a trustee of Roanoke College, whose daughter was enrolled in the course, protested to Roanoke's president, John Alfred Morehead, against the use of the book on the ground that it cast ignoble reflections on southern manhood and on Virginia and the South in general.

Moffett's ire was aroused by Elson's references to the Civil War as a "slave-holder's rebellion," to slavery, and slavery alone, as the cause of the war, to Virginia secessionists as "conspirators," to John Brown as not a criminal in the "motives and intents of his heart," and, most of all, to Elson's description of the "widespread" practice by masters of taking attractive slave women as mistresses, with the result that, "according to the inflexible rule of the slave states," children born of such unions became slaves and were sometimes sold by their own fathers (Elson, pp. 558, 607, 625, 645).

When Moffett demanded that use of the Elson textbook be discontinued, Morehead defended Thorstenberg's right to use it but assured the judge that Thorstenberg would rebut Elson's alleged misrepresentations in the classroom and had no intention of teaching anything unfavorable to the South. Not at all assured, Moffett insisted that the book was "pregnant with falsehoods" and on every page gave "birth to calumny, passion and slanders of the vilest character," and that it not only was "unfit for a text book of history, but from a moral and decent standpoint" was also "unfit to be read by any girl or young man, or to enter the home of any gentleman."

Late in February 1911, Moffett took his case to the press. Several Virginia newspapers, particularly the Roanoke *Times*, gave full coverage to the controversy and supported Moffett. The trustees of Roanoke sought to resolve the matter on March 7 by passing resolutions aimed at compromise. Stating that they could be true to the traditions and ideals of the college only "by fearlessly standing for the right, without undue regard to popular disfavor, which is certainly to some extent based upon incomplete knowledge of the facts," they affirmed their complete confidence in Thorstenberg "both as a man and as an acceptable and valuable teacher." At Thorstenberg's suggestion, they also voted to discontinue use of the Elson text in light of the fact that Thorstenberg had declared that he did not consider it of vital importance to his course in any case. Only Moffett and one other trustee voted against these resolutions.

Interpreting the vote as a vindication of Thorstenberg, Moffett resigned from the board on March 10 and proceeded to rally Confederate veteran groups and chapters of the United Daughters of the Confederacy to his cause. College officials remained silent in the face of this assault until the printing on April 10 of resolutions adopted by the Roanoke Camp of Confederate Veterans attacking Morehead for allegedly having broken his promise that the Elson text would no longer be used. In Morehead's absence, the Roanoke faculty adopted a resolution which was published in the Roanoke *Times* on April 16. In it, they condemned the "serious imputation" against the president's character. Morehead, they said, was "a man whom we know to be incapable of any dishonorable act and whom we regard as much with affection as with respect." The president's views, they continued, "are precisely the views of every regular professor in the College, and if odium attaches to his course of action, we share it equally with him." They added that the agreement of March 7 to withdraw the text had been scrupulously adhered to, and that in any event Elson's alleged errors had never been defended by Thorstenberg or anyone else on the faculty. "We hold," they concluded, "that the mistakes of an historian can be met and nullified only by clear reasoning and by the dispassionate presentation of the facts," and that "our chief duty is not to resurrect the bitterness and animosities of the past but to train young men for present day duties and to a patriotism that embraces the whole country."

Morehead issued a formal statement on May 11 reviewing the entire affair and defining the principles involved and their relation to educational work in the South. "There cannot be loyalty to the truth in scholarly work," he said, "without freedom to investigate, to think, to review all phases of a subject—the truths, the half-truths, and the untruths about it—and to form and to express independent judgments. This is the principle of academic freedom." Passions soon cooled, and the tempest subsided.

Wilson probably sent his "cheering word" to the Roanoke faculty soon after the publication of that body's statement defending Morehead. His letter is not extant among the many records relating to the episode.

The foregoing note is based upon William Edward Eisenberg, *The First Hundred Years of Roanoke College, 1842-1942* (Salem, Va., 1942), pp. 259-89.

ADDENDA

To Elgin Ralston Lovell Gould

My dear Gould,   Princeton, New Jersey, 22 September, 1898.

I am sincerely sorry to have missed seeing you when you were here. I was away visiting a distant friend. I shall hope for better luck next time,—for of course you must be coming again.

The trouble about addressing the Nineteenth Century is not disinclination, nor even modesty now, but that the time fixed would mean for me seven lectures in one week. My classes are so big that my college lectures are virtually public addresses; and I have, besides them, two addresses away from home that week. I really cannot in justice to myself add another. I should make them all poor, and should wear myself out. I am very sorry; and I should really enjoy speaking to the audience the Nineteenth Century gets together; but it is really out of the question.[1]

With warm regard,

Faithfully Yours, Woodrow Wilson

WWTLS (WC, NjP).
[1] Wilson spoke to the Nineteenth Century Club in New York on November 15, 1899. See the news item printed at Nov. 16, 1899, Vol. 11.

Two Letters to Hiram Bingham[1]

My dear Sir: Princeton, N. J. March 15, 1905.

I take the liberty of addressing you very frankly about a matter which is at present engrossing our attention here, and by which we set great store for the future of the University.

We are purposing to set up here a tutorial system, based as nearly upon the Oxford model as American conditions and our own local circumstances permit. Would you be willing to consider an appointment as Tutor in History and Politics under our new arrangement? "Tutor" is not the title we shall use; I simply use the word for the present in the Oxford sense.

A letter hardly furnishes suitable opportunity for setting forth exactly what we mean to do, but if you are sufficiently interested, I will be very glad indeed to see you here in Princeton, or to make an arrangement to meet you in New York for a short conference.

I am expecting to be away from home until Monday, the 20th, but should be pleased to hear from you at that time. I hope most sincerely that the idea will commend itself to you.

Very sincerely yours, Woodrow Wilson

[1] See WW to W. M. Daniels, March 14 and 15, 1905, Vol. 16.

My dear Mr. Bingham: Princeton, N. J. March 21, 1905.

I am very much obliged for your kind letter of March 16th, to which I would have replied sooner, had I not been obliged to be several days away from home.

I am sorry that I am not to be in Princeton on the 25th, but I am to be in New York on other business, and I would be very pleased if you would lunch with me at the University Club, 5th Avenue and 54th Street, at 2 o'clock that day. If this should not be convenient for you, telegraph me on receipt of this letter, as I must presently be away from home again.

    In haste,   Sincerely yours,   Woodrow Wilson

TLS (H. Bingham Papers, CtY).

INDEX

NOTE ON THE INDEX

THE alphabetically arranged analytical table of contents at the front of the volume eliminates duplication, in both contents and index, of references to certain documents, such as letters. Letters are listed in the contents alphabetically by name, and chronologically within each name by page. The subject matter of all letters is, of course, indexed. The Editorial Notes and Wilson's writings are listed in the contents chronologically by page. In addition, the subject matter of both categories is indexed. The index covers all references to books and articles mentioned in text or notes. Footnotes are indexed. Page references to footnotes which place a comma between the page number and "n" cite both text and footnote, thus: "624,n3." On the other hand, absence of the comma indicates reference to the footnote only, thus: "55n2"–the page number denoting where the footnote appears. The letter "n" without a following digit signifies an unnumbered descriptive-location note.

An asterisk before an index reference designates identification or other particular information. Re-identification and repetitive annotation have been minimized to encourage use of these starred references. Where the identification appears in an earlier volume, it is indicated thus: "1:*212,n3." Therefore a page reference standing without a preceding volume number is invariably a reference to the present volume. The index supplies the fullest known forms of names, and, for the Wilson and Axson families, relationships as far down as cousins. Persons referred to in the text by nicknames or shortened forms of names can be identified by reference to entries for these forms of the names.

INDEX

A. *Mitchell Palmer: Politician* (Coben), 409n1,2
Abbett, Leon, 173,n2, 281n1
Abbett, Leon, Jr., 281n1
Abbott, Lyman, 184
academic freedom, 604n2
Ackerman, Ernest Robinson, 474, 588
Adams, Alva, 584,n2
Adams, Frank, 584,n1
Adams, William H., 584,n1
Addams, Jane, 157n1
Adler, Felix, 91,n5, 157n1
Alabama Educational Association, 55, 95
Alderman, Edwin Anderson, 140, 595, 596
Alexander, Caroline Bayard Stevens, 530,n3
Alexander, Henry Eckert, 231
Alexander, James Waddel (Princeton 1860), 30, 510
Allen, Charles Sterling, Mrs. (Anjenett Holcomb), 100, 142, 295, 331, 334, 454, 501, 511, 520, 547, 572
Allen, Ethan, 39,n23
Allen, Lamson, M.D., 335,n1
Altland, Daniel Fickes, 581,n2
Alyea, Garrabrant R., 87n2
Amen Corner, 453, 453n1
American Academy of Arts and Letters, 27, 49
American Economic Association, 262
American Historical Association, 27, 49
American Insurance Union, 229,n2
American Magazine, 412n1
American Mail: Enlarger of the Common Life (Fuller), 427n1
American Political Science Association, 210,n4, 260, 262, 263
American Political Science Review, 272n
American Prison Association, 207
American Red Cross, 416
American Revolution, 474, 476
Amerika, S.S., 274, 393
Ames, James Barr (1846-1910), 213
Anderson, Donald F., 427n1
Anthracite coal strike of 1902, 215n1
Anti-Saloon League, 327n1
Anti-Saloon League of New Jersey, 599n1
arbitration treaties, 514, 514n1, 515
Arizona, 423, 433, 436, 438; state constitution, 291,n2, 592
Arizona, the History of a Frontier State (Wyllys), 291n2
Arizona Statehood League, 291n2
Arizona Territory, 1863-1912 . . . (Wagoner), 291n2
Asbury Park, N.J., 50n3
Associated Press, 197, 335

Association of American Universities, 35, 81,n11
Astor Hotel, New York City, 250n2, 410, 585, 588, 601
Atlanta, 206, 480; Atlanta Auditorium, 491n1; Capital City Club, 488; Piedmont Hotel, 489; WW in, 487-98, 500, 502, 507; Young Men's Democratic League, 488
Atlanta Journal, 491n, 506,n1,2
Atlantic City, N.J., 49, 300, 309, 384
Atlantic County, N.J., 300n4, 309
Atlantic Review (Atlantic City), 309, 309n1
Augusta (Ga.) *Herald*, 573, 573n1,2
Austin, Frank Rose, 375,n1
Axson, Stockton (*full name*: Isaac Stockton Keith Axson II), brother of EAW, 2:*386n1; 142n1, 186, 187, 234

Backus, Harry F., 253,n4, 481,n3
Bacon, Charles Reade, 50n2, 215,n1,2
Baer, George Frederick, 215-16,n1
Bagehot, Walter, 194,n4
Bailey, Joseph Weldon, 466,n2,3, 467
Bailey, Warren Worth, 409n1, 522,n1, 523
Baird, David, 250,n1, 300, 311n1
Baker, Curtis T., 516,n2
Baker, Ray Stannard, 142n1, 412n1,2
Baldwin, Simeon Eben, 15, 283, 453
Balentine, Edward D., 241, 242n2, 253, 281, 339
Ball, Alwyn III, 323
Ballinger-Pinchot controversy, 427n1
ballot reform, 351, 358
Baltimore, 139, 201; Civil Service League, 158; Woodrow Wilson Democratic Association, 523-24
Baltimore Sun, 158, 175
Barnes, William, 429
Bartlett, H. C., 173n1
Bathgate, James Edward, Jr., 72,n2
Battle Creek (Mich.) *Enquirer*, 238,n2
Battle Creek (Mich.) *Evening News*, 238n3
Battle Creek (Mich.) *Journal*, 238n
Beast (Lindsey and O'Higgins), 275,-n2, 388, 538
Beckwith, John F. B., 384,n7
Beechwood, Scarborough-on-Hudson, N.Y., 187n2, 234
Beggs, John Irvin, 57,n2
Bell, Theodore Arlington, 32n2
Bellevue-Stratford Hotel, Philadelphia, 148, 441,n1, 487n2
Belmont, August, 160
Belmont Hotel, New York City, 334
Bennett, James Gordon (1841-1918), 393,n1,2

Benny, Allan, 395,n1
Berea College, 48-49,n2, 172, 214, 417-21, 425
Berea Quarterly, 421n
Bergen County, N.J., 86, 87, 87n1,2, 124
Berlin, 604
Bermuda, 14, 100, 139, 141, 142, 204, 205, 209, 292, 294-95, 323-25, 329-30, 331-32, 396, 407-8, 440, 454, 500, 511, 517, 520, 533-34, 548, 569, 572; Girls High School, 331; Glencove, 141, 142, 204, 210, 407; Government House, 408; Hamilton, 331; Inwood, 210,n3, 330n1; Paget, 407; Salt Kettle Ferry, 141, 205, 364, 407, 454; Shoreby, 210,n3, 407
Bermudian, S.S., 407
Berry, William H., 409n2
Beveridge, Albert Jeremiah, 12,n4
Big Business, 540
Bingham, Hiram, 606-7,n1
Bipartizan Direct Primary League, 225
Birch, Thomas Howard, 231,n1, 307, 501, 502, 535n1, 536, 544, 545; Mrs. (Helen Barr), 544, 545
Birmingham, Ala., 206, 226
Bitter Cry of the Children (Spargo), 452n2
Black, Charles Clarke, 169,n1
blacklists, 291n2
Boardman, Mabel Thorp, 140,n3
Boettner, Frank A., 241, 242n2, 253, 281, 339
Bok, Edward William, 21
Bolterill, Samuel, 546n5
Bonbright, William Prescott, 202,n2
Booraem, John Van Liew, 328,n3
bosses, 26, 312, 326, 448, 586, 593, 594, 602
Bourne, Jonathan, Jr., 34-35,n1, 36, 248, 334
Bowdoin College, 165n1
Bracken, John Joseph, 223,n1, 253,n4
Bracken, John Joseph, Jr., 231n
Bradford, Gamaliel (1831-1911), 3:-*22,n1; 138,n6
Bradford, Gamaliel (1863-1932), 138-n6; Mrs. (Helen Hubbard Ford), 138n6
Bradley, William James Lee, 550n2
Breckinridge, Henry Skillman, 213-14, 236-37, 412, 523-24, 525-26
bribery, 359
Brice, Calvin Stewart, 113n2
Bridges, Robert, 1:*284,n1; 12, 287-88,n2, 332, 333, 361, 411-12
Briggs, Frank Obadiah, 226
Brodhead, Calvin Easton, 22,n1, 198, 199, 206, 232-33, 238, 243-44, 294, 308, 309
Brodhead, William M., 199n, 238n, 308n
Brooklyn Daily Eagle, 134,n1, 170,n1, 226,n4

Brooks, John Graham, 157n1
Brougham, Herbert Bruce, 581,n1
Brown, Charles W., 241, 253
Brown, John (1800-1859), 604n2
Brown, Oren Britt, 361-62,n1
Bruce, Philip Alexander, 254,n1; Mrs. (Elizabeth Tunstall Taylor Newton), 254,n4
Bruce, William Cabell, 384,n5
Bryan, Charles Wayland, 519n4
Bryan, Thomas Smith, 576-77,n1
Bryan, William Jennings, 115, 161, 217, 220, 221, 224-25, 231,n1, 255,n1, 284, 285, 285n3, 291n2, 307, 334, 409, 409n1, 435, 465-66n3, 466, 466-n4, 501, 502, 502-3, 519n4, 522, 535, 535n1, 536, 540, 541, 543-44, 545, 553,n1, 553, 554, 557,n4, 571, 587; WW on, 501
Bryan, William Swan Plumer, 327,n2
Bryce, James, Viscount Bryce, 33, 184, 211, 396n1, 483; Lady Bryce (Elizabeth Marion Ashton), 211,n2
Bulkeley, Frances Hazen, 37n
Bunnell, Jacob L., 378,n1
Burgan, J. A., 173n1
Burke, Eugene S., 253,n2
Burleson, Albert Sidney, 207,n5
Burlington, N.J., 307, 502, 544, 545; Auditorium, 535n1
Burlington County, N.J., 535
Burlington County Democratic Club, 535n1
Burnett, Curtis R., 367,n1
Burr, Aaron (1756-1836), vice-president of the U.S., 218
business, 64f, 74-76, 106f, 178-81, 196, 222, 268f, 315, 389, 391, 397-98, 470, 585-86
Butler, Nicholas Murray, 209
Byrd, Richard Evelyn, 20,n1

Cadwalader, John Lambert, 17, 436
Cady, Josiah Cleveland, 417n1, 424
Caldwell (Essex Fells), N.J., 413
Calhoun, John Caldwell, 40n25
Calhoun, Patrick, 39-40,n25
California, 318, 519, 524
California Progressives (Mowry), 32n
Cambridge, Mass., 138,n3
Camden, N.J., 300; Americus Club, 514,n3,4
Camden County, N.J., 50
Camden Courier, 249-50,n1
Campbell, John Alexander, 379, 380
Campbell, Thomas Mitchell, 123,n2, 422,n2
Canada: Conservative party, 478n3; Liberal party, 478n3; reciprocity with, 478n3, 486, 592, 601
cancer, 11
Cannon, Frank Jenne, 584
Cannon, Joseph Gurney, 226,n1
Cape May, N.J., 369

Cape May County, N.J., 203,n1, 516, 521
capital, 12
Carlyle, Thomas, 62
Carnegie, Andrew, 23, 514-15, 514n4, 515
Carnegie Endowment for International Peace, 514n1
Carnegie Foundation for the Advancement of Teaching, 23,n3, 24,n1, 53, 130-32,n2, 365-66
Carnegie Hall, New York City, 140, 412n2, 417n1, 514, 514n4, 515
Carrow, Howard, 25,n1
Cassatt, Alexander Johnston, 114, 115
Catchings, Thomas Clendinen, 226,n3
Central Railroad Co. of New Jersey, 215n1
Cerberus, 303,n5
Chamberlain, Alexander Francis, 379,-n1
Chamberlain, George Earle, 174-75,n1, 248
Chamberlains, 210
Chandler, Arthur Dickinson, 39,n7
Chapel Hill, N.C., 406, 499, 507, 509, 517, 520
Chaplin, Maxwell, 323
Charlottesville, Va.: Monticello, 558
Chautauqua, 327n1
Chesterton, Gilbert Keith, 442,n4
Chicago, 154, 533; Business Service Lecture League, 74; University Club, 71; WW in, 178-81, 210, 223; Young Men's Christian Association Hall, 74,n1
Chicago Evening Post, 388,n1
Chicago Tribune, 76n, 181n
Chicora College, 577n4
child labor, 11, 12,n4, 144, 152, 156-57, 157n1,3, 206-8, 291n2, 452n2
children, 594, 596
Childs, Richard Spencer, 197n2, 257-58
Childs, Starling Winston, 202,n2
Cincinnati Enquirer, 255n1
Civic Victories: The Story of an Unfinished Revolution (Childs), 197n2
civil service reform, 78-79
Civil War, 444, 445, 604n2
Clark, Champ [James Beauchamp], 198,n2, 285n2, 478n3, 479, 486, 487, 544
Clark, J. William, 546n5
Clark, William Andrews, 278,n2
Cleveland, Grover, 11-12,n3, 39n21, 113n2, 218, 221, 226,n3,5, 416, 489, 514
Cleveland, James Harlan, 362,n2
Clinton, N.J. library, 480
Coben, Stanley, 409n1,2
Cochran, Peyton, 96, 118
Cohalan, Daniel Florence, 602
Colby, Everett, 225n3, 366n2
cold-storage warehouses, 227-28, 260, 352-53, 438, 579n5, 591

Cole, Clarence Lee, 309, 413,n1
Collected Works of Walter Bagehot (ed. St. John-Stevas), 194n4
College for Women, Columbia, S.C., 577n4,5,6
Collier's Weekly, 73,n3, 181n1, 427n1
Collingwood Hotel, New York City, 87, 141, 230
Colorado, 388,n1, 405, 519, 537
Colquitt, Oscar Branch, 423,n4
Columbia, S.C.: Central National Bank, 507; Y.M.C.A., 576-77, 577n6
Columbia (S.C.) State, 507n1
Columbia (S.C.) Theological Seminary, 21n3
Columbia University, 172n1
Colvin, Fred H., Mrs. (Mary Loring), 289-90,n1
commission form of government for cities, 197n2, 551,n3, 574-75, 581, 591
Commoner (Lincoln, Neb.), 231,n3, 255n1, 285n2, 503, 503,n3
Congressional Record, 35n2
Conklin, Edwin Grant, 436
Conkling, Cook, 394-95,n1
Connecticut, 15
Connor, Henry Groves, 383,n1
conservation, 111-12, 205n2, 350, 371-n4, 371-72, 566-67, 594
constitutions, 102-3
Consumers' League of New Jersey, 157, 157n1
Cook, James E. W., 356,n1
Cornell University, 359
Cornish, Jonathan, 588,n1
corporations, 8, 18, 19, 63, 69-70, 75-76, 106, 107, 110, 114, 115, 121-22, 132-33, 185, 217, 219, 220, 221, 222, 223, 312-15, 346, 346-47, 347-49, 398, 485-86, 563, 586, 593
corrupt practices, 175, 255n2, 357n4, 358, 383n3, 455
corruption, 360
Cosgrove, John T., 546n5
Cothran, Perrin Chiles, 234,n1; Mrs. (Annie Wilson Howe), 234,n1, 293, 517n4
Coulomb, Harry R., 310,n2,3
Coxe, George S., 39,n14
Craiger, Sherman Montrose, 428-29
Cram, Ralph Adams, 375
Creelman, James, 216
Crimmins, John Daniel, 40,n28
Crisis (New York), 50n3
Croker, Richard, 167n1, 312
Cumberland County, N.J., 531, 532
Cupid, 218
Current History, 519n4
Cushing, George W. B., Mrs. (Juliet Clannon), 156-57,n1

Dabney, Richard Heath, 1:*685,n1; 13
Dallas, Tex., 576
Daly, Peter Francis, 294n2

Daniels, Josephus, 121, 406-7; Mrs. (Addie Worth Bagley), 121,n2, 406
Daniels, Winthrop More, 7:*205,n3; 25
David Harum: A Story of American Life (Westcott), 331,n5
Davidson, John, 573,n1
Davidson, Randall Thomas, 514,n2
Davidson College, 327
Davis, John David (Princeton 1872), 262
Davis, Robert, 26-27,n1, 73,n, 81, 81-n1,2, 86n1, 87n2, 98n1, 118-19n1, 128, 133, 200, 201, 223-24, 245,n1,2
Deal, N.J., 181n1
Dear, Joseph Albert, Jr., 98, 200, 357
Dear, Walter, 357
Declaration of Independence, 540, 560
deForest, Robert Weeks, 157n1
DeLong, George Washington, 393n2
democracy, 386, 420, 489, 604
Democratic party and Democrats, 3,n2, 6, 16, 17-18, 31, 32, 34, 44n3, 54, 61, 85, 94, 120, 125, 138, 167, 175, 181, 181n1, 189, 204, 207, 208, 213, 214, 215, 216, 217, 218, 219, 220, 221, 222, 223, 226, 229, 237, 250, 251, 255, 274-75, 277, 284-85, 291n2, 372, 376, 388, 409n1,2,3, 412n2, 423, 428-29, 441n3, 444, 465, 476, 478n3, 479, 480, 487, 488, 489, 491, 502, 534, 545, 554, 556, 557, 558, 559, 560, 561, 565, 567, 568, 569, 570, 573n2,5, 578, 584, 586, 587, 588, 591-92, 592, 594, 595, 601
Democratic party and Democrats in California, 31-32
Democratic party and Democrats in Colorado, 599
Democratic party and Democrats in Connecticut, 15
Democratic party and Democrats in Maryland, 158
Democratic party and Democrats in New Jersey, 10, 15, 16, 22, 25, 27, 29, 41-42, 47-48, 49, 52, 72, 77, 81n1,2, 86, 86n1, 86-87, 113n1,2, 114-16, 124, 125-26, 128-29, 136n1, 136, 137n3, 142n1, 153, 155-56, 163, 170n1, 173, 173n1, 181n1, 199, 205n2, 206, 217, 221, 230, 236, 239, 240, 242n2, 245n2, 248-49, 250, 251, 253, 257, 278, 278n1, 281, 283, 284, 285, 294, 296-307, 308, 310, 321-22, 334, 337, 339, 340, 365, 366, 367, 378, 415n1, 455, 458, 460, 463, 466n4, 474, 475, 477, 481-82, 483, 505, 505n1, 512, 513n2, 517, 518, 532, 535, 536, 537n4, 545, 550n2, 561,n5, 582, 588, 589, 602
Democratic party and Democrats in New York, 161, 161n1
Democratic party and Democrats in Ohio, 161, 161n1
Democratic party and Democrats in Pennsylvania, 408-9,n1,2,3, 522, 523
Democratic party and Democrats in Texas, 123, 409-10
Democratic party and Democrats in Virginia, 254,n2,3
Democratic Politics and the Presidential Campaign of 1912 in Tennessee (Link), 95,n1
Demosthenes, 451
Dennis, Samuel Shepard, 23,n1; Mrs. (Eliza Thomas), 23,n2
Denver, 276n1,2, 519, 521, 525, 533, 537, 584-85, 599; Chamber of Commerce, 527; Mile-High Club, 523, 527; Presbyterian Church, 577
Denver Express, 584
Denver platform, 307, 465
Depew, Chauncey Mitchell, 429
Des Moines, 533
Detroit Times, 229
Devine, Edward Thomas, 157n1
Devlin, Martin Patrick, 128-29
Dewey, Davis Rich, 139
Dickinson, Jacob McGavock, 478,n2, 500
Dickson, William, 546n5
Diefenthaler, John V., 242n2
Dillard, James Hardy, 140,n4
Dillow, Thomas H., 163-64
Dinsmore, Thomas H., 389,n2
Direct Legislation League, 247,n1
direct primary, 175, 197, 255n2, 335, 351, 371n4, 400,n2
Direct Primary League, 225n1
Dix, John Alden, 45,n2, 161n1, 250n2, 285n2, 287, 289, 338, 338n3, 359, 359n2, 361, 407n2, 421, 453
Dixon, John, 380
Dixon, Thomas, Jr., 4:*258,n1; 96,n1
Dodge, Cleveland Hoadley, 1:*210,n3; 29, 72-73,n3, 94, 232, 237-38, 377, 382, 412, 436-37, 438
Dodge, William Earl (1832-1903), 184
Donges, Ralph Waldo Emerson, 120-21
Donnelly, Frederick William, 455,n1
Donnelly, Thomas M., 136n1
Doubleday Page & Co., 433,n1
Dougherty, Hugh, 554,n1
Dreher, Julius Daniel, 604,n1
Dryden, John Fairfield, 416
Duffield, Henry Green, 165, 176, 186-87
Duke University, 489,n4
Dulin, Al, 229,n3
Duneka, Frederick A., 21,n1
Durham, N.C., National Religious Training School for the Colored People, 98-99
Dwight, Maitland, 150, 152, 323, 430, 430n1

East, Charles MaCaulay, 97
East Tennessee Historical Society's Publications, 95,n1
Eastwood, John Henry, 129-30,n1
Eaton, Frederick Heber, 39,n12
Economist (London), 209

Ecumenical Bearings of the Missionary Movement and the International Missionary Council (Latourette), 385n2

ecumenical movement, 385n2

Edge, Walter Evans, 481, 546n5, 588,n1

Edinburgh: World Missionary Conference, 1910, 385,n2

Eells, Stillman Witt, 331,n1

Egan, Charles Michael, 100, 133-34,n1, 481, 482,n4

eight-hour day, 291n2

Eisenberg, William Edward, 604n2

Eisenhart, Luther Pfahler, 436

Elder, William Simpson, 17-18,n1

Election of 1896, 307

election reform, 383n3, 430-32

electric chair, 238n1

Elgin-Marcy Reciprocity Treaty of 1854, 478n3

Eliot, Charles William, 78,n1, 78-79

Elizabeth I, 190-91, 196

Elizabeth (N.J.) Evening Times, 77n1, 117n1, 137,n1,3

Elliott, Orrin Leslie, 131n3

Ellis, Leroy J., 22,n2, 116-17, 244,n1

Ellis, Lewis Ethan, 478n3

Elson, Henry William, 604n2

Ely, Matthias C., 81n1, 85-86,n1, 98, 200, 201, 357

employers' liability, 291n2, 335, 357n4, 383n3, 455, 462f

engineering, 411

England, 604

Erdman, Charles Rosenbury, 466,n1, 503n2; Mrs. (Estelle Pardee), 503n2

Essex County, N.J., 117, 156, 164, 200, 201, 205n2, 212n1, 225n1, 232, 239, 239n1, 240, 241, 242n2, 245, 253, 281, 285, 286, 297, 335, 336, 340, 343, 378, 537n4; Direct Primary League, 245; Essex Eleven, 164

Essex Fells (Caldwell), N.J., 413

Everett, Wash., 395

Ewing, Joseph Neff, 323

experts, 359-60

Eypper, Charles Apffel, 344

Falconer, Robert Alexander, 45,n1

Farinholt, Benjamin L., 587,n1

Farrelly, Stephen, 602

federal regulation, 107

Feet of the Young Men (Kipling), 89,-n3

Feigl, George G., 376,n1

Fels, Joseph, 278-80,n1; Fels Fund, 258n1, 278n1

Ferguson, William T., 28

Fergusson, Harvey Butler, 563,n6

Fielder, James Fairman, 134, 157, 357

Fine, Henry Burchard, 7:*223,n3; 430, 436, 528,n2

Finlay, William Wilson, 140

Finney, John Miller Turpin, M.D., 158

First Hundred Years of Roanoke College, 1842-1942 (Eisenberg), 604n2

Fitzgerald, John Joseph, 16,n1, 207n6

Fitzhugh, Robert Hunter, 16:*336,n1; 587n1

Flanzman, David, 200

Flint v. Stone Tracy Co., 511n2

Florida tornado, 274

Folk, Joseph Wingate, 198,n2, 255n1, 275

football, 4-5

Ford, Cornelius, 546n5

Ford, Henry Jones, 11:*262,n2; 84-85, 399,n1

Fordyce, Alexander Robert, Jr., 225,n2

Fort, Franklin William, 27,n1

Fort, John Franklin, 27n1, 53-54, 294-n1, 402n3, 546n5; Mrs. (Charlotte Stainsby), 54,n5

Foss, Eugene Noble, 38, 74n2, 285n2, 335, 453

Foss, George Edmund, 74,n2

Foster, Solomon, 183,n1, 260

Fox, Austen George, 94

Fox, John, 167-68,n1

France, 514n4, 558

Francis, David Rowland, 198,n2

Frankfort, Ky., 102, 113, 126, 127, 132, 135n1, 135, 138n1

Franklin, Fabian, 32,n2

Franklin D. Roosevelt: The Apprenticeship (Friedel), 161n1

Fraser, Abel McIver, 96,n2, 118

freedom of the will, 530

Freehold, N.J., 50n3

Frelinghuysen, Joseph Sherman, 474,-n1, 532, 550n2

Friedel, Frank, 161n1

Frissell, Hollis Burke, 140,n1

frontier, U.S., 420

Frost, William Goodell, 48-49, 172, 214-15, 417,n1, 419, 421, 424, 425, 440-41

Fuller, Wayne Edison, 427n1

Gallagher, Charles Henry, 133

Gardiner, James L., 386

Garfield, Harry Augustus, 14:*486-87,n1; 14, 30-31

Garrett, Robert, 11:*113,n2; 84

Garrison, Harry J., 532,n4

Garrison, Lindley Miller, 40,n31, 210,-n1; Mrs. (Margaret Hildeburn), 210,n1

Gaskill, Nelson Burr, 546n5

Gaunt, George Washington French, 474,n1

Gaynor, William Jay, 255n1

Gebhardt, William Cavanagh, 101, 162, 257, 321, 357, 546n5

General Electric Co., 411n1

George, Henry, Jr. (1862-1916), 229,-n4

Georgia, 543

Geran, Elmer Hendrickson, 18-19,n1, 100-1, 280-81, 309, 430, 470, 482, 505, 569n1
German-American Alliance, 258
Germany, 514n4, 604
Gettysburg, Battle of, 302
Gladstone, William Ewart, 218
Glasgow, Joseph Anderson, 96,n2
Glazebrook, Otis Allan, 126,n3, 136
Glen Ridge, N.J., 242n2
Glenn, Robert Brodnax, 327,n1
Gloucester County, N.J., 164, 233, 321
Glynn, Martin Henry, 400n2
Goldmark, Josephine Clara, 157n1
Gollan, Henry Cowper, 14, 511,n1,2; Mrs. (Marie Louise Norris), 14,n1, 500,n3, 511n1,2
Goltra, Edward Field, 97, 197-98, 199
Gonzales, William Elliott, 507-8,n1
Goodwin, Elliot Hersey, 78, 256,n1
Gore, Thomas Pryor, 387,n1, 441, 441-n3, 442
Gorman, Arthur Pue, 113n2, 282
Gould, Elgin Ralston Lovell, 5:*41,n1; 606
Gould, Lewis L., 123n3
Governor Hughes and the Albany Gang (Hendrick), 85n2
governors, 108f
Governors' Conference, Frankfort and Louisville, Ky., Nov.-Dec. 1910, 54,-n4, 94, 95, 102-13, 126-27, 131, 132, 133, 133n1, 134, 134n1, 135, 138,-n1,4, 139, 141, 210; Proceedings of Third Meeting, 113n
Granges, 255
Gray, George R., 54
Gray, James Richard, 506-7,n1
Great Britain, 514, 514n4
Green, John Richard, 190
Green, Kate or Katheryne, 364,n1
Greer, David Hummell, 514,n3
Greet, Sir Philip Barling Ben, 36
Gregory, Julian Arthur, 225,n1, 245
Griffin, Thomas, 100, 280
Griffin, Thomas F. A., 574,n2,3, 575
Griggs, John W., 250,n2, 338
Grim, Webster, 409n2
Groesbeck, Ernest, 202-3,n3
Grosscup, Edward E., 321-22
Growth of American Foreign Policy: A History (Leopold), 514n1
Grubb, Edward Burd, 231,n2, 545,n3,4; Mrs. I (Elizabeth Wadsworth Van Rensselaer), 545,n4; Mrs. II (Violet Sopwith), 545-46,n3
Guffey, James McClurg, 409n1,2, 522, 522n1
Guigon, Alexander Barclay, 383-84,n1
Gurley, Boyd F., 584
Guthrie, George Wilkins, 409n1, 441n3, 443
Guttenberg, N.J., 344

Hadley, Arthur Twining, 130, 184, 187

Hale, William Bayard, 142n1, *414,n1, 414, 434, 438-39, 526
Hale, William Harlan, 414n, 526
Hamill, James Alphonsus, 72,n1
Hamilton, Alexander, 444-45
Hamilton, Lord Frederick Spencer, 392,n1
Hammond, John Hays, 478,n2
Hampton Normal and Agricultural Institute, 140
Hand, Robert, 476
Hanley, Edward W., 161n1
Hanson, Charles A., 61,n3
Hapgood, Norman, 131n4
Hardin, John Ralph, 37, 86n1
Harlan, John Maynard, 8:*179,n3; 74,n2
Harmon, Judson, 7, 15, 43, 133n1, 213-14,n3, 230, 255n1, 275, 285n2, 437,n2, 466, 466n3, 503, 503n3
Harper, Henry Sleeper, 39,n8
Harper, Joseph Henry, 38,n4
Harper & Brothers, 21n1, 38-39,n4,6,-7,8, 46,n1, 48
Harper's Weekly, 38,n3,5, 39,n9, 439
Harriman, Jefferson Borden, Mrs. (Florence Jaffray Hurst), 324,n3
Harrisburg: Central Democratic Club, 408, 409n3
Harrison, Charles Custis, 130,n1
Harrison, N.J.: West Hudson Board of Trade, 456
Harrity, William Francis, 487,n1
Hartzog, Henry Simms, 478,n2
Harvard Lampoon, 38n5
Harvard University: Law School, 213
Harvey, D., Jr., 173n1
Harvey, Dorothy, 39,n11, 46
Harvey, George Brinton McClellan, 11:*369,n2; 13, 38-41, 46-48, 72, 73,n3, 86n1, 143, 160, 181n1, 185, 214, 227-28, 237, 260, 274, 326-27, 393, 435, 435n1, 466, 466n3,4, 467,-n1, 479, 516, 532, 532n6, 543, 571; Mrs. (Alma Parker), 39,n10, 46, 260
Haussling, Jacob, 242n2
Hazen, Azel Washburn, 37
Hebrews, 317, 320
Heflin, James Thomas, 28,n1
Helping to Make a President (Inglis), 181n1
Hemphill, Charles Robert, 21,n1; Mrs. (Emma Muller), 21,n2
Henderson, Robert Randolph, 1:*270,-n1; 55
Hendrick, Burton Jesse, 81n1, 85, 85,-n4, 142n1, 504n1
Heney, Francis Joseph, 412n2
Hennessy, Charles O'Connor, 124,n1
Heyburn, Weldon Brinton, 368,n2, 371,n4, 372
Hibben, John Grier, 9:*125,n1,2; 77, 259, 426; Mrs. (Jenny Davidson), 573
Higbee, Enoch A., 310,n4

Higginson, Henry Lee, 38
High Court of Parliament and Its Su-premacy (McIlwain), 165,n2
Hill, David Bennett, 113n2
Hillyer, George, 488,n2
Hinchliffe, John, 312,n2
Hinners, William Henry, 87n2
Hirst, Francis Wrigley, 209, 234
History of the Ecumenical Movement, 1517-1948 (Rouse and Neill, eds.), 385n2
History of the Presbyterian Church in South Carolina since 1850 (Jones and Mills, eds.), 577n4
History of the United States of America (Elson), 604n2
Hoboken, N.J.: Board of Trade, 468; German Club, 468n1
Hoboken *Observer* (afterwards *Hudson Observer*), 77n1, 81n1, 86, 96,n1, 113n2, 129, 360n, 415n2
Hodge, Samuel Colgate, 259,n1
Hodges, LeRoy, 498n
Hoff, Joseph Stanislaus, 415,n1,2
Hohenzollerns, 399
Holley, A. T., 173n1
Hollis, Daniel Walker, 577n4
Holt, Hamilton, 11:*348,n1; 32,n1
Holt, Henry Winston, 96,n2
Homer, 218
House, Edward Mandell, 466,n1,3, 467
How Woodrow Wilson Won His Nomi-nation (Stockbridge), 519n4
Howe, Annie Wilson (Mrs. Perrin Chiles Cothran), niece of WW, 234,-n1, 293, 517,n4
Howe, Frederic Clemson, 412n2
Howe, George, Jr., Mrs. (Annie Jose-phine Wilson), sister of WW; 1:-*3,n6; 293, 517,n4
Howe, George III, nephew of WW, 33-34, 517, 520; Mrs. (Margaret Smyth Flinn), 34,n1, 517n2
Hudson, Virginia Tyler, 354
Hudson County, N.J., 26, 73,n3, 81n1, 98n1, 100-1, 101,n1, 119, 120, 133, 134, 135,n1, 137, 145, 200, 201, 245-n2, 249, 258, 280, 304, 344, 352, 353, 367, 404
Hudson Observer (Hoboken), 77n1, 81n1, 86, 96,n1, 113n2, 129, 360n, 415n2
Hudspeth, Robert Stephen, 119, 321-22
Hughes, Charles Evans, 85, 85n2, 140, 184
Hughes, Charles James, Jr., 388n1, 584,n3
Hughes, Gerald, 584,n3
Hughes, William, 18, 161, 173n1
Hulbert, Allen Schoolcraft, 142, 295, 334, 454, 501, 511, 520, 547, 572
Hulbert, Mary Allen, *see* Peck, Mary Allen Hulbert
Humphreys, Alexander Crombie, 39,-n24

Hunt, George Wylie Paul, 291,n1,2
Hunterdon County Democrat (Flem-ington), 162, 164n1
Hyde, Harriet, 361,n1

Illinois, 279
Illinois Manufacturers' Association, 71,n2, 178-81, 210
In Many Moods (Williams), 52,n2
In the Days of McKinley (Leech), 371-n5
income tax, 94, 144, 326,n1, 409, 434, 465, 511-12,n1,2,3,4, 534-35,n2, 591
Independent (New York), 32,n3
Indiana, 570, 571
Indianapolis, 523, 533, 571; Murat Temple, 557n1; University Club, 554; WW in, 554-56
Indianapolis News, 52n1, 466n3, 525, 554n, 556n, 557n3, 568n
Ingersoll, Charles Henry, 499,n1
Inglis, William Otto, 39,n9, 73,n3, 181n1, 228,n2, 260
initiative and referendum, 175, 208, 246-47, 255n2,3, 258, 279, 280, 291-n2, 315, 355, 376, 448-49, 521, 578, 592, 594, 597
Institute of Musical Art, New York City, 91n5
institution defined, 103
Insurgent Club, 412,n2
Interchurch Federation, 259
Inter-Church Federation of New Jersey, 385
"interests," 75, 255n1, 258, 261, 275, 278, 297, 298, 299, 300, 302, 303, 337, 341, 342, 375, 388, 429, 468-69, 495, 513, 540; *see also* Wall Street
intermediate state, 368,n3
Interstate Commerce law, 313, 316
Iolanthe (Gilbert and Sullivan), 298
Iowa, 519
Irvine, William Mann, 22,n1; Mrs. (Camille Hart), 22,n2
Isham, William Burhans, Jr., 519

Jackson, Andrew, 18, 215, 318,n2, 559
Jacobus, Melancthon Williams (Prince-ton 1877), 12:*400,n2; 44, 436
Jagels, Claus Henry Carl, 468,n2
James, Peter H., 352n3, 481,n3
Jamestown Exposition, 1907, 593,n1
Jefferson, Matthew, 516,n1, 521
Jefferson, Thomas, 18, 280, 530n6, 540, 545, 558-59, 570, 592
Jennings, Ryerson W., 284-85,n1,2
Jersey City, 98,n2, 118n1, 119, 229n1, 233, 286, 295, 508; Board of Trade, 359; Columbian Club, 400n1; Jersey City Club, 359; St. Patrick's Hall, 295-96,n1
Jersey Journal (Jersey City), 77,n1, 97, 211,n6, 245n2, 307n, 329n, 465n, 474n, 569n1

Jerseyman's Journal: Fifty Years of American Business and Politics (Edge), 546n5
Johns Hopkins University, 139, 523
Johnson, Hiram Warren, 32n2
Johnson, James A. Courvoisier, 87,-n1,2, 589,n2
Johnson, Robert Underwood, 98, 126-27, 406
Johnson, Tom Loftin, 161n1, 466n3, 557n4, 571
Johnson, William Mindred, 19-20,n1
Johnstown, Pa., 523
Johnstown Democrat, 522n1
Jones, Clarence Trimingham, 330n1
Jones, David Benton, 12:*288,n1,5; 71, 126, 223n1
Jones, Eugenius, Mrs. (Louise Lightbourn Trimingham), 330,n1
Jones, F. D., 577n4
Jones, Thomas Davies, 7:*614,n4; 48, 126, 154, 223,n2
Jones, William Atkinson, 282,n2
Jones, Winifred, 223,n1
Jordan, David Starr, 130-31,n3

Kane, Francis Fisher, 246-47, 409n1, 435, 441,n2, 486-87, 487n3
Kansas, 389-91
Kansas City, 519n4, 533
Kansas Society of New York, 389
Katzenbach, Frank Snowden, Jr., 47, 77n1, 415n2, 535n1, 540, 545
Kean, John, 113, 137n1, 153, 155, 199, 226, 240, 248, 250, 367
Kearny, N.J.: Disabled Soldiers' Home, 231n2
Keasbey, Lindley Miller, 422-23,n1, 433
Kelley, Florence, 157n1, 452,n3
Kelsey, Clarence Hill, 40,n26
Kelsey, Frederick Wallace, 146-47,n1
Kenny, Edward, 136n1, 357, 481,n1, 482
Kent, Charles William, 1:*588,n1; 326, 333
Kent, William, 31-32,n1
Kentucky: WW in, 210
Kentucky and Kentuckians, 421-22, 524
Kern, John Worth, 571n1; Mrs. (Araminta Cooper), 571,n1
Kerney, James, 86n1, 113n2, 142n1, 200, 201, 357, 357n2,4, 383n3, 503n2, 546n5
Kiefer, Daniel, 257-58,n1, 261, 576
Killgore, Anthony, 164,n1
Kinkead, Eugene Francis, 228,n1
Kipling, Rudyard, 89,n3
Kitchener, Sir Frederick Walter, 324,-n4, 331n2
Knox, Philander Chase, 478n3
Koelble, Alphonse G., 514n4
Kohn, August, 507
Kuehnle, Louis, 300,n4, 309, 310, 311-n1

labor, 12, 144, 163, 179, 221, 222, 255, 259, 291n2, 565
Laddey, Victor H. G., Mrs. (Clara Schlee), 289-90,n1
Laffan Press, 160
Lafferty, James, 233,n1
La Follette, Fola, 412n2
La Follette, Robert Marion, 18, 32, 234, 412n2, 461, 485; Mrs. (Belle Case), 412n2
La Monte, George Mason, 82-83, 174, 308-9, 481,n3
Lane, John J., 147,n1
Lankering, Adolph, 258
Lathrop, John E., 159,n1, 175, 237, 247-48, 255, 255n3, 292,n1, 404, 524; Mrs., 404
Latourette, Kenneth Scott, 385n2
Laurier, Sir Wilfrid, 478n3
law, 263f
Lawrence, R. V., 173n1
laws, uniformity of, 111
Laws of New Jersey, 157n3, 546n5, 550n2, 569n1, 575n5, 579,n3,4,5,6,7
leadership, 109f
Leavitt, Harry D., 53,n2, 574n1
Lee, Edward E., 31,n1
Lee, William Brewster, 14
Leech, Margaret, 371n5
Leigh, Frederick Tollington, 39,n6
Leland Stanford Jr. University, 130
Lentz, John Jacob, 228-29,n1
Leopold, Richard William, 514n1
Letters of Grover Cleveland (ed. Nevins), 226n3
Levey, Frederick H., 125-26,n1, 136
Lewis, Griffith Walker, 474,n1
Lewis, James Hamilton, 557,n2
Lewis, Vivian Murchison, 3, 9, 19, 27, 309
Libbey, William, 7:*176,n1; 415n2
liberals, 594, 596
liberty, 443-44
Life, 38n5
Liller, William C., 554
Linbarger, W., 173n1
Lincoln, Abraham, 4, 280, 419, 421, 429
Lincoln, Neb., 519n4, 587
Lind, John, 395,n2
Lind, Norman, 395,n4
Lindabury, Richard Vliet, 181n1, 225
Lindsay, Samuel McCune, 207n4
Lindsey, Benjamin Barr, 274-76,n1,2, 291n2, 387-88n1, 405, 525, 537, 584-85, 599
Link, Arthur Stanley, 95,n1, 123n2, 262n2, 282n1, 436n1, 447n5, 512n1, 575n2, 579n3,4
Lipper, Arthur, 39,n17
Lippincott, Job Herbert, 125
Littlehales, Thomas, 513,n1
Littleton, Martin Wiley, 192,n3
Lobb, Reginald Popham, 325,n6; Mrs. (Mary Beatrice Jackson), 325,n6

lobbying and lobbyists, 355, 541-42
Lobingier, Charles Sumner, 279,n4
local option, 599
Logue, William Augustin, 413,n3, 415
London, 604; Albert Hall, 514
Long Branch (N.J.) *Record*, 300
Los Angeles, 519n4, 533
Louisville, Ky., 102, 113, 138,n1
love, 528-29
Love, Thomas Bell, 25, 122-23, 224-25, 409-10, 422-23, 433, 434, 576, 583-84
Loveen, Michael, 253,n4
Lovejoy, Owen Reed, 157
Low, George Clark, 375,n2
Low, Seth, 172,n1, 214, 417n1, 424
Lowell, James Russell, 335
Lowell, Josephine Shaw, 157n1
Ludington, Arthur Crosby, 400n2
Lustgarten, William, 570,n1
Lyme, Conn., 534
Lyon, Adrian, 294,n1,2, 308

Mabie, Hamilton Wright, 172,n1
McAdoo, William Gibbs, 51, 188, 188,-n1
McAlpin, Charles Williston, 256, 293, 358; Mrs. (Sara Carter Pyle), 293,n1
McAlpin, David Hunter, M.D., 256,n1
McCarter, Thomas Nesbitt, 83-84,n1, 359
McClintock, Euphemia, 577,n5
McClure, Samuel Sidney, 85,n1
McClure's Magazine, 81n1, 85, 85n1,2, 142n1, 504n1
McCombs, William Frank, 518n3, 519-n4, 581
McCorkle, Walter Lee, 413-14,n1, 433, 518n3, 519n4
McCormick, Cyrus Hall, Jr. (1859-1936; Princeton 1879), 5: *767,n3; 29, 71, 388, 405-6, 436
McCormick, Vance Criswell, 408-9, 409n1
McCran, Thomas F., 575n2
McCutcheon, Samuel St. John, 550n2
McDermit, Frank M., 147,n2, 235-36,n1
McGovern, Francis Edward, 57, 61, 64
McGowan, Michael J., Jr., 253,n5,6, 367,n1
McGrath, James J., 136n1, 367,n2
machine politics, 593, 594, 602, 603
McIlwain, Charles Howard, 165-66,n1
McKelway, Alexander Jeffrey, 206-8,n1, 226
McKelway, St. Clair, 134-35, 170
McKinsey, Thomas, 238,n1,3
Macksey, William Pierce, 212,n1, 232, 241, 253, 330, 330n1
McLean, John Roll, 255n1
McPherson, James Rhoderic, 41,n3, 42
MacVeagh, Franklin, 396n1
MacVeagh, Isaac Wayne, 37, 39, 143-44, 205
Madison, James, 218, 532n6
Magie, William Francis, 1: *360,n6; 79

Magie, William Jay, 426,n4
Maine, 535, 556
Major, Elliott Woolfolk, 198,n2
Mallock, William Hurrell, 404,n1
Malone, Dudley Field, 45-46,n1
Manchurian relief, 416-17
Markley, Paul Hamilton, M.D., 356, 356n5
Marquand, Allan, Mrs. (Eleanor Cross), 426,n5
Marshall, F. A., 39,n16
Marshall, James William, 385,n1
Marshall, Thomas Riley, 554, 557, 571; Mrs. (Lois Kimsey), 571,n2
Martin, Edward Sandford, 38,n5
Martin, Lewis J., 378,n2
Martin, Thomas Francis, 136n1, 504n1
Martin, Thomas Staples, 282,n1,2
Martine, James Edgar, 36-37, 47, 52, 73,n3, 77n1, 81n1, 83, 86, 86n1, 87n2, 93-94, 100, 101, 113, 115-16, 124, 128, 133-34, 135, 136, 136n1, 137n3, 142n1, 145, 146, 147, 147n2, 153, 155, 160, 160n1, 162, 163, 164, 170n1, 173-74, 173-74n1, 175, 185, 198, 200, 205n2, 228, 230, 231,n3, 233, 235, 236, 238n1, 239, 240, 241, 242, 242n2, 243, 244n1, 245n2, 248, 251-52, 253, 263, 273, 278, 280, 281, 286n2, 303, 304,n6, 311, 311n1, 321, 330n1, 321, 330n1, 339, 340, 341, 344, 365, 365n1, 367, 378, 382, 387, 437, 524, 525, 535n1, 541, 544, 545-n2, 552
Martinique Hotel, New York City, 328-n1, 357, 357n4
Maryland, 16; Democratic banquet, 177
Massachusetts, 556
Massachusetts Institute of Technology, 139
Massey, John Edward, 338-39n4
Matthews, John Joseph, 357, 481,n3, 575n5
Maxwell, William Hunter, 214,n1, 290
Meldrim, Peter W., 543n2
Mercer County, N.J., 29
Mercersburg Academy, 22n1
merchant marine, 205n2, 371n4
Meyer, Charles Anthony, 253,n1, 378, 481,n3
Middlesex County, N.J., 145, 200, 201, 229n1, 294, 308
Milford, Pa., 144n3
Miller, Polk, 191,n2
Mills, Edward Kirkpatrick, 546n5
Mills, W. H., 577n4
Milwaukee, 55-71; City Club, 56, 57; Lecture Service League, 61; Press Club, 56; Schlitz Palm Garden, 56, 57; Schlitz Theater, 58, 61; University Club, 56
Milwaukee Journal, 56n, 61, 71n
Minneapolis, 519n4
Minnesota Railroad and Warehouse Commission, 122n2

Minnesota rate case, 122,n2, 313-14
Minton, Henry Collin, 311,n1
Mississippi, 16
Missouri, 519, 544
Mitchell, Samuel Chiles, 140
Moffett, William Walter, 604n2
monarchy in America, 541
money power concentration, 489,n3
Monmouth County, N.J., 200, 229n1, 309
Montana, 278
Monte Carlo, 393
Montgomery (Ala.) *Advertiser*, 96
Moody, John, 114-16,n1
Morehead, John Alfred, 604n2
Morehouse, Frederic Cook, 57,n1
Morgan, John Pierpont I, 39n21, 255n1
Morris, Roland Sletor, 285, 409n1, 435, 450
Morris County, N.J., 201, 229n1, 253
Morrow, William H., 550n2
Mott, John R., 159, 385n2
Mountjoy, Clifford Arnold, 384,n6
Mowry, George Edwin, 32n
Murfee, Hopson Owen, 55
Murphy, Charles Francis, 161n1, 602, 603
Murphy, Edgar Gardner, 157n1
Mutual Life Insurance Co., 39n12
Mylod, James P., 241, 242, 242n2, 253, 286,n2, 339

Narcissus, 218
Nashville (Tenn.) *Banner*, 376n1
Nast, Thomas, 59
Nation (London), 144n1
Nation (New York), 205
National Association for the Advancement of Colored People, 50n3
National Child Labor Committee, 157, 157n1, 206,n1,4, 226
National Civic Federation, 172n1
National Civil Service Association, 201
National Civil Service Reform League, 78-79, 256
National Conference of Charities and Corrections, 207
National Consumers' League, 157n1, 452,n1,3
National Democratic League of Clubs, 554, 557,n1
National Educational Association, 207
National Independent Democratic League, 428,n2
National Independent League of Colored Voters, 50
National Liberal Immigration League, 89,n4
Negroes, 31, 50, 50n3, 214, 290,n1
Neill, Stephen Charles, 385n2
Neville of Kensington, 143,n1
Nevins, Allan, 226n3
New Brunswick, N.J., 144
New Englands True Interest . . . (Stoughton), 89,n2

New Freedom (Wilson; ed. Hale), 414n1
New Jersey, 365f, 393, 466n4, 537, 538-39, 556, 562, 589, 602; Agricultural Experiment Station, 144,n2; Assembly, 232, 233, 239,n1, 240, 241, 242n2, 243, 253, 280, 301, 308, 352n3, 477, 481-82, 483, 504-5, 508, 518,n1, 534, 538, 539, 546n5, 569n1, 575, 575n2, 583, 591, Committee on Labor and Industries, 546n5, *Journal* . . . , 552n, Leavitt-Walsh bill, 575n5, *Minutes* . . . , 508n, 525n, 546n5, 548n, 575n2; automobile licenses law, 591; Board of Education, 550n2; Board of Equalization of Taxes, 322,n1; Board of Health (state), 579n5, boards of health (local), 510; Board of Pardons, 28; Board of Park Commissioners, 527; Board of Public Utility Commissioners, 579n4; Bureau of Roads, 144; city government reform, 549, 551-52; Civil Service Commission, 457, 569; cold storage warehouses, 227-28, 260, 352-53, 438, 579n5, 591; commission form of government for cities, 551,n3, 574-75, 581, 591; Constitution, 338, 504n1, 548; Corrupt Practices act, 481, 547,n6, 579,n3, 581; Court of Errors and Appeals, 54; determinate sentences for criminal offenses act, 579,n6; Edge Employers' Liability act, 481, 546n5, 579,n1; Egan Public Utility Ratemaking bill, 481; election law, 357n4, *see also* Geran Election Reform bill; election of 1910, 3-4; fire department employes, 508; Geran Election Reform bill and act, 430-32, 447n5, 455, 456-57f, 470-72, 481-82, 483-84, 484-85, 504, 504n1, 512, 513n2, 518,n1, 536-37, 537n4, 561,n5, 571, 579,n2, 581, 590, analysis, 569,n1; Governor's secretary, 328-29; indeterminate sentences, 591; inland waterway, 538-39, 591; Legislature, 155, 157, 162, 166-67, 171, 175, 182, 205n2, 206, 212, 226n1, 235, 240, 241, 242n2, 244, 249, 251, 252, 278, 279, 301, 303n5, 304, 311, 321, 328n1, 333, 339, 340, 343, 352, 353, 357n2, 365, 367, 382n1, 383n3, 396, 410, 430, 431, 432, 434, 436n1, 438, 454, 455, 459-60, 471, 476, 477, 481-82, 483, 484, 485, 504, 505, 508n2, 511, 531, 534, 547, 549, 550n2, 569, 571-72, 578-79, 581f, 583n4, 589, 590, 591, 597, 598, 602, 603, *Acts of the 135th Legislature*, 452,n4; *Laws* . . . , 157n3, 546n5, 550n2, 569n1, 575n5, 579n3,4,5,6,7; messenger boy bill, 452,n4; patronage, 262n2, 513, 513n2, 518; primaries, *see* Geran Election Reform bill

and act; public school reform, 549, 550n2, 579,n8, 581, 591; Public Service Commission, 11; Public Utilities act of 1911 and Public Utilities Commission, 447-48, 485, 547,n6, 579,n4, 581, 590; Public Utilities law (old), 84,n2, 349-50; railroads, 538-39; Road Commissioner, 415, 415,n1; Second Regiment, N.J.N.G., 230; Senate, 352n3, 474, 477, 482, 511n1,3, 531,n3, 534, 536, 538, 549, 550n2, 561,n5, 569n1, 574-75, 582, 583, 588-89, Committee on Corporations, 546n5, *Journal* . . . , 527n, 535n, 546n5, 552n4, *Report of Senate Committee to Investigate the Methods and Practices, Expenses and Disbursements of the Public Schools,* 549,n1,2; Simpson Corrupt Practices bill and act, 481, 547,n6, 579,n3, 581; State House, 230; State House Commission, 510; transportation, 538; Weights and Measures act, 579,n7, 591; Workingmen's Compensation act, 546, 579,n1, 581, 590

New Jersey Child Labor Committee, 156,n1,2, 157, 157n1

New Jersey Conference of Charities and Correction, 528; *Proceedings* . . . , 531n

New Jersey Consumers' League, 452

New Jersey Editorial Association, 455

New Jersey Federation of Labor, 546-n5

New Jersey Herald (Newton, N.J.), 378n1,2

New Jersey Society of Pennsylvania, 226n1

New Jersey State Bar Association, 50

New Jersey Tuberculosis Sanitarium, 356

New Jersey Woman Suffrage Association, 289-90

New Mexico, 563n6

New Nationalism, 9

New York American, 223n

New York City: Amen Corner, 453, 453n11; Astor Hotel, 250n2, 410, 585, 588, 601; Belmont Hotel, 334; Carnegie Hall, 140, 214, 412n2, 417n1, 514, 514n4, 515; Century Club, 209; Collingwood Hotel, 87, 141, 230; Free Synagogue, 585; German-American Citizens' League, 514n4; Henry Street Settlement, 207n4, 452n3; Insurgents' Club, 455; Kansas Society, 389, 392; Kentuckians of New York, 421; Martinique Hotel, 328n1, 357, 357n4; National Democratic Club, 167, 167n1, 208, 601; Nineteenth Century Club, 606; Plaza Hotel, 421, 425; Ritz-Carlton Hotel, 474, 477; Southern Society, 188-96, 202-3,n4, 210; Tammany Hall, 161-n1, 602; United Colored Democracy,

31; U.S. financial resources in, 603-4; University Club, 287,n1, 294, 333, 334, 391, 607; Waldorf-Astoria Hotel, 51, 274, 389, 392, 453n1; WW on, 489

New York *Evening Post,* 32, 83, 86,n1, 102n1, 181n1, 289, 308, 358n, 421n, 432n, 439

New York *Evening World,* 181n1, 235-36n

New York *Globe and Commercial Advertiser,* 356n

New York Herald, 41,n2, 50n3, 393

New York Southern Society, 51, 51,n1, 188-96; *Year Book for 1911-12,* 196n

New York state: Legislature, 602, 603; workmen's compensation act, 564,n7

New York Stock Exchange, 582

New York *Sun,* 160, 283n1,2, 311n1, 391n

New York Times, 24n1, 121, 122n1, 131n4, 168n, 186, 240, 243n, 261, 337-38,n1,2,3, 422n, 479, 514n4, 524, 524n1, 581n1, 604n; *New York Times Annual Financial Review,* 121-22, 186, 312, 313, 316n

New York Tribune, 77n1, 454

New York *World,* 10, 12n, 181n1, 421n, 454, 455, 546n5

Newark, N.J., 171, 199, 229n1, 242n2, 278n1, 280, 286, 333, 334, 343; Board of Trade, 373; Hebrew Benevolent and Orphan Asylum Society, 183,n2, 316,n1; D.L.&W.R.R. depot, 285; Jewish Community Council, 321n; Krueger's Auditorium, 285; New Auditorium, 285, 285n1, 335; Temple B'nai Jeshurun, 183, 316

Newark Advertiser, 300,n3

Newark Evening News, 4n, 73,n3, 77, 81n1,2, 87n2, 93n, 113n1, 133n1, 136n1, 142n, 167n, 180n, 181n1, 203n1, 205, 226n1, 230n, 234n1, 236n2, 242n2, 245, 250n2, 272, 274n, 284n, 344n, 357, 365, 371n4, 374n, 399n, 404n, 417, 432n, 465n, 474n, 513n, 514n2, 537n4, 542n, 543,n3, 546n5, 569n, 579n, 586n, 589n, 591n

Newark Evening Star, 300,n3

Newark *Morning Star,* 300,n3, 311,n1, 357, 357n1, 383,n2

Newark Sunday Call, 37n, 42n2

Newman, Harry Ellsworth, 145,n1

Newton, Richard Cole, M.D., 155-56,n1, 286

Nichols, Isaac T., 431,n1, 511n1, 531-32, 532, 571

Nike, 218

Nixon, Horace Franklin, 520,n2

Noel, Edmund Favor, 16,n1

Noonan, Joseph M., 133-34, 223-24, 245-46, 377

Norfolk, Va., 596, 597; Commission Form of Government League, 254n2;

Norfolk, Va. (*cont.*)
Democratic Club, 254,n2; Pewter Platter Club, 254,n5, 591,n1, 592, 593, 596, 597; Woodrow Wilson Club, 99; Woodrow Wilson Presidential Club, 254,n2
Norfolk Landmark, 591, 592n, 597n
Norfolk *Ledger-Dispatch*, 99n1, 254n2
Norfolk *Virginian-Pilot*, 594n
Norris, George Washington, 441, 441n3
North American Review, 467,n1, 479, 509, 532, 532n6
North Carolina, 327, 437, 499
North Carolina, University of, 20n1,2, 406, 517, 520
Nowrey, Joseph E., 413,n2
Noyes, LaVerne W., 180,n1
Nugent, James Richard, 49-50, 73,n3, 145, 171-72, 181n1, 201, 203, 203n1, 436,n1, 512-13, 513n2, 518, 548,n1, 575n2, 603
nullification, 68

Ocean County, N.J., 145
Oceana, S.S., 332
O'Gorman, James Aloysius, 16n1, 601, 602, 603
O'Higgins, Harvey Jerrold, 275n2
Ohio, 213, 214, 217, 229, 230, 255n1, 437, 524
Oklahoma, 247, 441, 442, 524n2
old age pensions, 143
Old Point Comfort, Va., 119
Optional Third Class law, 197,n2
Orange, N.J., 147
Oregon, 159, 175, 197, 247, 248n2, 255n2, 278, 334, 351, 352, 355, 357, 357n4, 433, 442, 458, 466, 521, 578
Orthodoxy (Chesterton), 442,n4
Osborn, William Church, 359,n2, 361
Osborne, Edmund Burke, 366,n1
Osborne, Harry Vliet, 157, 181, 181n1, 225, 229n1, 245, 285-86, 310-11, 312, 357
Outlook (New York), 172n1
Owen, Robert Latham, 208,n1, 247, 248, 524,n2, 526
Oxford University, 606

Page, Thomas Nelson, 30, 140, 377, 396n1
Page, Walter Hines, 413-14, 433-34, 439, 515, 518n3, 519n4, 520
Palmer, Alexander Mitchell, 26, 441n3
Palmerston, Henry John Temple, 3d Viscount, 360, 403
Panama Canal, 205n2
Parker, Alton Brooks, 285
Paterson Guardian, 77n1
patriotism, 493
Patten, Thomas Gedney, 39,n13
Patterson, Thomas MacDonald, 584, 599
Patton, Francis Landey, 3:*114,n3; 397,n2, 404, 425-26

Payne, George W., 531,n3
Payne-Aldrich Tariff Act of 1909, 478-n3, 511n2, 567
Pearson, Edward Clarence, 137,n3
Peck, Mary Allen Hulbert (Mrs. Thomas Harbach Hulbert; Mrs. Thomas Dowse Peck), 17:*29,n1; 100, 139, 141-42, 204-5, 209-11, 292-93, 294-95, 323-25, 329-30, 331-32, 333, 362-64, 382, 391, 396, 407-8, 424-27, 438, 453-54, 477, 500-1, 509-11, 517-20, 531-34, 543-47, 548, 570-72, 581-83, 583n1, 597-98
Peck, Thomas Dowse, 500,n1,4
Peel, Sir Robert, 194n4
Peirce, Mary Bisbing, 285,n4
Peirce, Thomas May, 285n3,4
Pennsylvania: Bryan Democratic League, 522
Pennsylvania Academy of Fine Arts, 329
Pennsylvania Railroad, 114, 154, 370, 377, 522, 523
Penrose, Boies, 409n2
People Awakened: The Story of Woodrow Wilson's First Campaign (Bacon), 50n2
People's Law . . . (Lobingier), 279,n4
People's Power League, 255n5
Periodical Publishers' Association, 51
Perkins, George Walbridge, 19, 72, 202
Perth Amboy, N.J., 294
Philadelphia, 215, 216; Baptist Temple, 486; Bellevue-Stratford Hotel, 148, 441,n1, 487n2; Democratic Club, 215,n2, 246-47, 435n1, 441, 450n, 451,n1; Peirce School, 285,n3,4; Princeton Club, 487,n2
Philadelphia and Reading Coal and Iron Co., 215n1
Philadelphia and Reading Railway Co., 215n1
Philadelphia *North American*, 43,n3, 149n, 231,n4
Philadelphia *Public Ledger*, 285n2
Philadelphia Record, 50n2, 367n
Philippines and Filipinos, 14
Phillips, Mark F., 253,n4, 367,n1
Phillipsburg, N.J.: Board of Trade, 590
Phinizy, Bowdre, 573,n1
Piedmont Hotel, Atlanta, 489
Pike County, Pa., 144
Pinchot, Amos Richards Eno, 383n, 412n2
Pinchot, Gifford, 32,n3, 144, 412n2
Pinchot, James Wallace, 144,n3
Pitney, Mahlon, 1:*360,n5; 28,n1
Plainfield, N.J., 22, 198-99, 238; Democratic Club, 117, 244n1
Platt, Dan Fellows, 86-87
Plaza Hotel, New York City, 421, 425
Plimpton, George Arthur, 209,n1
Poe, Clarence, 503n, 509n
Poe, Clarence Hamilton, 437,n1, 499, 503, 509

Political Education of Woodrow Wilson (Kerney), 86n1, 113n2, 142n1, 357-n2,4, 383n3, 503n2, 546n5

Political Predestination of Woodrow Wilson (Harvey), 467,n1, 479

politics, 264f, 398

Pollock *v.* Farmers' Loan & Trust Co., 535,n2

Pomerene, Atlee, 161n1

Poole's Index of Periodical Literature, 480

Populists, 220

Portland, Oregon, 519n4, 533

Post, George Adams, 484,n3, 485, 499

Post, Louis Freeland, 278n2

postal rates, 427

Pratt, Joseph Hyde, 517,n3, 520; Mrs. (Mary Dicus Bayley), 517,n3, 520

Presbyterian Church in the U.S. [southern], 577n4

Presbyterian Theological Seminary of Kentucky, 21n1

Present Crisis (Lowell), 335

Price, Jacob Cole, M.D., 325-26,n1, 378

primary reform, 357n4, 358, 383n3, 456f, 459f

Prince, John Dyneley, 476,n2

Princess (Tennyson), 71,n5

Princeton, N.J.: First Presbyterian Church, 234n1; Princeton Inn, 149, 329, 334, 358, 407, 501, 544, 600n1

Princeton Alumni Weekly, 79, 430n1, 487n3

Princeton Club of New York, 287,n1

Princeton Theological Seminary, 501, 544

Princeton University: Alexander Hall (9:*215,n5), 159, 501, 502, 528n1; Alligators (eating club), 28,n2; alumni, 17, 18n2; architecture, campus, 375; Catalogue, 358; Class of 1879, 28, 332n1, 519; Class of 1911, 149-52, 323, 430; Class of 1912, 323; Class of 1913, 323; Class of 1914, 323; Cleveland Memorial Tower, 416; Commencement, 1911, 430,n1; Committee on the Presidency, 436; curriculum reform, 487n3; *Daily Princetonian,* 5n, 152n, 160n, 323n, 332n1, 600-1; Faculty resolution on WW resignation, 79-81; Faculty Room, 425; Field Club, 4; football game with Yale, Nov. 12, 1910, 3-4,n1, WW talk to team, 4-5; Graduate College, 80, 487, 487n3; Graduate School, 80, 487n3; Mc-Cormick Professorship of Jurisprudence, 44,n1,2; Maryland Alumni Association, 158; Nassau Hall, 425,n1; Nassau Hall tigers, 332n1, 361; Philadelphian Society, 159-60; preceptorial system, 79-80, 150, 487n3, 606; presidency, 438; President's Report, 358; Princeton Alumni

Association of Western New York, 14; Prospect, 4, 6, 9, 44, 86n1, 136n1, 141, 216, 329, 334; Rocky Mountain Princeton Club, 375; St. Louis alumni, 262, 283; Stafford Little lectures, 11-12,n3; student parade following WW election, 3; Treasurer, 165; Trustees, 17, 18n2, 44, 186, 358; Curriculum Committee, 44,n2

Princeton University mentioned, 28, 29, 33, 36, 47, 52, 58, 118, 131, 151, 160, 165-66, 177, 209, 217, 375, 410, 436, 450, 525, 556, 557, 600-1, 606

Pritchett, Henry Smith, 23-24, 130-31,n4, 148, 283, 365-66, 548, 569-70, 572

progress, 91-92

Progressive Democrats of New York, 570, 570,n1

Progressive Farmer (Raleigh, N.C.), 437, 437n1

Progressive Republican League of New Jersey, 366,n2

Progressives, 387, 389, 390, 391

Progressives and Prohibitionists: Texas Democrats in the Wilson Era (Gould), 123n3

Progressivism in Ohio, 1897-1917 (Warner), 161n1

protection, *see* tariff

Providence, R.I., 390

Prudential Insurance Co. of America, 144

Public (Chicago), 278,n2

Public Service Corporation of New Jersey, 359, 462,n2

public service corporations, 110, 348-49, 448, 461, 469

public utilities, 310, 357n4, 455, 460f

Pulsifer, Frederick K., 117,n1

Purcell, William Edward, 226,n2

Pyne, Moses Taylor, 5:*132,n2; 17, 436,n2

radicalism, 449

Raleigh, N.C., 406

Raleigh *News and Observer,* 121,n1, 407,n2, 435, 499,n1, 509

Ramsay, William Ernest, M.D., 328,n2, 481,n3

Raphael, 218

rate-making, 84

recall, 175, 255n2, 291n2, 355, 412n2, 521, 592, 594

reciprocity with Canada, 478n3, 486, 592, 601

Reciprocity, 1911: A Study in Canadian-American Relations (Ellis), 478n3

Record, George Lawrence, 13, 77n1, 231,n3, 357n4, 357-58, 382-83n3, 546n5

Red Cross, 416

Reese, James Mitchell, M.D., 590

Reichner, Louis Irving, 450-51

Rentschler, Gordon Sohn, 214

representative government, 464, 595
Representative Government. Circular of the "Direct Legislation League" . . . , 247,n1
Republican party and Republicans, 7, 34, 61, 85, 164, 181, 207, 212, 214, 216, 217, 218, 219, 220, 221, 222, 225, 226, 274-75, 291n2, 334, 335, 372, 376, 378, 405, 423, 429, 442, 444, 445, 446, 465, 474, 475, 476, 478n3, 488, 491, 534, 536, 543, 556, 559, 565, 568, 573, 584n2, 587, 594, 595
Republican party and Republicans in California, 31-32, 32n
Republican party and Republicans in New Jersey, 22, 27, 47, 77n1, 125, 155-56, 164, 173, 204, 212, 216, 217, 219, 249, 250, 284, 294, 297, 298, 301, 308, 357-58, 366, 412,n2, 454, 455, 458, 460, 476, 513, 513n2, 517, 518, 531, 535, 537n4, 561, 569, 571, 582, 588, 589, 602; Board of Guardians, 249, 300; New Idea Progressive Republicans, 225n3, 297
Republican party and Republicans in Pennsylvania, 409n1,2
Review of Reviews (New York), 139,n2
Rhode Island, 390
Rhodes, James Ford, 27, 49
Rice, Richard Henry, 411,n1
Richardson, Hugh, 488,n1
Rideing, William Henry, 406
Rider, Frederic, 357,n3
Rise and Growth of American Politics (Ford), 399,n1
Ritz-Carlton Hotel, New York City, 474, 477
Roanoke Camp of Confederate Veterans, 604n2
Roanoke College, 604,n1,2
Roanoke *Times*, 604n2
Robb, James Hampden, 40,n29
Robert M. La Follette (La Follette and La Follette), 412n2
Robinson, Moncure, Mrs. (Lydia Biddle), 324,n2
Rocky Mountain News (Denver), 388-n1, 584
Roe, Gilbert E., 412n2
Roebling, Washington Augustus, 583,-n1; Mrs. II (Cornelia Witsell Farrow), 583n1
Roman Catholic church, 277, 305, 491
Roosevelt, Franklin Delano, 161n1
Roosevelt, Theodore, 44n3, 47, 48, 52, 59, 140, 164, 207n4, 209, 285, 375, 427n1, 429, 500, 536,n3, 562
Root, Elihu, 184, 514n1
Rosalsky, Otto A., 183,n3
Ross, Millard Fillmore, 101,n3, 145, 328
Rouse, Ruth, 385n2
Rowland, Reginald, 480,n1
Russell, Frank, Mrs. (May Pomeroy), 100,n1

Russell, Lucius Thompson, 137
Russell Sage Foundation, 177
Ryan, Thomas Fortune, 39,n22, 160,n2, 184, 274, 282n1, 393, 429

Sachs, Samuel, 39,n20
Sackett, Clarence, 50, 171, 200, 215
Sadler, Wilbur Fisk, Jr., 54, 482-83,n1, 532
"safe and sane," 594
St. John, William W., 73,n3, 76-77, 81, 86n1, 137,n2, 155, 200
St. John-Stevas, Norman, 194n4
St. Louis: City Club, 276; Princeton Club, 283; Southern Hotel, 262; WW in, 210,n4, 211, 260, 262-63, 263-72, 272, 276-77, 283, 292
St. Louis Post-Dispatch, 262, 263n
St. Paul, Minn., 519n4
St. Peter's College, Jersey City, 400n1
Salmon, J. R., 173n1
Salvation Army, 386
San Francisco, 519n4, 533
Santiago Bay, Battle of, 371,n5
Sato, Shosuke, 139,n1
Savannah, 543, 576; Hibernian Society, 466,n4, 532n6, 543,n2
Savannah Press, 466n4, 491n6, 516n1, 543,n1
Scarborough-on-Hudson, N.Y., 187n2
Scharnagle, Barbara, 356,n3
Schauffler, William Gray, M.D., 550n2
Schlesinger, Louis, 39,n15
Schmitz, Adolph John, 57
Schomburgk (Sir Robert) Line, 11
Schurman, Jacob Gould, 30, 130, 359, 399-400
Scotch-Irish, 418
Scott, Richard Carter, 383,n4
Scribner, Charles, 51-52
Scudder, Edward Wallace, 233-34
Scudder, Wallace McIlvaine, 225-26, 245, 357
Seattle, 519n4, 533; Commercial Club, 416
Seitz, Don Carlos, 455
Selden, Charles Albert, 101,n1, 127, 135, 287, 288, 307
Shafroth, John Franklin, 388n1, 584
Shakespeare, William, 270
Shalvoy, Frank P., 253,n4, 367,n1
Shannon, Thomas Berry, 598-99,n1
Sheehan, William Francis, 161n1, 359,n3, 361, 429, 429n1, 430n1
Sheldon, Edward Wright, 1:*240,n7; 13, 165, 176, 186-87
Shepard, Edward Morse, 125,n2, 161n1, 287, 289, 361
Shepard, James Edward, 98-99,n1
Shepherd, William Robert, 469n3
Shields, Charles Woodruff, 425,n2
Shoreham Hotel, Washington, 20
Short Ballot League, 258
Short Ballot Organization, 59, 197n2
Shreveport Rate Cases, 122n2
Shultice, Robert W., 99,n1

Silzer, George Sebastian, 243, 311-12, 328, 357, 550n2
Simpson, Charles E. S., 481
single tax, 2, 278n1
Sins of the Father (Dixon), 96,n3
Slattery, Daniel G., 283,n1
Slaughter, Evans Griffiths, 203,n1
slave women, 604n2
Sleeper, Charles F., 164-65,n1
Smathers, Frank, 310n5, 413,n1
Smith, George Doane, 142n1, 392,n2
Smith, Hoke, 2:*580,n1; 480,n1, 488, 489, 491n1
Smith, James, Jr., 15, 41-42,n2, 43,n2, 46, 47, 72,n3, 77n1, 81n1, 82, 83, 84, 86, 86n1, 94, 97, 98n1, 100, 101, 113,n1,2, 114-16, 117, 119, 120, 121, 126, 127, 128, 129, 132-33, 133-34, 134-35, 135-36,n1, 136, 137, 137n1,3, 141,n1, 143, 145, 146, 153, 154, 155-56, 160, 160n1, 162, 163-64, 166-67, 169-70, 170n1, 173-74n1, 175, 181, 181n1, 185, 197, 198, 199, 201, 204,n2, 206, 210, 212, 215, 217, 224, 225, 225n1, 226, 226n1, 229-30,n1, 231, 231n3,4, 232-33, 235-36,n2, 237, 238, 239, 240, 241, 242n2, 245, 245n2, 247, 248-52,n2, 253, 257, 258, 259, 260, 262, 272-74, 278, 280, 281, 283, 286n2, 287, 288, 289, 292, 295-307, 309, 312n1, 321, 325, 328, 331n1, 334, 336, 337, 339, 340, 357, 361, 363, 367, 376, 377, 382, 384, 392, 393, 435n1, 454, 513, 518, 582, 583
Smith, James III, 392,n2
Smith, John Henry, 392,n2
Smith, John Walker, 15-16,n1
Smith, Joseph Lyndon, 392,n2
Smith, Marie, 50n3
Smythe, Augustine Thomas, 34
Sobel, Herman, 100,n2
Socialism and the Child Labor Problem (Spargo), 452n2
Socialists and Socialism, 222, 280, 354-55, 452,n2
Somerset County, N.J., 532
Sommer, Frank Henry, 225,n3, 310
South, The, 189f, 419-20, 478, 490, 492f, 532n6, 598, 604n2
South and the Democratic Campaign of 1910-1912 (Link), 282n1
South Carolina, 68
South Carolina, University of, 140
South Carolina Presbyterian Institution for Young Ladies, 577n4
South Carolina Press Association, 499,-n2, 507
Southern Amusement Co., 96n1
Southern Commercial Congress, 478, 480; Proceedings . . . , 498n
Southern Hotel, St. Louis, 262
Southern Pacific Railroad, 32n2
Southern Railway, 140
Southwestern Historical Quarterly, 123-n3

Southwestern Life Insurance Co., 123, 422
Spanish-American War, 371
Spargo, John, 452,n2
Speer, Robert Walter, 388n1, 584
Speer, William Henry, 469,n3
Speir, Francis, Jr., 72,n1, 94
Sprigg, James C., 245, 413, 433
Springfield Weekly Republican, 604
Stahlman, Edward Bushrod, 376,n1
standpatters, 593, 594
Stanford University, 130
Stanford University: The First Twenty-five Years (Elliott), 131n3
state constitutions, 255n2
state insurance, 143-44
state vs. federal control of corporations, 312f
states, 104f
states-rights, 104
Staunton, Va., 9, 118; First Presbyterian Church, 118; Woodrow Wilson Democratic Club, 96, 118
Steck, David W., 199n
Steffens, Lincoln, 412n2
Stephens, Lawrence Vest, 198,n2
Sterling Hotel, Trenton, 583
Stetson, Francis Lynde, 39,n21, 121
Stevens, Edwin Augustus, 113, 173-74, 415n1
Stevens Institute of Technology, 39n24, 410-11
Stewart, John Aikman (1822-1926), 7:*602,n1; 436,n3
Stockbridge, Frank Parker, 519, 519,n4, 533, 581
Stockton, Bayard, Mrs. (Helen Hamilton Shields), 425,n3
Stoddard, Harry Galpin, 574,n4
Stoughton, William, 89,n2
Stovall, Pleasant Alexander, 491,n6, 516, 532n6, 543
Streitwolf, August C., Jr., 101,n2, 145, 233, 243-44, 308, 309, 328
Stubbs, Walter Roscoe, 180,n1
sugar trust, 113n2, 173, 177
Sullivan, Mark, Mrs. (Catherine Driscoll), 401,n1
Sullivan, Mark Anthony, 22-23, 87n2, 119, 228, 229n1, 304, 357, 400, 404, 413,n1
Sullivan, Roger, 74,n2
Sussex County, N.J., 253, 370, 378
Sutro, F. C., 173n1
Swackhamer, S. S., 173n1

Taft, William Howard, 32n3, 38n3, 44n3, 85n3, 88, 140, 184, 220, 248, 291n2, 362, 427n1, 478, 478n3, 486, 488, 491, 500, 514n1, 515, 573, 592n2
Talcott, Charles Andrew, 1:*240,n3; 12, 456
Tammany Hall, 161n1, 602
Tammany Times, 229, 376n1

tariff, 7, 32, 128, 138, 197, 205n2, 219, 220, 222, 223, 267, 301, 359, 478n3, 556, 567, 592, 601
Tarrant, Warren Downes, 56,n1, 61,n2
taste, 319, 386
Tawney, James Albertus, 207,n6
taxation, 349-50, 530-31
Tener, John Kinley, 409n2
Tennyson, Alfred, 1st Baron Tennyson, 71,n5
Texas, 122-23, 422-23, 466, 466,n3, 584; legislature, 422; State Fair, 576, 584
Thanksgiving Day, 87f
Theta Delta Chi fraternity, 250n2
Thilly, Frank, 35-36,n1
Thomas, Charles Spalding, 376, 388n1, 574, 584, 599
Thomas, Harvey, 309-10,n1
Thompson, Samuel Huston, Jr., 375-76, 405, 521, 523, 527, 574, 577-78
Thorstenberg, Herman Justus, 604n2
Thwing, Charles Franklin, 53
Tillman, Benjamin Ryan, 28,n1
Todd, Frederick, 121-22,n1, 185-86
tolerance, 91
Tories, 594, 596
Town Topics (New York), 324,n5
Treacy, John Joseph, 163,n1, 304, 357
Trenton, 379-82; Board of Trade, 483; Central Labor Union, 259; Chamber of Commerce, 482, 575n1; First Methodist Episcopal Church, 385, 386; First Presbyterian Church, 380, 452; Fifth Presbyterian Church, 259; Har Sinai Temple, 87,n1; Sterling Hotel, 583; Taylor Opera House, 53, 504n1; Trenton Country Club, 532, 582; Winkler's Orchestra, 380; Y.M.-C.A., 379
Trenton Evening Times, 9, 73,n3, 77,-n1, 99n, 129, 136n1, 142n1, 154n, 182, 216n3, 229n1, 252n, 382n, 416n, 455, 476n, 505n, 575n
Trenton Potteries Co., 379
Trenton True American, 73,n3, 81n1, 93n, 152n, 154n, 155, 238n1, 277n, 307n, 387n1, 399n, 427n, 453n, 474n, 484n3, 486n, 502, 503n, 504n1, 537n4, 546n5, 576n, 579n
Trinity College, Durham, N.C., 489,n4
Trotter, William Monroe, 50
trusts, 312
Tucker, Henry St. George, 282,n1, 287
Tuckerton, N.J., 375
Tumulty, Joseph Patrick, 81n1, 87n2, 98n1, 118-20, 134, 136n1, 142n1, 145-46, 200, 228, 229n1, 233, 245, 288,n1, 295,n2, 304, 312, 328-29, 356, 357, 439, 451-52, 510, 582, 588
Tweed Ring, 59

Underwood, Oscar Wilder, 95,n1
unemployment insurance, 144
Union County, N.J., 22, 114, 137, 153, 243, 278, 309

United Daughters of the Confederacy, 604n2
United States: Bureau of Education, 207; Children's Bureau, 207,n4; Commerce and Labor Department, 207n4; Congress, 102, 104, 316; Constitution, 10, 11, 12, 442, 511-n1,2, 535n2, 546n5, 562, 595-96, 16th Amendment, 511,n1,4, 534-35; farmer's free list bill, 592,n2; Interstate Commerce Commission, 96, 122n2; Library of Congress, 226; Post Office Department, 427n1; Senate, 514n4, 515, direct election of senators, 205n2, 355, 371n4, 578, 592, 601, 603; Supreme Court, 313, 314, 511,-n2, 535,n2, 546n5
United States Steel Corporation, 461
University of South Carolina (Hollis), 577n4
U'Ren, William Simon, 197,n1, 255n5

Vanderbilt, George Opdyke, 415n2
Vanderlip, Frank Arthur, 187,n2, 234
Van Valkenburg, Edwin Augustus, 44n3, 231,n4
Vardaman, James Kimble, 28,n1
Venable, Francis Preston, 20,n1, 517,-n1, 520
Venezuela Boundary Controversy (Cleveland), 12n3
Venezuelan controversy, 11-12,n3
Verdery, Marion Jackson, 201-3,n1, 257, 552-53
Villard, Oswald Garrison, 26, 83, 101-2, 127, 135-36, 287, 288-89, 307, 308, 454-55
Virginia, 282, 287, 604n2
Virginia, S.S., 597
Virginia, University of, 118, 140, 383-84, 558, 559; Glee Club (octette), 383,n3, 384; Jefferson Society, 383,-n2; Y.M.C.A., 326,n1, 333
Vroom, Garret Dorset Wall, 415n2

Wagner, Jay J., 291n2
Wald, Lillian D., 157n1, 207n14
Waldorf-Astoria Hotel, New York City, 51, 274, 389, 392, 453n1
Wall Street, 77n1, 199, 237, 261, 275, 292, 495
Walsh, Allan Bartholomew, 29,n1, 504n1, 546n5, 574n1,4
Warner, Hoyt Landon, 16in1
Warren County, N.J., 370
Washington, George, 4, 229, 389
Washington, D.C.: National Press Club, 377n1, 396, 404; Shoreham Hotel, 20
Washington Evening Star, 34,n3
Washington Herald, 160,n1
Washington Post, 255n1, 399n
Washington state, 395, 519
watered stock, 69, 461
Watterson, Henry, 140, 143, 160, 181n1, 184-85, 212, 274, 286, 393-94,

435,n1; Mrs. (Rebecca Ewing), 274, 393, 394
Wayland, Chandler Norton, 331,n3; Mrs. (Lucy Elton), 331,n4
Wayt, Hampton H., 9, 96
Webster, Daniel, 218
Weekly News (Palmyra, N.J.), 164n1
Welch, William Henry, M.D., 396n1
Werts, George, 173,n3
Wescott, John Wesley, 42-43, 169-70, 206, 261-62, 289, 394, 413, 414-15, 451-52, 516, 520-21, 548-49
West, Andrew Fleming, 6:*528,n3; 436, 438, 487, 487n2,3
Westcott, Edward Noyes, 331n5
Westcott, William Augustus, M.D., 261,n1
Westinghouse, George, 478,n2
Wheeler, Benjamin Ide, 54
Whitlock, Brand, 161n1
Wickersham, George Woodward, 600,-n3
Wilde, Edward Seymour, 41-42,n1
Wilder, William Royal, 1:*253,n2; 358-59, 361
Willcox, Thomas H., 596
William Howard Taft: A Conservative's Conception of the Presidency (Anderson), 427n1
Williams, Charles Richard, 52,n1, 525,n1, 557,n3
Williams, John Sharp, 93-94, 197
Williams, Thomas, 50,n3
Williams College: New York alumni dinner, 490,n5
Willson, Augustus Everett, 172, 214-15
Wilson: The Road to the White House (Link), 262n2, 436n1, 447n5, 512n1, 575n2, 579n3,4
Wilson, Eleanor Randolph, daughter of WW and EAW (*afterwards* Mrs. William Gibbs McAdoo), 6:*407,n1; 329, 501, 544
Wilson, Ellen Axson (Mrs. Woodrow Wilson I), 2:*334,n2; 21, 33, 45, 95, 131, 143, 187, 211, 232, 234-35, 274, 287, 293, 329, 356, 394, 425, 501, 502, 502n2, 507, 517, 534, 544
Wilson, Jessie Woodrow, daughter of WW and EAW (*afterwards* Mrs. Francis Bowes Sayre), 5:*565,n1; 329, 501, 544
Wilson, Joseph R., Jr., brother of WW, 1:*3,n8; 95-96
Wilson, Joseph Ruggles, father of WW, 1:*3,n1; 21,n3
Wilson, Margaret, daughter of WW and EAW, 329, 425, 454
Wilson, William Lawrence, 71,n1

WOODROW WILSON

APPEARANCE

He has the head and visage of a mediaeval scholar, 217

Woodrow Wilson, cont.

BIOGRAPHY

New Democratic Governors, 32,n3

FAMILY LIFE AND DOMESTIC AFFAIRS

Carnegie retirement pension, 130-32,n4, 148, 283,n2, 287n2
Income provided by friends, 333

GOVERNOR OF NEW JERSEY

Statement on the senatorship, 153-54
Proposed public statement on the candidacy of James Smith, Jr., 239,n1
Statement [on the senatorial candidacy of James Smith, Jr.], 248-52; mentioned, 257
Form letter to various correspondents on the senatorship, 252
patronage, 262n2, 513, 513n2, 518
Martinique Hotel conference, Jan. 16, 1911, 357-58
Inaugural address as Governor of New Jersey, Taylor Opera House, Trenton, Jan. 17, 1911; text, 345-54; mentioned, 53, 333, 363, 375, 521
appointments, 413, 414-15, 510, 516, 532
Statement on a proposed increase in postal rates, 427
Remarks at the annual dinner of the New Jersey Senate, Ritz-Carlton Hotel, New York City, March 3, 1911; news report, 474-76; mentioned, 477, 582
Conference with Democratic Assemblymen, March 6, 1911; news report, 481-82
Conference with Democratic Assemblymen, March 13, 1911; news report, 504-5
Veto message on Assembly Bill 163 on salaries of paid firemen, 508
Veto message on Assembly Bill 245 on fiftieth anniversary celebration funds, 524-25
Veto message on Senate Bill 148 on establishment of public parks, 526-27
Veto message on Assembly Bill 197 on legal commitment and reformation of wayward females, 548
Message to the House of Assembly on public school administration and city government reform, April 11, 1911; text, 549-52
Remarks about the commission government bill, 574-75
Statement on the work of the New Jersey legislative session of 1911, 578-79

HEALTH

bowel upset, 544, 546
attack of acute indigestion at banquet, 590

Woodrow Wilson, cont.

INTERVIEWS

5-12, 216-23, 235-36, 312-16 (mentioned, 186n1), 354-56, 554-56, 591-92

OPINIONS AND COMMENTS

I do not *want* to be President. There is too little play in it, too little time for one's friends, too much distasteful publicity and fuss and frills. I dote on going my way (Jan. 1911), 293

POLITICAL CAREER

Lawyers' Club conference, July 12, 1910, Editorial Note, 20:565-66n; mentioned, 181n1
Mentioned for president in 1912, 9, 14, 18, 20, 21, 22, 23, 27, 31, 32, 33, 38,n2, 43, 45, 52, 55, 78, 95, 96, 99, 117n1, 118, 123, 139, 143, 160, 161, 208, 213-14, 216-17, 237, 248, 254, 255, 258, 275, 292-93, 327, 334, 362, 375, 376, 393, 395, 410, 413, 437, 439, 454, 466n4, 466, 479, 483, 488, 489, 499n1, 500, 502, 509, 518-19,n4, 524, 533, 543n2, 545, 553, 554, 570, 573, 573n2, 576, 578, 587, 588, 592, 595, 598

PRINCETON UNIVERSITY

Talk to undergraduate demonstrators after election as governor, 3-4
Talk to football team, 4-5
Address at a dinner in his honor given by the Class of 1911, Princeton Inn, Dec. 7, 1910; news reports, 149-52
Remarks at a meeting in celebration of Princeton work in Peking, Alexander Hall, Dec. 8, 1910; news report, 159-60
salary, 165, 177, 186-87
Testimonial volume presented by Classes of 1911, 1912, 1913, and 1914; news report, 322-23
Response to a toast, Princeton Ideals, at the thirteenth annual banquet of the *Daily Princetonian*, Princeton Inn, May 1, 1911; text, 600-1

PROFESSIONAL ACTIVITIES

Elected vice-president of the National Civil Service Reform League, 256

PUBLIC AND POLITICAL ADDRESSES

Democracy, talk Aug. 31, 1901; mentioned, 395,n3; text in Vol. 12, 175-79
The Lawyer and the Community: address before the American Bar Association, Chattanooga, Aug. 31, 1910; mentioned, 68n4, 185, 315; text in Vol. 21, 64-81

Luncheon address to the City Club of Milwaukee, Schlitz Palm Garden,

Woodrow Wilson, cont.
Nov. 17, 1910; news report, 57-61; mentioned, 56
Lecture before the Milwaukee Lecture Service League, Pabst Theater, Nov. 17, 1910; text, 61-71
Development of the Business Conscience: address before the Business Service Lecture League, Young Men's Christian Association Hall, Chicago, Nov. 18, 1910; news report, 74-76; mentioned, 48,n2
The Spirit of America, Thanksgiving Day address at Har Sinai Temple, Trenton, Nov. 24, 1910; text, 87-93
Address to the Conference of Governors, Frankfort, Ky., Nov. 29, 1910; text, 102-13; mentioned, 185, 315,n3
Address to the Illinois Manufacturers' Association, Congress Hotel, Chicago, Dec. 12, 1910; advance text, 178-80; news report, 180-81; mentioned, 71,n2
Address to the New York Southern Society, Hotel Waldorf-Astoria, Dec. 14, 1910; text, 188-96; mentioned, 51, 51n1, 202-3,n4, 223, 257, 288
The Law and the Facts, presidential address to the American Political Science Association, Southern Hotel, St. Louis, Dec. 27, 1910; text, 263-72
Speech to the City Club of St. Louis, Dec. 29, 1910; news report, 276-77
Speech to the Princeton Club of St. Louis, Dec. 29, 1910; news report, 283-84; mentioned, 198
Address on the senatorial situation in New Jersey, delivered in St. Patrick's Hall, Jersey City, Jan. 5, 1911; text, 295-307; mentioned, 233,n1, 295, 309, 311, 311n1
Address at the golden jubilee of the Hebrew Benevolent and Orphan Asylum Society of Newark, Temple B'nai Jeshurun, Jan. 8, 1911; text, 316-21; mentioned, 183, 260
Address in New Auditorium, Newark, on the U.S. senatorship contest, Jan. 14, 1911; news report, 335-44; mentioned, 286,n1, 333, 335
Inaugural address as Governor of New Jersey, Taylor Opera House, Trenton, Jan. 17, 1911; text, 345-54; mentioned, 53, 333, 363, 375, 521
Remarks at the annual dinner of the Jersey City Board of Trade, Jersey City Club theatre, Jan. 19, 1911; news report, 359-60; mentioned, 399
Address to the Newark Board of Trade, Jan. 25, 1911; text, 367-74
Address in behalf of Know Your City Week, Y.M.C.A. auditorium, Trenton, Jan. 26, 1911; news report, 379-82
Address to the Inter-Church Federation of New Jersey at the First Methodist

Woodrow Wilson, cont.

Episcopal Church, Trenton, Jan. 27, 1911; news report, 385-87

After-dinner speech to the Kansas Society of New York, Waldorf-Astoria Hotel, Jan. 28, 1911; news report, 389-91; mentioned, 392

Address to the National Press Club, Washington, Jan. 31, 1911; text, 396-99; mentioned, 377, 396, 404

Tribute to Mark Anthony Sullivan at a banquet in his honor, Columbian Club, Jersey City, given by alumni of St. Peter's College, Feb. 1, 1911; text, 400-4

Address to a banquet of Stevens Institute alumni, Hotel Astor, New York City, Feb. 8, 1911; news report, 410-11

Address in behalf of Berea College, Carnegie Hall, New York City, Feb. 10, 1911; text, 417-21; mentioned, 49,n2, 172,n2, 214, 424, 425

Address to the Kentuckians of New York, Plaza Hotel, Feb. 10, 1911; news report, 421-22; mentioned, 425

Address to the Democratic Club of Philadelphia, Hotel Bellevue-Stratford, Feb. 21, 1911; text, 441-50; mentioned, 246-47, 435n1, 450, 451, 451,n1

Remarks at a meeting of the New Jersey Consumers' League, First Presbyterian Church, Trenton, Feb. 24, 1911; news report, 452-53

Remarks to the New Jersey Editorial Association, Trenton, Feb. 27, 1911; news report, 455

Address to the West Hudson Board of Trade, Harrison, N.J., Feb. 28, 1911; text, 456-65; mentioned, 477

After-dinner address to the Hoboken Board of Trade, German Club, March 2, 1911; text, 468-74; mentioned, 477

Address to the Trenton Chamber of Commerce, March 7, 1911; news report, 482-86; mentioned, 499

Remarks at a dinner in his honor given by Hoke Smith, Piedmont Hotel, Atlanta, March 9, 1911; news report, 489-91

The Citizen and the State: address to the Southern Commercial Congress, Atlanta Auditorium, March 10, 1911; text, 491-98; mentioned, 206,n2, 500, 506n2

Remarks to the New Jersey Conference of Charities and Correction, Alexander Hall, Princeton, April 2, 1911; text, 528-31

After-dinner political address at the Jefferson Day dinner of the Burlington County Democratic Club in the Auditorium, Burlington, April 5, 1911; text, 535-42; mentioned, 502, 543-44

Woodrow Wilson, cont.

Address at a banquet of the National Democratc League of Clubs, Murat Temple, Indianapolis, April 13, 1911; text, 557-68; mentioned, 466,-n3, 569, 570, 570-71, 576, 578, 604

Remarks at a dinner in honor of the fourth anniversary of the founding of the Free Synagogue, Hotel Astor, New York City, April 24, 1911; news report, 585-86

Remarks at a dinner given in his honor by Ernest Robinson Ackerman, president of the New Jersey Senate, Hotel Astor, New York City, April 26, 1911; news report, 588-89

After-dinner address before the Phillipsburg (N.J.) Board of Trade, April 27, 1911; news report, 590-91

Address to the Pewter Platter Club, Norfolk, Va., April 29, 1911; news reports, 592-97

Speech at a dinner of the National Democratic Club in honor of Senator James A. O'Gorman, Hotel Astor, New York City, May 2, 1911; news report, 601-4

Commencement address at the University of North Carolina, May 30, 1911; mentioned, 406, 517; text in Vol. 23

WRITINGS

Congressional Government (1885), mentioned, 138,n2

Constitutional Government in the United States (1908), mentioned, 12n4

Message to a banquet of the Sons of Delaware of Philadelphia at the Bellevue-Stratford, Dec. 7, 1910; text, 148-49

End of Woodrow Wilson entry

Wilson-Gorman tariff of 1894, 113,n2, 173, 226n3, 282, 535n2

Wilson Movement in Texas, 1910-1912 (Link), 123n2

Winchester, Caleb Thomas, 5:*753,n1; 35,n1

Winslow, John Bradley, 57

Wisconsin, 461, 485; Railroad Commission, 277

Wise, Stephen Samuel, 585,n1

Wittpenn, Henry Otto, 173n1

woman suffrage, 289-90, 356

women, 594, 596

Wood, Leonard, M.D., 396n1

Woodrow, James, maternal uncle of WW, 1:*41,n1, 507, 576n2; Mrs. (Felixiana Shepherd Baker), 1:*42-n1; 576,n2, 577

Woodrow Wilson: Life and Letters (Baker), 412n2

Woodrow Wilson: Political Leader
(Hendrick), 8n1, 142n1, 504n1
Woodrow Wilson: Possible President
(Hale), 414n3
Woodrow Wilson: The Story of His Life
(Hale), 142n1, 414n1
Woodrow Wilson and the New Jersey
Governorship, 139,n2
Woodrow Wilson as I Know Him
(Tumulty), 8n1, 142n1
Woodrow Wilson Democratic Associa-
tion, 213
Woodruff, John, Mrs., 415n
Woodruff, Timothy Lester, 429
Woods, Hiram, M.D., 1:*133,n3; 158,
175, 177; Mrs. (Laura Hall), 177,n2
Wooley, J. W., 39,n18
Wordsworth, William, 117n1, 408
workmen's compensation, 291n2, 347,
462f
World Missionary Conference, Edin-
burgh 1910, 385,n2

World Peace Foundation, 131n3
World's Work (New York), 414,n13,
439, 509, 520, 526
Wright, Henry Brooke Hagstromer,
500,n2; Mrs. (Helen Kirk), 500,n2
Wyeth, John A., M.D., 202
Wyllys, Rufus Kay, 291n2

Yale University: football game with
Princeton, Nov. 12, 1910, 3-4,n1;
School of Forestry, 144,n3; Yale
Lectures on the Responsibilities of
Citizenship, 184, 187
Yates, Frederic, 16:*437,n1; 187, 234-
35; Mrs. (Emily Chapman Martin),
235,n2
Yoakum, Benjamin Franklin, 40,n27,
466,n5
Young, George Washington, 39,n19
Young Men's Woodrow Wilson Demo-
cratic Association, 213
Youth's Companion, 406,n1